Litigation Technology

E. Allan Farnsworth
On January 31, 2005, Aspen Publishers lost a great author, colleague, and friend with the death of E. Allan Farnsworth, the Alfred McCormack Professor of Law at Columbia Law School and author of the seminal student treatise, Contracts, Fourth Edition, by Aspen Publishers.

Litigation Technology

Becoming a High-Tech Trial Lawyer

Mike Rogers

Chicago-Kent College of Law
and
Ronin Consulting Ltd.

ASPEN
PUBLISHERS

76 Ninth Avenue, New York, NY 10011
http://lawschool.aspenpublishers.com

Aspen Publishers
Attn: Permissions Department
76 Ninth Avenue, 7th Floor
New York, NY 10011-5201

Printed in the United States of America.

1 2 3 4 5 6 7 8 9 0

ISBN 0-7355-5290-8

Library of Congress Cataloging-in-Publication Data

Rogers, Michael G., 1963-
Litigation technology : becoming a high-tech trial lawyer / Michael G. Rogers.
p. cm.
Includes index.
ISBN 0-7355-5290-8 (alk. paper)
1. Trial practice--Technological innovations--United States. 2. Trial practice--United States--Data processing. 3. Trial practice--United States--Audio-visual aids. I. Title.

KF8915.R64 2006
347.73'70285--dc22

2006004153

About Aspen Publishers

Aspen Publishers, headquartered in New York City, is a leading information provider for attorneys, business professionals, and law students. Written by preeminent authorities, our products consist of analytical and practical information covering both U.S. and international topics. We publish in the full range of formats, including updated manuals, books, periodicals, CDs, and online products.

Our proprietary content is complemented by 2,500 legal databases, containing over 11 million documents, available through our Loislaw division. Aspen Publishers also offers a wide range of topical legal and business databases linked to Loislaw's primary material. Our mission is to provide accurate, timely, and authoritative content in easily accessible formats, supported by unmatched customer care.

To order any Aspen Publishers title, go to *http://lawschool.aspenpublishers.com* or call 1-800-638-8437.

To reinstate your manual update service, call 1-800-638-8437.

For more information on Loislaw products, go to *www.loislaw.com* or call 1-800-364-2512.

For Customer Care issues, e-mail *CustomerCare@aspenpublishers.com*; call 1-800-234-1660; or fax 1-800-901-9075.

Aspen Publishers
a Wolters Kluwer business

To my wife Cordelia Coppleson — for backing me and believing in me.

Summary of Contents

Contents

Contents

Contents

Preface

In August 1986, IIT Chicago-Kent College of Law was touting itself as a trailblazer in American legal education. Students were actually using computers to do their outlining and course work. Five years later, the same school put network hubs on a fiber optic network for every student in every classroom. Now the school has a secured wireless network and one of the few Litigation Technology classes in the country. Lawyers use computers in every aspect of their practices. Software programs and computer technology help lawyers manage their files, their client lists, their timesheets and billings, their calendars, and now their trials. While litigation technology is new now, in five years the majority of trial lawyers will use some type of technology in their trial presentation, and in ten years the lawyer who fails to use technology to present a case will commit malpractice.

This book was written with two purposes in mind. First, this book is the companion text for a Litigation Technology class. If you are taking a Litigation Technology class, you should have completed Evidence, Trial Advocacy I, and, if possible, Trial Advocacy II. From time to time, this book will revisit trial advocacy fundamentals while talking about using technology in the courtroom. This book does this because the trial advocacy fundamentals must be practiced while using technology in a courtroom. Simply put, one who cannot lay a foundation for a document during an examination will be unable to lay a foundation for a digitized document. By the same token, this book presumes that you have some passing familiarity with trial practice. If you used Mauet and Wolfson's Problems in Trial Advocacy for Trial Advocacy class, and used Mauet's Trial Practice book, you will be well prepared for a Litigation Technology class. This book builds on the things that you learned from those books because, after all, the art and science of trial advocacy is built on the principle of derivative thinking. (That means, steal good ideas if they work.) If you are using this book for a Litigation Technology class, then you should obtain the materials for the class from the Litigation Technology website, which is discussed at the end of this preface.

The second purpose of this book is to act as a resource book for attorneys and law students who want to learn something about using computer technology at trial *without* taking a Litigation Technology class. This book will help you learn to think about how to use technology in a courtroom or other adversarial hearing. The book talks about how to think about using computers at trial and then introduces you to three software programs that will become integral to trial presentation. If you are a lawyer who wants to learn how to integrate computers into your trial presentation or a law student who is interested in learning this skill to distinguish yourself from your fellow law students, then congratulations! You are now starting to read a book that is designed to demystify the field of litigation technology. After all, litigation technology is simply one more tool for a trial lawyer to use in his or her primary business, which is sales.

Trial lawyers are in the sales business. They cold call a bunch of strangers and lay the groundwork for their pitch during voir dire. Their opening statements, direct examinations, cross-examinations, and closing arguments are their sales pitches. They try to close every deal with a verdict. Judges and juries are the potential buyers. The sales job is made harder because the opposition is trying to obstruct the sale. Welcome to the adversarial system of justice: He or she who connects with the buyer wins.

With this idea of selling in mind, think about the would-be buyers. What is going to move the judge or jury toward closing the deal? What type of language and presentation style will reach your buyers? Think about how people think. When Aristotle talked about rhetoric, he encouraged his students to make appeals that would reach three kinds of people. He asserted that people tended to be logos-, pathos-, or ethos-driven in their decision making. People who are logos-driven in their thought process look to logic to solve problems. Aristotle recommended that arguments that targeted logos-driven people had to be justified with definitions, factual data, and statistics, along with literal and historical analogies. These arguments should evoke a cognitive rational response from the listener. Pathos-driven people make their decisions with their gut reactions to an event. Their instinct or intuition tells them to go in one direction, and they then rationalize their decision in order to follow their gut. By their nature, pathos-driven people respond to vivid language and descriptions. Appeals to these people are best made with emotionally loaded or figurative language. Ethos-driven people are those who make decisions because of their trust in the speaker. These individuals respond better to the restrained, sincere, and fair-minded presenter. They are likely to be impressed by the advocate's appropriate, accurate, and skillful use of language. Trial lawyers need to construct appeals that reach all three types of people.

Now consider how the majority of Americans receive their information, news, and entertainment: from televisions and computers. Both present information on a screen. Each medium, through a remote control or a mouse click, lets the viewer jump to other information. Think about television: It offers sounds, images, and differing vantage points every few moments. Television is the perfect selling tool. Consider how television as a presentation medium has evolved. If you grew up watching the *I Love Lucy* show, you were exposed to three-camera filming. Three movie cameras were positioned around the stage and captured the action from three different vantage points. One camera zoomed in on head shots. Another camera shot the entire stage, and the third camera focused on a particular actor or specific part of the set. During the editing process, the director decided which of the three different camera shots to splice together. That splicing process controlled the vantage point of the television audience. The director, then, controlled the television audience's point of view. In the *I Love Lucy* show, the image on the screen stayed on the screen for approximately 15 seconds, when the next bit of spliced film appeared. Viewers nowadays take the shift in focus for granted, but for the television audience in the 1950s, that extent of vantage point manipulation was completely new. Before *I Love Lucy*, the television camera functioned as nothing more than a member of the audience. Three-camera filming revolutionized its role. Now it became a tool of — and affected by — the whims of the presenter. The audience could now be forced to view the story from whichever vantage point the director chose.

Fast forward to today (a videotape reference that underscores how much Americans embrace video). Fifteen-second commercials are routinely shown on television. How many images are shown to a television audience in a 15-second commercial? Watch an MTV or a Nike commercial. Watch the images flash across the screen. As those images flash across the screen, consider how they impress themselves on your consciousness. Advertisers understand that we are now a society that gets the majority of our information from our eyes, and they use that understanding to make us feel that we need new cars, better vacuum cleaners, and new and improved deodorants and Spaghetti-Os. Advertisers also understand that we have been conditioned to accept such persuasion from our televisions. Advertisers use and reinforce this conditioning successfully to sell their products. These "masters" of the medium are usuallybetter at sales than trial lawyers are. It is time to learn from the masters, because the better you can sell your case, the better you can serve your client.

Access to Materials Online

How to Get a .pdf Copy of This Book

You can download a color .pdf version of this book to print or view on your computer. For full access to this useful feature, please fill out this form. No photocopies of this form will be accepted.

Make sure you include your e-mail address on the form because the serial number key for downloading and opening the .pdf will be e-mailed to you.

1. Complete the form.

Name			**Phone**
Address		**Apt. No.**	
City	**State**	**ZIP Code**	
Law School			**Year (check one)** ☐ **1st** ☐ **2nd** ☐ **3rd**

2. Cut out the UPC from the back of the book. It can be found on the lower left-hand corner of the back cover of the book. Staple the UPC inside this box. Only the original UPC from the book cover will be accepted. No photocopies or store stickers are allowed.

Attach UPC inside this box.

3. Mail the finished form to:

Aspen Publishers, Inc.
Legal Education Division
Litigation Technology Book Online
130 Turner Street
Waltham, MA 02453-8901

4. Upon receipt of this completed form, you will be e-mailed a URL and code so that you may download the Litigation Technology book in .pdf format. You may download the book once. The file will have a password that will be registered to you. The .pdf version of this book is nontransferable.

I understand that on-line access is granted solely to the purchaser of this book for the academic year in which it was purchased. Any other usage is not authorized and will result in immediate termination of access. Sharing of codes is strictly prohibited.

Signature ______________________________

How to Get Course Materials, Supplemental Materials, and Access to Web Boards

If you are taking a Litigation Technology class or are interested in getting supplemental materials regarding litigation technology, go to www.littech.org and sign up for a one-year subscription. You will get access to the following:

- Problems and exercises for a Litigation Technology course including video, audio, text, and image files for two full civil trials and two full criminal trials.
- Access to web boards where students and attorneys may network and exchange ideas regarding litigation technology.
- Access to quarterly updates regarding state and federal laws that affect the use and admissibility of technological evidence at trial.
- Access to motion forms regarding admissibility and impounding of evidence used in high-tech trials.
- Notification of updates regarding software changes and links to the respective sites.
- Tutorials and tips for different software packages and best practices. Tutorials will be available for how to use CaseMap, TimeMap, SmartDraw, PowerPoint, and other programs. You can watch the tutorial and follow along if you have a dual screen computer.

Acknowledgments

I Got By with a Little Help from My Friends ...

I would not have been able to create this book, the website, and the materials that are part of this project without the help, support, and advice of some important people. Justice Warren Wolfson and Judge David Erickson — thank you. These two men started me on my path to becoming a trial lawyer over 15 years ago when they put me on a trial advocacy team and took an interest in me. After that, they let me teach at Chicago-Kent College of Law and supported me when I came up with the idea of teaching a Litigation Technology class. Their enthusiasm and encouragement gave this nonacademic guy the courage to take the chance to write this book.

I must thank Dean Harold Krent and Associate Dean Stephen Sowle of Chicago-Kent College of Law of the Illinois Institute of Technology for supporting my effort to get this job done. Their support and resources made this project possible.

I would not have been able to conceive of this project had it not been for my involvement with the National College of District Attorneys. I was introduced to the prospect of using computers at trial by Jim Dedman, a former prosecutor from Memphis who was kind to me and supportive of me, even though I was from Chicago. The other people at the college who supported me and encouraged me were Candace Mosley and Dean Robert Fertita, who kept letting me come back to teach at the college.

I have to thank Mike Hahan, Dan Bowen, and Carp from Verdict Systems for sharing their time and their insight into Sanction with me. I would like to add Bob Wiss and Julie Parker from CaseSoft to this list because they put me through the CaseSoft Academy so that I would understand their case management software and TimeMap.

I would also like to thank Joan Coppelson, Barbara Roth, and Lisa Wehrle. Joan is my mother-in-law and was my first read-through editor. Chapters did not go out to others until they had been Joaned. Barbara, my editor at Aspen, then helped me further refine the book. Lisa did the final round of editing and got the jokes.

Now I must thank the practitioners, judge, and former students who proofread, brainstormed, appeared in videos, did legal research, and otherwise helped me get this project done.

Thank you:

Dan McCarthy from the Bronx
The Honorable Robert Holdman from NYC
Jacqueline Seely from Monmouth County, NJ

From Chicago
Rosanne McDonnel, Esq.
Brian Sexton, ASA
Ljubica Popovic, ASA
Adam Webber, ASA
Peter Benesh
Mathew Hamuddeh
Ida Nasser
Anthony Lucaffo
Steven Mayfield
Shannon Gomery
Blair Dawson
Susan Song
Daniel Hanichak
Andrew Cherkasky
Amy D'Addario
Lilanna Kalin
Stacey Manning
Robert Windon
Jason Kang
Jamie Goldstein
Craig Lawless
Demetrius Kottaras, ASA
Raymond Brogan, ASA

Acknowledgments

I am also grateful to the following sources for granting permission to use their materials in this work:

CaseSoft, for Time Map screen shots. All screen shots of TimeMap are copyrighted and reproduced with CaseSoft's permission.

Craig Lawless, for screen captures of the PowerPoint slides illustrating baselining diagrams in Chapter 4. Reproduced with the author's permission.

National District Attorney's Association, for "Cross Preparation Worksheet" that appears in Chapter 5: Based on the National District Attorneys Association approach point method of cross-examination, copyright the National District Attorney's Association. Permission to publish was granted by the National District Attorneys Association, Education Division, National College of District Attorneys No further reproduction or dissemination is allowed without written authorization of the College. For additional information please go to http://www.law.sc.edu/ncda/publications.sts.htm.

National District Attorney's Association, for screen captures of the following slides that appear in Chapters 1 and 4: "The Evidence Surround," "The Defendant in the Bullseye," "The Defendant Is Cornered," "The Relationship Triangles," and "Animated Walk Through a Shop and Rob." Copyright the National District Attorney's Association. Permission to publish was granted by the National District Attorneys Association, Education Division, National College of District Attorneys. No further reproduction or dissemination is allowed without written authorization of the College. For additional information please go to http://www.law.sc.edu/ncda/publications.sts.htm.

Sanction, for Sanction screen shots. All screen shots of Sanction are copyrighted and reproduced with Sanction's permission.

Litigation Technology

Chapter 1

The Visual Trial

This book teaches you three skill sets. First, it teaches you how to think about trying cases with the assistance of technology. Knowing how to think about using technology is the most important skill set you will develop from reading this book. An attorney who understands how technology affects the trial also understands when not to use technology in the courtroom because it could distract or annoy jurors. You do not have to be a master at making presentations to understand how to use them in the courtroom. If you know what you want but do not have the ability or inclination to create the visual yourself, you can get help from others, such as paralegals, IT people, and consultants.

The next two skill sets this book teaches you are how to use linear presentations and nonlinear presentations. It introduces you to PowerPoint, TimeMap, and Sanction, some software packages that you will use at trial to create linear and nonlinear presentations. You will see that the most powerful trial presentations occur when you use these software packages in conjunction. Linear presentations are the kinds of presentations that PowerPoint and TimeMap create. Linear presentations move sequentially through the presentation by either sliding a toolbar along a continuum or by moving through a sequential set of slides.[1] Nonlinear software allows you to pull up on the screen images of documents, digital photographs, transcripts, and video clips without having to move from slide to slide. You can even use nonlinear software to launch linear presentations and then return to the nonlinear software. Nonlinear software can be used at every

[1] In PowerPoint, a presenter can create hyperlinks that allow the presenter to jump to a specific slide or slides and then move back and forth between those slides and a menu slide, but the presenter is still working within a limited series of slides. This type of presentation can work, but it takes an inordinate amount of time to prepare, which is a shame because nonlinear software is so easy to use. Smart lawyers learn to use Sanction and PowerPoint together.

aspect of the trial, although it is ideal for most direct examinations, cross-examinations, and reactive arguments. (Reactive arguments are addressed in Chapter 6.)

In this chapter, we explore the notion of the visual trial. This chapter teaches you when to use a linear presentation, when to use a nonlinear presentation, when to use both, and when to use none. Chapters 2-6 cover how to prepare and use both linear and nonlinear presentations at each trial stage. In Chapter 7, you learn how to use PowerPoint, and in Chapter 8, you are introduced to Sanction. Finally, in Chapter 9, you get advice for equipping yourself and the courtroom, as well as for participating in computer-assisted trials.

Without further delay, let's turn our attention to the visual trial.

A visual trial uses digital media. Digital media are simply materials that have been converted into a computer readable format — for example, digitized video, digitized audio, and electronic images of the documents, photographs, and other types of physical evidence you intend to introduce throughout the trial. To prepare for a visual trial, first scan all your documents, photographs, physical evidence, and anything else you might have. It is also wise to digitize your videotapes (turn them into a computer-readable format) and to get or create ASCII[2] text file copies of transcripts from court reporters or whomever else you rely on for these types of things. (If you are a technophobe, just new to the game, or frightened by the last sentence, the things listed there are discussed later in this book.) Once you have gathered your raw material in a computer-usable format, you are ready to shape it with your software tools.

Screen Capture of PowerPoint Multiple Slide View

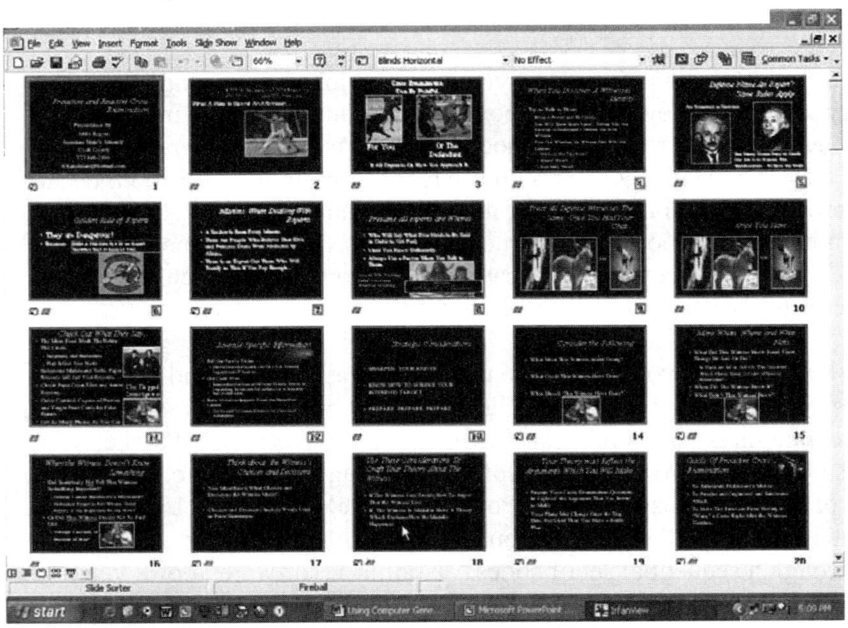

A linear presentation begins with slide 1 and moves sequentially through the slides until the last slide in the program has been shown.

The screen shot shows the multiple slide view of a PowerPoint presentation. Each slide looks like a thumbnail of the actual slide.

Linear presentations can be powerful if they are not interrupted.

---

[2] ASCII is an acronym for the American Standard Code for Information Interchange. Pronounced *ask-ee*, ASCII is a code for representing English characters as numbers, with each letter assigned a number from 0 to 127. For example, the ASCII code for uppercase M is 77. Most computers use ASCII codes to represent text, which makes it possible to transfer data from one computer to another. Court reporters often create their transcripts in ASCII text, which can be imported into Sanction and word searched.

Using Linear and Nonlinear Presentations

Ground Rules for Choosing Between Linear and Nonlinear Presentations

Linear slide presentation software is the ideal visual tool for opening statements, some types of direct examinations, and what we will call proactive closing arguments. Linear slide presentation software works best for presenting a choreographed presentation that is not likely to be interrupted or to involve an inexperienced witness. This is an important concept to embrace because linear software does not like to stop. Do not misunderstand. A presenter can stop the presentation, but doing that can interfere with the presenter's and the jury's concentration. Having to change a slide in the middle of a slide show and then resume, or having to stop the presentation altogether, can be disruptive if it has to be done in front of a jury.

The best way to avoid getting stopped in the middle of a linear presentation is to obtain a ruling on a motion in limine to be allowed to show your slide presentation. A motion in limine allows you to define the way that you will present evidence to the jury; it allows you to get a ruling on the motion before you put that information in front of the jury. Keep in mind that while you are arguing a motion in limine to introduce the presentation, you do not have to tell your opponent what you are going to say about the images in a presentation. You are simply showing the opposition and the court the slides and arguing that you have a good faith basis for showing them to the jury before any witnesses are called. Be prepared to tell the court that, during the trial, you will lay a foundation for the admissibility of the presentation images. The judge can rely on your assurance that you will lay a proper foundation and let you show the images to the jury, or the judge may choose to force you to authenticate the images. If you are forced to authenticate the images, then you will have to call witnesses to testify outside the presence of the jury to lay a foundation for the admission of the images. After a favorable ruling on a motion in limine, ask that your opponent be prohibited from interrupting your presentation in front of the jury since the issue has been preserved for appellate scrutiny. If your opponent objects to parts of your presentation outside the presence of the jury and the judge rules in your opponent's favor, then you should have an opportunity to make any changes to the offending slide or slides. If the presentation is barred absolutely, then you have created an appellate issue that may merit a reversal of an adverse jury verdict. If the judge rules that you must make a change to the presentation, then make the change and use your presentation. If the judge rules against your presentation in limine or mandates that you make changes to the presentation, ask that a copy of the presentation (burned onto a CD-ROM) be made a part of the record for appellate purposes. (Be prepared to renew your objection at the appropriate time during the trial.)

Although linear software is ideal for many aspects of a trial, certain aspects of every trial are better suited for a nonlinear presentation. Part of trial work is working with people who are not well suited to the witness stand. If you know that a witness is weak because he or she is forgetful or nervous, or you expect that the opposition will object frequently during a particular direct, then your computer-aided presentation should rely on nonlinear software or on software such as Sanction, which will allow you to launch a short linear slide presentation without presenting a full-blown slide presentation. For example, assume you are trying a civil rights case that involves, among other things, a witness's opportunity to observe the plaintiff while that individual is inside a store. One way to show a witness's vantage points for observation is to create a PowerPoint slide that shows the place in the store where the witness stood while watching the plaintiff. The movement of the plaintiff is recreated by creating a demonstrative slide that makes solid lines or shapes appear or move with animation effects on the slide. The animation symbolizes the plaintiff's path of travel within the store. This slide is actually a one-slide presentation that you can launch from the Sanction desktop with only a few keystrokes. Sit down with the witness before he or she testifies and create the slide together. Now the witness will be able to testify that he or she helped to create this piece of demonstrative evidence to show the jurors what happened. The witness can authenticate the slide by explaining how he or she helped to create the slide for demonstrative purposes. Once the witness has authenticated the slide, he or she may then testify about the information on it, and when the slide show ends, the computer returns to the black screen of the Sanction desktop, without drawing the jury's attention to the things that the computer did to launch the presentation. After that, the attorney can launch other exhibits that are simply digital images or other types of files without having to jump back and forth between the two programs.

There are also times when you should absolutely not use multimedia presentation during a trial. Using technology for technology's sake is foolish. Assume you have a wife of a decedent in a medical malpractice case who is going to testify about her last moments with her husband. Assume she and her husband came to the hospital because the husband was suffering from abdominal pain, and that a resident prescribed a lethal dose of medication that killed the man. This witness's demeanor and testimony will hold a jury's attention without any technology. It would be a mistake to flash images of the husband on the screen while the widow talks. A jury likely would find such images to be gratuitous or distracting if they were trying to observe and listen to the witness while also attending to the television monitor. After the witness has relayed her account, you could perhaps show the image of the man, but that too requires a careful judgment call on your part.

There may be other times when technology is especially important for the trial. For instance, an expert witness may use a timeline created by PowerPoint or TimeMap to underscore significant documents that appear in the decedent's chart. A blood gas report that explains what drugs were in the decedent's system before he was poisoned will make more sense to the jury during the direct examination of an expert witness if the expert can put the blood gas report into the context of time. The desire to use technology at trial must be tempered by this consideration: Does the technology help the case or hurt it?

Let's next address using linear and nonlinear presentations.

Ground Rules for Using Linear Presentations

A linear slide presentation can help or hurt a courtroom presentation. There is a right way and a wrong way to use linear software. Use a linear presentation the right way, and the jury sees the presenter as a trustworthy teacher. Use a linear presentation the wrong way, and the jurors are likely to become confused, or, worse, they may use the presentation as an excuse to find against the presenter. Does the prospect of defeating yourself with your own weapon frighten you? It should. That prospect should frighten *every* lawyer. Remember this rule: "Thou shalt not commit bad PowerPoint."

What is good PowerPoint? Good PowerPoint is a presentation that informs without drawing undue attention to itself. The best way to analyze good PowerPoint is to break down slides into their various components. (This chapter and others can be obtained in a .pdf format from the Litigation Technology website at www.littech.org. This format allows you to see this book's images in glorious color without having to bear the cost of purchasing a page printed in color.)

What is bad PowerPoint? You will know it when you see it. Bad PowerPoint fails to persuade or, worse, advocates against a position that a presenter is trying to take. Imagine being bombarded by slide after slide of pure text with print that is too small to read. Think of how tedious a presentation can be when the presenter simply repeats the information that is on the screen. Imagine watching a presentation in which the presenter talks at length but fails to advance his or her slides to keep up with the talk. The possible ways to torture a jury or audience with PowerPoint are limitless.

Considering color and the way it affects viewers

Begin developing your presentation with slide backgrounds. Everything that you add to a slide happens in front of the background. If the background does not contrast with text or lines that are placed on the slide, the information is hard to see and so gets lost. If you are going to project your slide or work with a big screen television on a cart, then you should use a dark slide background. Lots of white space on the screen or on a television monitor hurts jurors' eyes if they must look at it for a long time. It has much the same effect as looking directly at a light bulb. A dark background, on the other hand, is easy on the eyes. Use background colors like black, dark blue, dark brown, or dark green when projecting an image or when using a big screen television. There is another, almost primal reason for using dark backgrounds on slides: Dark background colors are the colors of chalkboards that the jurors grew up with. Think back to your grade school chalkboard. It was dark because the chalk was white or yellow. The contrast of the light text against the dark background shaped your education; it shaped your worldview. Capitalize on this. A dark background for a slide sends the message that you, the lawyer, and the witnesses are teachers. It says you are people who should be trusted because the colors you use for your presentation are the colors that the jurors were conditioned to get information from during childhood.

Dark green, deep blue, dark brown, or black are perfect backgrounds for slide presentations.

Light-colored text stands out extremely well against a dark background.

Once the dark background color is selected, pick text and line colors that contrast with it. Remember: Color combinations that look fine on a desktop or laptop computer screen may be too dark when they are projected or presented on a large screen television.

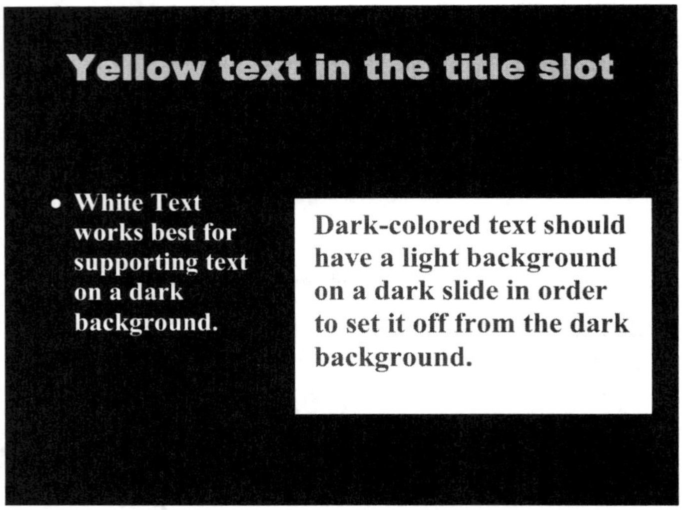

Text is most effective when it contrasts with its background.

Sometimes the lack of contrast does not become apparent until the attorney sees the image on the actual screen that the jury will see.

For this reason, make sure to dry run all presentations before showing them to a jury.

Do not use black text on a dark blue background; it is too hard to see. Similarly, a cream-colored box on a beige or brown background slide does not contrast well; the cream color appears very dim. Beige lines or text have the same effect when placed on a slide with a hunter green background. The beige-green combination may look nice on an Eddie Bauer edition Ford truck, but it disappears on a large screen.

Beige on hunter green or beige on cream are examples of bad color contrast. The beige does not have sufficient contrast to the background.

Selecting an appropriate font and font size

Fonts are the array of typeface styles in which a computer displays text. Before you put words on a screen, consider how long the slide will be in front of the jury. Different people read and comprehend at different speeds; if you are going to use words on a slide, use them sparingly or take into account the fact that the jurors will need time to read the slide. If you decide to put words on a slide, then use a font that is persuasive. A font is persuasive when it conveys information quickly and efficiently. Different fonts work with different types of messages. Long messages need one type of font, and short messages need a different type of font. So what type of font should you use? There are two types of fonts that you should use in presentations. The serif font is best suited for long sentences and paragraphs, and the sans serif font is effective for highlighting individual words or short phrases. A serif is a decorative element of a letter that makes it easier to read when it is in a sentence or paragraph.

Look at this letter: E ← Note the decorative strokes that finish the ends of the lines that make up the letter E. Those decorative elements are serifs. The serif font shown in the E (and in the main text in this book) is Times New Roman.

Now look at this letter: E This E does not have the decorative strokes. This font is the sans serif Arial.

When showing sentences on a visual, use the font of the local newspaper for jurisdiction where you are trying a case. That font is, after all, the font that the majority of jurors in the jurisdiction are used to reading when they get their daily information. "Literate jurors" who read newspapers are conditioned to "trust" the font of the local paper as a legitimate source of information. You can take advantage of this conditioning.

You can find different fonts for your visuals when you open the toolbar for Formatting in PowerPoint.

These are some of the fonts that are available for use in PowerPoint slides.

They appear in the Formatting toolbar.

The available fonts are in a drop-down menu that is activated when you click on this icon.

Later in the book you will learn to make custom toolbars in order to better navigate and control PowerPoint. Chapter 7 on using PowerPoint begins with an explanation for making a custom toolbar.

Present sentences, jury instructions, and longer quotations in serif text. Below are some examples of serif fonts that read easily on a text-heavy slide.

This book is written in Times New Roman.

Courier is the type of font that is commonly found in type-writers.

This font is Baskerville Old Face.

This font is Garamond.

This font is Book Antiqua.

Use sans serif fonts when the word itself is the message that you want to send to the jury. For example, assume you have evidence showing that an individual gave a number of inconsistent statements. Assume each statement was a lie or an attempt to obfuscate an investigation. To present your theory about these lies, you may want the word *manipulator* up on the screen while talking about an individual's attempt to obfuscate or deceive others. The message is conveyed with one word.

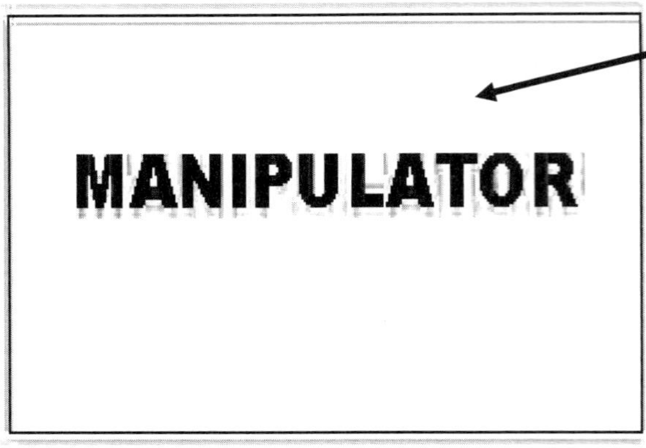

Use Arial font to annotate photos or to take center stage in a slide. It is bold and demands attention.

If this word looms on the screen while you are arguing to the jury about the credibility of a witness, then you are using a single word to encourage the jurors to draw a conclusion about that person.

Four score and seven years ago, our fathers brought forth, upon this continent, a new nation, conceived of liberty, and dedicated to the proposition that "all men are created equal."

Do not use Arial if you are going to place a lot of text on the screen. For a lot of text, use the serif font that resembles your local newspaper.

This is the first line from the first draft of Abraham Lincoln's Gettysburg address. It appears in the Times New Roman font.

Consider how your text appears on a screen. Generally a font size smaller than 32 points is too small to see clearly on a television monitor. With a 32-point size font as the minimum size to use for a slide, consider how much that will limit the amount of information you can put on a slide. There are 46 spaces across a PowerPoint slide when using a 32-point font size. You can fit seven bullet points onto a slide at 46 characters wide before PowerPoint will default to the next smaller font of 28 points.

Some fonts or capitalization styles can alienate jurors and should be avoided in presentations. Some are hard to read, and some contain visual elements that can distract certain readers. People who have dyslexia or other visual impediments are quickly frustrated with the "wrong fonts." Have you ever read a document or statement that was in all capitals? It is difficult to read, not to mention annoying. People who have problems with reversals (people whose brains switch letters around in words) will find reading all capital letters to be an even more frustrating experience. Other people dislike swirling or garish fonts and may resent you for forcing them to look at these. Using any one of these fonts or capitalization styles puts you at risk for alienating a juror who suffers from these disabilities; it may even turn that juror against you, your argument, and your client.

Sans serif text like Arial does not have the hooks and swirls mentioned above, but can be difficult to read in long sentences or paragraphs. For example, look at the visual with the black background that has the line "Yellow text in the title slot." That line is in the Arial font. It is visually separated from the rest of the text on the slide by black space. A short phrase in Arial has authority. It has authority because it is the font used in street signs. If a slide contains a lot of text, say, a long quotation or passage, the authority of the sans serif face is diminished. Arial is easy to read if it gives "short bursts" of information, such as the text seen through a car windshield as the viewer travels toward the sign. A wordy sign in Arial is hard to read in a long sentence because Ariel lacks the serifs that provide a kind of visual flow between the letters of the words.

Here are examples of fonts that should not be used in presentations because they are distracting:

This is Bernhard FashionBl.

This is Comic Sans MS.

THIS IS ALGERIAN.

This is Allegro BT.

This is Bernard MT Condensed.

This is Blackadder ITC.

By this time, you get the point. Save the fancy text for people who has time to decipher your notes on their own time.

Capitalization can also defeat a visual. ALL CAPITAL LETTERS in a long passage are also hard for most people to read, as are sentences that Capitalize Each Word In A Sentence. All capital letters also can mean "SHOUTING" to people who use text messaging or who are frequent computer chat room visitors. Capital letters in a phrase are fine for emphasis or for titles, but if they appear in each slide, capitalization loses its impact and can even become distracting.

Avoiding wordiness and visual clutter

Once you have selected your colors and your font, make a conscious effort to avoid killing your message with text because wordiness and visual clutter can affect a slide presentation adversely. As a trial lawyer, you have good oral skills. Let your slides enhance your verbal presentation, not duplicate or substitute for it. The purpose of your slide presentation is to corroborate your story, to illustrate a point, or to orient the jury to time or place. Use your slides to explain timelines or to illustrate connections between witnesses and evidence. Put bullet points on a slide to give your jury a checklist of facts or conclusions that they can copy down and use throughout the course of the trial. Avoid showing a large number of slides that contain paragraphs of information. Slides filled with text are hard for groups to read and retain when the slides are projected on a screen or presented on a video monitor for a limited amount of time. And jurors who are concentrating on reading all your text are not listening to all your words. So use these types of slides sparingly. If your proof absolutely demands the use of paragraphs or complex charts as trial visuals, then consider presenting the jury with an exhibit book that contains copies of the documents. This exhibit book can be admitted into evidence and can contain the printed paragraphs or other complex exhibits. With an exhibit book, jurors may review the exhibits and read at their own speed. Jurors will want to read ahead, so ask the judge to order the jurors not to look through the book until they are instructed to look at it.

Cutting the amount of text on the screen does not mean you should dumb down a presentation. Indeed, the object of this book is to help you to create smarter, more compelling presentations.

Ground Rules for Using Nonlinear Slide Presentations

A number of types of nonlinear software are available. This book teaches you to use Sanction, a software program that is sold by Verdict Systems. Go to www.sanction.com to download a fully functioning version of Sanction and test it yourself. The software launches 30 times before you have to buy it. Or, if you are a student who is taking a litigation technology class, have your professor verify this information for the company in order to get an extended license.

Sanction includes many useful features. Imagine you are doing a direct examination of a witness. Assume the witness decides to talk about details regarding the scene that you had not anticipated; however, these details are relevant and helpful to your case. With Sanction, you can simply call an aerial photograph or a scene photograph to the desktop and then let the witness mark the photograph with an electronic pen. An electronic pen is a pen used with art or graphics software. It allows you to make lines and markings on a computer screen with a great deal of control. Think of the electric pen as the kind of telestrator that is used on *Monday Night Football* to mark plays on the video screen. You can do the same thing with documents. You can zoom in on any portion of the document or photo and then highlight, annotate, or put a box around it, as you please. You can show an image of a document on one side of the screen and then a photograph or other exhibit referred to by the document on the other side of the screen.

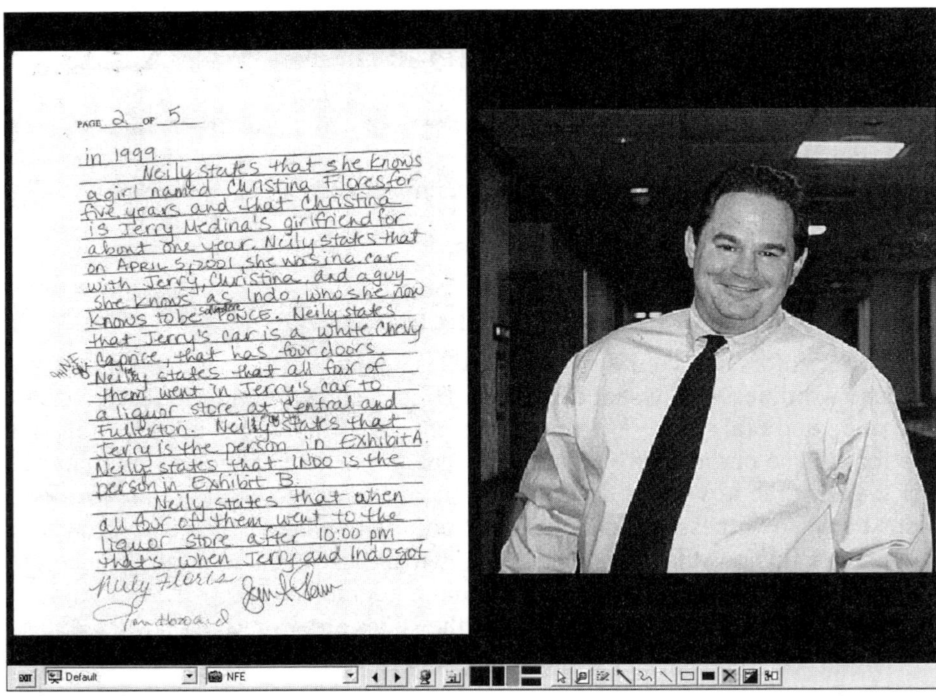

The document on the left side of this screen capture is the first page of an individual's handwritten statement. In Presentation mode in Sanction, the document image can be on one side of the screen and a photo, video clip, or other document image may be placed on the screen.

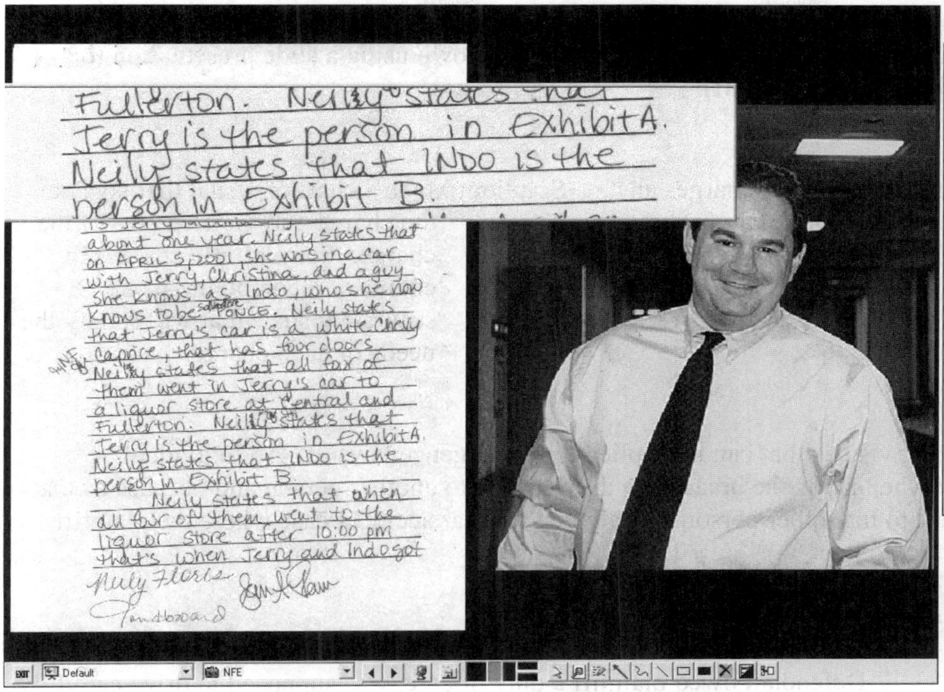

The callout box that appears on top of the document can be produced with the zoom function of Sanction. This controls the jury's focus while showing where the information is found in the original document.

Sanction is excellent for presenting digitized video evidence in a courtroom. Most of us think of videotape as linear. While an analog videotape is linear in that it begins at the beginning of the tape, moves through the middle, and ends at the end of the tape, *digitized video is not linear:* It may be started at any point without needing to play through the entire video. A digitized video allows a presenter to jump around within the video without having to wait for the videotape recorder to advance or rewind the tape. Sanction has a video clip feature that allows the trial lawyer to make custom clips that can be played in any order.

You can begin with any digital video, synchronize it with a transcript, and then create video clips based on the transcript. Each video clip can be coded so that it can be called to the screen with either a keystroke or with a toolbar. You can also use the Dual Monitor feature and literally drag the clip from the desktop to the presentation desktop. (Either of these methods is actually faster ways to launch an object than using a bar code scanner.) This feature allows a trial lawyer to control every word that comes out of a hostile witness's mouth. Simply tell the witness what he or she said during the video and play the clip if the witness equivocates or disagrees.

Another feature of Sanction allows you to call up from within the Sanction desktop an entire PowerPoint presentation or individual PowerPoint slides that are launched at different times as you address the jury. This capability means that you never have to shuttle back and forth between software programs in front of the jury. Simply type in the keystrokes to call up the slide or the full-blown presentation, and Sanction runs the presentation.

Deciding What Kinds of Visual Problems You Need to Solve

What follows are a number of problems that can arise for attorneys trying to explain things in their trials. Next to the problem is a solution that uses linear and nonlinear presentations.

One effective approach to developing a presentation is to decide what kind of visual problem needs to be solved. Any of the following visuals can be shown using a slide presentation (or, of course, a piece of paper or a flip chart).

Problem: How can I explain what charges an individual faces or explain the counts alleged in a complaint?

Solution: Make a chart or visual that lays out the charge and the elements of the charge. For multiple charges or counts of a complaint, make separate visuals that will satisfy the needs of each charge.

Look at the following visuals that can be applied to a negligence lawsuit. An individual is negligent for a tort when he or she breaches a duty of care to another person and because of that breach causes injury to that other person. Apply that to a car accident case where the plaintiff gets rear ended in a collision.

Negligence

Defendant owed plaintiff a duty of care: was supposed to drive carefully and attentively.

Defendant breached the duty of care: failed to keep a lookout while driving down the street.

Defendant proximately caused plaintiff's injury: defendant drove into the rear of plaintiff's car as plaintiff waited to turn right.

Damages suffered as a result of defendant's actions: lost wages, medical bills, pain and suffering.

The above negligence visual breaks up a paragraph into separate elements for a negligence argument. To turn this section into a visual checklist, simply put a box next to each point and check them off as you argue them.

☐ Defendant owed plaintiff a duty of care: was supposed to drive carefully and attentively.

☐ Defendant breached the duty of care: failed to keep a look out while driving down the street.

☐ Defendant proximately caused plaintiff's injury: drove into the rear of plaintiff's car as plaintiff waited to turn right.

☐ Damages suffered as a result of defendant's actions: lost wages, medical bills, pain and suffering.

Another way to create this visual is to split the slide in half by putting a vertical line down the middle. On the left side of the line, list the legal requirement; on the right side of the line, have the fact that satisfies the requirement appear. When you show this to the jury as a slide presentation, you set the order of animation so that the legal requirement appears first and then the factual satisfaction of the legal requirement appears on the next mouse click. Finally, a check mark appears in the box on the next mouse click.

☑	Owed a duty of care	Defendant was supposed to drive carefully and attentively.
☑	Breached the duty of care	Defendant failed to keep a lookout while driving down the street.
☑	Caused plaintiff's injury	Defendant drove into the rear of plaintiff's car as plaintiff waited to turn right.
☑	Damages suffered as a result	Lost wages, medical bills, pain and suffering.

Problem: How do I make a forensic scientist's testimony interesting for a jury?

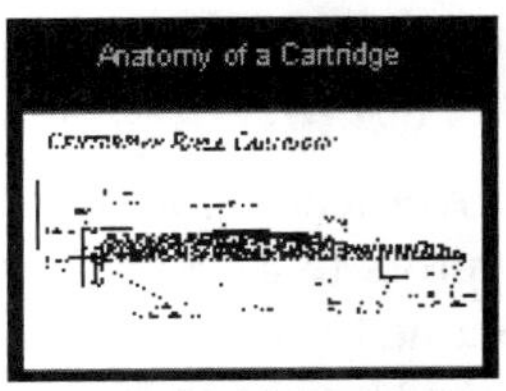

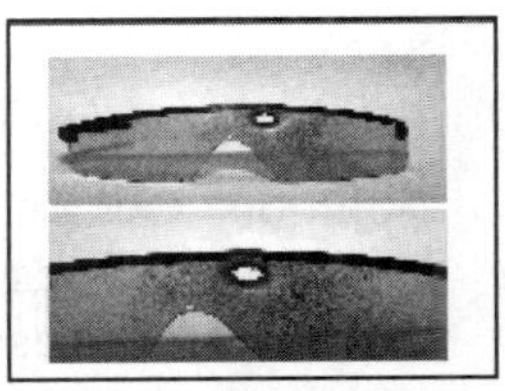

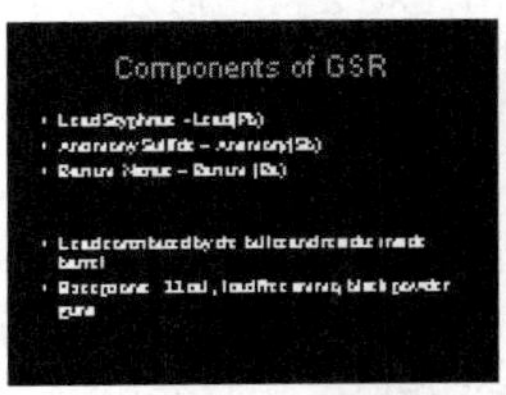

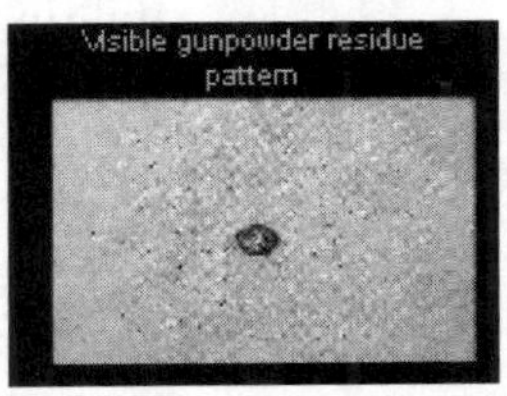

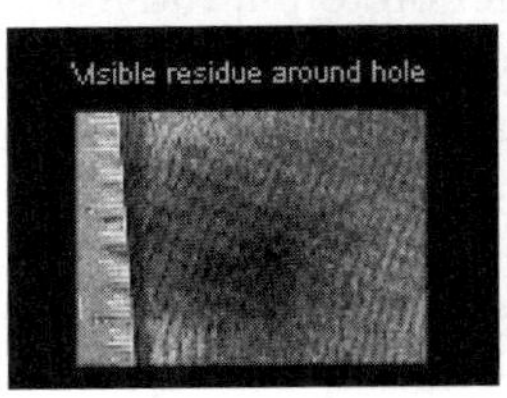

These are slides that were created to explain gunshot residue evidence to a jury. Look at how the slides illustrate the science.

Solution: Forensic science evidence is often hard for jurors to grasp. Think of ways to supplement an expert witness's testimony with graphics that define terms and help explain the science. Ask yourself how you will make witnesses with deficits or problems make sense. How will you explain complicated concepts? Will you create a slide presentation that your expert witness can use to educate the jury about terms that are relevant to his or her opinions? Will you have your expert build his or her opinion before the jury by having the expert use a slide that continues to add images to the master slide as he or she explains each aspect of the opinion? How can you use presentation software to create chronologies that do not confuse or bore jurors"?

Problem: How can I underscore a key clause in a contract dispute case? For example: On page 5 of the contract at the middle of the dispute, there is the pivotal clause in the dispute, "Clause 40." How can you make that clause important in the juror's minds?

Solution: You could simply put the clause on a slide and talk about it. But, without showing the context of this type of floating clause within the document, you risk causing jurors to distrust you. The best way to show this clause is to tell the jurors that they will be learning all about clause number 40, which is on page 5 of this contract. Show the jurors a scanned page of the first page of the contract bearing the appropriate exhibit number using Sanction or PowerPoint. Next tell them that you are moving to page 5 of the contract. Show page 5. Either use Sanction to create an instant callout of the page or use PowerPoint to make a red box around the clause on the fifth page. Then show the exact text of the clause with an enlarged image. Jurors will see for themselves and will have no doubt about your veracity.

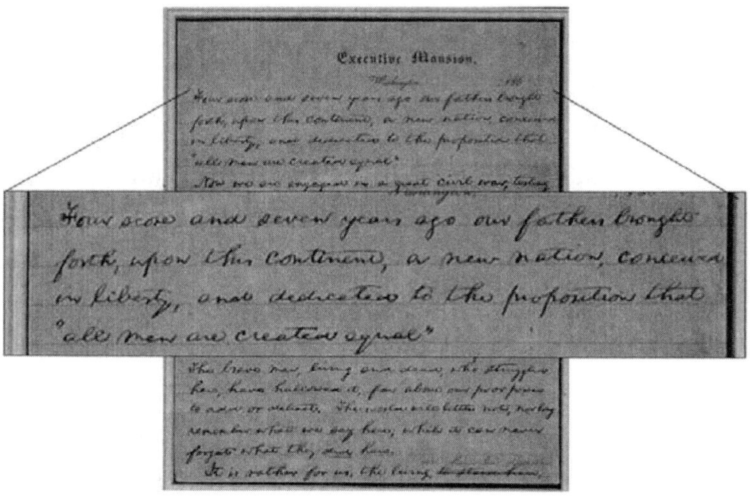

This is the Gettysburg address with a callout button that appears to wipe out from the first page of Lincoln's draft.

The lines show the jurors where the sentence comes from on the page.

Problem: How do I explain where events take place to simplify a story about action that occurred in different places?

Solution: Get a map or overhead photo that orients your jurors to a scene. These are easily obtained from the Internet. Now use a shape like a triangle to show how the photo corresponds with the map. Use a text box and a block arrow to show where another place is on the map. Put these on a PowerPoint slide and then use Sanction to put the image on one side of the screen and show the other image on the other side, or use PowerPoint to create the same effect.

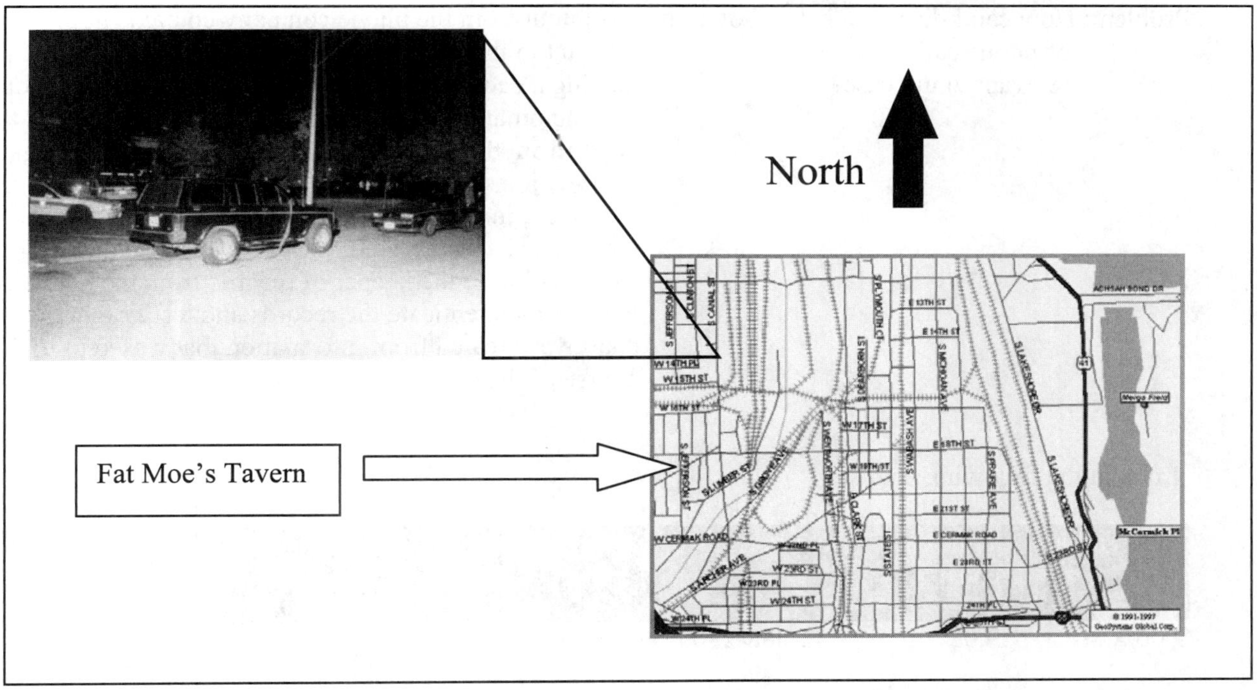

Problem: How do I help the jury keep the players straight? Multiple individuals are relevant to the story.

Solution: Make an organizational chart showing a photo of each individual and listing each person's name, role in the case, and any other relevant information. Make a PowerPoint slide and launch it with Sanction.

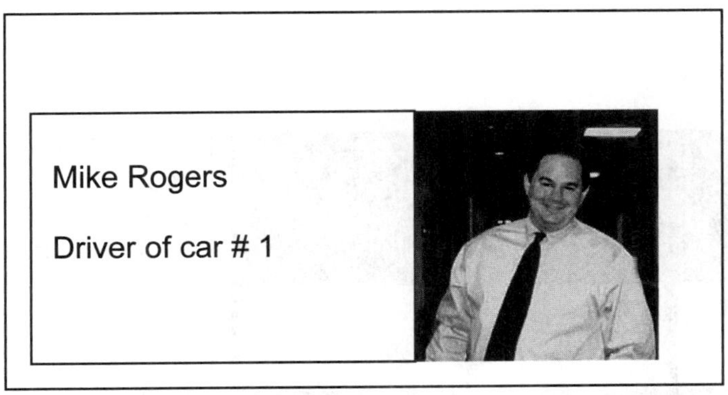

If you create this type of visual, you must have some witness during your trial be able to testify about the accuracy of the information on the chart.

Consider organizing information into tables or other visuals that will make the information easy to understand.

Problem: How can I display a list of phone calls that are relevant to my case?

Solution: A printout from the phone company contains information that is relevant to the phone company but of little relevance to a jury making a decision. The records can be used as the foundation for a summary chart that distills the information that the jury needs from the phone records. Make a table that organizes the information, decide which information is relevant to the issue before the jury, and put only that information into the visual. Once the chart is created, it can be introduced during the examination of the keeper of records from the phone company, who will authenticate the records and testify that the summary chart was created from information that was kept in the ordinary course of the phone company's business.

Look at the following charts.

Time call is made	Time call ends	Number called	Length of call	Third party call brought in?
9:00 A.M.	9:02	312-588-2300	2 mins	No
9:25	9:40	312-588-2300	15 mins	Yes 312-555-1212
10:15	10:20	312-588-2300	5 mins	No
11:00	12:05	312-588-2300	65 mins	No

TIME CALL IS MADE	TIME CALL ENDS	NUMBER CALLED	LENGTH OF CALL	THIRD PARTY CALL BROUGHT IN?
9:00 A.M.	**9:02**	**312-588-2300**	**2 mins**	**No**
9:25	**9:40**	**312-588-2300**	**15 mins**	**Yes 312-555-1212**
10:15	**10:20**	**312-588-2300**	**5 mins**	**No**
11:00	**12:05**	**312-588-2300**	**65 mins**	**No**

This first chart has no visual competition.

This allows an observer to think about and absorb the information readily.

Now look at the next chart.

Why is the second chart more annoying than the first? The second chart is full of chart junk. The font is ugly and hard to read. The underlining and borders around the sections of the table are visually busy and constitute undesirable distractions.

Using Tables to Explain Complex Sets of Facts

Tables are excellent visuals for explaining evidence that fits into a F.R.E. 404(b) other crimes or conduct motion. A 404(b) motion allows a proponent to introduce other crimes or conduct offered to show identity, intent, modus operandi, common design, absence of mistake, motive, and so on. In the following figure, the first column shows the charged crime, and the columns to the right apply to the other cases or factual situations that are being introduced under F.R.E. 404(b). The top cell of each column labels the type of evidence that appears in the cells below it.

Charged case	Pre-mortem conduct — Victims who survived defendant's attack	Post-mortem conduct — Defendant's other murder victims
Victim's hands bound at the wrists.	Defendant binds victims' hands in front of their bodies, as he tries to control them.	Victim's hands are bound at the wrists.
Victim's hands pulled over her head.	Victim got away.	Victim's hands pulled over her head.
Victim's body posed with legs spread, pants at the ankles, hands above her head.	Defendant tells victim he wants to see her naked.	Victim's body posed, legs spread, pants off, hands above her head.
Victim's vagina mutilated by stick or other found object.	Defendant tells victim he's going to tear her up.	Victim's vagina mutilated by tent pole.

This information is organized to underscore F.R.E. 404(b) or other crimes evidence to show an individual's modus operandi. Phrases are repeated to underscore the message that the defendant's method of treating his victims is the same. There are no borders around these columns for a reason. The observer's brain is now allowed to do the organizing of the information. An exhibit like this should be used during opening statement, closing argument, or both.

Using Bullet Points to Break Up Text

Another way to break up blocks of text into a visually appealing format is to divide complex thoughts and concepts into bullet points. Bullet points act as headings for jurors. They impose order on language and give a natural sequence to each point. Your bullet points should be the main points of your slide. The main point can be numbered, and the subpoints can be marked with a shape or dot. The bullet points function as a visual checklist as you talk about the things that apply to each bullet point. In jurisdictions that allow jurors to take notes, tell the jurors to write down the bullet items so they will be able to use them as a checklist when they analyze the evidence in the case. Below is the language from the Illinois Pattern Jury Instruction for Accountability. The first box shows the instruction as it reads; the next box contains the same language broken into bullet points. Notice how much easier the bullet points are to comprehend.

Illinois Pattern Jury Instruction for Accountability

> A person is legally responsible for the conduct of another person when, either before or during the commission of an offense, and with the intent to promote or facilitate the commission of an offense, he knowingly solicits, aids, abets, agrees to aid, or attempts to aid the other person in the planning or commission of an offense.
>
> The word "conduct" includes any criminal act done in furtherance of the planned and intended act.

> A person is legally responsible for the conduct of another person:
>
> 1. When, either before or during the commission of an offense,
> 2. And with the intent to
>   - Promote or
>   - Facilitate the commission of the offense,
> 3. He knowingly
>   - Solicits,
>   - Aids,
>   - Abets,
>   - Agrees to aid, or
>   - Attempts to aid the other person
> 4. In the planning or commission of an offense.
>
> (The word "conduct" includes any criminal act done in furtherance of the planned and intended act.)

Presenting this instruction in an argument is simple to do. Show the jury the first box so the jury knows what the law looks like, and then go the next box and break down the instruction. If you come from a jurisdiction where the judge does not give out a written copy of the instruction, skip publishing the first box.

Here is another way to animate the accountability instruction. Simply animate different words and phrases of the instruction so that you can explain the instruction in parts and then add more information as you progress through the explanation. So the first part of the sentence — "A person is legally responsible for the conduct of another person when, either before or during the commission of an offense" — would appear on the screen for you to explain how it applies to the facts of the case. After you have finished talking about that point, you would click your mouse and the next clause — "and with the intent to promote or facilitate the commission of an offense, he knowingly" — would appear on the screen for you to talk about.

Using Symbols with Text

You can eliminate even more text by using familiar images and symbols to replace text.

This symbol means stop: 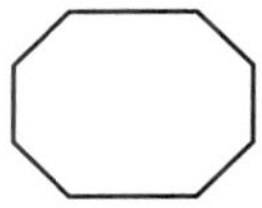 This symbol means don't: 

Check out the various shapes and symbols that can be placed on a slide. Go to the Draw menu at the bottom of your PowerPoint desktop.

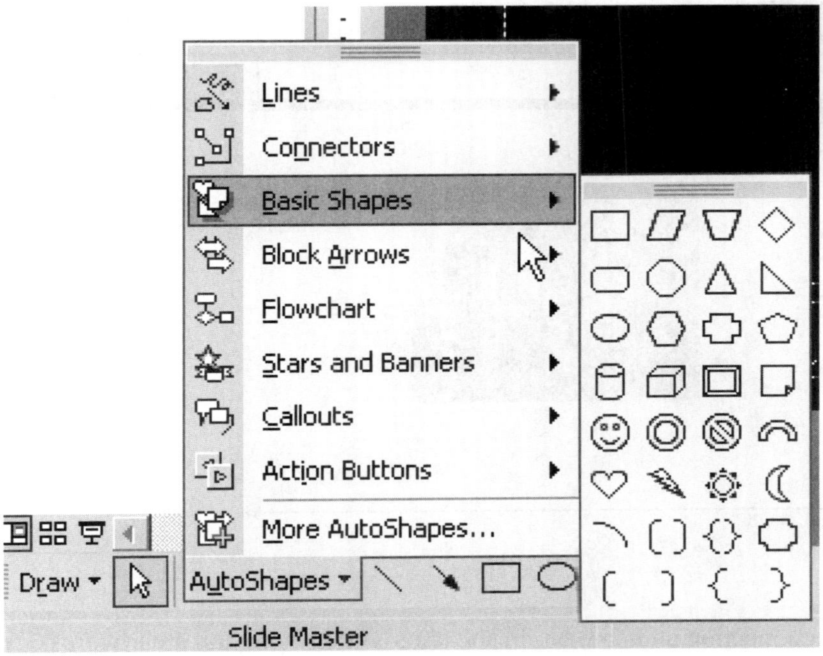

Under the Basic Shapes menu from the AutoShapes menu, you can find universal road sign symbols and other shapes that can be placed on a screen.

You can use the triangle shape to create a relationship triangle by positioning a photo of the defendant and another person, place, or thing at the other points of the triangle. Then list the facts that connect the person, place, or thing to the defendant.

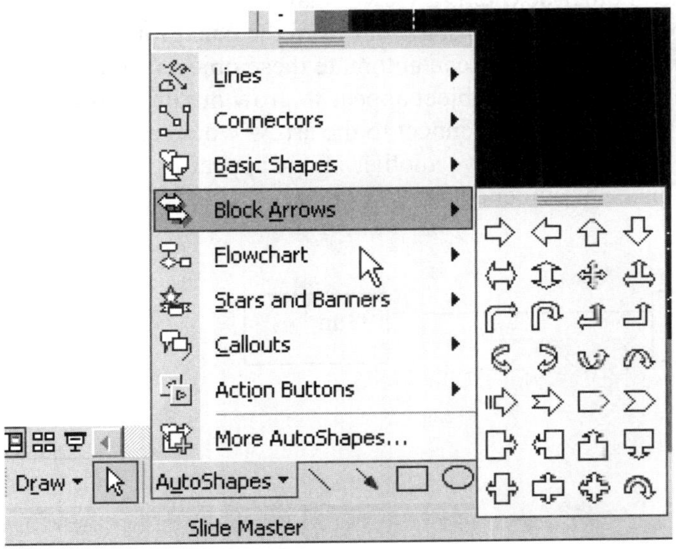

Block arrows from the same AutoShapes menu are excellent devices for annotating photographs. The top rows of block arrows work well to show directions or connections between individuals or places.

The bottom two rows of the block arrows have boxes that can be expanded so you can insert text in the arrows. You can place a series of these block arrows in a row and then animate them to show a progression of ideas, activities, or elements from a jury instruction.

Combining symbols and other concepts to create lasting impressions

We have been conditioned to understand that symbols, lines, arrows, and shapes emphasize specific information in the slide. Underlining tells a reader that the text is important. This is important!

An arrow next to a photograph sends the message, “Pay attention to this particular object.” An arrow between two dates says that events occurred chronologically. An arrow that has thumbnail photographs connotes connections between different places and chronology.

The attorney can explain the connection and context for the photographs with his or her words.

A box around a word, with a line drawn to another box, tells a viewer that there is a connection between the two boxes. The lines must be thick enough to stand out from the background and must be in colors that contrast from the background. You can automate these objects so they wipe left, right, up, or down. The wipe effect makes the object appear to grow out of another object. In the image above, the photos and the lines that connect to the arrow would appear to grow up from the arrow when animated. You can then have another image appear right at the base of the arrow to show the source of a piece of evidence.

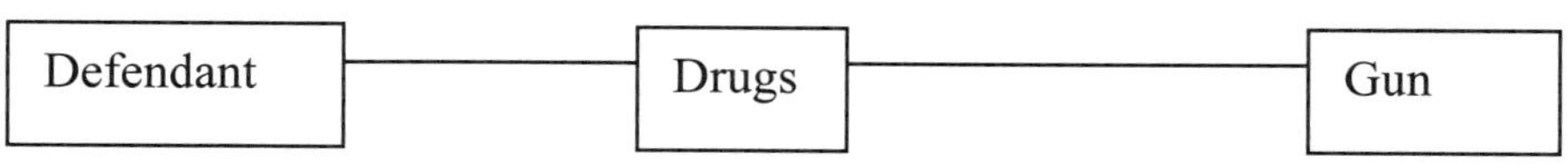

Making "the evidence points to" visuals

Perhaps you need a device that illustrates a concept of a defendant or party's culpability or innocence. Use shapes like arrows, circles, squares, and boxes to create visual analogies. The following visuals were developed by Jim Dedman from the National College of District Attorneys. Note how the defendant or party is literally surrounded. The defendant's name or photo is placed in the middle of the visual with arrows and evidence characterization placed all around the defendant.

What happens if you turn the arrows in the opposite direction? How does that change the visual message? If you are a defense lawyer in a criminal case, you may want to show a visual that has the arrow pointing at other witnesses and away from the defendant. These are things you must consider as you get ready to create your visual.

"All Evidence Points to…" Visual

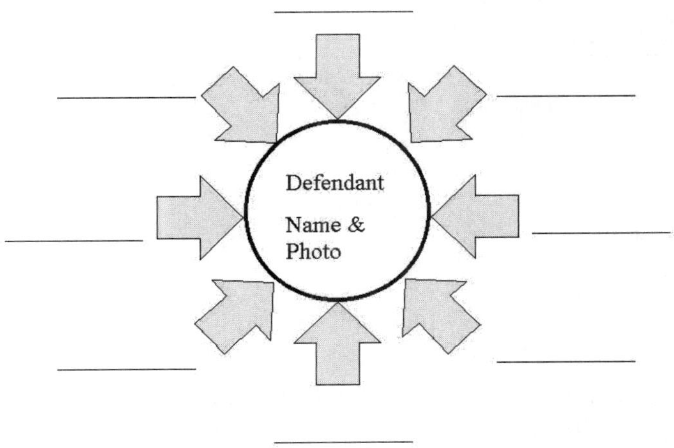

You can insert words, phrases, or photos on the lines behind the arrows.

Simply point the arrows in the opposite directions and the evidence does not point to the defendant.

Visually cornering a party

In the figure below, the defendant or party is cornered. By placing the defendant's name or photo in the corner of the document with the evidence cornering the defendant, you show the jury that the defendant is surrounded by his or her guilt.

A plaintiff or a prosecutor now has the defendant physically cornered by the evidence that has been admitted.

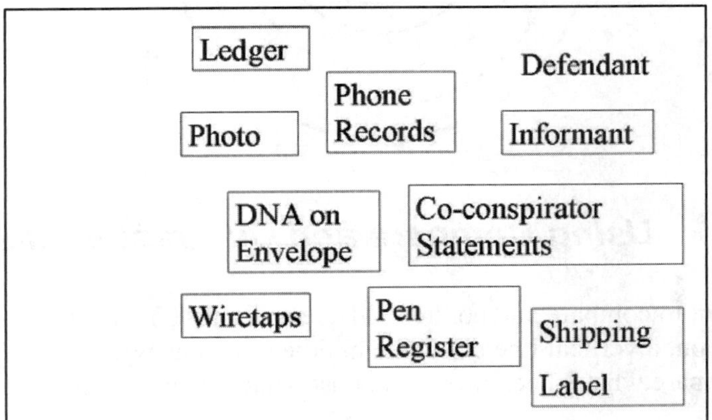

"Surrounded or cornered Visual"

Using relationship triangles

Maybe you need to show that a defendant or party is connected to a place, person, or thing and another place, person, or thing. Make a triangle, and then put a photo of the defendant or witness at one point of the triangle. Next, list facts on the sides of the triangle that link the individual to other objects, places, or people, as shown below.

A triangle is an excellent visual for connections. The shape is appealing and it connects the pieces in a way that makes visual sense. You can place a photo of the connected object, person, or thing at each point of the triangle.

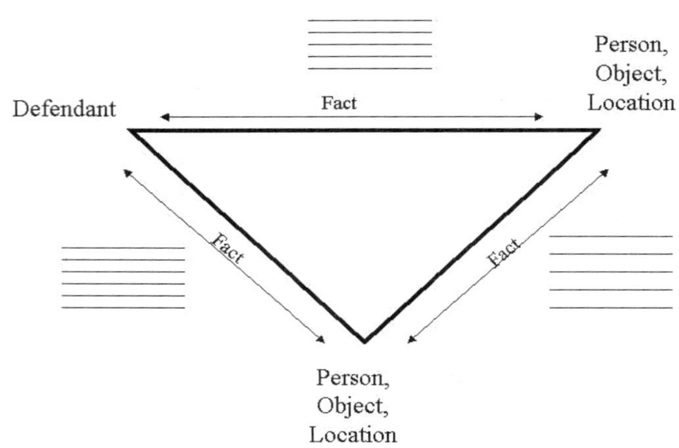

Typical Relationship Triangle

Put a photo of a defendant or a party in the middle of a bull's-eye, and then list the facts with corresponding arrows that point to the circle of the bull's-eye that surround the defendant.

Target Visual

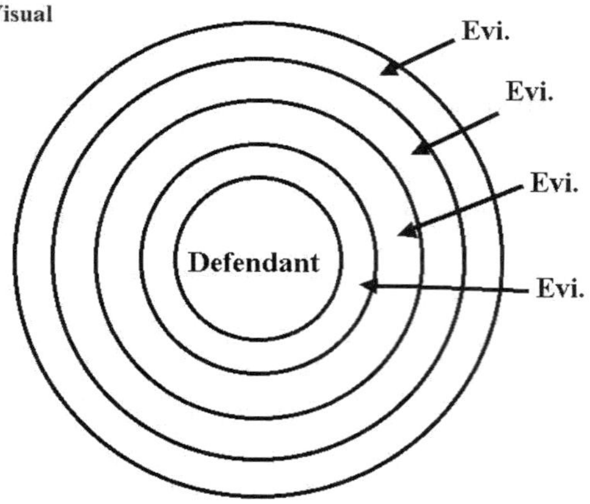

Placing an individual's photo in the center of the target is another way of surrounding the individual.

Using Compare and Contrast Visuals

Want to compare and contrast different visuals? You can achieve this in a number of ways. You can put a vertical line down the middle of a page with lists on each side of the line. You can then compare what's been proven against what's been charged.

Things we know about the thief:	Things we know about Murray Mope:
Was familiar with the business.	Worked at the store for three years as the assistant manager.
Had access to the safe.	Knew the safe combination and had been seen putting cash into and taking cash from the safe.
Entered the store after 9:00 P.M., when the store had closed.	Is seen standing in the shadows across the street around closing time at 9:00 P.M. by Pricilla Prim.
Got away with $50,000.	Bought a $30,000 car with cash. Paid off $15,000 in credit card debt with money orders bought with cash.

Controlling the Jury's Attention Without Being Obvious

Ever sit through the telling of a joke when the joke teller has already told you the punch line? That is what jurors feel like when a lawyer puts new information up on a screen and then talks about something else leading up to it. Given the opportunity, people read ahead. When they do, they lose your point because they have stopped paying attention to what you are saying. If you display text before you're ready to discuss it, jurors are likely to read it while you're talking about something else and perhaps then take the text out of context or draw false conclusions about it. The communication process is thus short circuited. However, you as the attorney are able to control the jury's attention by controlling when information appears on the screen simply by using animation and secondary effects.

Most slide presentation packages include effects that allow the user to bring text, images, and other information onto the screen. Take advantage of these to control the jury's focus. You begin by bringing text onto the screen incrementally. Once the initial text is on the screen, you may wish to move to another point on the same screen by employing a secondary effect to dim the text already on the screen. In this way, jurors taking notes can write down the first piece of information while you are focusing their attention on the next piece of information to go onto the screen. Do not be afraid to darken the screen during your presentation. (If you want to darken a screen while you are using PowerPoint, simply press the B button on your keyboard. Press the B button again, and the image on the screen comes back.)

You now have an overview of the concepts and skills that this book presents. You will find that using technology at trial changes the way you think about storytelling and about presenting evidence at trial. Good luck!

Chapter 2

Technology and Case Themes

A computer presentation should underscore the case theme that a trial lawyer can marshal. A case theme is the fundamental concept or message that the trial lawyer wants jurors to connect with. It is the story of the case crafted in such a way that the jurors feel compelled to look past a particular side's problems to find in that side's favor. The case theme must be consistent with the evidence in the case, or the case theme and the client's cause fail. This case theme should be the legal and moral reason that jurors will point to as their justification for deciding the case in a particular side's favor. For a plaintiff, the case theme should explain why jurors are justified in making a finding in the plaintiff's favor despite any flaws or problems with the evidence. For the defense side, the case theme must supply jurors with a justification for saying the plaintiff or prosecution has not met its burden of proof.

This chapter talks about organizing computer files and developing case themes. We begin with computer file storage and organization because (1) the computer must know where information is before it can use it; and (2) for exactly this reason, attorneys working on a case must agree on where and how to store the files and on file naming conventions before they can begin developing case themes to present on computers. After discussing computer storage and organization, we examine ways to analyze the facts of a case to develop a case theme from them. Finally, we look at how to use available computer technology to demonstrate and highlight the case theme.

Storing and Organizing Files

Technology is useless unless it is used to convey messages that resonate with jurors. Technology's sole purpose in a courtroom is to emphasize specific evidence, but for this process to work, a computer needs to know where to find an exhibit so that it can get the exhibit and display it on a screen. Once a computer knows where to find an exhibit, all it needs to know is when to put the exhibit onto the viewing screen. A computer finds a file by following a path. In the figure that follows, the path to the Carter file is C:\Carter.

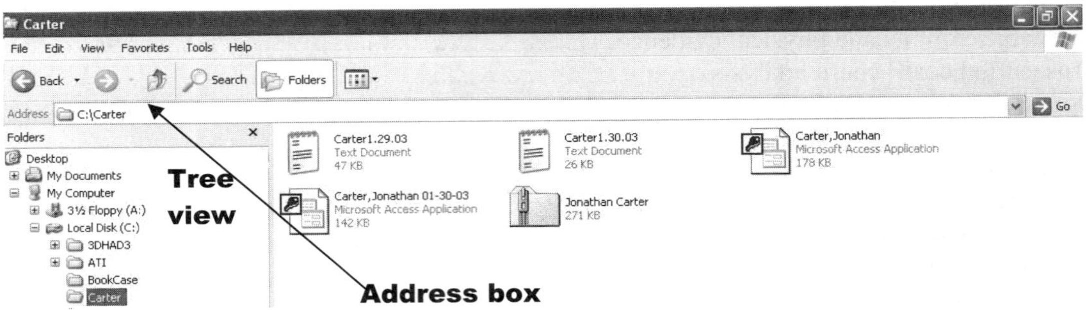

Most Windows-based computers save their files in the My Documents folder. This is Window's way of making it easy for people to find things on their computers. But the ways that Windows creates paths to your computer files varies depending on how you have configured your computer. If you are logged onto your computer as an administrator, your file path might look like this: **C:\Documents and Settings\Administrator\My Documents**. On the other hand, it might not. If you are logged in under your name, then your computer path would look like this: **C:\Documents and Settings\Username\My Documents**. This variation in path can cause problems for PowerPoint and Sanction if you copy case files onto other computers without duplicating the same file-path structure.

Here is a simple way to go about organizing your exhibits (particularly video exhibits) so that Sanction and PowerPoint will be able to find exhibits that they need.

Right click on the Start button of your desktop. 

You should see a menu that looks something like this.

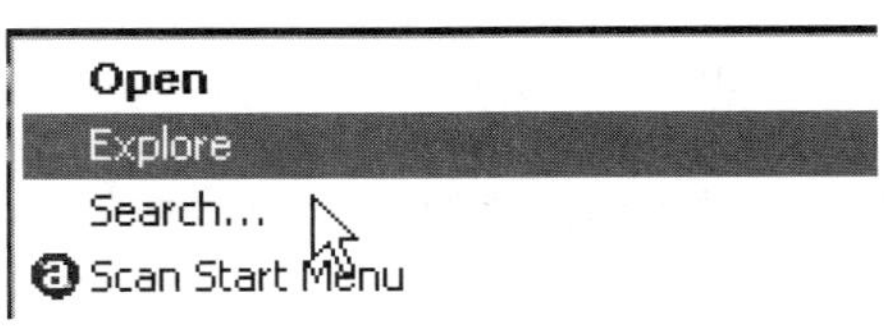

Left click on Explore.

This launches Windows Explorer.

Windows Explorer shows you the way folders and files are saved on your computer.

When a folder has a + sign in a box next to it  that symbol means that the folder has subfolders within it. Folders contain files. Files can be the actual programs that your computer uses or the images, videos, and other types of files that will evenually make up your presentation. Sanction and PowerPoint rely on folder placement on your computer to summon images and videos to the presentaion. If two lawyers working together on a case create their own Sanction files on their own computers but use the same filing naming conventions and have identical paths to the files on their respective computers, those lawyers can import each other's Sanction presentations so that they can both run their presentations from one machine with no problems. In the following screen capture, the Carter file is opened with Windows Explorer. The Tree view shows where the Carter file is saved in the C directory. The Address box shows the path that the computer will follow to open the files saved in the Carter directory. Sanction and PowerPoint will use this path to call files onto the screen during a presentation. If, for example, you want to call the file Carter1.30.03 to the desktop with Sanction or PowerPoint, both programs will follow the path C:\Carter\Carter1.30.03 to find the file.

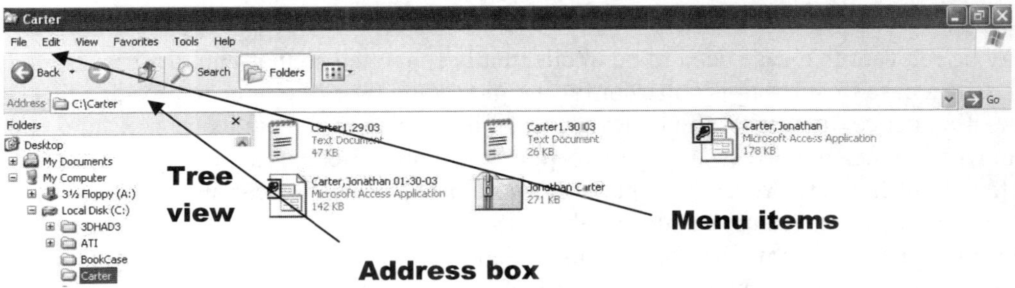

An easy way to manage your files is to make a practice of saving them in a folder that is saved in the root directory of your computer like the file Carter was. To create a file in the root directory, click on the File menu, select New, and then select Folder. Now make a folder for your particular case in the C drive. Once you have created the new folder, save all of your files for this case in this folder. This convention of keeping the file in the C directory simply makes it easy for you to transfer your files from one computer to another since each computer that you save these files on will look for the path of C:\.

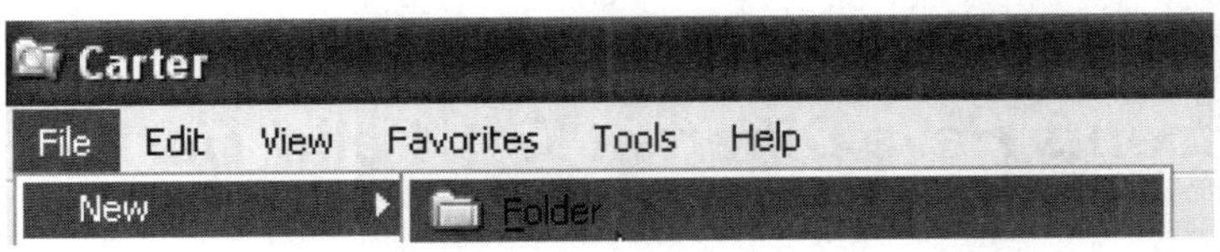

This is a close-up of the File menu from Windows Explorer. Click on File, put your cursor on New, and the next window will open. Select Folder.

If you want to learn more about paths or about Windows functions, look at the excellent section in the Sanction manual called "Windows Terms You Ought to Know," which launches from the Sanction Help Topics menu.

When you decide about naming conventions for your files, be aware of how Sanction searches for exhibits. Sanction can search for exhibits in four ways: It can search for an ID/file name, a description, an exhibit number, and a trial number. The search by ID function is the default for Sanction, which make sense since every file that is added to Sanction is given an ID. It is the easiest to work with since every item in a case will be given an ID when it is created, while you, the user, will have to decide whether to add things like descriptions, an exhibit number, or a second set of trial numbers. When you link a file to Sanction, a drag and drop screen comes up that lets you choose whether to use a file name as an ID for Sanction. When you select this option, you can launch the file out of Sanction by simply typing the filename. If your file is relatively small with, say, 50 exhibits, then spend time thinking about your filenames. Short names are easy to type when you are looking for something or when your adrenaline is pumping because you know you can find something that impeaches a witness. For that reason, consider naming files with short names. For example assume that Carter gave a handwritten statement. A file name of CHW.tif is a good short name. You know it means “Carter handwritten statement,” but typing CHW will launch the file quickly. If you are working collaboratively with another attorney and you both agree on the filenames, then you can import each other’s databases and have the databases launch files that use identical paths and names.

Organizing Your Facts to Craft a Case Theme: Identifying Tier 1 and Tier 2 Evidence

Facts that may be relevant to a case need to be intellectually separated so that you, the trial lawyer, can create a case theme that is coherent for the jury. One type of evidence proves a fact; the other type of evidence diminishes the believability of the source of the evidence. Assume you have a case in which a teenage driver, trying to keep up with some friends, ran through a yellow light and hit the plaintiff’s car. Assume the plaintiff was a passenger in the car and that the driver died instantly when her neck was broken during the collision. Assume that the plaintiff has been able to obtain statements that show that the defendant lied about following anyone through the light, and in fact lied when he claimed that the driver of the plaintiff’s car ran a red light. Assume that the defendant is still maintaining that he had the right of way. In a wrongful death case, the plaintiff must prove that the defendant owed the plaintiff a duty of care in that the defendant should have been driving safely. To win the lawsuit, the plaintiff must prove that the defendant breached the duty of care by driving into the intersection without yielding to oncoming traffic and thus caused the death of the deceased. The evidence that proves the elements of the tort fall into the first category. The evidence that diminishes the defendant’s credibility falls into the second category because although it is important to the outcome of the case, it does nothing to establish the elements of the tort. In this book, these two categories of evidence are called Tier 1 and Tier 2 evidence. The best way to make a case theme is to separate your evidence into the two distinct categories to better focus on the case theme that you want to create.

Plaintiffs and Defendants Have Different Tier 1 and Tier 2 Evidence

The very nature of our adversarial system requires that every story have two sides. Each side will try to capitalize on the strength of its evidence to win. For a plaintiff or prosecutor, all evidence that attempts to establish the elements of the charged crime or tort is Tier 1 evidence. A case theme that is built around highlighting Tier 1 evidence presents the jury with an affirmative or “nondefensive” portrayal of the plaintiff’s case. A plaintiff becomes defensive when his or her case theme tries to explain away problems with the case instead of going on the offensive and attacking the defense with the strongest portrayal of the plaintiff’s case. Tier 1 evidence is affirmative evidence that proves identity, a culpable mental state like intent or negligence, and action. Tier 1 evidence should be talked about during opening statement, introduced on direct examination, elicited from defense witnesses during the factual concession section of cross-examination, and argued during closing argument.

For the defense lawyer, Tier 1 evidence proves the defense attack on the plaintiff’s evidence or tells the story that explains away the plaintiff’s case. Tier 1 evidence can also support an affirmative defense or provide information obtained from the plaintiff’s or prosecution’s witnesses by forcing those witnesses to conceed facts that support the affirmative defense. For the defense, Tier 1 evidence may have to be mentioned during opening statement to underscore the jury's need to wait and see what all the evidence in the case will be. This is evidence that will be elicited at the beginning of cross-examinations of the plaintiff's or prosecution's witnesses before attacking the witnesses. It is wise to seek concessions that corroborate the defense theory of the affirmative defense before attacking a witness's believability. Jurors are more willing to embrace concessions from witnesses if the concessions come before the defense attorney attacks the witness. Tier 1 evidence should be introduced during the defense case-in-chief on direct examination of defense witnesses. It is evidence that should corroborate the concessions that the plaintiff's or prosecution's witnesses admitted during the concession-based cross-examination section of the cross. The defense lawyer should argue this information when he or she is talking about why the jury can trust the defendant's evidence.

Tier 2 evidence for a plaintiff or prosecutor is impeachment and rebuttal evidence. It impeaches the believability of defense theories and defense witnesses. Tier 2 evidence should not be mentioned in opening statement because it does not establish the defendant's guilt or liability. During the presentation of the plaintiff's or prosecution's case, Tier 2 evidence should be mentioned only during redirect examination since the purpose of this evidence is to undermine the defense attorney's attempt to elicit favorable information for the defense. Tier 2 evidence will provide the basis of the attack portion of the plaintiff's or prosecutor's cross-examination because it sets out to impeach the believability of the defendant and his or her witnesses. Tier 2 evidence should be introduced in a rebuttal case to perfect impeachment or to attack the believability of the defendant's evidence.

Prosecutors and plaintiffs should be wary of evidence that appears to fall into Tier 1 evidence but is really Tier 2 evidence. Consider the defendant who repeatedly tells lies during the interview process or who gives a series of inconsistent statements. Evidence of repeated lies is not necessarily an admission of culpability. Evidence of lies and self-serving statements are not Tier 1 evidence because they do not affirmatively prove the charged crime or tort. All this evidence proves is that the jury should not trust the defendant because the defendant is either trying to manipulate people or to tell lies to protect him- or herself. Although it may be tempting to introduce this type of evidence in the plaintiff's or prosecution's case-in-chief, it might better serve the plaintiff's or prosecution's interests by waiting to introduce the inconsistent statements in rebuttal to the defense case. The foundation for impeachment can be laid in the defense case and then perfected in the rebuttal case. Evidence of the defendant's lies could make a nice line of cross-examination. If the defendant admits that he or she told lies, then the defendant is an admitted liar. If the defendant denies telling the lies, then he or she is a liar who calls others liars to protect him- or herself. In either case, the lies can be pointed out during rebuttal argument as an explanation as to why the jury should not trust the defendant.

For the defense, Tier 2 is evidence that perfects impeachment or blunts the impact of the plaintiff's or prosecution's evidence. Tier 2 evidence attacks the believability of the oposition's case. It is the portion of the defense case where the defense attorney establishes the claim that the prosecution's or plaintiff's witnesses are biased, mistaken, or lying. Tier 2 evidence is the backbone of an attack cross and should come after the consessions since it is an effort to undermine the witness. A defense lawyer should handle this information in the section of the argument where the believability of his or her opponent's case is attacked.

Analyzing Your Two Tiers of Evidence to Figure Out How to Tell Your Side of the Story

Once you have analyzed the facts, turn your attention to refining the case theme for courtroom presentation. Each side in a lawsuit must address special considerations when constructing a case theme. For a plaintiff or prosecutor, the case theme must anticipate all possible defenses, inconsistencies, and unexplained matters. It must attempt to fashion a story that resolves all these considerations so as to secure a favorable verdict. For a defense attorney, who does not bear any burden of proof, the case theme should attack the sufficiency of the evidence being offered by the prosecution or plaintiff to satisfy the elements of the charged crime or tort or to support the allegations in a complaint. The defense case theme should also advance any affirmative defenses that nullify the plaintiff's claim.

One of the best ways to craft a case theme that forwards your side's objectives is to conduct a form of cost-benefit analysis of the facts of the case. Such an analysis identifies those facts that will rally jurors to your side's cause as well as any problem areas that may alienate jurors. Take a blank sheet of paper and draw a line down its middle. Put a plus sign on the left side of the page and a minus sign on the right side. On the plus side, list facts that you believe will evoke positive responses from jurors for your side of the case. On the minus side, list the facts of the case that may alienate jurors or any factual weaknesses of your case that you expect your opponent to exploit.

Ask yourself the following questions while composing the list. If the answer helps your case, list that fact on the plus side; if it hurts your case, list it on the minus side.

- What kinds of people are the witnesses in this case? Are they employed? Are they innocent victims or people with a degree of unclean hands? Are they smart or stupid? Are they streetwise or naive?
- Does a witness have a series of arrests where he or she used aliases?
- Are there arrest photos that may be obtained for each time the witness used a false name?
- Does a witness have some other vulnerability that may be exploited in a challenge to that witness's credibility?
- Has a witness lied in a job application, on his or her resume, or in any other document?
- Has the witness given conflicting accounts? Is there a good explanation for the discrepancy?
- Do the witnesses corroborate each other?
- Does physical evidence exist? If physical evidence does not exist, be ready to explain why it does not if your side was supposed to preserve it. If your side was not required to preserve evidence, decide how you will attack your opponent for this failure.
- Where does physical evidence in this case fit into this analysis?
- Are there photos in the case that help the cause or hurt it?
- Are there tape recordings or other audio or video evidence that must be presented or attacked?

The process of identifying favorable and unfavorable facts of the case forces you to view your case from the opponent's vantage point. By doing this, you can see that what appears to be a strength of your case may not be, and what appears to be a problem can be turned to an advantage. When using this process, you must ask how you would try to dismantle the case if you were on the other side. The lawyer who anticipates the opponent's attacks is better able to counter those attacks.

As an example, assume you are a defense attorney who is considering the different ways that your opponent's choices could affect your defense case. Ask yourself the following types of questions. The answers will reveal the strengths and weaknesses of your case.

- How will my opponent's decision to hold back certain evidence for a rebuttal case affect my defense case?
- How will my opponent's decisions about the order of witness presentation or about cutting witnesses from the order of proof affect my defense case?
- Are there witnesses that my opponent can cut from an order of proof and still possibly prevail?
- How will I perfect impeachment of a witness if a detective, police officer, or insurance investigator is called to testify before a civilian witness is called? (You would have to serve that witness with a subpoena after he or she testifies or ask the judge to order the witness to return for your case.)
- After I have retained jurisdiction over the witness, how will my opponent cross-examine that witness when I recall the witness? (That consideration should affect your choices about how to cross that witness; you must ask whether you can lay a foundation for impeachment with this witness or whether you will have to recall the witness in your case-in-chief.)
- If the witness is to be recalled, how will my cross-examination of the detective or investigator be affected if I later have to rely on the same witness to prove up a prior inconsistent statement?

Once you have identified the strengths and weaknesses of your case, find ways to turn the negatives about the case into positives. Ask yourself these types of questions.

- How can I blame my opponent for the problems in the case?
- Can my opponent argue that my argument "that the plaintiff failed to mitigate damages" is due to depression that was caused by my client's negligence in a civil case where the dispute is over the amount of damages to be paid where liability has been admitted by the defense?
- Is physical evidence missing? Was it mishandled in any way? Was physical evidence not analyzed because a party lost or destroyed it?
- Can I blame my opponent for mishandling or destroying physical evidence? Did my opponent, for example, have an aggressive shredding policy that I can cast as a conscious effort to conceal wrongdoing? Did a gun used in the commission of a crime or tort disappear after having been in the exclusive control of a party?

Figure out how to blame your opponent or third parties for blunders, oversights, and mistakes. Has the prosecutor spotted the things that a defense attorney must say or do to secure a lesser-included offense jury instruction? Is there a way to blunt this attempt? All these issues come into better focus if you take the time to think about them before the battle heats up.

Juror Value Analysis

We will use case analysis on a criminal case and then ask you to analyze the civil case in order to walk through the value analysis process.

Criminal Case

Factual scenario

Victim is a local athlete who takes his mother's car to run an errand and is never seen alive again. A week later, the car is found by a former military man who recognized the smell of rotting flesh. In the backseat of the car is the victim's maggot-covered body. The car is littered with bottles and debris, which the victim's mother says were not in her car when her son left. The mother will testify that she cleaned out the car with her son just before he left on the errand. The police find defendant's fingerprints on multiple bottles from the car.

Police arrest defendant and find the murder weapon in defendant's house. Police find another witness who puts defendant near the victim's car while the victim was sitting in the front seat of the car.

The pathologist determines that the cause of death was multiple gunshot wounds. One bullet, still in the body, entered the victim's abdomen and traveled directly backward, severing the victim's spine so that, if he had survived, he would have been paralyzed from the waist down. This wound was not an immediately fatal wound. The victim suffered two other gunshot wounds that entered his back above the kidneys and traveled upwards toward the front and into the victim's heart.

There is a blood stain on the rear seat of the car consistent with the abdomen wound, but the blood pooled in one place. This indicates that the victim died quickly and was not moving around in the car. Had the victim been moving around after he was shot, there would have been more blood splattered on the interior of the car.

While in custody for 48 hours before he was charged, the defendant gave no inculpatory statements. The defendant gave different accounts for his whereabouts, but no one is supporting the defendant's claims. Defendant starts giving accounts that conflict with his prior statements after he is told no one is supporting his claims.

The defendant has a history of mental illness. The defendant has been involuntarily hospitalized for depression and schizophrenia. The defendant appears dirty and disheveled at the police station. Defendant admits touching a bottle but has no idea how the bottle got into the victim's car. Defendant denies ever being near the victim's car.

The defendant is married with two children and has a spotty employment history. The defendant's wife cannot account for the defendant's whereabouts at the time of the victim's disappearance. The defendant's wife says that the defendant sometimes goes off and gets drunk and disappears for days at a time. She also says that the defendant is not violent. The defendant's wife does not know where the murder weapon came from or how it got into their house.

Available exhibits and physical evidence

- Life photo of the victim
- Scene photos of the car that contained the victim's corpse
- Scene photos of the area surrounding the victim's car
- Close up scene photos
  - Of the victim's body
  - Of the bottles found in car
  - Of the overall interior photos
- Diagrams of various locations shown in the photographs
- The bottle that has the defendant's latent print
- The latent print lift
- The murder weapon
- The bullets and casings from the murder weapon
- Photos of the defendant's house
- Photos of the interior of the defendant's house where the weapon was found
- Autopsy photos
- Videotaped police statements taken from witnesses at the time of charging
- Consent to videotaping from witnesses
- Photographs and diagrams referred to during the videotaped statements
- Videotaped statements taken by defense investigators
- Photographs taken by the forensic odontologist who identified the victim's remains
- Psychiatric records from defendant's prior hospitalizations
- Psychiatric evaluations of the defendant

Prosecution cost-benefit analysis

+	–
Victim had no known vice that could get him mixed up with defendant.	Potential insanity defense? • It would put defendant in the car. • This defense makes the defendant commit the act but excuses his mental state. Potential some other guy did it defense? • Makes defendant out as a victim. • Are there other unsolved armed robberies or murders from this area? • Defendant can claim he got the gun from a stranger. • Defendant can claim he was afraid of the stranger and hid the weapon. • Defendant can claim that told lies to the police out of fear.
Eyewitness puts defendant near car. Eyewitness puts defendant in car after the time victim was dead. Macabre Rolling coffin Twisted trophy Defendant's prints on bottles in car.	No one sees defendant shoot into the car.
Defendant repeatedly gives alibis. The police then break these alibis.	Only know bottles got in the car sometime after the victim left his house. Defendant never confesses to the killing. Defendant professes his innocence.
Victim's mother never sees son again. Horror Fear Nightmare Helplessness	Physical evidence tells only so much.
Murder weapon in defendant's house Path of victim's wounds say victim was laying down on his stomach or on all fours.	Shock can distract from facts contained in the photos.
At some time the victim is shot in the back after bleeding from his stomach wound on the backseat of the car. Grisly photos Maggots Decomposition fluid	No single piece of evidence points directly to defendant as the shooter.

Defense attorney value analysis

+

No eye witnesses to the crime.
Witness identification of the car defendant is near is tenuous. There is no identification of a license plate, just a car type and color.
Witnesses who put defendant in a car don't see a dead body in the car.

Prints on a bottle mean only that the defendant touched a bottle.
Prints don't say when the defendant touched the bottle.
Know only that bottles got in the car sometime after victim left his house.

Defendant repeatedly gives alibis.

> No videotape of alibis.
> No audiotape of alibis.
> No handwritten statement signed by defendant of these alibis.

Fact that a person doesn't remember where they were is a big "so what?"
Defendant never confesses to the killing.
Defendant professes his innocence.
Police are unpopular right now due to things in the press.

Murder weapon — mere presence of the weapon doesn't mean defendant pulled the trigger.
Can the defense claim that the police planted evidence?

No single piece of evidence points to defendant's guilt.

Insanity defense? Who but a "crazy person" would drive around with a dead body in the car?
Reasonable doubt defense?

—

One witness puts defendant near the car.

Witness can say he never got close enough to the car to see inside of it.

Prints on the bottle found in the car with the victim's body are circumstantial evidence of defendant being in contact with the victim after he disappears since the victim's mother claims to have helped clean out the car.

Police claim they broke alibis.

> Officers are articulate.
> Officers have no obvious motive to lie.
> Potential rebuttal is if the police wanted to frame the defendant, how could they have done a better job? Create a confession etc.

Murder weapon in defendant's house is good circumstantial evidence that defendant controlled the weapon around the time of the murder.
Defendant or some other must account for the weapon's presence.
Grisly photos — more prejudicial than probative. Try to keep them out.

No history of prior mental illness.

A case based on circumstantial evidence is a hard case to beat.

Civil Case

Factual scenario

A young woman getting off of a train on a local commuter line is horribly injured when she gets pulled under the train's wheels. The woman was carrying a briefcase slung over her shoulder. As the woman was exiting the train, the doors closed with the woman's briefcase trapped inside. There was no conductor standing on the platform assuring that the doors were clear. The woman tried to pull her briefcase free as the train began to move. Before she could wriggle free from the shoulder strap, the woman tripped and stumbled under the wheels of the train. The woman lost her right leg and almost lost her left leg. A commuter who got off the train before the woman turned around after hearing the woman scream and witnessed her being pulled under the wheels. A witness inside the train saw the woman trying to pull her briefcase through the door before losing sight of the woman when she fell. This witness will testify that it appeared that the woman was unwilling to let go of the briefcase. The woman was horribly injured and underwent an amputation just below her right knee. She then endured three months of rehabilitation, which she attended sporadically. She missed appointments. She refused to do exercises that were designed to help her with her rehabilitation and was less than cooperative with the people trying to help her get better. At the woman's depositions, she appeared aloof and confrontational. During the discovery process, the plaintiff learns that the railroad company has had 5 incidents of passengers being caught in the doors and injured, and 25 incidents of passengers who got caught in the doors and were nearly injured. A plaintiff's expert witness on commuter line management will testify that having a conductor step off the train and monitor passengers as they board or leave the train could easily prevent this injury.

Available exhibits and physical evidence

- Photographs of the train platform
- Photographs of the train doors
- Photographs of the wheels that ran over the plaintiff
- Photographs taken from the vantage point of the witness who was outside the train at the time of the plaintiff's injury
- Photographs taken from the vantage point of the witness who was inside the train when the plaintiff was injured
- Photograph of the plaintiff's injuries taken at different times during the healing process
- Photographs of the healed stump and scars
- Photographs and exhibits referred to during the depositions
- Medical records
- Hospital bills
- Photographs of the plaintiff taken during the course of rehabilitation
- Videotaped depositions of the plaintiff and witnesses
- Photographs and exhibits referred to during the depositions
- Videotaped deposition of the CEO of the railroad
- Surveillance video taken by a railroad investigator of the victim walking with a less pronounced limp than the one in the videotaped depositions
- Forensic economist's report
- Attendance logs from the rehabilitation institute

Plaintiff cost-benefit analysis

Apply the same methodology for case analysis from the criminal case to the civil case. List the strengths and weaknesses from a plaintiff's lawyer's perspective. How and when should the notice of prior incidents be introduced to the jury? How should the plaintiff treat the witness who will testify about watching the plaintiff struggle with her briefcase? Where is the plaintiff's case vulnerable? How will the plaintiff address the surveillance video should the defense decide to introduce it? Does the plaintiff want to introduce this video? How can the negative facts about the plaintiff's case be turned around?

Defense attorney value analysis

Consider how a defense attorney would analyze the facts of the civil case. What defense theory is guaranteed to outrage the jury and increase the amount of damages awarded to the plaintiff? What defense theory will help to minimize the damages award? What is the wisest theory for the defense attorney representing the railroad to proceed with?

Technology Considerations

Once you have analyzed your facts, think about how you want to show the jury your case.

Criminal Case Prosecutor

Opening statement

An excellent choice for presenting the opening statement is a linear slide presentation. There are multiple exhibits that may be introduced during the course of the presentation. Suggestions for crafting an opening statement are addressed in the next chapter, but consider here the exhibits that are available for an opening statement in a criminal case with the factual scenario given above. A photograph of the victim when he was alive is a good exhibit to show the jury because it gives a face to the victim. The jurors will identify with the image of a living, breathing human being as the prosecutor talks about the circumstances of the victim's death.

Time is important in this case. You must underscore the relationship between the victim, the defendant, and time. Use a timeline slide that can be woven into the presentation. A timeline that has callout boxes that wipe up and down from a central line is a good device for driving the presentation. This timeline can show how the investigation unfolded and how the investigation led the police, and ultimately the jury, to the defendant.

There are grizzly photos that may eventually be admitted in evidence; these exhibits can overwhelm jurors. These photos are likely to draw objections from the defense with a claim that they are overly prejudicial. Also, the prosecutor faces the prospect of desensitizing the jury to the photos if the grizzly photos are shown too often. One solution to this dilemma is to use a diagram that shows the locations of evidence without dwelling on the physically repellent aspects of the crime. A diagram of the inside of the car showing where the victim bled on the backseat counterpointed with a diagram of the victim's injuries is a good way to introduce the horror of the victim's death without unnecessarily dwelling on gory photos.

Some scene photos and evidence photos may be helpful to the story. The photo of the car is important because the car contained the victim and the bottles that held defendant's latent prints. A slide that shows the photograph of the outside of the car that then has a smaller photograph of the bottle appear with an arrow that wipes toward the interior of the car is a effective visual to underscore the connection between the bottle and the victim. The photo of the defendant's house where the murder weapon was found is important. A slide showing the house that has a smaller photo of the gun with an arrow that wipes toward the house is another effective way to show the connections between the gun and the defendant's house.

The jury will want to see the latent finger print lift from the bottle and defendant's known prints at some point in the trial. If you show this during opening statement without having a witness explain loops, whorls, and the other things that are important to fingerprint examination, its importance may be lost on the jurors. On the other hand, the bottle that yielded the print should sit on the prosecutor's table, while a photo of the bottle inside the car is shown to the jurors.

The fact that the defendant gave numerous inconsistent statements can be used as evidence of consciousness of guilt in an opening statement or where you want to focus on the defendant's attempts to lie his way out of responsibility. A prosecutor can argue that these lies are important evidence of defendant's guilt should the defense pursue an insanity defense because the conscious attempt to deceive investigators can indicate consciousness of guilt. One way of introducing this evidence in an opening statement is to take a photo of the defendant and put it on a slide. Then take callout balloons and show the lie told by the defendant. Next show a slide that lists the things that the detectives did to check out the defendant's account. This will show that the defendant is manipulative and deceitful. Another way to do this is to take one slide and put a line down the middle of it. On one side, list the defendant's claim; on the other side, list the thing that shows that defendant's claim is a lie.

Direct examination

Here are some suggested visuals to use during direct examination.

Direct of Witnesses	Evidence and Type of Presentation
Victim's mother — life photo of the victim	Life photo document camera or nonlinear software
Man who smelled the victim's decomposition and found the body	Car photo and document camera or nonlinear software
Crime scene officers	Multiple photos and physical evidence — document camera
Fingerprint examiner	Lifts and physical evidence use a document camera or nonlinear software
Medical examiner	Linear slide show — document camera or nonlinear software for publication of autopsy photos
Detectives	Multiple scene photos

Cross-examination

You must use Sanction as the platform for execution of your cross-examination. Every statement and document that can be tied to a witness should be digitized. If video- or audiotaped statements were taken of a witness, then the attorney should make sure that the video statements are synchronized with transcripts in order to create the video clips that can be recalled in any order that he or she chooses. If there are demonstrative slides that can be used during cross-examination, then these can be built in PowerPoint and launched from Sanction. Additional exhibits that should be incorporated for a cross-examination of the defense psychiatrists or psychologists are scanned pages of the DSM-IV TR in the event that the defense pursues the insanity defense. For cross-examination of the defendant, the prosecutor must be prepared to confront the defendant with the photos and physical evidence.

Closing argument

Use linear software for a proactive closing argument and nonlinear software for a reactive closing argument. There are really two kinds of closing arguments in trials, despite the fact that every jurisdiction has unique rules about how closing arguments can be conducted. In some jurisdictions, the plaintiff has an opportunity to present a closing argument and then a rebuttal argument that responds to the defense closing argument. In other jurisdictions, the plaintiff speaks last after the defense presents its closing argument. But when one gets down to it, the two kinds of closing arguments that exist are proactive closing arguments and reactive closing arguments. Proactive closing arguments go first in the order of argument. Reactive closing arguments go second in the order of argument (or third when the third argument is a rebuttal argument). A proactive closing argument allows the attorney to explain either why he or she has satisfied the elements of a particular cause of action or why the plaintiff or prosecutor has failed to prove his or her case. All reactive closing arguments must be fluid to allow the attorney presenting this argument to adjust his or her argument to respond to the arguments presented by the first attorney.

Think about how a prosecutor should argue the facts from the criminal case. He or she should weave photos with jury instructions to make a powerful closing argument. The jury instructions that are necessary for a prosecutor in the criminal case we've been discussing to explain are circumstantial evidence, elements of aggravated kidnapping, elements of armed robbery, elements of first degree murder, and elements of felony murder. The circumstantial evidence instruction needs to account for almost every piece of evidence, like the murder weapon in the defendant's house and the prints from the bottle that link the defendant to the victim. The defendant's broken alibis could also be argued as circumstantial evidence of defendant's consciousness of guilt.

The victim's nonfatal stomach wound and the fatal wound to his back are circumstantial evidence of defendant's intent to kill, which satisfies the mental state element of first degree murder.

Use one of the argument concept slides like the "evidence points to" slide or one of the other slides to show how the defendant is trapped by the evidence. Any of these are effective ways for summing up the evidence against the defendant.

Nonlinear software allows the prosecutor to pull up exhibits without being tied to a format.

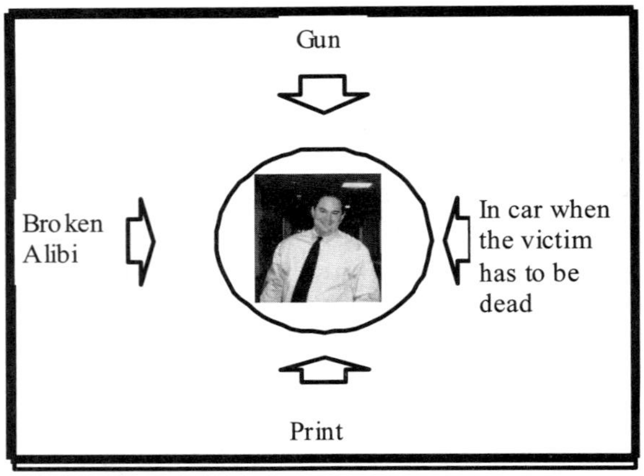

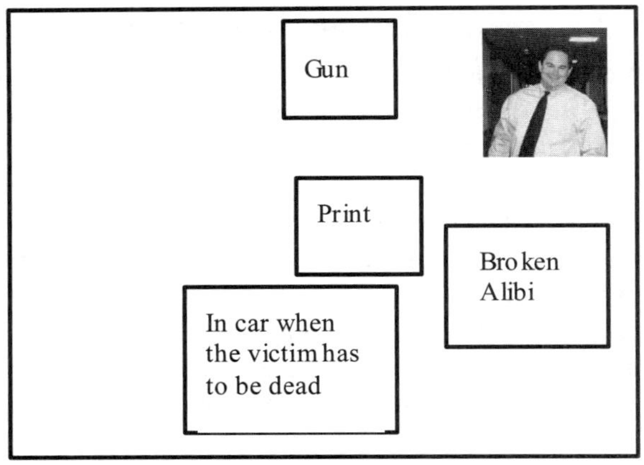

Defense Attorney

Opening statement

If you are the defense attorney in the criminal case we've been discussing, you should consider a series of mini-linear presentations that you can launch from Sanction. These slides must stress the burden of proof. The introductory slide may include a photo of defendant and his family as you take time to introduce the jury to defendant. You might list favorable facts about the defendant's background on a slide as a checklist, which should send the message that "it would be unlikely that a person like this defendant would do something like this." If the jurisdiction has a definition for the burden of proof, then you should use key words and phrases from the burden of proof slide in your visuals when talking about why the jury should have doubts. Remind the jurors of their promise to apply the law to the facts that they hear during the trial. Other exhibits that you as the defense attorney may want to show include a clock that illustrates the passage of time that the defendant endured in police custody before making any of the statements that the prosecution has mentioned. If the prosecution wins a motion in limine to introduce the gory photos, then you may want to introduce those photos yourself to desensitize the jury to the photographs.

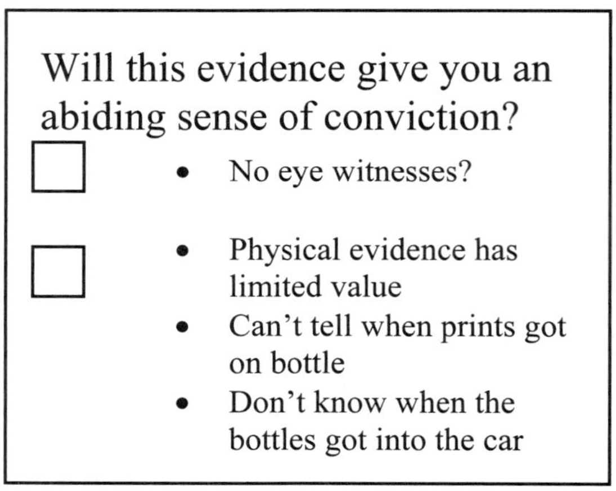

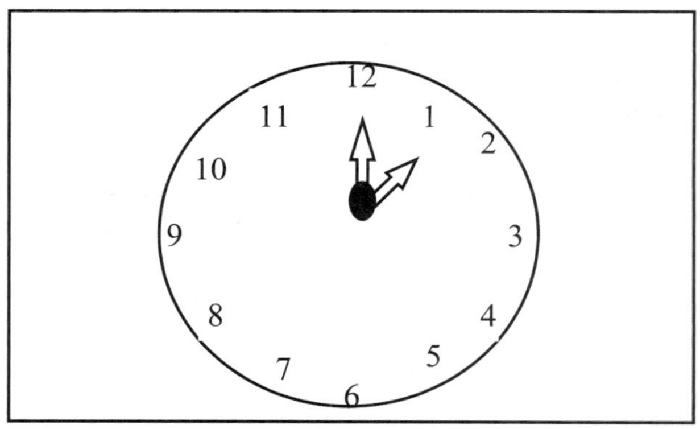

Direct examination

If you choose to present any evidence in the defense case-in-chief, it would be wise to use photos of the defendant and his family, which give the subliminal message that a person with a family would not do such a thing.

Cross-examination

You must use Sanction as the platform for execution of your cross-examination. Every statement and every document that can be tied to a witness should be digitized. Detective notes should be scanned so they can be put up on a screen to corroborate impeachment or to impeach by omission. If video- or audiotaped witness statements were taken, then you should synchronize those statements with transcripts to create the video clips that you can recall in any order you choose. If there are checklists of information that should be elicited from witnesses and introduced during cross-examination, then you can build these in PowerPoint and launch them from Sanction. If there are witnesses who do not identify the defendant, then showing a photo of the defendant as he appeared when he was out of custody is an effective exhibit to put up on the screen.

Closing argument

You must use slides that illustrate the witness credibility instruction and the shortcomings that each prosecution witness has exhibited. You must use slides that prompt the jury to use common sense. You must also use slides that highlight the presumption of innocence and that explain how monumental the task is of overcoming the burden of proof in criminal cases. If your jurisdiction allows you to define the burden of proof, then you should take that language and put it up on the screen. Then take choice words and phrases from the instruction and explain how they have not been satisfied.

Civil Case Attorneys

What about the commuter train civil case? Think about how you would use visuals to drive your case if you were a civil plaintiff or defense attorney. There are a myriad of problems that come up in civil trials that you can solve using visuals. All you have to do is think about and anticipate the problems and then experiment with visuals that capture or explain your concepts. Ron Bowers of the Los Angeles District Attorney's Office developed the following checklist for the attorneys in his office, who were encouraged to think about visuals that they could use to solve whatever problems they anticipated. Bowers's questions and answers talk about charts that can be created for a jury, but the same concepts can be translated into slides that are shown to the jury either during the direct examination or during argument when a witness's testimony is put into the context of the rest of the case for the jurors.

Bowers has also written a book called *Visuals for Today's Prosecutors* (National College of District Attorneys, 2003). It is worth looking at if you are looking for ways to communicate ideas. In the book, Bowers comes up with visuals that address some of the many problems that prosecutors face as they meet their burdens of proof. Bowers's suggestions are good springboards for any attorney who faces the prospect of creating a visual to explain a concept. Simply substitute *count*, *cause of action*, or *tort* for the word *crimes* to see how the question may be answered. Then think about your own ways to articulate the answers to the questions.

Questions How to explain	Answers Charts to use
Multiple crimes and when they occurred?	Charges chart
Who are all the parties?	Witness list chart
What's the connection between all the parties?	Relationship of the parties chart
All the key events that occurred over a long period of time?	Timeline of events chart
When and what investigation occurred?	Timeline of investigation chart
When a statement was made?	Timeline of statements chart
A period of abuse?	Timeline of abuse chart
Various business transactions?	Timeline of paper case chart
Lengthy descriptions of events?	Vertical timeline chart
Events that occurred over short period of time?	Clock timeline chart
A pattern of events on certain days of a week or month?	Calendar chart
Frequency of phone calls?	Timeline of calls chart
Who the calls are made to and from?	Relationship of calls chart
Witnesses gave the same or similar description of a suspect?	Similarities of description chart
The similarities between various crimes?	Similarities of crimes chart
The number of times the witness identified the suspect?	Similarities of ID chart
The testimony of each of the prosecution witnesses?	Facts by witness chart
The defendant had reasons to commit the crimes?	Motive chart
That all the incriminating evidence points to the defendant?	Arrow chart
That each element of the crime has been proven?	Elements/facts chart
Felony murder in simple language?	Definition chart
Aiding and abetting in lay terms?	Definition chart
Various levels of homicide?	Homicide chart
The difference between reasonable and unreasonable interpretation of the evidence?	Circumstantial evidence chart
Various legal terms?	Legal terms chart
Argue the prosecution's witnesses are credible?	Credibility chart
The defense claims are inconsistent with the facts?	Comparison of sides chart
The defense argument does not make sense?	Hmm chart
Make memorable ending to an argument?	Pull-down chart
Scientific tests or numerous transactions?	Legend type chart

Chapter 3

Using Computer Presentations in Opening Statement

Shanachie (Sha-na-kee) is a Celtic word that means "storyteller." A Shanachie would travel from town to town telling stories and sharing recent news. A good trial lawyer is a Shanachie. An opening statement, if performed artfully, feels just like a good story. An opening statement corroborated by a computer presentation lets jurors hear a good story *and* see it.

There are three advantages to using computer presentations for opening statement. First, the trial lawyer is better able to control jury focus because the trial lawyer decides when to show an image on the video screen. The control over *when* the jury gets to learn information dictates the jury's point of view. If this disclosure is executed properly, it underscores the theme of the case. The second advantage is organization. A trial lawyer who uses a presentation for opening statement is better organized because the process of preparing a computer presentation forces a trial lawyer to organize his or her thoughts about the case. That process forces the attorney to consider the order and structure of the presentation. Computer presentations also force an attorney to pick a vantage point to tell the story from. This vantage point, or point of view, determines whether the jury's introduction to the story is intimate, distant, or somewhere in between. An intimate story talks about the facts of the case from the vantage point of a person who is actually experiencing the event. A distant telling of the story steps back from the facts and attempts to emotionally distance the jury from the event. The third advantage to using a computer slide presentation is confidence. The attorney who seamlessly introduces slides or images of the evidence appears better prepared than the attorney who does not. That feeling of confidence can also translate into credibility in the eyes of the jury simply because the advocate who uses the computer presentation shows the jury the sources of the evidence that they will consider.

After analyzing the facts of a case and deciding what case theme best suits these facts, a trial lawyer must decide what point of view to tell the story from. All stories are told from a point of view. In Thornton Wilder's play *Our Town*, the story is narrated by the stage manager. This character creates an aesthetic distance from the story because he repeatedly injects himself into the story as he introduces the town and the characters. He further removes the audience from the story by watching the play along with the audience. The stage manager comments on the action in the play and, through this literary device, keeps the audience at an emotional distance from the characters. In plays, the voice of the narrator and the vantage point that the narrator chooses to tell the story from directly affect the reaction of the audience. This same principle applies to trial work. For this reason, it is imperative that the trial lawyer locate a point of view to tell the case's story that will paint the best picture for the lawyer's cause.

This chapter introduces you to a methodology for preparing opening statements. It will show you how to identify a point of view for telling the story of the case. Next it will offer suggestions for starting the opening statements, and then introduce visual and rhetorical devices that can help you tell the story.

Locating Points of View

Every person who experiences an event has a different perspective. An accountant who audits a company's books and discovers a fraud scheme will tell a story differently than a person who is defrauded by the scheme. The young woman who is pulled under the wheels of a train and loses her leg will tell a story differently than a person who witnesses the incident. A person's physical condition, emotional state, or relationship to an event directly affects that individual's ability to perceive or recount that event. As you, the trial lawyer, begin to think about telling your case's story, stop and think about what the people in the case were doing before, during, and after the event that is now in dispute in a lawsuit. Imagine telling the story of the case from each person's perspective. Which perspective will best narrate your facts and your case theme?

Using a Timeline Progression

An excellent way to identify vantage points for narrating an opening statement is to analyze the case's timeline progression. Make a timeline progression diagram that maps out the pivotal facts of the case and identifies the different perspectives that witnesses in the case had at different times throughout the case. This device allows you to spot perspectives of the case that otherwise might not be noticeable.

TIMELINE PROGRESSION

LEAD-UP EVENTS	POST-CRIME EVENTS
Victim or plaintiff did something pre-event.	Victim or plaintiff did something post-event.
Witness did something pre-event.	Witness did something post-event.
Defendant did something pre-event.	Defendant did something post-event
Investigator did something pre-event.	Investigator did something post-event.

CRIME/EVENT

Witness Point of View
Plaintiff Point of View
Investigator Point of View
Defendant Point of View
Scene
Time
Things

Each witness listed above has a perspective that is unique to the case. Since you, the trial lawyer, are the playwright who shapes the telling of the story, you now have different perspectives that you can touch on to make the witness into a narrator for the opening statement.

Consider the criminal case from Chapter 2 about the local athlete who is found murdered in the backseat of his mother's car.

- Which vantage points could the prosecutor choose to tell the story from?
- Which vantage point is the strongest one to tell the story from?
- Which vantage point is most likely to grab the jury's attention and keep it?
- Which vantage points could alienate the jury?
- Which vantage points could a defense attorney in the same case tell the story from?

Now think about the civil case from Chapter 2 about the young woman who loses her leg after falling under the wheels of a train. Identify places in the timeline progression for a plaintiff's lawyer to begin telling the story in this civil case. Which vantage point should the defense attorney who chooses to litigate liability tell the story from? Where should a defense attorney who conceded liability but is contesting the extent of a damage award begin the story from?

Locating Points of View in the Criminal Case of the Murdered Athlete

Let's next analyze more carefully the points of view in the criminal case introduced in Chapter 2.

Prosecution points of view

PRE-CRIME

Victim tells his mother he is going to run an errand.

Police on patrol, oblivious to what happens to victim.

Witness sees victim in car talking to defendant and another.

Later witness sees defendant driving around in the car that victim had been seen sitting in.

Defendant complains to a witness that he is broke and needs a gun to go do an armed robbery.

POST-CRIME

A passerby who notices the smell discovers victim's maggot-covered body in the backseat of the car.

Police begin their investigation:
- Start processing scene.
- Collect physical evidence.
- Canvass neighborhood looking for clues.
- Learn of defendant's prints on the bottles.
- Find the murder weapon at defendant's house.

The defendant gives many inconsistent statements.

Pathologist catalogs victim's wounds:
- Does autopsy on victim's body.
- Collects bullet from victim's body.

Witness watches television and recognizes the car.

CRIME/EVENT
Second witness sees car outside his house.
Witness hears gunshots.
Witness calls the police; they don't come for 30 minutes.
Victim receives gunshot wound to the abdomen.
Victim bleeds out and dies in the backseat of the car.
Police have no idea anything has happened to the victim.
Defendant's perspective unknown.
Scene: Area outside second witness's house 2:00 A.M.

If you are the prosecutor in this case, you could begin your opening statement from a number of different vantage points. You could begin the story from the victim's mother's perspective. She is a sympathetic character since she has to face the horror of never seeing her son again. You could tell the story from the victim's perspective. This opening could focus on the victim's terror as he dies in the backseat of his mother's car. You could tell the story from the vantage point of the witness who was watching television and realized what he had seen or from the vantage point of the passerby who noticed the smell. Another perspective to consider is that of the medical examiner who conducted the autopsy on the victim. You could begin by talking about the damage that had been inflicted on the victim before looping back to the facts that you intend to show. Or you could tell the story from the different police perspectives that exist in the case: the detective looking for witnesses who could help solve a horrible crime, or the crime scene or crime lab personnel who gathered and then processed the physical evidence.

Defense points of view

Think about perspectives that you could use for beginning the opening statement if you are the defense attorney in this case. If you pursue a defense that incorporates a theme of a "police/prosecution rush to judgment," then you could begin the opening by reminding the jury of the fact that this brutal crime was mentioned on television. You could then talk about community shock and outrage and how that created an environment in which the police felt pressured to solve the crime. Another vantage point for beginning the defense opening statement is to focus on things that will challenge the credibility of the witness who will claim that he saw the defendant driving the victim's car. If you choose to pursue an insanity defense, then your opening statement should begin by portraying defendant's battle with mental illness and how that demon drove the defendant to commit this crime. If you choose to pursue a reasonable doubt defense, which says there is simply not enough evidence to merit taking away the defendant's freedom, then you could begin the story from the defendant's vantage point of every citizen's worst nightmare. You could talk about how the defendant was simply walking down the street on his way to buy a newspaper when he was suddenly arrested; then you could explore how a bottle the defendant drank from came back to haunt him.

Consider how juror value analysis (explained in Chapter 2) and point of view selection affects jury selection. Taking the time to conduct cost-benefit analysis and to select different perspectives from which to begin the opening statement will make you an advocate who is better able to think about the types of jurors that will give you the outcome you want — and to think about the types of jurors who are not acceptable. Using these two types of analysis will also make you better able to identify juror types who could be sympathetic to the opposition's case because you will have already analyzed the strengths of the opponent's case. It is wise to read the jury instructions for any case you are trying. Take the time to identify words and phrases in the instructions that you can stress in voir dire. Stress these same words in opening statement.

Presentation Suggestions for the Criminal Case of the Murdered Athlete

Once you have identified the vantage point from which to begin your opening statement, you should select visuals that will drive the story. Let's return to the criminal case from Chapter 2.

Presentation Suggestions for the Prosecutor

You could use the first series of visuals below if your opening was starting from the victim's mother's perspective. These slides should paint the picture of every parent's worst nightmare before moving into the justification for having the defendant sit in the courtroom to face the charges resulting from the crime. The second and third series of slides are examples of presentations you could use if you were starting from the medical examiner's or the police investigator's point of view. (Remember that a blank slide with no graphics should come between the slides with images in case you want to talk about something with no images on the screen.) Think about how a change in order of the below slides alters the entire feel of the presentation. As you look at the selection of slides, think about how you would narrate each opening statement.

Telling the story from the mother's point of view

This opening should begin with the life photo of the victim that the mother will identify. Use a headline regarding the last time the victim's mother ever saw the victim alive. There is a section about headlines later on in this chapter.

Show the jury the photograph of the car that the mother helped the victim clean before sending the victim off to run an errand.

It becomes a base line for what was in the car before the victim disappeared.

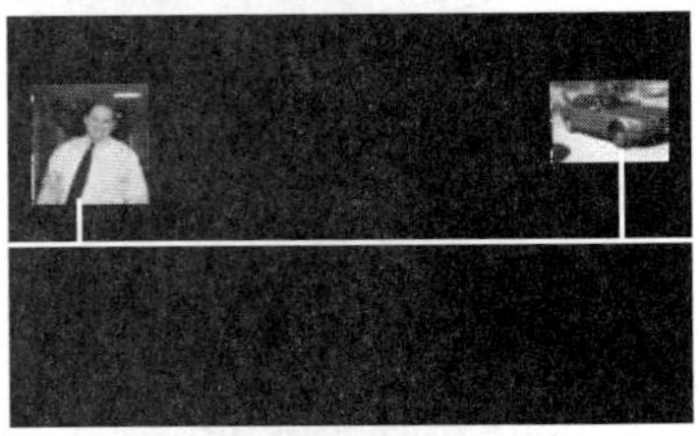

The next slide could be a timeline. This is an image-driven timeline that will be filled in as the events forming the case unfold. For the rest of the opening statement, you could go back to this slide to fill in the blanks of what happened to the victim or what happened with the evidence. Making timelines like this one is explained in Chapter 7 on using PowerPoint.

Another effective slide is one that has the bottle appear with an arrow that points toward the car. This should underscore the relationship between the bottle and the car. It is the piece of evidence that will lead to the defendant and solve the mystery. Now talk about fingerprint analysis and explain how the defendant is identified as the person who touched the bottle.

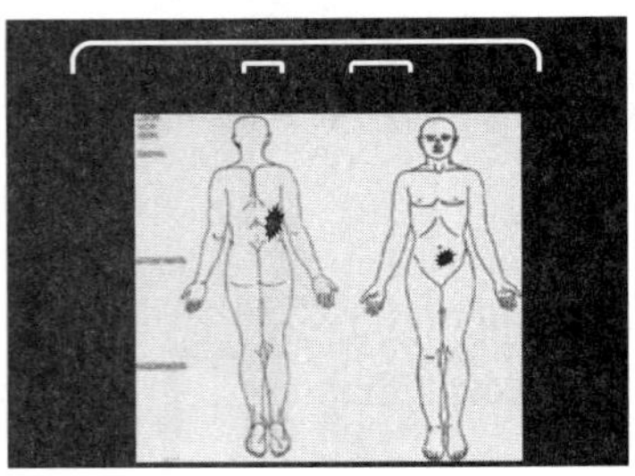

Since blood spatter in the backseat of the car is important, now is a good time to use a diagram that shows where the blood stains will appear in the actual scene photographs. This blood spatter without any drag marks tends to show that the victim had not been moved in or out of the car. This will become important to the jurors when the witness who saw the defendant in control of the car is introduced.

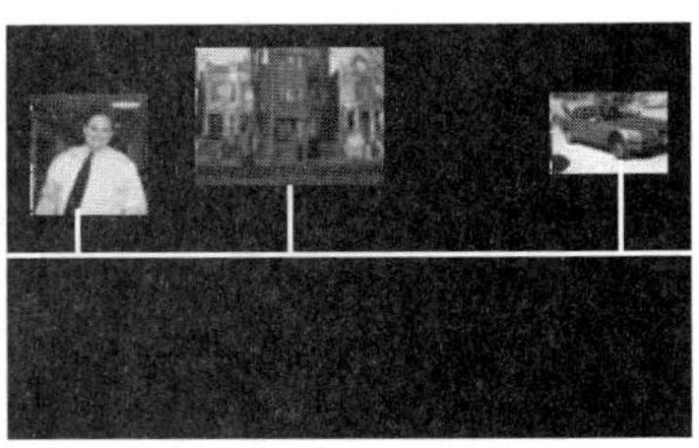

With the baseline for the physical evidence established, it is now a good time to loop back to the police investigation or to the witness who will identify the defendant as being in control of the car. Here is a good place to return to the timeline.

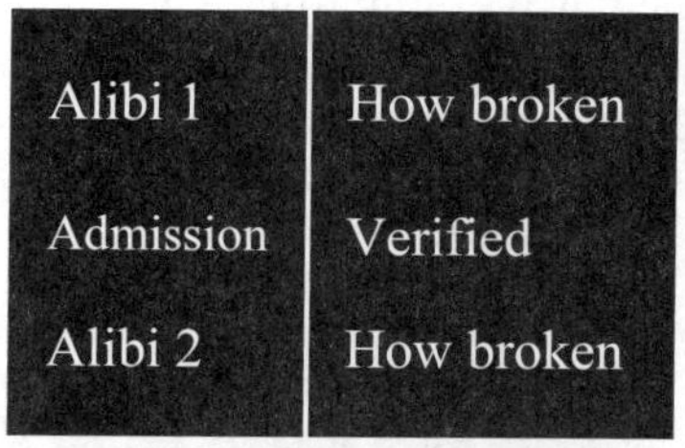

Since the defendant gave statements that were either damaging because they were discredited or were verified and proven to be true, a compare and contrast slide is a good device to characterize the statements before they have been introduced.

Once the statements are addressed, it is a good time to show the gun that matches the bullets from the victim's body next to a photo of the defendant's house where it was recovered.

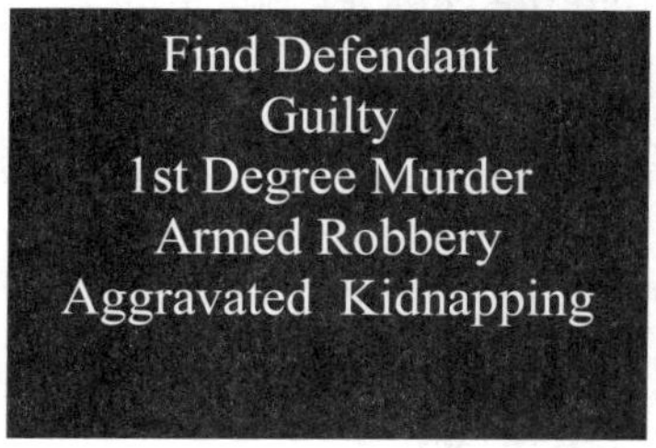

End with a prayer slide asking the jury to find the defendant guilty.

Telling the story from the medical examiner's point of view

This opening begins by focusing the jury's attention on the horror and inferential terror that the deceased victim endured. Tell this story by starting with the medical examiner, the doctor who stared down at the helpless body of the deceased and began to deconstruct the ways that the deceased suffered. An opening like this is ideal for a prosecutor who wants to underscore a catalog of injuries and suffering.

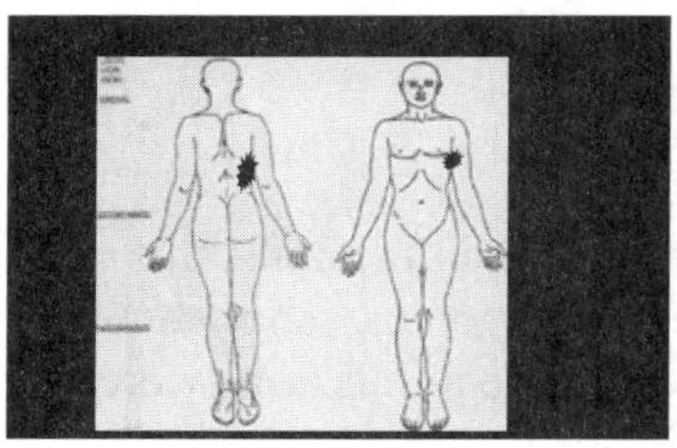

This opening could start with the body chart. It tells a story that begins with solving the mystery of who the victim was and how the victim was injured. The medical examiner's theories regarding the length of time the victim suffered before dying and the significance of the maggot evidence are underscored since the maggots help forensic pathologists and entomologists establish approximate times of death based on the gestation of the bugs.

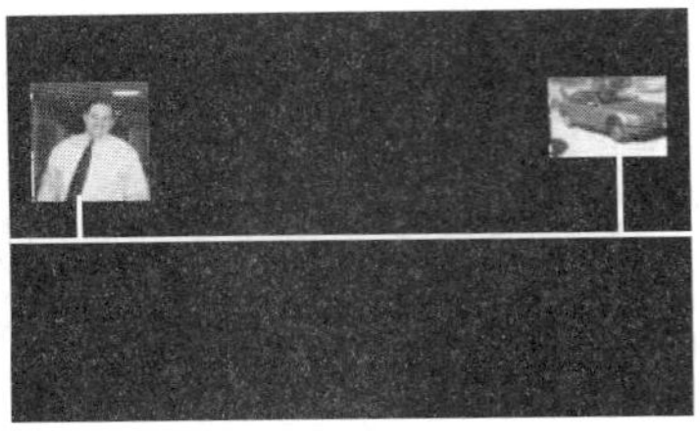

The next image could introduce the victim and the car with the timeline that symbolizes the passage of time between discovery and disappearance.

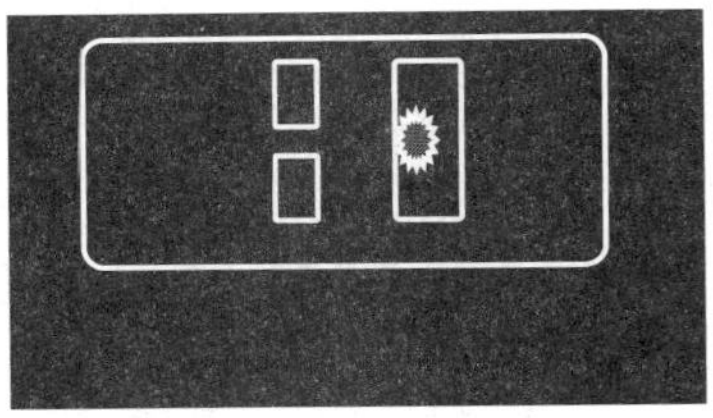

A diagram of the car helps underscore the significance of the blood spatter in the backseat. It indicates that the victim did not appear to have moved around much in the car after being shot. This means it is more likely that the victim died in the backseat and was in the car around the time that the defendant was seen near the car.

The next slide can talk about the other evidence that the car yielded.

The bottle bearing the defendant's fingerprints should appear next to the car with an arrow pointing from the car to the bottle. It is the piece of evidence that you will argue leads to the defendant and solves the mystery of who hurt the victim.

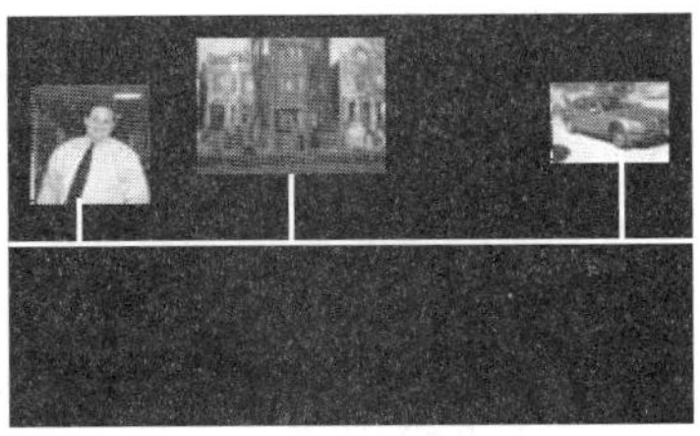

This is a good place to introduce the investigation that led the police to finding the witness who identified the defendant and another man as being in control of the car. The visual of the area where the witness saw the defendant in control of the car is an effective addition to the timeline.

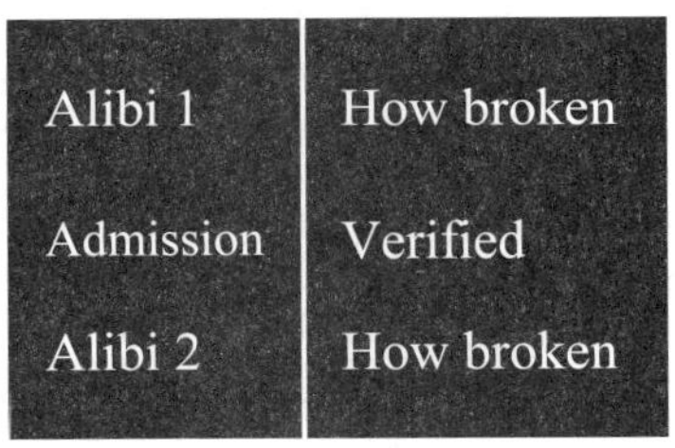

If you want to talk about the defendant's statements and admissions, this is a good place to use a compare and contrast slide. Here you can show how the defendant's accounts do not make sense or where the admissions were verified.

From your point of view as prosecutor, the fact that the location where the witness saw the defendant near the victim's car turns out to be the defendant's house, where the murder weapon was then found, further underscores the defendant's guilt, so include a visual that reinforces this for jurors.

You should then use a life photo and talk about seeking justice for the victim.

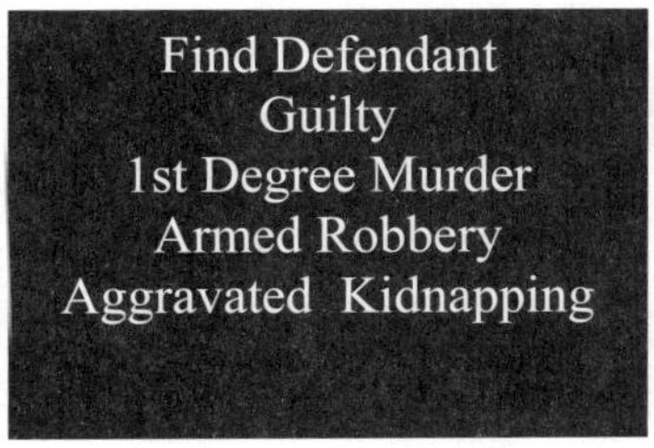

End with a prayer slide asking the jury to find the defendant guilty.

Telling the story from the investigator's point of view

This presentation could start with the car, yielding an unknown human body with horrible injuries, covered with maggots. This sets the stage for the detectives trying to seek justice for the unknown dead person in the car.

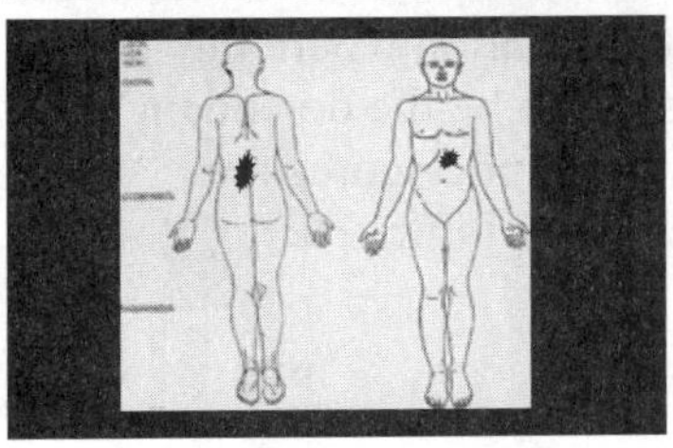

Tell a story that tries to identify the unknown victim. Underscore the medical examiner's theories regarding the length of time the victim suffered before dying and the significance of the maggot evidence since the maggots help forensic pathologists and entomologists establish approximate times of death based on the gestation of the bugs.

With identity determined, introduce the victim by showing a life photo and talk about what the detective was able to learn regarding when the victim died, where he was last seen alive, and what he was driving.

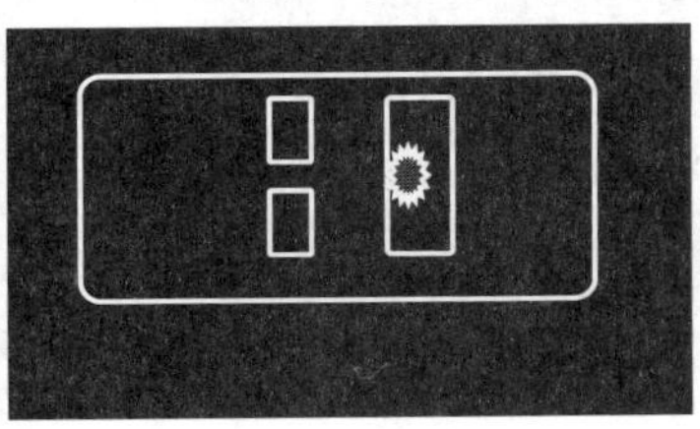

Turn to the significance of the blood spatter in the backseat of the car. It indicates that the victim did not appear to have moved around much in the car after being shot. This means it is more likely that the victim died in the backseat and was in the car around the time that the defendant was seen near the car.

The next image could introduce the victim and the car with the timeline that underscores the passage of time between discovery of the victim and his disappearance.

The bottle bearing the defendant's fingerprints should appear next to the car with an arrow pointing from the car to the bottle. It is the piece of evidence that leads to the defendant and solves the mystery of who hurt the victim.

This is a good place to introduce the investigation that led the police to finding the witness who identified the defendant and another man as being in control of the car. The visual of the area where the witness saw the defendant in control of the car is an effective addition to the timeline.

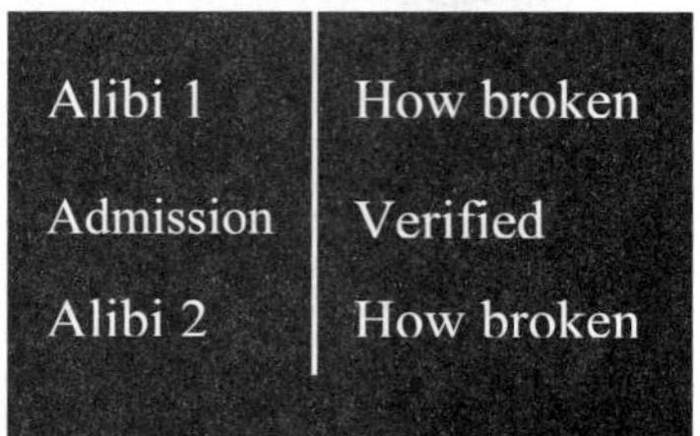

If you want to talk about the defendant's statements and admissions, this is a good place to use a compare and contrast slide. Here you can show how the defendant's accounts do not make sense or where the admissions were verified.

From your point of view as prosecutor, the fact that the location where the witness saw the defendant near the victim's car turns out to be the defendant's house, where the murder weapon was then found, further underscores the defendant's guilt, so include a visual that reinforces this for jurors.

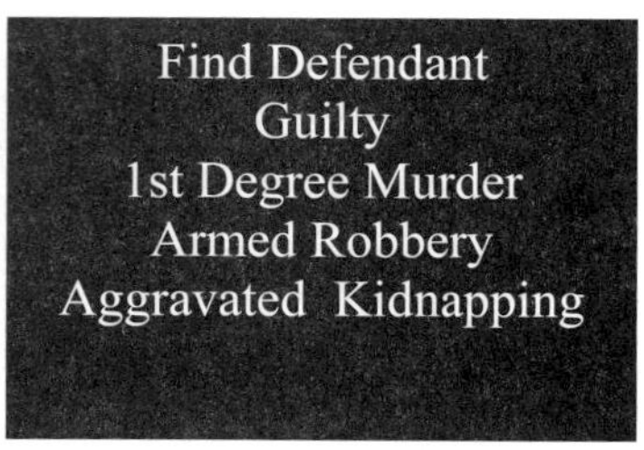

End with a prayer slide asking the jury to find the defendant guilty.

This exercise simply shows some of the different ways that an opening statement can be told. These types of organizations help the trial lawyer "storyboard" the case to create the maximum impact on the jury. Before reading on, consider the types of visuals and the different orders that could be used in the plaintiff's case in the civil personal injury case about the woman who loses her leg after falling under the wheels of a train.

Presentation Suggestions for the Defense Attorney

A defense presentation need not be linear, although PowerPoint does create visuals that can be launched in Sanction. As a defense attorney, you should avoid having to stick to the script of a linear presentation since you may want to address specific things that the prosecutor addressed in his or her opening statement. For that reason, you should create a series of mini-slide presentations that address defense themes. These mini-presentations can be launched from Sanction. This way, you have visuals that you can use in any order that you believe is right at the time of the opening. In addition to this concern, you must decide which defense to use before deciding which visuals to stress. There are three basic defenses to the criminal case from Chapter 2. The first holds the prosecution to its burden of proving its case beyond a reasonable doubt, the second mounts an affirmative defense, and the third attempts to negate a conviction by pursuing an insanity or diminished capacity defense.

Creating visuals for a burden of proof defense

There are a number of ways to pursue the first defense, which asserts that the prosecution cannot prove its case beyond a reasonable doubt. This defense can attack a specific element or all elements of the charged crime. The reasonable doubt defense is the most common defense pursued by defense attorneys. It attacks the weight and reliability of the prosecution's evidence without putting the defense in the position of having to offer evidence. If you decide to pursue a reasonable doubt defense, you must ask whether this defense will offer an alternative theory for the jury to embrace. For instance, are you going to attack identity and offer an alternative offender as a suspect, or are you simply going to hope that the jury will simply believe that the wrong guy may be on trial? The prospect of claiming that the defendant is an innocent man or woman is an attractive prospect, and the chance of blaming a third party for the crime certainly makes jurors more comfortable with signing a verdict in a particular defendant's favor.

One way to underscore this path is to offer a visual that puts a photo of the defendant next to a photo of the alternative suspect. For the purposes of the following visuals, assume that the photo we've been using for the victim now represents the defendant.

The alternative suspect in the visual with the question mark can be introduced by superimposing the alternative photo over the defendant photo. Simply make the photo appear on a mouse click, and the second picture will replace the first.

On the other hand, the third party may not be readily available or discernable from the defense investigation of the case. If this is the case and you still want to pursue the "wrong guy" defense, then the visual you choose should focus on the details in the witnesses' description of the offender that do not match the defendant.

This first slide puts a photo of the defendant on the screen and then lists the things from the witnesses' descriptions that do not match the defendant. The question marks emphasize the discrepancy.

This next side has arrows that point away from the defendant. These arrows appear as the attorney lists the description characteristics that do not apply to the defendant.

Or, you could use a linear presentation for attacking identity that does not offer an alternative suspect.

On X date, the victim was found dead in the backseat of his mother's car. The victim was a college basketball star, from all accounts a good and decent kid. People in the community were outraged. The victim had been missing for a week.

The press ran photos of the victim and his car on the news. They asked the public for information about the car. A man watching the news remembered seeing the car. He remembered something else, seeing my client, the defendant, standing near the car.

Use a blank slide and talk about the burden of proof or use some of the burden slides that appear throughout the chapter.

Use a photo of the defendant and the defendant's house to show that he is not afraid to be put near the car.

Explain how the defendant had a beer with an old friend as the defendant stood outside the car. Talk about how the defendant must not have noticed the victim's body in the back seat. Speculate about it being covered up. Talk about the defendant accepting the gun from his friend, putting it in his house for safe keeping. Now you have accounted for all the physical evidence in the case.

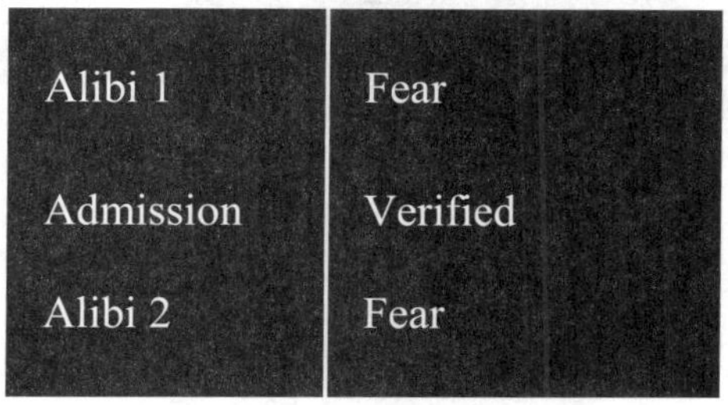

Explain how the defendant was arrested and how he foolishly concealed his friend's whereabouts. Front the fact that defendant told untruths because of his fear of being implicated since defendant had accepted a weapon from the same person who drove the car.

End with a prayer asking the jury to find defendant not guilty.

Another slide that is imperative is a burden of proof slide. Some jurisdictions do not define the burden of proof, while others give jurors their definition of a reasonable doubt. Although it is improper to talk about the law during an opening statement, nothing stops you from reminding the jury that the burden exists or from using selected words and phrases from the jury instruction.

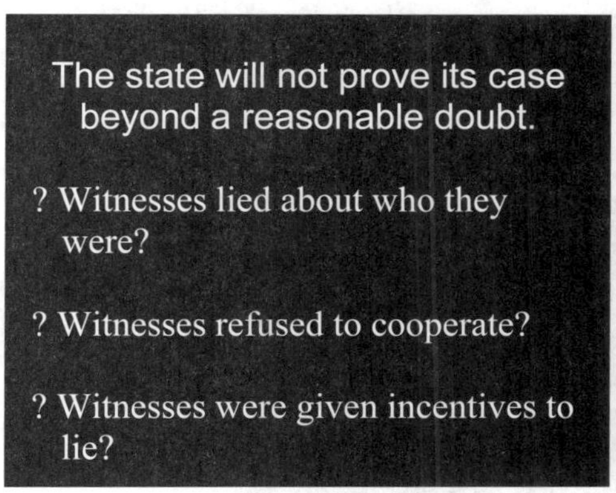

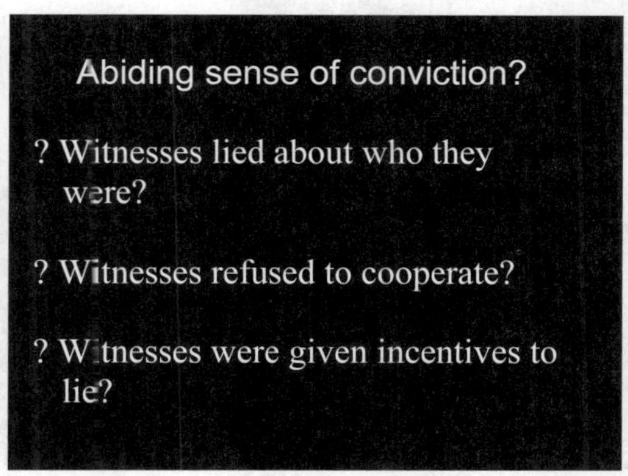

You can narrate these slides by asking rhetorical questions about whether the jurors want to be in the position of having to rely on evidence that comes from witnesses who have these problems. If you are pursuing a reasonable doubt defense that infers that the defendant was framed by police officers who have crafted their stories to implicate the defendant, or who intimidated the defendant into confessing to a crime that he did not commit, time and prior allegations of misconduct against the officers must be stressed.

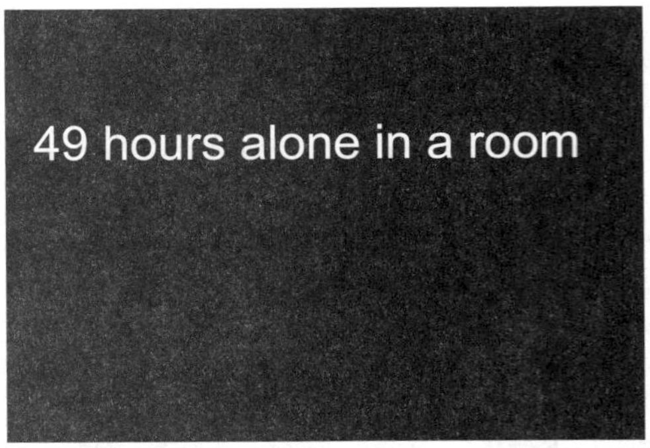

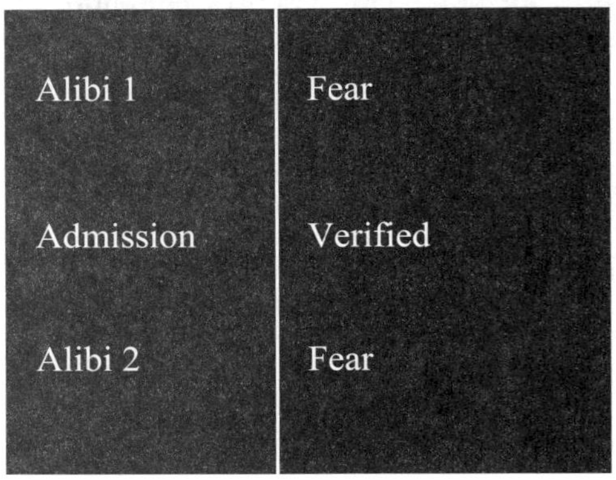

Explain how the defendant was arrested and how the defendant foolishly concealed his friend's whereabouts. Front the fact that the defendant told untruths because of his fear of being implicated since defendant had accepted a weapon from the same person who drove the car.

Here are some universal reasonable doubt visuals.

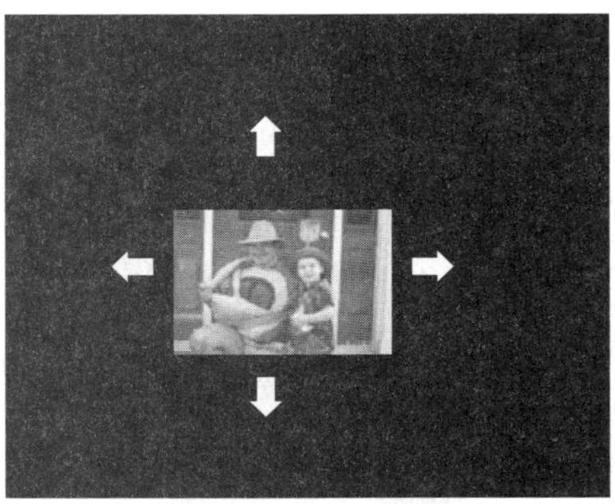

The arrow pointing away from the defendant is a good device for saying the state does not have enough evidence to point at the defendant. It is a visual that underscores the fact that the evidence points at someone or something besides the defendant.

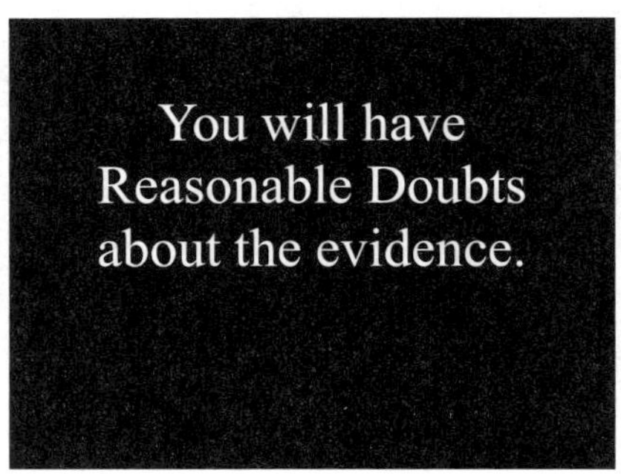

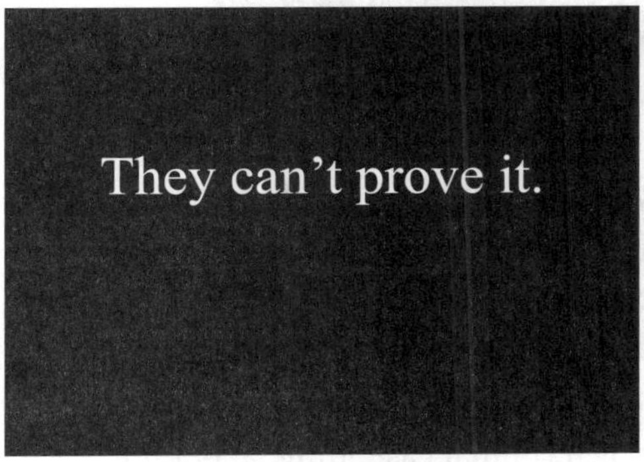

Creating visuals for a legal justification defense

Turn now to the second defense, which offers a legal justification for the activity that has resulted in the defendant being charged with a crime. For example, the defense of self-defense concedes that a defendant has committed the acts that caused injuries to an individual; however, the defense maintains that the force used by the defendant was justified. This defense concedes much of the evidence, but claims that the victim somehow provoked the defendant, who then felt compelled to defend himself.

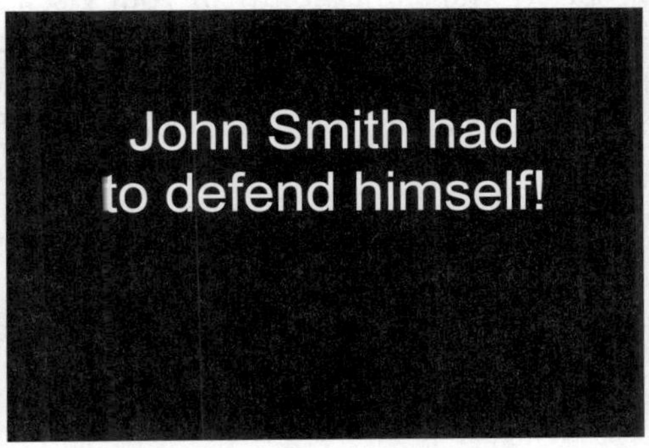

Creating visuals for an insanity or a diminished capacity defense

The final defense you could pursue in this murder case is the insanity or diminished capacity defense, where you claim that the defendant's lack of ability to form the necessary mental state to commit the charged crime should absolve him from criminal responsibility. Although you cannot argue the law during the opening statement, nothing stops you from explaining your theory for a defense. You should use carefully chosen phrases that set the stage for some of the themes that you will introduce. This particular sequence needs four slides.

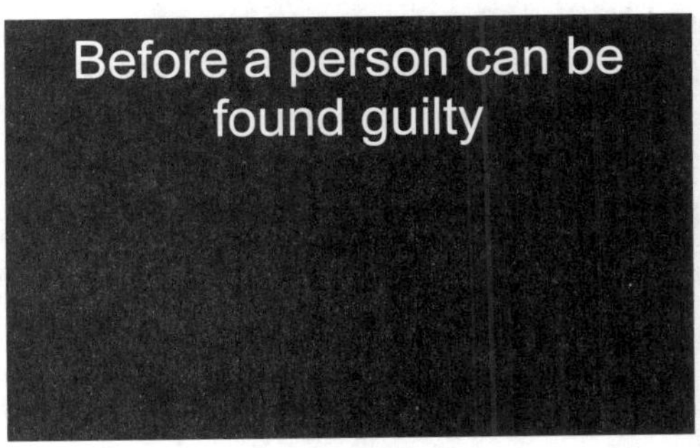

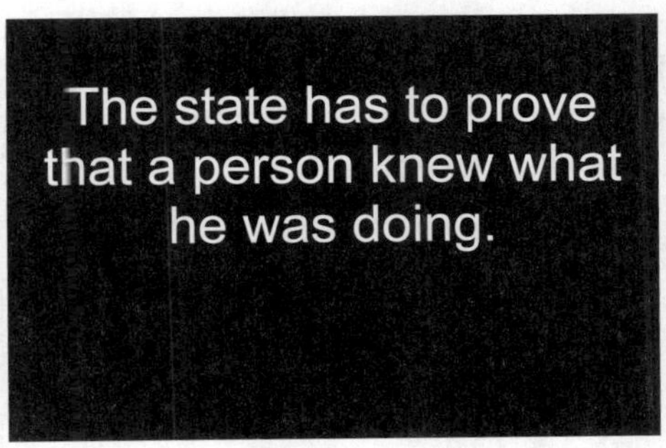

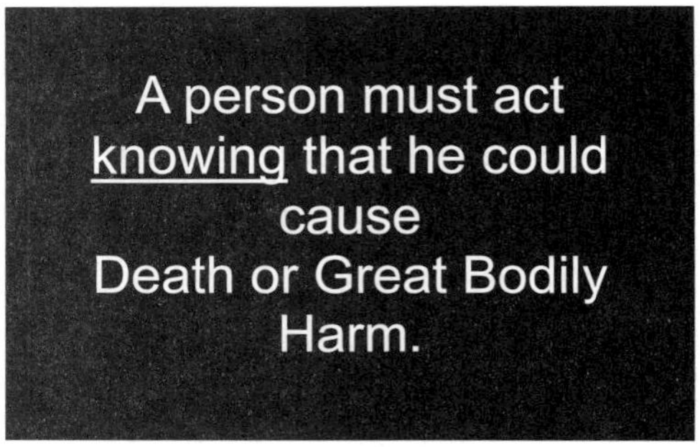

After considering the different ways to mount a defense for the criminal case, think about how you might use visuals in the defense of the civil case from Chapter 2.

General Suggestions for Opening Statements

Launch your presentation from Sanction. Sanction lets you run a PowerPoint show or a TimeMap presentation on top of the Sanction desktop. If you are a plaintiff's or prosecution's attorney, stick to a linear presentation for opening. You should have obtained pretrial rulings regarding the propriety and admissibility of your visuals before beginning the presentation. The advantage of using a PowerPoint show for opening statement is that you can use a cordless mouse or other presentation device to advance through the slide show without having to stand by the keyboard. This freedom allows you to activate a slide from any place in the courtroom. If you are a defense attorney, create mini PowerPoint shows that can be launched from the Sanction desktop in any order that you deem appropriate.

Assume again that you are the defense attorney in the criminal case from Chapter 2. You want to address the following topics in your opening statement:

1. the burden of proof — the state hasn't met it;
2. the witness who will claim he saw the defendant near the victim's car is not believable;
3. the things the police did not do during the investigation that could have or should have been done to ensure a full fair and complete investigation;
4. the prospect of the existence an unknown offender who will be identified by the defense; and
5. the prayer slide.

You could simply run a linear presentation, but you risk being locked into a script that you may want to change after hearing the prosecution's opening statement. For example, imagine how you would feel about a linear presentation that talked about all five of the above topics if you learned during the prosecution's opening that the witness covered in point 2 *is now not going to be called.* You would now be put in the position of talking about the witness because that witness was simply part of the script. The solution to this dilemma is to create five individual presentations that you can launch independently of each other. You can still use a cordless mouse to advance slides, but you will need to launch the slide shows from the keyboard, the Sanction toolbar, or a bar code scanner.

Tactical Considerations for Opening Statements

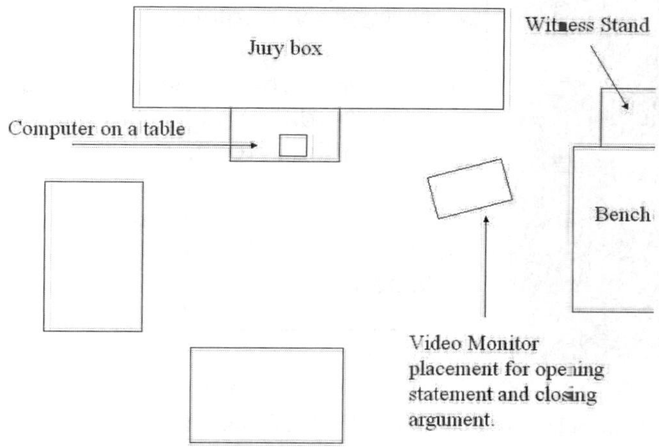

Set your equipment up in the following positions.

You want the monitor off to the side during your opening statement or closing argument. In this location, a right-handed person can gesture toward the monitor naturally

Jurors can look at the lawyer and then look at the information that is on the screen. This position puts the lawyer in the position of teacher while doing the presentation.

Visual Suggestions for Opening Statement

Timelines

A timeline is simply a slide that helps jurors keep evidence in context. The screen capture that follows shows a simple timeline that appears between other evidentiary slides. You can put as many evidentiary slides between the master timeline slides as you like because the timeline simply keeps the story grounded to a time sequence. Once you give a jury a context for time, you can move backward or forward through the timeline to explain things or put things into context. A timeline is a powerful tool that lends itself to any story. You can create a timeline like the one that follows in TimeMap and then export the timeline to PowerPoint or set up Sanction so you can launch the timeline from Sanction. Either device allows you to take the jury through the story while keeping the individual events in context.

The case that follows was a medical malpractice case that claimed that the defendant doctors failed to provide acceptable medical care when they prescribed a lethal dose of medication for the plaintiff and then failed to counteract the poisoning. The case was a circumstantial evidence case in which the plaintiff went into arrest after his doctor's order was written. The timeline for the opening was designed to get the jury comfortable with the general idea of a timeline because an expert witness was going to use a similar timeline to put the hospital's medical chart into an understandable context for the jury. So one timeline was used in the trial as an orientation for a second, more complex timeline. This TimeMap timeline shows supporting documents for each of the boxes on the timeline.

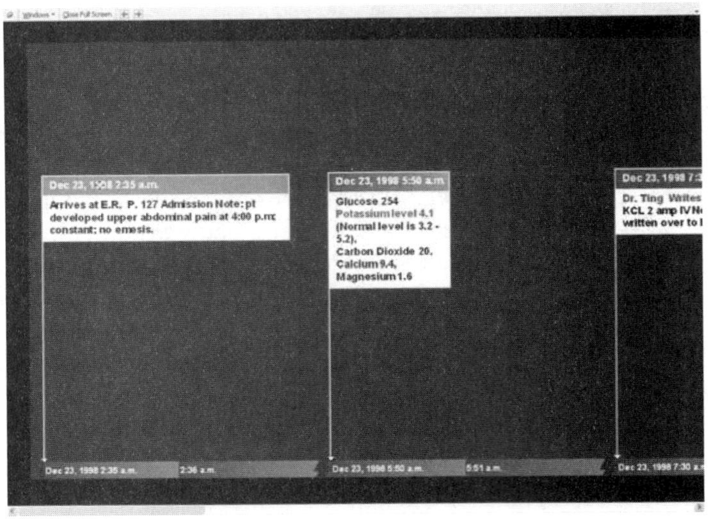

This is a screen capture of a TimeMap timeline. It was created by attorney Mark Bodner of Mark L. Bodner PC for an opening statement for a medical malpractice wrongful death case.

In TimeMap, you can scroll through the timeline by dragging the blue bar at the bottom of the screen.

The case settled for a multimillion dollar settlement after the jury was selected.

Next is a timeline that was created for a criminal case and run from PowerPoint. The animation for this slide has the text box wipe up or down from the center line. The master timeline continues to appear as the attorney progresses through the story of the opening statement. The attorney can insert slides with photos videos or other visuals between the timeline slides. This lets the attorney give a context to each exhibit because the timeline imposes a structure on the presentation. Jurors expect the story to unfold as each box wipes up or down from the center line. Once the boxes for a slide are completed, the final slide can be saved as a .jpg slide and then inserted on top of another timeline slide.

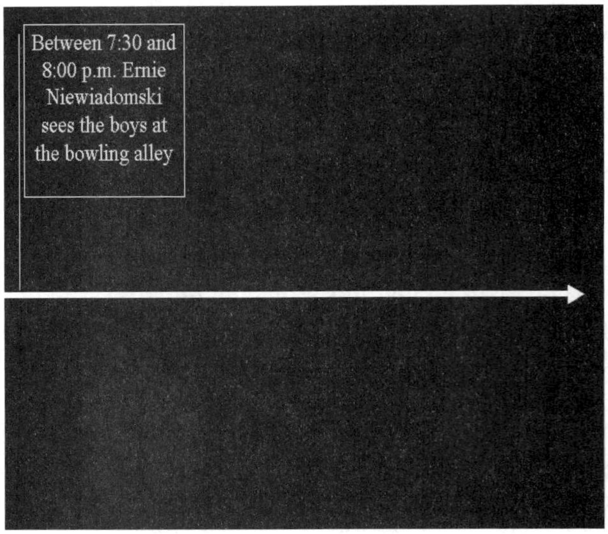

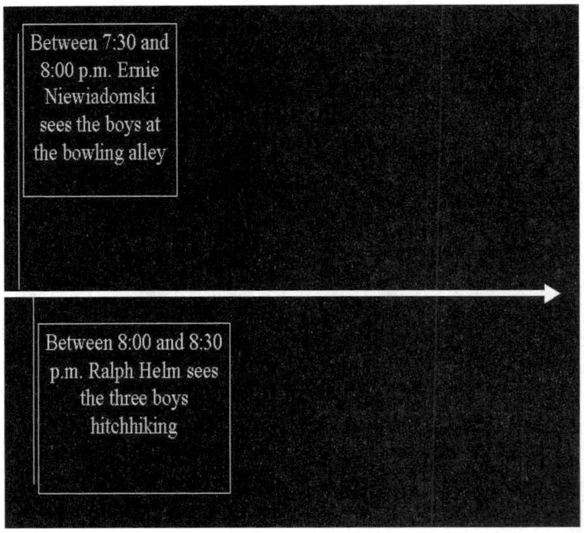

The type of timeline shown next was used in the case of *People v. Hansen*, as illustrated in the following visual. Hansen was accused of murdering three boys in 1955 and was being prosecuted in 2002. Hansen had made a series of admissions to different individuals. The objective of this timeline was to focus the jury on the empirical facts of the case by showing that Hansen lived close to the boys and had to travel past the place where the boys were last seen alive. Hansen also worked at a stable that was near the horse path where the boys' bodies were dumped. Then the timeline was used to put Hansen's admissions into perspective for the jurors.

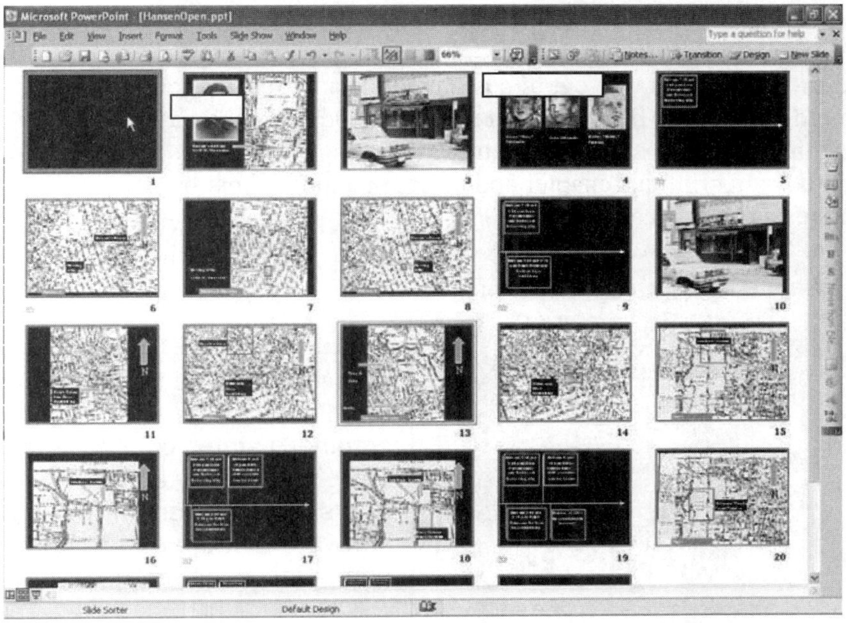

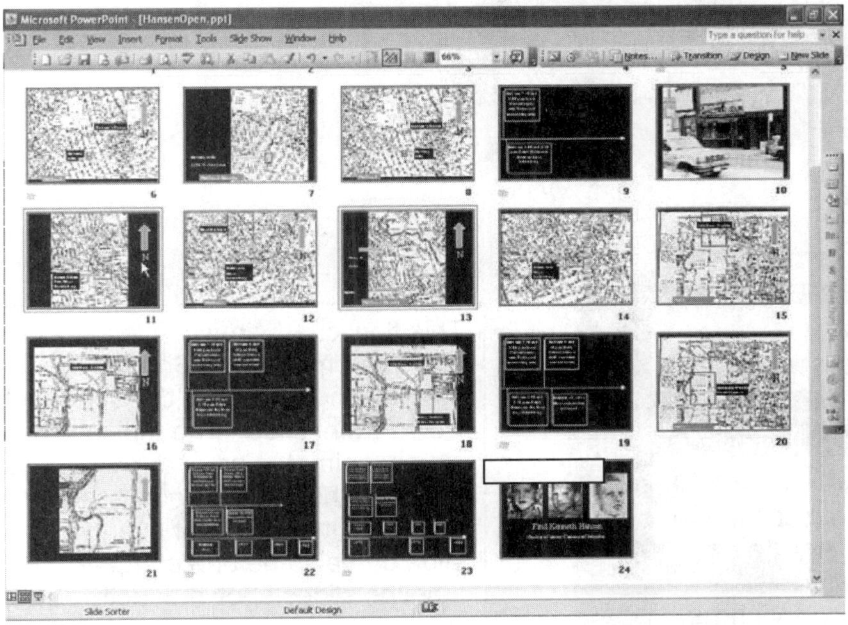

This is a screen capture of a timeline that integrates maps and photos into the story.

The presentation moves back and forth between the timeline and the exhibits to give the jurors a sense of time and place, since Chicago in 1955 did not look like Chicago in 2002.

The first 22 slides of the timeline track some of the important facts surrounding the disappearance of the three boys.

The twenty-third and twenty-fourth slides simply list years. These years showed the jury that Hansen continued to brag about this unsolved case.

Each time the prosecutor, Linas Kelecius, advanced through the timeline to another year, he talked about a conversation that a witness was expected to testify about.

PowerPoint has a calendar template that lends itself to the next visual. When working in Windows, you can capture a screen on the computer desktop by pressing the Alt + Print Screen keys. Then you can paste that screen capture onto a PowerPoint slide by pressing Ctrl + V. In this capture, the green means the defendant was out of custody while an arrest warrant was pending. The medium-colored blue means the defendant was in custody at the jail after the execution of the warrant, and maroon means the defendant was in prison serving his sentence. (Remember: You can download and print this chapter and others in a .pdf format by going to the Litigation Technology website at www.littech.org.)

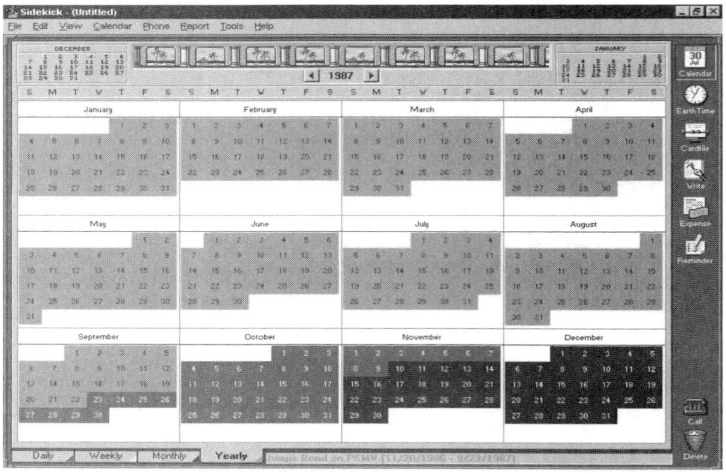

This is a timeline that uses color on top of a calendar to show a criminal's status over a period of time. It is simply a screen capture of a sidekick calendar (the calendar software that the author had on his computer at the time).

Flow charts

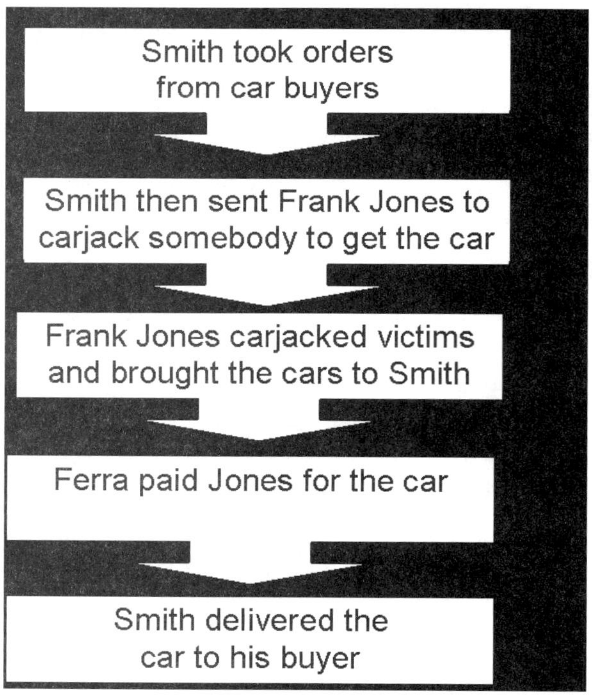

This flow chart simply takes block arrows from the AutoShapes menu on the drawing toolbar at the bottom of the PowerPoint slide. The trial lawyer simply animates each arrow to wipe down as the attorney addresses the next step in the flow of events. This slide can also be broken up like the timeline slides shown directly above.

Other visual devices

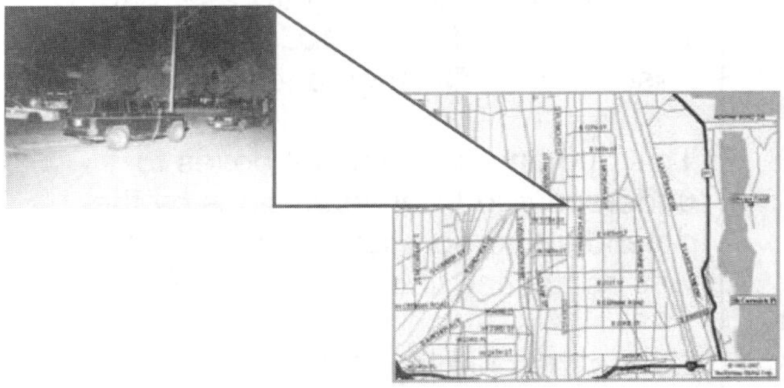

This visual uses a solid triangle to show where a photograph corresponds to a point on the map.

The triangle is layered on top of the map and simply touches the side of the photograph. Later, a witness can authenticate this visual during direct examination.

1 2 3

This series of slides shows how a photograph can become a baseline for a simple diagram. In PowerPoint, this entire effect can be achieved on one slide by having the lines appear and then change color, and then by having the photograph fade out with a mouse click. This visual is effective because it removes visual clutter from the information that the attorney wants to focus on.

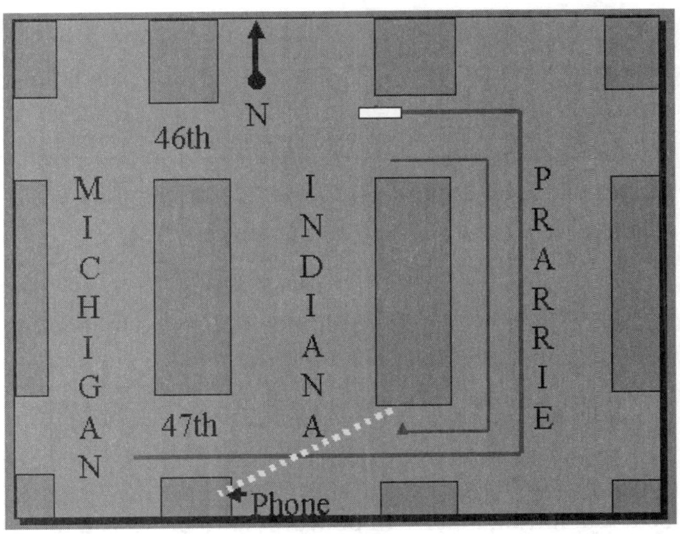

This slide was used to demonstrate a witness's vantage point for a drive-by shooting in Chicago. The witness (indicated by the blue line) walked from 46th Street and Indiana down Prarrie to 47th Street. The witness then crossed kitty-corner to the southwest corner and stood there when he saw the defendants in the white car (indicated by the red line) stop at the street light. At that point, the witness was merely 30 feet from the defendants. Then the defendants turned the corner and were next seen at 46th and Indiana, where they then shot and killed the victim. This diagram was prepared with the assistance of the witness and later authenticated during direct examination.

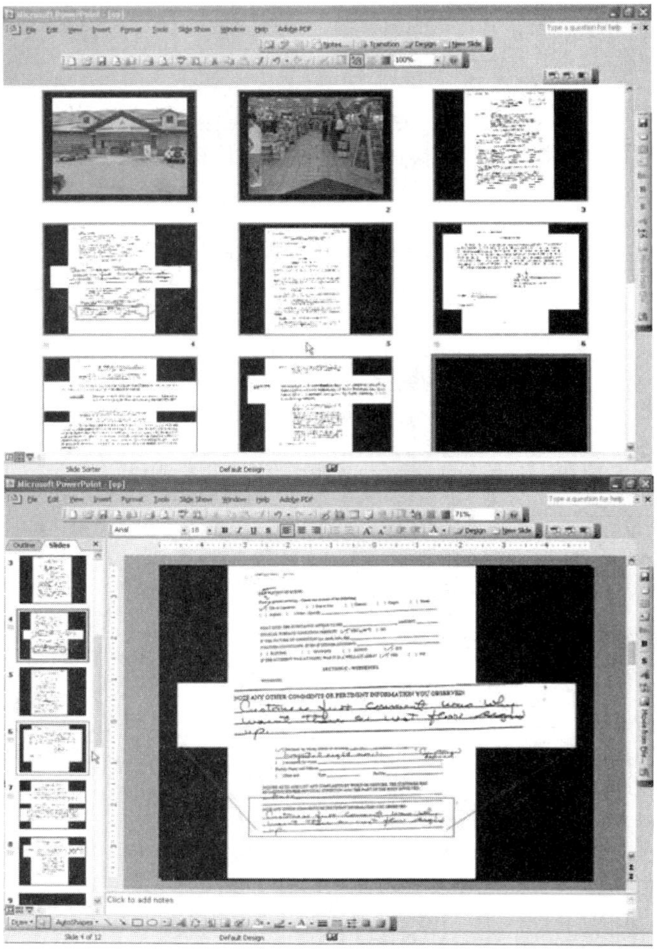

These are screen captures from a civil personal injury slip and fall case tried by Tom Kelliher of Gary McCallister and Associates of Chicago and Kansas.

This opening used callout boxes to underscore judicial admissions by the defendant corporation where the defense was contesting liability.

During the opening statement, Tom was able to show the jury that the witnesses they were going to meet were going to be corroborated by the pleadings and other documents that were filed during the pending litigation.

Tom used callout boxes to show the jury exactly where the admissions appeared on the documents.

In this case, the plaintiff had a preexisting back injury that was further injured when the plaintiff slipped and fell on a wet floor that had no warning signs around the wet area.

Tom and the McCallister firm were able to secure a jury verdict in excess of $1 million at trial.

Things to Keep in Mind About Opening Statement

The Don'ts

Don't waste the first 30 seconds on needless ritual: "May it please the court, counsel, and members of the jury (curtsy or bow) . . ." This filler type of activity serves no purpose. It simply diminishes the message that you are delivering to the jury.

Don't start your opening statement with a fawning thank you. "Before I begin, I'd like to thank each and every one of you for taking time out of your busy schedules to be here today." (Why not serve tea?)

Don't do the worthy Centurion.

> "Ladies and gentlemen, this will be a tough trial, and I will be working to bring you the evidence that I have available to me."
>
> "I'm the prosecutor, and it is my duty to present the evidence in this case. It will be a long and hard trial, but you will see . . ."

"I represent the plaintiff, and it is my duty to present the evidence in this case . . ."

"I am the defense attorney, and it is my duty to represent my client to the best of my ability (putting your hand on the defendant's shoulder). This will be a long, hard trial, but you will see . . ." Go jump in a phone booth, Clark.

Don't do the Julie from the *Love Boat* routine: "Before I tell you what the evidence is, let me tell you a little bit about what we can expect at trial Opening statement is like a road map or an outline of what we expect the evidence is going to show . . ." Just tell the story.

Don't do the "what I say isn't evidence" shuffle: "Now what I say isn't evidence, and what the lawyer over there says isn't evidence . . ." You this might as well tell the jury to ignore everything you're about to say.

Don't read a speech. This kills communication. Imagine how hard it would be to sit through the experience of hearing an attorney who simply reads his or her argument. Instead, script a headline and an exit line, and then outline the rest.

Don't do a book report. Opening statement is not your chance to list the name of every witness or to give a catalog of every piece of evidence or event that occurred during the investigation.

The Dos

Clear the decks from objections to the use of technology during opening statement. Don't be afraid to show your slide presentation to the opposition. The only exhibits that should be contained in the presentation are those that you will seek to admit at trial. The proponent of the slide show must have a good faith basis for the use of the exhibit or should be prepared for the sanction of a mistrial with prejudice for showing exhibits that were not admitted in evidence. Once the opposition has viewed the presentation and indicated that he or she is objecting to the presentation, make a motion in limine seeking judicial permission to use the presentation and any other exhibits as visuals during opening statement. Be prepared to make a proffer regarding the foundation for the exhibit and, if necessary, be prepared to call a witness to testify outside the presence of the jury regarding the facts needed to lay the foundation for the exhibit. This motion forces the opposing attorney to articulate all of his or her objections to the presentation outside the presence of the jury. Once the opposing attorney has articulated his or her objections, the judge has the opportunity to rule on the propriety of the presentation. If the judge sustains any objections to the presentation, you should make any changes or corrections to the presentation and then seek permission to publish the modified presentation. If the trial judge continues to find an image objectionable, then you should be prepared to remove the image or hide (turn off) the offending slide.

Using Headlines

Plan to begin an opening statement with a headline that grabs the jury's attention. If a theme has been clearly presented and properly underscored with appropriate visuals, and if the case has been laid out logically while at the same time connecting with juror value judgments that support signing the verdict form in a party's favor, then the opposing attorney will face the monumental challenge of getting the jurors to change their minds. It is fair to say that many jurors have made up their minds regarding the outcome of a case by the end of the opening statement phase of the trial. First impressions matter. Although people try not to judge a book by its cover, they often do. For that reason, it is wise to use the first 30 seconds of opening statement to seize the jurors' attention and to begin juror indoctrination.

"This is a case" headline

This headline is a raw distillation of a case theme. It should contain the essence of whatever fundamental concept you want your jurors to seize on as they begin to decide in your favor.

Examples

Prosecution theme: A gang-affiliated youthful offender is just as deadly as a big one. "This is a case about a cold-blooded gang murder on the south side. It is a case about a 16-year-old assassin who shot a young man in the back five times as the young man tried to run away. This is a case about a defendant who told two people about coming back to the scene of this shooting to watch his victim bleed, so he could make sure the 'worthless piece of garbage was gone . . .'"

Defense theme: Rush to judgment. "This is a case about a rush to judgment by detectives anxious to clear a high-profile case. It is a case about investigators who chose to ignore evidence that pointed at other possible suspects and instead to focus on an easy target. It is a case about a person who was at the wrong place at the wrong time . . ."

Civil case: Personal injury. "This is a case about negligence, about not paying attention. It is a case about a woman whose life was forever changed by the defendant's carelessness when driving a 5000 pound automobile. It is a case about a defendant who drove a shiny new Lincoln Town Car through a red light on a rainy Friday evening, into the woman who sits here today in that wheelchair . . ."

Civil case: Wrongful death. "This is a case about people who tried to unring a bell. It is a case about a group of doctors and nurses who tried frantically to reverse a horrible mistake. It is a case about medical malpractice — about failing to provide adequate medical care for a patient. But before we talk about how Robert Johnson got poisoned in the hospital, I want to talk about antidotes. Because you're going to see how the way Robert Johnson was given those antidotes will tell you that the doctors and nurses realized just how grave a mistake was made in this case . . ."

Appropriate visuals

Use a slide that shows a word or a phrase that captures the essence of the case theme.

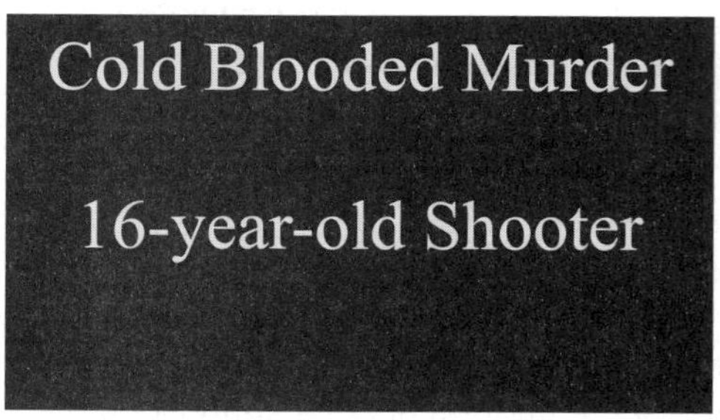

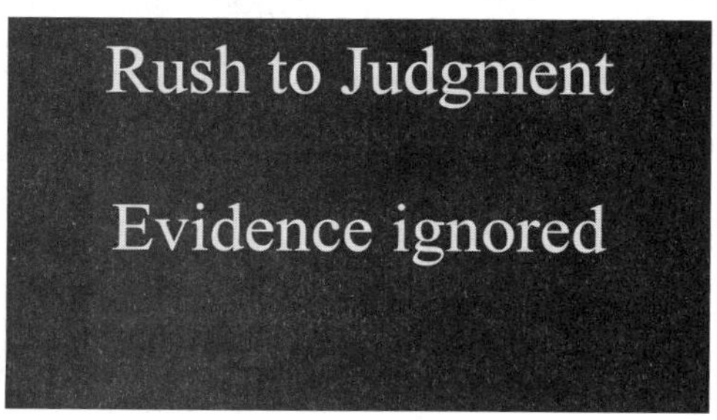

"First words" headline

This headline is ideal when an individual's words distill the theme of a case. This kind of opening theme uses ironic phrases or telling phrases that were uttered by a party about the incident that is at the center of the lawsuit.

Examples

Prosecution attorney in a criminal case. "'Where's the money?' Those were the defendant's first words to 78-year-old Martha Wake. The defendant said those words as he stood over Ms. Wake in her bedroom. At first she thought she was dreaming; then she looked into the defendant's dead white eye. She saw the scars on his face. His distorted mouth, his hands just inches from her throat. She saw these things because the light spilled into her room from the street lights outside her window . . ."

Civil plaintiff's attorney in a personal injury lawsuit. "'Man, am I loaded!' Those were the defendant's first words as he staggered from his car after he collided with the Emerson family car. Defendant said those words as he spoke to Mr. Emerson as Emerson was trying to help his wife who had been injured in the car crash. Those words tell you everything you need to know about this defendant's ability to drive safely on March 15, 2004 . . ."

Civil plaintiff's attorney in a medical malpractice case. "'I'm sorry, I tried my best.' Those were Dr. Robert Johansen's first words to the family of Edith Brown as he spoke to them about her death. Words designed to comfort them. Words designed to make them feel there was nothing more he could do for Edith Brown. Words that you will soon know were designed to conceal Dr. Johansen's carelessness . . ."

Civil defense attorney in a personal injury lawsuit. "'I'm sorry, it was all my fault.' Those were the plaintiff's first words to Robert Townsend as she got out of her car after the collision. Words that she said before she had time to reflect, time to change her story, time to file her lawsuit trying to get money from Mr. Townsend . . ."

Appropriate visuals

Use the "first words" phrase or the images of the people who were affected by the defendant's conduct and *no other text*. Tell a story about the people who were affected by the person who spoke the words.

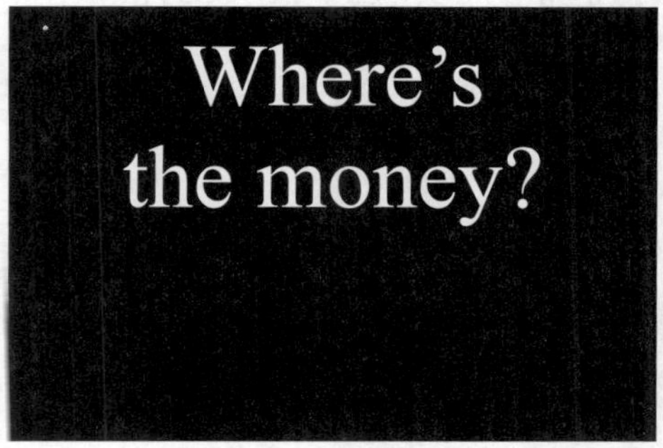

"Dark and stormy night" headline

Edward George Bulwer-Lytton began his novel, *Paul Clifford*, with this sentence: "It was a dark and stormy night; the rain fell in torrents — except at occasional intervals, when it was checked by a violent gust of wind which swept up the streets (for it is in London that our scene lies), rattling along the housetops, and fiercely agitating the scanty flame of the lamps that struggled against the darkness." That sentence is now sighted as an example of the overly flowery, contrived writing that personified bad writing in the Victorian era. On the other hand, almost every horror movie begins with some variation on that sentence. The "dark and stormy night" headline sets the stage for the victimization of an unwitting person who didn't know something, or didn't realize something, or who disregarded something and got hurt.

Examples

Prosecution attorney in the murdered athlete criminal case. "On March 8, 2004, at 2:00 in the afternoon, Marcia Pomeroy thought her son was just driving her car to run an errand. She didn't know as her son pulled away that this would be the last time she would ever see him. She didn't know that her car would become her son's rolling coffin. She couldn't have known that her son would have the great misfortune of meeting this defendant and his friend Henry Miller. She had no idea that after her son met these men, that the first ones to find her son would be the flies . . ."

Defense attorney in the murdered athlete criminal case: Defendant's nightmare. "At 8:15 A.M. on March 13, 2004, Henry Miller stepped out of his front door and headed out looking for work. But before Mr. Miller could reach the corner, he felt the barrel of the gun being shoved into the side of his head. Before he knew it, Henry Miller was handcuffed, fingerprinted, and charged with murder. Henry Miller is living a nightmare that continues today. So to understand the reason why he is unjustly charged with this case, I need to take you back . . ."

Appropriate visuals

Consider beginning the presentation with a photo of a place or a photo of the person who is encountering the nightmare. Now the jury can associate a face with a name, which should make them care more about the person who is the subject of the story.

Greek chorus

This literary device imitates the voice of the stage manager from *Our Town*. These headlines work best when used in cases that involve multiple injured parties or patterns of injury that create a community of injury or the collision of two radically different worlds. These headlines are ideal when trying large-scale personal injury lawsuits or prosecuting serial rapists, serial murderers, or financial fraud cases in which numerous people were impacted by the defendant's conduct. These types of openings also work well with "innocent victims" who are victimized because of the defendant's choices alone.

Example

Plaintiff's opening for a wrongful death lawsuit. Theme: The defendants just didn't care, the bar let the drunk driver drive, and the drunk driver put an innocent person in danger.

"At 4:00 A.M., the bartender at the Bucket of Blood Lounge woke the man sitting across this room from you and told him he had to leave the lounge. The defendant had been drinking shots and fell asleep at the bar. The bartender asked the defendant if he wanted a cab. The defendant said, 'No, I'm going to walk,' and left the bar. The defendant got into his red 1974 Plymouth station wagon and started the engine. He pulled away from the Bucket of Blood Lounge as the bartender walked out after locking the front doors. The defendant drove westbound down North Avenue.

Some time around that moment, a man named Arthur Kane walked into his bedroom holding a cup of coffee. He set the cup down on the night stand next to his wife Maria and kissed her. Arthur Kane told his wife to wake up, and then said he would call her later to make sure that she had gotten up. He got into his car, pulled out of his driveway, and drove toward Division Street. Arthur Kane reached Division Street and turned right. He drove to Harlem and turned right again. Arthur started driving north toward North Avenue.

The defendant sideswiped the first car at Austin Boulevard. That car was being driven by a man whom you will meet. The man was Horace Lockerman. Mr. Lockerman pulled over, expecting the defendant to do the same. Instead, the defendant sped away. Mr. Lockerman began chasing the defendant west down North Avenue. At Oak Park Avenue, the defendant accelerated to 80 miles an hour. Mr. Lockerman got on his cell phone. He called the police. Mr. Lockerman was telling the officer the defendant's license plate when the defendant reached the Sears at Harlem and North. Arthur Kane had the green light and started through the intersection. Within moments, Arthur Kane was dead, and this man earned his place in that seat."

Appropriate visuals

Consider using photos of the plaintiff and the defendant on opposite sides of the slide with a line drawn down the middle of the slide separating the parties.

Using Loop Backs

Use a loop back as a transition to explain a problem or to put the rest of case into a context that the jury will follow. Use the words "to understand" to either set the stage for the story you will unfold or to front a problem fact before telling the rest of the story.

Examples

Prosecution attorney in a criminal case. "To understand the facts in this case, to see how this defendant earned his chair at the defendant's table, I need to take you back to the facts of that bloody night. It all started when . . ."

Plaintiff's attorney in a civil tort case. "To understand the facts in this case, I need to tell you something before I go any further. You are not going to meet Gaddis Johnson: He passed away a few weeks ago. These defendants had nothing to do with his death. But you will get to hear what Gaddis had to say because he had the opportunity to testify against this defendant in another proceeding before he passed away . . ."

Plaintiff's attorney in a civil medical malpractice case. "To understand why Paul Hankerman is paralyzed, I need to tell you something about charting procedures in hospitals . . ."

Defense attorney in a criminal case. "To understand why I am telling you that the wrong person is sitting at the defendant's table, I need to tell you some things about the way investigations are supposed to be conducted in this state. What was supposed to happen, didn't happen in this case, and that is why the government has chosen to charge the wrong guy . . ."

Using Movement Purposefully in the Courtroom

Unless the court requires an attorney to remain at the podium, get as far away from it as possible. When talking about what one expects a witness to say from the witness stand, move toward the witness stand, point at it, and stand next to it.

Underpromising and Overdelivering

In short, leave something for the jury's imagination. Do not present an opening statement that is highly detailed and that shows your entire hand. If you can hold some of your evidence back, do it.

Explaining How Different Types of Evidence Fit into the Case

There are many different types of evidence and cases that juries get to make decisions about. When a case involves scientific evidence, refer to it briefly, but leave the heavy science to the expert witness who will teach the jury about the science later on during the case. When a case involves circumstantial evidence, tell the jury that it exists, tell them briefly what the circumstantial evidence will show, and talk about how it corroborates your other evidence. When a case relies on the introduction of F.R.E. 404(b) evidence, consider not mentioning it in opening statement. If an advocate has won the right to introduce such evidence because of a ruling on a motion in limine, the jury that does not hear about the evidence in opening will see that the advocate has underpromised and overdelivered his or her evidence. The jury will learn about "super corroboration" when the victim or witnesses from the 404(b) incidents testify. This evidence will tell the jurors that they can trust your witnesses who are testifying about the charged crime or complaint.

Final Tips

Project confidence and sincerity during opening statement; eliminate verbal crutches, like repeating "ladies and gentlemen" every time you have a lull in the action.

Don't look at the presentation on the video monitor unless you are referring directly to the image that is on the screen. Make sure that your laptop is set up in a place where you can see the computer while speaking to the jurors. Avoid the impulse to watch the video monitor or the screen where the image is being projected.

Create blank slides for those times in the presentation when the jurors should be focusing on something in the courtroom besides the video screen.

Chapter 4

Using Computer Presentations in Direct Examination

A trial lawyer's job on direct examination is like the job of a ring master in the circus. The ring master in a circus drives the show; he or she keeps the show on schedule and makes sure that performers are in place before asking the audience to direct their attention to the performer. Once the performer is ready, the ring master steps out of the spotlight and lets the audience watch the show. A trial lawyer on direct should do the same thing. He or she should disappear into the background while the information that the attorney elicits from the witness holds the jury's attention. If the attorney does his or her job right on direct examination, the jurors will remember the evidence. Put another way, a lawyer's job is to choreograph the performance of a witness so that the truthful testimony of the witness will persuade the members of the jury to sign the verdict form in the client's favor. Linear and nonlinear presentations help the trial lawyer to achieve these results because they give the jury visual corroboration of the witness's account — the witness describes something, and the technology shows that the witness knows what he or she is talking about.

This chapter discusses ways to integrate computer presentation into direct examination. Tim Tomasik, a former prosecutor with the Cook County State's Attorneys' office and now a distinguished attorney with the Clifford Law Offices, says that plaintiffs' lawyers win their cases on direct examination, and he is absolutely right. Direct examination is an attorney's opportunity to shape a jury's perception with choreographed presentations. This chapter discusses strategies for preparing witnesses so they can maximize their impact on the jury. It then suggests techniques for identifying and creating presentations that underscore the story that you want your witnesses to tell. Finally, it discusses ways to handle witnesses with special challenges and ways to manage the passage of time for the presentation.

Tactical Considerations for Direct Examination

Start analyzing a case by knowing which jury instructions will affect the ways a jury should scrutinize a witness's testimony. Most jurisdictions use pattern jury instructions that are put together by jury instruction committees. Sometimes these instructions are easy to understand; sometimes the instructions are confusing. A winning trial lawyer capitalizes on the law that the jurors will read in the jury room by identifying concepts and limitations that the law imposes on jurors in the decision-making process and then crafting his or her case to use the concepts and limitations to his or her advantage. To begin, you should assemble a full set of jury instructions from the judge's opening comments to the verdict forms. Next, identify words and phrases from the instructions that you can weave into a direct examination and into the graphics that you will present to the jury.

Ask yourself questions like these:

- What other instructions are relevant to my case?
- How can I use the jury instruction about witness demeanor? Are there words and phrases in that instruction that I can use to buttress a witness's believability?
- How can my opponent use these instructions against my witnesses?
- What can I do or say to this witness in the testimony preparation phase to prepare the witness for the attack?
- Are there special instructions that define mental states that apply to my case?
- Is there an instruction for willfulness or wantonness that my opponent will try to give the jury to insulate an insurance company from liability?
- Are there things that my witness can testify about that will block the opposition from getting a particular instruction?
- Are there special hearsay instructions that jurors must consider, like evidence of identification procedures, spontaneous declaration instructions, or instructions regarding the substantive use of prior inconsistent statements?
- How should I structure a direct examination to satisfy the requirements of the instruction in the minds of the jury?
- How should a jury be instructed about F.R.E. 404(b) evidence when witnesses are going to testify about these incidents on direct examination?
- Should the judge instruct the jurors about the limited ways to consider evidence before and after a witness testifies as well as at the close of the trial?
- Are there other limiting instructions that will affect the ways that jurors are allowed to scrutinize the evidence?

Answering these questions strengthens your case by helping you to identify types of visuals that can help the witness testify.

Along with knowing which jury instructions apply to the jury's scrutiny of the witnesses, you should consider the biases, prejudices, and any other baggage that each witness will bring to the witness stand. A witness's limitations directly affect the believability of his or her evidence. Some people are shy, or some cultures teach people that it is rude to make eye contact when speaking. Witnesses like these may appear aloof or incredible, even though they are telling the truth.

Here are more questions you should ask yourself before putting a witness on the stand:

- Does the witness have some character trait, cultural restriction, or physical disability that will inhibit the witness's ability to communicate in a courtroom?
- Has the witness engaged in conduct that will make the witness's testimony suspicious? For example, has the witness used alias names?
- Does a witness have convictions for a felony or theft that can be used for impeachment purposes under F.R.E. 609 or some other standard?
- Is the witness testifying in exchange for a benefit of some kind, like a reduced sentence or a promise from a party to a lawsuit that the witness will not be joined as a party?
- Is the witness a child? How can I make a jury see that the child understands the meaning of the particular words that he or she is using? For example, how can a child demonstrate that he or she knows the true meaning of the words *in*, *on*, and *touching*?
- How can I bolster a witness's credibility before my opponent argues that this witness cannot be believed?
- Is there going to be an instruction regarding expert witnesses and their opinions? Can I create presentations that can capitalize on these instructions?

If you have answers to these questions, you will be better prepared for the fight that is coming because you will know which visuals to use to strengthen the witness's believability.

These considerations will help you decide whether to use nonlinear visuals or linear visuals with the witness. Some witnesses should be presented with no exhibits, while others should use only tangible exhibits like photos that can be marked in court. Budget will be a factor, so you must know whether the client will pay for a bill from a copy center, photography store, or professional exhibit shop. You must know whether there is technology like document cameras available for evidence presentation. Assuming a document camera is available, you must then decide whether to publish photographs with the document camera or with Sanction or PowerPoint. If an exhibit is complex because it contains a great deal of relevant information, then you should put the exhibit on a board to allow the jurors to scrutinize the exhibit at their own paces. Some attorneys put together exhibit books for each juror so that each one has his or her own copy of the exhibit. Each of these considerations will affect the way you approach the use of exhibits during the trial.

Preparing for Witness Testimony

Keep a witness's limitations firmly in mind when you are organizing your thoughts about each witness's presentation before meeting him or her. Make yourself familiar with all statements that are attributable to the witness. It is a good practice to make a file insert that contains all of the statements that were generated by the witness or that are attributable to him or her. These statements must be addressed when preparing that witness to testify. Pre-preparation organization — specific elements of which are discussed in the sections following — shows a witness that you are serious about the case and that you expect the witness to be serious too about what he or she testifies to in court.

Creating a Witness Prep Sheet

One effective way to get ready for the pre-testimony meeting is to prepare an outline of the topics that you will address with the witness. This outline should list the facts and the exhibits that you want to have the witness authenticate during the testimony. This prep sheet keeps you and the witness focused on the things that are important to the case. What follows is an example of a prep sheet that an attorney in a negligence case involving a car crash might use.

Name/Background		**Item ID/Codes for Sanction.** (Type these to launch in Sanction)
Car ownership	Photo of car Title documents	C1
Familiarity with the area	Diagram and photos of intersection	AP
Collision	Show automated diagram on TV monitor	Di1
Damage to car	Photos of repair bills	Med1–41
Injuries	Photo of plaintiff at hospital Body chart of surgeries Day-in-the-life video of plaintiff at home getting bathed and cared for	H1 Di2 DL1

Reviewing Prior Statements

During the testimony preparation session, make sure the witness acknowledges all of his or her prior statements, whether testimonial or otherwise. Sometimes you have to be ready to impeach your own witness, so you need to show the witness's prior statements to the jury. This is why there should be a third person present to witness the conversation between you and a witness whenever possible. This third person can testify at trial, if necessary, that the witness did acknowledge the statements. This third person is commonly called a prover because that individual can prove up any admissions made by the witness to you without putting you in a position of having to withdraw from representation of a client to perfect impeachment. This prover can authenticate the statement that you used to confront the witness for the purposes of proving up impeachment with your technology in front of the jury.

Explaining a Witness's Role

During the pre-testimony interview, make certain that the witness understands his or her role. The witness is your partner in the evidence presentation of a direct examination. A witness who understands how he or she fits into a case can be a great asset to a case presentation. Explain how you will be laying evidentiary foundations during the course of the witness's testimony so that the witness can help you establish the authenticity of the exhibits while explaining what happened. A witness who understands his or her role in a case is better able to connect with a jury because the witness understands why he or she is being asked particular questions. Put another way, a witness who understand why he or she is being asked a series of questions is more likely to answer those questions readily and help explain the significance of the exhibits. A witness should be made aware of how the opposition will attack witnesses. When you talk to your witness, avoid coming off as aloof, erudite, or pithy. Keep your language simple when talking to "civilians" and save the *plethoras* and *priors* and *subsequents* for your appellate practice. Speaking in plain English with your witnesses better prepares you for speaking with the jury in plain English. Seemingly arrogant lawyers alienate witnesses and jurors and lose trials. If you talk over your witnesses' or jury's heads, you will lose them or alienate them, perhaps making them hostile to your client's side.

Example

"All I want you to do is tell the truth on the stand. Now you and I know this is an identification case. Let's face it — the guy didn't grab you, so we've got no prints. So it pretty much is going to come down to your word against the bad guy." (Tell the witness this so that the witness sees you as an ally in the mission to convince the jury to believe the witness. When the witness believes that you believe him or her, the witness will be more willing to embrace your suggestions.) "I need you to help me show the jury how it is that they can trust what you say. So here are a couple of things that I have been thinking about."

"We've got to make this jury understand just how good a look you got at the defendant. We're going to have to talk about lighting and the different times that you got to see his face. That is why I am going to put photos on the television to show the lights that are visible at night. I will show you the photograph and ask if it accurately shows the street as it appeared at night. I will then ask you if you had the chance to look at a scanned image of this photo." (You show the witness the image on your laptop.) "I will ask you if the scanned image fairly and accurately depicted this photo. I will ask that the photo be admitted and ask leave to publish the scanned image. I will then ask you to look around the room and tell the members of the jury whether you see in this courtroom the man who accosted you. I will ask you to point to that person and describe something the person is wearing. I will then ask you to mark on the electronic photos with the mouse. I will ask you to circle the areas in the photos that show where you were able to see the defendant during the attack."

"I'm then going to ask you questions about how you were able to identify the defendant in the lineup. I am going to ask you to describe how the lineups were run. I will ask you to describe how the lineup procedure was run. I will show you the lineup photo and ask you to tell the members of the jury where the defendant stands in the lineup. I will then show you the electronic image after I lay the same type of foundation that I did for the scene photos. When the defendant's picture is on the television screen, I will ask you if there is any doubt in your mind about the man on the screen and the man in the courtroom being the guy who attacked you. I am doing this because the jury gets to consider your level of certainty during the ID procedure and here in court."

"Keep in mind that an ID case also means that the defendant needs to show that your identification of him can't be trusted, if he wants to win. This means the defense lawyer may ask what you think are ridiculous questions like, 'How many seconds did you get to look at the defendant's face?' You know an honest answer to that question is, 'I looked at his face long enough to remember his face for the rest of my life.' So if you can give that answer and it is the truth, then go ahead and say it if the defense lawyer asks you the question. That lawyer wants to get the bad guy off by saying that you weren't paying attention at the time of the crime. The way a defendant does this is to let his lawyer get real cute with her questions. She'll ask you silly stuff like, 'You weren't expecting to be attacked, were you?' She'll do this to make you look like you got bum-rushed. Now if your gut told you that something was going to happen right before the defendant pulled the gun, the honest answer to the question is, 'I was hoping I wouldn't, but something about the defendant told me he was up to no good.' So go ahead and give that answer. One more thing: Just because you think the defense lawyer is acting like a jerk doesn't mean you should be defiant or cop an attitude with her. Sometimes lawyers try to get witnesses mad to make them look stupid or ridiculous or not credible. So don't let the lawyer get you mad because if you get angry, you are helping the bad guy. Just tell the truth. You're going to be fine."

Avoiding Scripting a Witness

Making a witness understand his or her role does not mean that you should give that witness a script. Scripted witnesses look overprepared. When a witness answers questions before the attorney asks them or repeatedly volunteers information that goes beyond the scope of an attorney's questions, jurors start to distrust that witness's testimony. If a witness looks spontaneous and credible, the jury is more likely to trust or even like the witness. The more a jury trusts or likes a witness, the more they believe the witness. With that in mind, you should prepare witnesses to look spontaneous. If a witness understands what topics he or she will be asked about and understands that there will be times when he or she will be asked sequential questions versus open-ended questions, the witness will do fine on the stand.

During the preparation session, you must teach witnesses the importance of differentiating between descriptions and conclusions. Witnesses should be taught to describe observations of demeanor and actions instead of testifying about conclusions that they have drawn from observing demeanor or actions. For example, a witness is giving a conclusion when he or she says that someone was upset. In some circumstances, a conclusion about someone "being upset" could be objectionable because that conclusion is speculative. If instead the witness describes his or her observations of the other individual, then the jury can draw their own conclusions.

Witnesses must understand why the attorney is asking sequential questions. Tell the witness that you will ask questions that are designed to break up the action. Explain that you are doing this to slow down the action so that the jury hears everything. Later in this chapter is a section on handling the passage of time in direct examination that addresses strategic ways to use sequential questions.

Make sure that a witness understands that "I don't know" or "I'm not sure" are fine answers to questions when the witness indeed does not know or is not sure about an answer. A witness should be assured that it is perfectly acceptable to admit that he or she doesn't understand a question. A witness must understand that he or she should admit discussing the case with you. A witness needs to know that it is all right to ask a lawyer to repeat a question. Witnesses should be prepared to say that the only thing the attorney told them to do was to tell the truth.

Putting a Witness on the Stand (or Jumping Out of the Plane)

Preparing Every Witness for an Introduction to the Jury

Get the witness ready to introduce him- or herself to the jury. Use introductory questions and loop-backs to give the jury a context for every witness. Plan on beginning the direct examination with an introductory question. This introductory question gives you a context for the rest of the case by telling the jury why the witness is on the stand and why the witness is important to the case. After the introductory question, use a loop-back question to better introduce the witness to the jury. A loop-back question is simply a device that lets a direct examiner humanize the witness before having to move to the meat of the witness's testimony.

> ***Examples***
>
> "Are you the woman who was awakened in her bed by a voice at two o'clock in the morning? Before we talk about what happened to you, ma'am, I'd like the jury to know something about you."
>
> "Are you the doctor who examined the body of Deborah Prescott? Before we talk about that, I'd like the jury to know more about your background."
>
> "Were you the officer who went to a collision at 48th and Homan in Chicago on March 15, 2004? Before we talk about that, I'd like the jury to know a little bit about your background."

Marshalling Exhibits for the Direct Examination

During witness preparation, you should have decided which exhibits to use with the witness and what order to introduce those exhibits in. It is a good practice to make a central exhibit list to keep track of all of the exhibits that you will use throughout the trial. On the insert that was created to gather all of a witness's statements, list the particular exhibits that apply to the witness. If you are working without a trial partner, the list on the witness file insert will ensure that no exhibits are missed. On the other hand, if you are working with a trial partner, your partner can track exhibits off of the central list, and the examiner can keep track of exhibits off of the list that are unique to the particular individual.

Use your word processor's Table function to create an exhibit list. The first row of the column should track the information shown in the list below. Since slide shows and individual exhibits can be launched from the Sanction desktop, it is important to make a column for the Sanction item/page ID on the exhibit list. This way, you know what item/page ID code to type on the keyboard to call the exhibit to the screen. Keep Sanction codes short to minimize the likelihood of making a mistake while typing the code. One method for creating a coding scheme is to use the first initial from the witness's name. Then use an abbreviation for the type of statement the witness gave and a page number. For example, the first page for John Doe's handwritten statement could have a Sanction item/page ID of "JH1." When you decide to publish this page of Doe's statement while in Presentation mode, you simply type "jh1" and hit the Enter key. Or, if you are working with the Dual Monitor mode, simply drag the item to the desktop. At that point, Sanction will launch the page.

Example

Exhibit number	Description of the exhibit	Witnesses who will use the exhibit	Sanction item/page ID	Foundation	Admitted	Published
1	Diagram of the crash scene	Smith, Jones, and McMillan	D1 (Short codes will allow you to call the exhibit up to the screen with few key strokes.)	Yes	Yes	Yes
2	Photo of crosswalk	Smith, Jones, McMillan, and Henry	Cw1	Yes	Yes	Yes

Preparation Tips

Go to the Scene So You See What the Jury Should See

See the vantage points that witnesses had at the time of an incident. When you know what the scene looks like, you have greater insight into the different vantage points that the witnesses had. That insight will directly affect your ability to recreate those vantage points in the courtroom.

When visiting a scene, go to the scene around the same time of day that the event occurred. Places look different in morning light than they do in evening light. Shadows that exist on the east side of a street in the morning are gone in the late afternoon or evening. The appearance of shadows in photographs can obscure the way a scene really appeared at the time of an event. That is why it is a good idea to have photos that show what the lighting conditions were like at the time of an event. Photos taken at the proper time can answer many questions about a witness's perceptions. A photo can show whether a person was driving into the sun at the time of a collision. If an event occurred at night, then you should stay at the scene long enough for your eyes to adapt to the darkness. Then you can have the witness explain how his or her eyes had adapted to the darkness.

When taking photos of a nighttime scene, always document light sources. Take photos that show the actual lights in the scene, including store lights, vestibule lights, and residential lights. When creating diagrams for trial, make sure that the light sources appear in any diagrams. In cases in which only natural light was available at the time of the event, you can check with the U.S. Naval

Observatory Astronomical Department (www.USNO.navy.mil) for sun and moon rise data to document the light that existed.

These illustrations show why scene photos should be taken around the time that the event in dispute occurred. The left-hand image shows where shadow falls at 9:00 A.M., while the right-hand image shows where shadow falls at 3:00 P.M. A 9:00 A.M. photo used in a trial that interprets a dispute at 3:00 P.M. will radically impact a jury's judgment of a witness's and attorney's credibility.

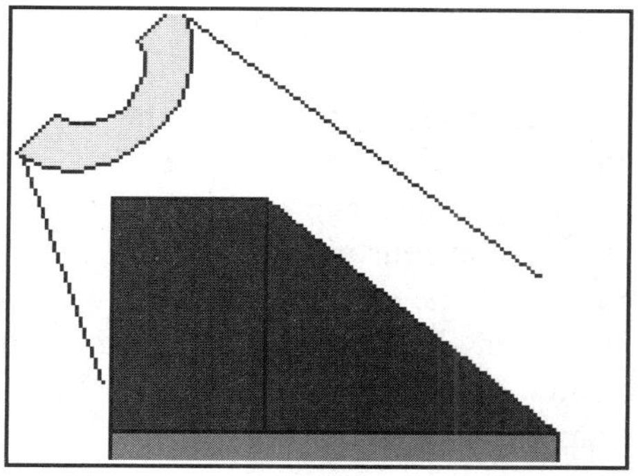

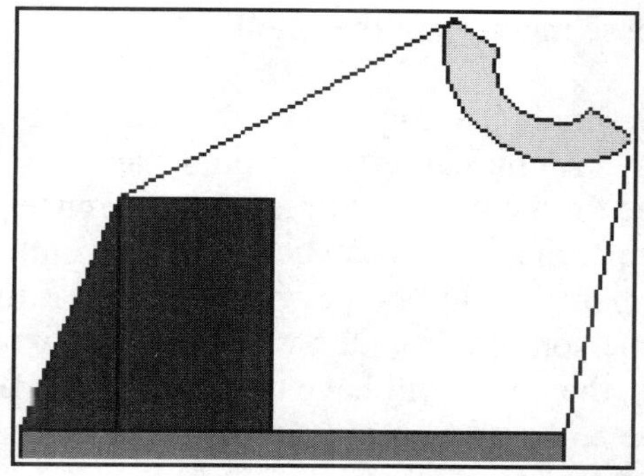

Integrate Charts and Diagrams into Your Direct

Use charts and diagrams to underscore strong witnesses and to divert attention from weak witnesses. When a strong witness is testifying about information that is important to the cause of action, that witness should stand in front of the jury to explain his or her testimony. If a witness is explaining something on the video screen, have the witness point away from his or her body. If the witness is working with a chart or diagram, use the same rule regarding pointing; however, the witness should write across his or her body when marking the diagram. When a witness is weak but still must be relied on for important information, then have the witness remain on the witness stand while he or she directs you to indicate where important information is contained in the exhibit or where on the exhibit you should mark. By joining in the presentation, you divert attention from the witness and focus it on the information that the witness is talking about.

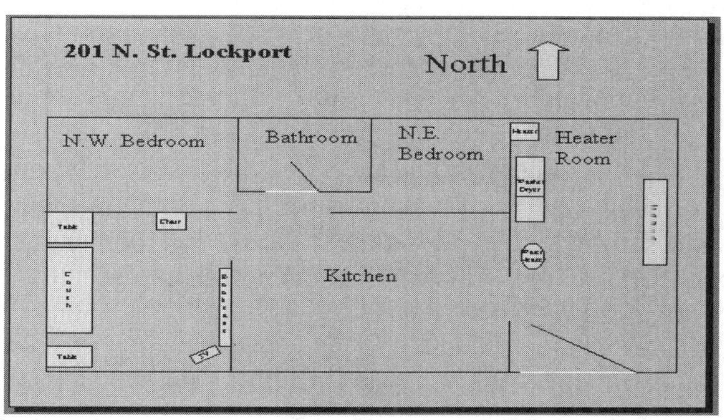

When a witness steps down from the stand to work with an exhibit, the witness should know how to include the jurors. A right-handed witness standing on the right side of this diagram or video screen while facing a jury will be able to point at things on the diagram or screen with his or her right hand without shutting out the jurors.

Use Empirical Reference Points

Devise ways to engage multiple juror senses when a witness is testifying. If a witness recreates how the defendant threw a punch, the jurors will use both their eyes and ears to internalize the evidence. Often when witnesses describe smells, jurors will physically react to the description. For example, a witness talking about smelling a burning gasoline smell at the scene of a traffic collision will physically react to the smell with his or her facial expressions as he or she describes the smell. At the same time, witnesses who are familiar with the smell will also physically react to their sense memory of the smell.

Witnesses should use empirical reference points during their testimony even when working with technology. Empirical reference points are simply reference points that jurors can see or experience for themselves. Empirical reference points can apply to distance and time. The distance reference points can be inside the courtroom or around the courthouse. These types of reference points let jurors see what the witness means when he or she talks about how far away an object or person was from the witness. If the witness points to an object in the courtroom to show a distance, the jurors will have empirical information on which to make their decisions. When time matters, the witness can simply sit in silence for the length of time that the witness remembers the event taking.

The witness who points at an object in a courtroom eliminates debate over his or her ability to gage distance. This empirical reference point helps the direct examiner since it gives the jury a baseline for distances. Empirical reference points also frustrate cross-examiners since a cross on a choice of words is nullified when the witness shows the jury just how long something took or just how far away something was.

Use Expert Witnesses

If a witness is going to testify as an expert, then you will face some additional preparation tasks. You must have all reports generated by the witness and by any opposition witnesses. You should assemble a collection of treatises and other writings that are recognized in the particular forensic field and provide them to the witness. You and the witness should meet and make sure that you have a meeting of the minds regarding the opinions and the foundations for those opinions. Once that meeting of the minds occurs, you and the prospective expert witness should collaborate over the way the witness will present his or her expert opinion. One of the most powerful places for the use of a linear slide show in a trial is with an expert witness.

When an expert witness testifies about the scientific tests that he or she performed on a piece of evidence, that witness has a perfect opportunity to win a jury's confidence. Jurors trust an expert witness who explains scientific principles with plain language. Scientific principles become less abstract when they are illustrated or explained with a visual presentation. A forensic economist who creates a spreadsheet that is used to support assertions in a visual that gives a jury a bottom line for the amount of damages that a plaintiff will need is more compelling than the witness who simply takes the stand and talks. The same witness can convert the data from the spreadsheet into a bar graph or pie chart to give the jury a picture of what effect the injury will have on a plaintiff. You can create visuals to accompany any expert witness's testimony. You simply have to sit with the witness and brainstorm about ways to make the testimony come alive.

In medical malpractice cases, Mark Bodner, the attorney from New York who was mentioned in the previous chapter, has his expert witnesses make a timeline that cross-references different entries in the medical chart. Mark uses a timeline developed in TimeMap and launched out of Sanction to help his expert witnesses better explain how they reached their opinions regarding facts in the medical chart. The timeline becomes an index for the medical record, and that index helps the expert justify his or her presentation. The visual cues in the timeline put the admission in the medical chart into context for the jury.

Tom Kelliher and Gary McCallister from Chicago have used a timeline to make an expert witness economist show the jury their client's solid work history up until the plaintiff was injured. They used a vertical timeline that scrolled down through the chronology to better illustrate the plaintiff's history.

When you are using an expert witness to explain complex theories or science, make that testimony easier to understand with a linear slide presentation that addresses the fundamentals of the science. A slide show that defines key terms and explains the methodology for reaching an opinion has great persuasive power with a jury. Sit down with the expert and draw up a rough sketch of the things that you and the expert agree are important for explaining the opinion. Make a rough draft of the presentation, and then bring it to the expert to select appropriate text and graphics. Call the witness to testify and establish the fact that the witness is here to give some expert opinions, but do not illicit the opinions until after you establish the witness's qualifications for an expert opinion. Once you have established that the witness has the training and experience necessary to testify as an expert, ask the judge to find that the witness may testify as an expert witness. Once the judge finds that the witness is an expert, ask the witness whether he or she has prepared a slide show to help the jury understand the field and the basis for the opinions that the expert has reached. Move to have the presentation admitted and ask that the expert be allowed to make the presentation. If your opponent objects to a narrative, ask the witness to explain the significance of each slide. The following is a screen capture of just such a presentation that was prepared for the presentation of STR DNA evidence.

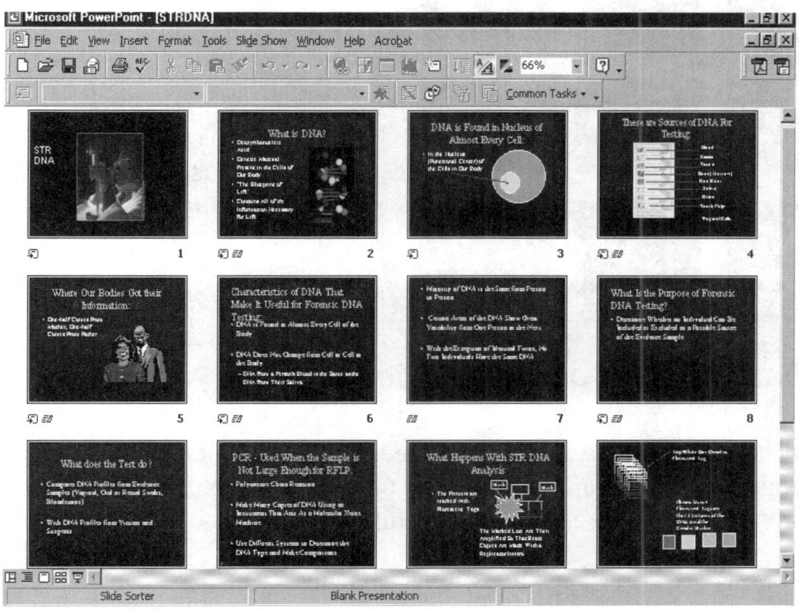

Attorney: "Mr. DeFranco, did you help create a slide presentation that will help the jurors understand how STR DNA analysis works?"

DeFranco: "Yes."

Attorney: "Does this slide presentation contain images, animation, and text?

DeFranco: "Yes."

Attorney: "Did you show me what you wanted animated and how you wanted this slide show laid out?"

DeFranco: "Yes."

Attorney: "Will this help you to explain your testimony?"

DeFranco: "Yes."

Attorney: "Motion to admit the presentation and to allow Mr. DeFranco to step down so he can explain STR DNA analysis to the jury."

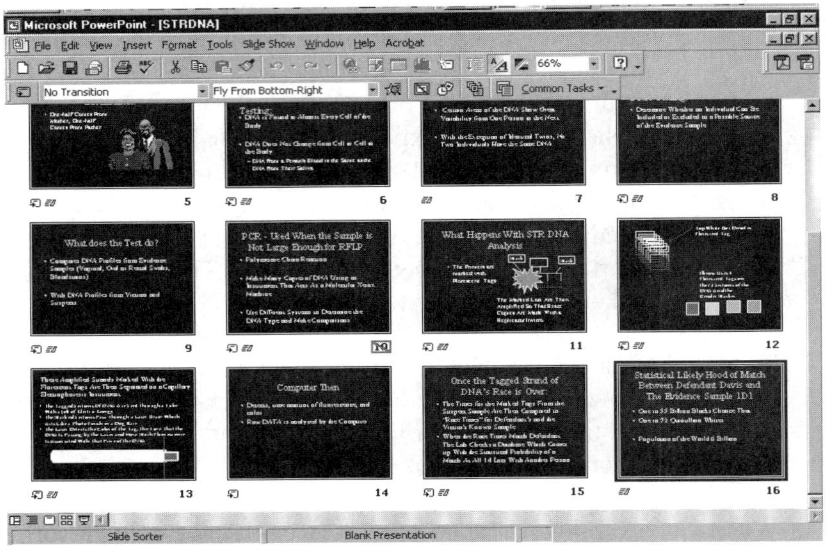

Use Visual Layering

Visual layering is a technique that uses images on a master slide to drive the presentation. It is a graphic storyboard for the examination. Take a master slide and continue adding to it as you progress through the presentation. This effect can be used with any expert witness.

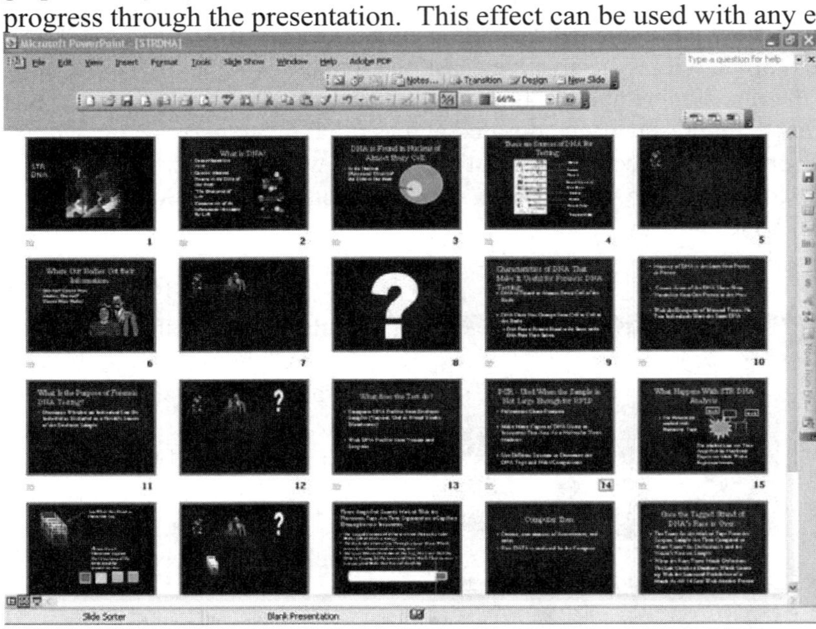

This example shows a visual layer being attached to the DNA on the previous page. The master graphic is a blue slide that has a graphic added on completion of the topic in each previous slide. It is a visual reminder of the subjects covered previously.

Create Special Visuals for Special Witnesses

Be prepared to create visuals that enhance witness testimony. Remember to consider disabilities or mannerisms of a witness that could distract jurors. Try to come up with ways to turn an infirmity or impediment into an advantage. When establishing a child's competence to testify about the difference between "touching on" and "touching in," for example, why not take a picture of the child and place it in and on a box. You would then ask the child to tell the judge and jury what the child's picture is doing to the box. When the child says it is *on* the box and then *in* the box, the jurors will see that the child understands the difference between these two concepts.

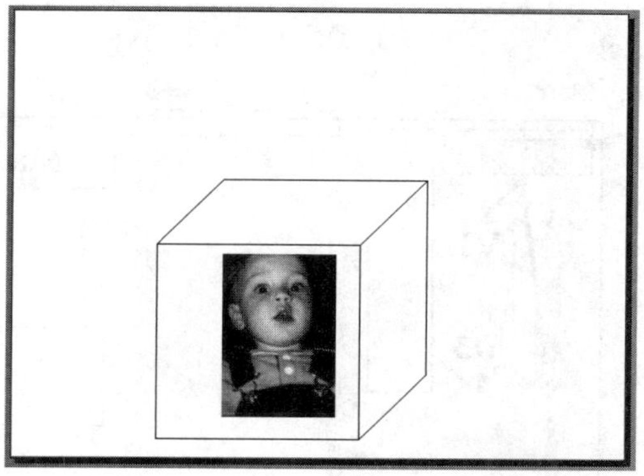

Create Visuals That Become Reminders During Argument

Robert Baizer from Baizer Kolar P.C. in Highland Park, Illinois, is a successful personal injury attorney. When Bob is trying wrongful death cases, he uses a technique to underscore damages for loss of society. Bob has witnesses make lists of words to describe the impact the deceased individual had on the witness. For example, a little brother might call his dead brother a role model, a hero, or a good friend. During the direct examination of the witness, Bob asks the witness to pull out this list and then publishes the list on a document camera during the direct examination. He then scans the document and pulls it onto the screen during closing argument when he is talking about the damages jury instruction and how the jury should construe the instruction on loss of society.

Use Text Boxes and Symbols in Visuals

Some visuals are best created with combinations of text and symbols. Assume you are trying a case in which identification of an individual is important to the facts of the case. The jury instruction in Illinois for a criminal case requires that a jury consider (1) the opportunity the witness had to view the offender at the time of the offense; (2) the witness's degree of attention at the time of the offense; (3) the witness's earlier description of the offender; (4) the level of certainty shown by the witness when confronting the defendant; and (5) the length of time between the offense and the identification confrontation. One of the most important factors that the attorney who wants the identification believed must underscore is factor number 1. The reliability of in-court identification by a witness in court hinges on the witness's opportunity to view the offender at the time of the offense.

The following visual helps to illustrate a witness's opportunity to view the offender. This slide was created by Jim Dedman from the National College of District Attorneys to help a witness show the jury when the witness was able to see the offender's face. The solid light-colored lines represent the witness's opportunity to see the defendant's face; the broken lines symbolize the time that the defendant turned his back on the witness. The witness must testify that he or she helped to create the presentation by showing the attorney where the solid arrows should appear. The attorney launches the slide from Sanction while the witness testifies that the solid arrows show when the offender was facing the witness and the broken arrows symbolize the time when the offender turned away.

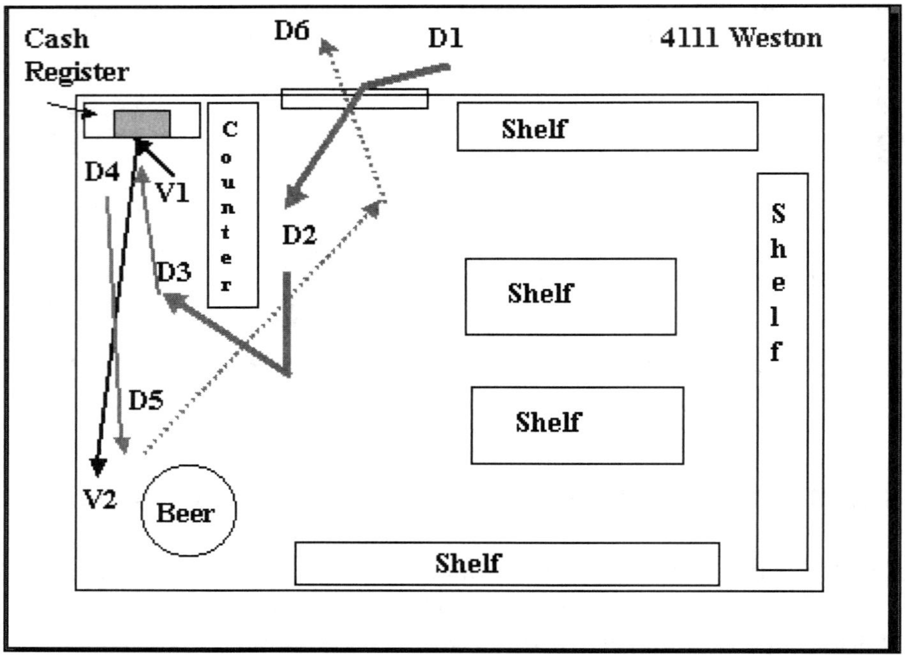

To automate a slide set, the arrows should animate automatically on .5 second intervals after the first mouse click.

Each arrow appears and shows the path that the offender and the victim took.

The witness then testifies that this slide will help the members of the jury to understand his or her testimony. The lawyer asks that the slide be admitted for demonstrative purposes. The slide then animates the lines so that they appear in one-second intervals. Once the jury has seen the visual that recreates the vantage point that the witness had, the attorney should then have the witness sit in silence for the amount of time that he or she was able to view the offender. Now the jury has seen two empirical reference points that they can consider as they scrutinize the witness's testimony with the jury instruction.

The next slide was created to allow an evidence technician to explain where shell casings were found when he was investigating a drive-by shooting.

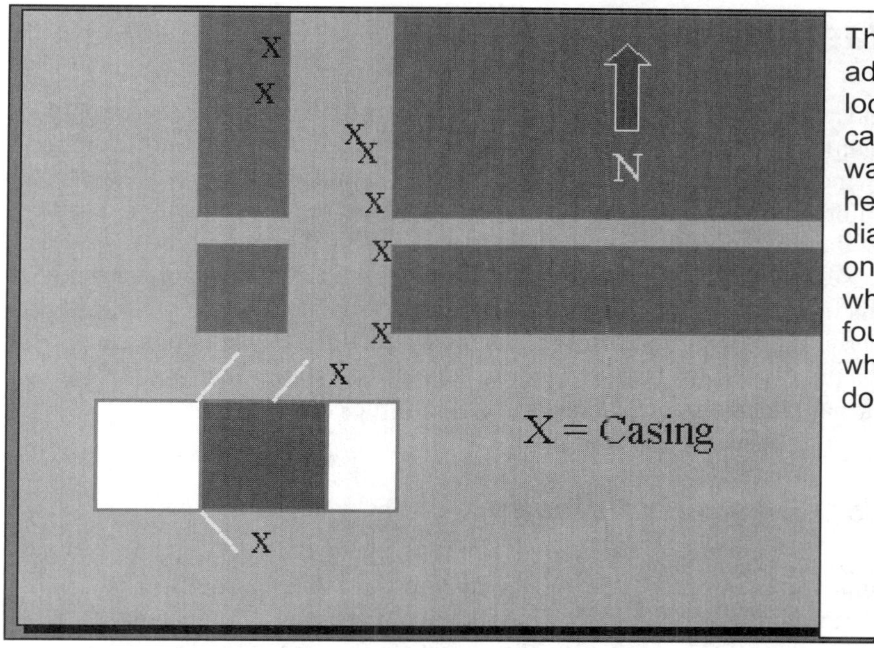

The scene photos did not adequately show the locations of the individual casings, so the witness was able to testify about helping to prepare the diagram and placing the X on the diagram to indicate where the casings were found in relation to the white car with the open doors in the slide.

Baseline Diagrams on Photographs

You can baseline a diagram from a photograph by using an underlying photograph to authenticate a diagram. These are excellent demonstrative exhibits for showing how a series of events occurred because they remove extraneous information from the photograph but maintain its vantage point. The following visual is a series of slides that were created by Craig Lawless when he was a student at Chicago-Kent College of Law. The first slide started as a photograph that then had text boxes superimposed on it. On the next slide, Craig created shapes and lines that covered the photograph. On the third slide, he filled the boxes and shapes, but set them to be transparent as they sat on top of the photograph. On the fourth slide, Craig removed the photograph, which allowed him to remove all background information from the slide. With PowerPoint 2003, all of the effects from these six slides can occur on one slide. The cost to the client is merely the time that the lawyer or his or her support staff put into creating the visual.

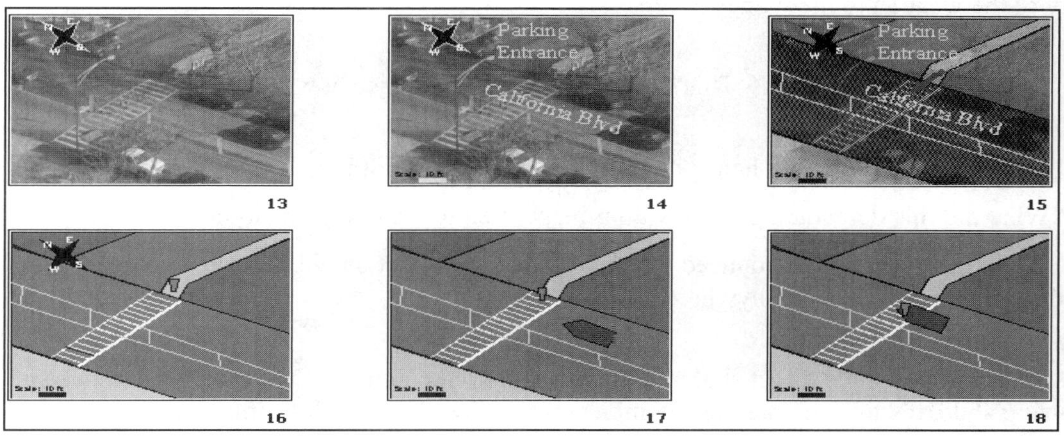

Handling the Passage of Time

Any lawyer can get up and ask a witness what happened next. Direct examinations that simply repeat this question are painful to watch. After a while, the question becomes as monotonous as the sound of windshield wipers. Some attorneys believe that they should simply give witnesses scripts and prompt them along with what happened next, but those attorneys can run into trouble when the witnesses forget their scripts. Instead of conducting windshield wiper direct examinations, have witnesses testify in a chronological fashion, in an episodic fashion, or in a hybrid of the two. Time is important only if you decide to make it important: Remember, just because a case evolved chronologically doesn't mean that the evidence in the case must be presented that way. When there are gaps in the story or when there are things that you want to avoid with a witness, a chronological direct examination can hurt the case.

Chronological Direct Examination

Chronological direct examinations are the perfect tool when you want to tell a short, straightforward story. Chronological accounts work best when a witness is talking about a specific event like an armed robbery or a car crash. This direct starts at the beginning of the story and moves forward through time. A well-executed chronological direct uses rhetorical devices to highlight a sequence of events and to control the witness's rendition of the story. A witness's retelling of an event can be controlled by simply asking the witness to talk about the first thing that he or she saw before asking about the next thing that he or she saw. The more you sequence the events by asking a witness to break down the action of the things that the witness experienced, the more controlled the witness's testimony will be. When you want to speed up the narrative, simply skip the sequential questions. Another device that works with nervous witnesses is to let a witness recount the action in his or her own words before looping back to fill in any details with sequential questions about details that the witness may have missed during the initial account.

For example, a good way to slow time down during a direct examination of an armed robbery victim or witness is to talk about where the gun was and how far the gun was from the victim, while asking the witness to talk about the robbery. An ideal direct examination of this type of witness jumps back and forth between the defendant's words and actions and the physical proximity of the weapon to the witness.

> "When the defendant said, 'This is a stickup,' did you notice how far the gun was from your head?"
>
> "Show the jury with your hands how this defendant was holding the gun."
>
> "What did this defendant do or say after he pointed the gun at your stomach?"
>
> "When the defendant announced that he wanted you to get on your knees, did the defendant point the gun anywhere else?"

A witness in a chronological direct should use a presentation to annotate his or her testimony. In the following slide, the light-colored arrow indicates the direction that the witness was traveling before the defendant approached her. The dark-colored arrow shows where the defendant came from, and the circles show the sources of light that were in the area that the witness is testifying about. This exhibit shows that the light had to be illuminating the defendant's face at the time of the robbery. If these arrows are shown in a linear presentation, then the arrows should be automated on a mouse click. If the arrows are made with a mouse or a light pen in Sanction, then the photo, after it is marked, can be saved and, if need be, printed for the jury to have in their possession during deliberation.

Episodic Direct Examination

An episodic direct examination controls a jury's focus just like a director in television or the movies. An episodic direct examination directs the witness's attention to a specific event and then moves from event to event, either forward or backward through time.

> "On March 15, 2005, at about 4:00 A.M., did you hear something that upset you?"
>
> "Before you heard that scream, where were you standing?"
>
> "Did there come a time when you smelled something burning?"

Episodic directs are ideal when a witness is summarizing an investigation or explaining the different steps that he or she had to go through while working on a case. Use questions that flag or headline the topic for the witness to talk about; once you identify the topic, use nonleading questions to explore the topic. "Did there come a time when you checked defendant's phone records? Let's talk about that . . ."

Note that the Federal Rules of Evidence and many local rules of practice allow for the use of leading questions when the advocate believes they are necessary to develop the witness's testimony. F.R.E. 611(c). This simply means that an attorney may lead a witness to a particular event to develop the witness's testimony. Once the topic is identified, you should flesh out the account with nonleading questions.

Illustrating Passage of Time

Timelines are strong aids for a direct examination in which a witness has to narrate a complex account, such as a physician talking about a sequence of treatment for an individual who is suffering from a degenerative disease that is at the center of a legal dispute. A timeline that integrates photographs or videos of the afflicted person at different stages of deterioration will become a powerful exhibit. The timeline would show either the image or the video while allowing the doctor to talk about specific dates and times. This device should be either a linear slide show or launched from a Sanction bullet list.

A timeline is introduced on direct by asking the witness if he or she helped to create the timeline. The rest of the foundation for the timeline is the same as for a demonstrative exhibit; the witness must explain that he or she thinks that the exhibit will help the witness explain his or her testimony. In the following illustrations, the horizontal timeline can carry only so much information before a second line has to be added and the first line has to be decreased in size. Where a timeline covers numerous events, a vertical time line that travels diagonally across a slide is a good device because you can add many more events to the timeline. You should animate the boxes so the jury does not read ahead; you can simply click a mouse button or on the space bar of the keyboard to move to the next callout box.

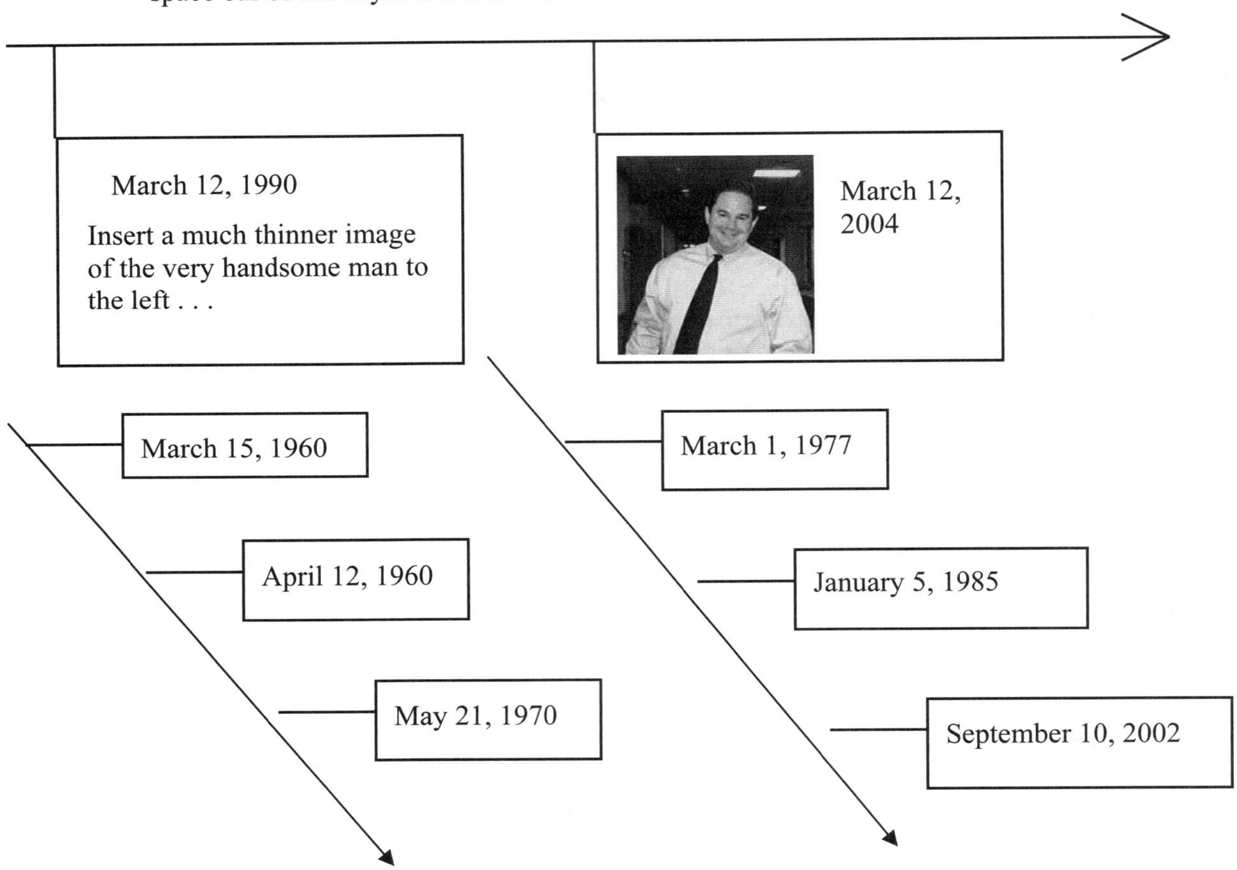

Each of these callout boxes should be animated. Callout boxes are found on the AutoShapes menu in PowerPoint. (Chapter 7 contains more information about using PowerPoint.)

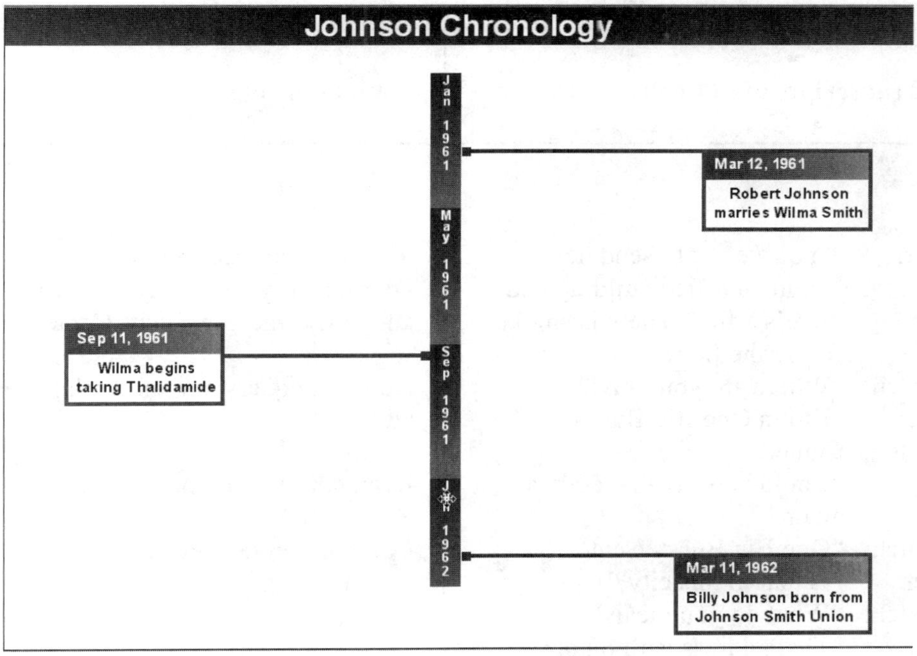

This is a TimeMap timeline that has been exported to PowerPoint.

You can call a witness and proceed through the timeline as you tell the story.

A clock is another good visual for passage of time. If there are documented times in the case, then you can animate the hands on the clock and have the witness testify about the times that are important to the matter in dispute.

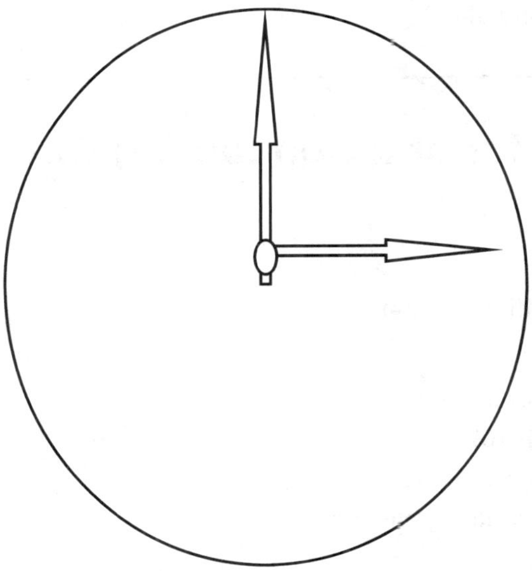

Consider creating a timeline that cross-references a witness's accounts with empirical data like computer queries.

The next diagram is a table that can be authenticated by a number of witnesses. The first section of the table should be authenticated by the person who prepared the transcript. The next section should be authenticated by the witness who can authenticate the computer logs. You can use Sanction or PowerPoint to block out part of the diagram until you lay the foundation for that particular part of the diagram. The first witness can testify about the authenticity of the 911 transcripts, and the next witness can testify about the records gleaned from the computer logs.

Time	Transcripts of 911 calls	Computer logs
9:00 P.M.	Caller: "You've got to send help. I'm in an office building and there's a fire. There is smoke filling the floor." Dispatch: "Where are you, miss?" Caller: "I'm in One Big Bucks Dispatch: Center." "Could you say that address Caller: again?" Dispatch: "One Big Bucks Center." Caller: "Is that in this city?" Dispatch: "What do you mean?" "That address isn't on our Caller: map. Do you know a cross street?"	911 dispatch receives the call. Dispatcher types in a query for the address, "One Big Bucks Center." Computer query says no such address. Dispatch types in the query again. Computer gives same answer.
9:07 A.M.	Caller: "Did you find me yet?" Dispatch: "I'm sorry, no." Caller: "I can't breathe."	

Checklist: Preparing for and Conducting Direct Examination

1. Compile jury instructions.
2. Have pre-testimony preparation session with witness.

    Prover present.
    Prior statements addressed.
    Witness understands role.
    Witness knows about attacks.
    Witness and attorney have gone over exhibits.

3. Create exhibit list.
4. Listen to the witness's answers in the event that the witness talks about something unexpected. Be ready to incorporate "good answers" into the next question.
5. Avoid the windshield wiper direct examination style: "What happened next? What happened next? What happened next?"
6. Use sequence questions when appropriate.
7. Introduce exhibits and have the witness annotate them where appropriate.
8. Sit back down with confidence.

Chapter 5

Weaving Computer Presentations into Cross-Examination

While we may execute only one actual cross-examination of each opposing witness, in reality, three occur. First, there is the cross-examination that you compose before actually confronting the witness. This is the cross-examination that you carefully plan based on all the information you possess before the witness testifies. Second, there is the cross-examination that you actually execute in the courtroom, warts and all. Third, there is the replay of the cross-examination in your mind when you think of all of the things that you wanted say or meant to say, but did not. Inevitably, it is the third cross-examination that is the best one that you do — but it is always a fiction.

There are two keys to performing effective cross-examination: preparation and self-control. These two tools enable you to control a witness during cross-examination. The only way you will be able to exert control over a witness in a courtroom is if you control your organizational choices, line of questioning choices, word choices, and technology choices.

This chapter addresses the first two cross-examinations that occur in every trial. (Sadly, there is nothing that can be done about the third one.) We begin by discussing strategies for composing the pre-cross-examination. The first section addresses a methodology for forcing witnesses to concede information that

- bolsters the trial lawyer's theory of the case,
- destroys the witness's believability, and
- exposes lies and inconsistencies.

We focus on the cross-examination that is based on both the information the trial lawyer has gathered (including video files, audio files, and images of documents) and the inferences that he or she draws from that information. The chapter also addresses ways to organize the media and exhibits that are actually used for the cross-examination. Next, the chapter discusses techniques and considerations for the second kind of cross-examination, the one that takes place in front of the jury. Naturally, the success of this cross-examination relies heavily on the preparation that goes into the first cross-examination *and* the attorney's ability to control the witness. Witness control is directly related to the questions asked and the attorney's ability to force the witness to answer those questions.

The First Cross-Examination: Preparing for the Courtroom

You are an advocate, and as such, it is your responsibility to "go the extra mile." You cannot simply sit back and wait to see what opposing counsel throws at your client during the trial. To be a true advocate, you must thoroughly prepare for the cross-examination you will execute later in the courtroom.

Gathering Information About Witnesses

Before doing anything, make sure you thoroughly understand your jurisdiction's discovery requirements to determine how much of the information that you discover must be disclosed before trial. After you're certain that you've done this, make an effort to find out who the potential opposition witnesses will be in a case as soon as possible. Once you learn the witnesses' identities, gather as much information as possible about them so that you are better able to manage any damage that these witnesses will inflict on your case. To begin, gather all of the witnesses' statements (taped, written, and oral). Next, gather all the relevant records you can about each witness. You should also talk to any of your witnesses who know the opposition witnesses, and ask the following questions.

- What do you think this witness knows about this case?
- Why do you think the other side is calling this witness?
- What did the witness say when he or she was first interviewed?
- Did this witness come forward voluntarily, or did someone have to go find this witness?
- Did this witness conceal or withhold any information after being discovered by the police or by a party to the litigation?
- Can the witness give a plausible reason for concealing or withholding information?
- Should you make an effort to interview this witness again now that you have seen what others say this witness has said? Remember that witnesses who are represented by counsel cannot be interviewed without the lawyer's permission in many jurisdictions.
- Did the witness make any contradictory statements in subsequent interviews or depositions?

- Do other witnesses in the case say things that you can use to impeach or corroborate the things that the targeted witness is now saying?
- Has the witness refused to be interviewed?
- Assuming you can take depositions in your state, can or should you depose this witness before trial?

Videotaping Witness Statements

If discovery tools like depositions are available for the particular type of litigation you are pursuing, there are a number of things that you should do before conducting a deposition. First, find out if the witness is represented by counsel. *Do not interview people who are represented by attorneys without the attorney's permission!* If the witness is not represented by an attorney and your jurisdiction's rules allow you to contact witnesses, then make an effort to contact the witness *before* conducting depositions. Once the witness has been interviewed, you have a baseline for what the witness will say and for what can be used to confront this witness during cross-examination or during a deposition should the witness vary from what he or she told you at the earlier interview.

Assume that a witness agrees to be interviewed. Under optimum circumstances, you want to bring a video camera with you to an interview in addition to a prover, who can testify about the substance of the conversation or can authenticate any written or videotaped statements. Leave the video camera out of sight while you conduct your preliminary interview. You want to hear what the witness has to say and avoid making the person anxious. Once you have had a chance to talk to the witness, make the decision about asking for the videotaped statement. This decision about whether to take a videotaped statement should be made on a witness-by-witness basis. If a person will not agree to give a videotaped statement, do not force the issue. See if the person will give you a videotaped interview where he or she stays off camera or will let you take a handwritten statement in which he or she acknowledges the fact that you gave them the option of giving a videotaped statement. Witnesses who refuse to be videotaped will look like they are hiding something when they are asked about it on the stand, and the prover can testify to any admissions and/or the circumstances of the interview should the witness make any false claims. Although some credible witnesses may prefer to not be videotaped or recorded, most people will agree. If the witness agrees to be videotaped, your prover can testify regarding the foundation of the video if the witness later declines identifying him- or herself on the video or if the witness claims that he or she was coerced into giving the video statement.

When a witness agrees to a videotaped interview, the ideal place to tape it is on the witness's home turf. The more comfortable the witness appears during a video statement the harder it will be for the witness to disavow the statement. Where the witness is being forced to testify pursuant to a subpoena for a deposition, you should have a court reporter present and a video camera with a microphone that can be placed in front of the witness. The court reporter will create the transcript that will later be synchronized with the video on Sanction, while the video camera will catch the witness's voice, physical appearance, and demeanor while being questioned. When depositions are taken, they should take place at the attorney's office in a room that has few visual distractions.

Remember that while an analog videotape is linear in that it begins at the start of the tape, moves through the middle, and ends at the end of the tape, *digitized video is not linear*. It may be started at any point without needing to play through the entire video. With this in mind, it is not necessary that you use the conventions that are common in a direct examination, or even in a cross-examination. Although an attorney taking a written statement or a court-reported statement from a witness may want to recommit a witness to a prior statement, such a recounting of a prior conversation on a videotaped statement can make it look like the attorney is coaching or threatening the witness. Be mindful of how your opponent will try to use videotaped evidence against you. While you may want to use only two or three questions or answers from an interview, your opponent may try to play other parts of the video to rehabilitate the witness or to impeach the circumstances surrounding the taking of the video statement. For this reason, you should make an effort to let the witness tell the story in his or her own words before pinning the witness down on details or before confronting the witness with prior statements that were made before the video statement was taken. In the event that the video is played from beginning to end, a jury will see that the witness was given an opportunity to express him- or herself before you began challenging things that the witness said. While recording the video, ask the witness to show how or explain why he or she knows something. Use rhetorical devices in the interview room for the measurement of distance, and have the witness sit in silence to show how much time passed. It is important that you assemble a collection of exhibits that will be referred to during the course of the interview to lock the witness into an account. The more things a witness explains on the video, the more comprehensive the cross-examination can be later on when you turn the video into clips.

When a video statement is taken pursuant to a subpoena or is a consensual encounter, begin the video statement by having the witness acknowledge that he or she understands that the interview is being videotaped. When the interview is a consensual encounter, go further and ask the witness to consent to having his or her statement videotaped. When the video is taken pursuant to a court order, you should have the witness acknowledge the order. Simply ask, "Do you understand that the court has ordered you to submit to a videotaped deposition?" Once the witness acknowledges the video camera, have him or her talk about background information. From there you should have the witness explain where he or she was at the time of the event by having the witness mark on a diagram or an aerial photograph of a location. Use the first portion of the interview to ask the witness to recall all that he or she knows about the case. By beginning the interview with this technique, you lock the witness into his or her account without forcing the witness into a confrontation on the video. Whenever possible, you should ask open-ended, nonleading questions during this portion of the interview to show that you are trying to get the witness to recall everything he or she remembers about the incident.

Once the witness admits that he or she has told you everything he or she knows about the topic, then you should summarize the things that the witness has testified about. The witness's answers to these summary questions are a good source for future video clips to use during cross-examination. These summary questions are leading questions that force the witness to agree or disagree with the summarization of the witness account.

After you have summarized the witness's account, explore the witness relationship to the party, litigation, or opposing attorney. If the witness is a friend or relative of a party, have the witness hold up photographs and other mementos that demonstrate the witness's relationship to the party. Ask if any photos of the witness and the party exist. Later you can serve this witness with a subpoena duces tecum listing the described photos as items that must be produced. Every answer a witness gives on videotape regarding a relationship to the party is a concession that demonstrates either a motive to help the party, a bias in favor of the party, or an interest in the outcome of the case on behalf of the party.

Finally, during the last hour of the interview or deposition, test out lines of cross-examination, and try to obtain concessions that attack the opposition's case. Try for these lines of cross-examination because they are unlikely to be seen by a jury unless they work. If a court reporter was present during the videotaping, give him or her a copy of the videotape at the conclusion of the process to ensure that the transcript is accurate. You should get a copy of the deposition transcript in ASCII text format that has page numbers and line numbers in order to synchronize the video with the transcript. See Chapter 8 on Sanction for instructions on synchronizing video and transcripts; see Chapter 9 on the equipment you will need for instructions on doing a video capture.

Using fallbacks if videotaping is not possible

When a witness will not consent to a videotaped interview but will consent to signing a statement, the written statement should contain a number of points to make it more valuable for cross-examination. First, give the witness an opportunity to write the statement him- or herself. If the witness declines to write the statement, then document the fact that the witness was given the choice. The statement should contain biographical information that is important to the witness's background. Statements that contain biographical information or other facts that are important to the witness are hard to challenge as being the product of the statement taker's imagination since they contain information that is known only by the witness. In the statement, the witness should acknowledge that he or she understands that the statement is a summary and not word for word. The witness should initial all exhibits and refer to them throughout the statement. This way, the exhibit can be called to the screen while the page of the statement that refers to the exhibit is also on the screen. The witness should initial any changes or additions that he or she makes or wants made to the statement. This process locks the witness into the account that he or she has given. Later, the witness will have to acknowledge every signature and correction should the witness deviate from this account.

Crafting Theories About Witnesses

Once you gather your information and disclose the things that you are required to disclose, craft a theory about each witness. A trial attorney must ask why the witness is going to walk into court and say the things that he or she is expected to say. What does this witness have to say to help the opposition? What facts must the witness concede? Is there anything that you can make this witness say that will discredit the witness's information? What can you do to prove that a witness should be discredited? By knowing the answers to these questions, you will be able to craft a theory about this witness that will support arguments about this witness to the jury. If a witness lies, why did that person lie? If a witness is mistaken, how did the mistake happen? You must prepare your cross-examination questions so that the questions reflect the argument that you will make.

Digitizing Exhibits

If you are truly going to use technology to its full advantage in advocacy, then you should digitize or scan all statements, be they written, audiotaped, or videotaped. Do the same for all photographs, diagrams, or other exhibits that witnesses refer to in their statements or that you plan to use during cross-examination. All of these exhibits should be saved in a folder on the C drive under the case name. If, for example, you save all the files for the Carter case in a folder named Carter on your C drive, then you can simply link the files to Sanction. When you want to launch the files during your examination, Sanction will know to go into the Carter folder to get the exhibits.

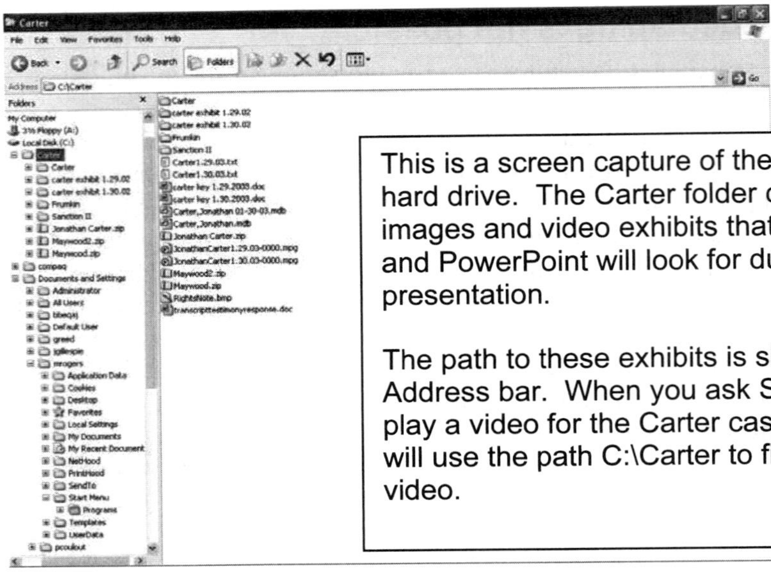

This is a screen capture of the author's hard drive. The Carter folder contains the images and video exhibits that Sanction and PowerPoint will look for during a presentation.

The path to these exhibits is shown on the Address bar. When you ask Sanction to play a video for the Carter case, Sanction will use the path C:\Carter to find the video.

If all the exhibits for a case are saved in the Carter folder, then a backup copy of the case files can be created and installed on another computer with ease. Simply make a duplicate folder named Carter on the new computer and copy the exhibits into that folder. Then when you install Sanction or PowerPoint on the backup machine and open the Carter folder, Sanction will know where to look for the exhibits that are saved. Chapter 2 instructs in more detail about how to organize your computer files.

Coding Your Exhibits

In Chapter 8 on Sanction, you will learn how to code your exhibits — give them short names — so that you can launch them quickly during a cross-examination. Although coding your exhibits may seem like a strictly mechanical exercise, it helps you get ready for cross-examination in several ways. It helps you get organized because it allows you to list your exhibit codes on your cross-examination notes next to the questions that you intend to ask. For example, say you want to launch a 14-second clip of questions and answers from a video of Carter. A simple naming convention for clips from Carter's video is to use C for Carter and then a number 1. C1, then, would be the first clip that you intend to play during Carter's cross-examination. This process of naming the exhibits forces you to prepare strategically because it helps identify those things that a witness must admit based on the material that you have. Instead of naming every question-and-answer sequence in the video, name only the ones that you think you need or that you intend to use. Sanction has the capacity to search through exhibits on the fly, so you can create other clips as needed. If you have a written statement that Carter gave, then use the ID of CH1 for page 1 of Carter's handwritten statement. This way you can simply type the ID and launch it as needed during the cross-examination of Carter. This coding process also helps you keep control over the tenor of a cross-examination because the short exhibit codes you create will ensure that you are able to quickly launch exhibits in Sanction during your cross-examination. To help prepare for cross-examination, make a list of the exhibits that are available for an attack.

Once you have coded your exhibits, you can use the Sanction duration list to make a list of the video/audio clips that you want to launch, and you can use the Print function to print a text file that contains a thumbnail image of the exhibit and the ID of the other exhibits that you intend to use. You can then import that text file into your notes by simply cutting and pasting them into your notes.

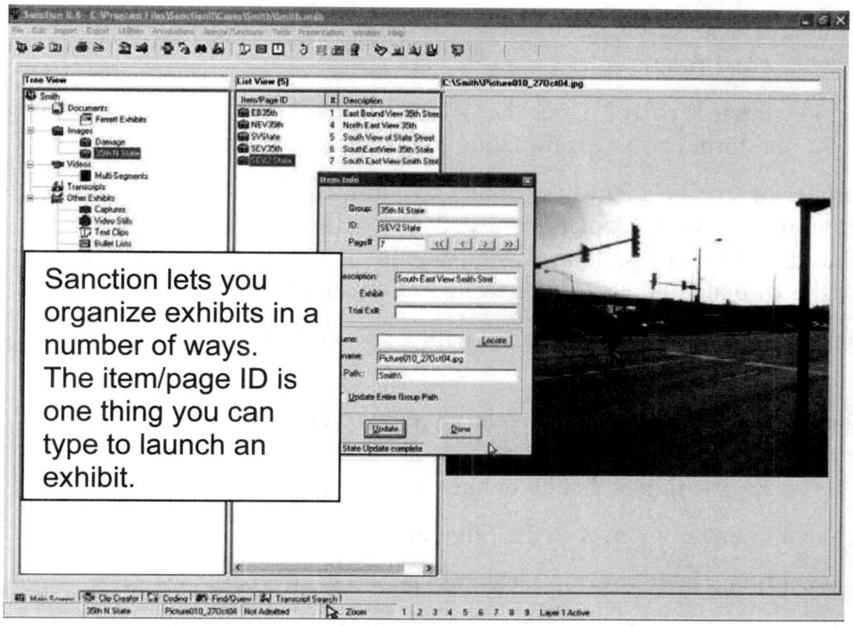

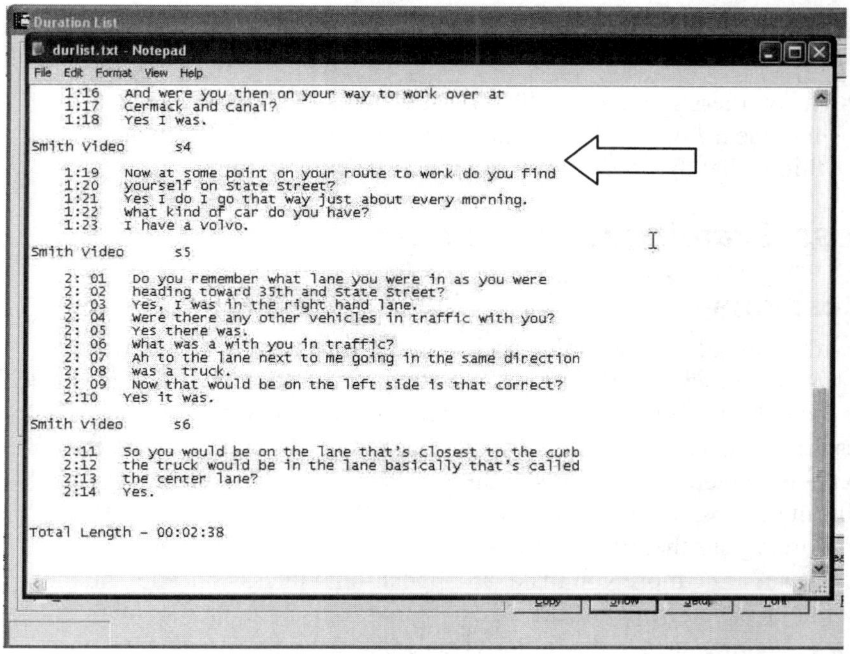

Sanction has a duration list for managing video and audio clips that helps you track ID codes and line and page numbers for cross-examination. You can copy and paste these clips into your notes.

The duration list tells you that the clip with the ID s4 will show the clip starting with "Now at some point …"

In the Sanction chapter, you will learn how to blind type, drag and drop, and use other methods to launch exhibits.

Reviewing Final Pre-Cross-Examination Considerations

Remember those questions that you were told to ask yourself in the "Gathering Information About Witnesses" section earlier in the chapter? Here are some additional questions that you should ask about a witness to craft an effective cross-examination.

- What are all of the things the witness did? What must the witness admit doing? The answers to these questions must be based on the information that you can tie that witness to.
- What are all the things the witness knew? When did the witness know these things? Again, this is based on what the witness said or did.

- Based on the information you have discovered, what are *all* the things the witness did not do that the witness *could have* or *should have* done?
- Does the witness have a relationship to a party? Does the witness have a relationship to an issue in the case that can be brought out during cross-examination to discredit the witness?
  - Is the witness a member of a party's family or someone similarly situated? For example, if the witness is the mother of the defendant's baby, what kinds of things can you make a person concede about this woman's feelings for the defendant at the time the baby was conceived, or about the woman's hopes for her child's relationship with the father?
  - Is the witness a party's friend? If so, how long have they known each other? How close are they?
  - Does this witness have an ideological bias, such as an avowed anti-capital punishment stance, or does the witness testify only for plaintiffs who sue doctors? Ask yourself what motivates the witness to say the things that he or she chooses to say on the stand.
  - Does the witness have a financial interest in the litigation?
  - Does the witness have a financial interest in pleasing the opposing side's lawyer?
- What are all the things the witness did not know? Did the witness not know things because no one told him or her? Or did the witness not know something because he or she decided not to find out through laziness, disinterest, or bias?
- What are all of the decisions the witness was faced with? What choices did the witness make? Those choices and decisions include *all* words the witness chose to use in prior statements. After all, those words are the very things that the trial lawyer can force the witness to repeat.

Planning Your Cross-Examination Questions

Seeking concessions

Plan to begin a cross-examination with a line of questions that seeks concessions that try to neutralize facts being disputed by the opposition. When witnesses for the opposition agree that facts are indeed true, any dispute about the truth of those facts disappears. These factual concessions can be called neutralization or corroboration questions, and should be talked about during closing argument, when you are trying to underscore the fact that even the opposing side's witnesses corroborate your case. To spot those facts that can be neutralized during a cross-examination, ask whether there are things this witness must admit that can be used to corroborate your theory of this case. Does this witness have to admit something that helps your side of the case? The more you make an opposition witness concede, the more the evidence from your case-in-chief is insulated from attacks. Be prepared to use Sanction to launch exhibits such as relevant scene photos, documents, and any other visuals that the witness can corroborate.

There are two reasons why beginning cross-examination with neutralization or corroboration questions is effective. First, witnesses are more comfortable agreeing with an attorney at the beginning of a cross-examination. Witnesses who have not yet been accused of bias or lying are not yet defensive and therefore are more willing to concede facts. Take advantage of this comfort level and try to get the witness into a pattern of agreeing with you. The more the witness gets comfortable saying yes, the more likely he or she is to say yes to something that may hurt the opposition later on during the cross-examination.

The second reason for beginning cross-examination with neutralization or corroboration questions is that you want to get concessions before attacking the witness's truth-telling ability. At the beginning of a cross-examination, a cross-examiner should want the jury to believe *some* of the things that the witness says. The jury will be more willing to embrace the witness's concessions if you get those concessions before exposing the flaws in the witness's believability.

Assume you have a witness who has given a videotaped statement wherein the witness admits that he was on a corner at the time of a collision. The witness is locked into an account in which the witness says he heard a screech, turned and looked in the direction of the sound, and saw the plaintiff flying to the side. The witness believed that the plaintiff was out of the crosswalk at the time that the plaintiff was hit. You have the following text available for you:

> "I was standing on the corner, you know, trying to catch a taxi. It was the southeast corner of Adams and Jefferson in Chicago. I was trying to catch a cab to the west side. I heard the screech. I turned around and I saw the lady lying in Jefferson. The lady was south of the crosswalk. Her feet were out of the crosswalk."

This witness must admit:

> "Before the collision, you were looking for a cab?"
>
> "On Adams?"
>
> "Wanted to go west?"
>
> "Adams is one way?"
>
> "Runs westbound?"
>
> "Heard the screech?"
>
> "The screech made you turn around?"
>
> "By the time you turned around, the lady was already on the ground?"
>
> "Saw her feet were out of the crosswalk at that time?"
>
> "Did not notice her before the screech?"
>
> "You were looking for that cab?"
>
> "Do not know where she was standing before the car hit her?"
>
> "Only saw where the lady landed?"

Exposing bias, motive, and interest

The next phase of a cross-examination should seek to expose any bias, motive, and interest that the witness may have in the outcome of the litigation. To achieve this end, make a list of the facts that each witness must concede that reflect a bias, motive, or interest. Bias, motive, and interest can influence a witness to lie or otherwise shade his or her testimony in the opposition's favor. Work these facts into concession-based questions so that the witness is forced to acknowledge that they are true. These factual concessions will support arguments that the witness cannot be trusted because of his or her obvious bias. For this block of cross, be ready to launch Sanction codes for every exhibit that underscores the witness's bias toward helping the opposition.

Building up and perfecting impeachment

Finally, you must be prepared to explore any logical inconsistencies in the witness's account or statements. Impeachment lines of cross must accentuate details about the witness's making of the prior statements to make those prior statements resonate with jurors. Among the things that this line of cross-examination must address are:

- Where did this conversation take place?
- Who was present for the conversation?
- When did the conversation occur?

You must be prepared to address all the considerations that were discussed in the bullet list of questions above regarding the things the witness knew and did. This cross should be prepared to force the witness to concede all of the things that should have been going through the witness's mind at the time the witness made the prior statement. This line of cross lets you use inferences to show what was going through the witness's mind. If the witness disagrees with you, you can then loop back to focus on things that the witness knew or should have known at the time the witness made this statement. For example, assume you have a witness who claims to be a close friend of the complaining witness in a criminal case. Assume that this person claims to have been a witness in a case but chose not come forward to the police until months after the complaining witness was injured. Analysis of the witness's actions should focus on what should have gone through the witness's mind when he or she saw the complaining witness get hurt. The witness should have wanted to do something; he or she should have wanted to help the police catch the person who injured the complaining witness. Common sense says that the witness would have come forward if the witness really saw what he or she claims to have seen.

Assume a witness is trying to imply that he was tricked into making a statement against his will by an investigator. Force the witness to admit that he knew that the investigator was talking to the witness because she was investigating a case. The witness must admit he understood that the investigator was asking the witness questions to learn information. By gaining these concessions, it makes it harder for the jury to believe the witness's claim that he didn't make the statement. When the witness first talked to the investigator, the witness knew the person he was talking to was an investigator. If the witness denies this, the investigator will testify that she had identified herself as an investigator. The witness knows where this conversation with the investigator took place. The witness has to know that the investigator is asking questions because the investigator wants to know what the witness knows about an incident. The witness may have observed the investigator writing down the things the witness said. A witness can be forced to admit all of these things so long as you ask the questions.

Watching your word choice

During cross-examination, choose your words carefully. A cross-examiner's word choice directly affects jury perception of a witness's ability to tell the truth. Generalities and imprecise language in a question posited to a witness during a cross-examination can destroy a cross-examination. Assume an attorney can prove that a witness was at the 7-11 on Division Street and Harlem Avenue in River Forest, Illinois, on two specific occasions. A question that asks the witness if the witness "*always* goes to the 7-11 on Division and Harlem" can be honestly answered in the negative. The witness may not always go to the 7-11. A question that asks if the witness "*often* goes to the 7-11 on Division and Harlem" can also be honestly answered with no. However, the question "you *have* been to the 7-11 at Division Street and Harlem Avenue" *must* be answered with a yes or the witness will be vulnerable to impeachment. Should the witness deny going into the 7-11, then the attorney can simply call a witness in the attorney's rebuttal case to prove that the witness had indeed been to the 7-11.

Create leading questions because those questions control a witness's options for answering them. Leading questions suggest an answer by limiting a witness's response to yes or no. Leading questions do not call for a discussion or dissertation. One can create leading questions by stating the fact to a witness. For example, the statement "You were in a car" can be posed as a question: "You were in a car?" If you like, you can follow this factual statement posed as a question with a tag line. Tag lines simply finish the factual statement with a question. Ask the question by first listing the fact that a witness must acknowledge or look foolish denying and then add a tag line that turns the fact into a question. The tag line can be either before or after the fact. The fact can be "The car was blue." The tag line that turns the fact into a question is "wasn't it?" The question becomes "The car was blue, wasn't it?" There are other tag lines that can be used to turn a fact statement into a question. "Is it true that the car was blue?" "The car has always been blue, hasn't it?"

Another effective tag line for a leading question is the voice inflection tag line. You can use your tone of voice and inflection to make a factual statement into a question. Assume the italicized words in the following questions are the words that the attorney stresses when saying the question. "*The car* was green?" "The car *was* green?" "The car was *green*?" An interrogator can use his or her voice to stress the words in this short sentence three different ways.

Once you isolate facts and come up with your tag lines, keep the questions short and simple. The best way to do this is to elicit one fact per question. Assume the following facts are true: On March 12, 2005, at 2:00 A.M., a witness was seated in the front seat of a green car on the corner of Division and Marion Streets at the time of a shooting. Here is one way to turn the preceding sentence into a leading question.

> "On March 12, 2005, at 2:00 A.M., you were seated in the front seat of a green car parked on the corner of Division and Marion Streets when the shooting happened, weren't you?"

Think about how many ways a witness can answer that question without lying. If the witness does not think that the car was green, or if he or she was not in the front seat, then the witness can answer no to the whole question. By breaking the question down, you can limit any wiggle room the witness may have and ensure that the question must be answered. Rework that last question about the shooting. Start the line of cross-examination with an introductory question that telegraphs the topic of the examination. Call this type of question a "chicken feed" question because you are using the question to introduce a topic and inviting the witness and the jury to follow along, like a chicken following feed on the ground. After introducing the topic, the attorney moves to short factual statements with tag lines.

> "I'm going to ask you some questions about where you were on March 12, 2005, at 2:00 in the morning, understand?" (The witness must say yes or look foolish for not understanding such a simple question.)
>
> "About 2:00 A.M., you were in a car?"
>
> "The car was green, right?" (If you have a picture of the car, move to admit it and publish it.)
>
> "The car was at the corner, true?"
>
> "The corner of Division and Marion Streets, right?" (Publish the map of the intersection with Sanction.)
>
> "You sat in the front passenger seat?"
>
> "The shooting happened?"

The multifact question became seven questions that no witness can elude on the stand. That kind of tight question construction comes from repeatedly refining questions so that the witness's options for answering are limited.

Using the Cross-Examination Worksheet

On the last page of this chapter is a blank cross-examination worksheet that is based on one created by the National College of District Attorneys for its approach point method of cross-examination. You can download a copy of this cross-examination worksheet from the Litigation Technology website at www.littech.org. Make multiple copies of it because you will use multiple sheets for each witness and topic. The top box of the worksheet is labeled Type. The purpose of the Type box is to let you keep track of the types of concessions that you will seek with this line of questioning. Label this box as either factual, witness theory, or impeachment. This label will come in handy when you organize the cross-examination because it will help you place this line of cross within the overall structure of the cross-examination. Remember that the most effective cross-examination begins with factual concessions, moves to introducing witness bias, and ends with impeachment.

Use the Point of This Line of Cross box on the worksheet to distill the conclusion you want the jurors to draw from the line of questioning. This is a note to yourself about why you want to ask this series of questions. This box comes in handy when you are responding to objections because it helps you articulate a response to your opponent's objection.

The Transition Question box is for the introductory question that you want to use to introduce this line of cross-examination.

On the left side of the worksheet, list the facts that the witness must concede based on the things you can prove. Use the right side of the worksheet to list the exhibit and Sanction ID code for launching the exhibit. Keep this ID code short because it is the code that you must type on the computer keyboard to call the exhibit to the screen. If you are using a bar code to launch your exhibits from Sanction, you can put the bar code on the worksheet. Once you have composed a series of approach point worksheets, you can physically move the worksheets around to organize the order of your cross-examination.

Applying the technique to a witness who refuses an interview

When using this methodology, think about some of the different situations that may arise with witnesses and ways in which you can prepare for proactive cross-examination. What do you do about witnesses who refused to be interviewed? You may assume that you cannot prepare a proactive cross-examination if the witness refuses to be interviewed before trial. This is not true. A witness who refuses to talk to you is actually helping you. A witness's refusal to answer questions can give rise to the inference that the witness has a motive to lie, is biased toward the opposition, or is biased against you. Use a witness's refusal to talk to you or to your investigator to argue that the witness is trying to hide something or to help the opposition. This refusal to be interviewed sets a witness up for the following line of cross-examination:

> "On X date, I came to your house, didn't I?" (Launch a photo of the house.)
>
> "That's your house, isn't it?"
>
> "I brought an investigator, right?" (Launch a photo of the investigator.)
>
> "That is the woman who was with me, true?"
>
> "I asked you who you were?"
>
> "You told me?"
>
> "I told you who I was, didn't I?"
>
> "I told you I was a trial lawyer and was representing ____________?"
>
> "I told you your name had been given to me by the opponent's attorney as a witness, true?"
>
> "That was the first time we met, wasn't it?"

"You had previously talked to that lawyer over there, hadn't you?"

"*Previously* means you had talked to that lawyer before we ever met, true?"

"But our meeting was your first time to tell someone who represented ___________ what you knew, wasn't it?"

"You decided that you weren't going to talk to me?"

"You said you were refusing to talk to me?"

"You refused to answer my questions?"

"Didn't you want to know what my questions were?"

"Had you already decided you were going to help __________?"

"Did you think that refusing to talk to me might help ____________ get out from under this case?"

"Did you think that refusing to talk to me made you look like an unbiased witness?"

Applying the technique to a witness who reviewed his or her statement

The following is an example of how one might cross-examine a witness who, after having reviewed and approved his or her statement, testifies inconsistently at trial.

"On X date, I came out to your house with an investigator, true?" (Show a picture of the house.)

"We sat in your living room and talked about the case?"

"I asked you questions, correct?"

"After a while, I asked you if you would give a videotaped statement?" (Show the camera.)

"You chose not to do that?"

"Then I asked you if you would sign a written statement, true?"

"You did agree to do that, didn't you?"

"I asked you if you wanted to write the statement out yourself?"

"You said you did not want to do that?"

"So I wrote it out in your presence and in my investigator's presence, didn't I?"

"After I wrote it out, we asked you if you wanted to make any corrections, true?"

"You did want to make some changes, didn't you?"

"You took the pen? You made some changes?"

"You initialed the corrections, didn't you?"

"Let me show you your statement." (Approach and hand the original to the witness.)

"That's your statement, isn't it?" (Move to admit the statement and ask leave to publish the digital image of the first page of the document. Be ready to argue that the statement is being used to lay the foundation for impeachment purposes.)

"This is a scanned version of that document, isn't it?"

"Look here." (Point to the screen.)

"These are your initials here and here, aren't they?"

"Look at the bottom of each page. Your signature is on each page, isn't it? Look at the video screen. That is a picture of the first page of the document that you are holding in your hand, isn't it?"

"Let's look at the places where you made corrections on this document. Every place on the document where your initials appear is a place where a correction was made, true?"

"I asked you if there was anything else that you wanted to add to what you told us, true?"

"You said you were satisfied?"

"In fact, you signed your name after the sentence that says, 'I have had an opportunity to make changes and corrections to this statement and there is nothing more that I wish to add to it. I have told you everything I know about the case and the defendant and have signed this statement in order to indicate that these notes are true and accurate,' didn't you?"

Preparing a litany for publication of a video clip

The final worksheet that you should prepare is the litany for the publication of a video clip with Sanction. There is a model litany at the end of the impeachment section below.

The Second Cross-Examination: Executing in the Courtroom

It is now time to address the cross-examination that an attorney actually performs in the courtroom in front of the jury. Before beginning, ask: "Has this jury been conditioned to react to cross-examination?" If your opponent has cross-examined before you, ask: "Was he or she a skilled examiner?" If the opposing attorney was skilled, then your jury is conditioned to expect succinct or purposeful cross-examinations. On the other hand, if your opponent was not skillful, he or she may have damaged the jury's expectations. If so, jurors may watch you begin your first cross-examination with a sense of dread because they do not want you to annoy them as much as your opponent did. In any case, do not allow yourself to sink to a bad advocate's level. Be the voice of reason, the professional, the person whom the jurors will later look to for guidance during closing argument. This means that you must control your line of questions, your demeanor, and your tone during the execution of the cross-examination.

Gathering Your Thoughts

Before you begin a cross-examination, take a moment to gather your thoughts about what the witness has just said on the stand. Ask yourself these questions:

- Were there really any surprises, or did I anticipate most of what was said?
- Can I use anything the witness has said to corroborate the evidence in my case?
- Is there anything the witness has said that I can turn against the opposition?
- Put another way, if what the witness says is true, what else must be true?

If the witness has said things that you can turn to your advantage that do not involve an attacking line of cross-examination, stick to the concession-based format to ask about those things at the beginning of your cross-examination.

Beginning

Once you have gathered your thoughts, it is time to begin your cross. Start an examination with an even tone of voice. Impress the jury as a professional who is not being tricky or manipulative. Appear as someone who is listening to the witness and giving the witness an opportunity to explain him- or herself. Your questions and tone should appeal to common sense and common juror experience to allow jurors to perceive you as the voice of reason in the trial.

Using Transition Questions

A good transition or introduction for a line of cross-examination is a device called a chicken feed transition. Chicken feed transitions tell the witness the topic that will be addressed with the next series of questions. The chicken feed leads the witness and the jury to the line of questioning the attorney wants to ask. For example, the question, "I'm going to ask you some questions about where you say you were on March 15th at four o'clock," is virtually impossible for a witness or a jury to misunderstand.

Once you have asked the transition question, ask whether the witness understands. Once the witness indicates that he or she understands, it is time to use the short tight questions that you developed on the approach point worksheet. This way, the jury can see that you are not trying to confuse the witness (or jury) with your questions.

Being Ready for Difficult Witnesses

Every attorney encounters difficult witnesses. One type of extremely difficult witness is one who has been coached or prepared by the opposition to evade answering questions or to inject things that are designed to hurt your case. If a witness starts to flip or waiver, give the illusion of disappointment before showing anger. If you think that there will be a confrontation where you will have to show anger or sarcasm, then the jury must believe that the witness has earned your harsh treatment. Set a witness up for jury scorn by repeating questions when a witness tries to be evasive. A question that is repeated *slowly* cannot be misunderstood. A witness who refuses to answer the repeated question looks evasive. Try to remain courteous for as long as possible because the witness may honestly be mistaken or confused, and more importantly, you may gain points with the jury, who will believe that you are being fair by repeating a question. If a cross-examiner gets confrontational before the jury is ready (that is, before they are fed up with the witness's behavior), then that lawyer risks not only alienating the jury, but also encouraging their sympathy for the witness.

Other difficult witnesses give absolutely ridiculous answers to simple questions. When dealing with this type of difficult witness, simply stop after receiving the ridiculous answer, pause, turn, and look at the jury. If the cross-examiner can recreate a John Belushi eyebrow raise, then he or she should do it. The jury will laugh at the reaction to the ridiculous answer and at the fact that the attorney sees the ridiculous answer for what it is. The jury who laughs at the witness for saying something stupid does not believe the witness.

Some difficult witnesses use the answer "I don't recall" in response to questions in an effort to avoid getting impeached with a prior inconsistent statement. When a witness tries to do this, ask: "Are you saying that you might have said it and you forgot, or are you saying you didn't say it?" This question forces the witness to choose. In either circumstance, you may now call a witness to perfect impeachment of the evasive witness.

Another type of difficult witness tries to avoid answering questions, tries to talk about everything except the answer to the question, or asks the attorney to rephrase the question. Here are some suggested witness control techniques.

- Ask the witness if he or she understood the question. When the witness indicates that he or she indeed understood the question, repeat the *exact* same question.
- Or ask, "Now, why don't you try answering the question I asked you?"
- Ask the witness to repeat your question: "What was my question?" or "Would you repeat my question?" or "What did I ask you?"
- Ask, "Was there a word in that question that you didn't understand?"
- "Are you through?"
- "Is there something else you want to say before you answer my question?"
- "Could you tell me what that last answer had to do with the question I just asked?"
- "You came to tell the truth, correct? If the simple truth is yes, can't you tell us yes?"

Make well-coached witnesses expose their testimonial preparation. Make witnesses who have been prepped to look at the jury stand up and hold an exhibit or diagram. Assuming you work in a jurisdiction that allows you to move around the room, move to a position where the witness has to look away from the jury. This tactic forces the well-coached witness off balance and underscores the fact that the witness has been trained to choreograph his or her presentation. If your movement in the courtroom is restricted by court or practice rules, you should, if appropriate, have the witness hold up the scene diagram or another exhibit while answering questions. This forces the witness to look away from the jury and perhaps gives you an advantage during cross-examination by making the well-coached witness uncomfortable.

Handling Impeachment

As this chapter draws to a conclusion, it is time to address maximizing impeachment during reactive cross-examination. Prior inconsistent statements are effective credibility-attacking weapons *only* when the jury catches the significance of the prior statement. Impeachment should be handled in steps. Like everything else in cross-examination, break it down. Assume the witness claims that a car was yellow when earlier the witness told the police the car was green.

- *Never be afraid to pause* between any of these questions. Silence is a powerful tool. Most witnesses are uncomfortable with it.
- *Never begin an impeachment question with the words "Do you remember."* A witness who answers the question about memory with an answer of no could arguably be telling the truth. Instead, use an accusatory question that states the point as a fact that must be admitted or denied rather than "remembered."
- *Recommit the witness to the inconsistent statement* that the witness has made in open court. "Did you just tell this jury that the car was yellow?"
- *Confront by tracking the language of the prior statement* to underscore the fact that you have information that contradicts the witness's statement in court today. Do not immediately divulge the source of the statement; you will get to that later. "The car was green, wasn't it?"
- *Build up the circumstances of the prior inconsistent statement* before going into the substance of the statement. Once the conflict is underscored, introduce the bias concessions while building up the circumstances of the making of the actual prior inconsistent statement. The bias information will show why the subsequent change of testimony should not be trusted before you perfect your impeachment with the actual prior inconsistent statement. It also builds up the importance of the prior inconsistent statement.

Applying the technique

"When you were at the police station, they asked you to wait in a room for a while, true?"

"While you waited, one of the officers brought in food?"

"You had something to eat?"

"In fact, you had a burger, fries, and a ginger ale, right?" (Show a picture of the type of food.)

"Nobody prevented you from going to the bathroom, did they?"

"In fact, you were able to smoke while you were at the station, weren't you?"

"Smoked Newports, right?" (Show a pack of Newports.)

"Then the police officer came to interview you?"

"You knew the person in the room with you was a police officer, didn't you?"

"The two of you sat in a room?"

"Was there a table in there?" "Chairs?"

"The officer sat next to you or across from you?"

"Anybody else in the room?"

"The officer started asking you questions?"

"Ever tell the officer you were having problems understanding the questions?"

"When that officer started asking questions, you knew that the officer wanted to know what you knew, true?"

"You gave him answers to those questions, didn't you?"

"Answered those questions because you had been at the scene of the collision?"

"You didn't refuse to answer those questions, did you?"

"That police officer, when he asked you about the color of the car . . ."

Perfect the impeachment by now confronting the witness with the prior inconsistent statement. Unless the witness admits the truth, be prepared to call a witness in your rebuttal case to impeach the witness.

"You told that police officer the car was green?" (If this statement is on video, launch the clip.)

"Not yellow?"

"You said green?"

When the witness is confronted with a video clip, the perfection looks like this:

"On X date, I came out to your house with an investigator, true?"

"We sat in your living room and talked about the case?"

"I asked you questions, correct?"

"After a while, I asked you if you would give a videotaped statement, true?"

"You agreed to do that?"

"After that, we got a video camera?"

"We set it up in your house?"

"My investigator turned on the camera?"

"You were interviewed on video, weren't you?"

"During that interview on video camera, you were asked this question and you gave this answer." (Launch the Sanction clip.)

"That was you, wasn't it?"

"You said green, in response to that question?"

CROSS PREPARATION WORKSHEET

Type

Point of This Line of Cross

Transition Question

Concession Points:

Source of Information: ⇓

Chapter 6

Using Computer Presentations in Closing Argument

Every jurisdiction has unique rules about how closing arguments can be conducted. In some jurisdictions, the plaintiff has an opportunity to present a closing argument and then later a rebuttal argument that responds to the defense's closing argument. In other jurisdictions, only two arguments are allowed, so the plaintiff speaks second after the defense presents its closing argument. Regardless of the procedure, there are really only two kinds of closing arguments in trials: proactive and reactive. Proactive closing arguments go first in the order of argument. Reactive closing arguments go second in order (or third, if the third argument is a rebuttal argument). A proactive closing argument allows you to explain either why you believe you have satisfied the elements of a particular cause of action or why you believe that the plaintiff or prosecutor has failed to prove its case. All reactive closing arguments must be fluid to allow the attorney presenting the argument to adjust his or her argument to respond to the arguments presented by the first attorney.

This chapter talks about methodologies for creating effective proactive and reactive closing arguments that can be presented with Sanction, PowerPoint, or a combination of the two programs. It addresses considerations for organizing both proactive and reactive arguments and for creating visuals that advance a party's case theme.

Choosing a Methodology

How you use PowerPoint and Sanction to present a closing argument is determined by a number of factors, including your argument preparation style, your argument style, and your choice of making a proactive or reactive argument. A proactive argument can be presented almost exclusively with PowerPoint so long as you are the type of presenter who is willing to stick to the script. If you are a methodical type who likes to choreograph every phase of a closing argument, you will love using PowerPoint for closing argument. It is magnificent for presenting complex ideas, elaborate visuals, video clips that have been previously viewed with Sanction, and jury instructions. On the other hand, if you are presenting a reactive argument or are the type of attorney who handles closing argument like it is more of an extemporaneous presentation, then you will need the flexibility offered by a nonlinear presentation software such as Sanction.

Sanction is flexible because it can act as a platform for launching mini-PowerPoint slide presentations or can launch its own exhibits and video clips in any order you choose. Sanction also has a built-in bullet point function and can integrate CaseSoft's TimeMap timelines that can be used to launch exhibits. Mini-slide presentations are simply presentations that are restricted to a short topic. Mini-slide presentations can be launched quickly from the Sanction presentation screen and, once launched, can be advanced from slide to slide with a cordless presenter until the slide show concludes. At the conclusion of the mini-slideshow, PowerPoint will return to the black Sanction presentation screen. The Sanction presentation screen also allows you to launch individual exhibits from the presentation screen a number of ways. The quickest way to launch an exhibit in Sanction if you are not using Dual Monitor mode is with a couple of keystrokes by typing in an item's page/item ID, exhibit number, or description.

Creating an Effective Closing Argument

An effective closing argument needs three things. First, the argument must have an attention-grabbing beginning. Next, the argument needs an interest-holding middle that explains how and why the jury is justified in making a decision in your favor. Finally, the argument needs a powerful and compelling ending. These three components make up the global structure that must exist in all successful proactive and reactive arguments. The specific components for proactive and reactive closings are detailed below.

Proactive Arguments

The global structure for a good proactive argument includes having a beginning that grabs the jury's attention. Next the proactive argument must explain how the law should be used to interpret the facts that were adduced at trial. This is the section of the argument that you will use to teach the jury how to filter the evidence. The proactive argument should then move to why the case has either satisfied or failed to satisfy the legal requirements for the tort or charged crime.

When the attorney giving the proactive argument is entitled to present a rebuttal argument, then you may want to have a section of the proactive argument that goads the defense into presenting its closing argument. Although it happens only rarely, if the defense attorney waives closing argument, the plaintiff or prosecutor does not get to present a rebuttal argument.

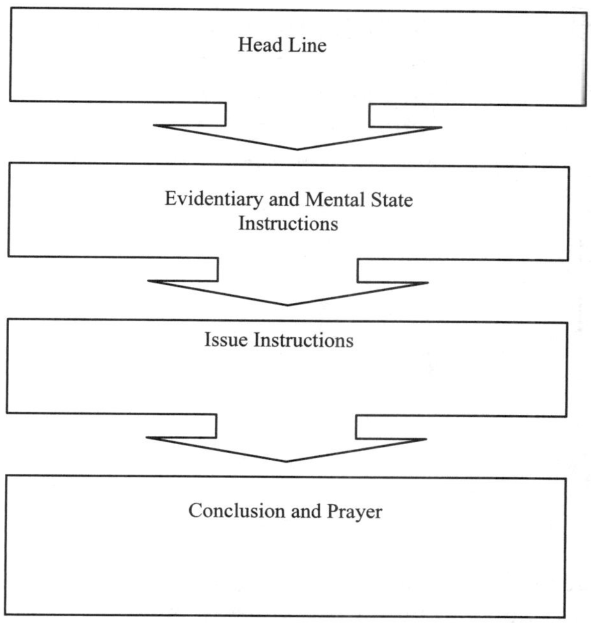

This visual lays out a structure for a proactive closing argument.

When the argument flows like this, you make the argument easy for the jury to follow.

The prayer slide is simply the last slide in your argument presentation where you tell the jury what to do. For example, it can say: "Sign the verdict that says we, the jury, find for the Plaintiff."

Reactive Arguments

A reactive closing argument necessarily has a different global structure. A reactive argument should be more malleable to allow you to adjust the argument in response to your opponent's arguments. If you are presenting a reactive closing argument, you may want to have a number of different potential headlines or lead-off arguments that you can use in reaction to the things that your opponent said. Let's face it: Many lawyers forget to argue things, miss things that they should have argued, or make misstatements. If you are following someone who did one of these things, you may want to adjust your argument to capitalize on your opponent's failure. For example, you may come up with a headline that challenges the misstatement or that adds or drops an argument depending on the needs of the moment. You should always have a block of argument that addresses the relevant burden of proof. The argument must explain how jury instructions should be applied to the facts of the case from your perspective. Once the principles are defined, the argument should then move to why your case has either satisfied the legal requirements or why your opposition has failed to satisfy the legal requirements for the tort or charged crime. When a defense argument is sandwiched between the plaintiff's or prosecutor's proactive and reactive arguments, the defense argument must attack the prosecution's or plaintiff's case. The defense argument must present the defense theory that explains why the defendant should not be convicted or should not be found liable, and should challenge the plaintiff or prosecution to explain the unexplainable.

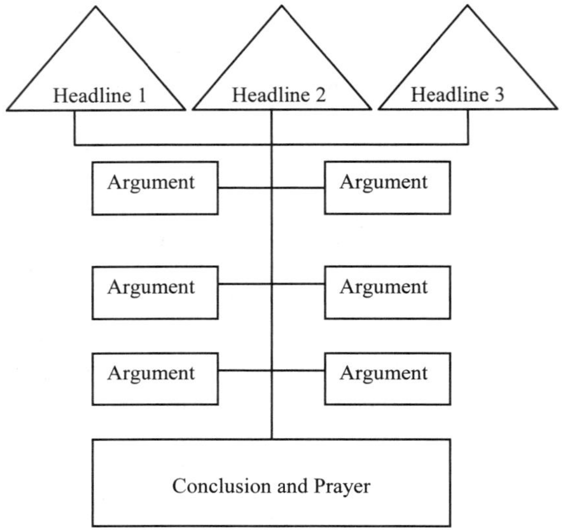

This graphic illustrates the adjustability that a good reactive argument needs.

With Sanction, you can launch any of the headlines or arguments in any order you choose.

Tactics for Both Sides

Plan to use visuals

Both argument types should choreograph the use of photographs, diagrams, physical evidence, and witness testimony with appropriate jury instructions. Quotes from witnesses must be highlighted and then corroborated so that the jurors trust that the quotes are accurate. Consider blowing up direct quotes from the trial testimony and putting them in a visual.

Anticipate your opponent's move

The attorney for either the proactive argument or reactive argument must think through the opponent's argument before creating his or her own. Find the holes in the opposition's theory, and then anticipate how the opposition is going to try to get around the holes. When the holes are spotted in your case, try to close them; and when you spot holes in your opponent's case, plan to blow them wide open. Plaintiffs and prosecutors should make sure that they do not chase the defense theory during their proactive argument, especially when they are getting an opportunity to present a rebuttal argument. When you will have an opportunity to present a rebuttal argument, you should talk about your own evidence in your proactive argument and save your attack on the defense evidence for your rebuttal argument. Stick to this rule unless the defense did something *really stupid* during the trial, like have the defendant confess to the crime, admit liability on the stand, or present witnesses who were so incredible that you must capitalize on these failings at the outset. The proactive argument should focus on the Tier 1 evidence that you identified during the cost benefit analysis discussed in Chapter 2. When you are presenting a reactive argument without the right to rebuttal, you must be prepared to attack your opponent's case with Tier 2 evidence at some point during the argument.

Plot an exit line

Both proactive and reactive arguments should have a choreographed ending that includes a conclusion and a prayer. The conclusion is that portion of the argument in which you rally the jury to your cause. It is a plea for the jury to "do the right thing" by signing a verdict form in your favor. The prayer is where you tell the jury what to do during the deliberation. A prayer should tell the jurors which jury interrogatories to sign and which verdict form to sign.

Make your visuals sell your theory

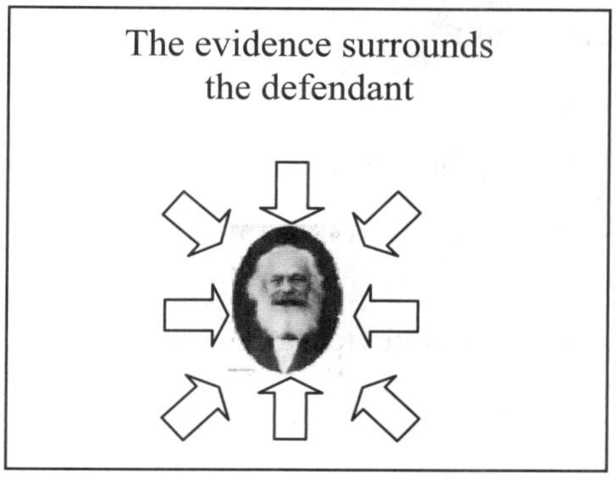

Plaintiff or prosecution slide

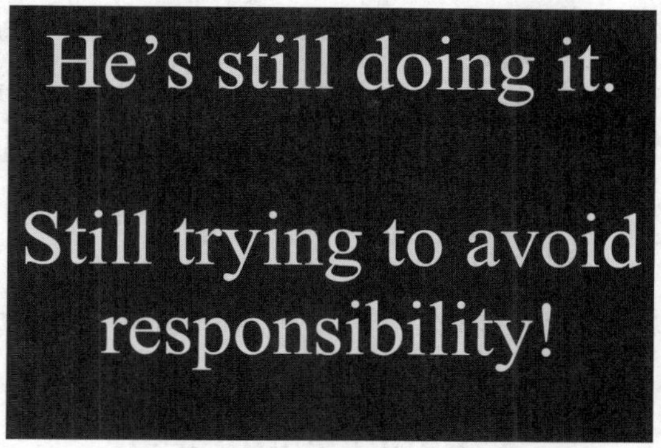

Plaintiff or prosecution headline slide

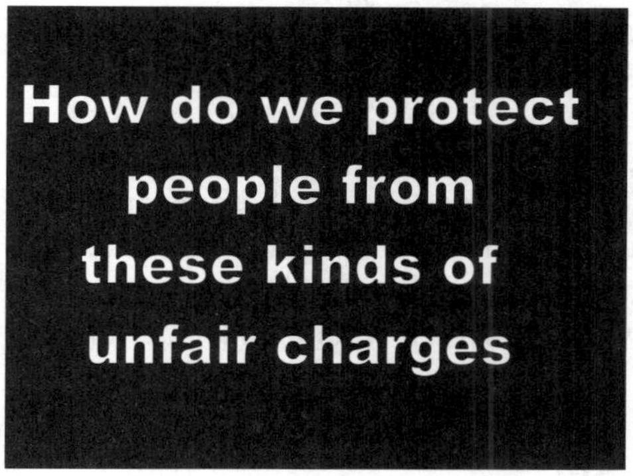

Defense headline or introductory headline for a block of argument

Plaintiff or prosecution headline for a breach of contract or a fraud case where the agreement was struck over a handshake

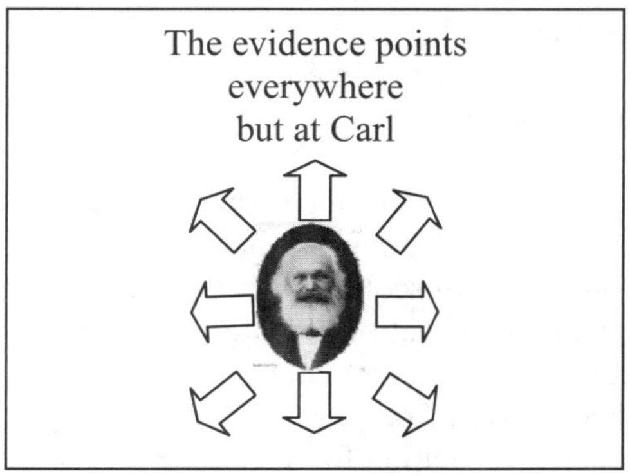

Defense slide that supports your argument that the evidence points away from the defendant

This slide simply uses the question mark to loom in the background while the defense lawyer talks.

Weigh pre-argument considerations

Ask yourself these questions as you prepare for the closing argument:

- What kind of visual is going to advance my case theme?
- Can I make rhetorical devices that will help me get my point across to the jury?
- Where can I weave these specific slides, video clips, and sound files into my presentation?
- Can I use phrases, images, shapes, and lines to create rhetorical devices that will enhance an argument?

Avoid self-defeat

Keep the following in mind while preparing any kind of an argument. Do not plan on writing a speech and then reading it. Reading an argument to a jury is the fastest way to bore them. If you must use notes, make an outline and leave it next to your laptop. Set your laptop up in a place where you can see the screen while facing the jury. This way you can present your argument while being able to keep track of what is on the viewing screen for the jury. This will also help keep you from falling behind or speaking ahead of the presentation. One additional advantage to having the computer in front of you is that you can get to the keyboard and launch items or remove them from the screen. PowerPoint will go to a black screen when a presenter hits the B key on the keyboard. This blacks out the screen until the presenter touches another key to advance a slide. Sanction will remove an object from the viewing screen when a presenter clicks on it with a mouse or hits the Esc key.

Do not make needless objections

You should object to an opponent's misstatements of the law. An attorney does not have the right to mislead a jury regarding the meaning of the law. However, needless objections have the potential to create juror resentment toward the lawyer making the objections. Objections are often perceived as rude, especially if your opponent has not been objecting during your closing remarks. This perception is enhanced when the judge overrules your objection. Another by-product of needlessly objecting during your opponent's argument is that your opponent may choose to retaliate with some needless objections of his or her own, just to interrupt your flow or momentum. Although this is not necessarily ethical conduct, it happens.

Avoid objecting to misstatements of fact or factual overstatements by your opponent if you still have the opportunity to argue. These are the things that reactive argument was made for. Objections only invite a judge to cure the record or give you a judicial scolding for whining. Where the judge has cured the record by sustaining an objection and cautions the jury to disregard the argument, there is a good appellate argument that an advocate who later makes a reactive argument to the "judicially cured" argument should have been barred from making the otherwise invited comments before the jury. Tactically, you may be better off letting these comments come before the jury without objection, and then responding to these intellectually dishonest arguments in reactive argument. Where you have already argued and will not get a chance to respond to intellectually dishonest arguments, you should object to misstatements of law, violations of motions in limine, and material misstatements of fact. You should do this for a number of reasons. First, since you do not have another opportunity to speak to the jury, it is your only means of cluing the jury into the fact that your opponent is not being intellectually honest. In addition, it is the only way you can obtain any curative action on the part of the court.

Write sound bite arguments

When composing a reactive argument, you should write "sound bite" arguments that address potential arguments that the other attorney may raise. While a reactive argument must be fluid and cannot be scripted, 90 percent of the argument can be anticipated. You know where the holes in your case are, and you know where your opponent's weaknesses in his or her case are; so you should have short arguments that defend your weaknesses and that attack your opponent's weaknesses. Of course, some things you cannot anticipate since lawyers sometimes go off on tangents. Your opponents may offer bizarre theories, inappropriate or gratuitous bible quotes (meaning they have nothing to do with the case), appeals to sympathy and prejudice, and other types of courtroom antics. Those completely unanticipated things that come up during your opponent's argument are things that you will have to address on the fly after you hear them. However, if you have planned for the other 90 percent of your argument, you will be better able to think through the rest of your argument as you listen to your opponent.

Each sound bite argument can have its own series of slides or images that launch during your argument. Each sound bite argument should have a caption that you keep track of on a key sheet. Make a key sheet that lists the captions of all of your sound bites. List the Sanction page/item IDs for these exhibits and slide presentations next to the caption on the key sheet, so you will know where to find the IDs when you want to type them into the keyboard. As you listen to your opponent's argument, circle the captions for your sound bite arguments on the key sheet. This process frees you from composing your reactive argument as your opponent argues. Because you will have done this work ahead of time, you will be able to listen for overstatements, misstatements, and other types of arguments that you can turn against your opponent.

Know when to darken the screen

Use a blank screen or the B key on a slide presentation or the black Sanction presentation desktop when you do not want the jury looking at the screen. If you are using a series of slides and do not want to return to the Sanction desktop, but want to talk about something that is not supported by a visual or if you simply do not want to use visuals at every step of the argument, then you should insert blank slides at the appropriate places in the presentation.

Making Your Closing Argument in the Courtroom

Using Headlines to Begin the Argument

When you begin the argument, you will have the jury's undivided attention. You must capitalize on this attention. One of the most successful ways of doing this is by using a headline that drives the case theme or that tries to resonate with the jurors.

Where a cause of action involves a status crime (think *malum prohibidum* crime) or a complaint that alleges a statutory or contractual violation that did not cause a personal injury, you should use a headline that underscores the defendant's conscious decision to defy the law or violate the law or contractual provision.

Examples

Possession of a controlled substance with intent to distribute: "When defendant decided to go stand on that porch with his pockets lined with money, when he chose to carry this cell phone and this pager, when he decided to hold onto this strip of tape with the bags of cocaine stuck between them, he decided to begin his journey to this courtroom. He put himself in this chair because of his choices and his decisions alone."

Breach of contract: "It's time to put integrity back into a handshake. When that defendant put out his hand and shook Robert Jones's hand and said, 'We've got a deal,' that was a contract, a promise, a pledge to carry out his word. So when that defendant decided not to keep his word, he decided to begin his journey to this courtroom."

Visuals: A picture of the controlled substance and a picture of a handshake.

Assume you want to use a symbolic slide like the handshake slide. It is fairly unlikely that a photograph of two people shaking hands will be admitted into evidence in a contracts case unless it happens to be a picture of the parties shaking hands. If earlier in the trial the judge would not admit such a photo into evidence, then your opponent will object to your using it during your closing argument. What a judge will do with the argument to exclude the handshake is an unknown decision. For that reason, a smart trial lawyer will have a backup slide like the integrity slide that can be used if a judge excludes the handshake slide.

In the case in which a human being was injured physically, emotionally, or financially, consider beginning your opening with a headline that makes the jury both sad and angry — sad for the injured party and angry with the defendant for causing the injury. A headline that begins by making the jury feel sad for the circumstances of the victim's suffering gives them a "Kodak moment" that they can collectively refer to as they work toward their verdict of guilty. This headline allows you to blame the defendant from the outset for everything in the case.

Examples

Injured victims and plaintiffs: "When Simon Chee opened his front door and saw the damage" (publish a photo of the outside of Chee's house), "when he realized that a stranger had touched his things, gone through his drawers, opened his closets, and scattered his possessions across the floor of his house, he was robbed of more than his possessions. He was robbed of his piece of mind. His house, his castle, his place where he had a right to do whatever he wanted, where he had a right to be private, was violated, debased. And why? Why did this have to happen? Because this defendant wanted something to steal, because he was greedy, because he felt he had the right to invade another person's world. Let's look at what this defendant did to Mr. Chee's castle . . ." (Publish the scene photos of the damage.)

Personal injury: "When Hanna Jones felt what it feels like to be too tired to breathe, when she felt the fluid filling her lungs drowning her with the by-product of the staph infection, when she felt her skin stretching from the fluid seeping into her tissue, she had no idea that this had been caused by a careless resident who didn't keep his examination gloves clean. She didn't know that carelessness conducted just 18 hours earlier was now threatening her life as the staph infection raced from her uterus into her blood stream and then into her lungs. She just wanted to breathe."

Use a photo of the plaintiff or victim. If a photo has been admitted, depicting the victim in the hospital or showing the victim's injures would be ideal. Let that person's photo stay on the screen while you talk about the impact of the crime or incident on your plaintiff or victim.

Defense headlines should be crafted to connect with juror values that reward or absolve the defendant.

Examples

Failure to mitigate damages: "Everything my opponent just said is very important. Hanna Jones was horribly injured. No one should have to suffer like that. But how much of her suffering was her own fault? Who was it who didn't follow up on physical therapy? Who failed to make her appointments? Who aggravated her own condition? You know who it was . . ."

Visual: Use a close-up of the plaintiff's face.

A face shot gets the jury to focus on the decisions made by the person in the photo. It helps underscore the irony of an individual asking for money when the individual is at least partially responsible for his or her own suffering.

Reasonable doubt or plaintiff did not meet burden of proof: "How does a man defend himself from these kinds of allegations? What mechanism steps in and gives a person a fair shot? A chance for justice? What kind of shield does the law provide for a person on the receiving end of such unfair and unjust accusations? I'll tell you what it is. It is the burden of proof, the law's demand that the person who accuses must prove his charge. And when he can't or he doesn't, the law says that you, the jurors, must say so with your verdict. So let's look at how the plaintiff has failed to prove his case . . ."

Visual: Blank screen lets the jury focus on the advocate.

Self-defense: "Robert Wilson was justified in using deadly force. He believed that Colleen Brown was going to kill him, and that is why Robert pulled his gun and fired. Robert understood the same thing that we all understand. A man has the right to defend himself when he believes he is facing deadly force. And that is all that Robert Wilson did."

Visual: Blank screen stands next to the client.

The empty chair defense: "You know, the argument the plaintiff's lawyer just gave sounds pretty compelling, except for one thing — one very important thing. Do you know what it is? Here it comes — the wrong people are sitting at the defense table. This plaintiff had the right to sue anyone that she wanted, but why did she sue us? We had nothing to do with her getting hit on the head with the clock. We just own the train platform. How could we expect a bunch of people to set off fireworks and make the people on the platform stampede? How could we foresee that a crowd of people would knock over the clock and make it hit Mrs. Palsgraf in the head? I'm deeply sorry she was injured, but she picked us because she thought we were the deep pocket. That's all. That's why . . ."

Visual: Use a photo of a train station showing the station clean and clear of debris or hazards, or use a question mark.

Plotting How to Explain the Whys

After spending so much time tinkering with your theory, it is time to use the exhibits and testimony to demonstrate how your theory is the intellectually honest path for the jurors to take. The argument should explain how "we" can know things, in light of the evidence that has been presented. Let the jurors know that you have discussed the instructions with the judge. Tell them when you are going to paraphrase instructions.

Explaining the whys for proactive arguments

For a plaintiff or prosecutor, the advocate presenting the proactive argument should shape the jury's thought process by using a transition that moves the argument to the evidentiary and mental state jury instructions that need particular emphasis, in light of the facts of the case. Structurally it makes sense to do this because those types of instructions help the jurors understand how they are supposed to use the instructions to interpret the evidence. Simply put, the evidentiary and mental state instructions help to focus the jury's analysis. When you incorporate the evidentiary and mental state instructions into the second block of the argument, you step into the role of teacher. The hope is that the jury will take your lead and use the instructions to filter the evidence the way you have told them.

If you come from a jurisdiction that gives jurors written jury instructions that are taken into the jury room during deliberation, show the jury the instruction that they will see before explaining it or turning it into a visual. This way, the jurors will be able to go into the stack of jury instructions and pull it out when they are deliberating. If you come from a jurisdiction that does not allow the jurors to have the instructions in the jury room during deliberation, read the exact jury instruction to the jurors. This way, the judge will corroborate you when he or she reads it, and you will be showing the jury how your analysis of the instruction is intellectually honest. Always tell a jury when you are paraphrasing an instruction; otherwise you risk creating needless error in your argument or risk looking like you are being sneaky. After telling the jury what the law is, use the facts of the case to illustrate how these facts should be interpreted in light of the law. Too many advocates rely on the use of clichés such as sports analogies or rainstorms to explain concepts like circumstantial evidence or accountability. The best way to illustrate a legal principle is to use the facts of your case to show the jury how to interpret the evidence. A trial lawyer's argument is more powerful when it takes the facts of the case and explains how the jury instructions should be applied to them.

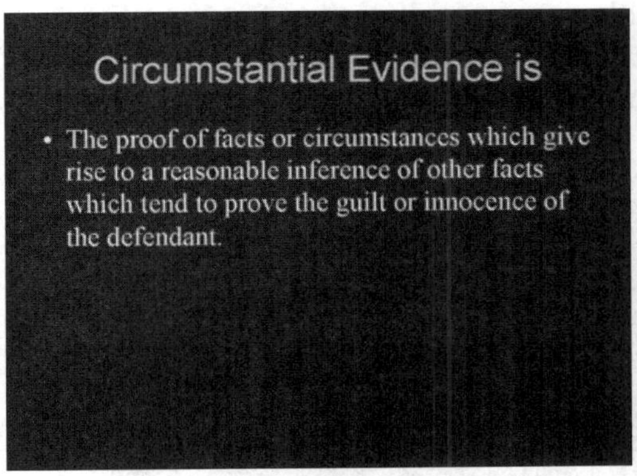

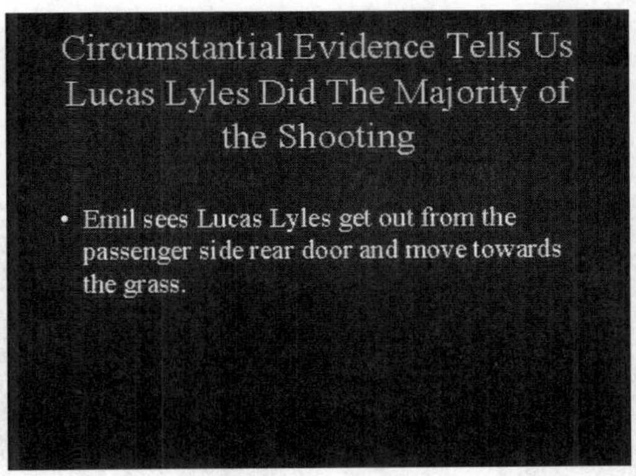

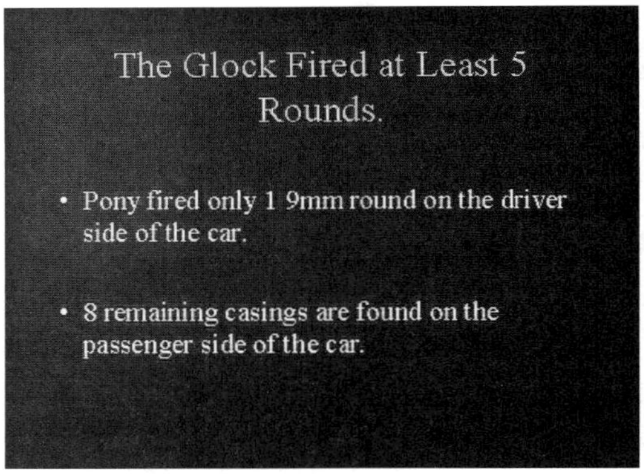

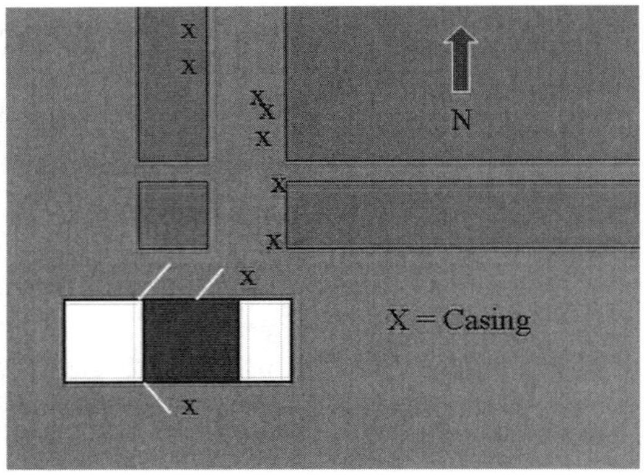

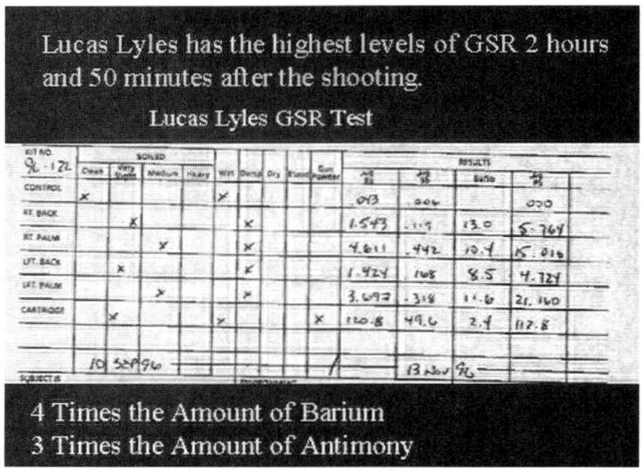

Every scene photo contains some type of circumstantial evidence. Either recite or paraphrase the language from the instruction and then go to the photos to show how the jury can infer things from them. Use the circumstantial evidence that you are able to glean from the photos to corroborate trial testimony. This shows the jury how to consider the evidence in light of the instruction. Show slides that explain how the evidence fits together.

This series of slides shows how the jury can use the circumstantial evidence instruction to find that one individual actually did the majority of the shooting in light of the testimony of the witnesses and the physical evidence that was recovered at the scene or that was later found by the crime lab.

Explaining the whys for reactive arguments

For the reactive argument, the same principles apply, although you will want to focus on different jury instructions. Assume you are a defense attorney from a jurisdiction like Illinois, which does not allow attorneys to define the burden of proof, but instead leaves that job to the jurors. Here are some things that you can do:

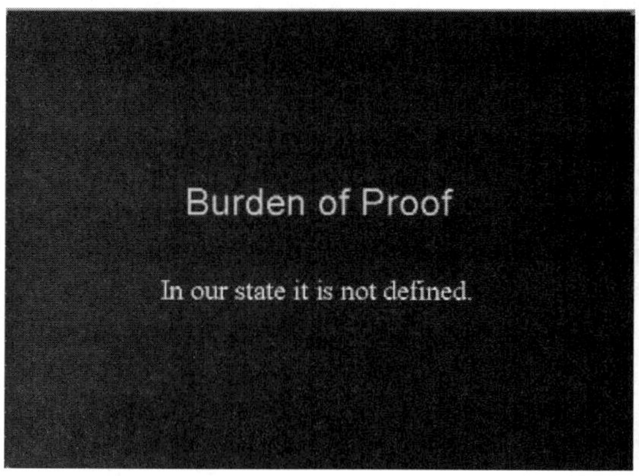

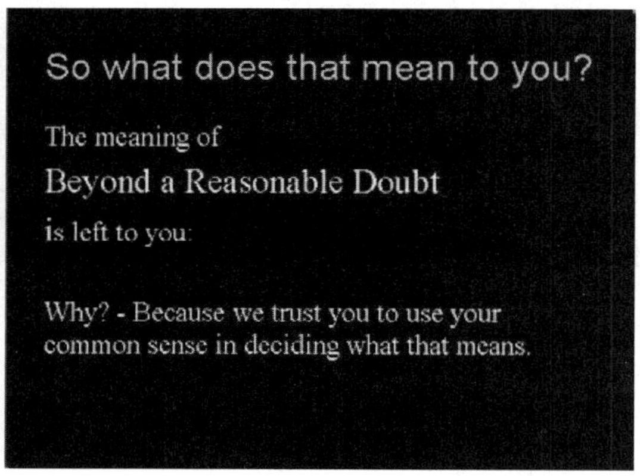

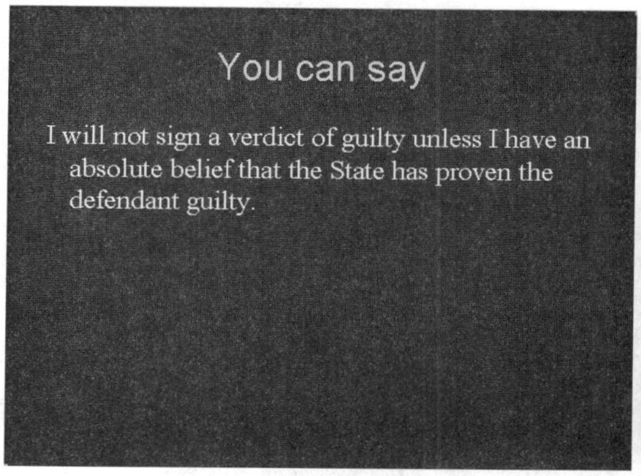

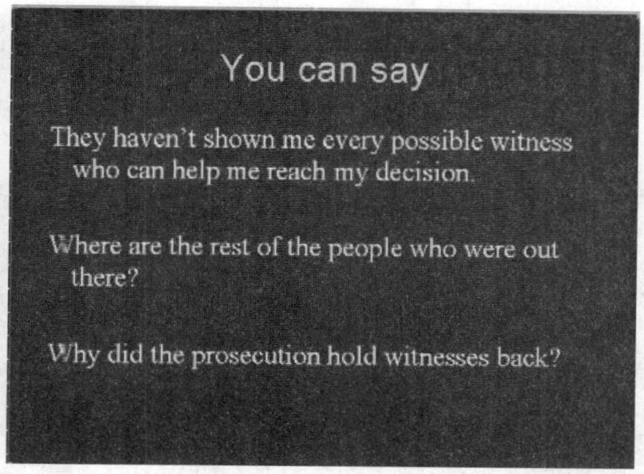

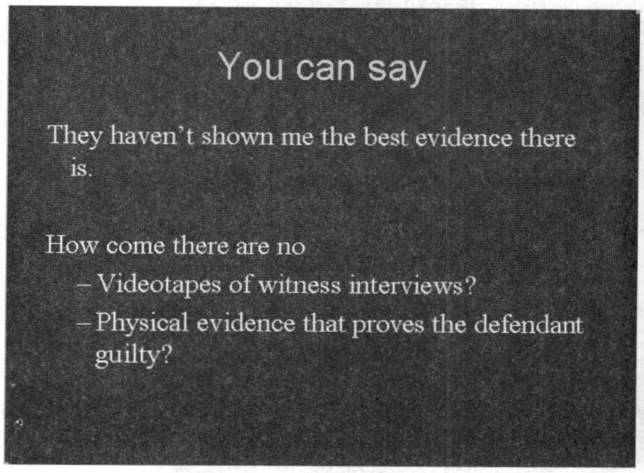

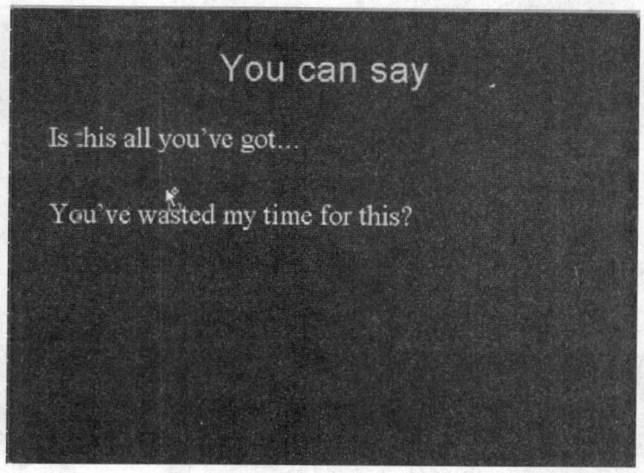

Both proactive and reactive arguers must talk about "how we know things." Instead of rehashing the evidence and risking the possibility of boring the jury, talk about the conclusions that the jurors can draw from the things that they have heard. Talk about what witnesses knew and what they didn't know as you use the evidentiary instructions like circumstantial evidence, other crimes' instructions, and identification instructions.

Using visual tools and devices for explaining the whys

When explaining how an injury was caused, use counterpoint diagrams and photographs to explain how injuries were inflicted.

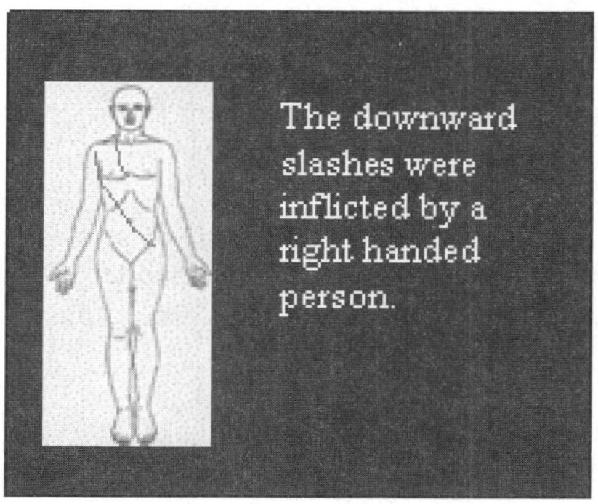

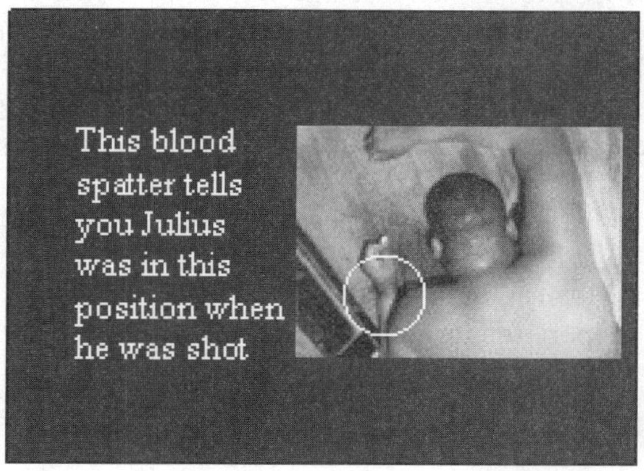

Use a checklist or an equation visual for arguing credibility instructions. Consider how to choreograph the use of photos and other physical evidence with the circumstantial evidence instruction and the portion of the jury instructions that talk about corroboration of testimony.

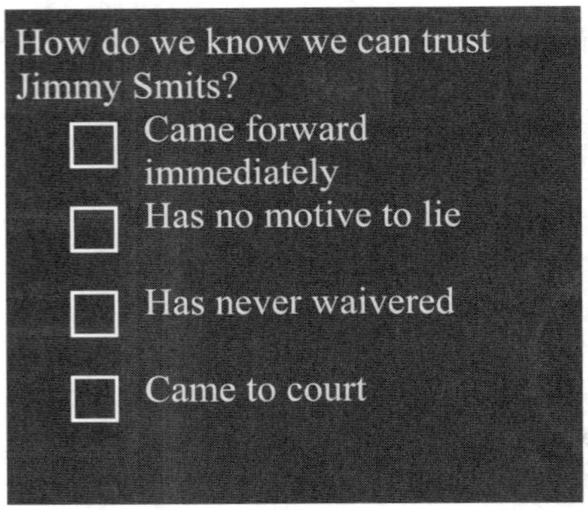

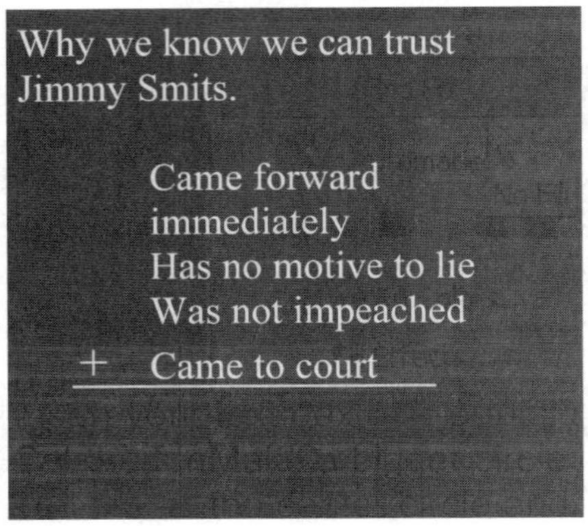

Defense attorneys should use circumstantial evidence instructions and credibility instructions when illustrating why it is that the jury should not trust the other side's witnesses.

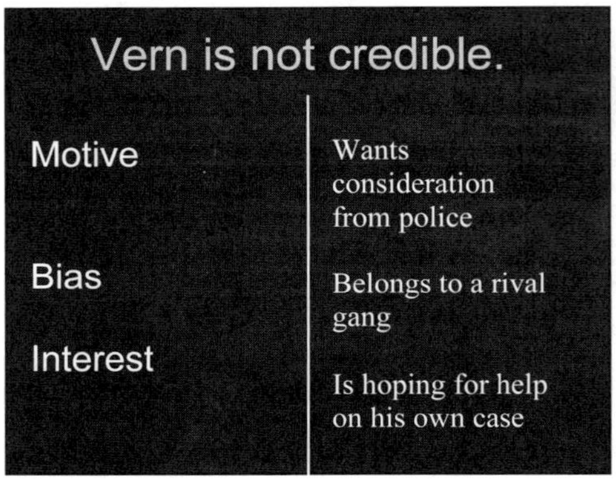

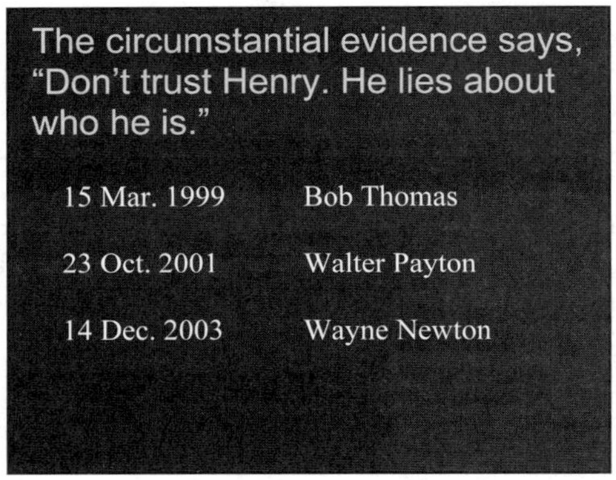

The line down the middle of the screen or the simple text box that follows the jury instructions corroborates the defense attorney as he or she attacks the believability of the witness. This slide can also be followed by a rhetorical question that asks, "Do we want someone like that guy to help prove a case beyond a reasonable doubt?" If there are a number of reasons for distrusting a witness, consider making a slide that puts a photograph of the witness in the middle and surround the witness with text boxes containing the reasons for not trusting him or her.

When arguing about a specific witness's credibility, ask the jury to remember when a witness was in the witness chair (walk over and touch it or even sit in the witness chair yourself for added emphasis) and talk about that witness's demeanor and physical gestures. Use these descriptions to support your argument that the witness was or was not believable.

Take a digital photograph of a witness on the day he or she testifies. Ask the judge to have it admitted before presenting your closing argument since it merely captured how the witness appeared at the time of testifying. When it is time to argue about that witness, put that witness's photograph on the screen or monitor.

When a witness's picture is on the screen, the jurors will know exactly who you are talking about when you walk over to the witness stand and talk about when that person testified.

Using Visuals in Your Closing Argument

Making Jury Instructions into Visuals

You can make slides that contain the key words from the jury instructions. If possible, incorporate evidentiary facts like "Defendant destroyed evidence" or "Defendant's words to witness A, witness B, etc." These provide jurors with a visual checklist that you can physically fill in with a check that is animated with a mouse click or that you can simply refer to when you are arguing.

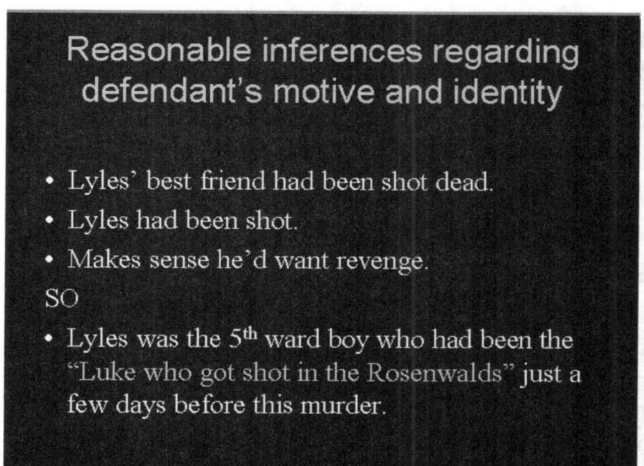

This slide is designed to apply to the other crimes or conduct instruction that is given when that type of evidence is introduced against a defendant. But the font is wrong, and this slide is fairly wordy. How would you edit some of the text out of this slide?

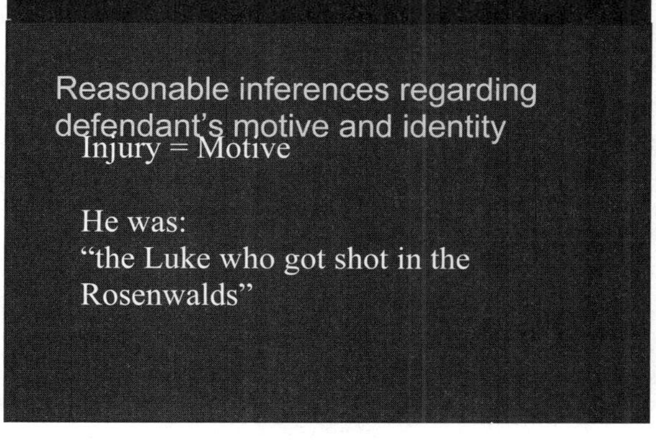

Perhaps the first two injury bullet points could be shortened to say:

Injury = Motive

Now how can the next bullet point be distilled?

Using Evidence Boards

Some visuals are better off being printed and placed on evidence boards.

Charged Case	Pre mortem Conduct	Post mortem conduct
Victim's hands bound with buckskin string.	Defendant binds victim's hand with buckskin string before she escapes.	Victim's hands bound with buckskin string.
Victim's hands posed above her body.	Victim escaped.	Victim's hands posed above her body.
Victim posed with shirt pulled up, pants pulled down.	Defendant tells victim he wants to see her naked.	Victim posed with shirt pulled up, Pants pulled down.
Victim's vagina mutilated, abdomen is eviscerated.	Defendant tells victim he is going to tear her up.	Victim's vagina mutilated, abdomen is eviscerated.

This slide is a table that merely lists similarities between the charged crime and the other crimes cases. It is an extremely effective device for explaining F.R.E. 404(b) evidence.

However, when dealing with this much information, it is probably a better idea to have this table printed and mounted on an evidence board. This way, jurors can take it back into the jury room during deliberation.

How could this device be used with the civil case from Chapter 2?

Using PowerPoint Slides

The visuals described next work well on slides.

Relationship triangles

Create relationship triangles wherever they are applicable. The template below is a perfect device for explaining circumstantial evidence, accountability, or any concept that requires showing connections between people, places, and/or things.

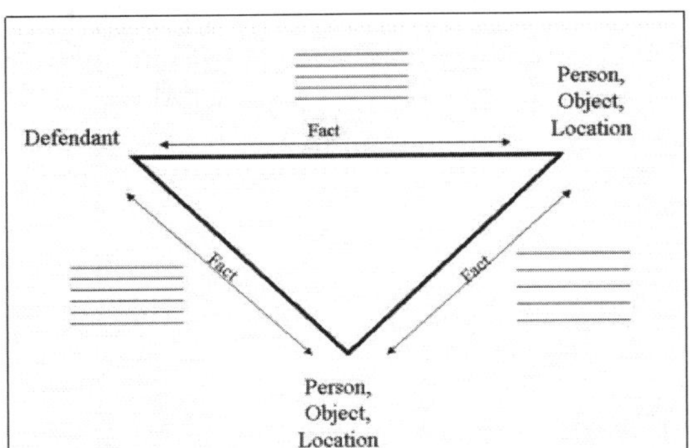

Typical Relationship Triangle

A relationship triangle like this was used in the prosecution of serial killer Ted Bundy to show connections linking Bundy, a van used by Bundy, and victim Kimberly Leach, who Bundy had killed in the van. The prosecutors who used this visual were Bob Deckle and Jerry Blair of the State Attorney's Office for the Third Judicial Circuit in Florida. The same device can be used in a personal injury, medical malpractice, or contract case to identify the relationships and draw the connections between them.

The relationship triangle in the next visual shows connections among three defendants. The defendants are charged under an accountability theory since the victim received only one injury as a result of a shooting in which each offender fired in the victim's direction. The legal requirements of the accountability instruction are shown on the first slide, and then the relationship triangle shows how the prosecution has satisfied the legal requirement.

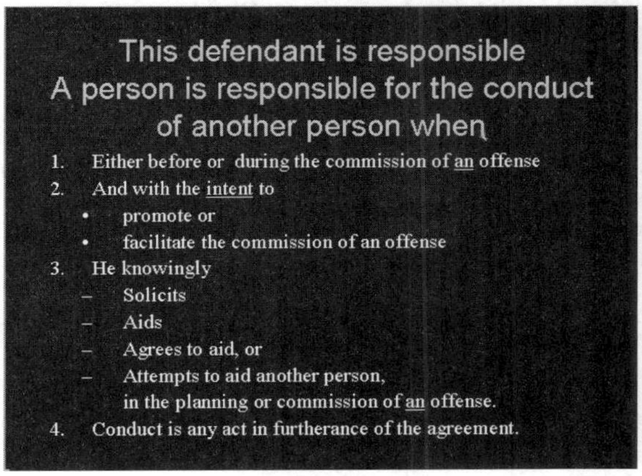

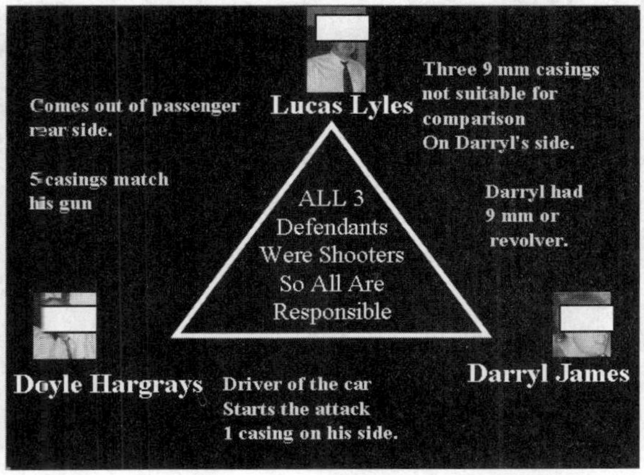

Top ten lists

Make top ten lists to capitalize on pop culture's influence on the jury pool. Modern television and some of the devices that exist in the entertainment world can be used effectively in the courtroom. A slide that flashes the 10 reasons in support of your point cannot be crossed out by your opponent like a flip chart can.

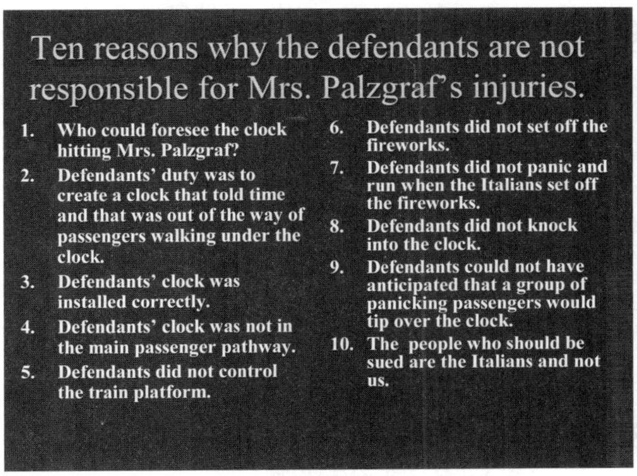

Mrs. Palzgraf got hurt when the group of "Italians" set off fireworks at the railroad station. The crowd panicked at the sound of the explosion and, during its flight from the exploding fireworks, pushed over a clock that was standing on the station platform. Palzgraf's lawyer went after the deep pocket instead of the "fleeing Italians." One wonders what the outcome of the case would have been if the defense had used PowerPoint.

Checklists

Move back and forth between visuals and the checklist. The more you illustrate how you have satisfied the requirements of the checklist, the more the jury is going to be comfortable with deciding the question in your favor. Use the checklist slide as a rhetorical device that constantly reminds the jury of their duty to make a decision based on the law and the evidence. The more you keep your presentation focused on this concept, the easier you are making it for the jury to agree with you.

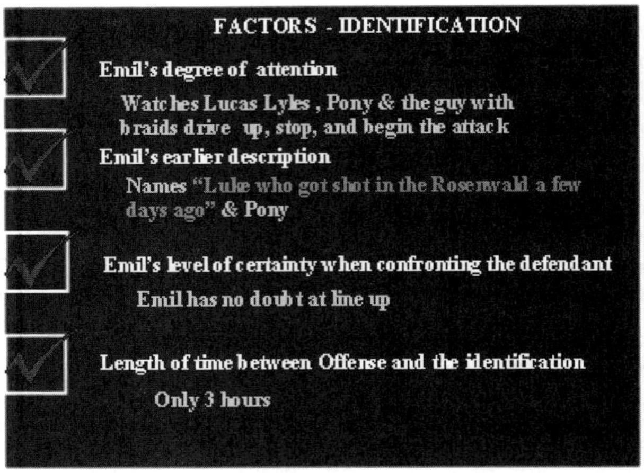

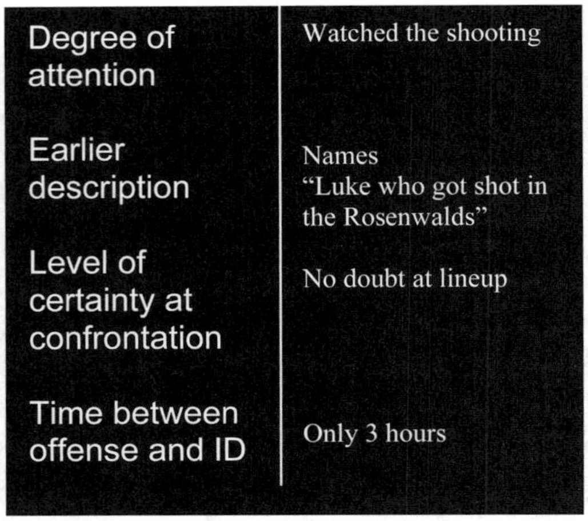

Callout boxes

When using a callout box, a blowup of a specific part of an exhibit, remind the jury that they will get the entire exhibit during their deliberations. The following is a callout box using the U.S. Constitution. When using Sanction, simply use the Magnify function. Left click and drag your cursor across the segment of the document that you wish to enlarge; then release the mouse button, and Sanction creates an instant callout box.

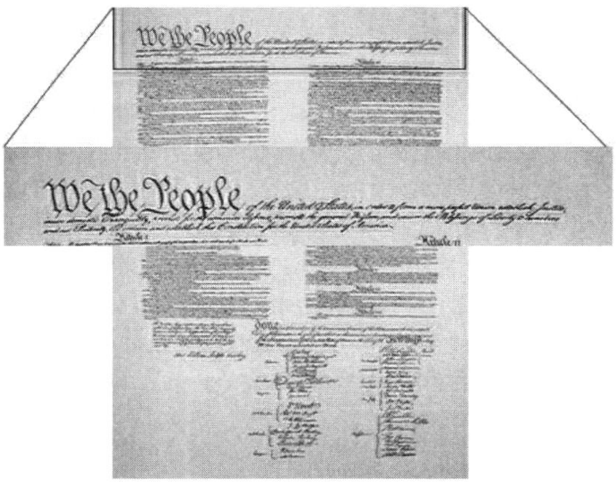

Lesser included instructions

When having to prove disjunctive mental states or other types of conditional elements, the easiest way to create this visual is to bring the elements onto the slide before having the check appear on the box. The following slide accomplishes this by bringing the mental states propositions into the slide one at a time. The yellow and orange text lists the legal requirements, and the white text contains the facts that satisfy the requirement. Of course, the red check marks mean you have satisfied the requirement.

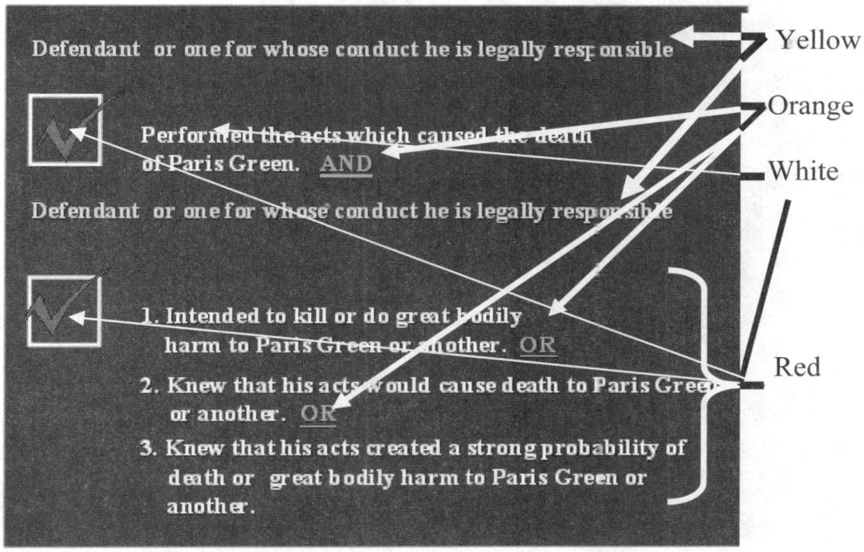

Prayer slides

Make a prayer slide that tells the jury what you want them to do.

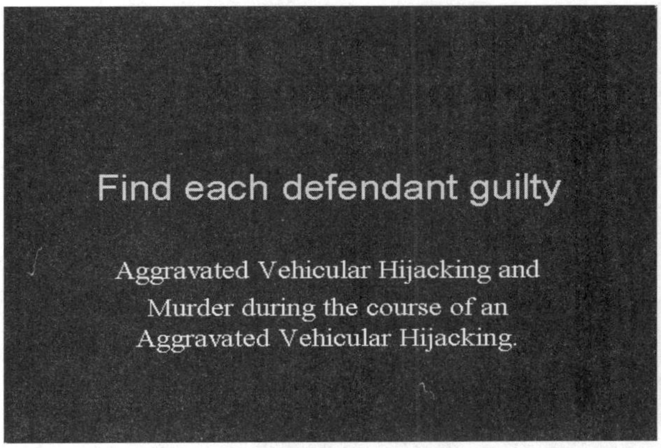

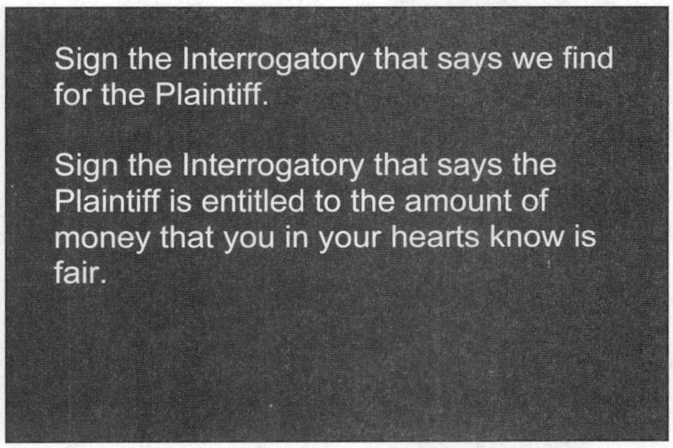

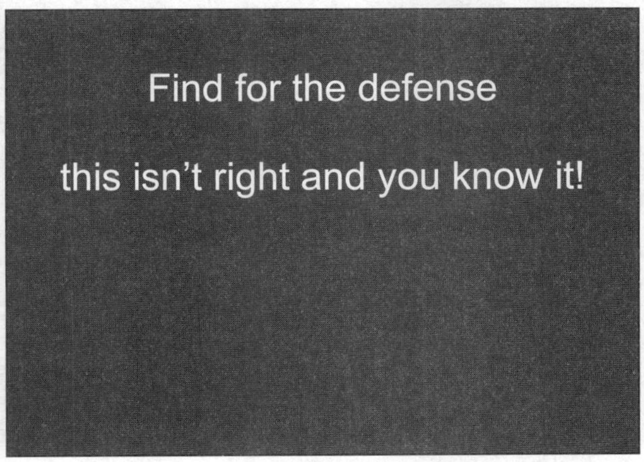

Chapter 7

Using PowerPoint 2003

This chapter is written and designed so that you can follow the basic functions of PowerPoint step by step. The many screen captures and examples in this chapter show PowerPoint screens, commands, and directions exactly as the software shows them, so place this chapter under or next to your computer screen as you read. Think of this chapter and Chapter 8 on Sanction as comic books designed to give you a skill set. They will teach you techniques that you can use to create other visuals.

If you are already familiar with PowerPoint but want to learn how to accomplish specific tasks, you can use this chapter that way also. If you want to see or print this chapter in color, download it in a .pdf format from the Litigation Technology website (www.littech.org).

This chapter does not pretend to substitute for an introduction to PowerPoint book. Some of those books are great, and if you want to get one, you should. Each book teaches its reader to use the software a different way. PowerPoint has some incredibly powerful features, but many of these features are unnecessary when it comes to putting together a slide presentation for courtroom use. The focus in this chapter, then, is to teach you the following things.

- **How to create a custom toolbar.** A custom toolbar simply collects the icons that you need to handle the majority of the tasks that are explained in the chapter.

  These icons will help you work quickly and efficiently with PowerPoint.

- **How to use toolbars, menus, and other functions.** These toolbars are explained in the context of creating different types of visuals. An index at the back of this book lists where these toolbars and commands are found in the book. One toolbar that you will use often in this chapter is the Draw toolbar at the bottom of the PowerPoint desktop. It contains icons and submenus that are often used in the demonstrative slide creation process.

For a quick way to learn what an icon's function is, let your cursor hover over the icon for a moment. PowerPoint shows you a text box that tells you what the icon symbolizes.

For example, this text box 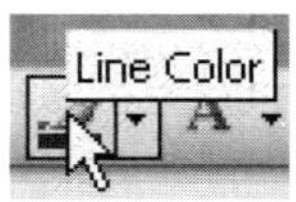

tells you that by clicking on this icon, you can change the color of a particular line. If you click on the inverted triangle  next to the line icon, you can see the other options that will appear for assigning line color. When you click on a submenu, it will expand.

If you click on the Draw or AutoShapes menu, you will see the following options.

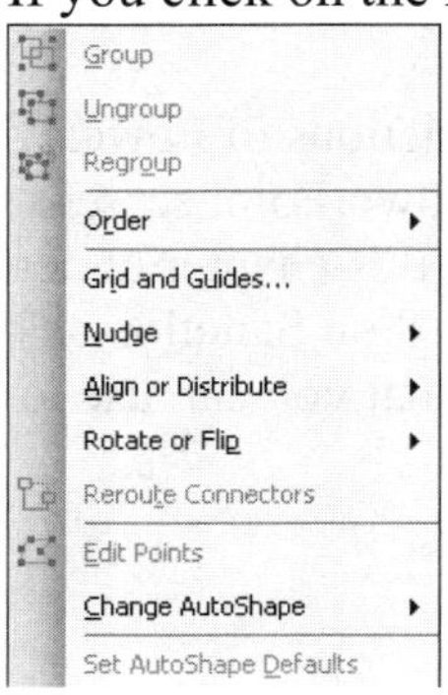

Draw lets you manipulate objects or group them together. AutoShape lets you insert different objects into a slide.

If you click on the triangles for the AutoShapes, you will see all the different shapes that can be placed on a slide.

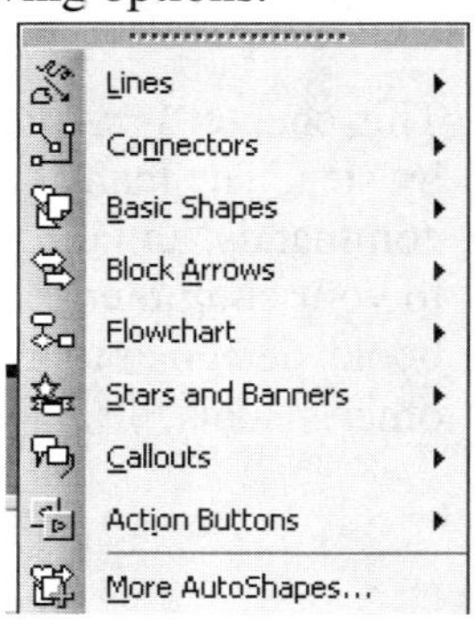

- **How to use the Slide Master function to change font and font size.** You can find the Slide Master menu in the View menu. It looks like this:

- **How to select colors for slide backgrounds, headlines, and supporting text.** The icon for Slide Design is found when you right click while your cursor is on a slide. This icon looks like this: 
.

- **How to insert text and animate the text and bullet points.**

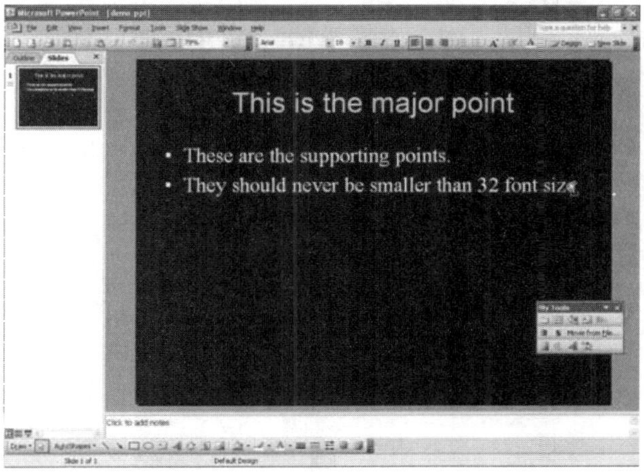

- **How to create many of the visuals that appear throughout the book.** You will learn how to make compare and contrast slides, the evidence points to or away from slides, and similar demonstrative slides.

- **How to create timeline templates.** This template allows you to move back and forth between a master timeline and the information that fills in the blanks of the timeline.

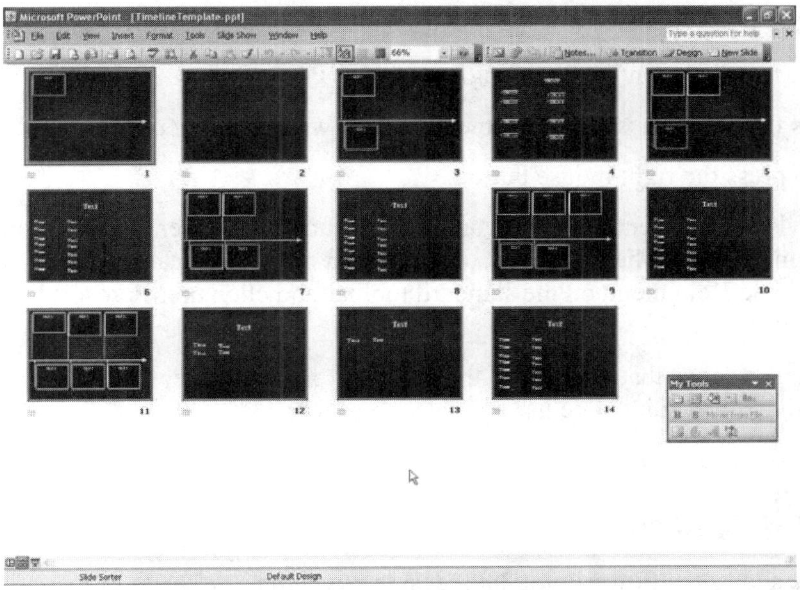

- **How to use a photograph as a baseline for a diagram.** You may then animate the diagram, if you wish.

1

2

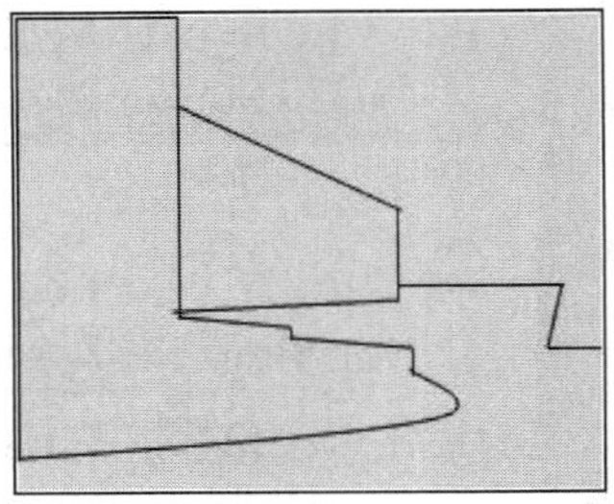
3

- **How to insert photos with this icon , video files with this icon , and audio files with this icon .**
- **How to save presentations as PowerPoint slide shows.** You may then launch the PowerPoint slide show in Sanction.
- **How to launch a PowerPoint presentation.**
- **How to turn off a slide in PowerPoint.**

Getting Started

PowerPoint uses many of the same menus, commands, functions, and icons that you use in other Microsoft software products, such as Word. But for those who may benefit from a summary of the most important of these, we begin by defining basic terminology. We then take a look at PowerPoint's opening screens.

Terminology

Here are the terms we use most often in describing how to use PowerPoint:

- *Click*: To press the left mouse button; sometimes also written as *left click.*
- *Right click*: To press the right mouse button.
- *Icon*: A small visual representation of a command or function. When you click on the icon, PowerPoint executes the command. (If you want more information about what an icon does, go to the Help menu on the standard toolbar and click on Microsoft Office PowerPoint Help.)
- *Toolbar*: Groups of icons that are related to one other. For example, the Draw toolbar at the bottom of the PowerPoint slide has a collection of icons.
- *Menu*: Listing of related commands.

PowerPoint Desktop

The screen that follows shows the PowerPoint 2003 desktop, which has a series of menus. Each menu has commands or submenus.

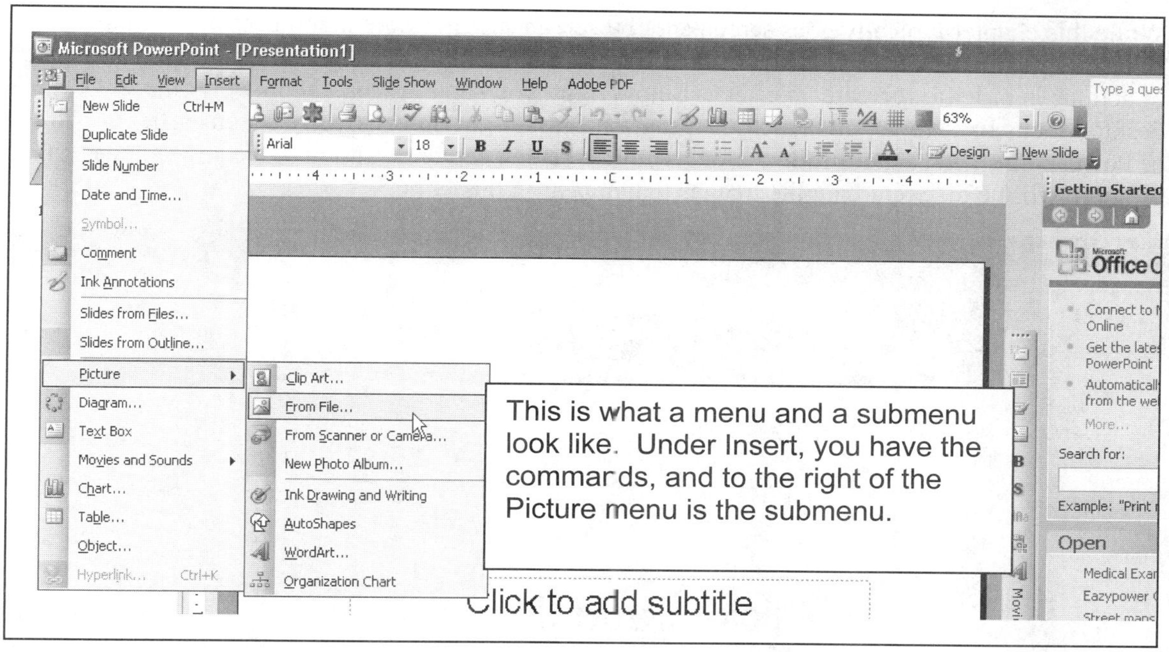
Microsoft PowerPoint - [Presentation1]
This is what a menu and a submenu look like. Under Insert, you have the commands, and to the right of the Picture menu is the submenu.

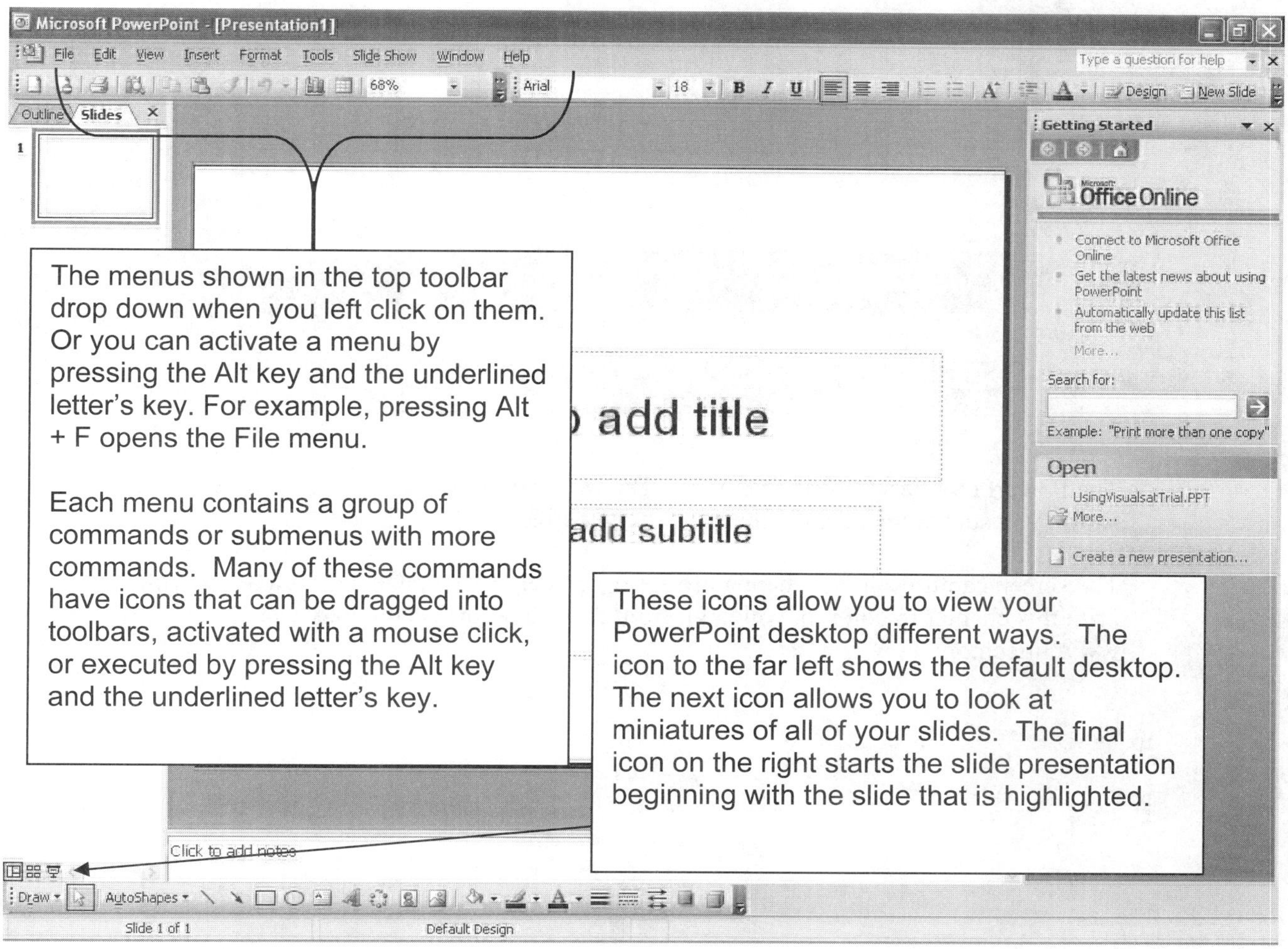
Microsoft PowerPoint - [Presentation1]
The menus shown in the top toolbar drop down when you left click on them. Or you can activate a menu by pressing the Alt key and the underlined letter's key. For example, pressing Alt + F opens the File menu.
Each menu contains a group of commands or submenus with more commands. Many of these commands have icons that can be dragged into toolbars, activated with a mouse click, or executed by pressing the Alt key and the underlined letter's key.
These icons allow you to view your PowerPoint desktop different ways. The icon to the far left shows the default desktop. The next icon allows you to look at miniatures of all of your slides. The final icon on the right starts the slide presentation beginning with the slide that is highlighted.

While this chapter typically goes screen shot by screen shot through the process of creating a visual, sometimes the specific parts of the desktop are highlighted to take you through a sequence of actions in order to recreate an effect. Below right, you can see what the PowerPoint 2003 desktop looks like when you launch the program for the first time. If you own an earlier version of PowerPoint, you can still follow along with the screen captures, although the appearance of the program will be different than the images that appear in this book.

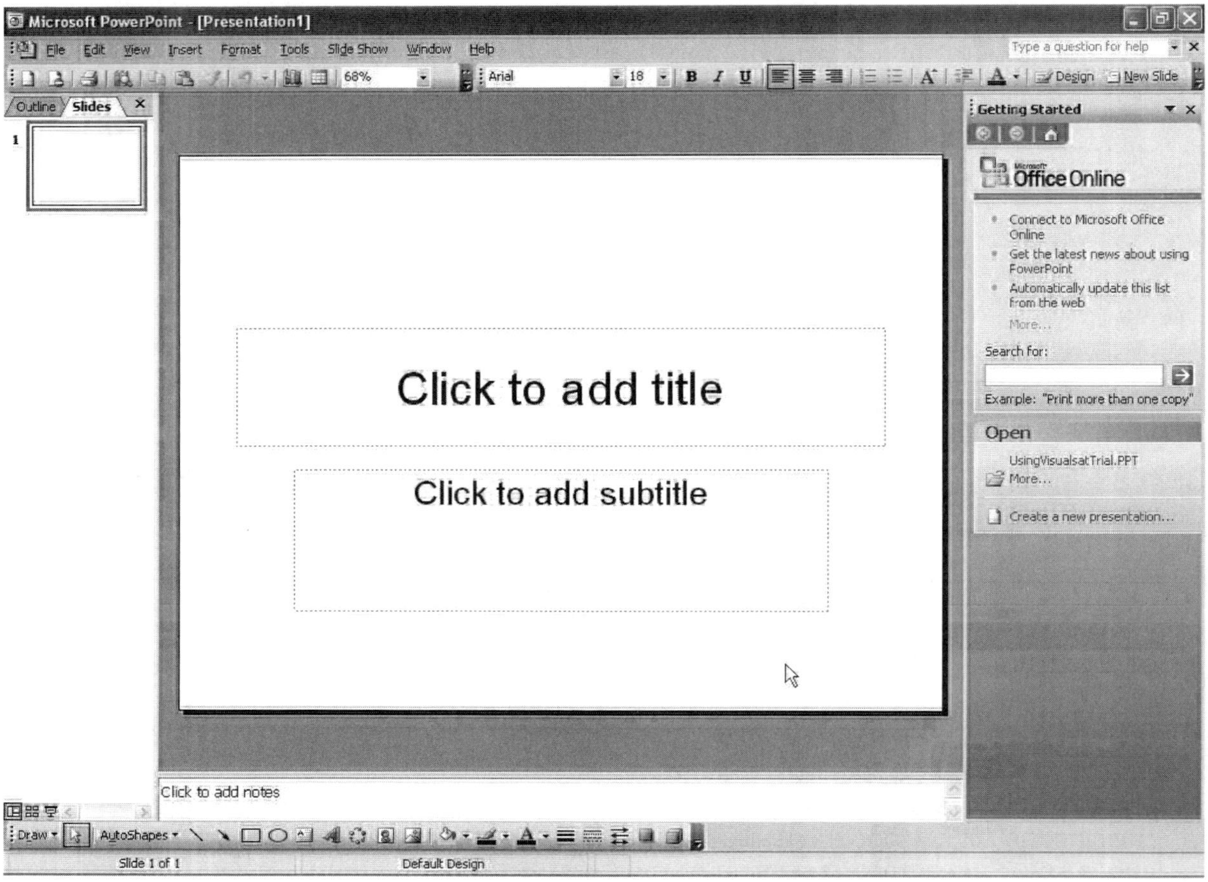

The PowerPoint desktop has five parts. The work space is in the middle, and each side either shows you subcommands of a menu or smaller slides.

The screen captures in this chapter are approximately half a page. Remember: If you want to print this chapter in color, download it from the Litigation Technology website at www.littech.org.

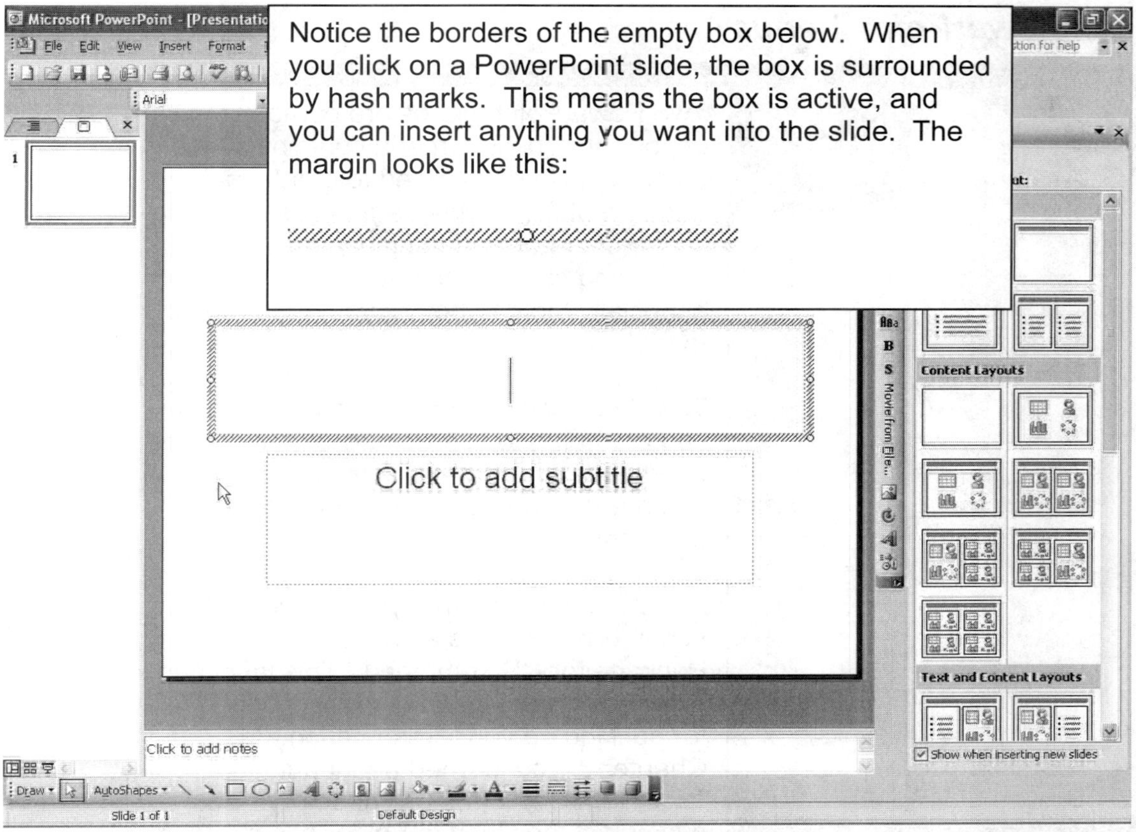
Microsoft PowerPoint - [Presentatio
Notice the borders of the empty box below. When you click on a PowerPoint slide, the box is surrounded by hash marks. This means the box is active, and you can insert anything you want into the slide. The margin looks like this:
Click to add subtitle
Content Layouts
Text and Content Layouts
Show when inserting new slides
Click to add notes
Slide 1 of 1
Default Design

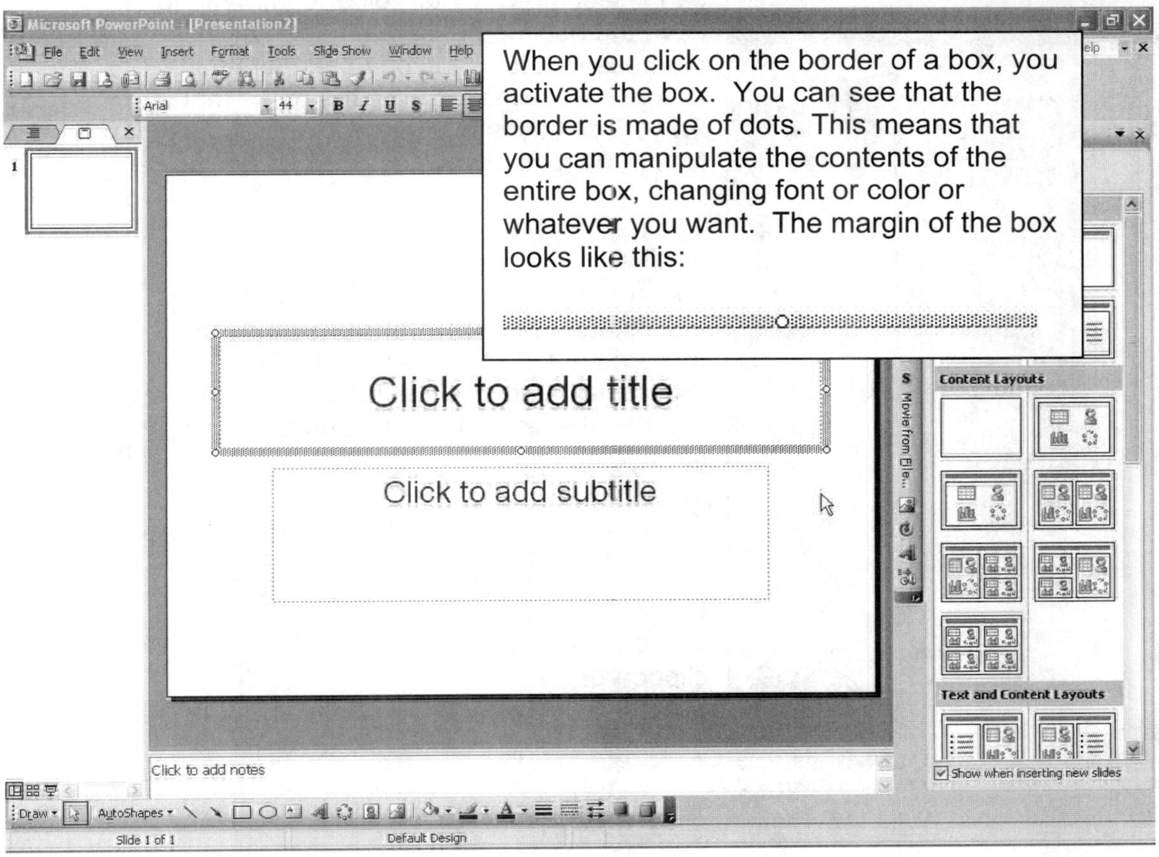
Microsoft PowerPoint - [Presentation2]
When you click on the border of a box, you activate the box. You can see that the border is made of dots. This means that you can manipulate the contents of the entire box, changing font or color or whatever you want. The margin of the box looks like this:
Click to add title
Click to add subtitle
Content Layouts
Text and Content Layouts
Show when inserting new slides
Click to add notes
Slide 1 of 1
Default Design

PowerPoint Menus

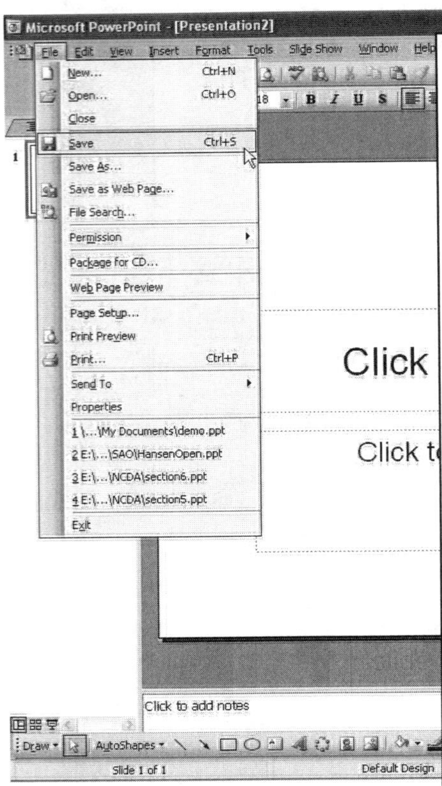

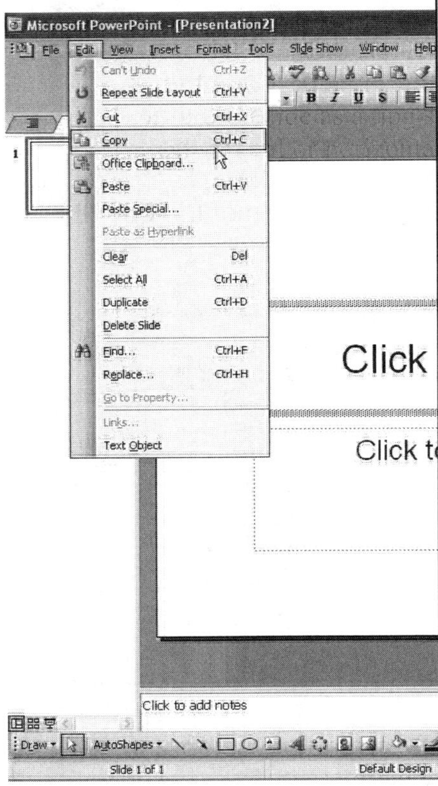

Two PowerPoint menus are particularly important. The File menu contains all the commands that you need to create, save, and format files. Make a practice of saving your work often. Nothing is more frustrating than losing your work, especially the day before you're due to go to trial.

The Page Setup command is important if you are going to use PowerPoint to create overheads or other low-tech visuals that use a document camera or an overhead projector.

Another command that you may want to use in order to have a backup is the Package for CD command. This launches a series of menus that gives you options for backing up your presentation. In Chapter 2, you learned about putting a folder for a case in the C directory. You can select the Copy to Folder command to have the backup put in that folder, and then use Windows to copy the entire folder to a CD. This makes sure the paths that PowerPoint uses to find video and audio files remain constant.

The next menu is the Edit menu. Copy and Paste are important commands. If you are importing data from different types of files, the Paste Special command lets you strip out format codes that other programs insert into the data. This lets you use the text without adding any strange effects.

If you cut and paste a lot, activate the Windows clipboard. This command is just below Copy: Office Clipboard... . You can save up to 24 items on this clipboard.

Making a Custom Toolbar

PowerPoint allows you to customize toolbars to place the icons that you use frequently in one place.

You can, of course, add any icon that you want to your custom toolbar. For our purposes in this chapter, we will place the following icons on the custom toolbar:

New Slide: Inserts a new slide into an existing presentation.

Slide Layout: Changes the layout for a slide. A layout refers to the way things are arranged on a slide. A layout is a template for a particular type of slide that has placeholders (these are boxes with dotted or hash-marked borders) that are part of the slide layouts. These boxes hold titles and body text or can preformatted for text, photos, media, and other objects.

Fill Color: Changes the background for a specific slide.

Text Box: Inserts a text box anywhere on a slide.

Case: Changes the capitalization of selected text.

B **Bold:** Makes text bold.

S **Shadow:** Adds a shadow to text, which gives the text greater contrast from the background of a slide.

Movie from File... **Movie from File:** Inserts a movie into your slide, which can be launched automatically or on a mouse click.

Insert Picture: Inserts a photo into your presentation.

Free Rotate: Rotates an object or photo on a slide.

Insert WordArt: Inserts preformatted text effect by inserting a Microsoft Office drawing object.

Custom Animation: Adds or changes animation effects on a current slide. Animation effects include sounds, text and object movements, and movies that occur during a slide show.

The following screens walk you through the process for creating a custom toolbar for PowerPoint. To begin, open the PowerPoint desktop.

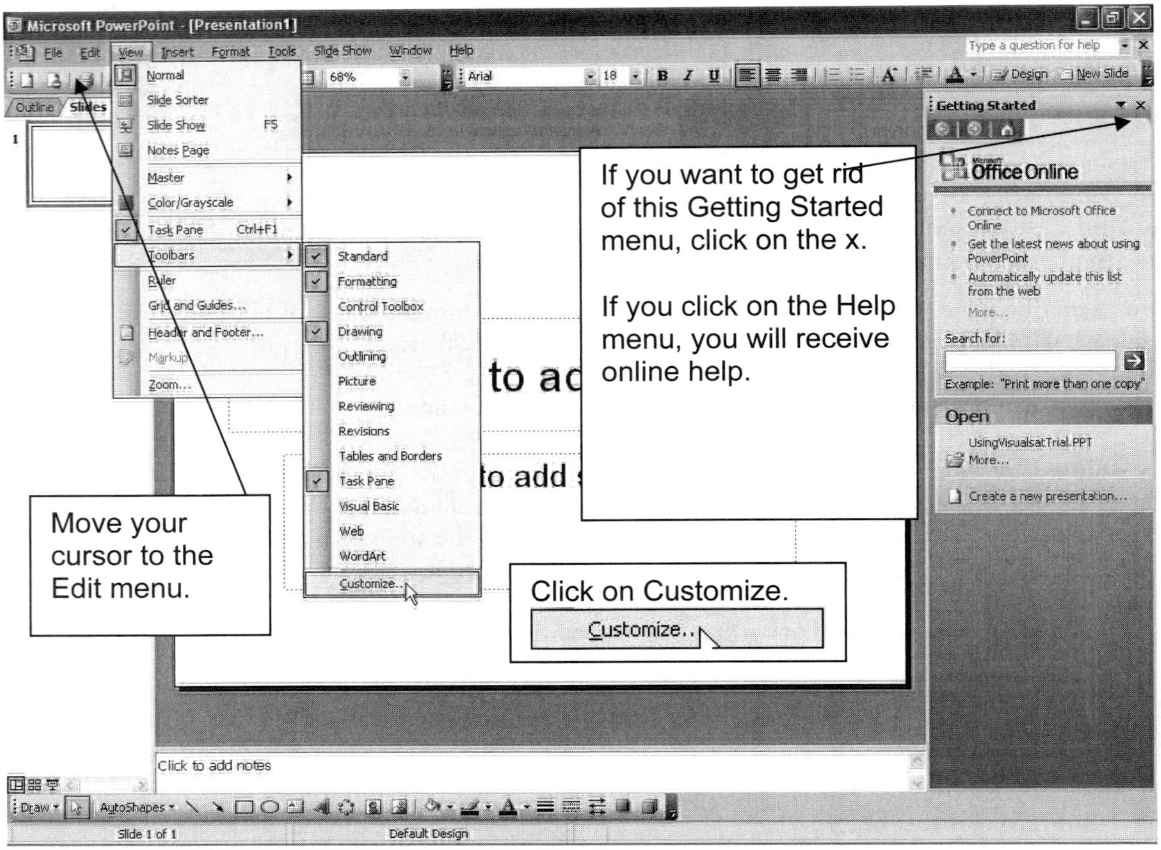

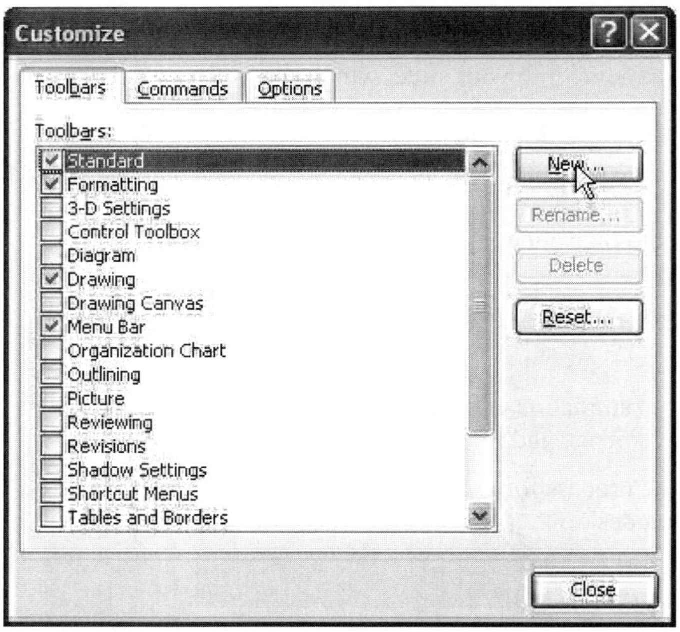

This Customize box lets you create your own toolbar or customize any existing PowerPoint toolbar or menu.

Click on New, and then name your toolbar in the box that appears.

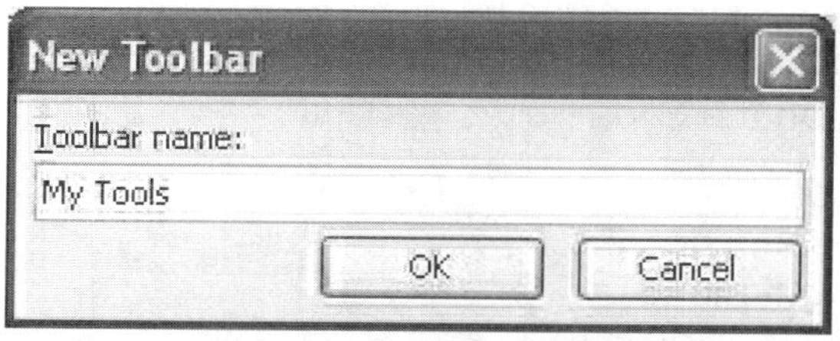

Use the name My Tools. Your desktop will now look like this.

Click OK.

This toolbox will appear next to the Customize box.

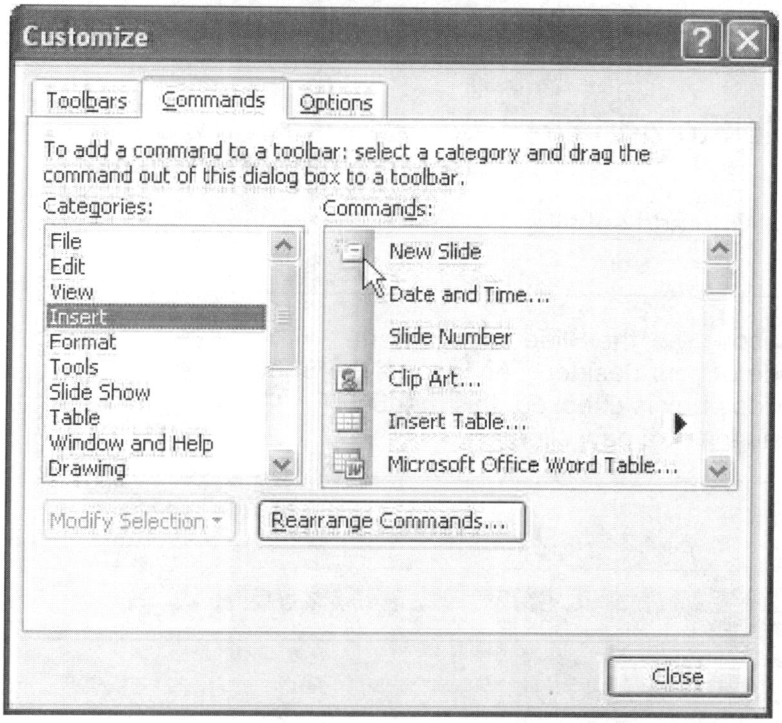

Click on the Commands tab, and then left click on the icons that appear in the toolbar in the menu. Hold the button down with your index finger and drag the icon to the My Tools box until you have all of the icons that appear in the toolbox below. Release your left finger, and the icon will stay in the My Tools box. Now drag the icons above from the Insert, Format, Slide Show, and Drawing categories.

These icons will help you do the majority of the work needed to create effective visuals for trial.

Basic PowerPoint Functions

Next we will create a slide presentation. Consistency is important for slide presentations that are being used in a courtroom.

Using the Slide Layout Function

The next screen shows the default slide that PowerPoint puts on the desktop when it opens a blank slide presentation. A title slide is a good default choice for an ordinary presentation, but it is not much help for a courtroom presentation. So we will change the default slide's layout to make a blank slide. Remember: The first and last slides in a presentation should be blank slides that have the default background color that you chose for the presentation.

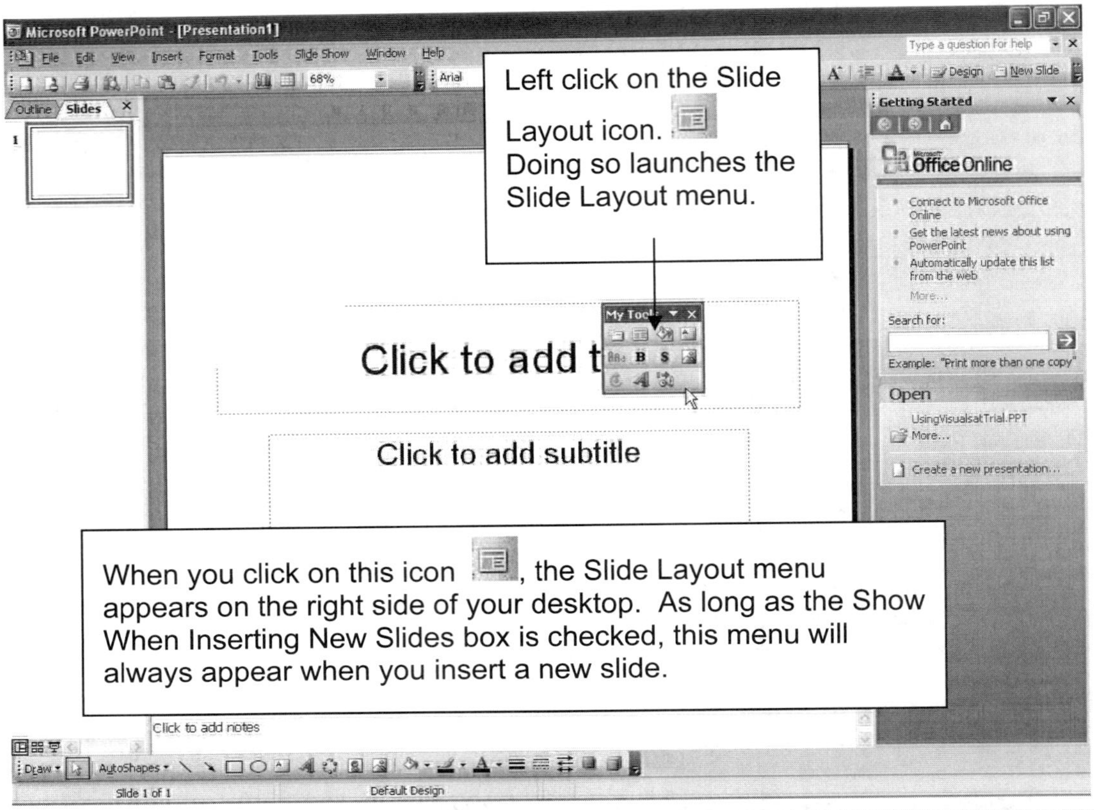
Microsoft PowerPoint - [Presentation1]
Left click on the Slide Layout icon. Doing so launches the Slide Layout menu.
Click to add title
Click to add subtitle
When you click on this icon, the Slide Layout menu appears on the right side of your desktop. As long as the Show When Inserting New Slides box is checked, this menu will always appear when you insert a new slide.
Getting Started
Office Online
Open
Click to add notes
Slide 1 of 1
Default Design

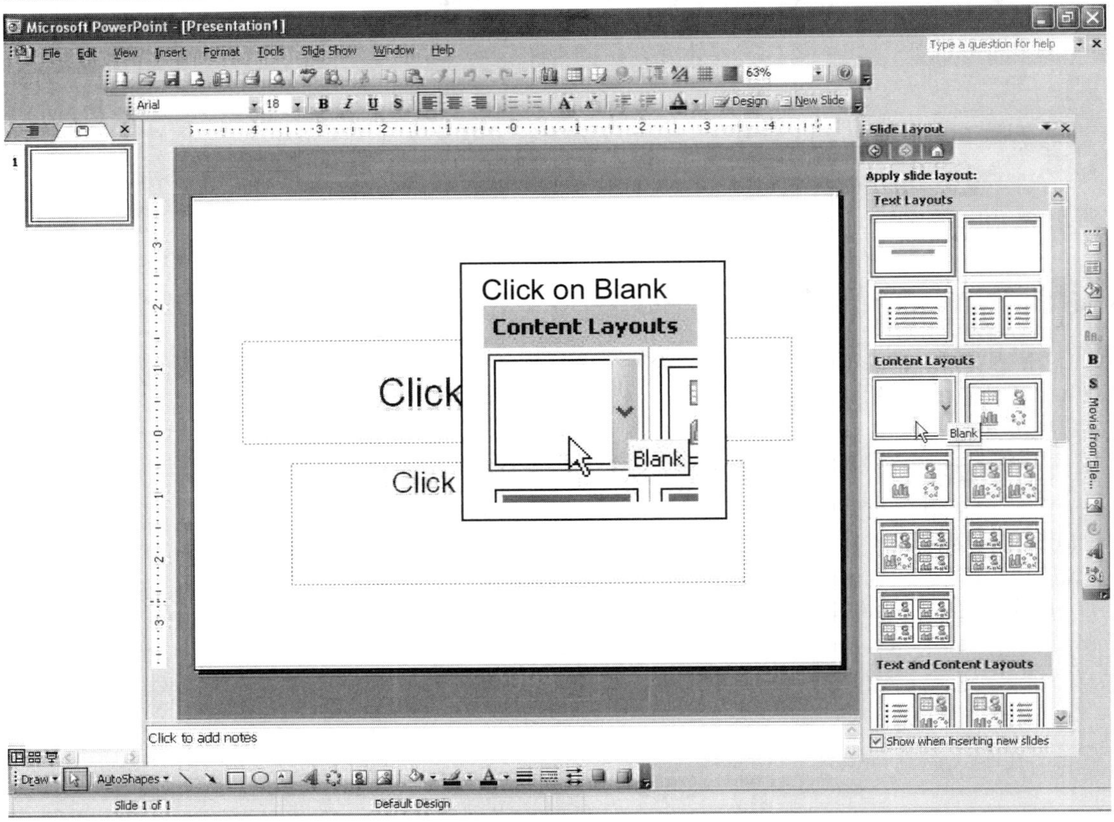
Microsoft PowerPoint - [Presentation1]
Click on Blank
Content Layouts
Blank
Slide Layout
Apply slide layout:
Text Layouts
Content Layouts
Text and Content Layouts
Show when inserting new slides
Click to add notes
Slide 1 of 1
Default Design

Using the New Slide Function

Now that we've created our opening blank slide, using the background color we're planning to use for all the slides in our presentation, we're ready to create our first text slide.

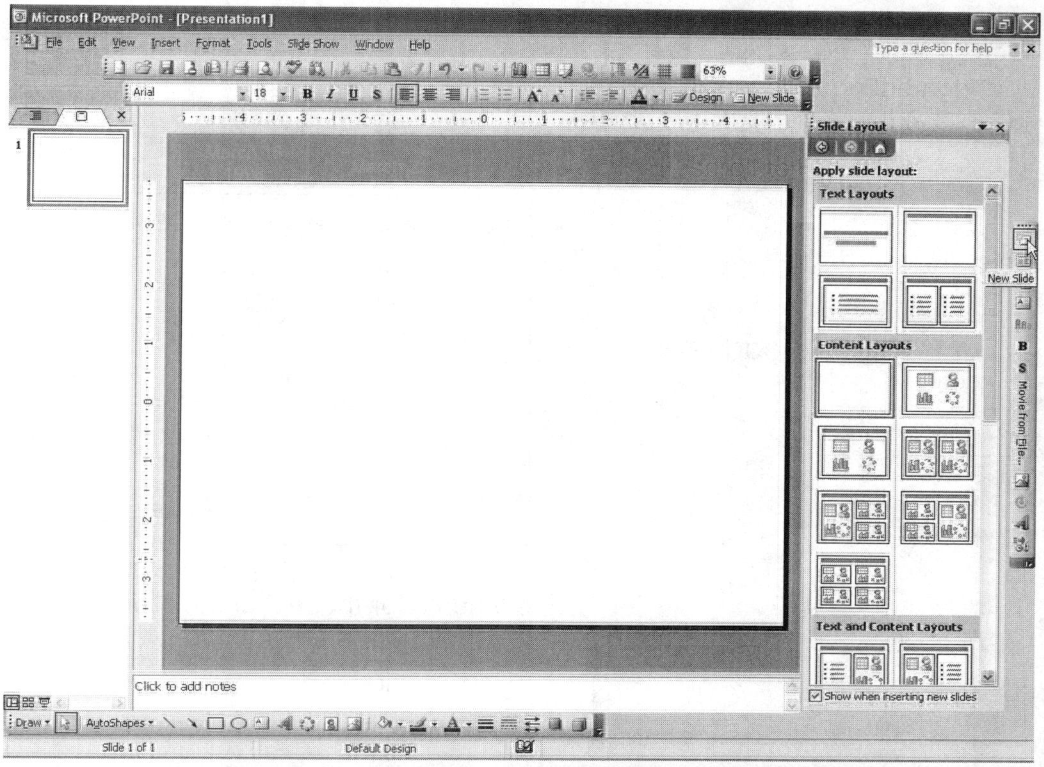

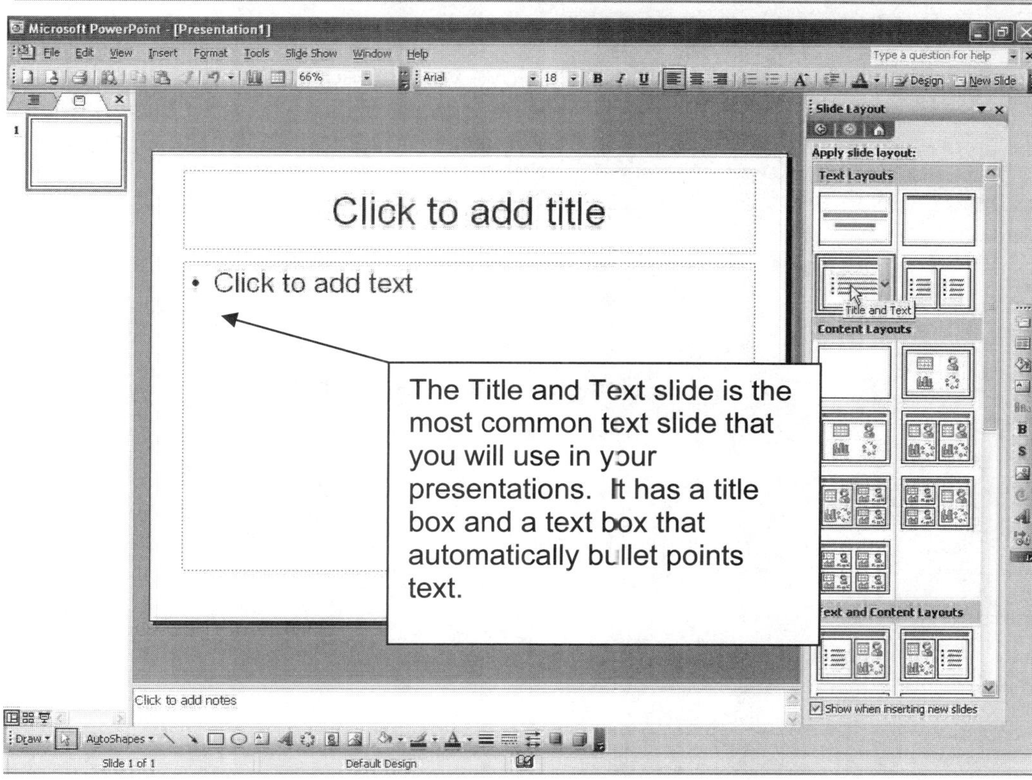

Using the Slide Master Function

PowerPoint has a Slide Master that sets a format for the entire presentation. The Slide Master lets you set font and font size, background color, and text color in one place for the series of slides.

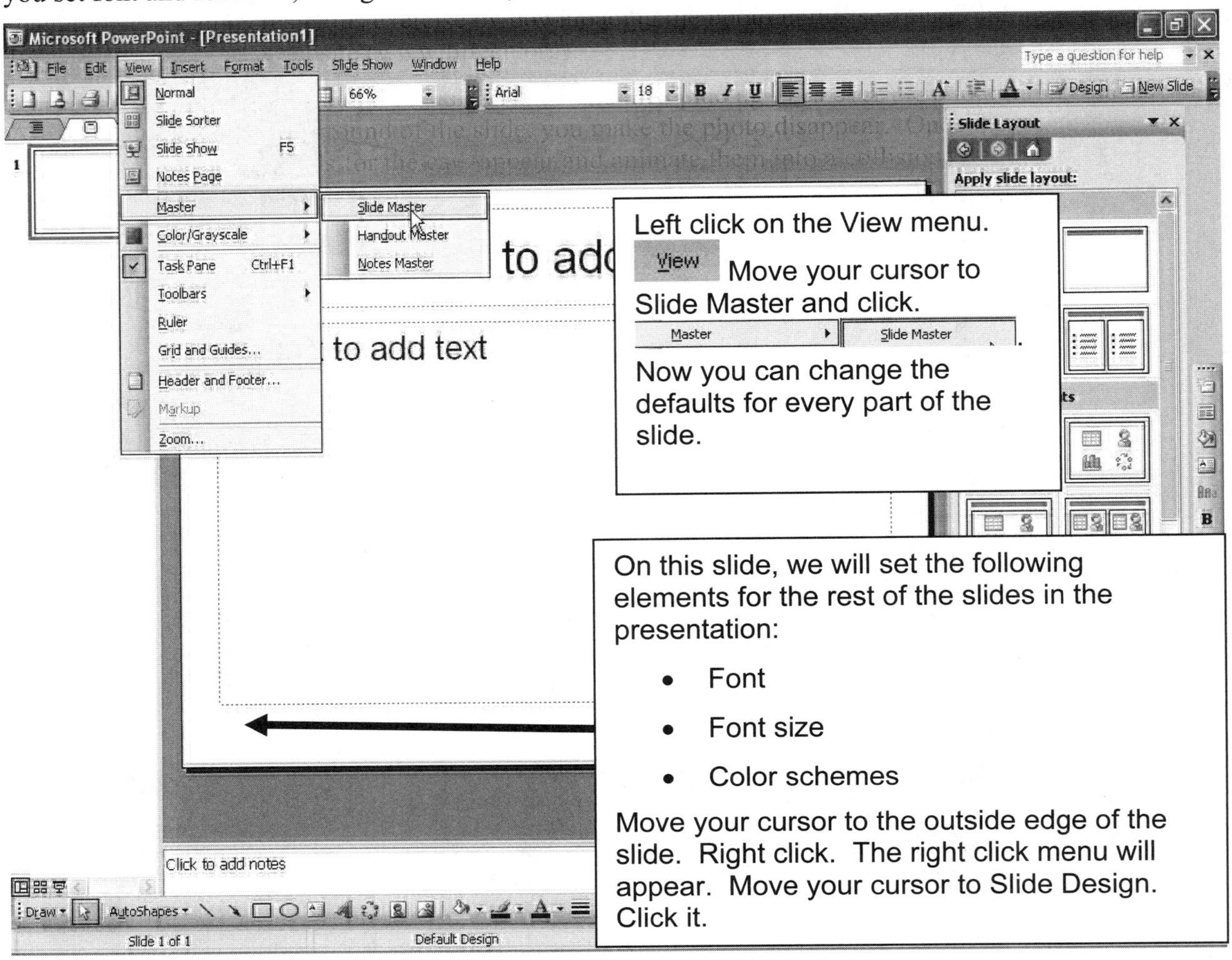

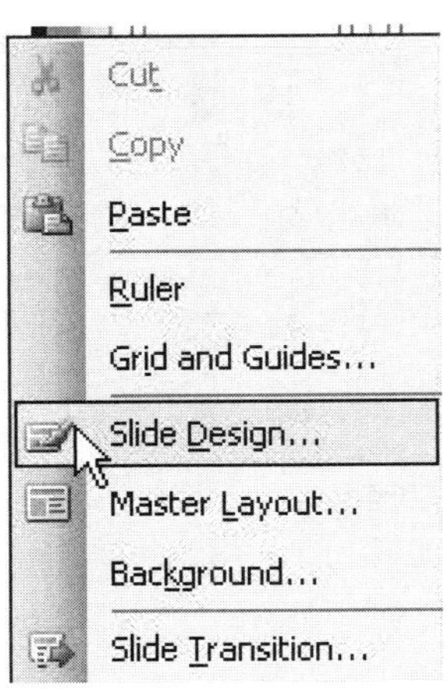

The Slide Design menu will appear.

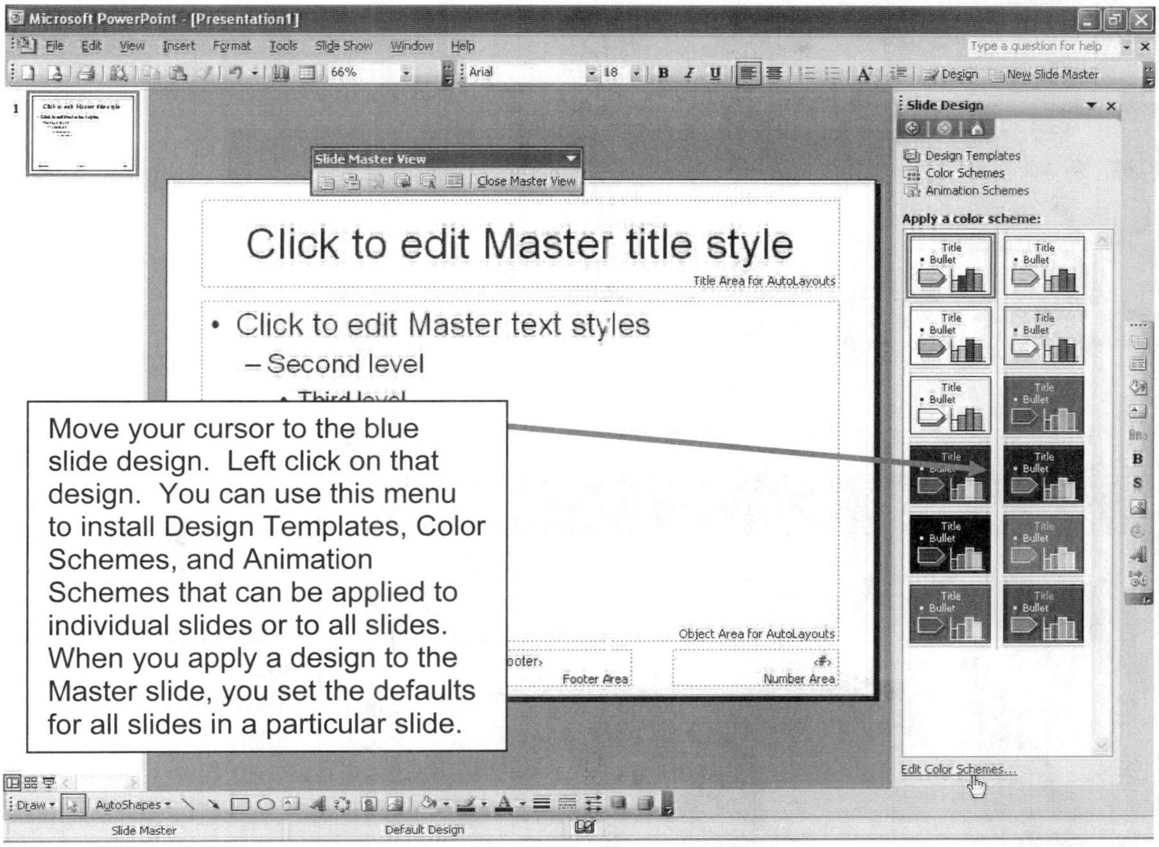

Set the color schemes for this presentation. The default color is dark blue with a light blue headline. In the following screen captures, we will change the headline color to yellow and leave the supporting text color as white. By looking at the rectangular box at the top of the Master slide, you can see that the font for this box is Arial. That font is fine for a headline, but we will change the font for the box that says Click to Edit Master Text Style. For now, let's change the font from Arial to Times New Roman, and then set the font size for all of the text in this box at 32 points. (A font size of 32 is the smallest text that you should use on a video screen.)

Put your cursor on the edge of the Master title box and double left click. The little white circles that appear along the margins of the box appear to be a series of dots. When the box looks like this, you can now manipulate the entire content of this box. Move your cursor down to the Draw menu and click on the inverted triangle next to the Font Color icon, which gives you the drop-down menu.

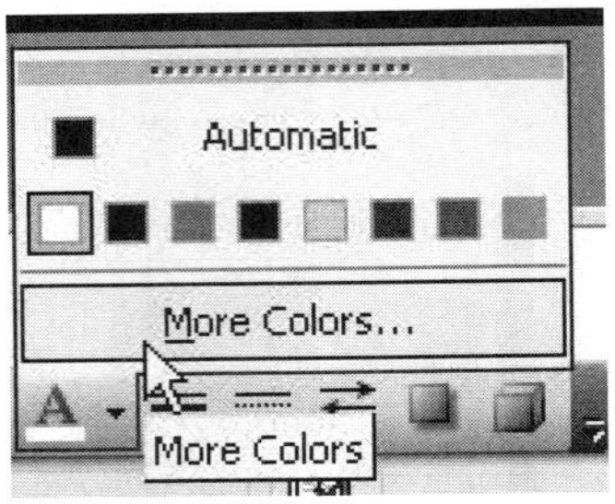

Click on More Colors and choose the color yellow. Yellow shows up well against a blue background. It is a powerful color for the title style. Use white for the text in the text box.

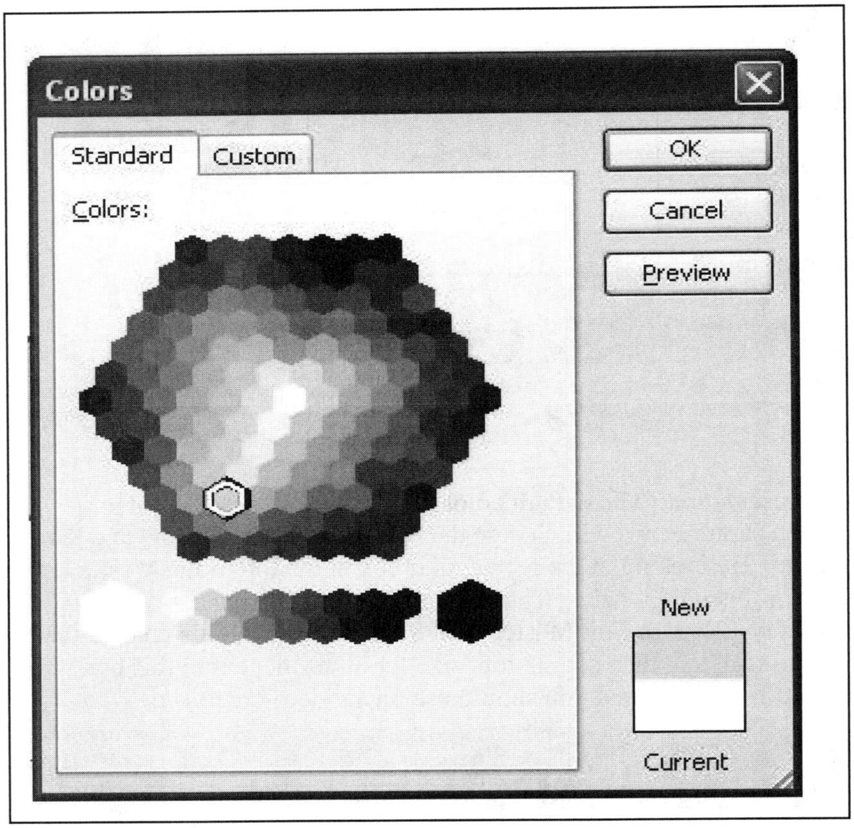

This More Colors menu can be used at any time. In fact, PowerPoint will let you change colors for lines, background fills, and many other commands.

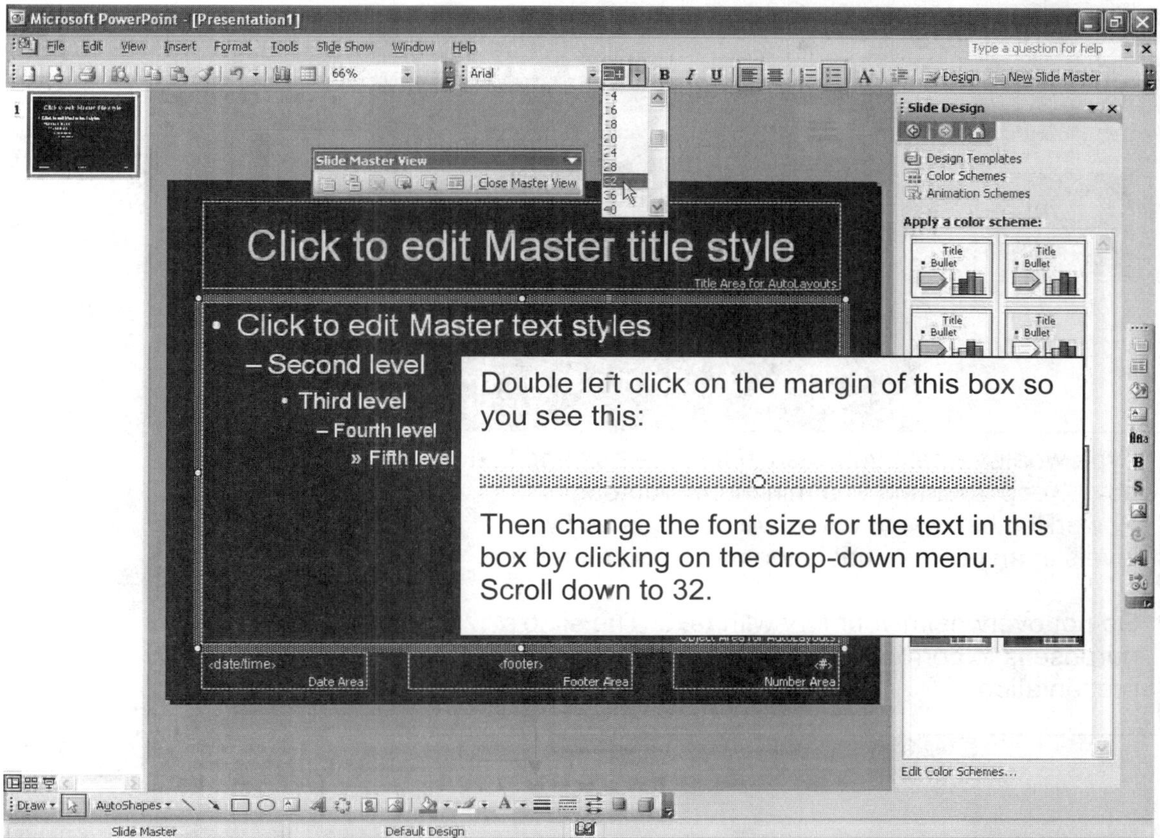
Microsoft PowerPoint - [Presentation1]
Slide Master View
Close Master View
Click to edit Master title style
Click to edit Master text styles
– Second level
• Third level
– Fourth level
» Fifth level
Double left click on the margin of this box so you see this:
Then change the font size for the text in this box by clicking on the drop-down menu. Scroll down to 32.
Slide Design
Apply a color scheme:

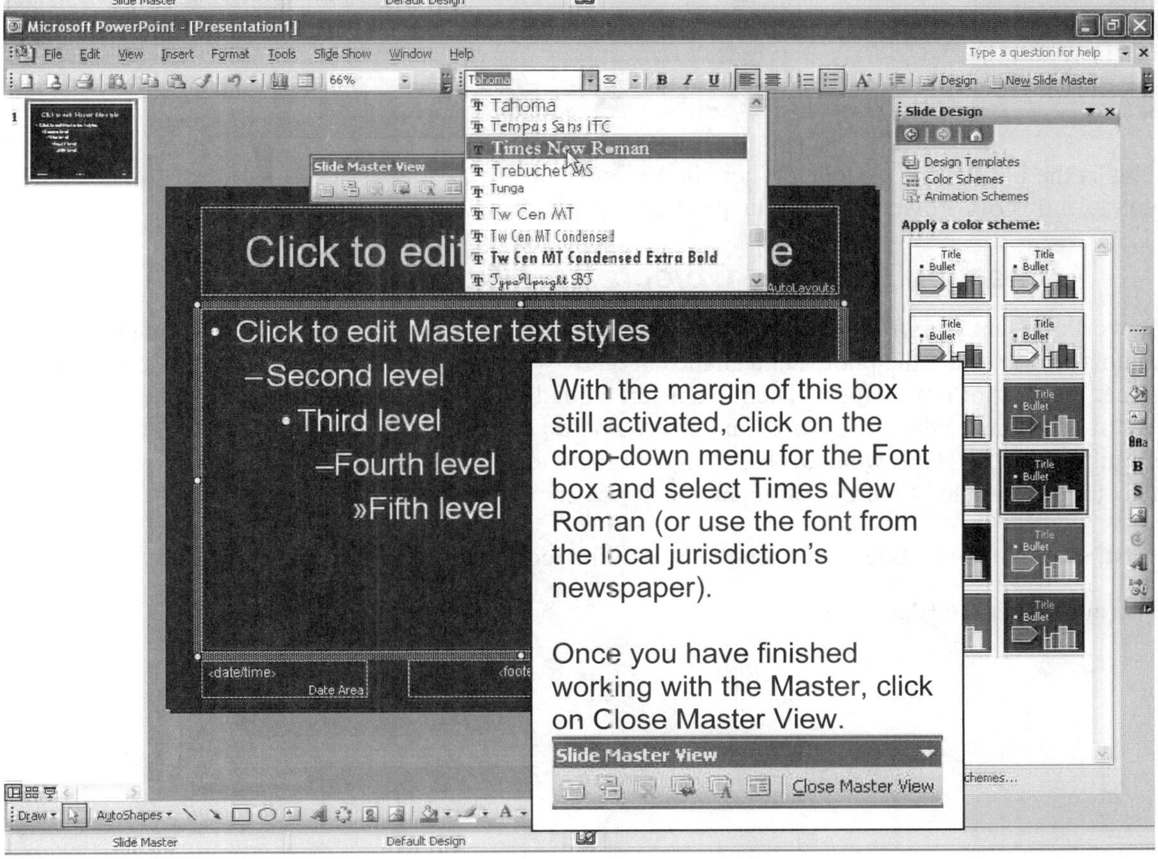
Microsoft PowerPoint - [Presentation1]
Tahoma
Tempus Sans ITC
Times New Roman
Trebuchet MS
Tunga
Tw Cen MT
Tw Cen MT Condensed
Tw Cen MT Condensed Extra Bold
Click to edit Master text styles
–Second level
•Third level
–Fourth level
»Fifth level
With the margin of this box still activated, click on the drop-down menu for the Font box and select Times New Roman (or use the font from the local jurisdiction's newspaper).
Once you have finished working with the Master, click on Close Master View.
Slide Master View
Close Master View

Inserting Text

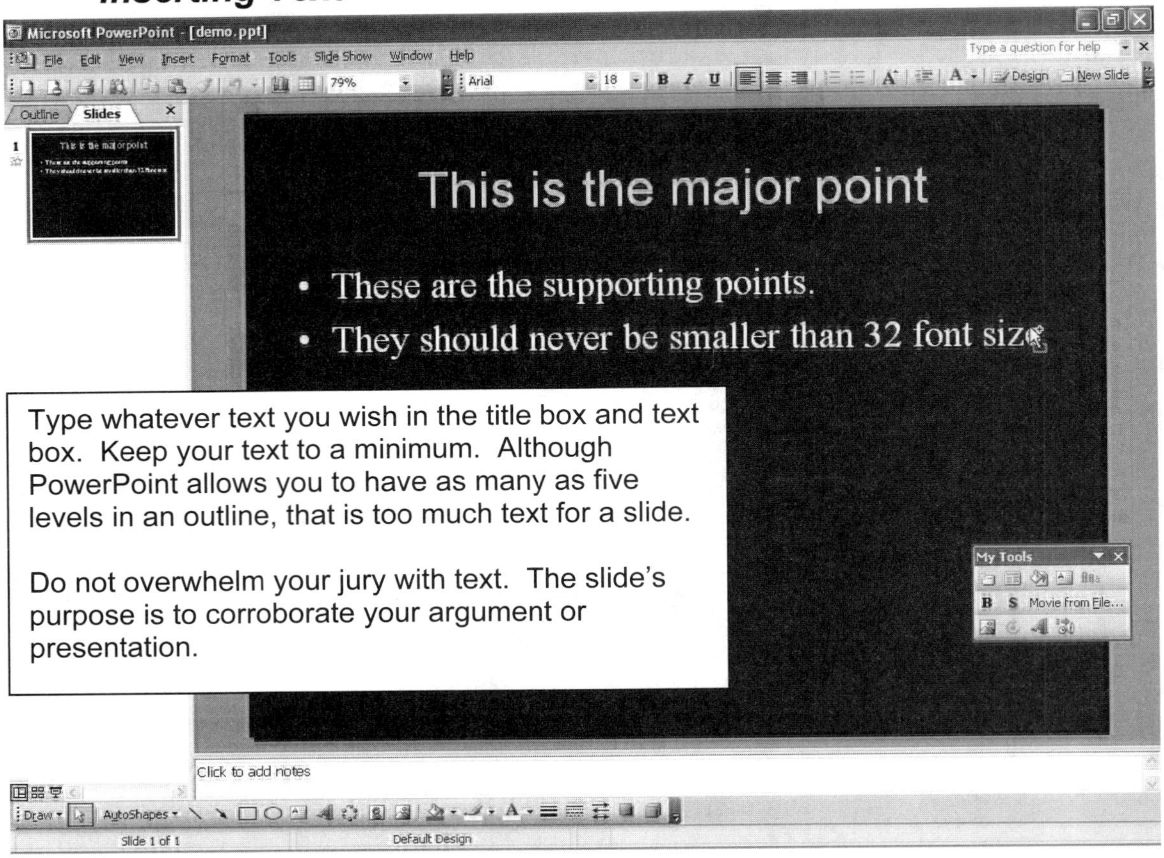

This is the Formatting toolbar. When the Bullets icon is activated, it looks like this: . When you turn this off, PowerPoint eliminates bullet points from the visual.

Inserting Drawing Objects and WordArt

PowerPoint lets you insert photos and shapes onto slides. This is handy because you can then annotate or animate the photos and shapes in many ways. In the next screen captures, we create a street map out of box shapes. Then, we insert a quad arrow for the direction north. Next, we use WordArt to create the word *North* and insert a photo of a police car on our map. We will then shrink it to size. Next, we use the Group command to link two rectangles together to create a two-tone rectangle. Later, we animate the police car and the two-tone rectangle.

First, create a blank slide. Click on the New Slide icon . Then click on the Slide Layout icon  and select the Blank icon.

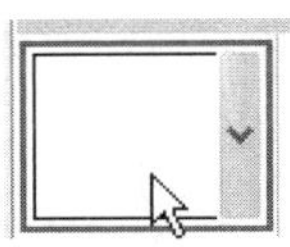

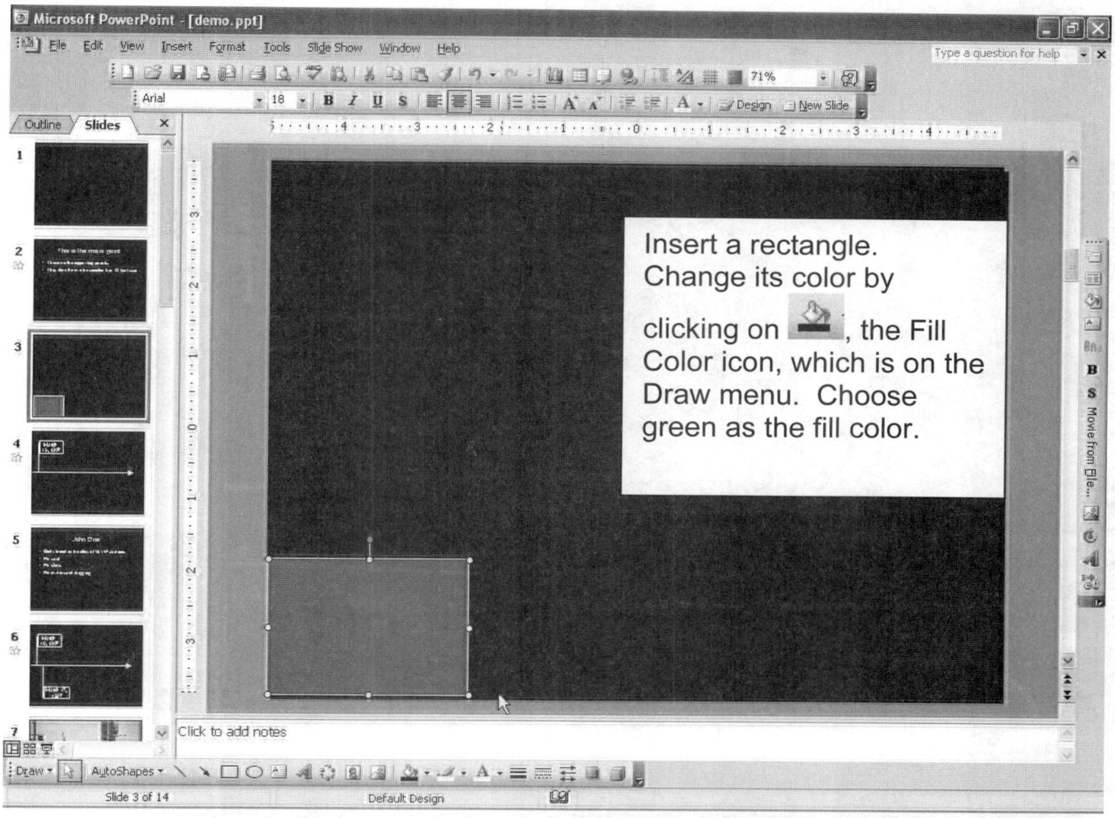
Microsoft PowerPoint - [demo.ppt]
File Edit View Insert Format Tools Slide Show Window Help
Type a question for help
Outline Slides
Insert a rectangle.
Change its color by
clicking on , the Fill
Color icon, which is on the
Draw menu. Choose
green as the fill color.
Click to add notes
Draw AutoShapes
Slide 3 of 14
Default Design

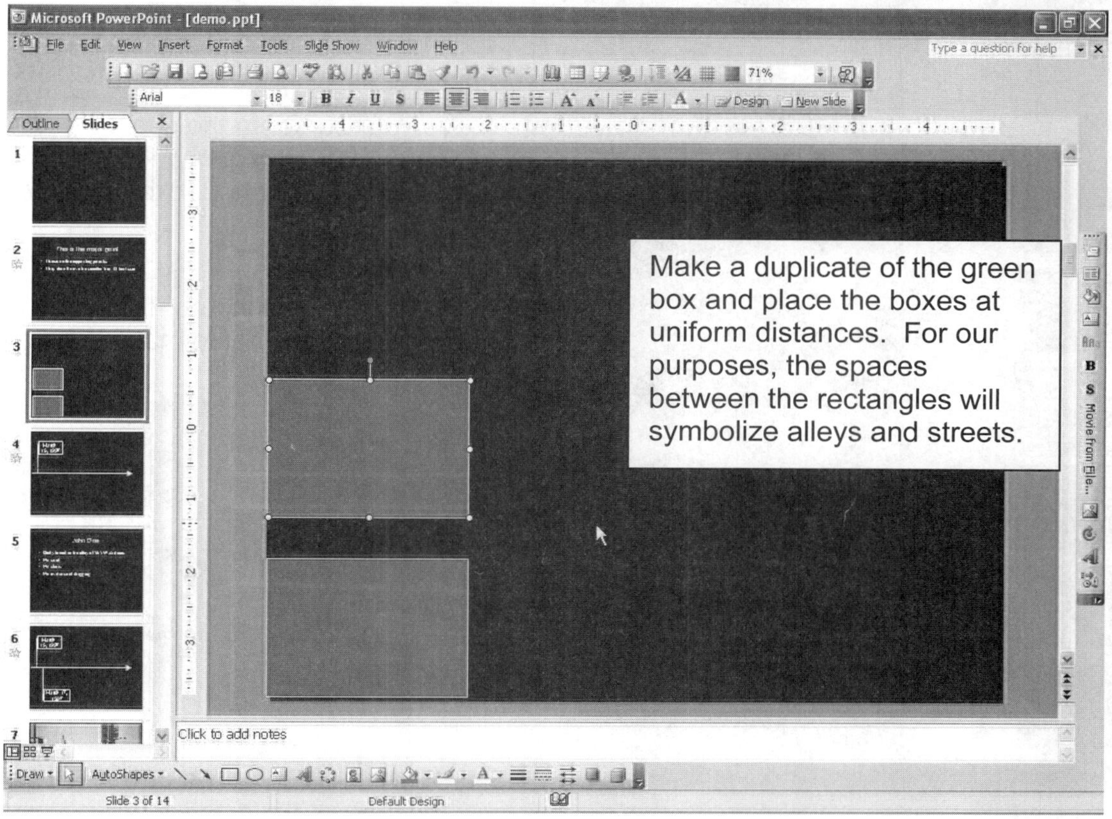
Microsoft PowerPoint - [demo.ppt]
File Edit View Insert Format Tools Slide Show Window Help
Type a question for help
Outline Slides
Make a duplicate of the green
box and place the boxes at
uniform distances. For our
purposes, the spaces
between the rectangles will
symbolize alleys and streets.
Click to add notes
Draw AutoShapes
Slide 3 of 14
Default Design

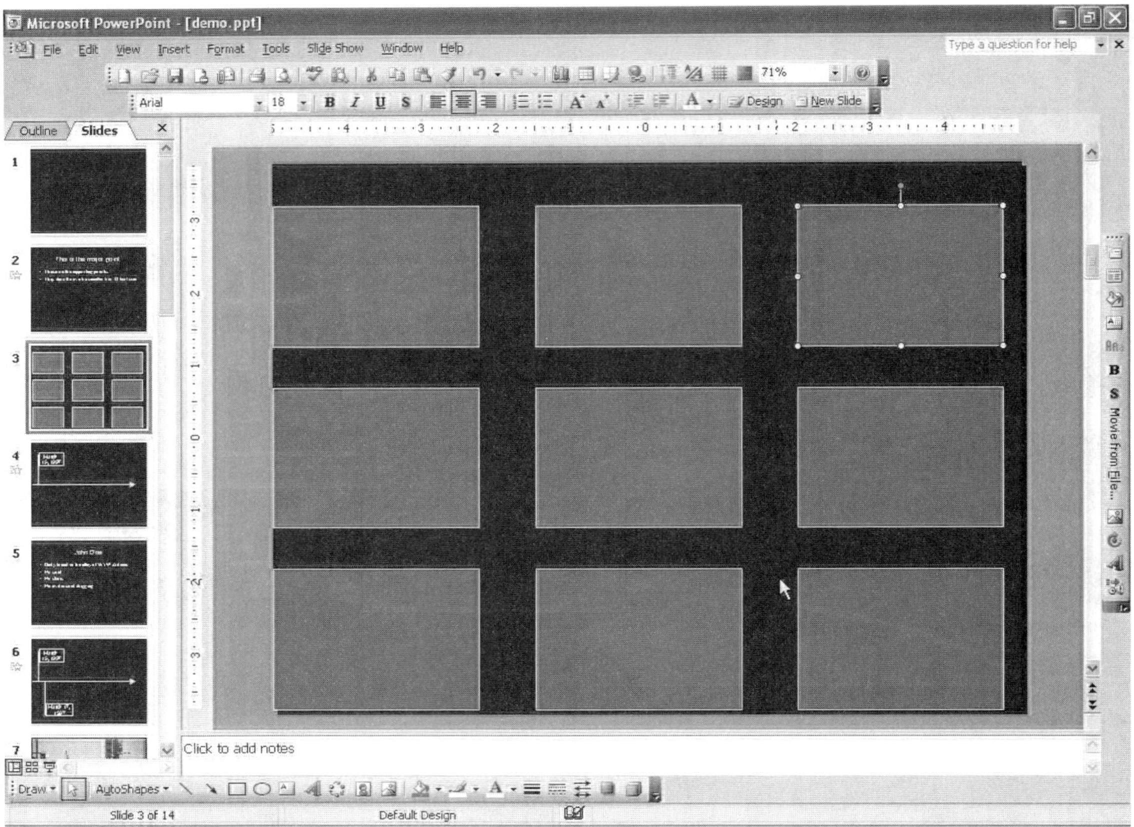
Microsoft PowerPoint - [demo.ppt]
Click to add notes
Slide 3 of 14
Default Design

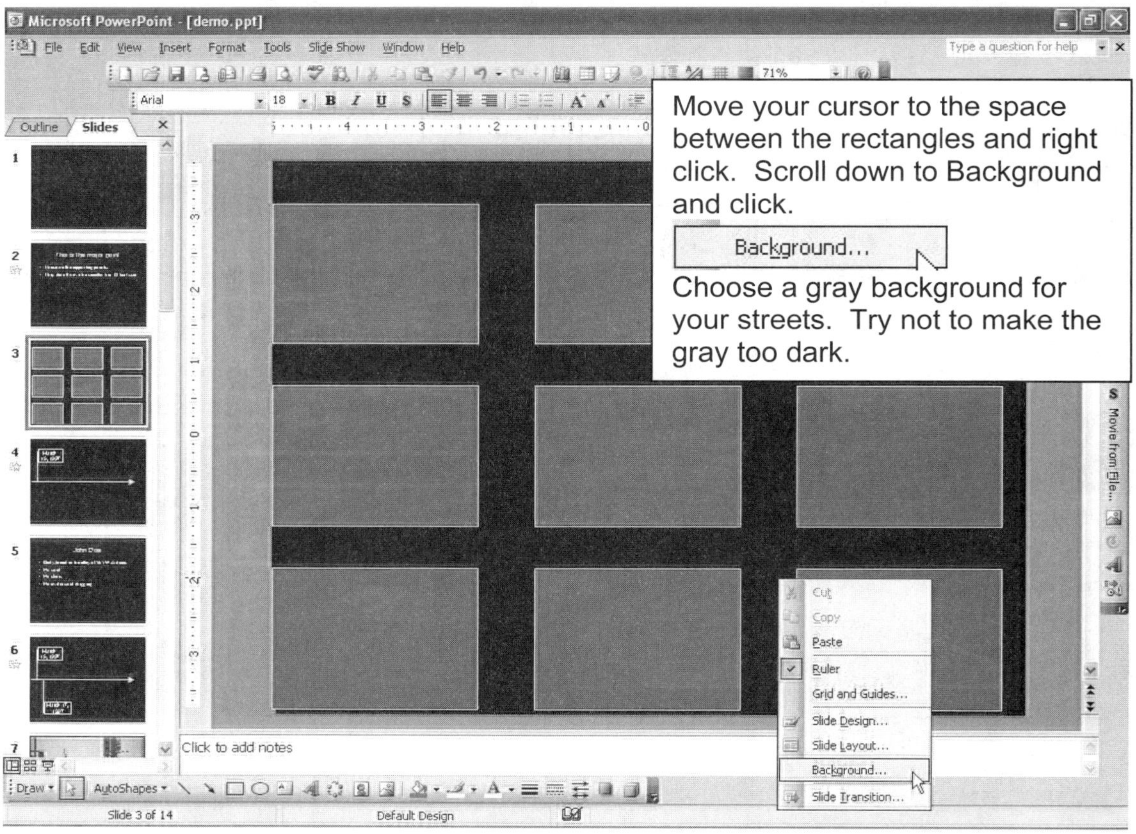
Microsoft PowerPoint - [demo.ppt]
Move your cursor to the space between the rectangles and right click. Scroll down to Background and click.
Background...
Choose a gray background for your streets. Try not to make the gray too dark.
Cut
Copy
Paste
Ruler
Grid and Guides...
Slide Design...
Slide Layout...
Background...
Slide Transition...
Click to add notes
Slide 3 of 14
Default Design

Microsoft PowerPoint - [demo.ppt]
File Edit View Insert Format Tools Slide Show Window Help
Type a question for help
Arial 18 71%
Design New Slide
Outline Slides
Background
Background fill
Title of Slide
Bullet text
Apply to All
Apply
Cancel
Preview
Automatic
More Colors...
Fill Effects...
Movie from File...
Click to add notes
Draw AutoShapes
Slide 3 of 14
Default Design

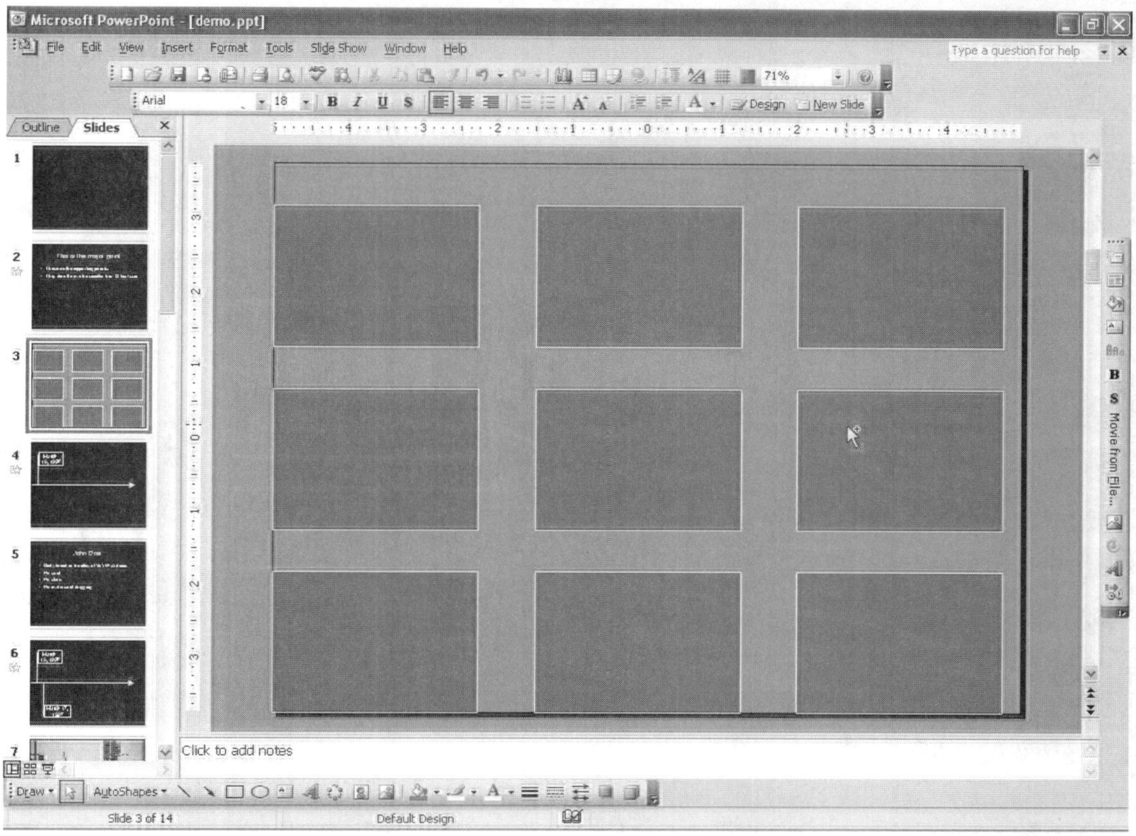
Microsoft PowerPoint - [demo.ppt]
File Edit View Insert Format Tools Slide Show Window Help
Type a question for help
Arial 18 71%
Design New Slide
Outline Slides
Movie from File...
Click to add notes
Draw AutoShapes
Slide 3 of 14
Default Design

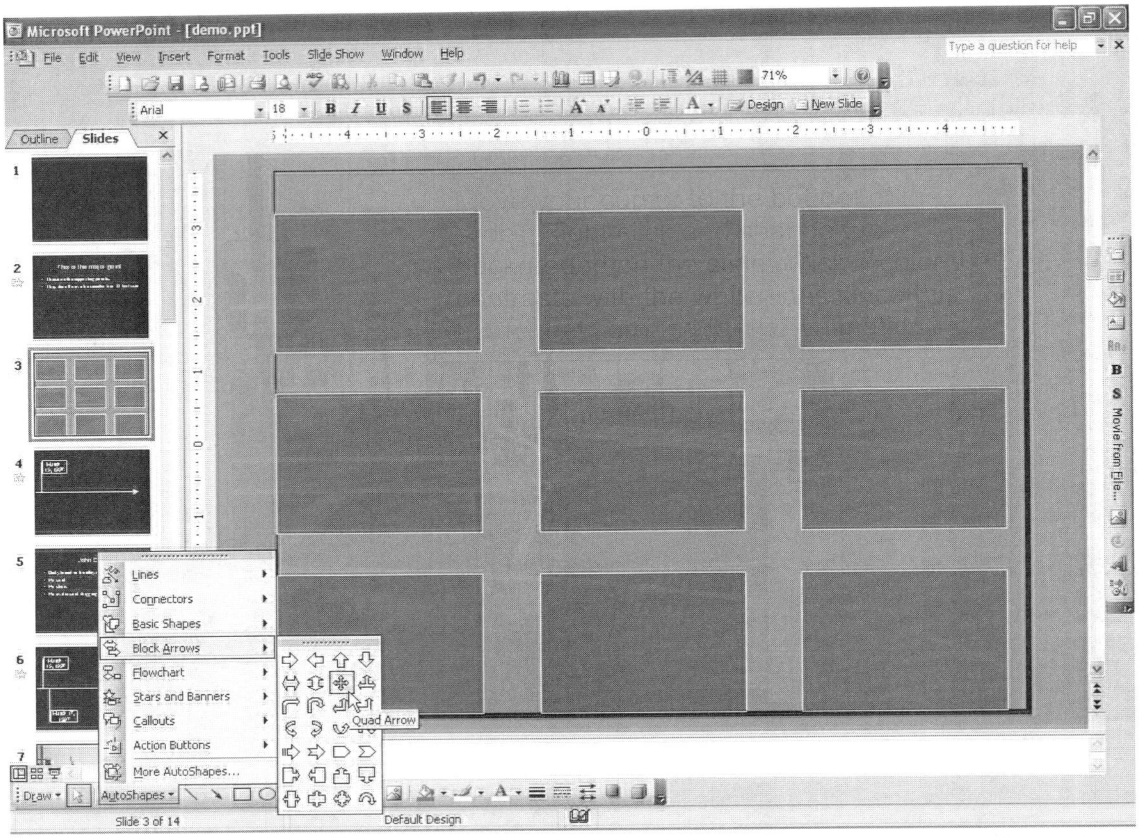
Microsoft PowerPoint - [demo.ppt]
File Edit View Insert Format Tools Slide Show Window Help
Type a question for help
Arial
18
71%
Design
New Slide
Outline
Slides
Lines
Connectors
Basic Shapes
Block Arrows
Flowchart
Stars and Banners
Callouts
Action Buttons
More AutoShapes...
Quad Arrow
Draw
AutoShapes
Slide 3 of 14
Default Design

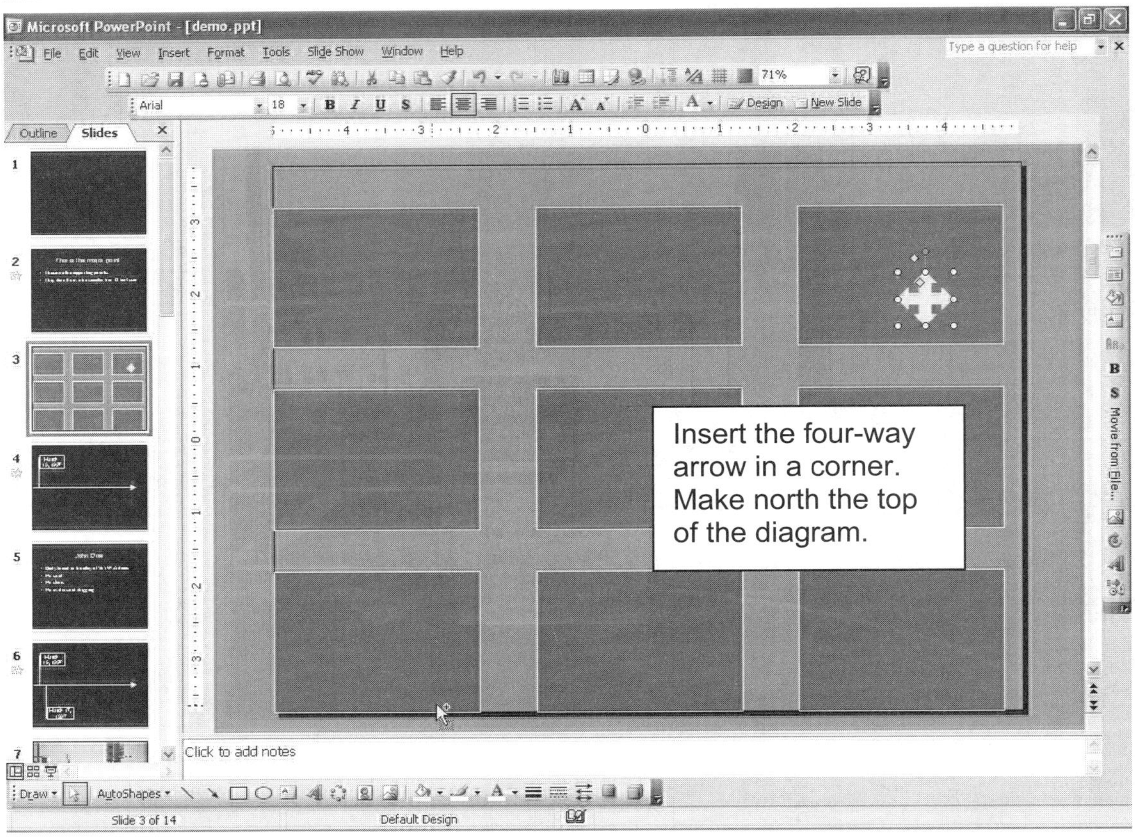
Microsoft PowerPoint - [demo.ppt]
File Edit View Insert Format Tools Slide Show Window Help
Type a question for help
Arial
18
71%
Design
New Slide
Outline
Slides
Insert the four-way arrow in a corner. Make north the top of the diagram.
Click to add notes
Draw
AutoShapes
Slide 3 of 14
Default Design

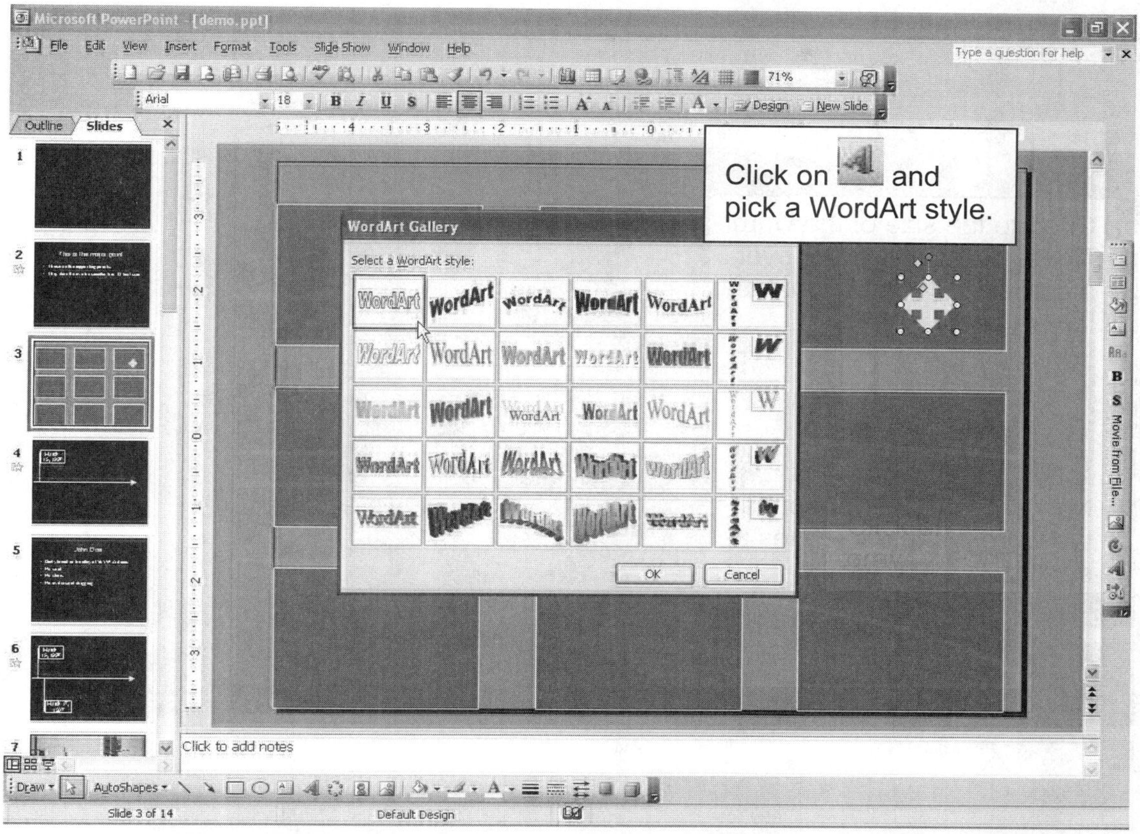
Microsoft PowerPoint - [demo.ppt]
Click on and pick a WordArt style.
WordArt Gallery
Select a WordArt style:
OK
Cancel
Click to add notes
Slide 3 of 14
Default Design

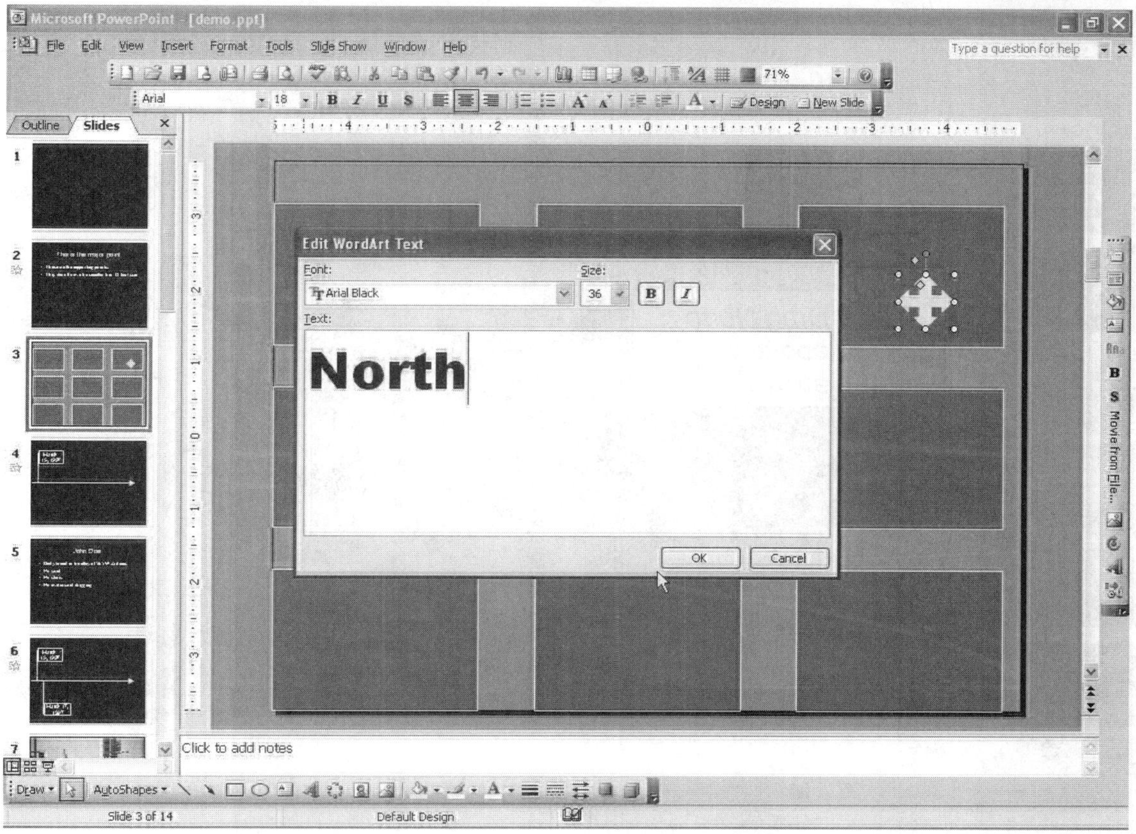
Microsoft PowerPoint - [demo.ppt]
Edit WordArt Text
Font:
Arial Black
Size:
36
Text:
North
OK
Cancel
Click to add notes
Slide 3 of 14
Default Design

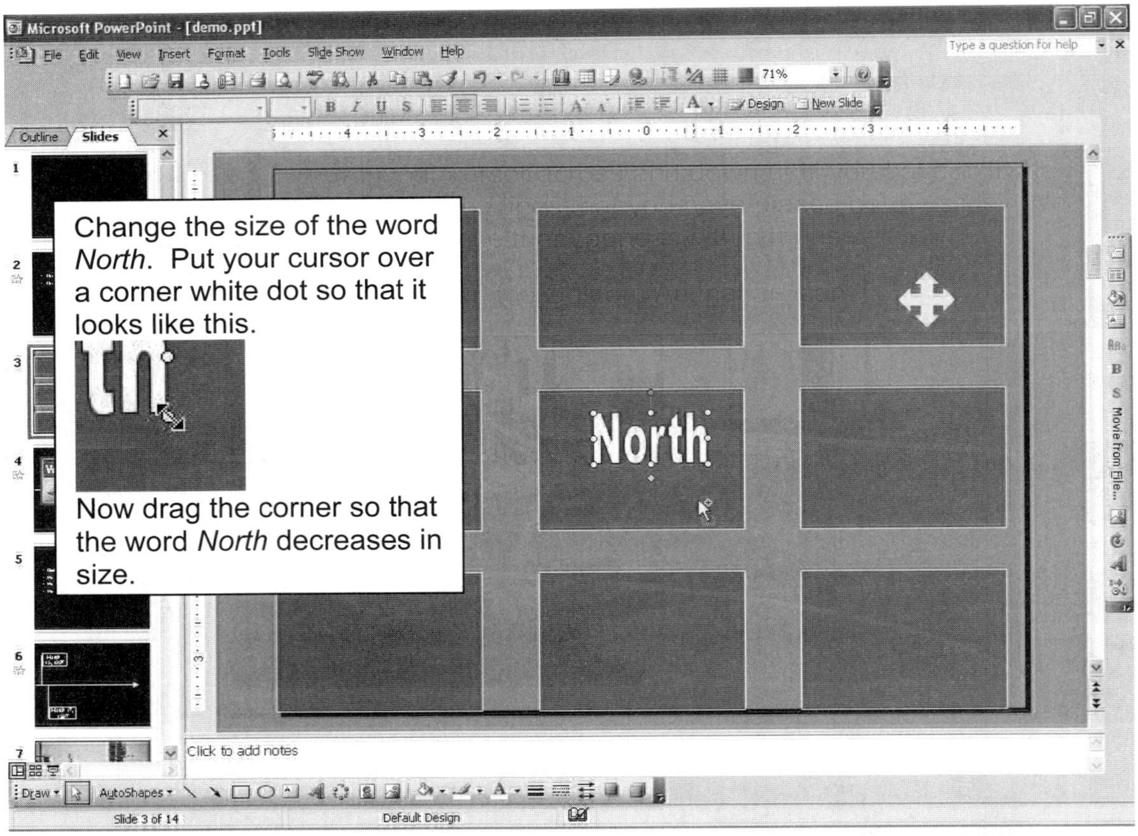
Microsoft PowerPoint - [demo.ppt]
Change the size of the word *North*. Put your cursor over a corner white dot so that it looks like this.
Now drag the corner so that the word *North* decreases in size.
North
Click to add notes
Slide 3 of 14
Default Design

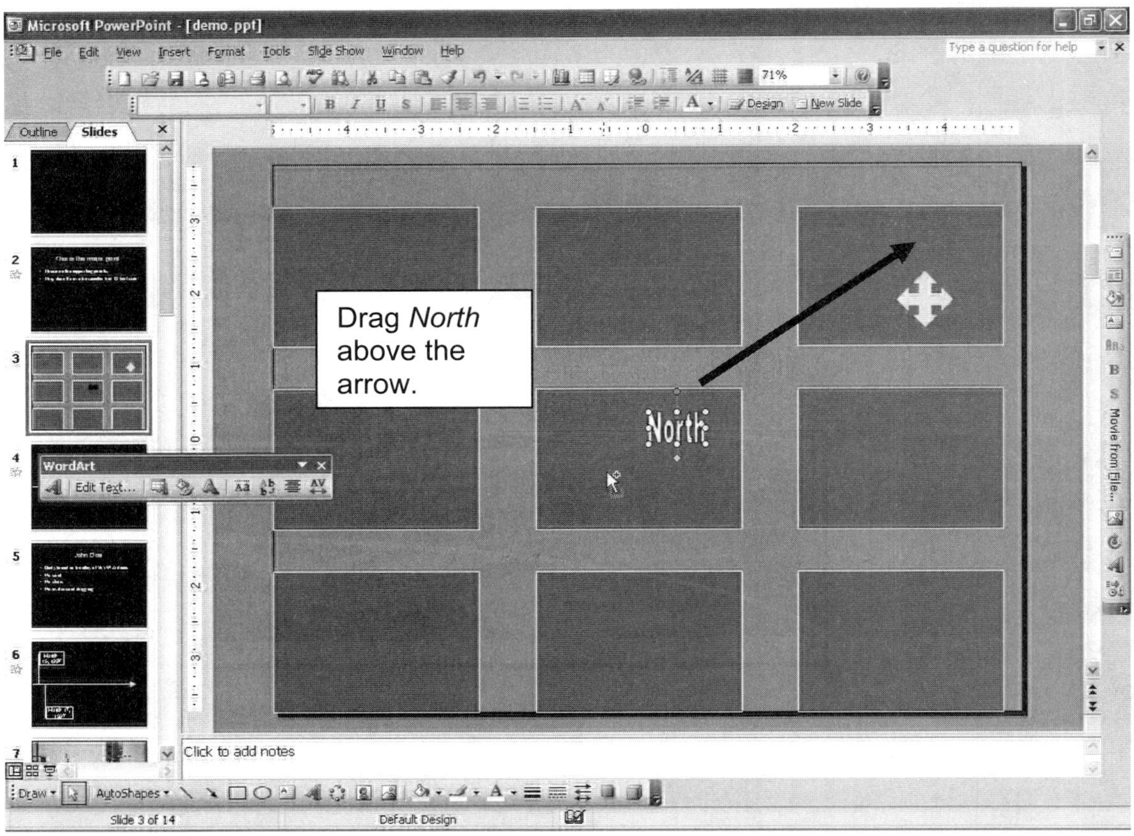
Microsoft PowerPoint - [demo.ppt]
Drag *North* above the arrow.
North
WordArt
Edit Text...
Click to add notes
Slide 3 of 14
Default Design

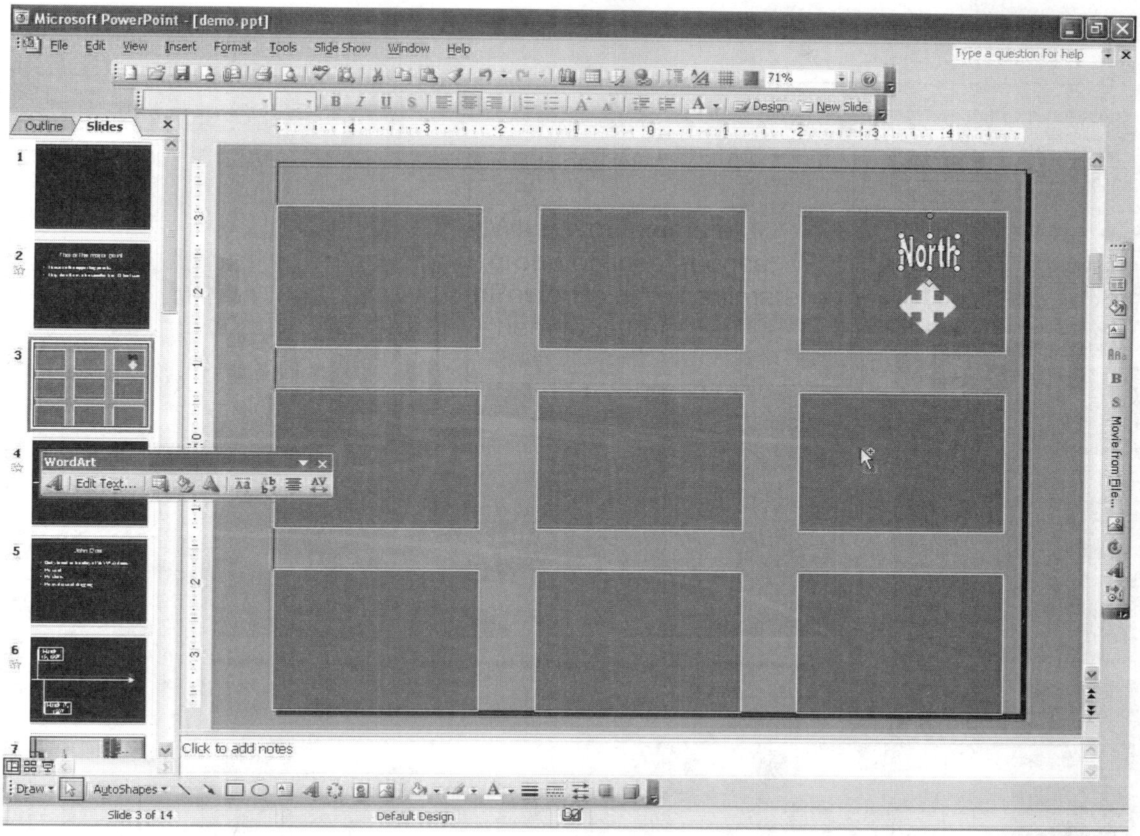

Inserting Photographs

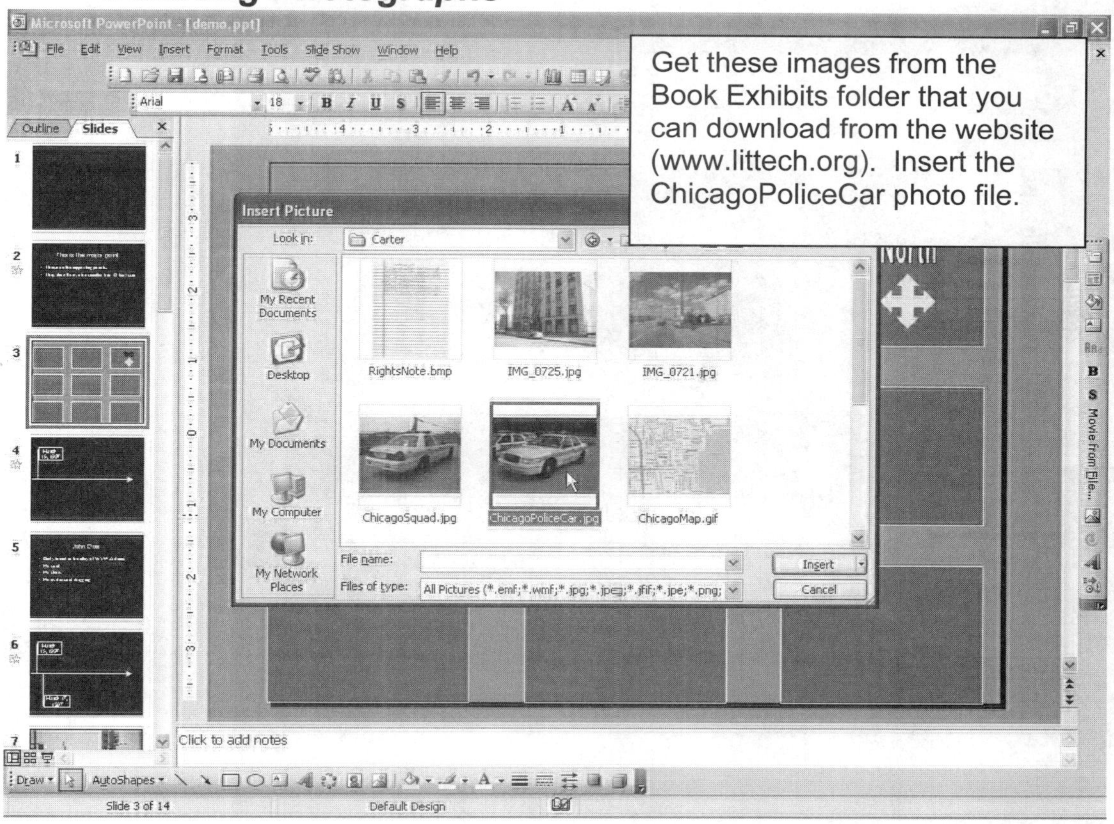

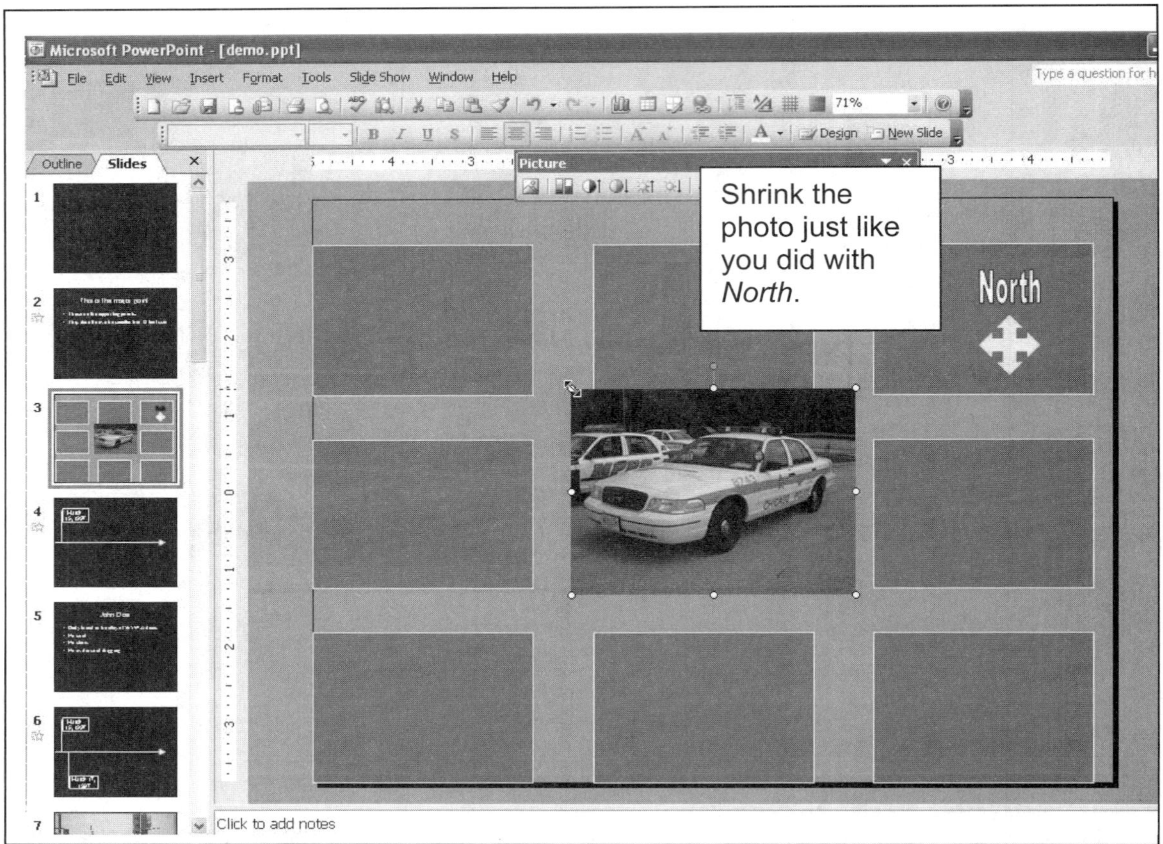
Microsoft PowerPoint - [demo.ppt]
Shrink the photo just like you did with *North*.
North
Click to add notes

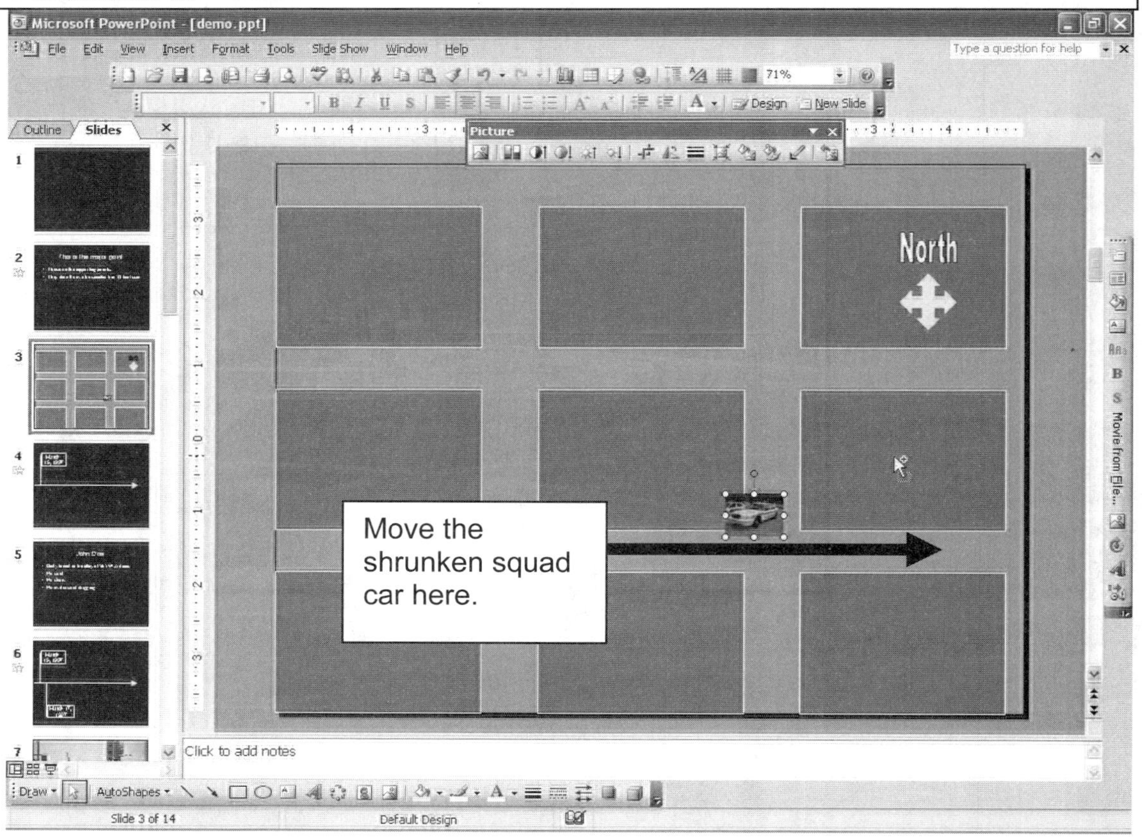
Microsoft PowerPoint - [demo.ppt]
North
Move the shrunken squad car here.
Click to add notes
Slide 3 of 14
Default Design

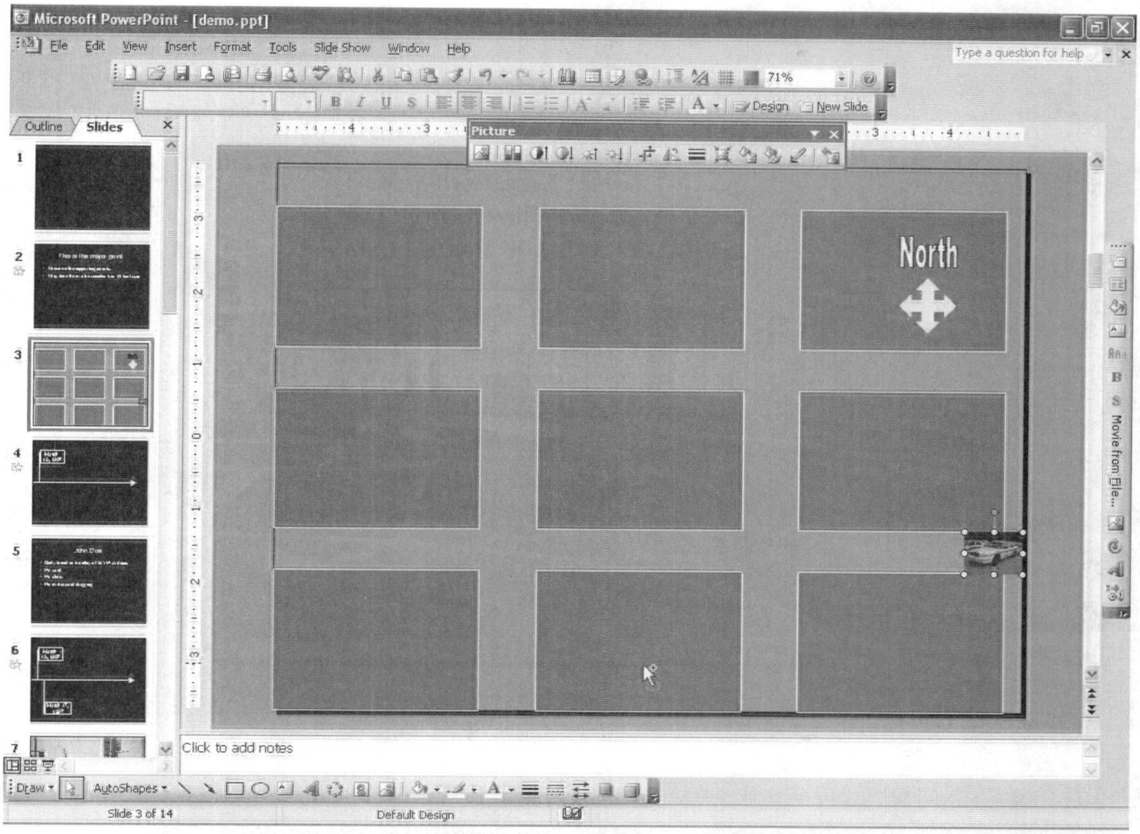

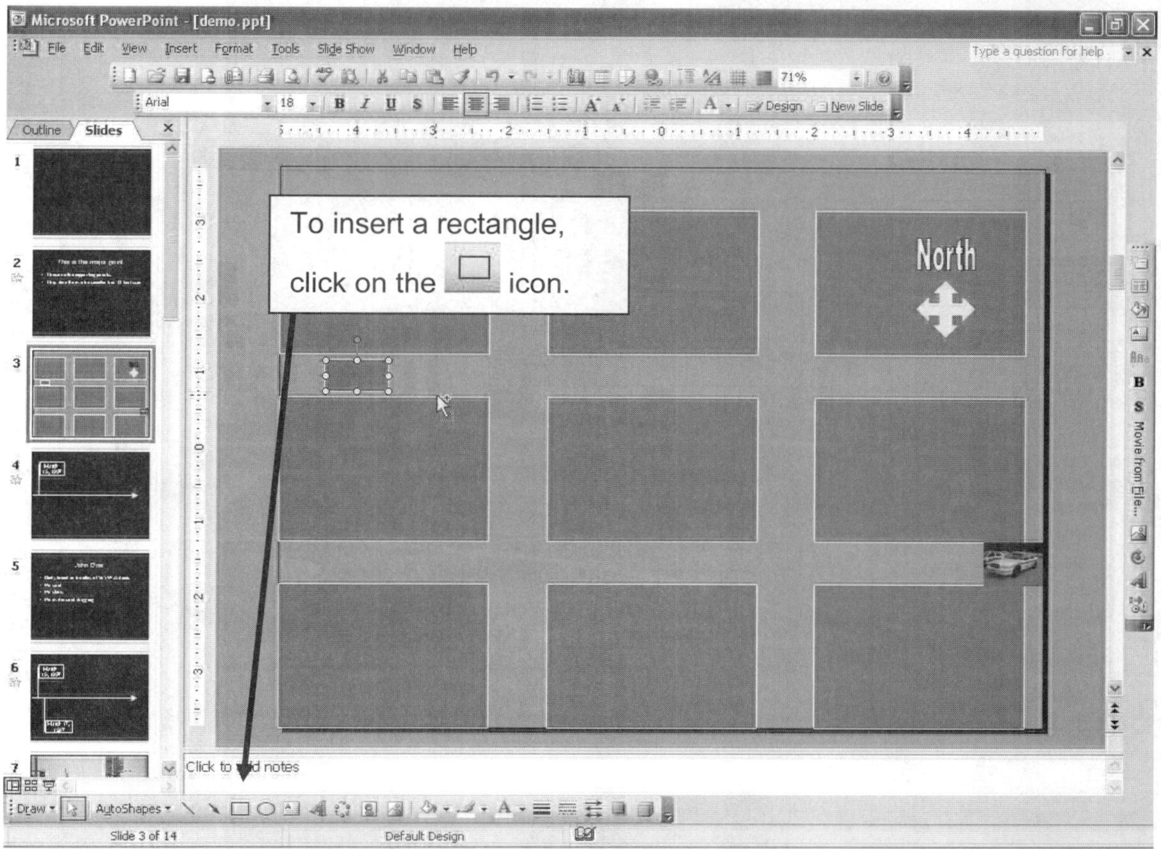
To insert a rectangle,
click on the icon.

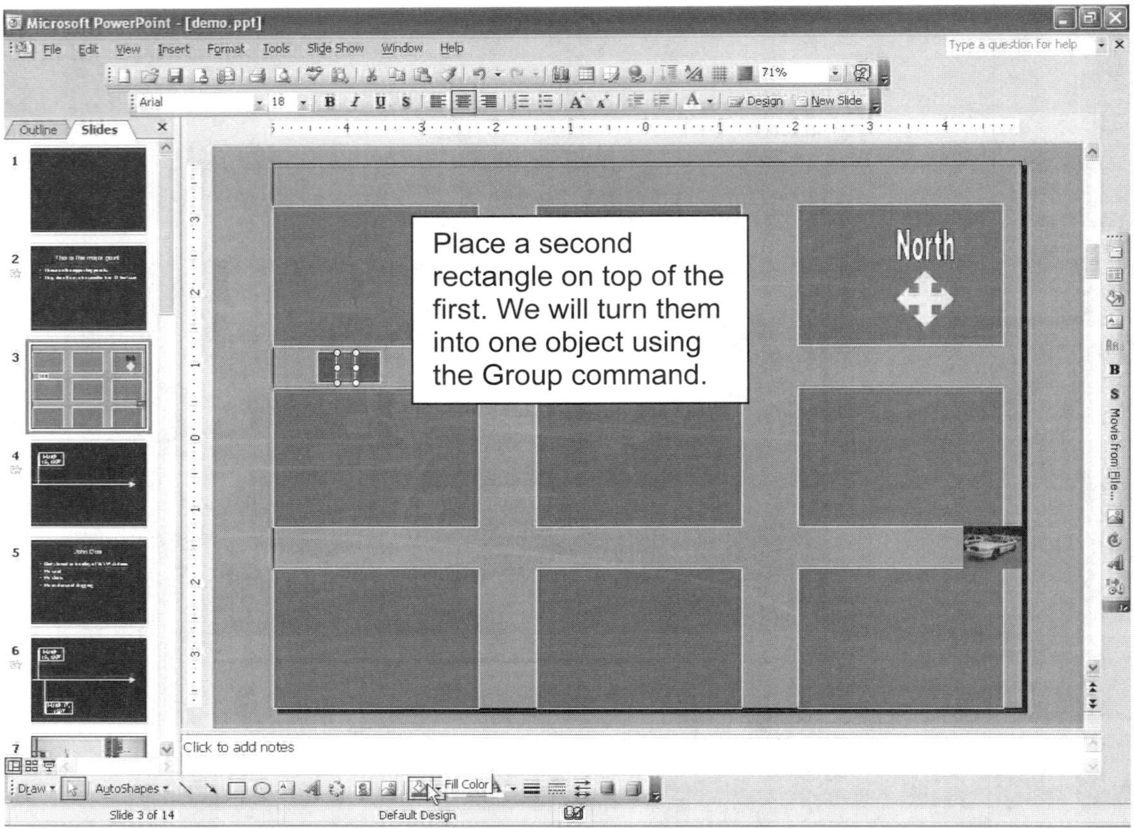
Microsoft PowerPoint - [demo.ppt]
Place a second rectangle on top of the first. We will turn them into one object using the Group command.
North
Click to add notes
Fill Color
Slide 3 of 14
Default Design

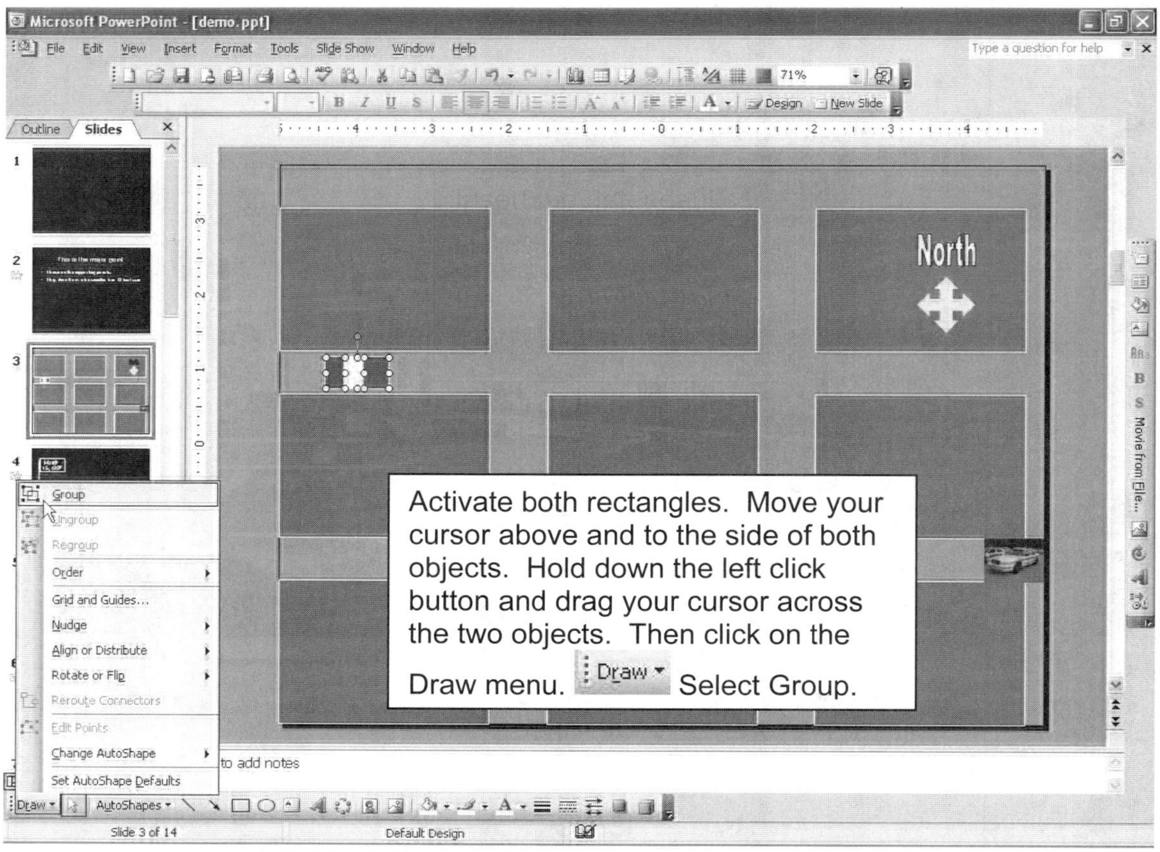
Microsoft PowerPoint - [demo.ppt]
North
Activate both rectangles. Move your cursor above and to the side of both objects. Hold down the left click button and drag your cursor across the two objects. Then click on the Draw menu. Draw Select Group.
Group
Ungroup
Regroup
Order
Grid and Guides...
Nudge
Align or Distribute
Rotate or Flip
Reroute Connectors
Edit Points
Change AutoShape
Set AutoShape Defaults
Slide 3 of 14
Default Design

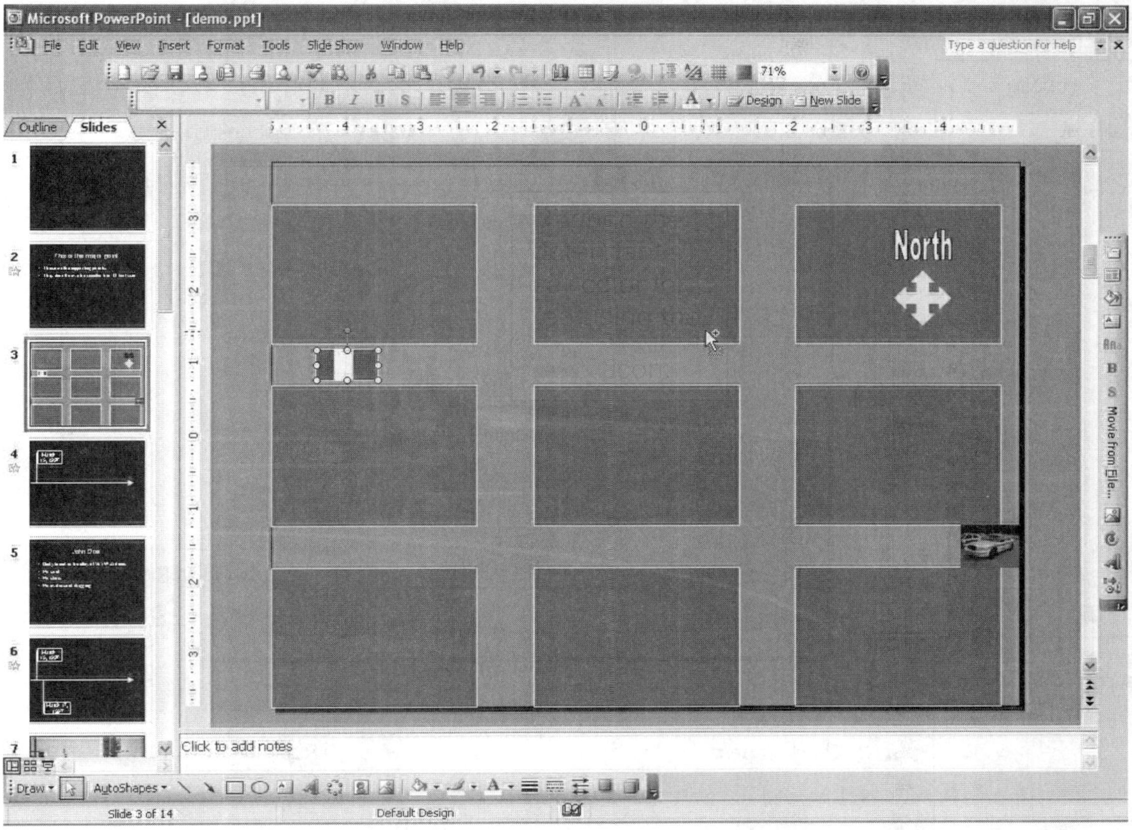

Advanced PowerPoint Functions

Animating Text and Objects

Text

PowerPoint has a number of effects available to animate images, text, and objects. You can make objects appear, move around the slide, receive emphasis, and finally disappear.

To begin, click on , which we placed on our custom My Tools toolbar:

The menu, with a prompt of 

, will appear on the right side of the slide. You will then see these menu options:

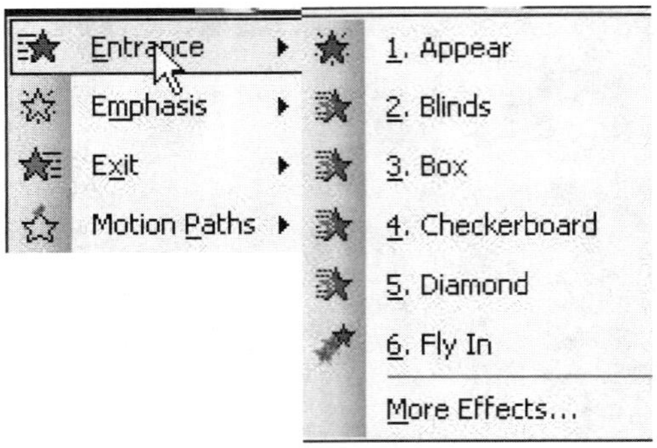

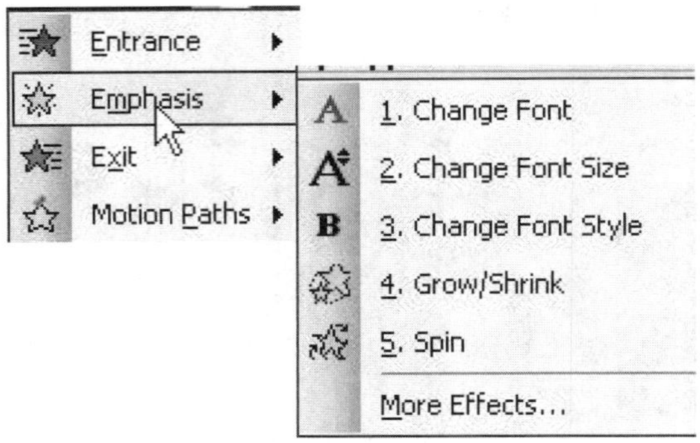

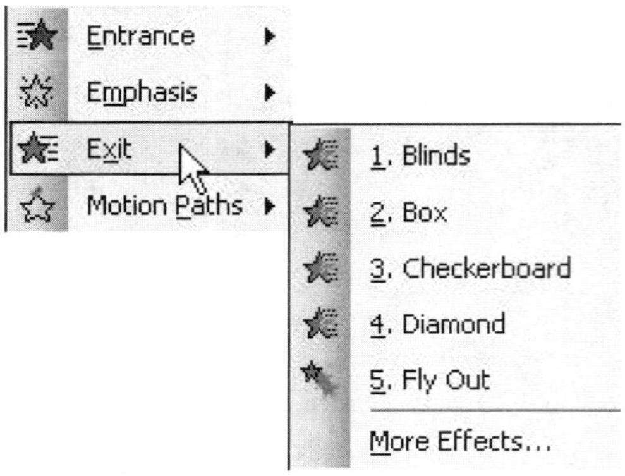

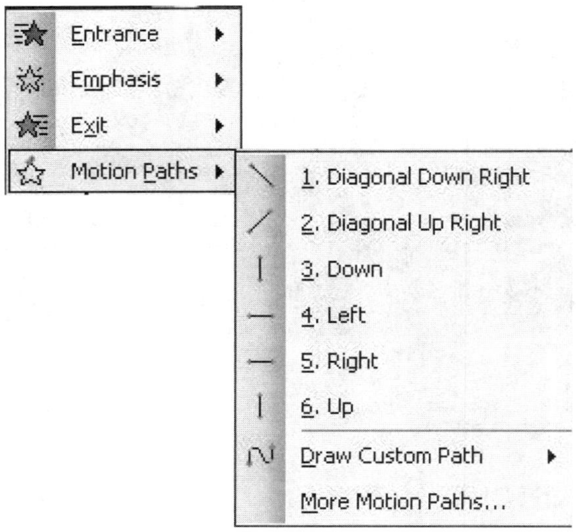

If you click on the More Effects tab for each submenu, you will find even more types of animation that can be worked into the presentation.

You can make effects appear on mouse clicks or as part of animation sequences with this menu.

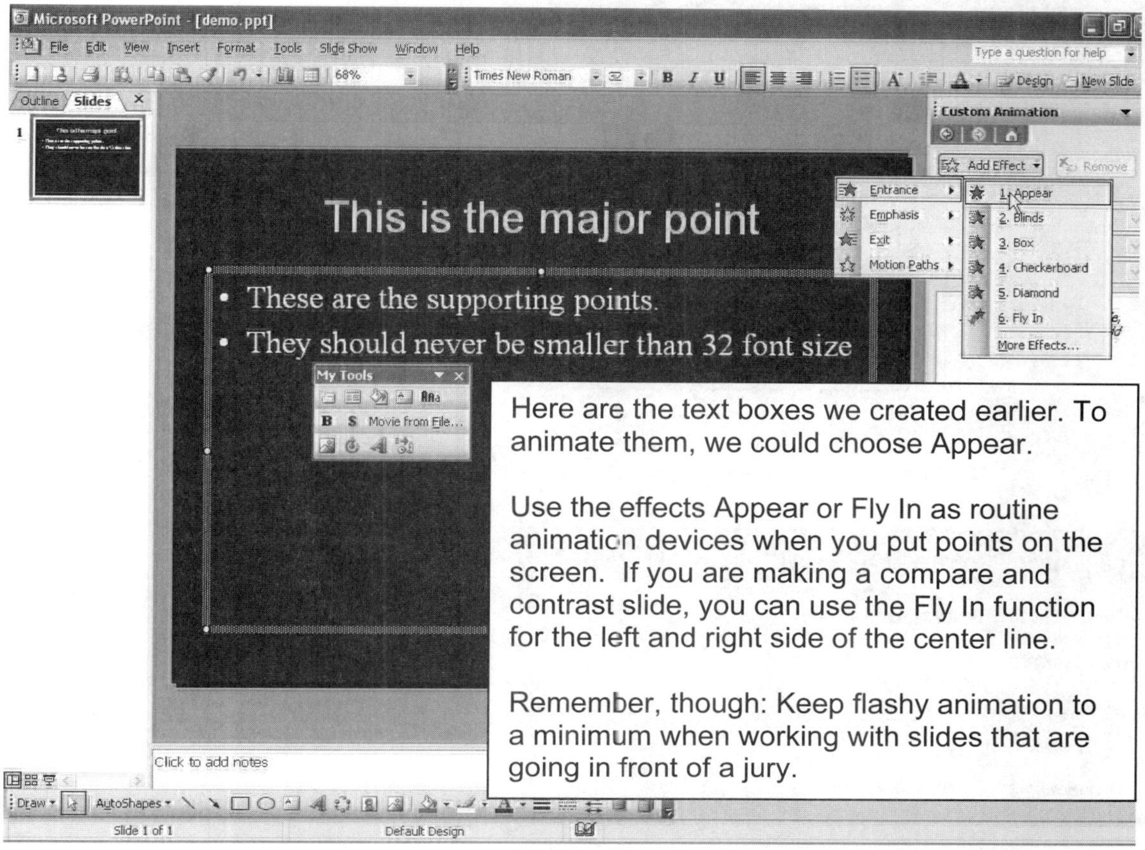

After you have selected the animation for these text boxes, "These are supporting points" and "They should never be smaller than 32 font size" will appear individually. If you want to animate them separately, click on the two arrow tips: 

. This will separate the two text lines. If you want to animate the group of objects, click on the single arrow tip in the number 1 box. When you click on the single arrow tip, you see the following menu. If you click on Effect Options, you will be able to insert a secondary effect like dimming.

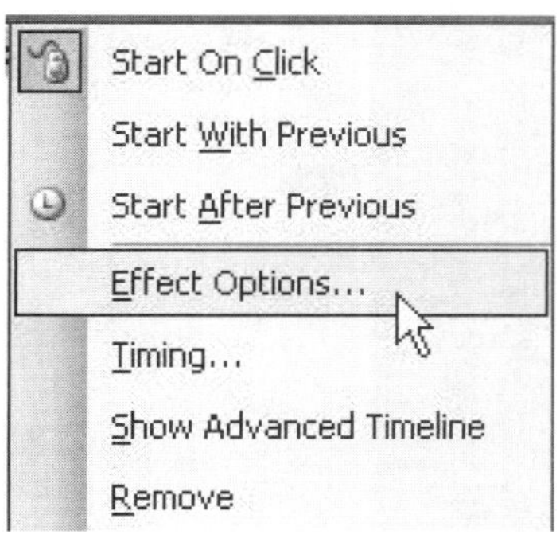

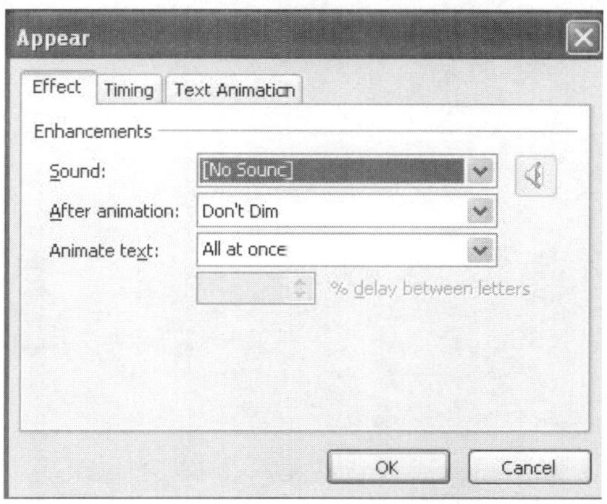

Click on the arrow tip next to Don't Dim. This box will appear.

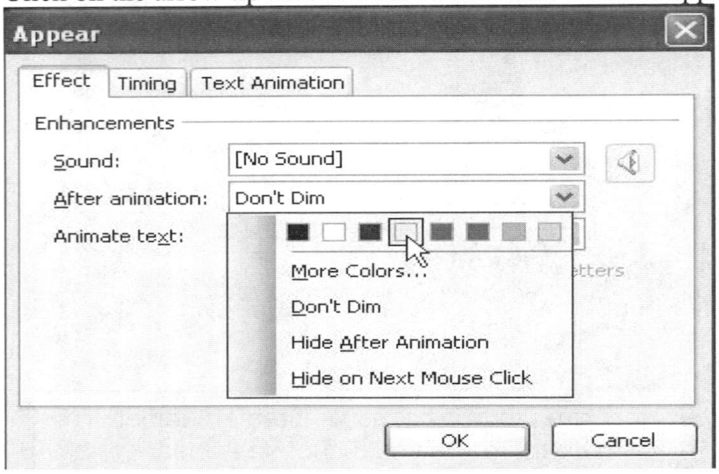

If you want, you can click on one of the available colors or you can select more colors.

You can also use the Hide After Animation effect to make something disappear right after it comes on to the screen, if you do not want to use an Exit function. Use the Hide on Next Mouse Click if you want the object to remain on the screen until your next prompting with a mouse click.

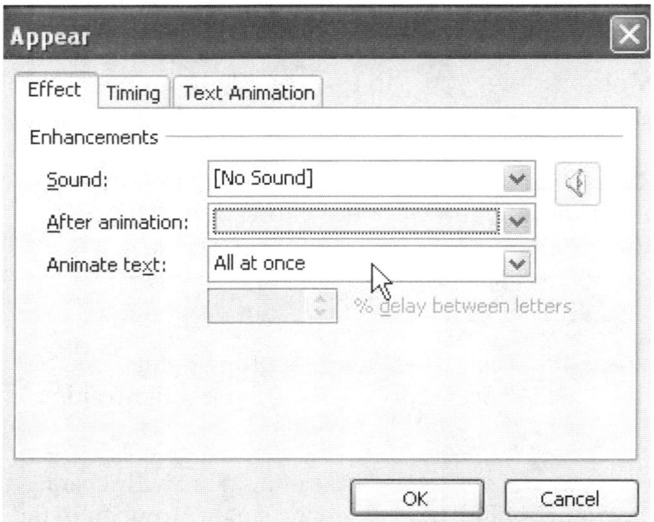

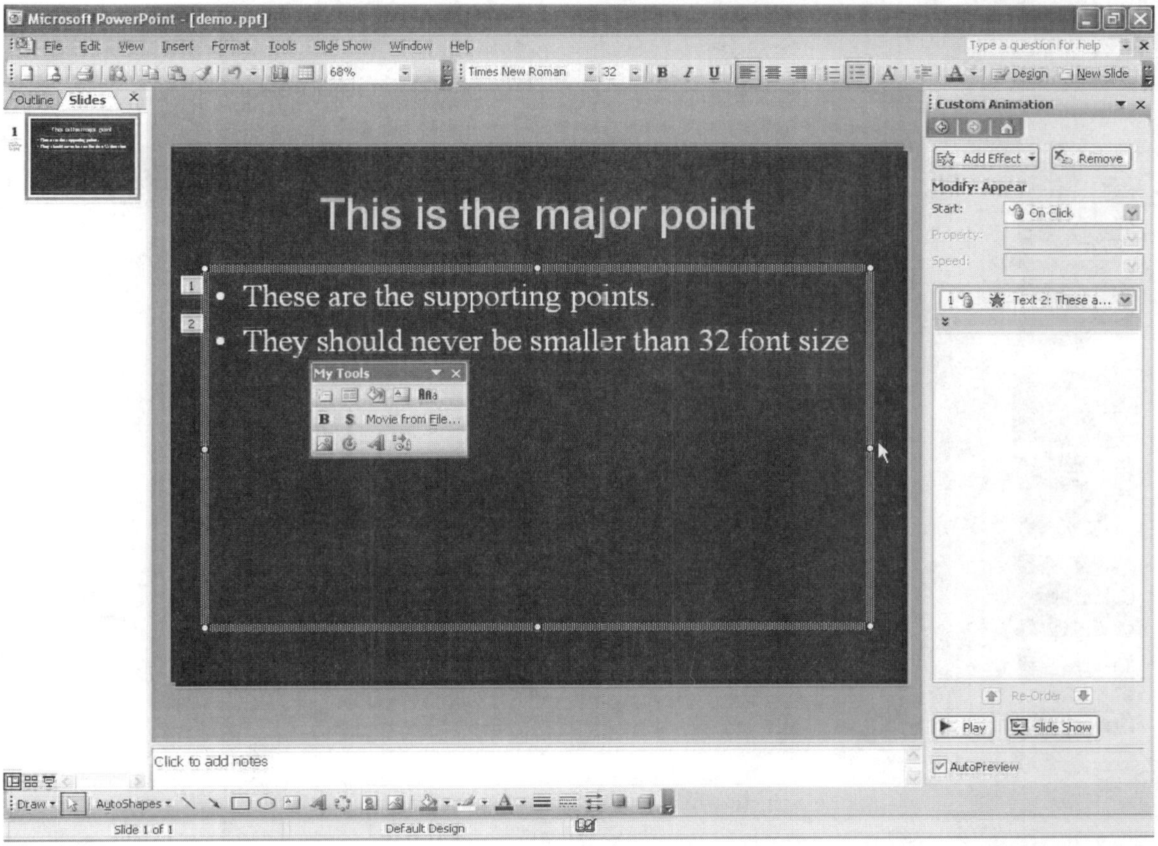

When this slide is played in a presentation, the jury will start by seeing the headline "This is the major point." On the first mouse click, the line "These are the supporting points" will appear. On the next mouse click, the line "They should never be smaller than 32 font size" will appear.

Photos and objects

Now it is time to animate the diagram with the photo of the police car and the two-tone rectangle. First, we will animate lines to simulate paths of travel before a crash. Next, we will animate the objects themselves.

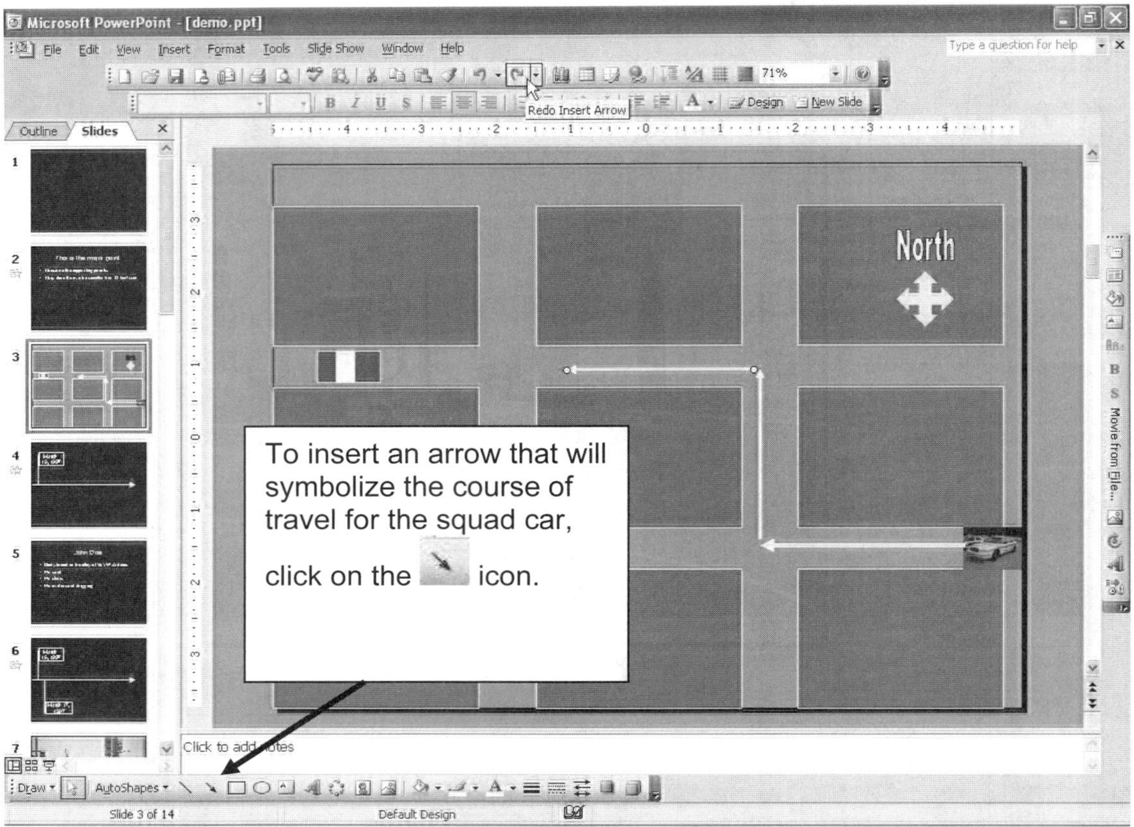
Microsoft PowerPoint - [demo.ppt]
File Edit View Insert Format Tools Slide Show Window Help
Type a question for help
Redo Insert Arrow
Design
New Slide
Outline
Slides
North
To insert an arrow that will symbolize the course of travel for the squad car, click on the icon.
Click to add notes
Draw
AutoShapes
Slide 3 of 14
Default Design

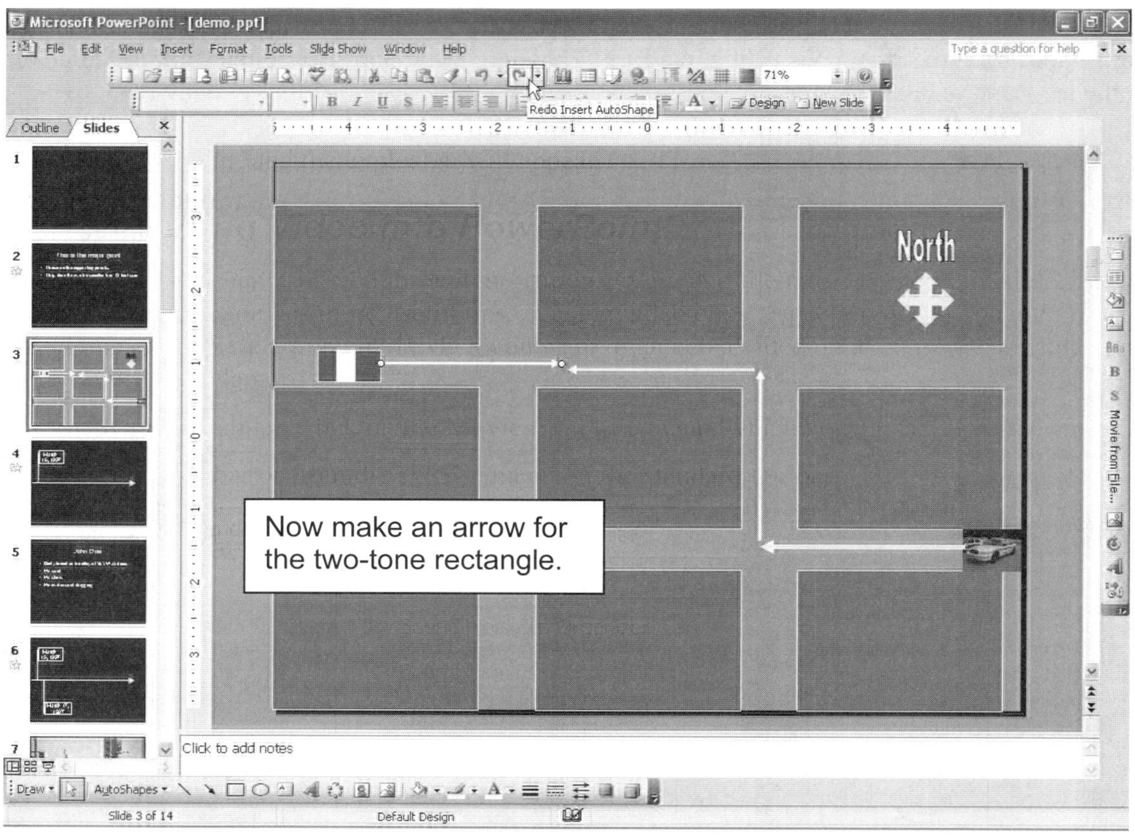
Microsoft PowerPoint - [demo.ppt]
File Edit View Insert Format Tools Slide Show Window Help
Type a question for help
Redo Insert AutoShape
Design
New Slide
Outline
Slides
North
Now make an arrow for the two-tone rectangle.
Click to add notes
Draw
AutoShapes
Slide 3 of 14
Default Design

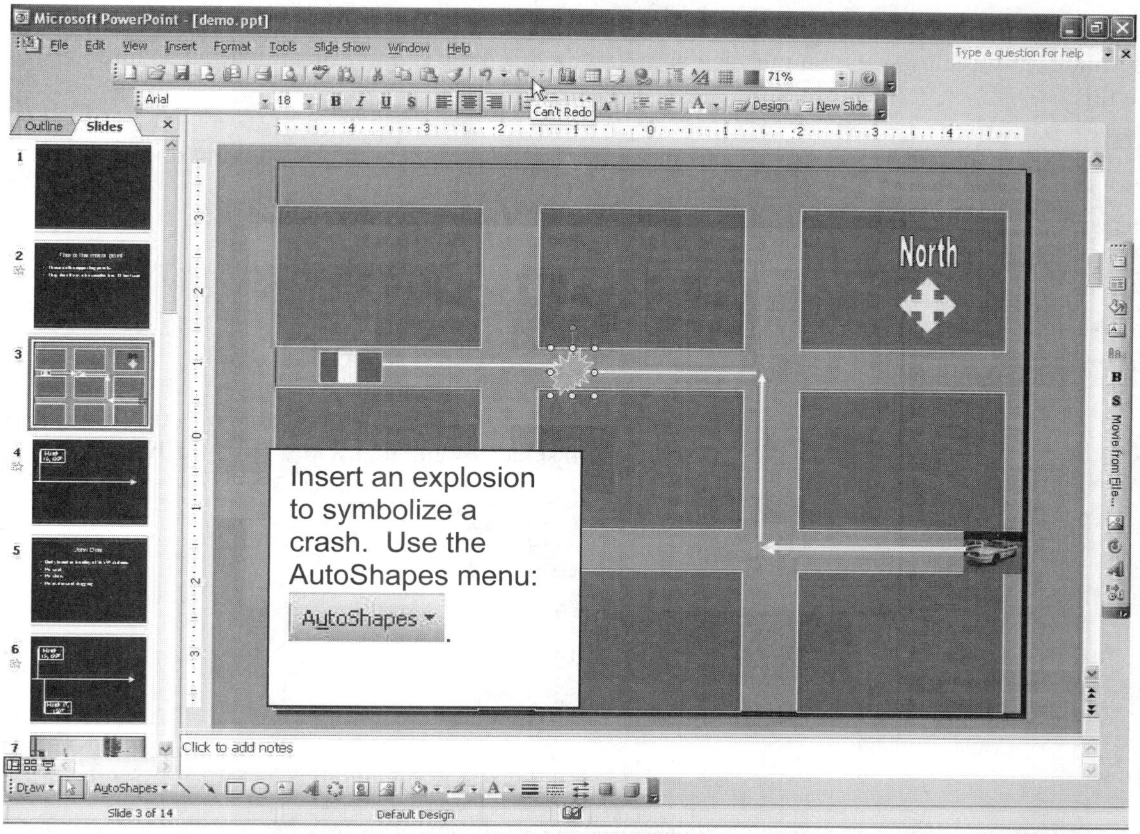
Microsoft PowerPoint - [demo.ppt]
File Edit View Insert Format Tools Slide Show Window Help
Type a question for help
Can't Redo
Design New Slide
Outline Slides
North
Insert an explosion to symbolize a crash. Use the AutoShapes menu: AutoShapes .
Click to add notes
Draw AutoShapes
Slide 3 of 14
Default Design

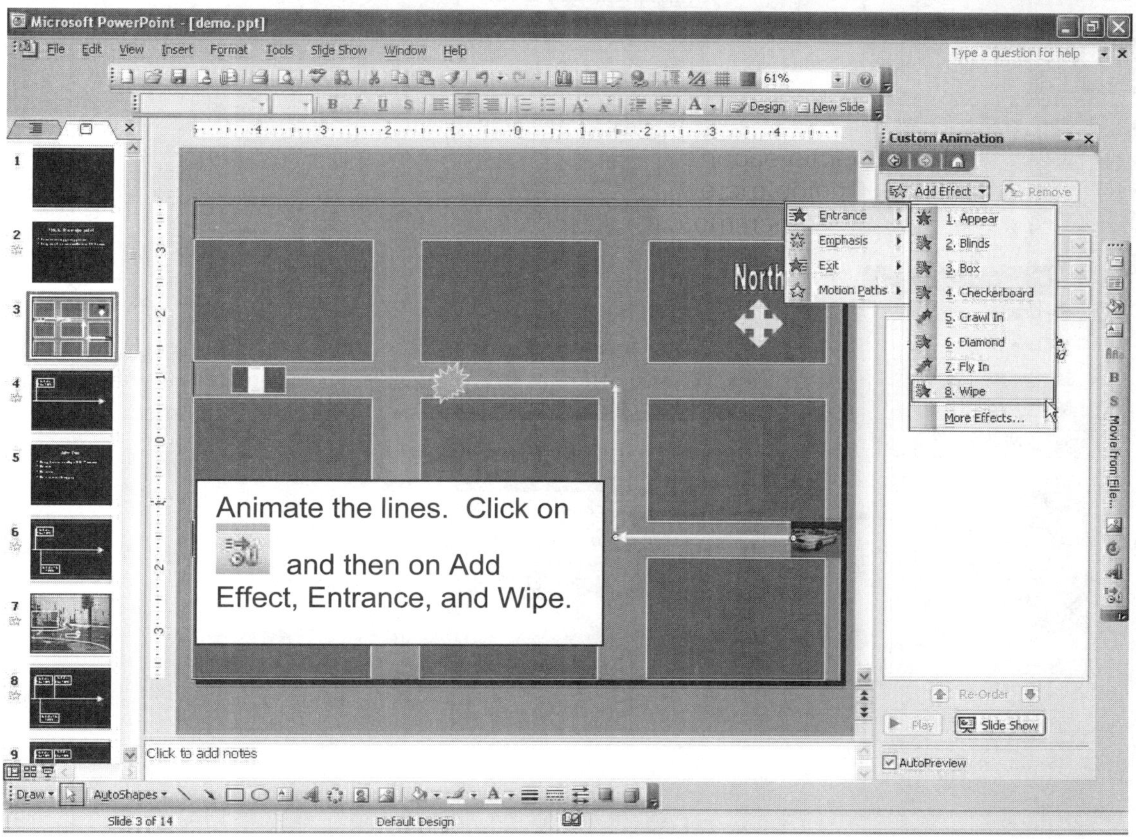
Microsoft PowerPoint - [demo.ppt]
File Edit View Insert Format Tools Slide Show Window Help
Type a question for help
Custom Animation
Add Effect
Remove
Entrance
Emphasis
Exit
Motion Paths
1. Appear
2. Blinds
3. Box
4. Checkerboard
5. Crawl In
6. Diamond
7. Fly In
8. Wipe
More Effects...
North
Animate the lines. Click on and then on Add Effect, Entrance, and Wipe.
Re-Order
Play
Slide Show
AutoPreview
Click to add notes
Draw AutoShapes
Slide 3 of 14
Default Design

Animate each arrow so that it wipes from a particular direction. The arrows showing the path of the police car traveling west on our map should wipe from the right. The animation should look like this:

Control the direction of the wipe by clicking on the next to the direction.

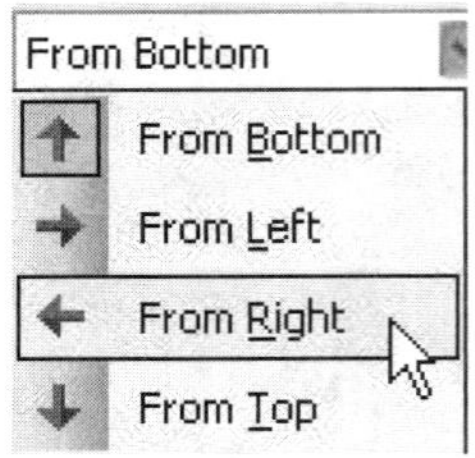

For the arrow that shows travel north on the diagram, select a wipe that wipes from the bottom.

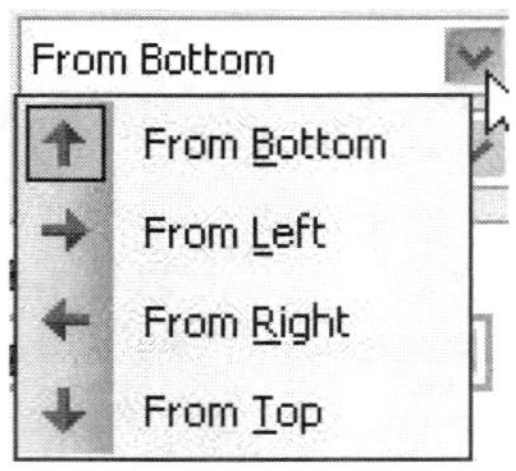

For the red and white rectangle, make it wipe from the left.

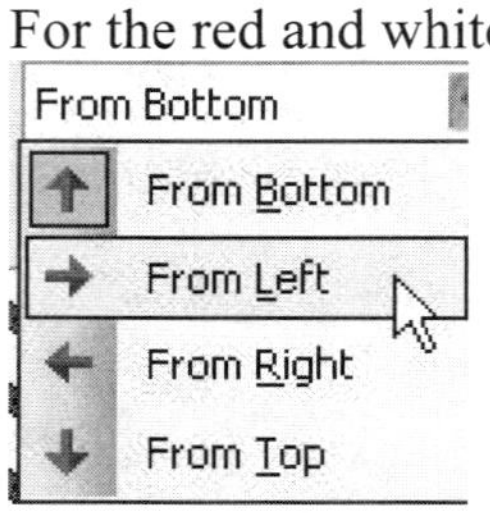

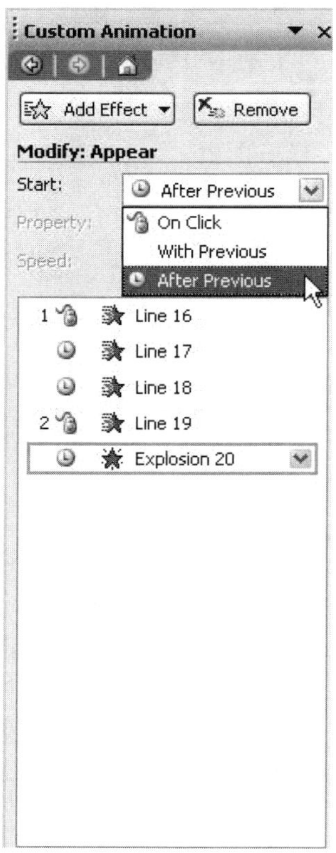

Choose the animation effect of

for the explosion.

Make sure your animation effects are set correctly by choosing whether the lines or explosion will animate on, with, or after another effect. Make these choices with this menu:

Motion paths

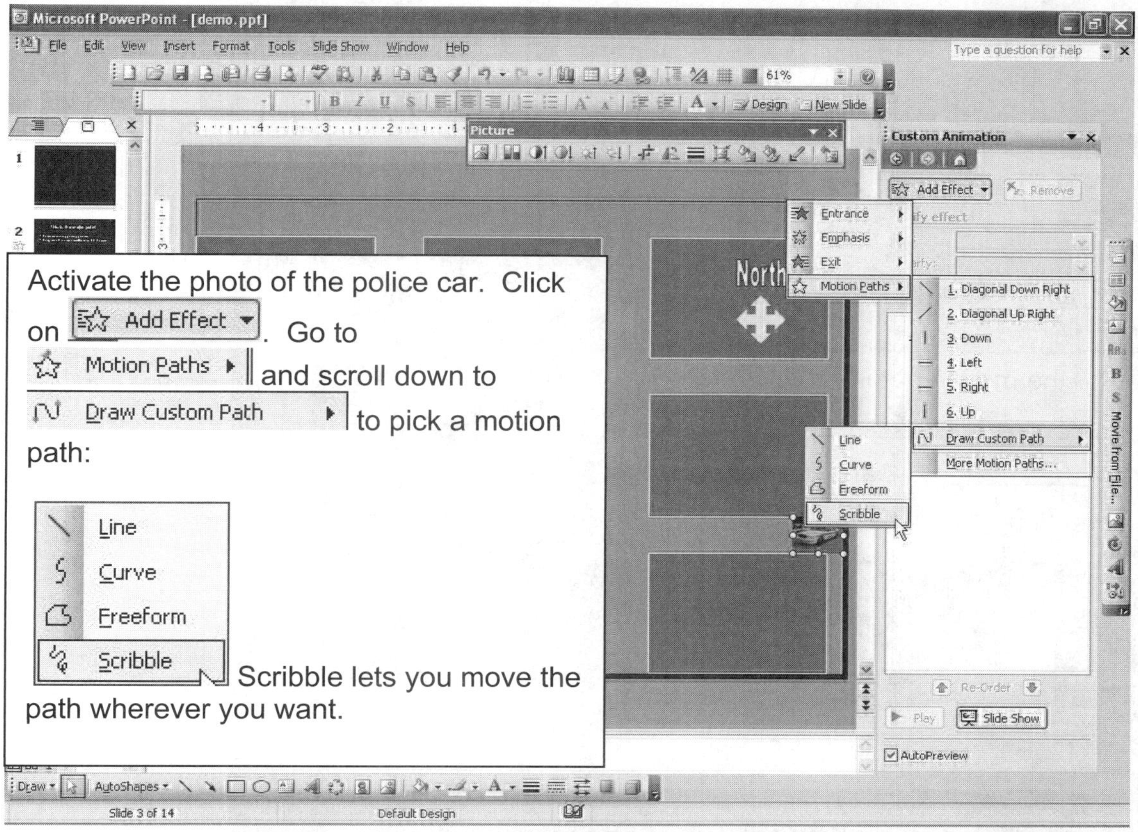

Activate the photo of the police car. Click on [Add Effect]. Go to [Motion Paths] and scroll down to [Draw Custom Path] to pick a motion path:

Line
Curve
Freeform
Scribble

Scribble lets you move the path wherever you want.

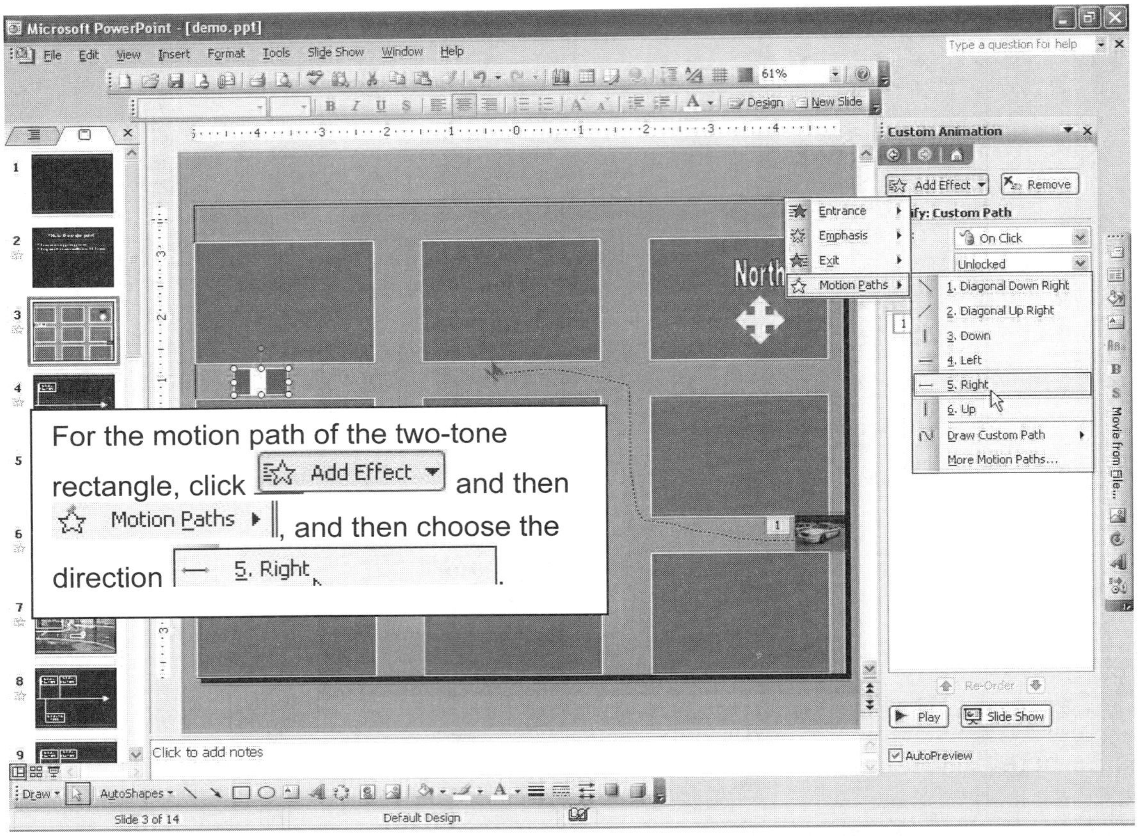
Microsoft PowerPoint - [demo.ppt]
For the motion path of the two-tone rectangle, click Add Effect and then Motion Paths, and then choose the direction 5. Right.
Custom Animation
Entrance
Emphasis
Exit
Motion Paths
1. Diagonal Down Right
2. Diagonal Up Right
3. Down
4. Left
5. Right
6. Up
Draw Custom Path
More Motion Paths...
North
Click to add notes
Slide 3 of 14
Default Design

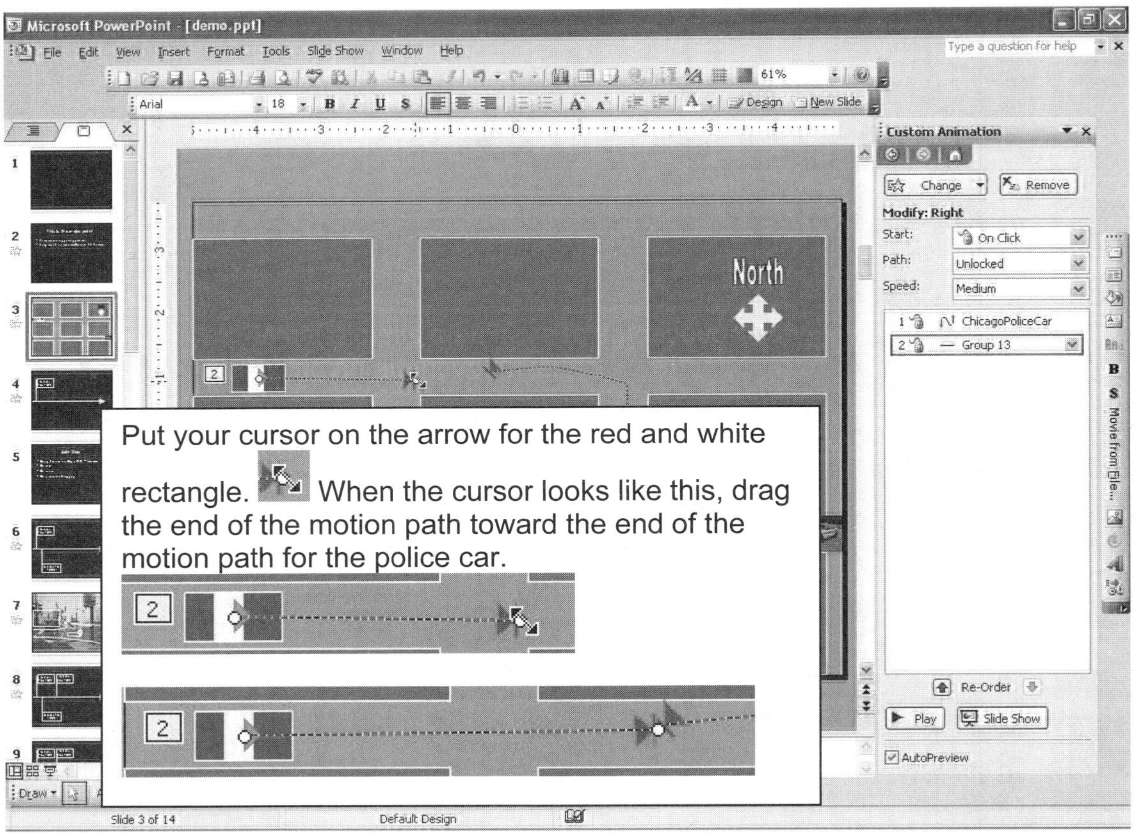
Microsoft PowerPoint - [demo.ppt]
Put your cursor on the arrow for the red and white rectangle. When the cursor looks like this, drag the end of the motion path toward the end of the motion path for the police car.
Custom Animation
Modify: Right
Start: On Click
Path: Unlocked
Speed: Medium
1 ChicagoPoliceCar
2 Group 13
North
Slide 3 of 14
Default Design

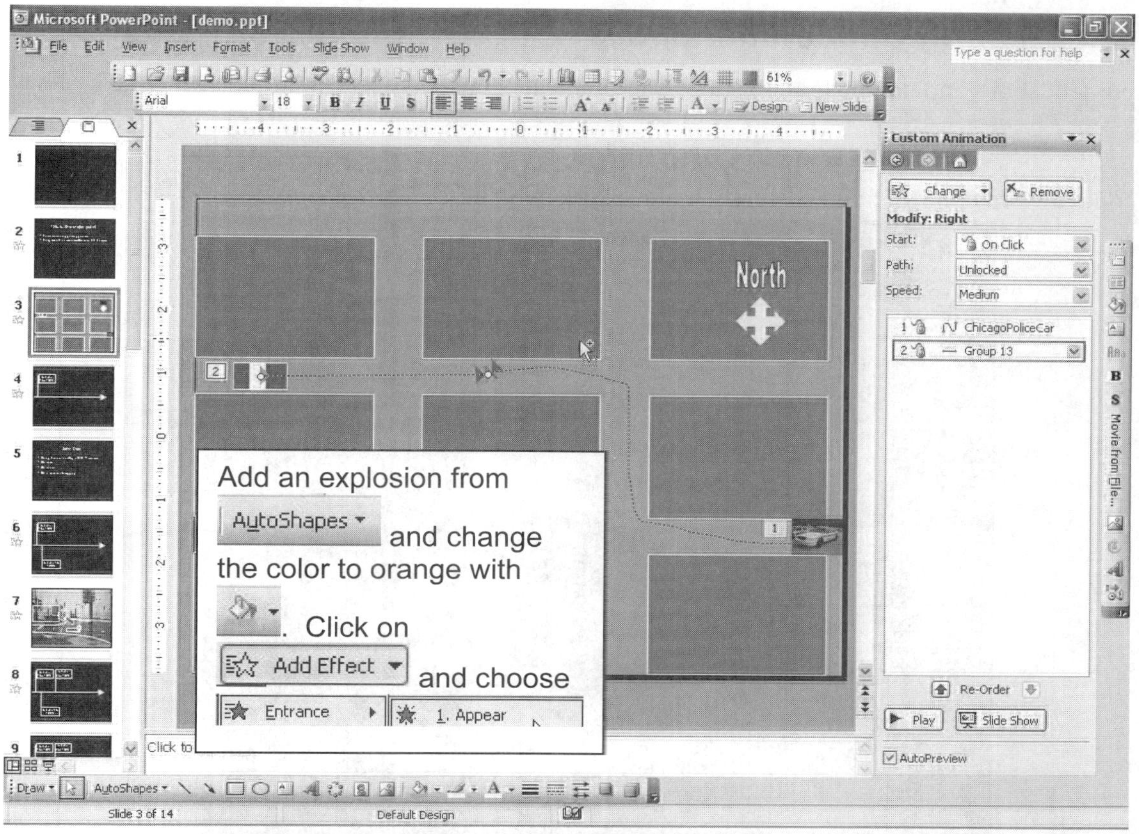
Microsoft PowerPoint - [demo.ppt]
Add an explosion from
AutoShapes
and change the color to orange with
. Click on
Add Effect
and choose
Entrance
1. Appear
Custom Animation
Modify: Right
ChicagoPoliceCar
Group 13
North

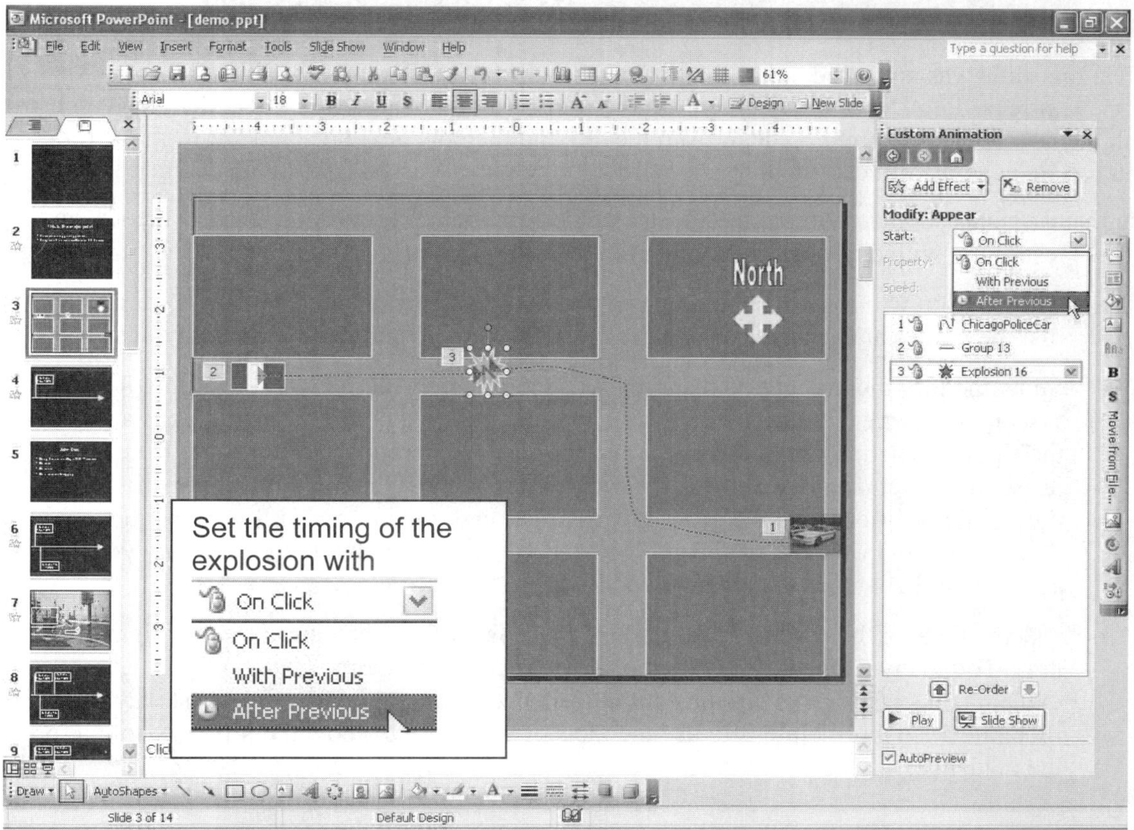
Microsoft PowerPoint - [demo.ppt]
Set the timing of the explosion with
On Click
On Click
With Previous
After Previous
Custom Animation
Modify: Appear
ChicagoPoliceCar
Group 13
Explosion 16
North

Creating Conceptual Slides

Argument slides and demonstrative slides communicate concepts and explain ideas.

Compare and contrast

A compare and contrast slide is simply a blank slide with a line down the middle.

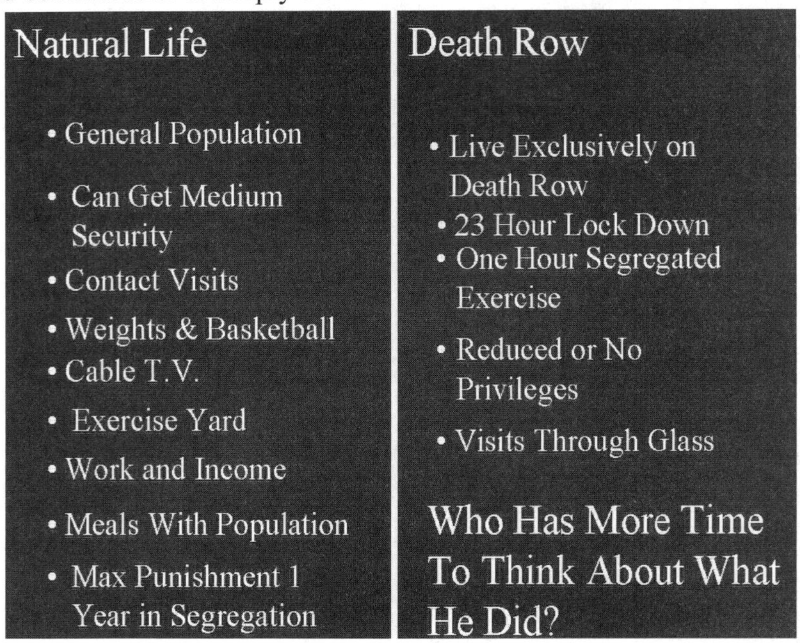

When this slide was animated, all of the text came in from the left regarding Natural Life. And all the text regarding Death Row came from the right. Another animation effect that you can use with this is to have one point come in from the left and then the next one come in from the right. You can manage the effect with animation order, which is discussed later in the chapter.

Argument visuals should choreograph the use of photographs, diagrams, physical evidence, and witness testimony with appropriate jury instructions.

- Quotes from witnesses must be highlighted and then corroborated so that the jurors trust that the quotes are accurate. Consider blowing them up and putting them in a visual.
- Show the jury the instruction that they will see before breaking it up or turning it into a visual. This way the jurors will be able to go into the stack of jury instructions and pull the right instruction out of the pile when they are deliberating. If you come from a jurisdiction that does not allow the jurors to have the jury instructions in the jury room during deliberation, read the exact jury instruction to the jurors. This way the judge will corroborate you when he or she reads it, and you will be showing the jury how your analysis of the instruction is intellectually honest.
- Use the facts of the case to illustrate how these facts should be interpreted in light of the law. Too many advocates rely on the use of clichés like sports analogies or rainstorms to explain concepts such as circumstantial evidence or accountability. The best way to illustrate a legal principle is to use the facts of your case to show the jury how to interpret the evidence.

Bull's-eye

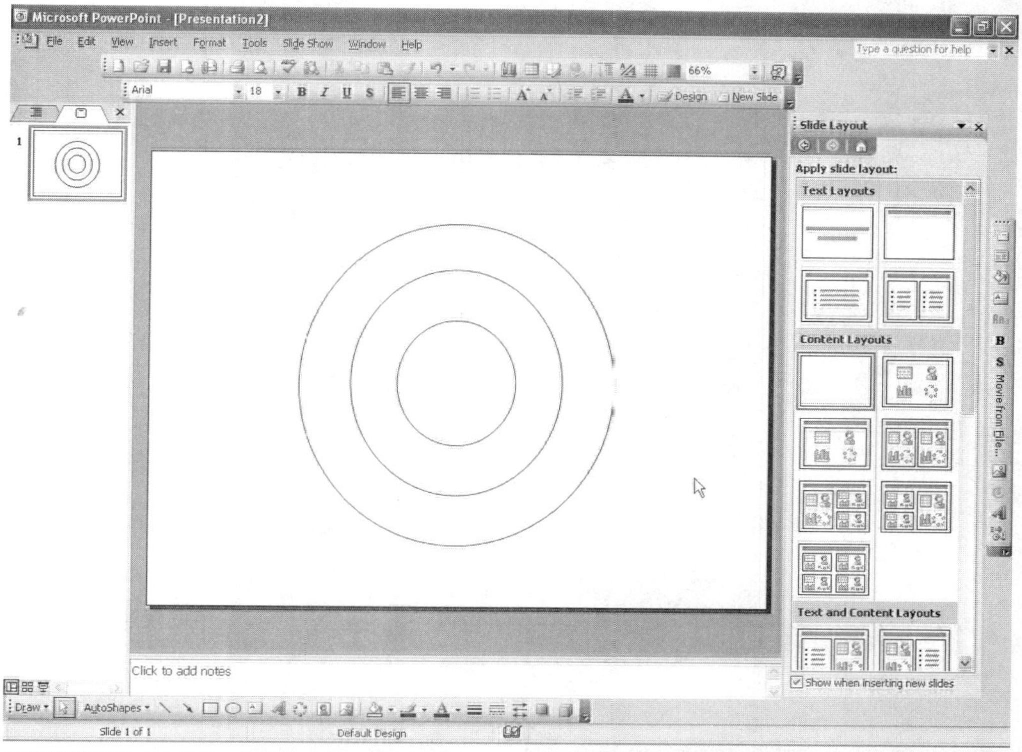
Microsoft PowerPoint - [Presentation2]
File Edit View Insert Format Tools Slide Show Window Help
Type a question for help
66%
Arial 18
Design New Slide
Slide Layout
Apply slide layout:
Text Layouts
Content Layouts
Text and Content Layouts
Show when inserting new slides
Click to add notes
Draw AutoShapes
Slide 1 of 1
Default Design

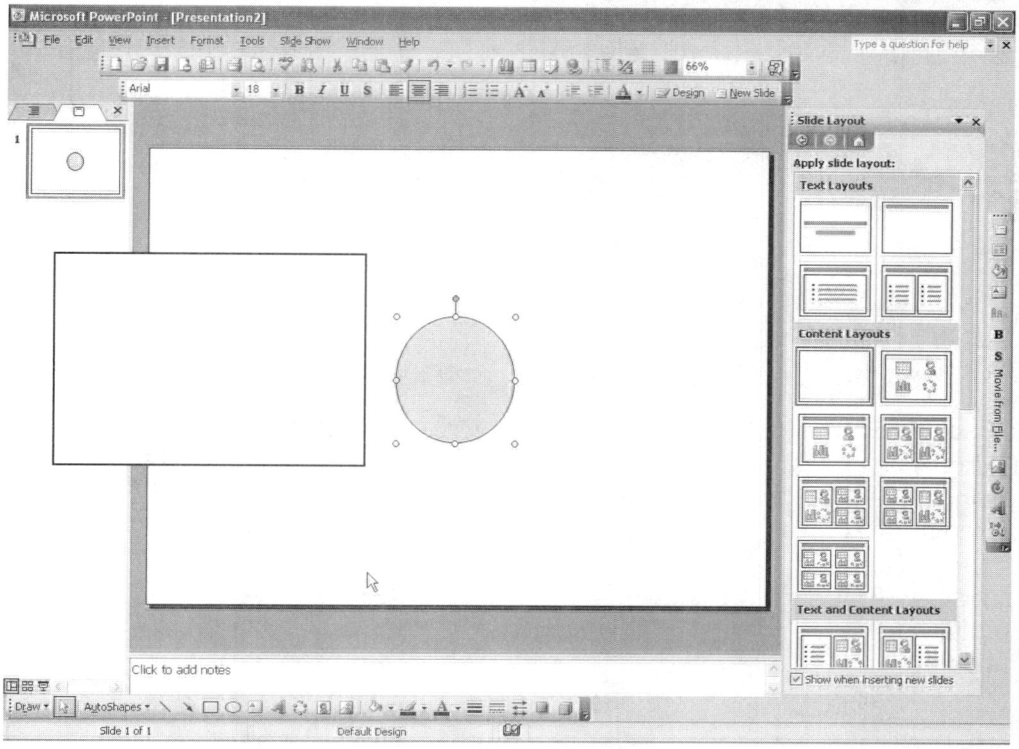
Microsoft PowerPoint - [Presentation2]
File Edit View Insert Format Tools Slide Show Window Help
Type a question for help
66%
Arial 18
Design New Slide
Slide Layout
Apply slide layout:
Text Layouts
Content Layouts
Text and Content Layouts
Show when inserting new slides
Click to add notes
Draw AutoShapes
Slide 1 of 1
Default Design

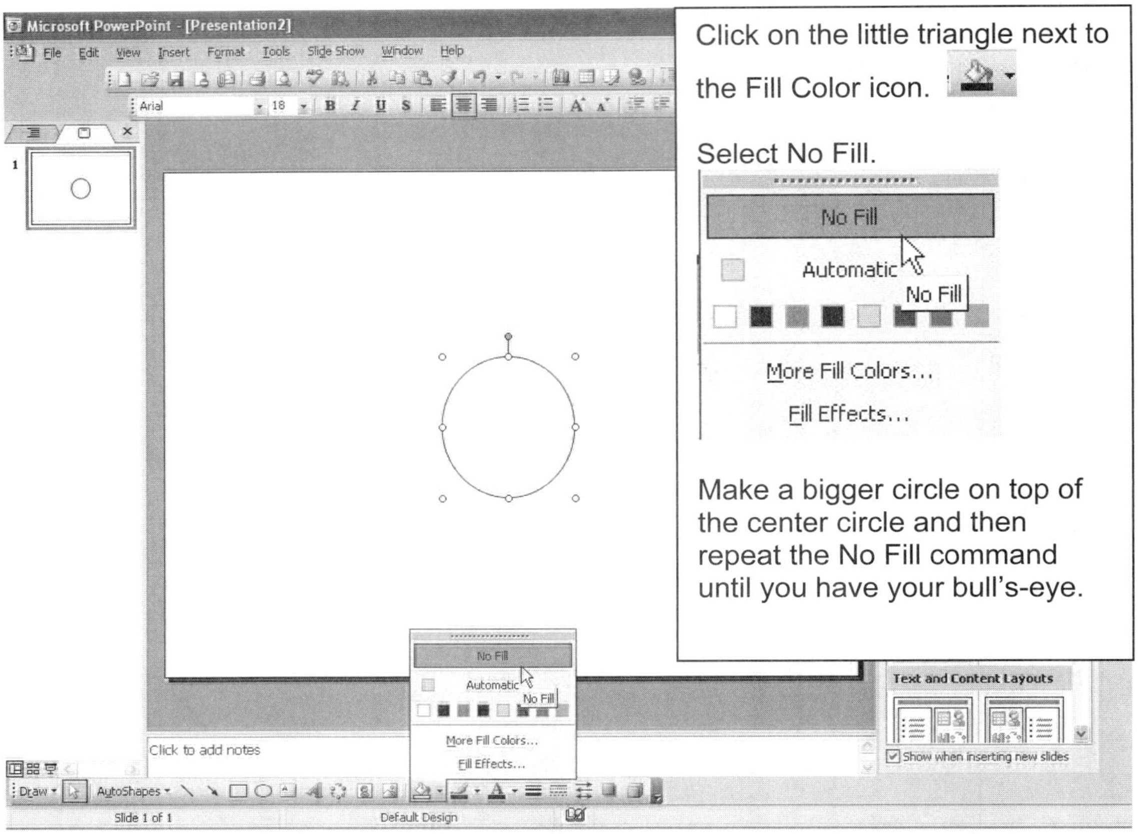

Click on the little triangle next to the Fill Color icon.

Select No Fill.

Make a bigger circle on top of the center circle and then repeat the No Fill command until you have your bull's-eye.

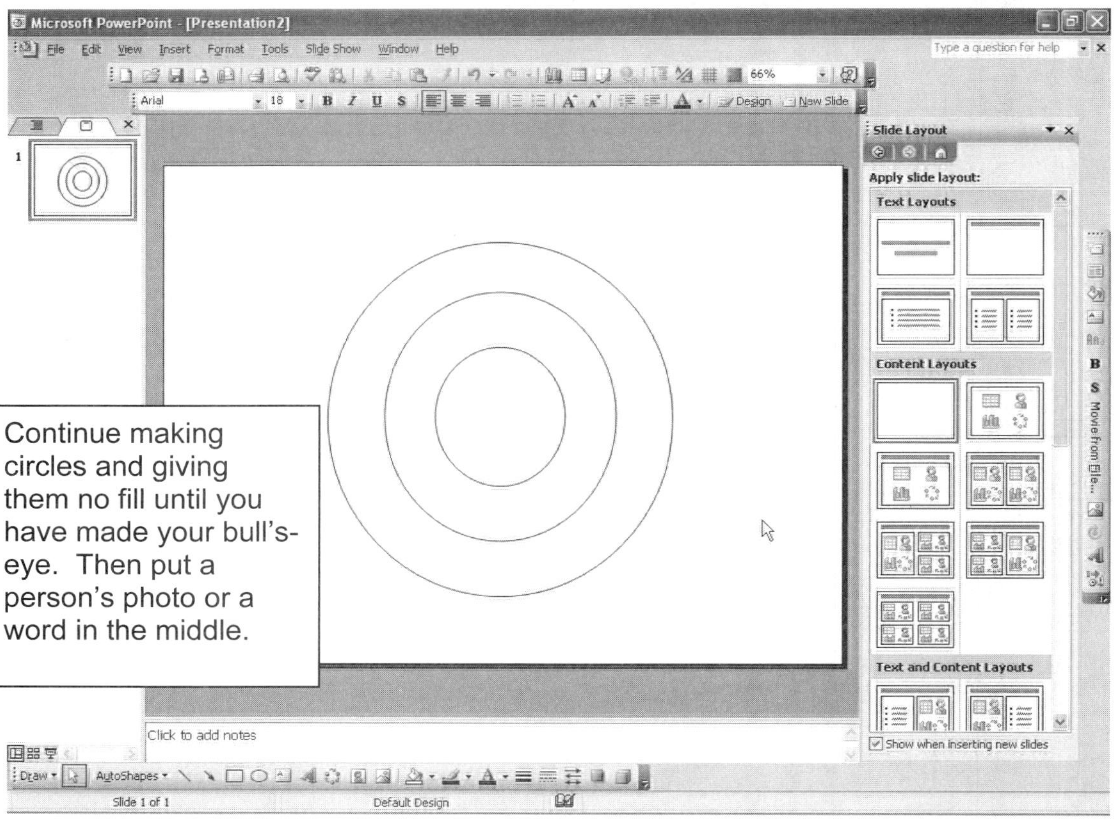

Continue making circles and giving them no fill until you have made your bull's-eye. Then put a person's photo or a word in the middle.

Evidence points to or away from

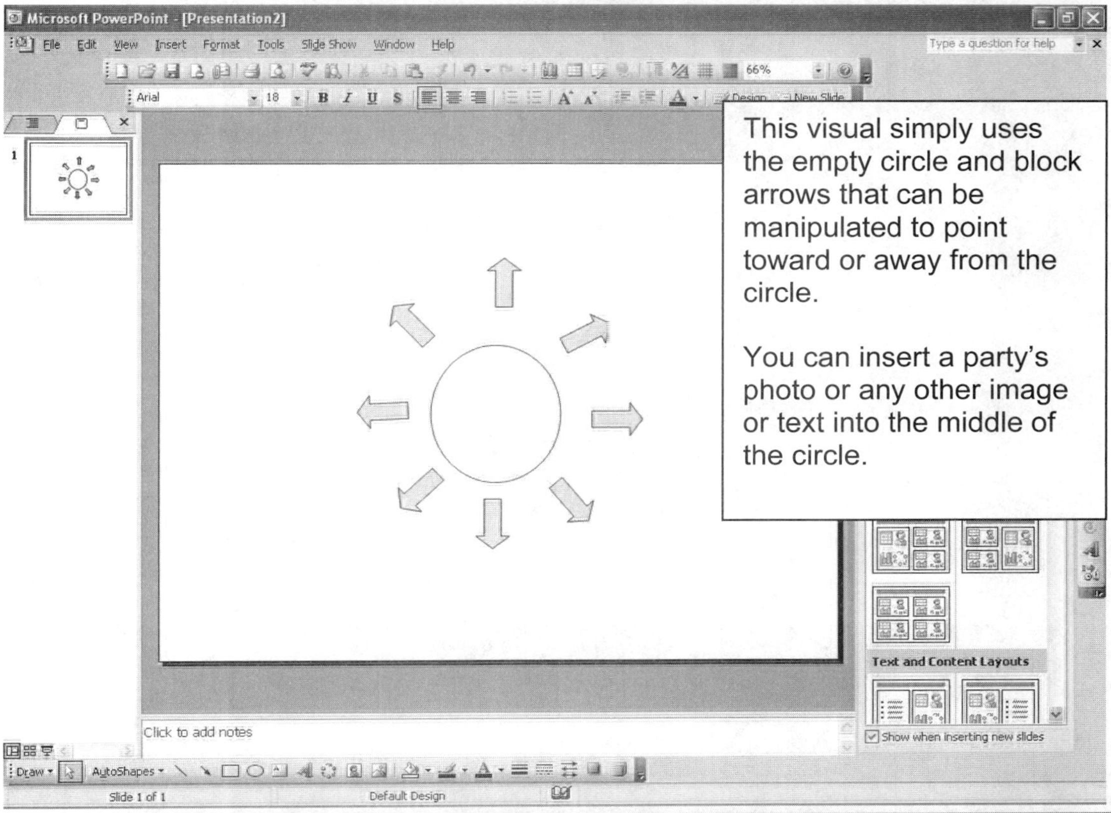

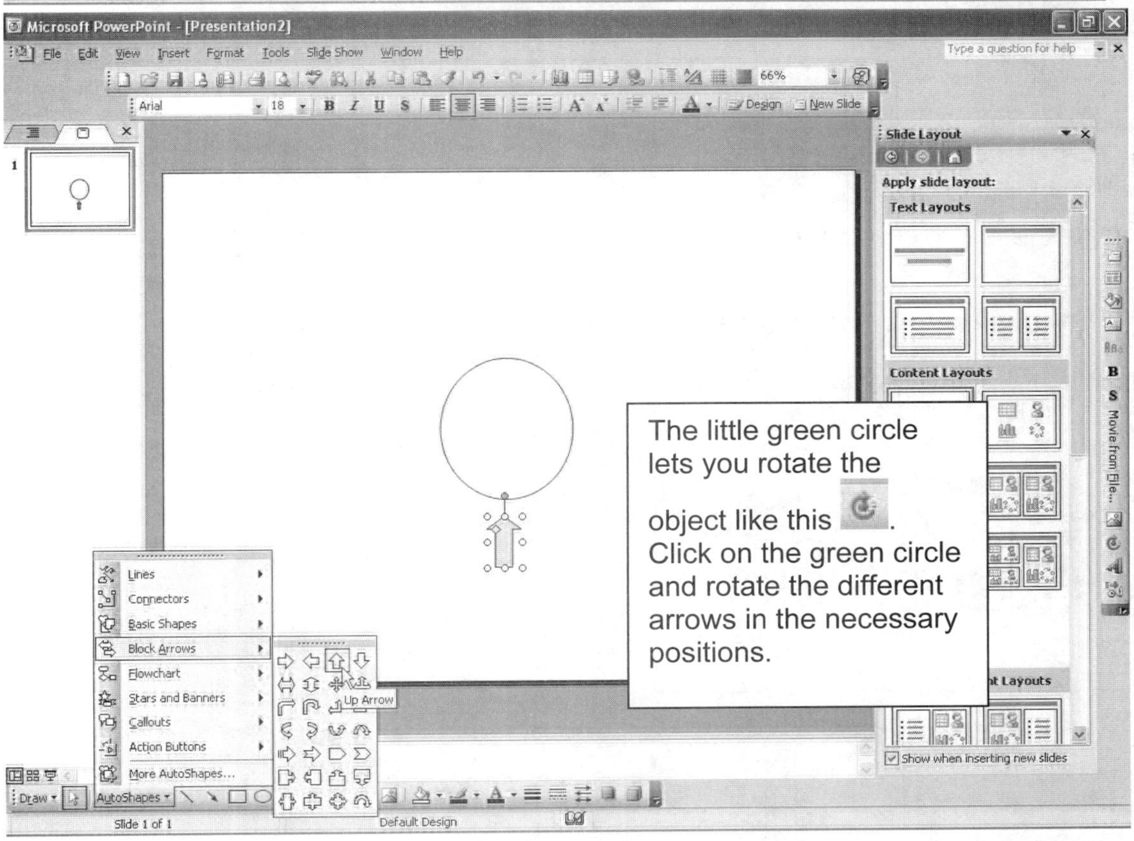

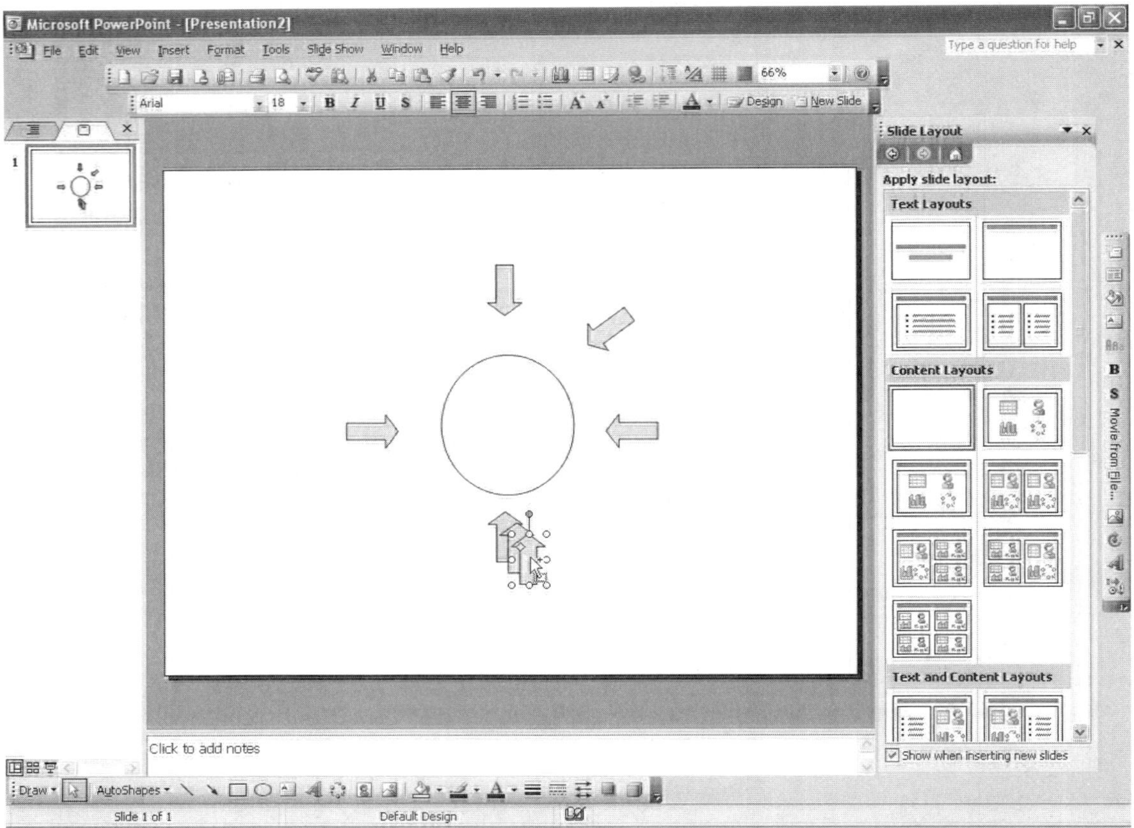
Microsoft PowerPoint - [Presentation2]
File Edit View Insert Format Tools Slide Show Window Help
Type a question for help
Slide Layout
Apply slide layout:
Text Layouts
Content Layouts
Text and Content Layouts
Show when inserting new slides
Click to add notes
Slide 1 of 1
Default Design

Cornered

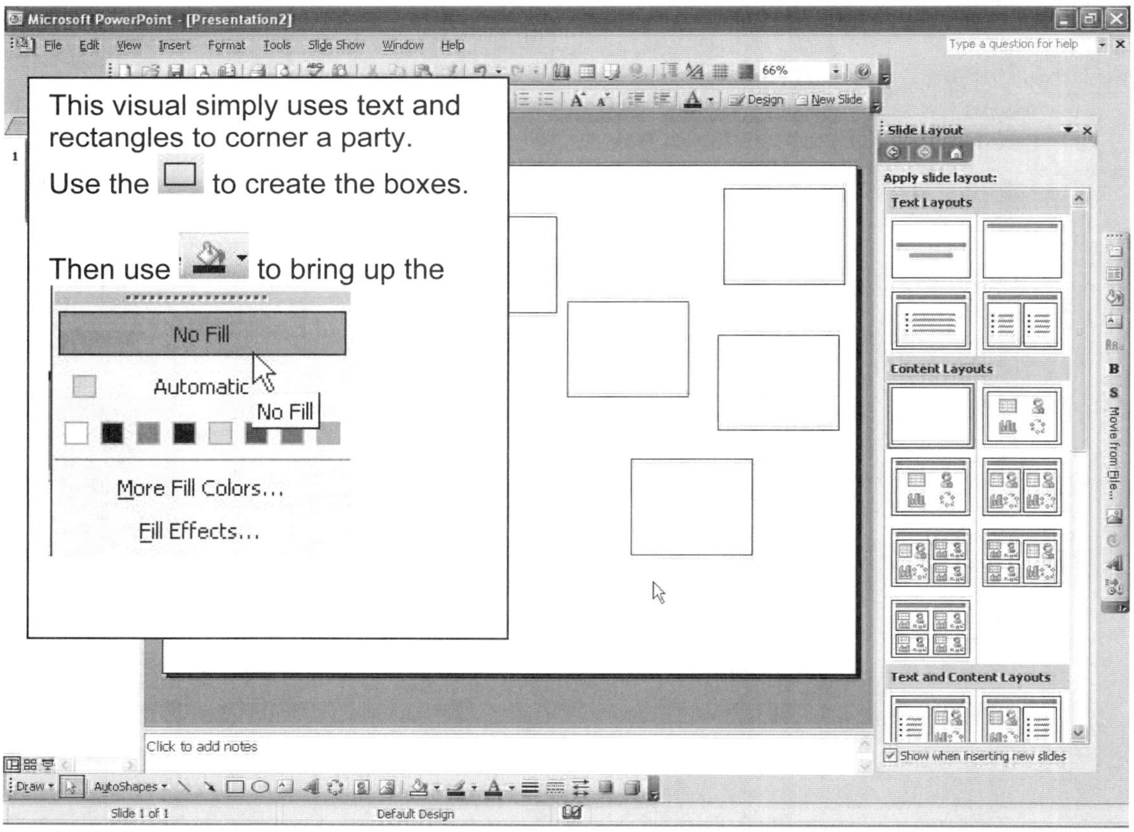
Microsoft PowerPoint - [Presentation2]
This visual simply uses text and rectangles to corner a party.
Use the to create the boxes.
Then use to bring up the
No Fill
Automatic
No Fill
More Fill Colors...
Fill Effects...
Slide Layout
Apply slide layout:
Text Layouts
Content Layouts
Text and Content Layouts
Show when inserting new slides
Click to add notes
Slide 1 of 1
Default Design

Making Timelines

The key to making a timeline that allows you to go back and forth between the timeline slides is to make the last slide first and to delete unnecessary information from copies of the final slide.

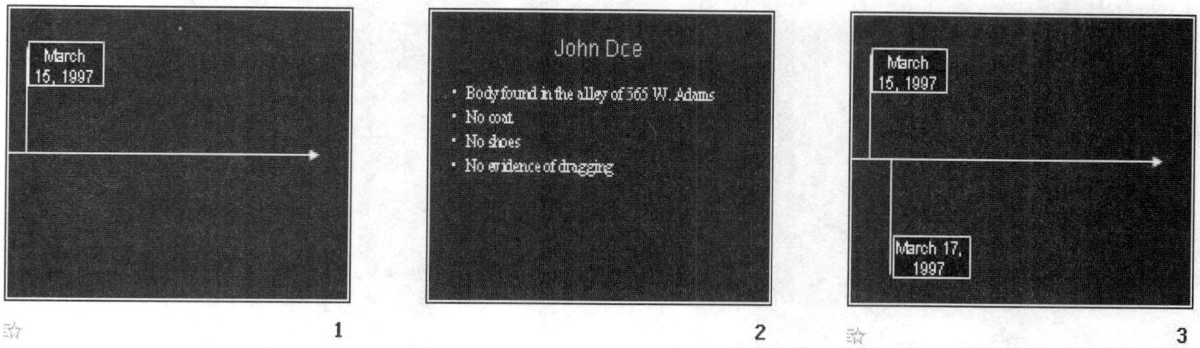

The following screen captures take you step by step through the process for making a timeline. If you are going to make a timeline for a specific case, make a new slide presentation and format the Master slide the same way as explained earlier in this chapter. For this chapter's purposes, we will simply add a blank slide by clicking on the New Slide icon on your toolbar.

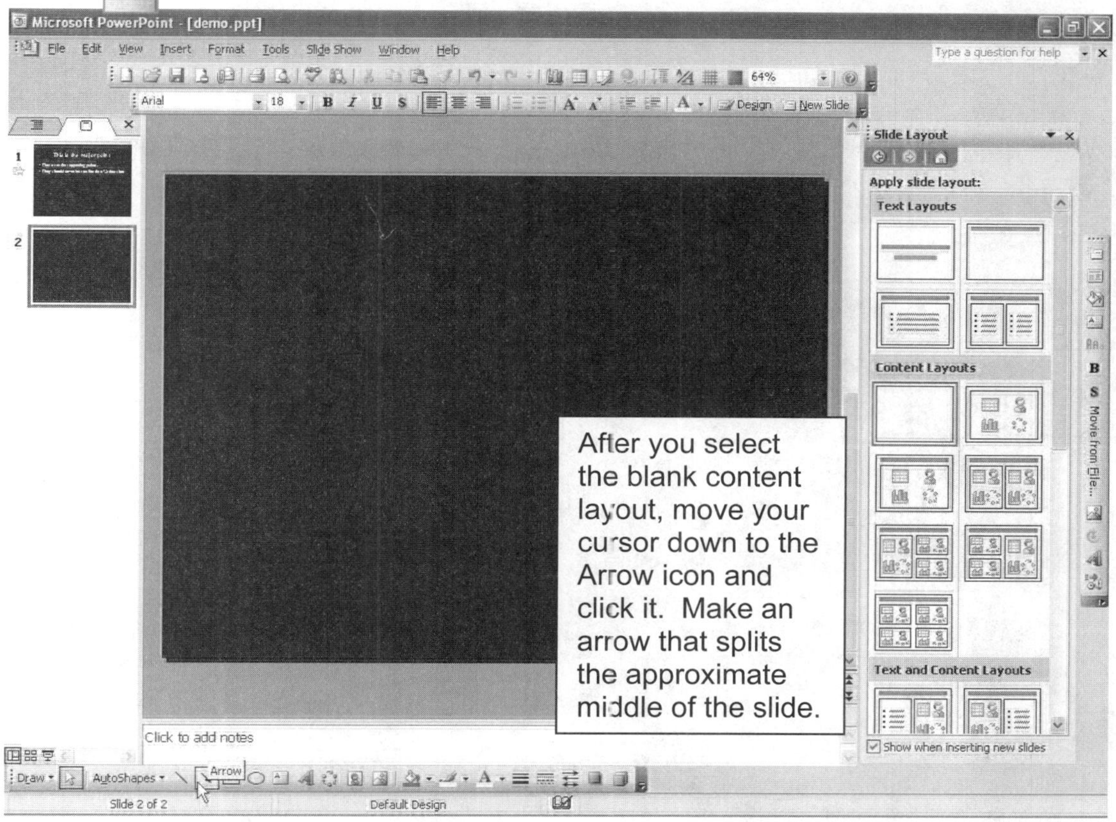

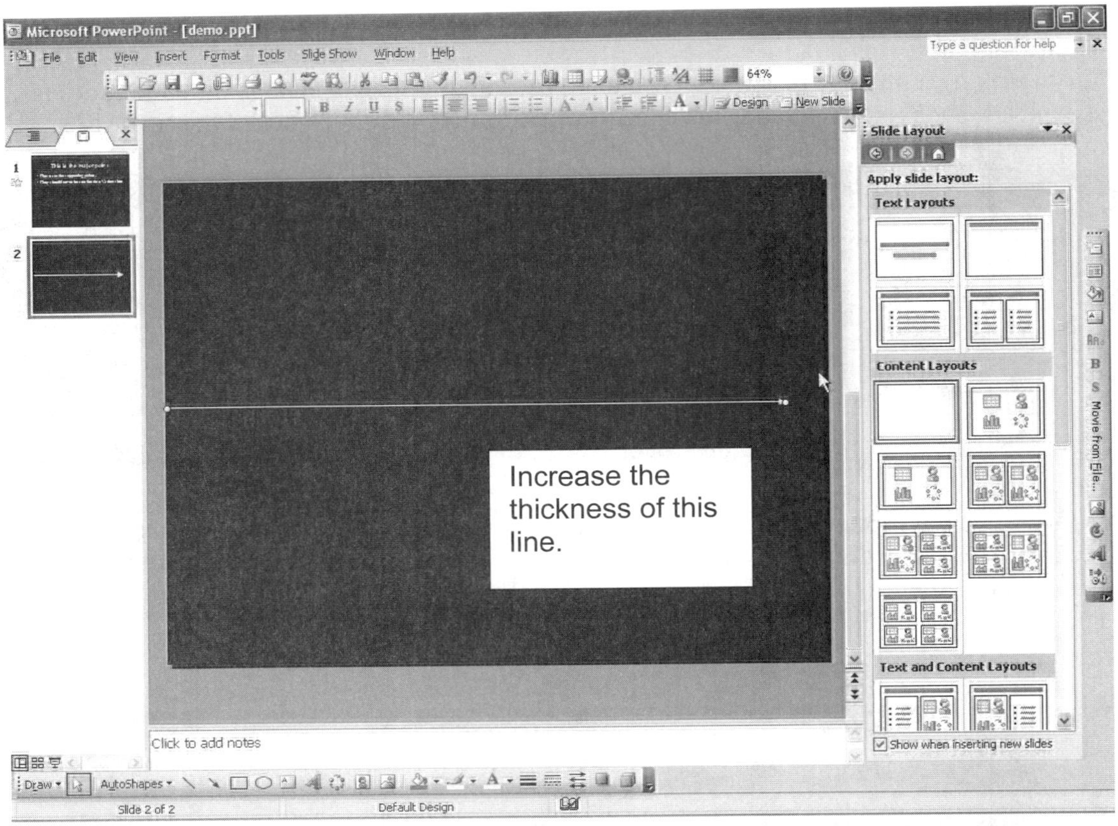
Microsoft PowerPoint - [demo.ppt]
Slide Layout
Apply slide layout:
Text Layouts
Content Layouts
Text and Content Layouts
Increase the thickness of this line.
Click to add notes
Show when inserting new slides
Slide 2 of 2
Default Design

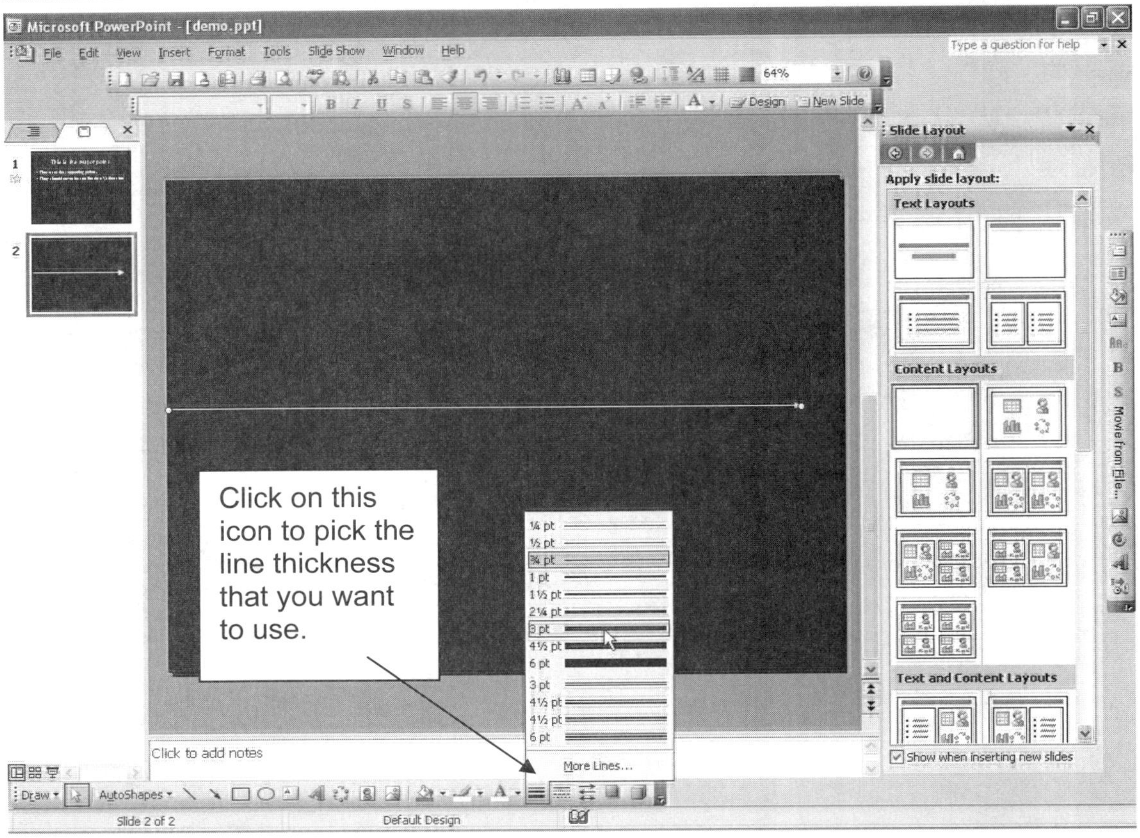
Microsoft PowerPoint - [demo.ppt]
Slide Layout
Apply slide layout:
Text Layouts
Content Layouts
Text and Content Layouts
Click on this icon to pick the line thickness that you want to use.
¼ pt
½ pt
¾ pt
1 pt
1½ pt
2¼ pt
3 pt
4½ pt
6 pt
3 pt
4½ pt
4½ pt
6 pt
More Lines...
Click to add notes
Show when inserting new slides
Slide 2 of 2
Default Design

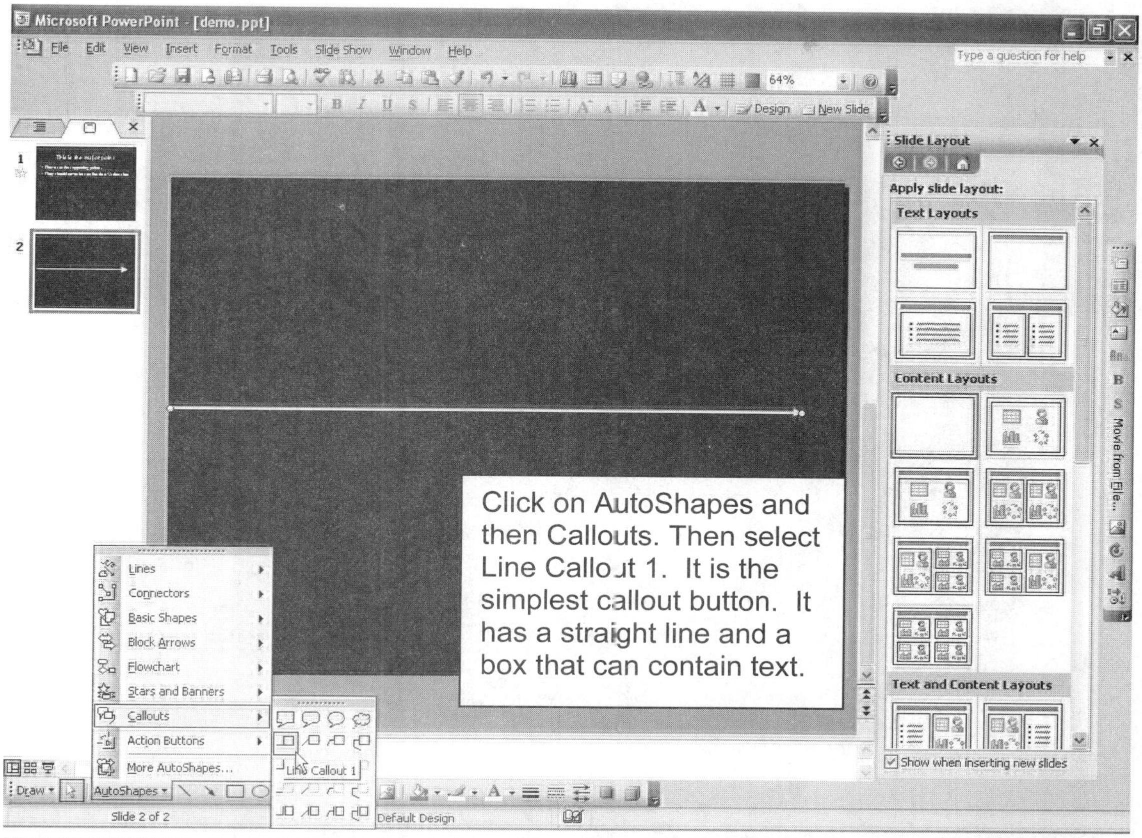
Microsoft PowerPoint - [demo.ppt]
Slide Layout
Apply slide layout:
Text Layouts
Content Layouts
Text and Content Layouts
Show when inserting new slides
Lines
Connectors
Basic Shapes
Block Arrows
Flowchart
Stars and Banners
Callouts
Action Buttons
More AutoShapes...
Line Callout 1
AutoShapes
Slide 2 of 2
Default Design
Click on AutoShapes and then Callouts. Then select Line Callout 1. It is the simplest callout button. It has a straight line and a box that can contain text.

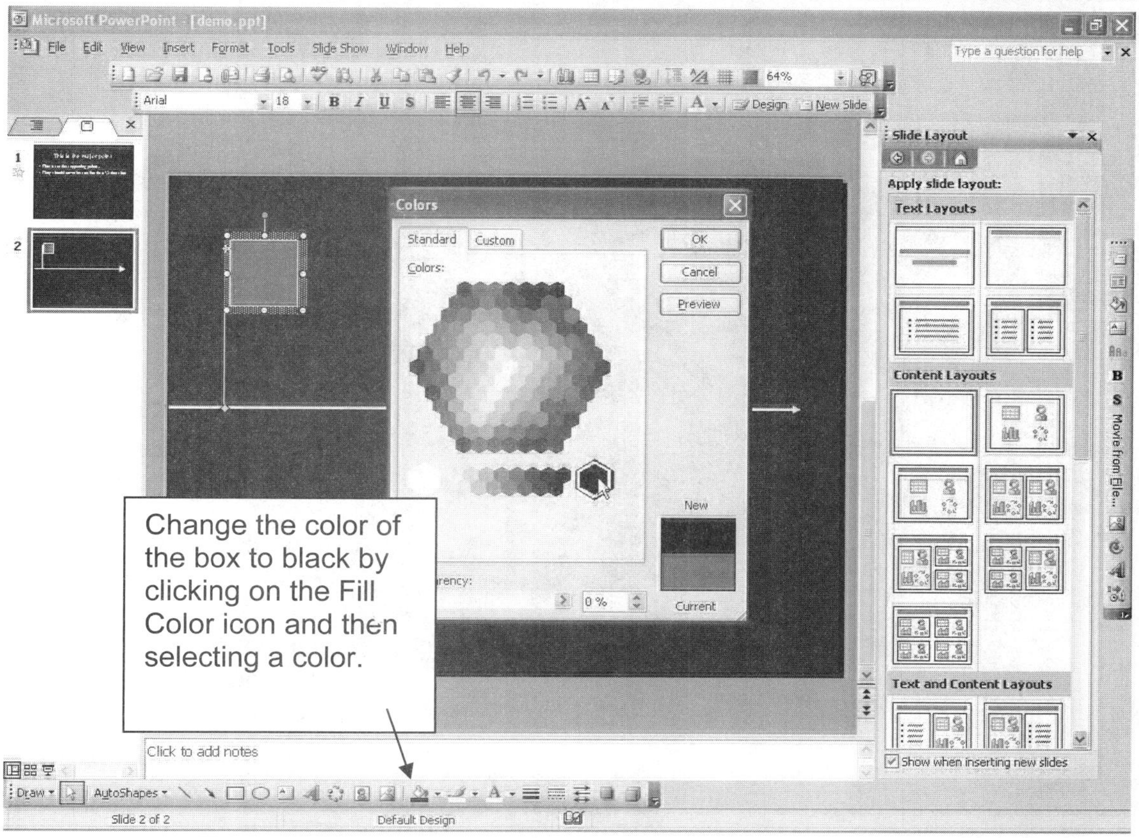
Microsoft PowerPoint - [demo.ppt]
Colors
Standard
Custom
Colors:
OK
Cancel
Preview
New
Current
Slide Layout
Apply slide layout:
Text Layouts
Content Layouts
Text and Content Layouts
Show when inserting new slides
Click to add notes
Slide 2 of 2
Default Design
Change the color of the box to black by clicking on the Fill Color icon and then selecting a color.

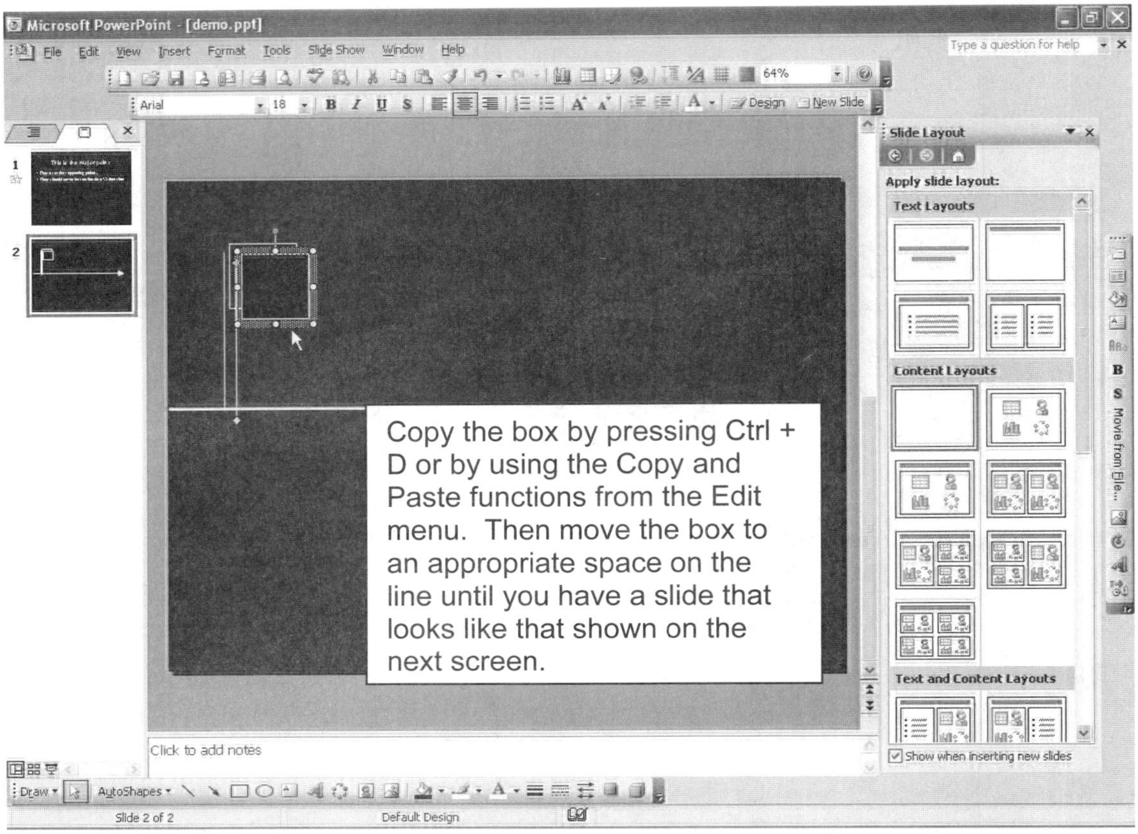
Microsoft PowerPoint - [demo.ppt]
File Edit View Insert Format Tools Slide Show Window Help
Slide Layout
Apply slide layout:
Text Layouts
Content Layouts
Text and Content Layouts
Copy the box by pressing Ctrl + D or by using the Copy and Paste functions from the Edit menu. Then move the box to an appropriate space on the line until you have a slide that looks like that shown on the next screen.
Click to add notes
Show when inserting new slides
Slide 2 of 2
Default Design

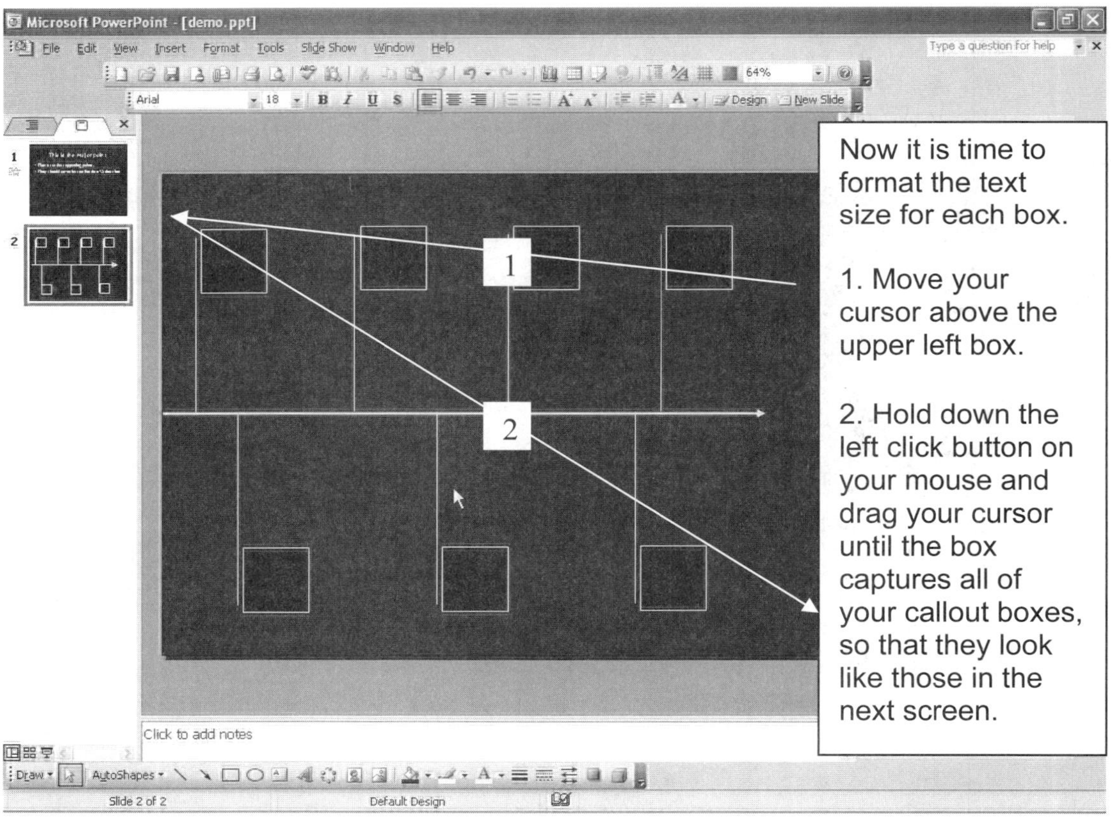
Microsoft PowerPoint - [demo.ppt]
File Edit View Insert Format Tools Slide Show Window Help
Now it is time to format the text size for each box.
1. Move your cursor above the upper left box.
2. Hold down the left click button on your mouse and drag your cursor until the box captures all of your callout boxes, so that they look like those in the next screen.
1
2
Click to add notes
Slide 2 of 2
Default Design

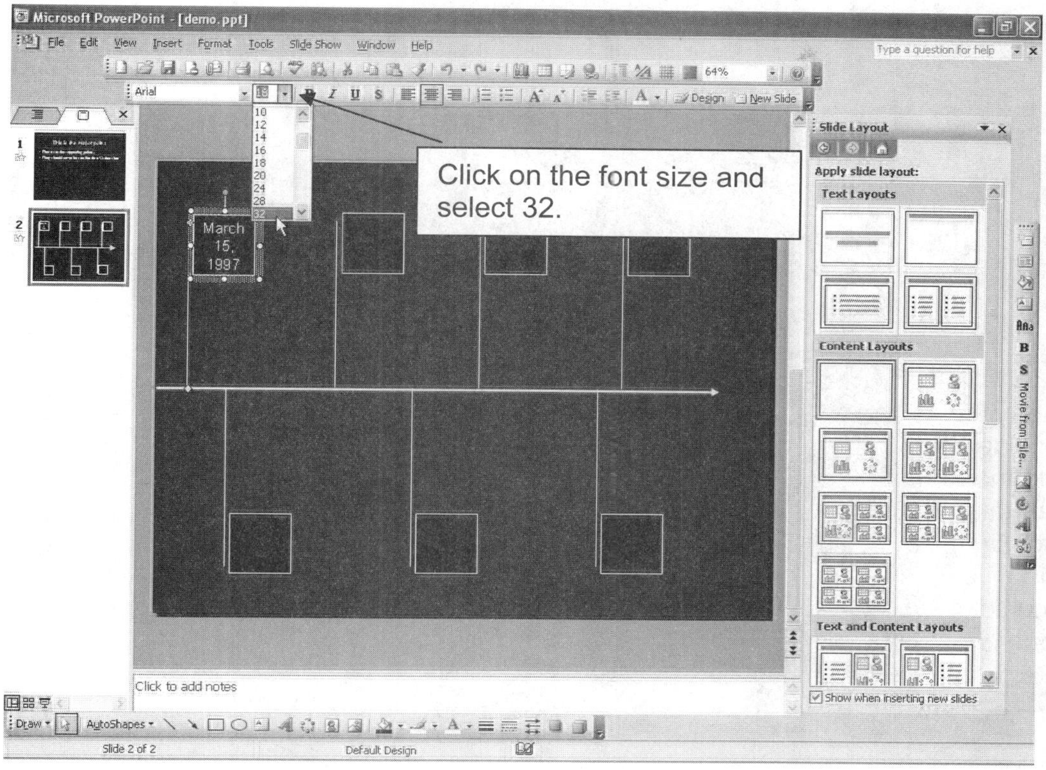
Microsoft PowerPoint - [demo.ppt]
Click on the font size and select 32.
March 15, 1997
Slide Layout
Apply slide layout:
Text Layouts
Content Layouts
Text and Content Layouts
Show when inserting new slides
Click to add notes
Slide 2 of 2
Default Design

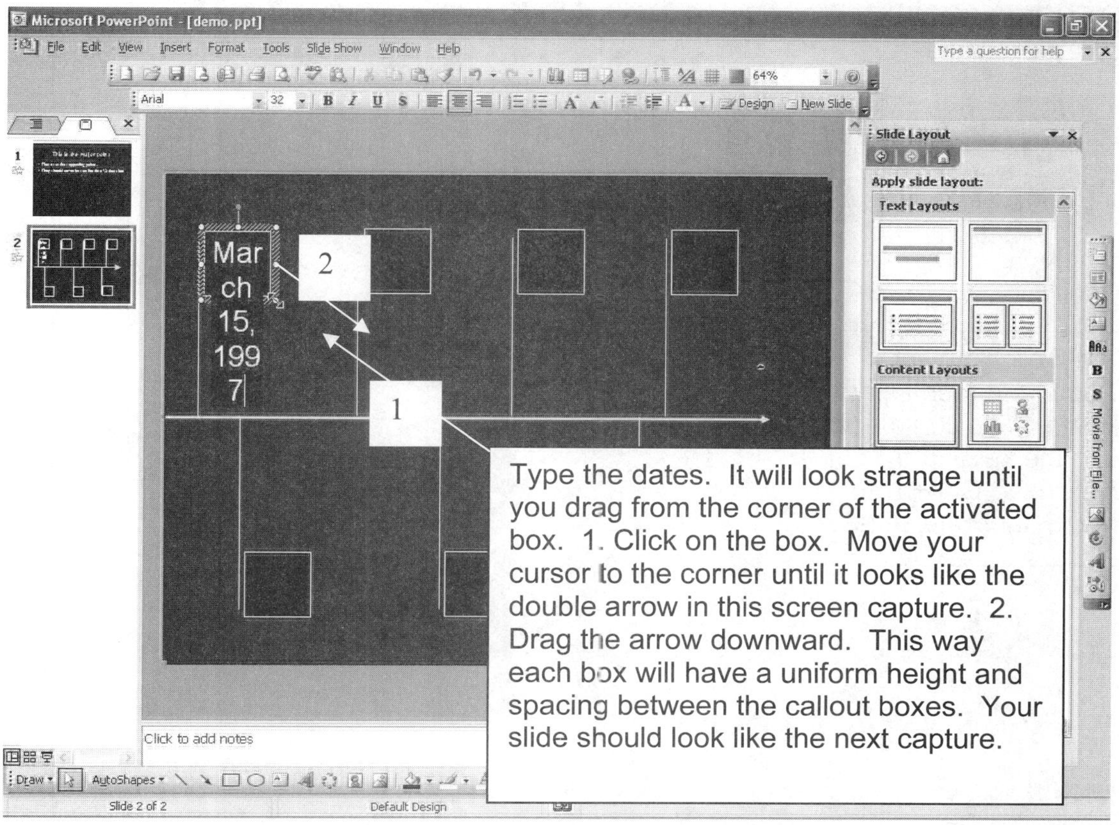
Microsoft PowerPoint - [demo.ppt]
Mar ch 15, 199 7
2
1
Type the dates. It will look strange until you drag from the corner of the activated box. 1. Click on the box. Move your cursor to the corner until it looks like the double arrow in this screen capture. 2. Drag the arrow downward. This way each box will have a uniform height and spacing between the callout boxes. Your slide should look like the next capture.
Slide Layout
Apply slide layout:
Text Layouts
Content Layouts
Click to add notes
Slide 2 of 2
Default Design

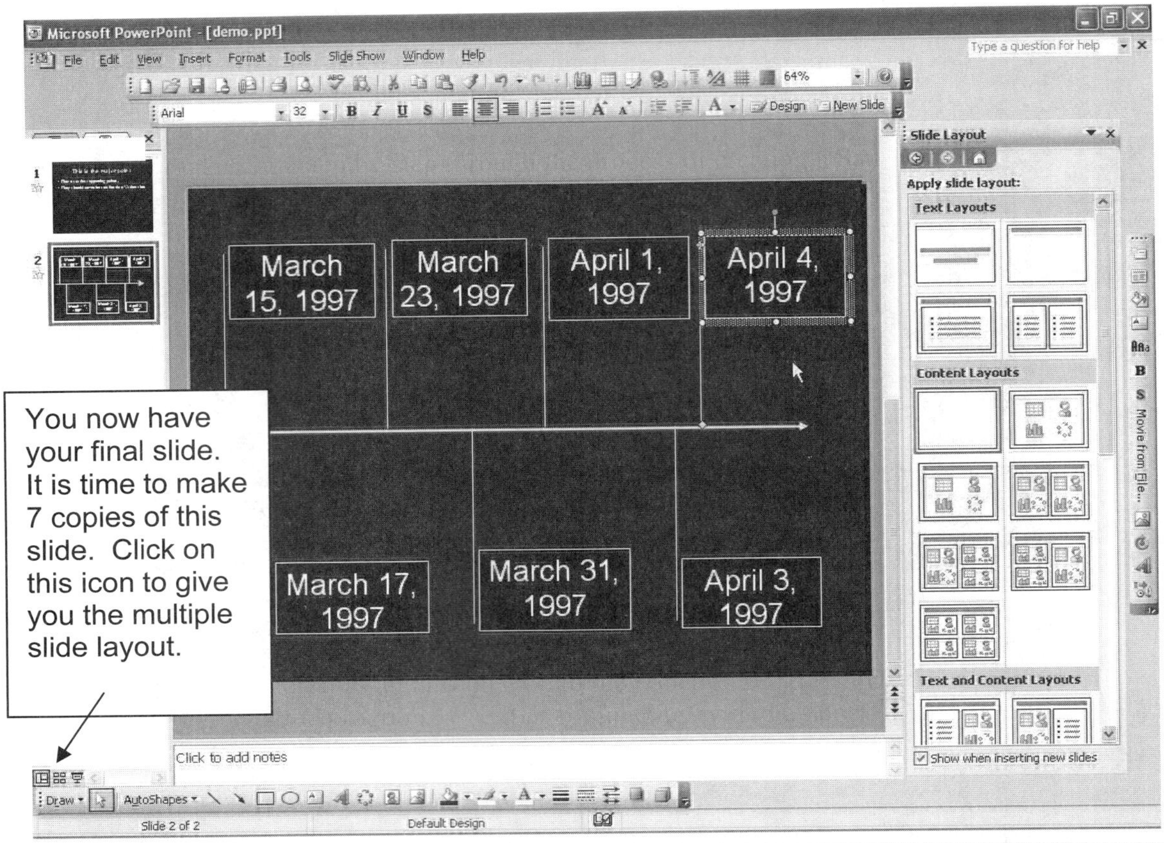
Microsoft PowerPoint - [demo.ppt]
File Edit View Insert Format Tools Slide Show Window Help
Slide Layout
Apply slide layout:
Text Layouts
Content Layouts
Text and Content Layouts
March 15, 1997
March 23, 1997
April 1, 1997
April 4, 1997
March 17, 1997
March 31, 1997
April 3, 1997
You now have your final slide. It is time to make 7 copies of this slide. Click on this icon to give you the multiple slide layout.
Click to add notes
Show when inserting new slides
Slide 2 of 2
Default Design

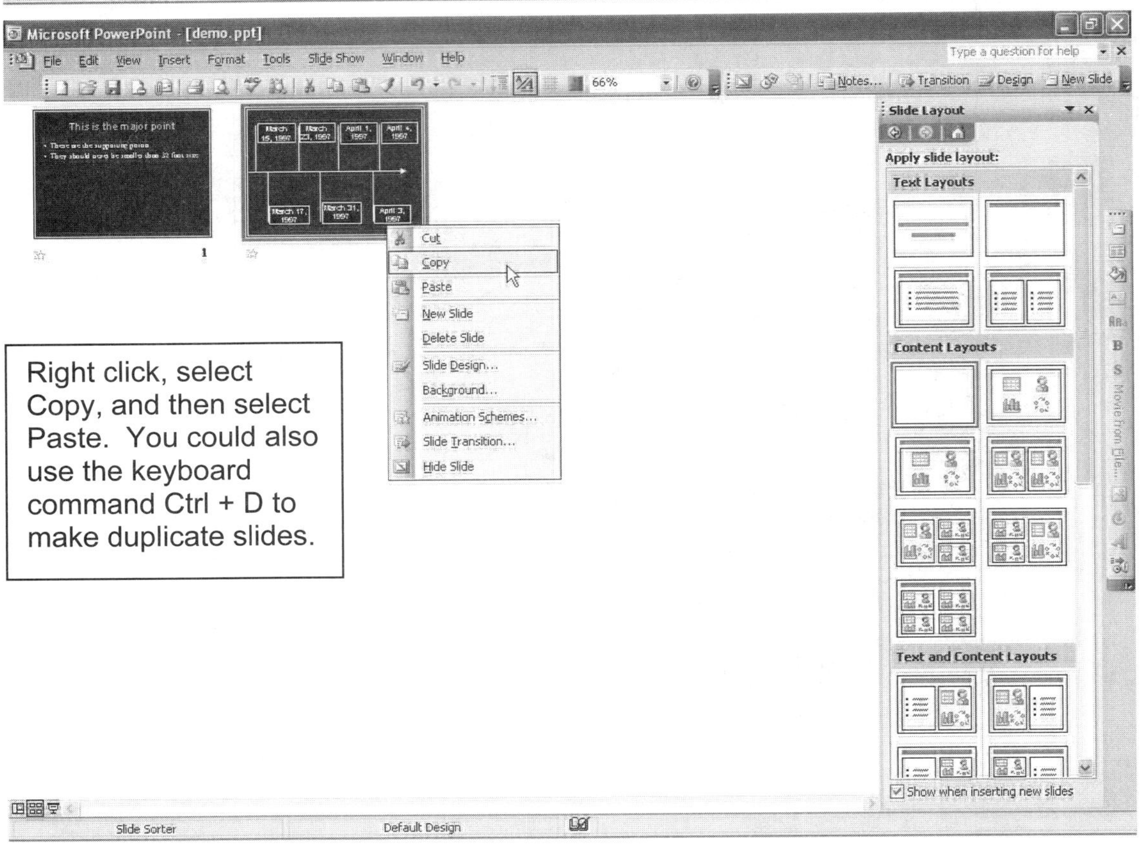
Microsoft PowerPoint - [demo.ppt]
File Edit View Insert Format Tools Slide Show Window Help
This is the major point
Cut
Copy
Paste
New Slide
Delete Slide
Slide Design...
Background...
Animation Schemes...
Slide Transition...
Hide Slide
Right click, select Copy, and then select Paste. You could also use the keyboard command Ctrl + D to make duplicate slides.
Slide Layout
Apply slide layout:
Text Layouts
Content Layouts
Text and Content Layouts
Show when inserting new slides
Slide Sorter
Default Design

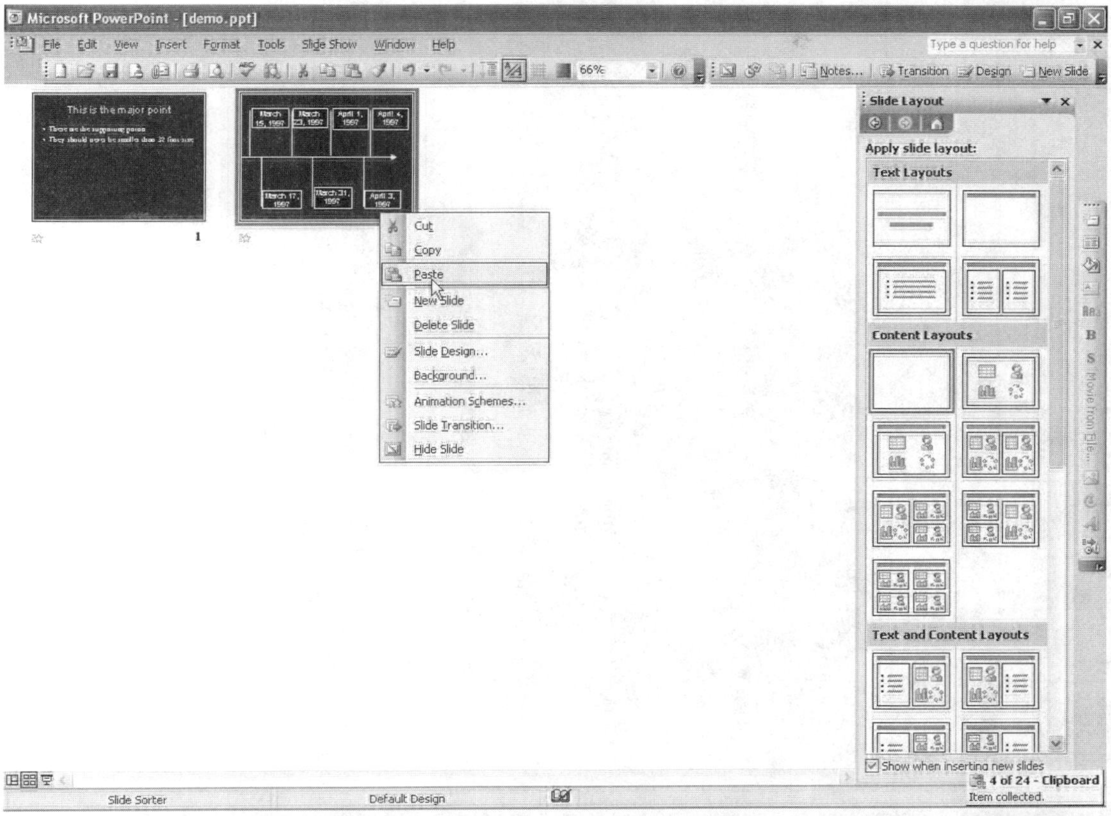
Microsoft PowerPoint - [demo.ppt]
File Edit View Insert Format Tools Slide Show Window Help
Type a question for help
Notes... Transition Design New Slide
This is the major point
Cut
Copy
Paste
New Slide
Delete Slide
Slide Design...
Background...
Animation Schemes...
Slide Transition...
Hide Slide
Slide Layout
Apply slide layout:
Text Layouts
Content Layouts
Text and Content Layouts
Show when inserting new slides
4 of 24 - Clipboard
Item collected.
Slide Sorter
Default Design

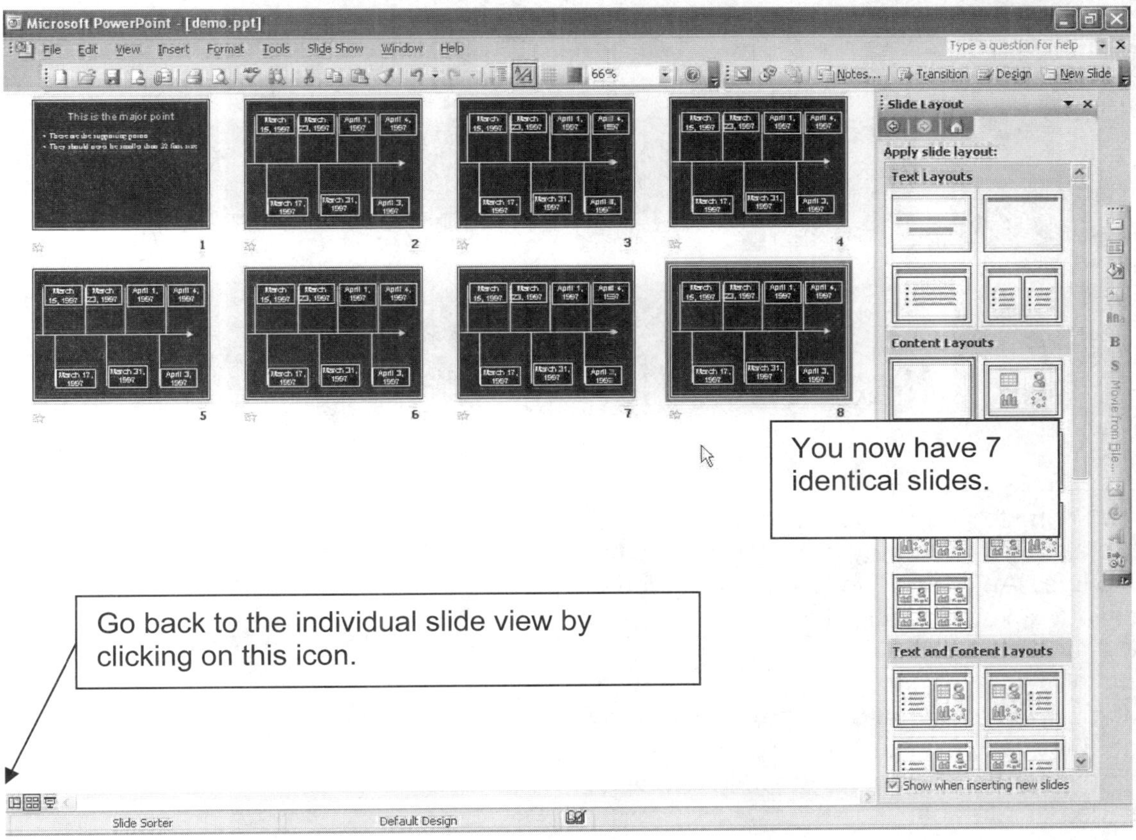
Microsoft PowerPoint - [demo.ppt]
File Edit View Insert Format Tools Slide Show Window Help
Type a question for help
Notes... Transition Design New Slide
This is the major point
Slide Layout
Apply slide layout:
Text Layouts
Content Layouts
Text and Content Layouts
Show when inserting new slides
Slide Sorter
Default Design
You now have 7 identical slides.
Go back to the individual slide view by clicking on this icon.

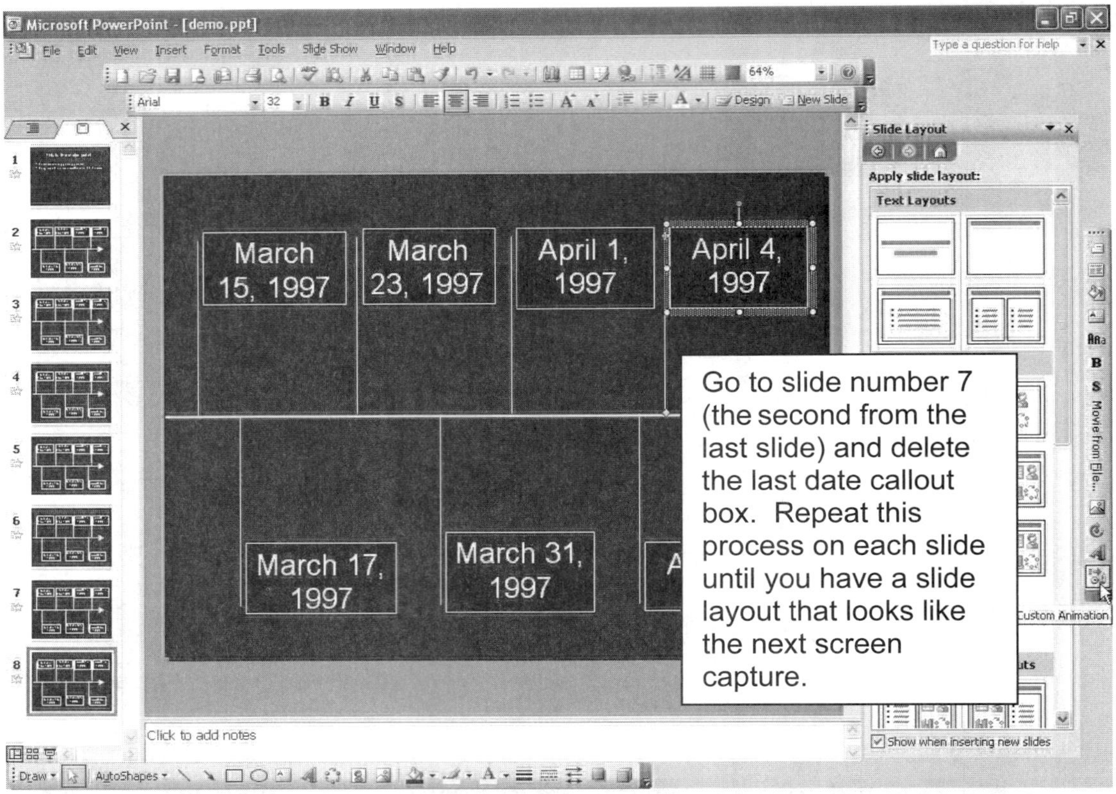

Go to slide number 7 (the second from the last slide) and delete the last date callout box. Repeat this process on each slide until you have a slide layout that looks like the next screen capture.

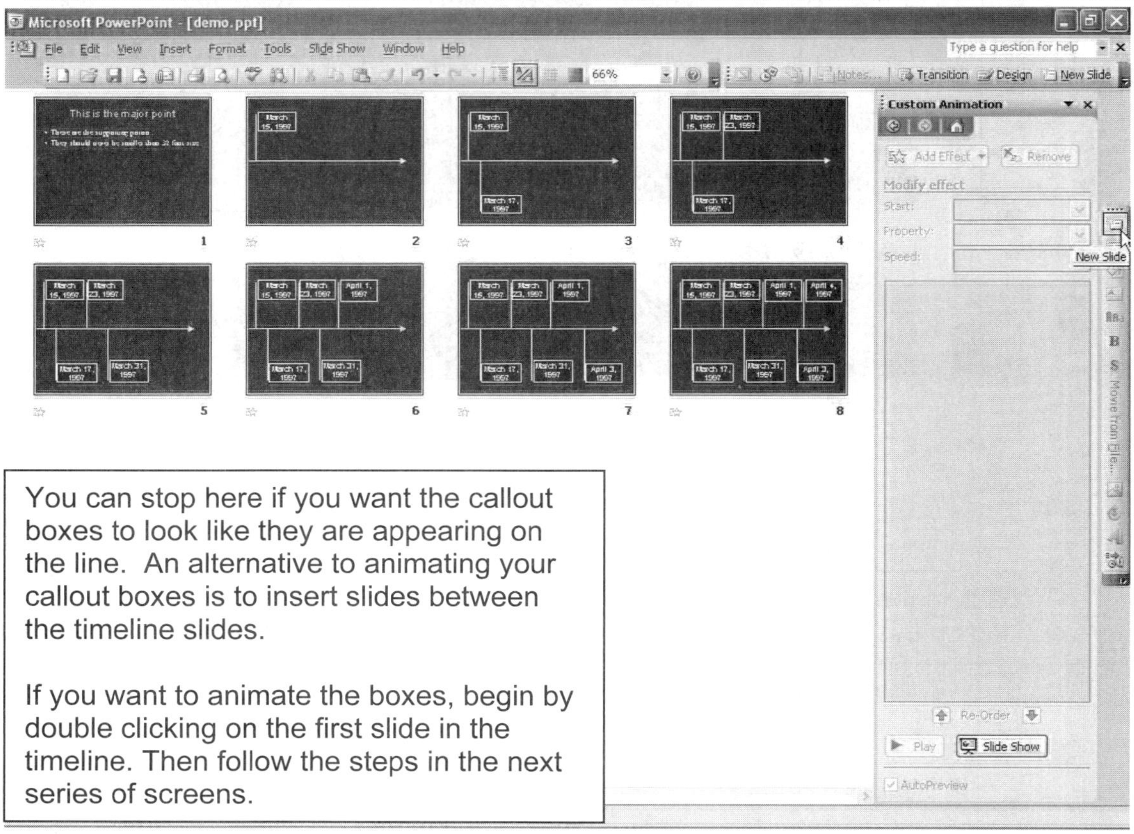

You can stop here if you want the callout boxes to look like they are appearing on the line. An alternative to animating your callout boxes is to insert slides between the timeline slides.

If you want to animate the boxes, begin by double clicking on the first slide in the timeline. Then follow the steps in the next series of screens.

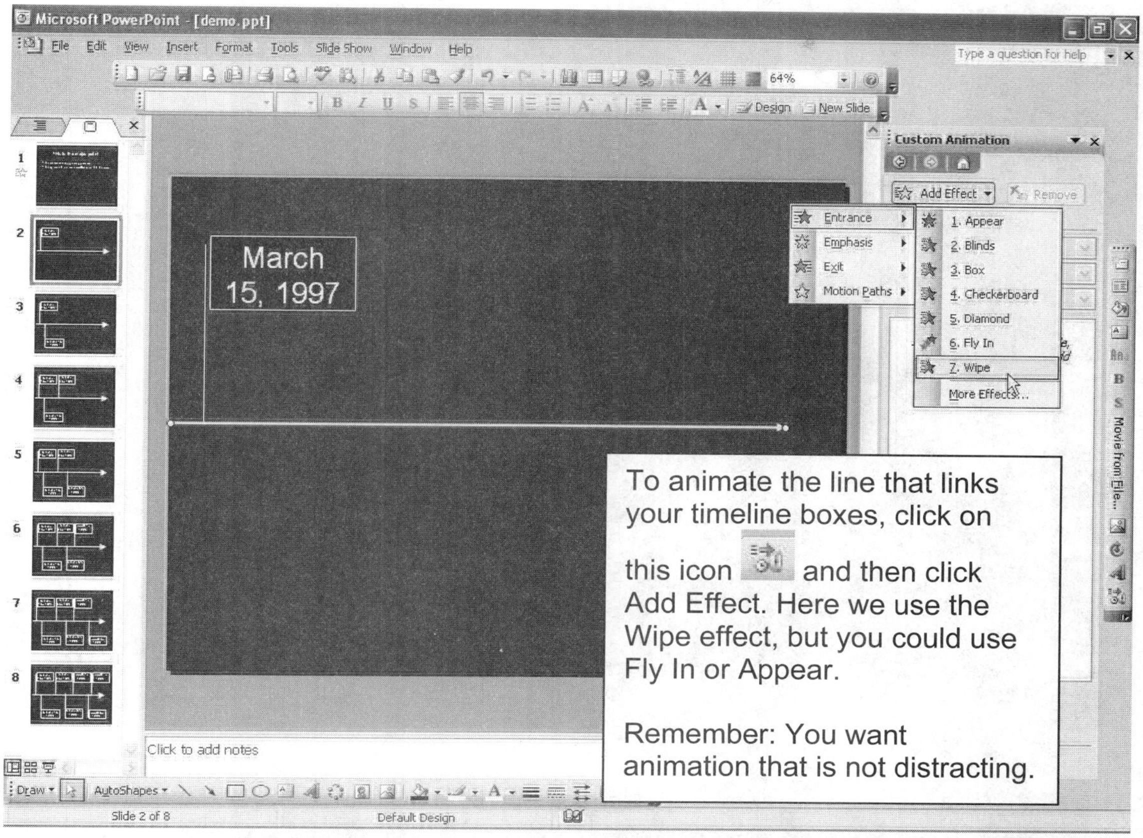
To animate the line that links your timeline boxes, click on this icon and then click Add Effect. Here we use the Wipe effect, but you could use Fly In or Appear.
Remember: You want animation that is not distracting.

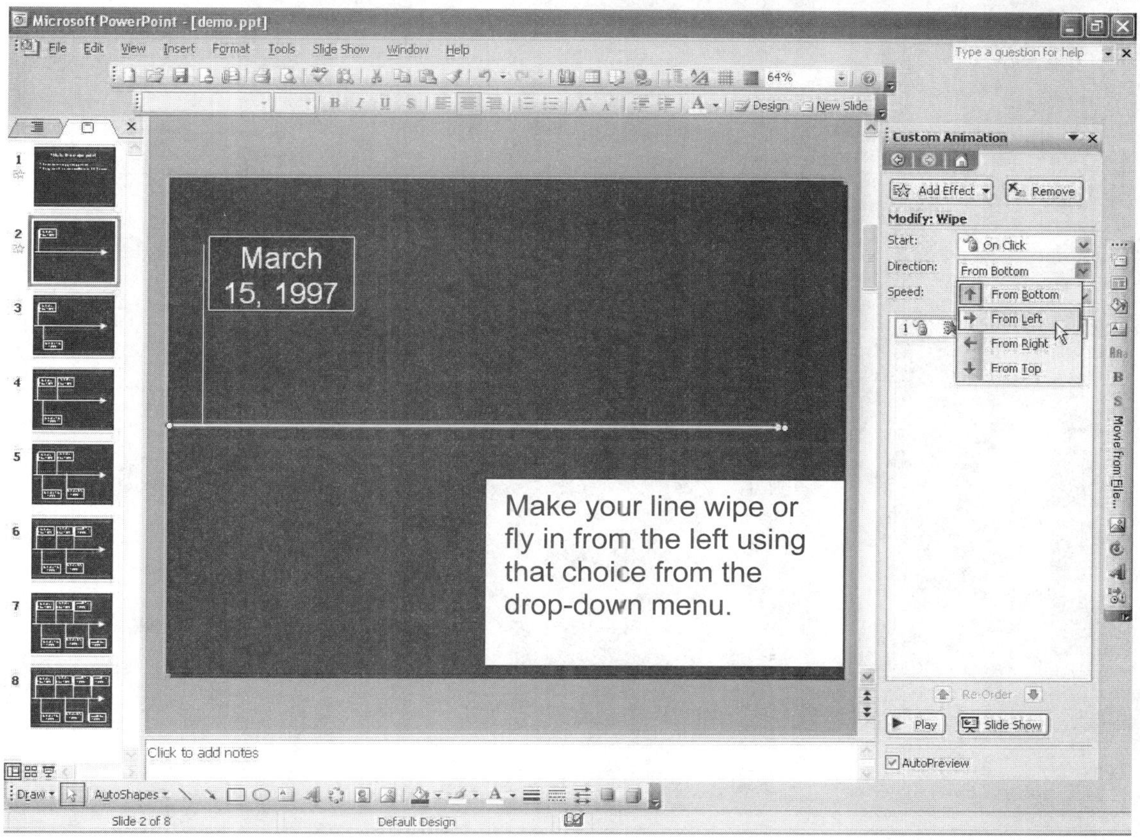
Make your line wipe or fly in from the left using that choice from the drop-down menu.

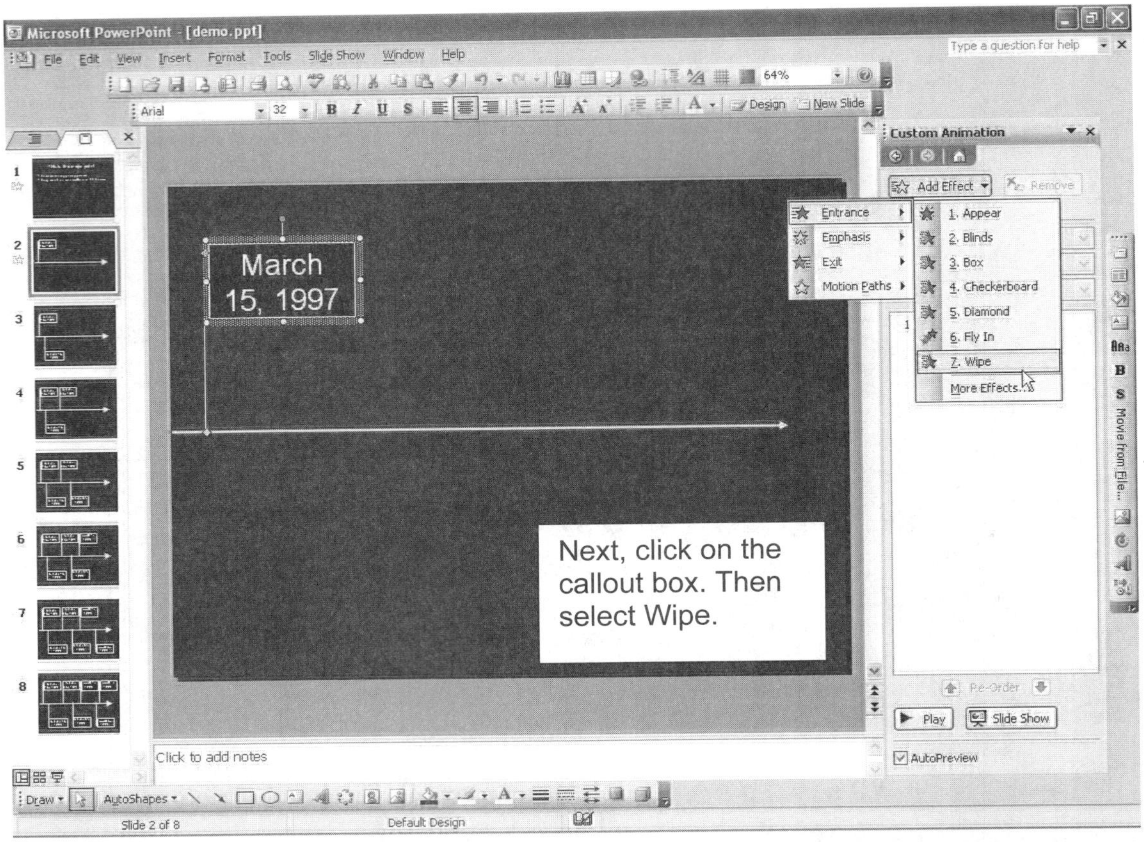
Microsoft PowerPoint - [demo.ppt]
Custom Animation
Add Effect
Remove
Entrance
Emphasis
Exit
Motion Paths
1. Appear
2. Blinds
3. Box
4. Checkerboard
5. Diamond
6. Fly In
7. Wipe
More Effects...
March 15, 1997
Next, click on the callout box. Then select Wipe.
Click to add notes
Play
Slide Show
AutoPreview
Slide 2 of 8
Default Design

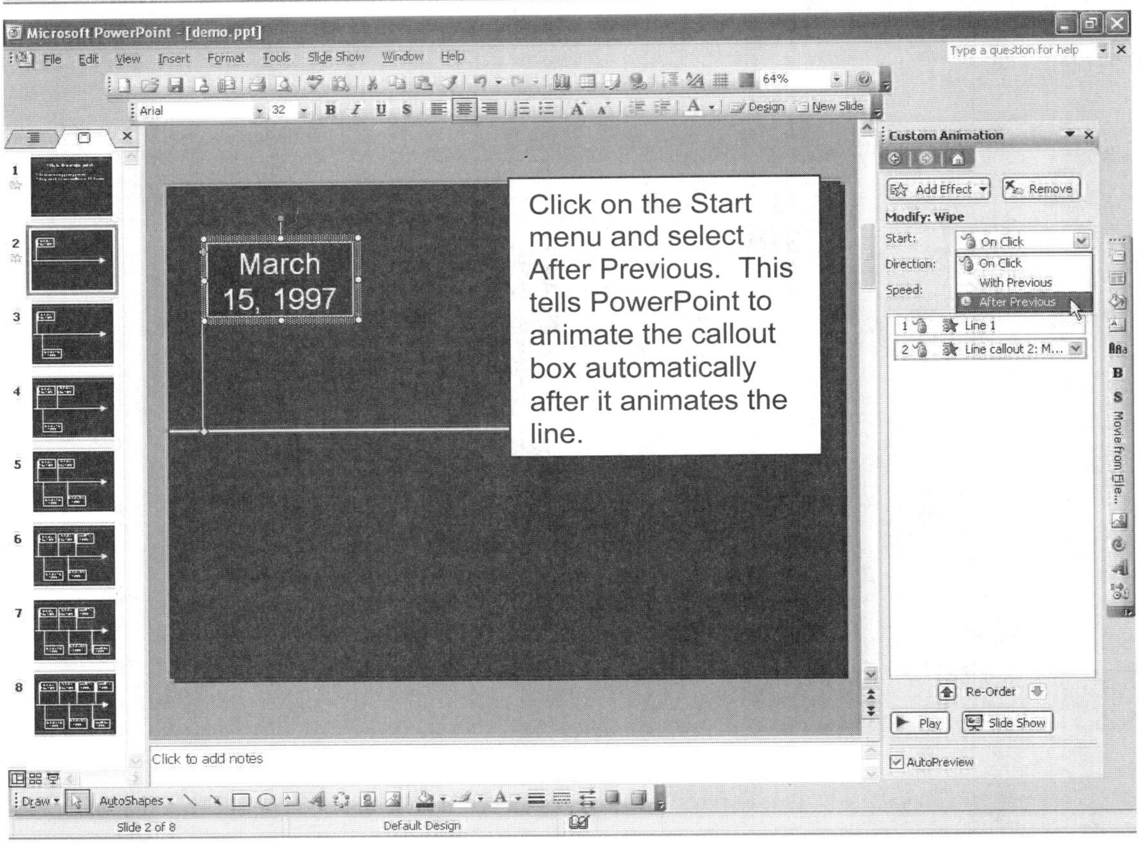
Microsoft PowerPoint - [demo.ppt]
Custom Animation
Add Effect
Remove
Modify: Wipe
Start:
Direction:
Speed:
On Click
On Click
With Previous
After Previous
Line 1
Line callout 2: M...
March 15, 1997
Click on the Start menu and select After Previous. This tells PowerPoint to animate the callout box automatically after it animates the line.
Click to add notes
Re-Order
Play
Slide Show
AutoPreview
Slide 2 of 8
Default Design

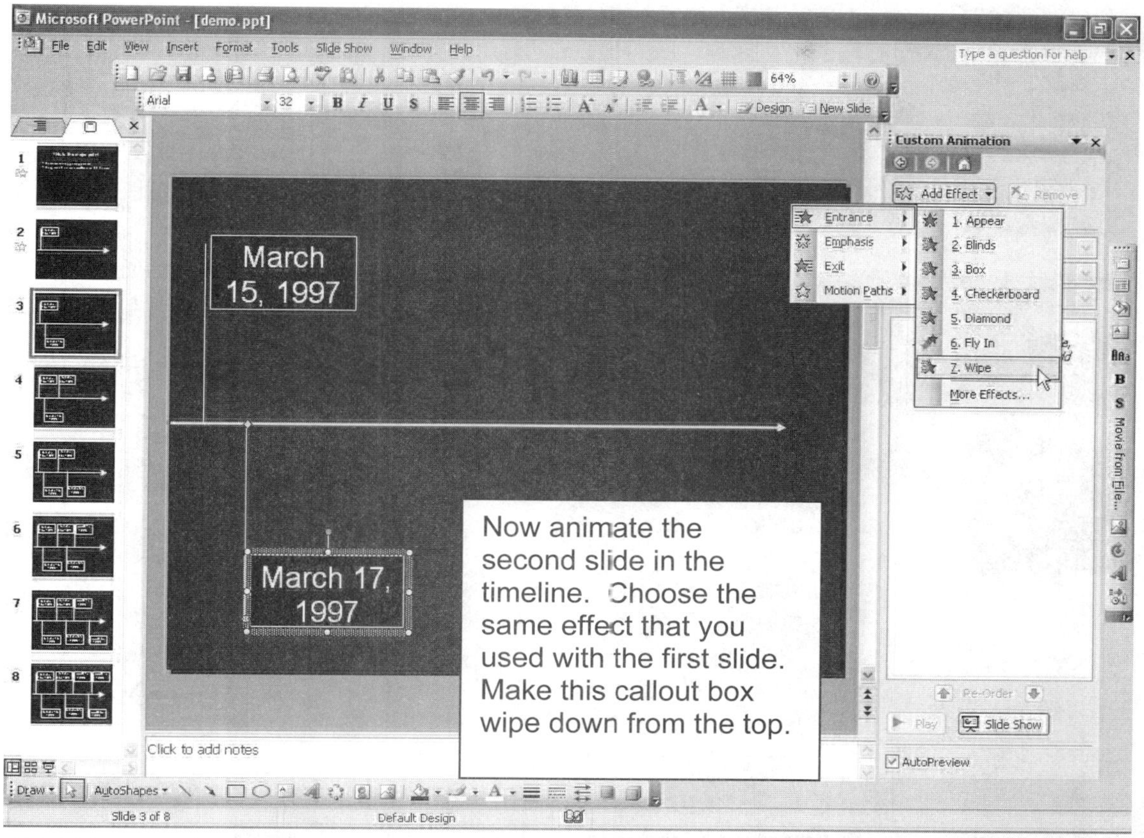
Microsoft PowerPoint - [demo.ppt]
Custom Animation
Add Effect
Entrance
Emphasis
Exit
Motion Paths
1. Appear
2. Blinds
3. Box
4. Checkerboard
5. Diamond
6. Fly In
7. Wipe
More Effects...
March 15, 1997
March 17, 1997
Now animate the second slide in the timeline. Choose the same effect that you used with the first slide. Make this callout box wipe down from the top.
Click to add notes
Slide 3 of 8
Default Design

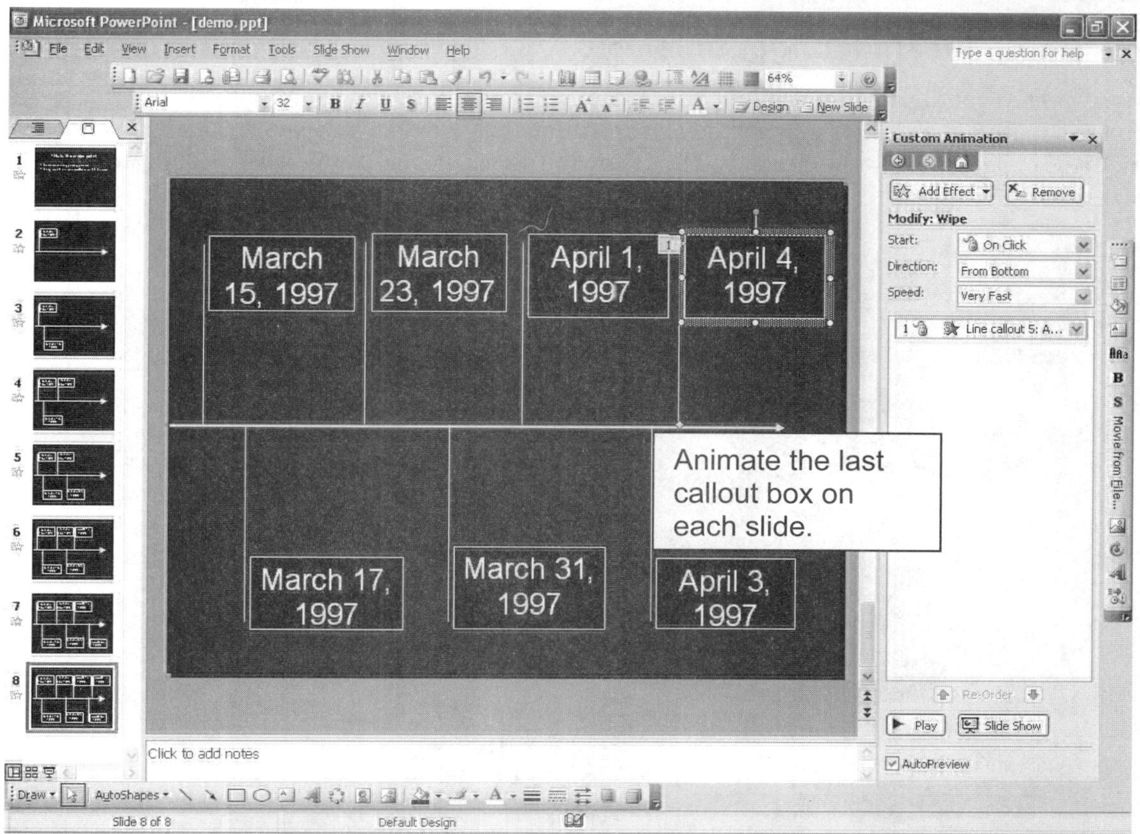
Microsoft PowerPoint - [demo.ppt]
Custom Animation
Modify: Wipe
Start: On Click
Direction: From Bottom
Speed: Very Fast
March 15, 1997
March 23, 1997
April 1, 1997
April 4, 1997
March 17, 1997
March 31, 1997
April 3, 1997
Animate the last callout box on each slide.
Click to add notes
Slide 8 of 8
Default Design

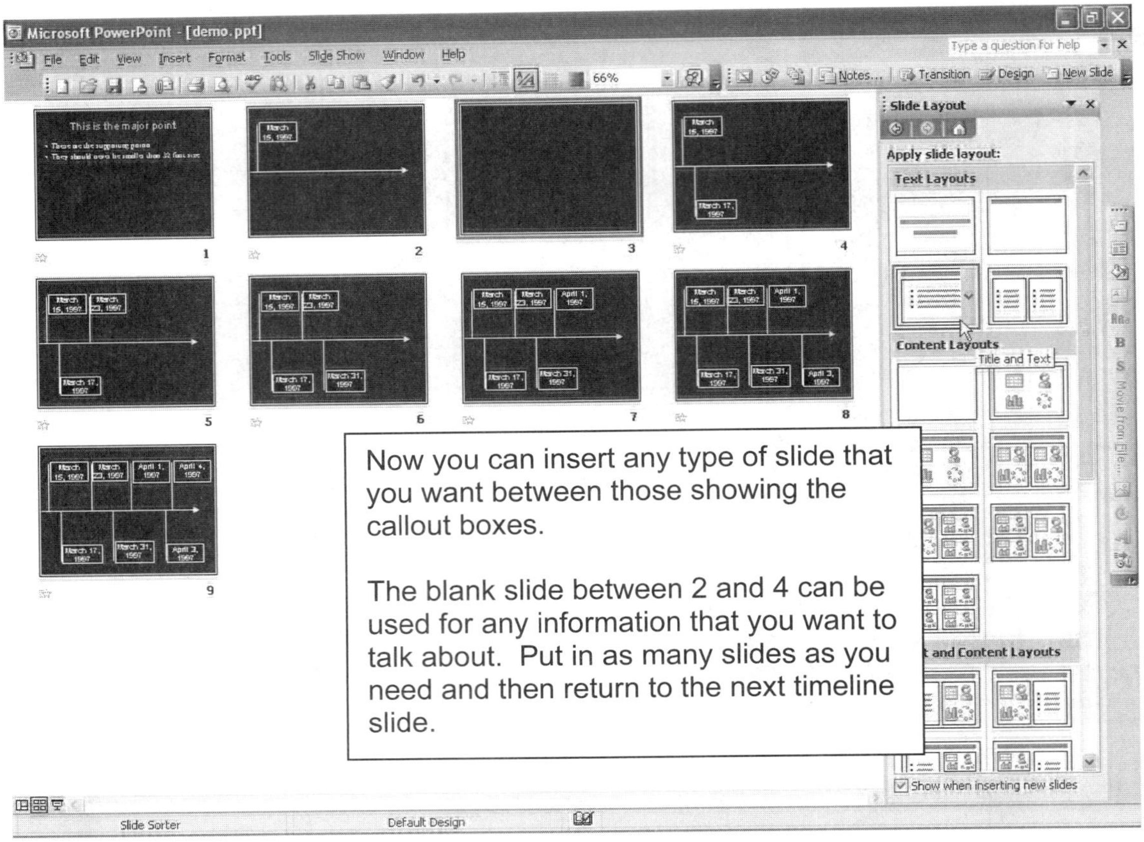

Making longer timelines

If you want to continue adding callout boxes after you have filled the boxes on your first slide, you have to save the slide as a .jpg slide and insert the image onto a new slide. This type of timeline can be vertical or horizontal. The following screen captures will walk you through that process.

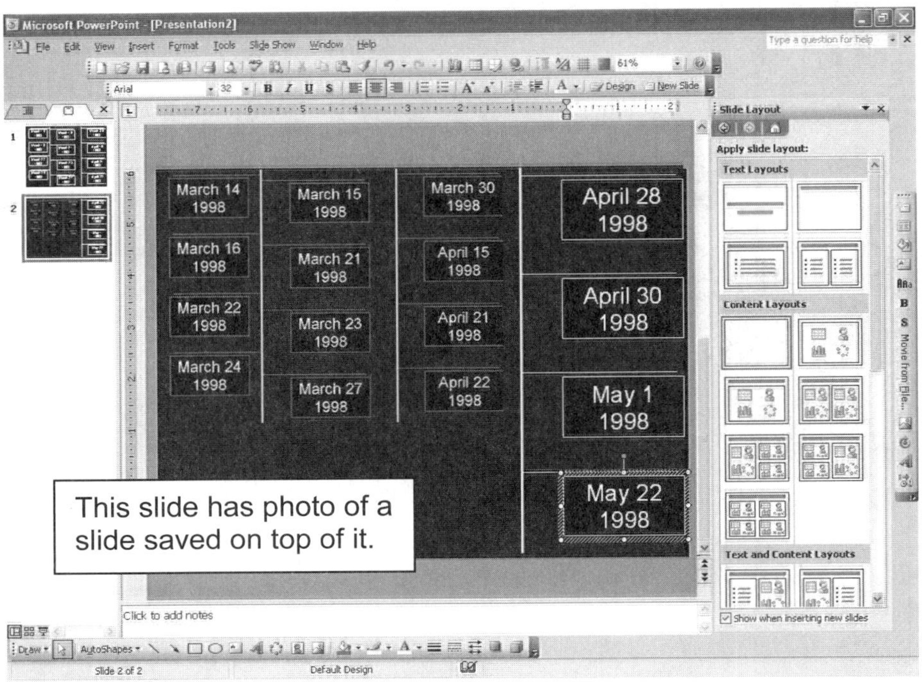

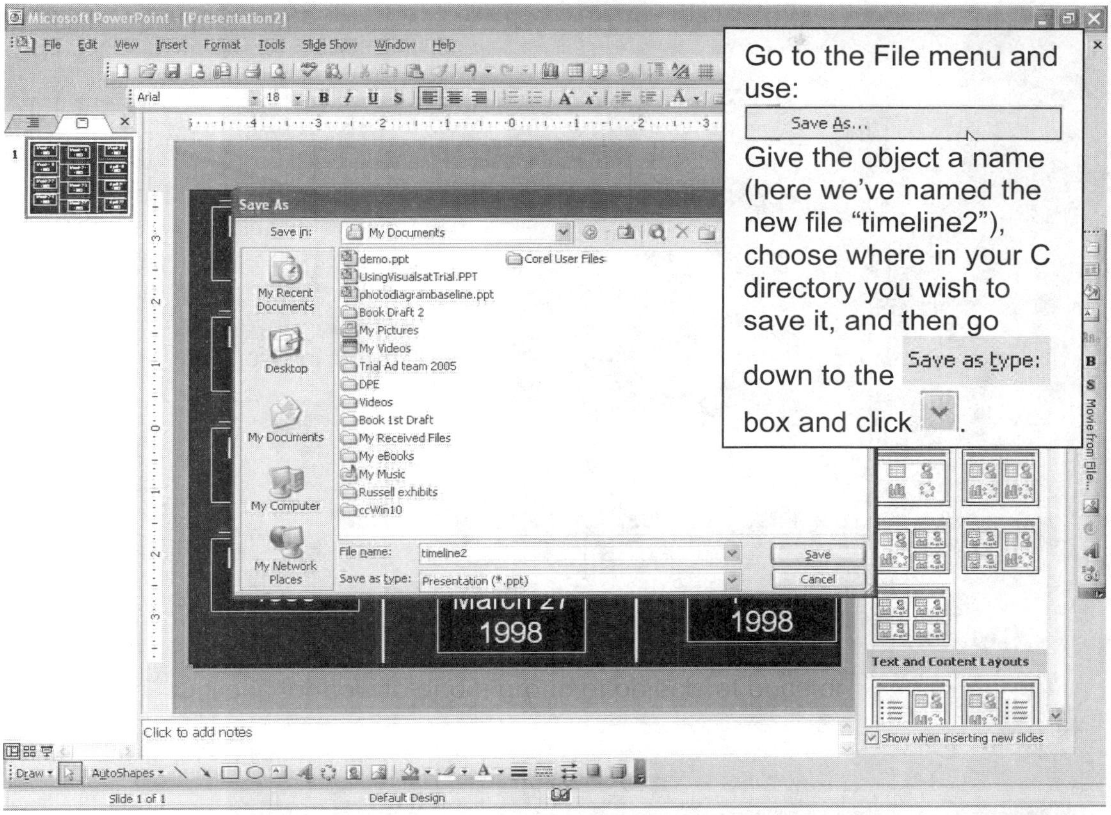
Go to the File menu and use:
Save As...
Give the object a name (here we've named the new file "timeline2"), choose where in your C directory you wish to save it, and then go down to the Save as type: box and click .

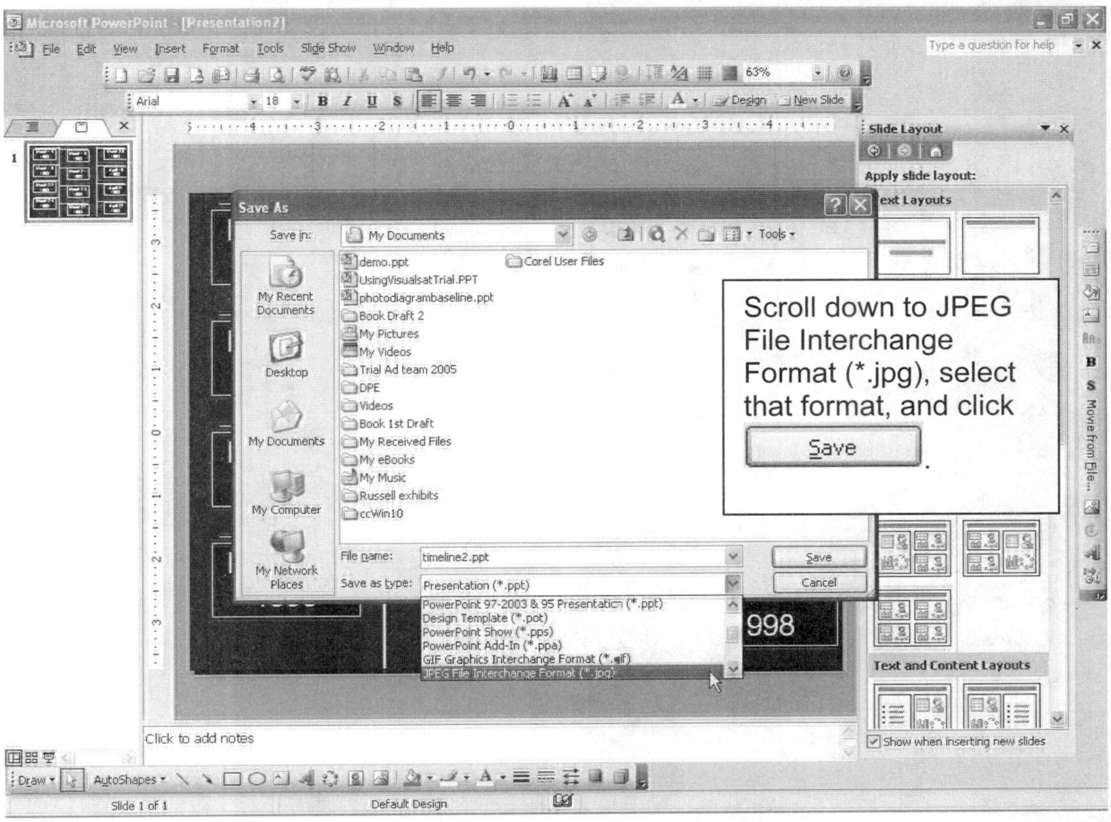
Scroll down to JPEG File Interchange Format (*.jpg), select that format, and click Save .

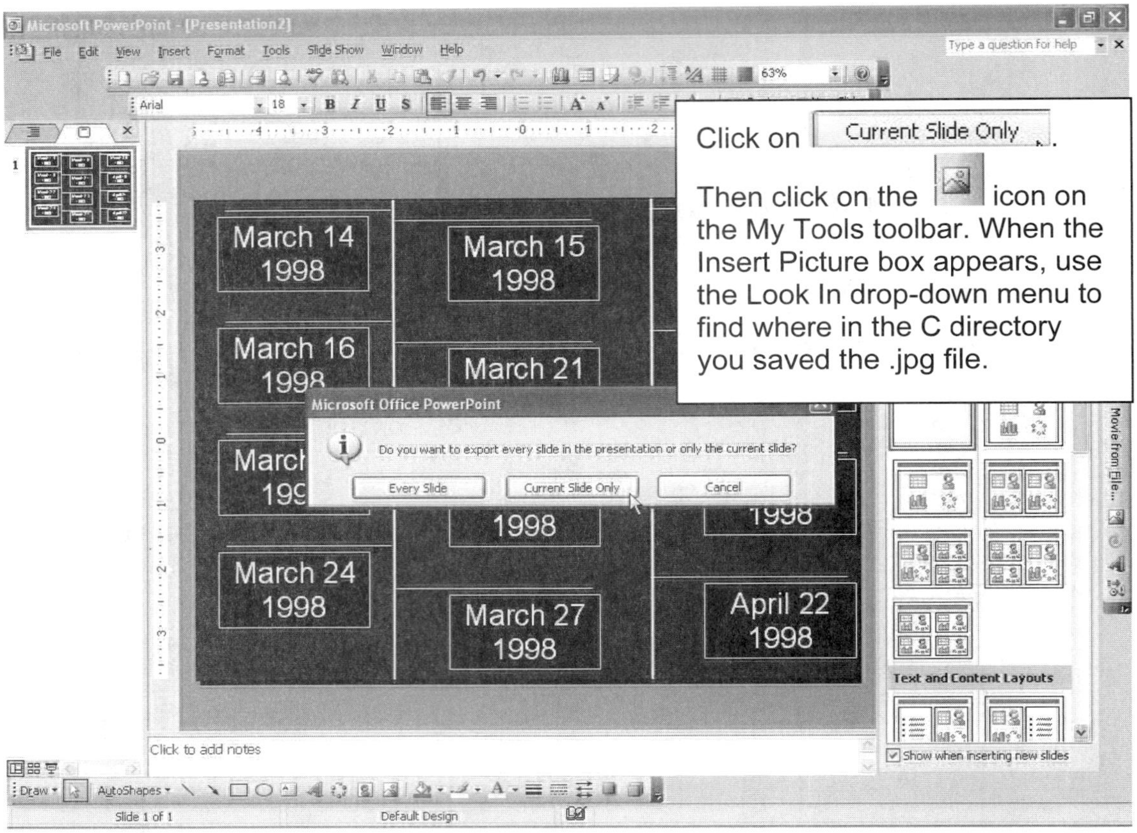
Click on Current Slide Only.
Then click on the icon on the My Tools toolbar. When the Insert Picture box appears, use the Look In drop-down menu to find where in the C directory you saved the .jpg file.
Microsoft Office PowerPoint
Do you want to export every slide in the presentation or only the current slide?
Every Slide
Current Slide Only
Cancel
March 14 1998
March 15 1998
March 16 1998
March 21
March 24 1998
March 27 1998
April 22 1998

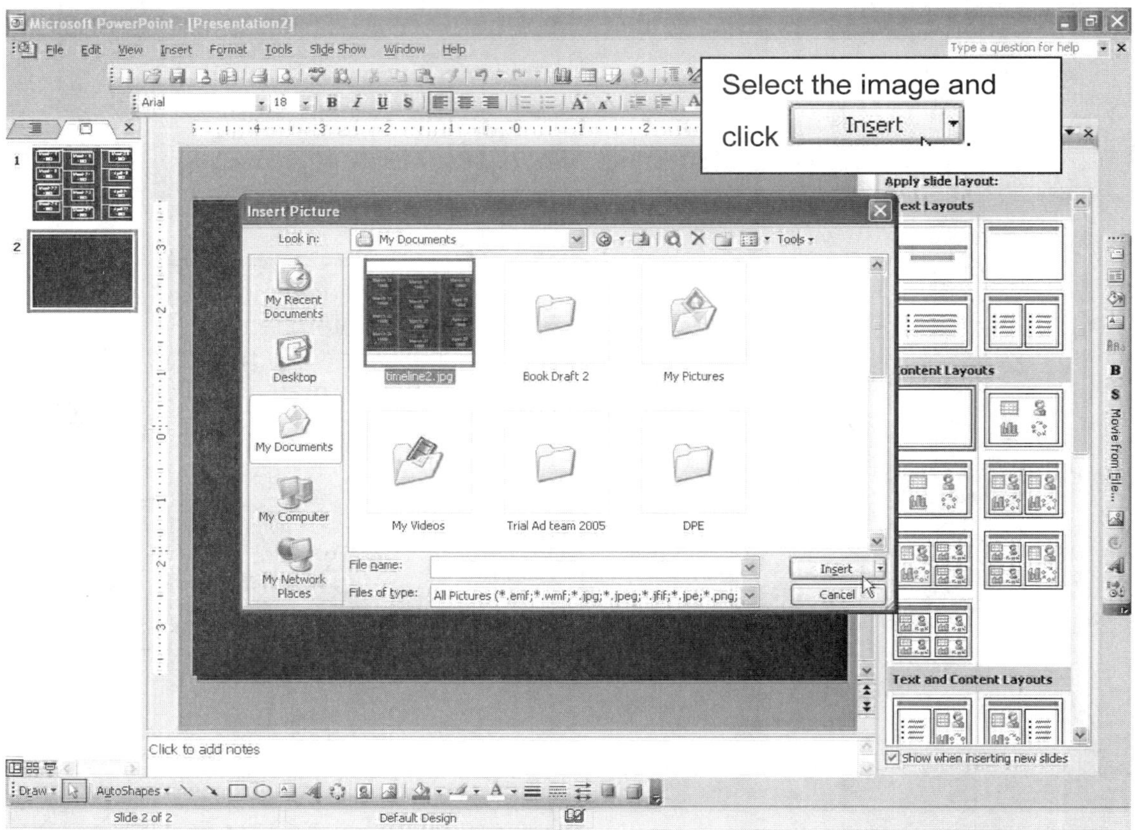
Select the image and click Insert.
Insert Picture
Look in: My Documents
My Recent Documents
Desktop
My Documents
My Computer
My Network Places
timeline2.jpg
Book Draft 2
My Pictures
My Videos
Trial Ad team 2005
DPE
File name:
Files of type: All Pictures (*.emf;*.wmf;*.jpg;*.jpeg;*.jfif;*.jpe;*.png;
Insert
Cancel

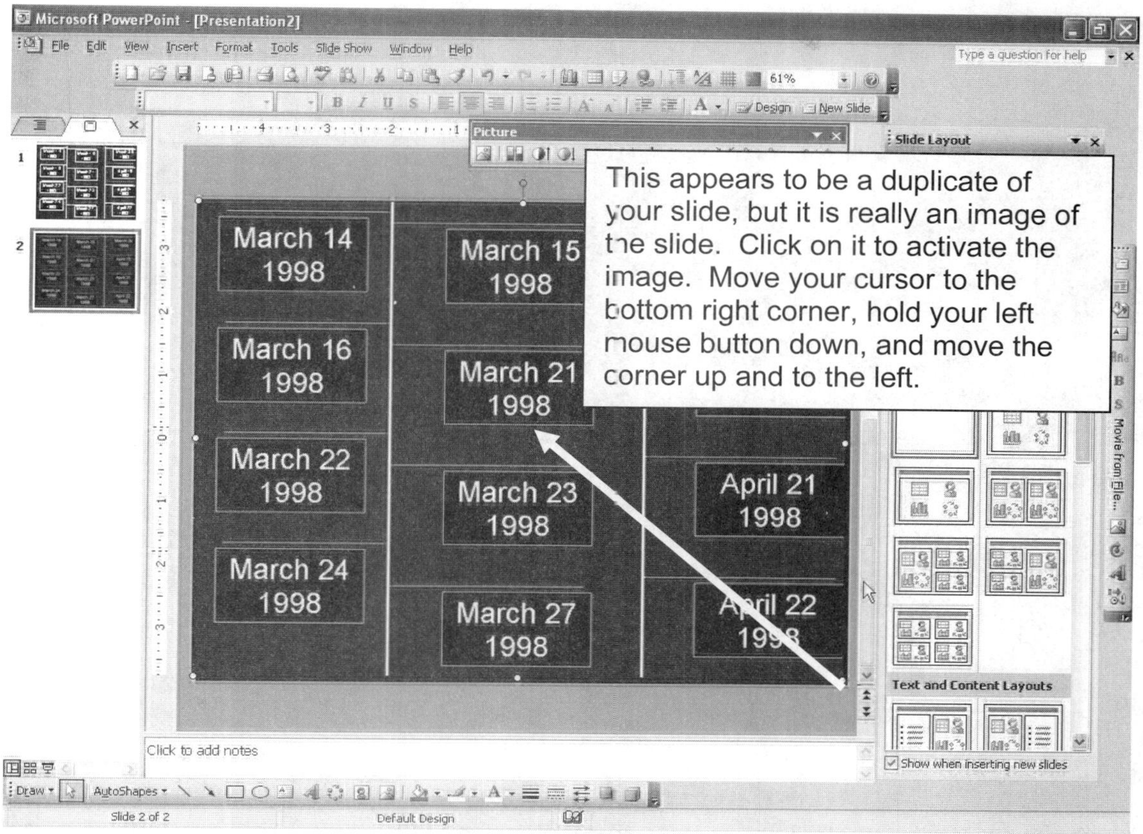
This appears to be a duplicate of your slide, but it is really an image of the slide. Click on it to activate the image. Move your cursor to the bottom right corner, hold your left mouse button down, and move the corner up and to the left.

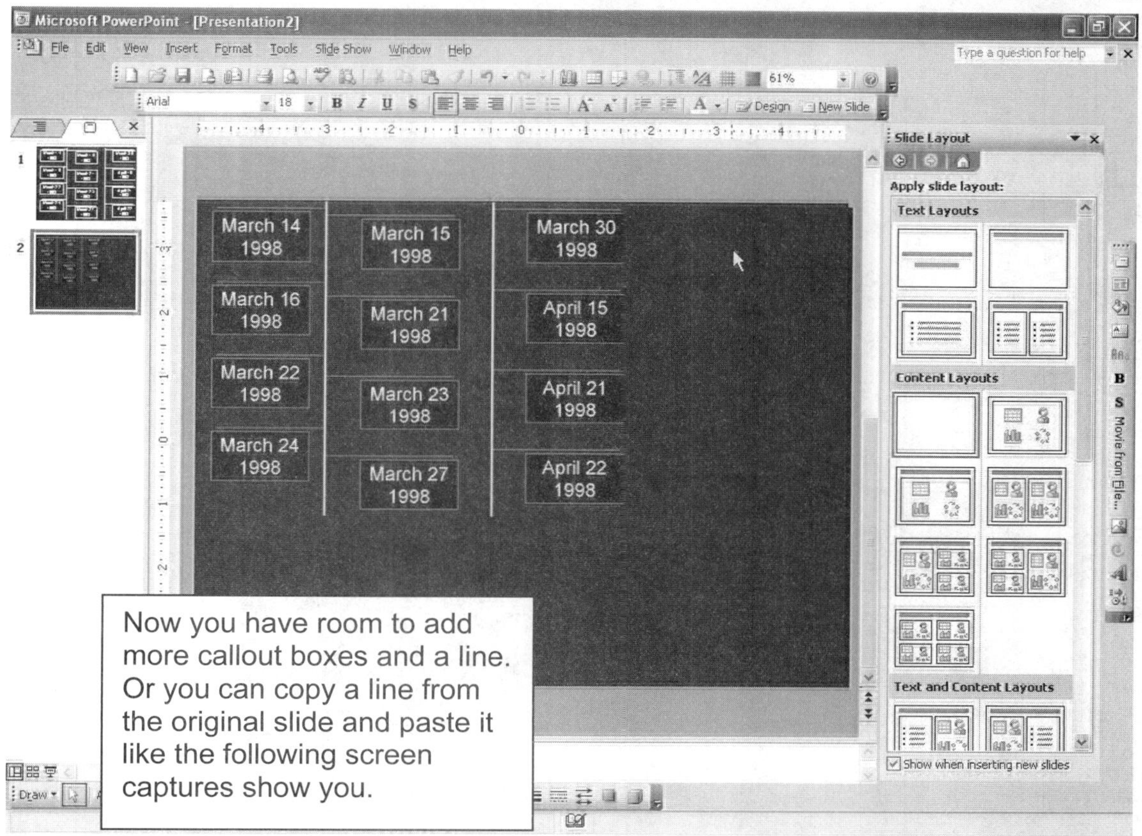
Now you have room to add more callout boxes and a line. Or you can copy a line from the original slide and paste it like the following screen captures show you.

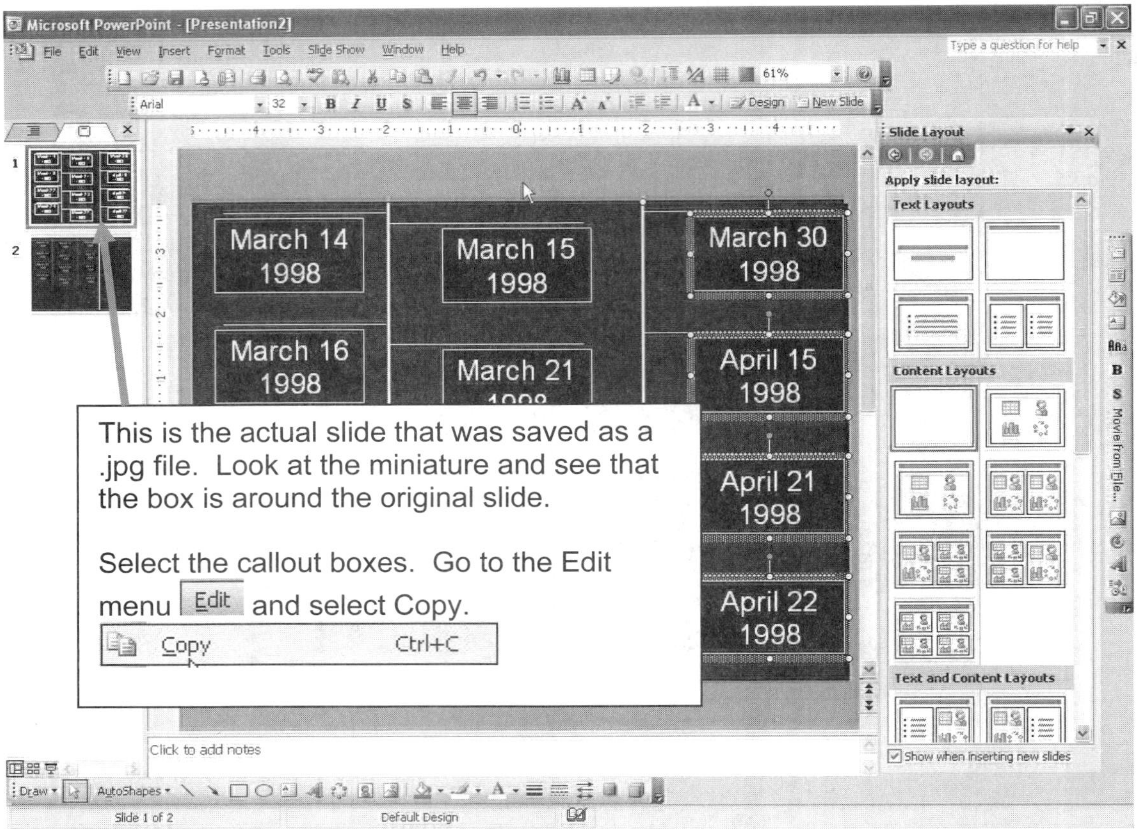
Microsoft PowerPoint - [Presentation2]
March 14 1998
March 15 1998
March 30 1998
March 16 1998
March 21
April 15 1998
April 21 1998
April 22 1998
This is the actual slide that was saved as a .jpg file. Look at the miniature and see that the box is around the original slide.
Select the callout boxes. Go to the Edit menu Edit and select Copy.
Copy Ctrl+C
Slide Layout
Apply slide layout:
Text Layouts
Content Layouts
Text and Content Layouts
Show when inserting new slides
Click to add notes
Slide 1 of 2
Default Design

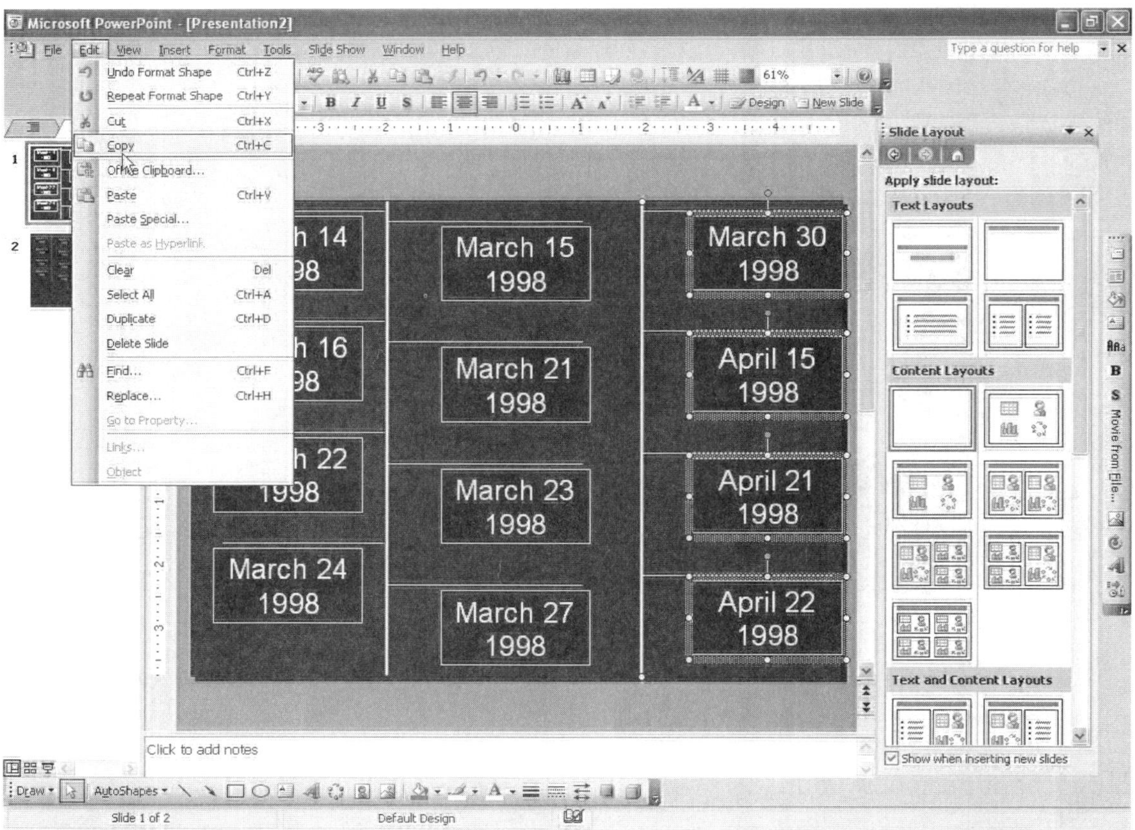
Microsoft PowerPoint - [Presentation2]
Undo Format Shape Ctrl+Z
Repeat Format Shape Ctrl+Y
Cut Ctrl+X
Copy Ctrl+C
Office Clipboard...
Paste Ctrl+V
Paste Special...
Paste as Hyperlink
Clear Del
Select All Ctrl+A
Duplicate Ctrl+D
Delete Slide
Find... Ctrl+F
Replace... Ctrl+H
Go to Property...
Links...
Object
March 15 1998
March 30 1998
March 21 1998
April 15 1998
March 23 1998
April 21 1998
March 24 1998
March 27 1998
April 22 1998
Slide Layout
Apply slide layout:
Text Layouts
Content Layouts
Text and Content Layouts
Show when inserting new slides
Click to add notes
Slide 1 of 2
Default Design

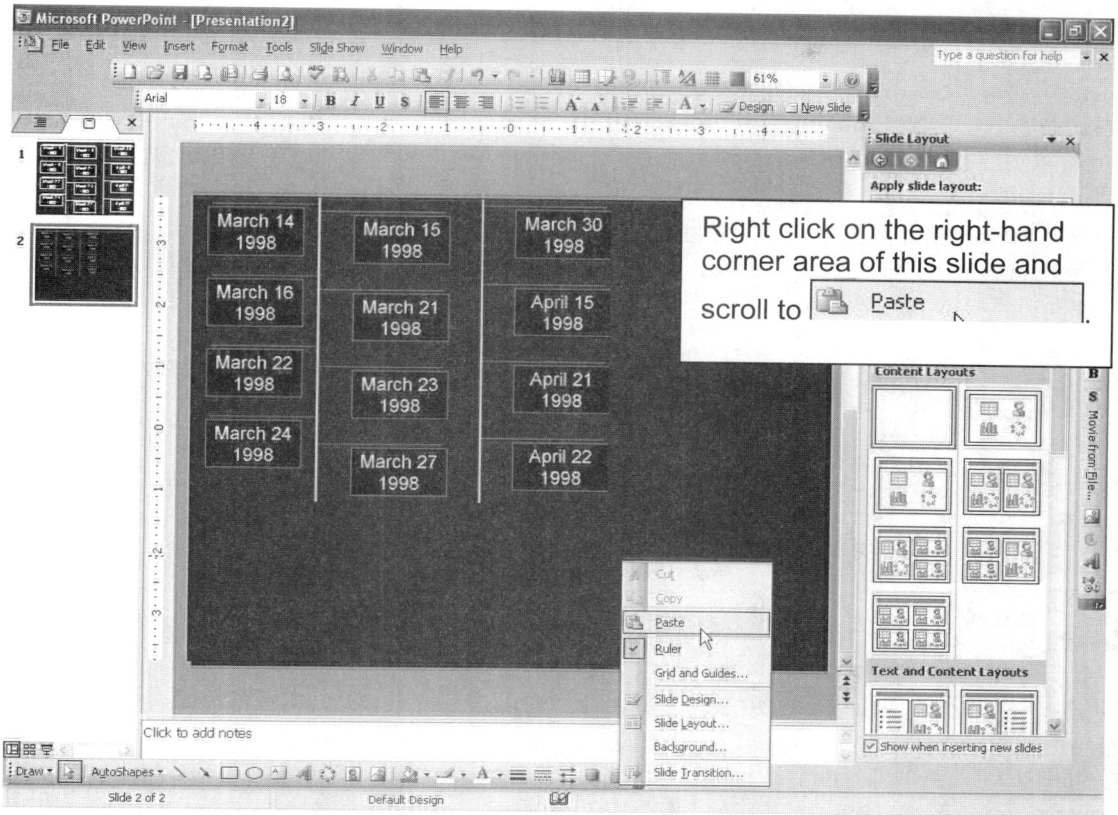
Microsoft PowerPoint - [Presentation2]
March 14 1998
March 16 1998
March 22 1998
March 24 1998
March 15 1998
March 21 1998
March 23 1998
March 27 1998
March 30 1998
April 15 1998
April 21 1998
April 22 1998
Right click on the right-hand corner area of this slide and scroll to Paste.
Cut
Copy
Paste
Ruler
Grid and Guides...
Slide Design...
Slide Layout...
Background...
Slide Transition...
Slide Layout
Apply slide layout:
Content Layouts
Text and Content Layouts
Show when inserting new slides
Click to add notes
Slide 2 of 2
Default Design

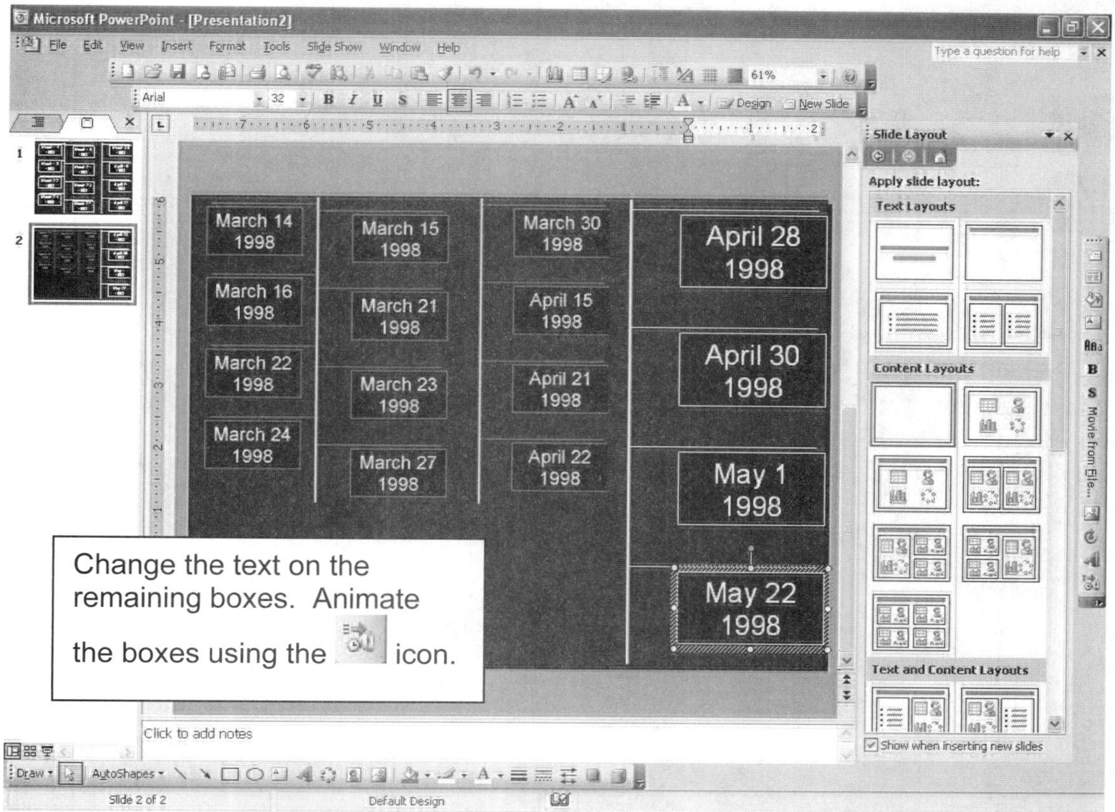
Microsoft PowerPoint - [Presentation2]
March 14 1998
March 16 1998
March 22 1998
March 24 1998
March 15 1998
March 21 1998
March 23 1998
March 27 1998
March 30 1998
April 15 1998
April 21 1998
April 22 1998
April 28 1998
April 30 1998
May 1 1998
May 22 1998
Change the text on the remaining boxes. Animate the boxes using the icon.
Slide Layout
Apply slide layout:
Text Layouts
Content Layouts
Text and Content Layouts
Show when inserting new slides
Click to add notes
Slide 2 of 2
Default Design

Creating Diagrams from Photographs

This section teaches you how to make a diagram that takes its baseline from a photograph. The following exercise creates a diagram of a car collision using a photograph to authenticate the diagram. You can recreate this exercise by downloading the photo in this section from the Litigation Technology website (www.littech.org).

You begin by inserting a photo into a blank slide and then placing lines over the photograph. After you change the background of the slide, you make the photo disappear. Once the photo is gone, you make the symbols for the cars appear and animate them into a collision.

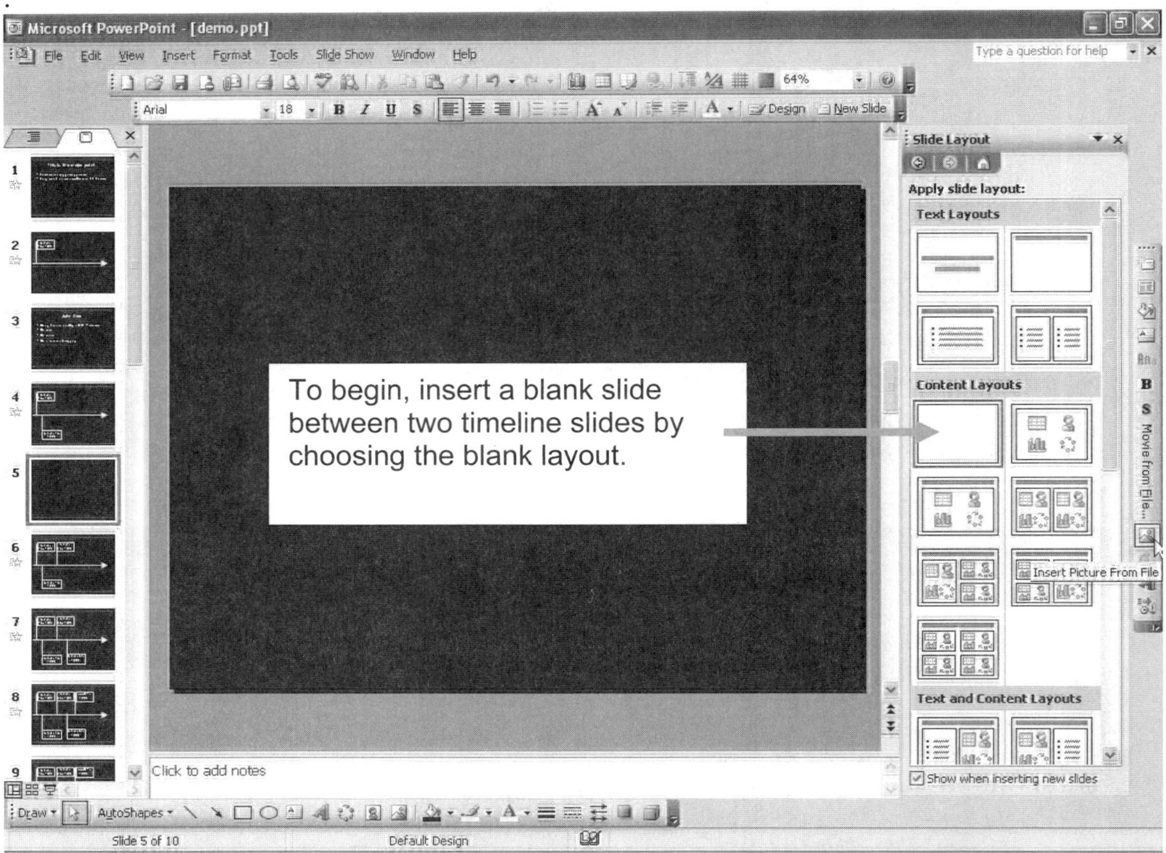

PowerPoint will by default open your My Pictures folder. If you have the images for your case saved in a different place in the C directory (for instance, in the C:\Carter file that we keep referring to in this case), simply type the path to the folder or navigate through Windows until you find the folder and files. Then, click on Insert to have PowerPoint insert the file onto your blank slide.

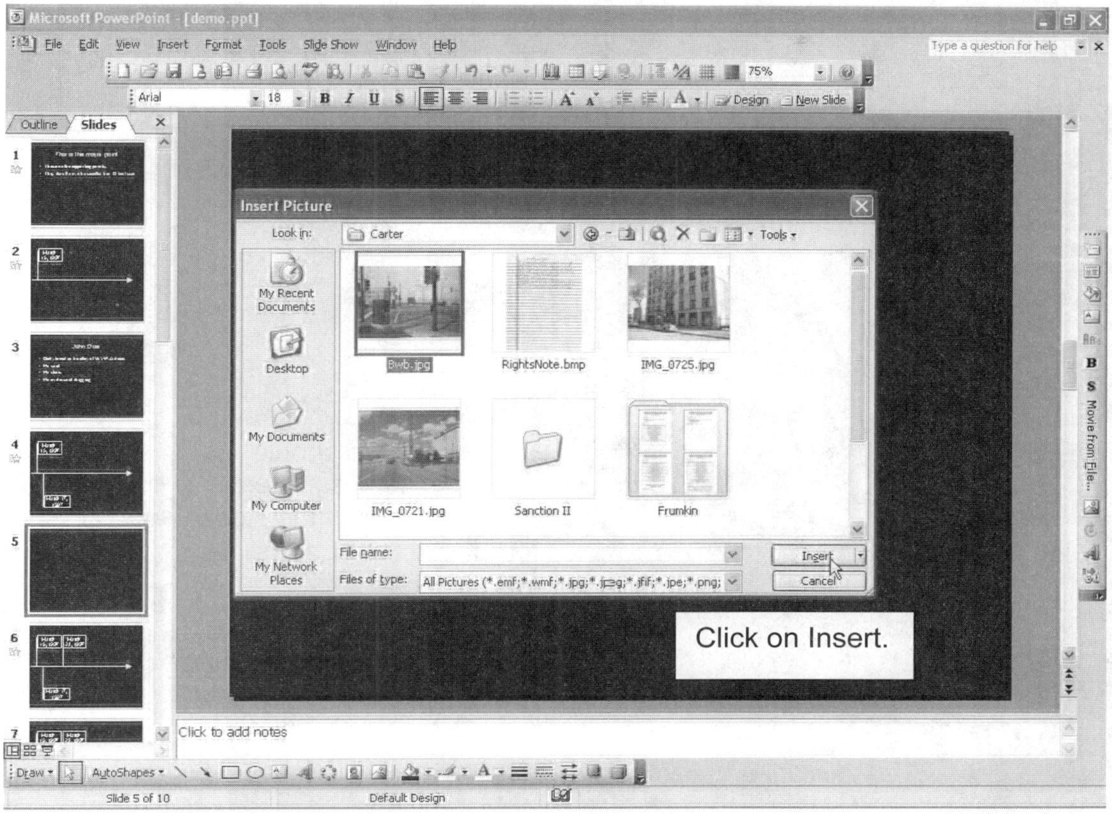
Microsoft PowerPoint - [demo.ppt]
Insert Picture
Look in: Carter
My Recent Documents
Desktop
My Documents
My Computer
My Network Places
Bwb.jpg
RightsNote.bmp
IMG_0725.jpg
IMG_0721.jpg
Sanction II
Frumkin
File name:
Files of type: All Pictures (*.emf;*.wmf;*.jpg;*.jpeg;*.jfif;*.jpe;*.png;
Insert
Cancel
Click on Insert.
Click to add notes
Slide 5 of 10
Default Design

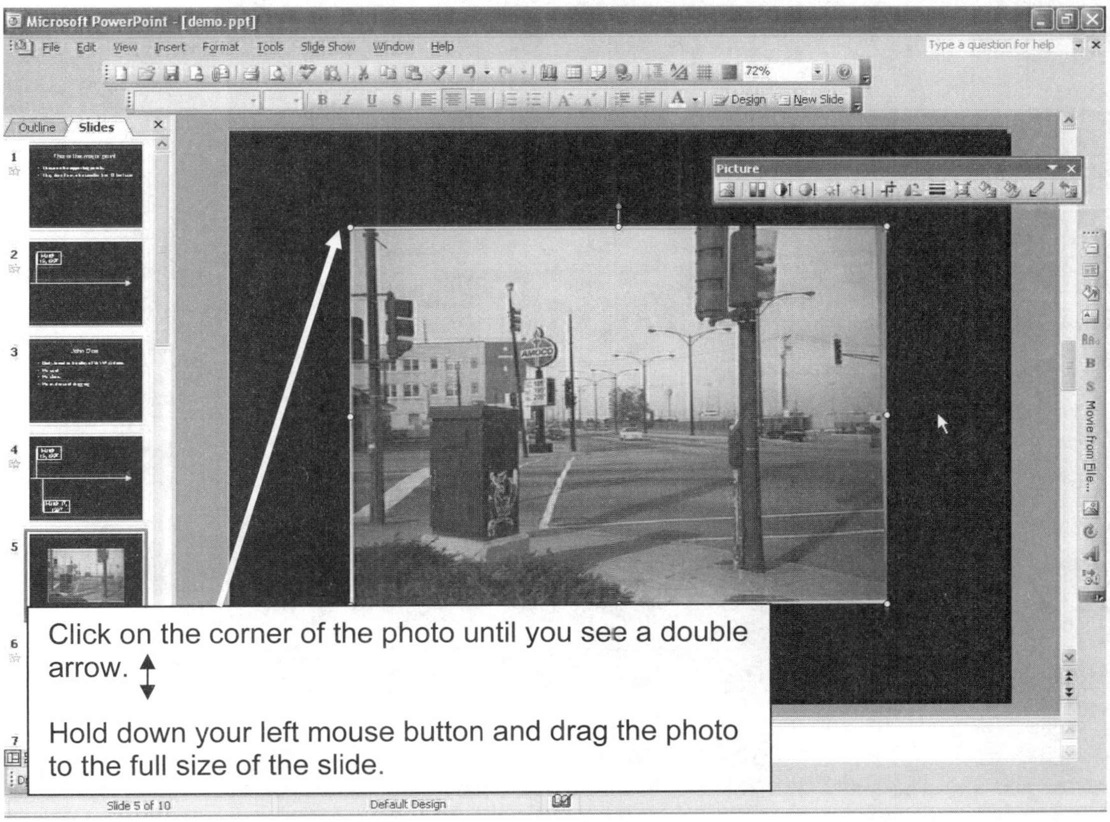
Microsoft PowerPoint - [demo.ppt]
Picture
Click on the corner of the photo until you see a double arrow.
Hold down your left mouse button and drag the photo to the full size of the slide.
Slide 5 of 10
Default Design

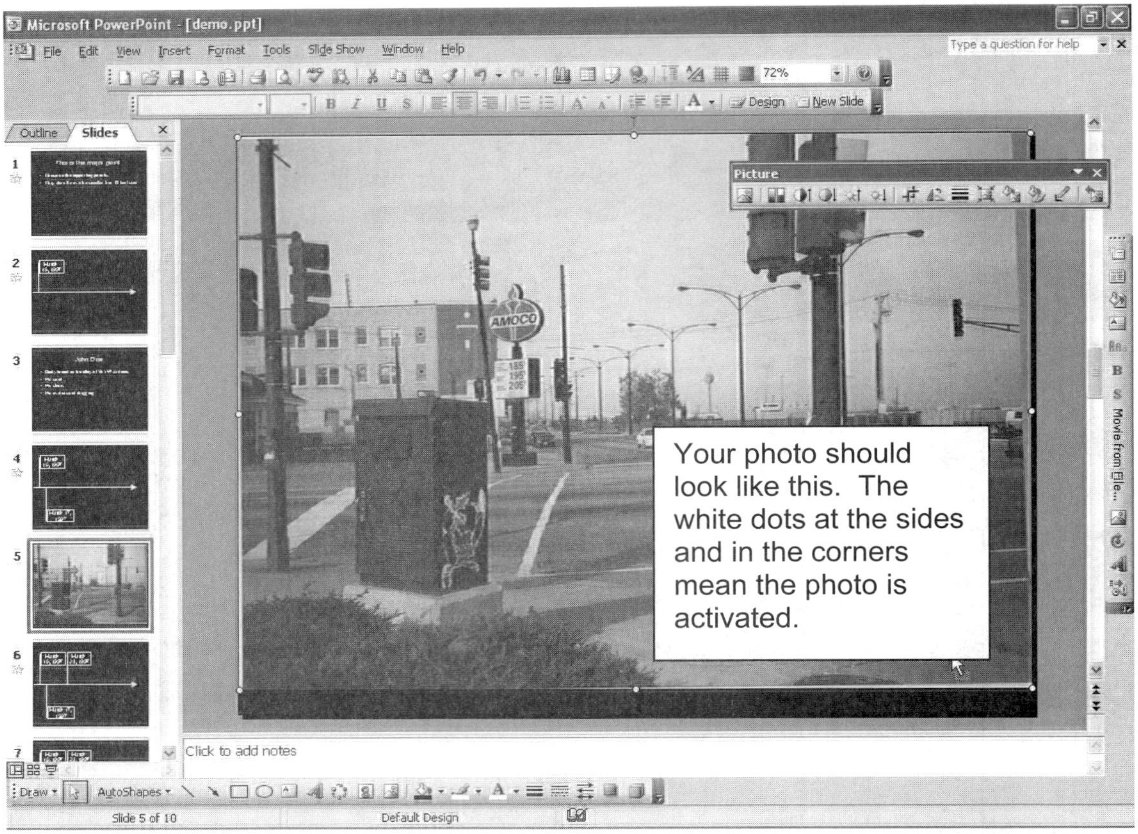
Microsoft PowerPoint - [demo.ppt]
File Edit View Insert Format Tools Slide Show Window Help
Type a question for help
72%
Design New Slide
Outline Slides
Picture
AMOCO
Your photo should look like this. The white dots at the sides and in the corners mean the photo is activated.
Click to add notes
Draw AutoShapes
Slide 5 of 10
Default Design
Movie from File...

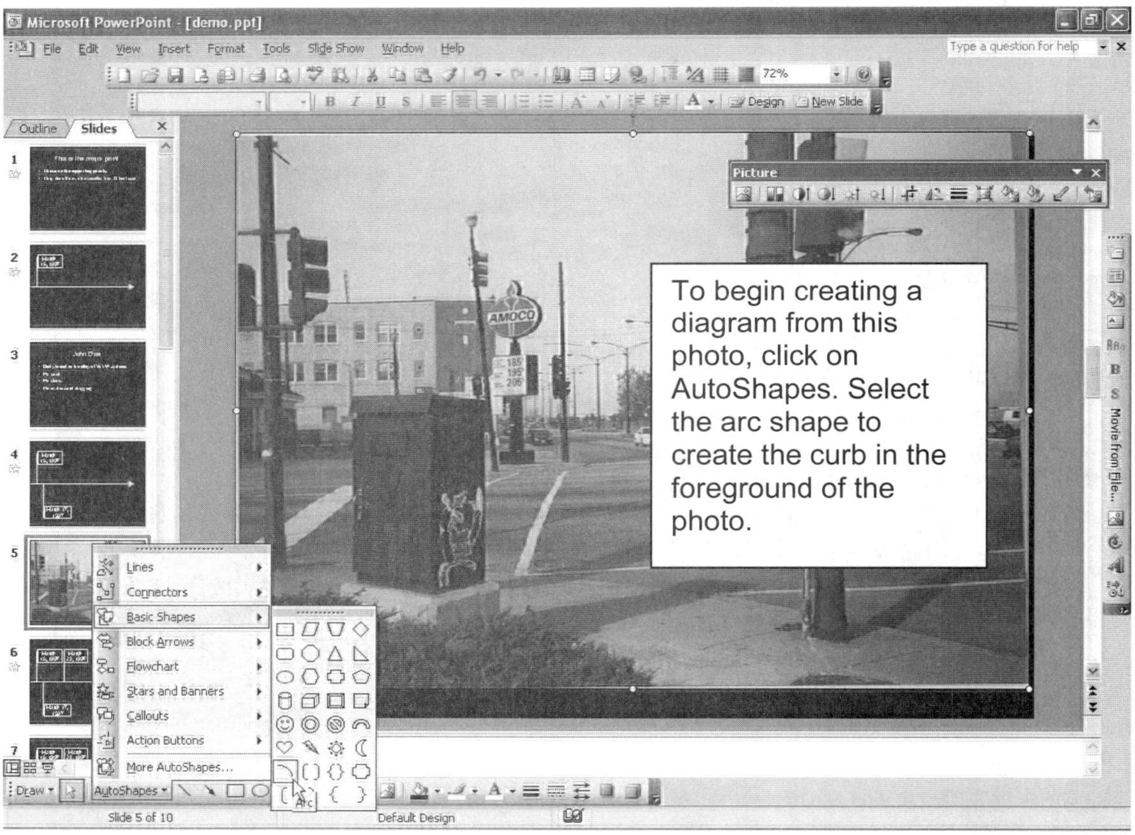
Microsoft PowerPoint - [demo.ppt]
File Edit View Insert Format Tools Slide Show Window Help
Type a question for help
72%
Design New Slide
Outline Slides
Picture
AMOCO
To begin creating a diagram from this photo, click on AutoShapes. Select the arc shape to create the curb in the foreground of the photo.
Lines
Connectors
Basic Shapes
Block Arrows
Flowchart
Stars and Banners
Callouts
Action Buttons
More AutoShapes...
Arc
Draw AutoShapes
Slide 5 of 10
Default Design
Movie from File...

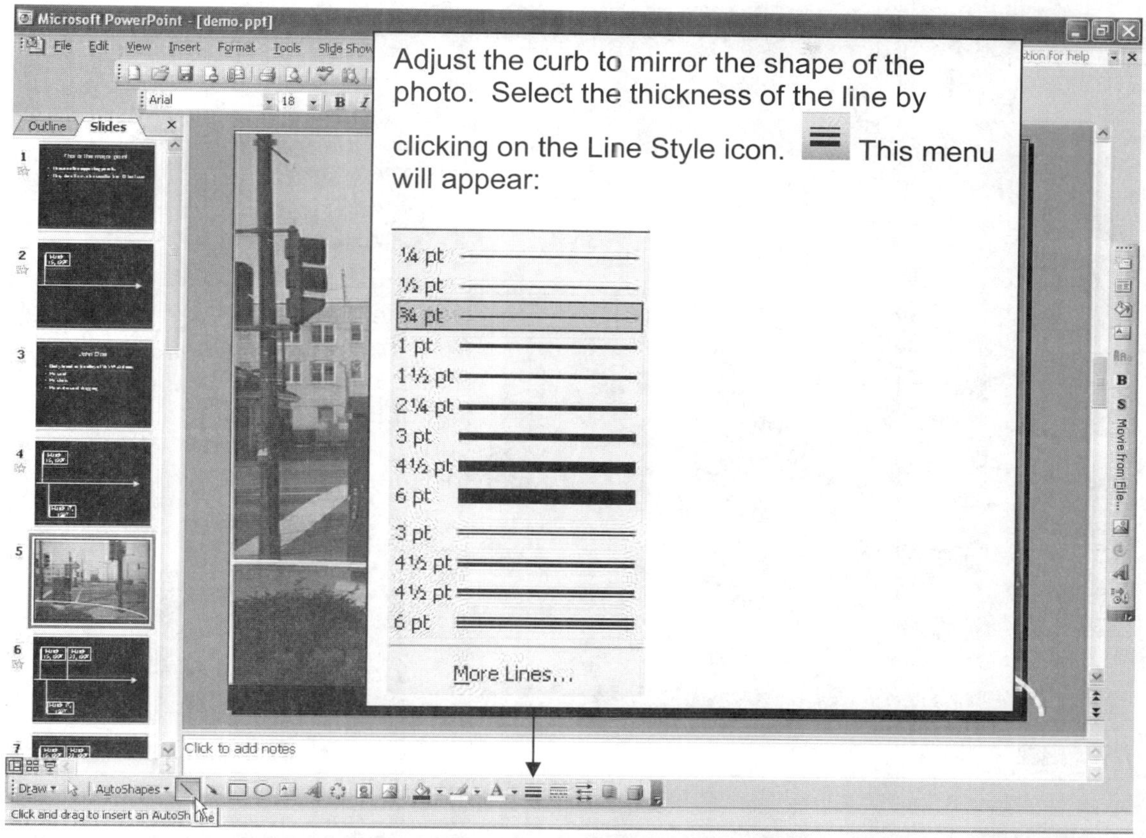
Microsoft PowerPoint - [demo.ppt]
Adjust the curb to mirror the shape of the photo. Select the thickness of the line by clicking on the Line Style icon. This menu will appear:
¼ pt
½ pt
¾ pt
1 pt
1½ pt
2¼ pt
3 pt
4½ pt
6 pt
3 pt
4½ pt
4½ pt
6 pt
More Lines...
Click to add notes
Click and drag to insert an AutoShape

Microsoft PowerPoint - [demo.ppt]
Insert a straight line to mirror the opposite side of the street. Use the Line and Line Style icons.
Click to add notes
Slide 5 of 10
Default Design

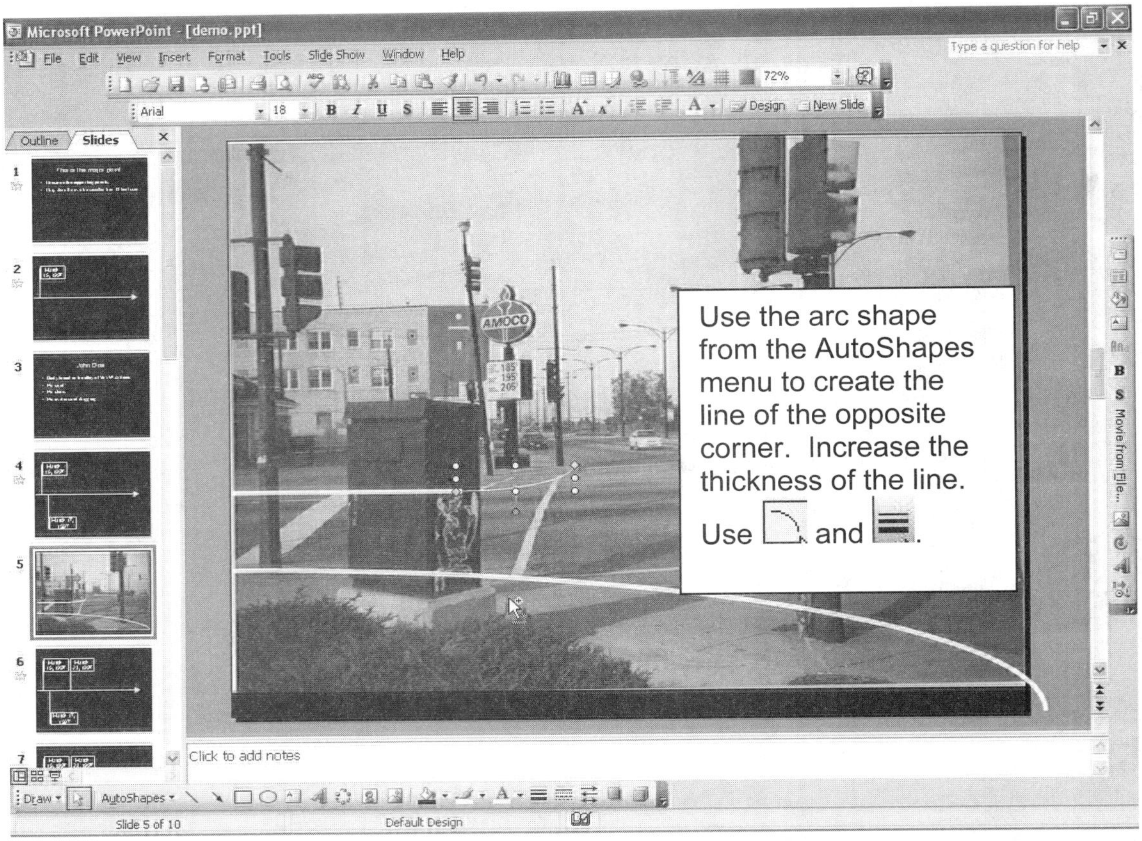

Use the arc shape from the AutoShapes menu to create the line of the opposite corner. Increase the thickness of the line.
Use and .

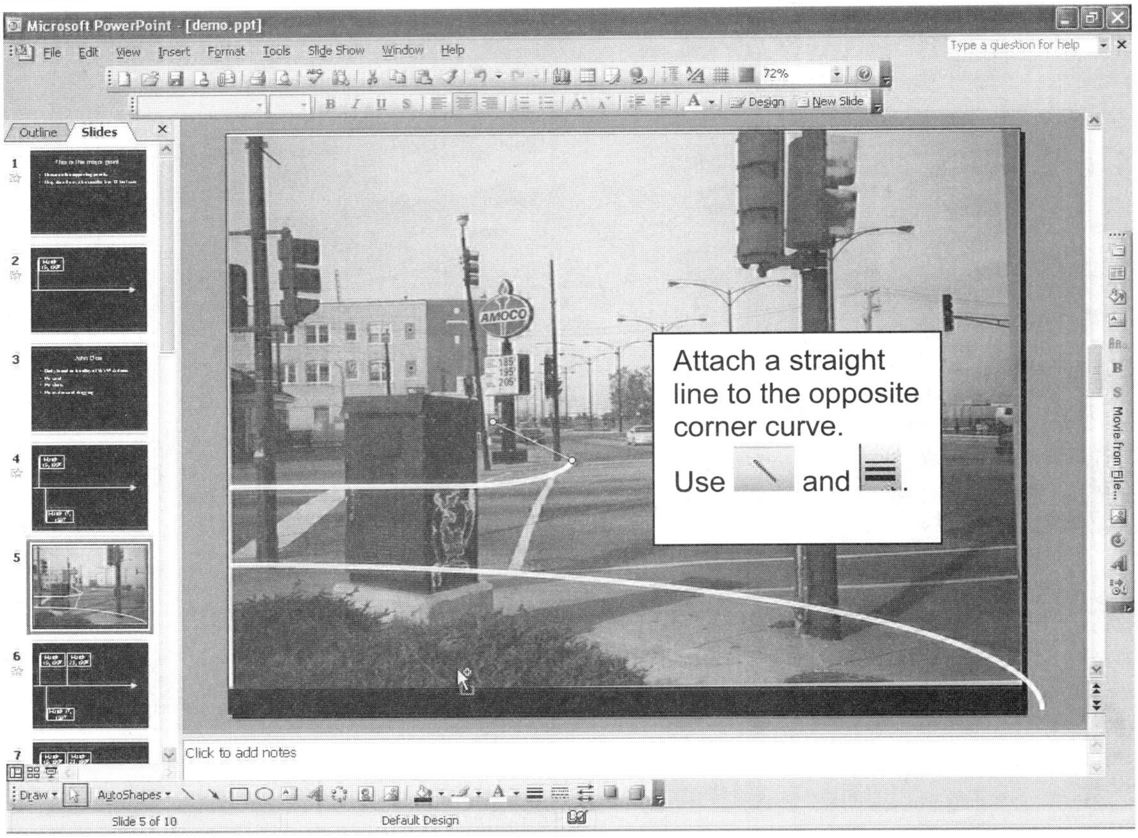

Attach a straight line to the opposite corner curve.
Use and .

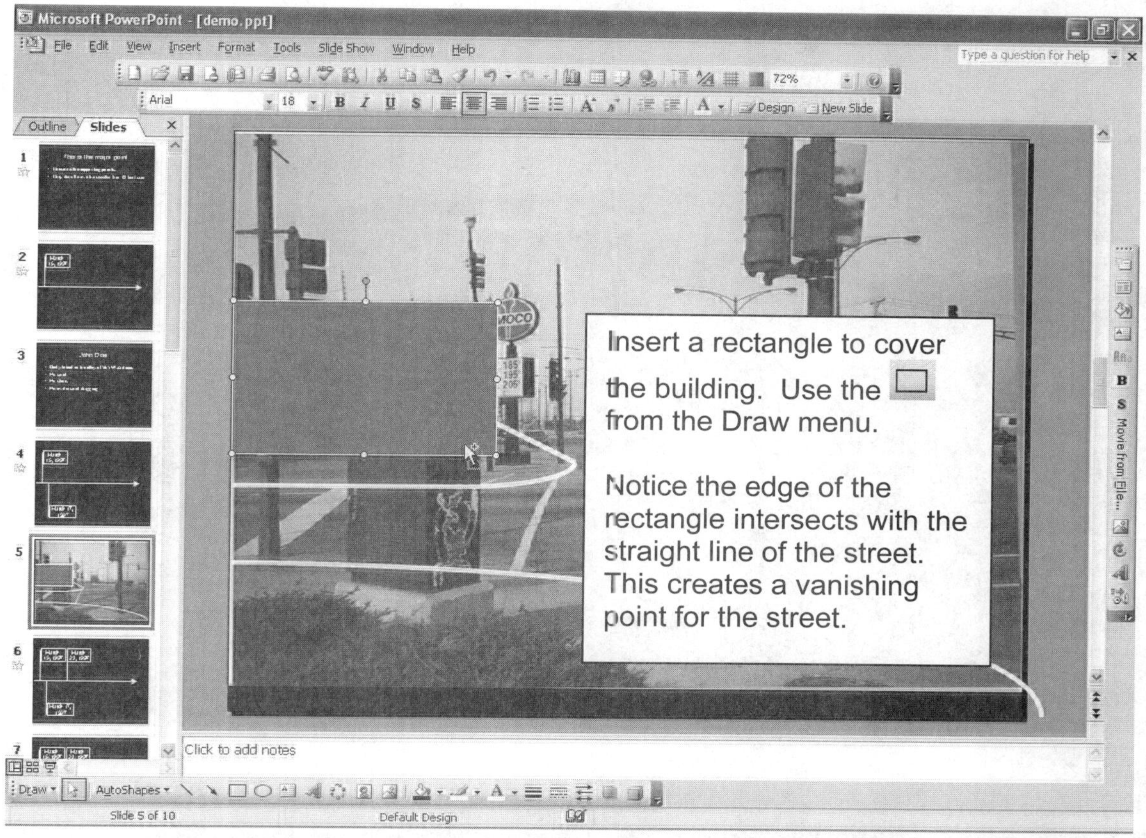
Microsoft PowerPoint - [demo.ppt]
Insert a rectangle to cover the building. Use the from the Draw menu.
Notice the edge of the rectangle intersects with the straight line of the street. This creates a vanishing point for the street.
Click to add notes
Slide 5 of 10
Default Design

Microsoft PowerPoint - [demo.ppt]
Use No Fill to eliminate the fill from the rectangle. It is found on this icon .
No Fill
More Fill Colors...
Fill Effects...
Click to add notes
Slide 5 of 10
Default Design

Microsoft PowerPoint - [demo.ppt]
File Edit View Insert Format Tools Slide Show Window Help
Type a question for help
Outline Slides
Insert lines for the opposite side of the street.
Use and .
Click to add notes
Draw AutoShapes
Slide 5 of 10
Default Design

Microsoft PowerPoint - [demo.ppt]
File Edit View Insert Format Tools Slide Show Window Help
Type a question for help
Arial 18
Outline Slides
Use the arc shape for the corner.
and .
Click to add notes
Draw AutoShapes
Slide 5 of 10
Default Design

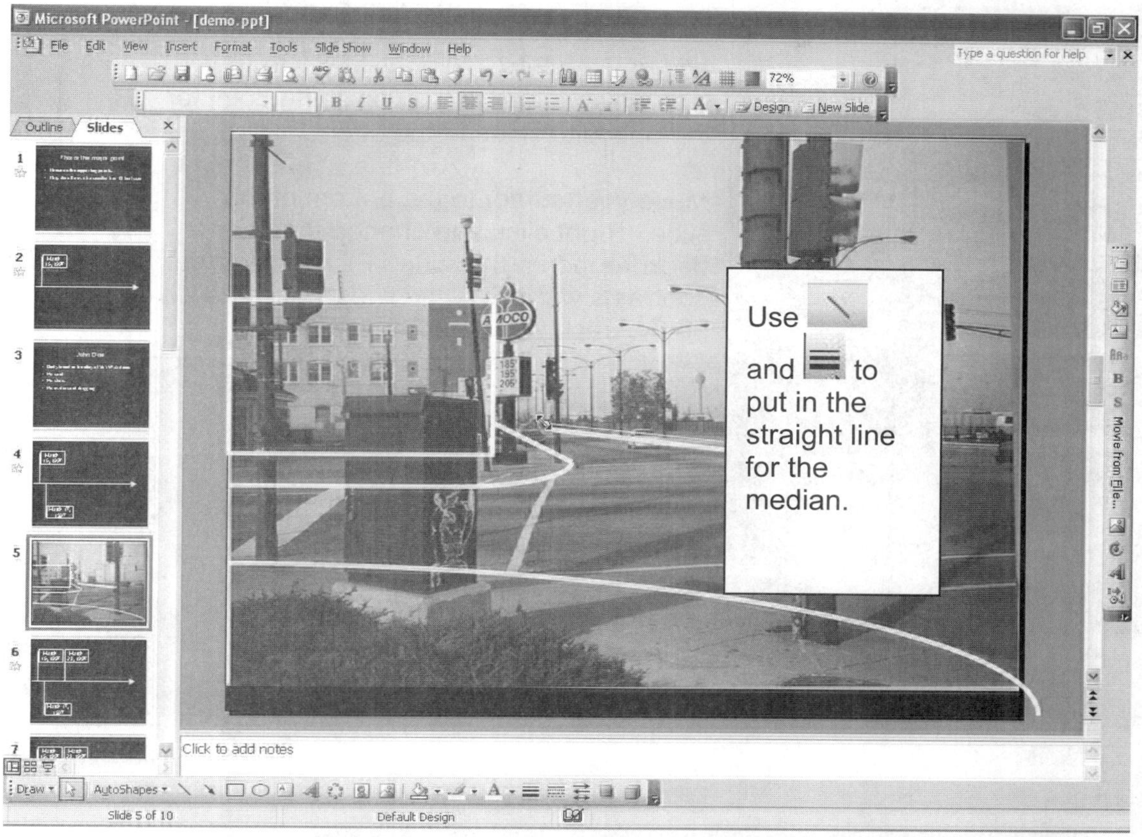
Microsoft PowerPoint - [demo.ppt]
Use
and
to
put in the
straight line
for the
median.
Click to add notes
Slide 5 of 10
Default Design

Microsoft PowerPoint - [demo.ppt]
Use
and
to
complete the
opposite side
of the street.
Click to add notes
Slide 5 of 10
Default Design

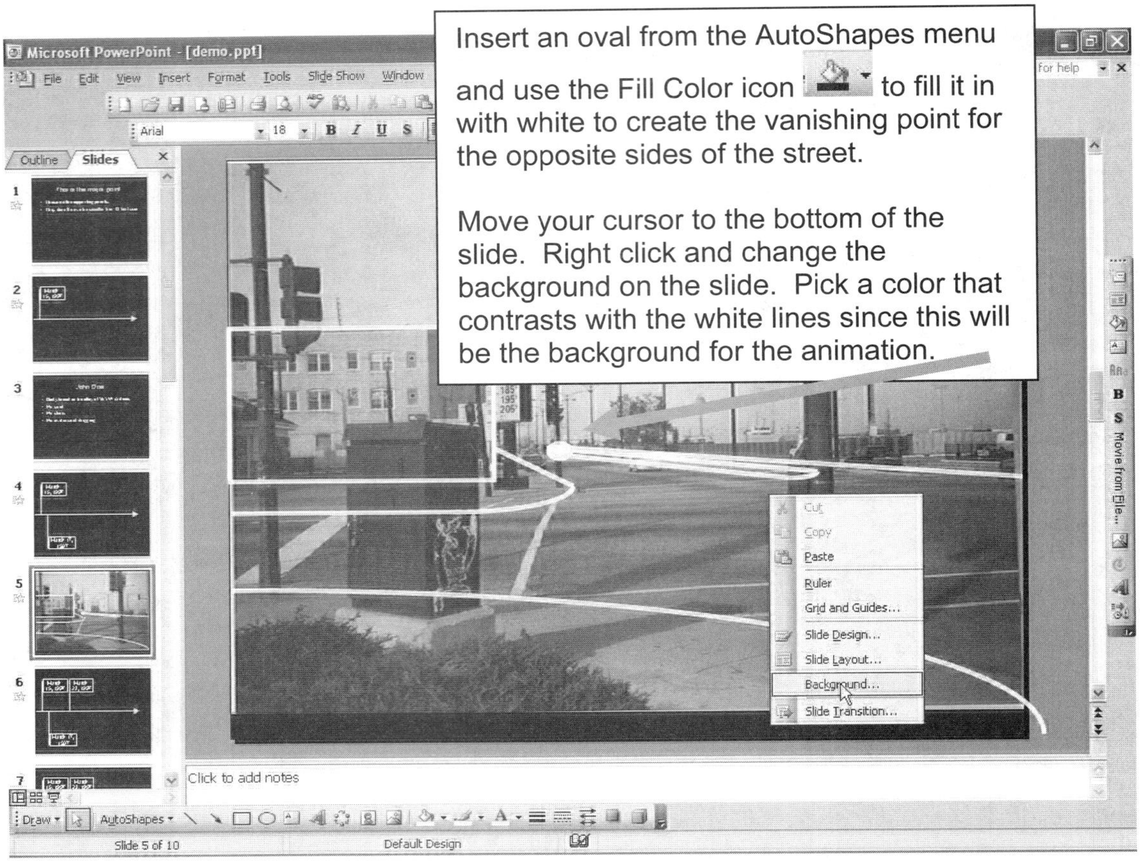
Insert an oval from the AutoShapes menu and use the Fill Color icon to fill it in with white to create the vanishing point for the opposite sides of the street.
Move your cursor to the bottom of the slide. Right click and change the background on the slide. Pick a color that contrasts with the white lines since this will be the background for the animation.
Microsoft PowerPoint - [demo.ppt]
Cut
Copy
Paste
Ruler
Grid and Guides...
Slide Design...
Slide Layout...
Background...
Slide Transition...
Click to add notes
Slide 5 of 10
Default Design

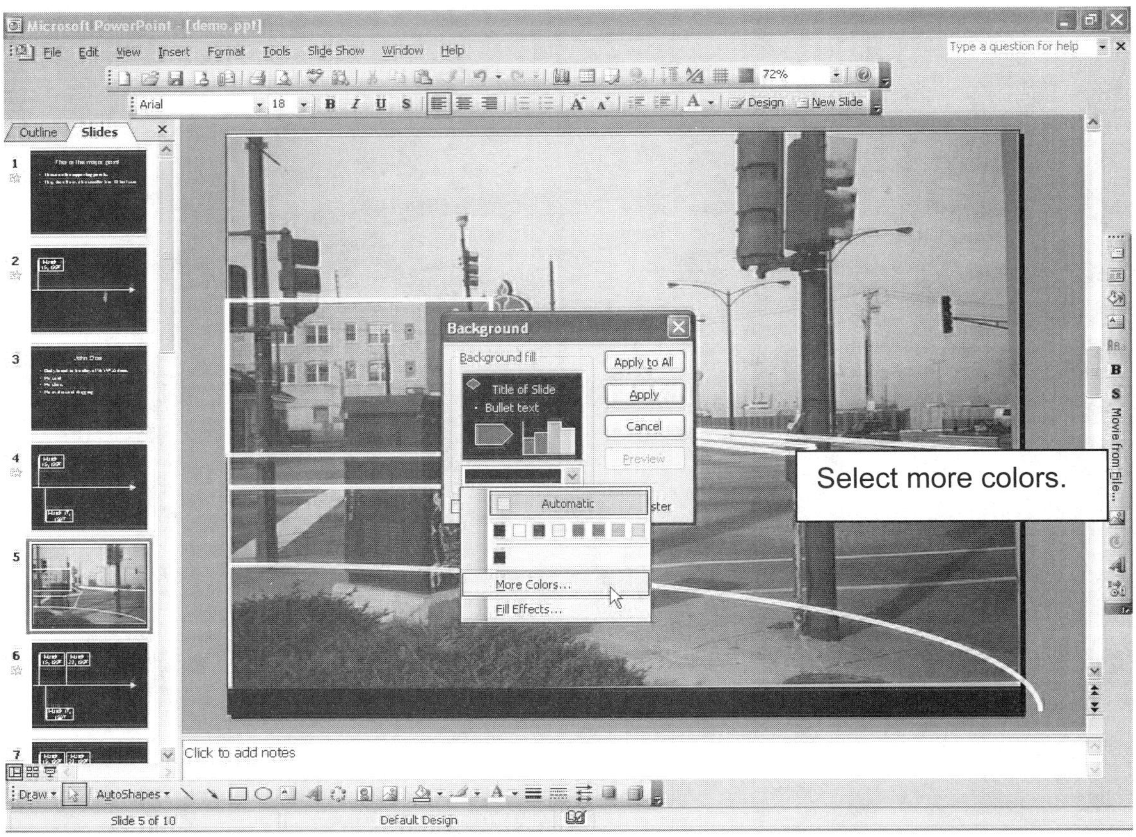
Microsoft PowerPoint - [demo.ppt]
Background
Background fill
Title of Slide
Bullet text
Apply to All
Apply
Cancel
Preview
Automatic
More Colors...
Fill Effects...
Select more colors.
Click to add notes
Slide 5 of 10
Default Design

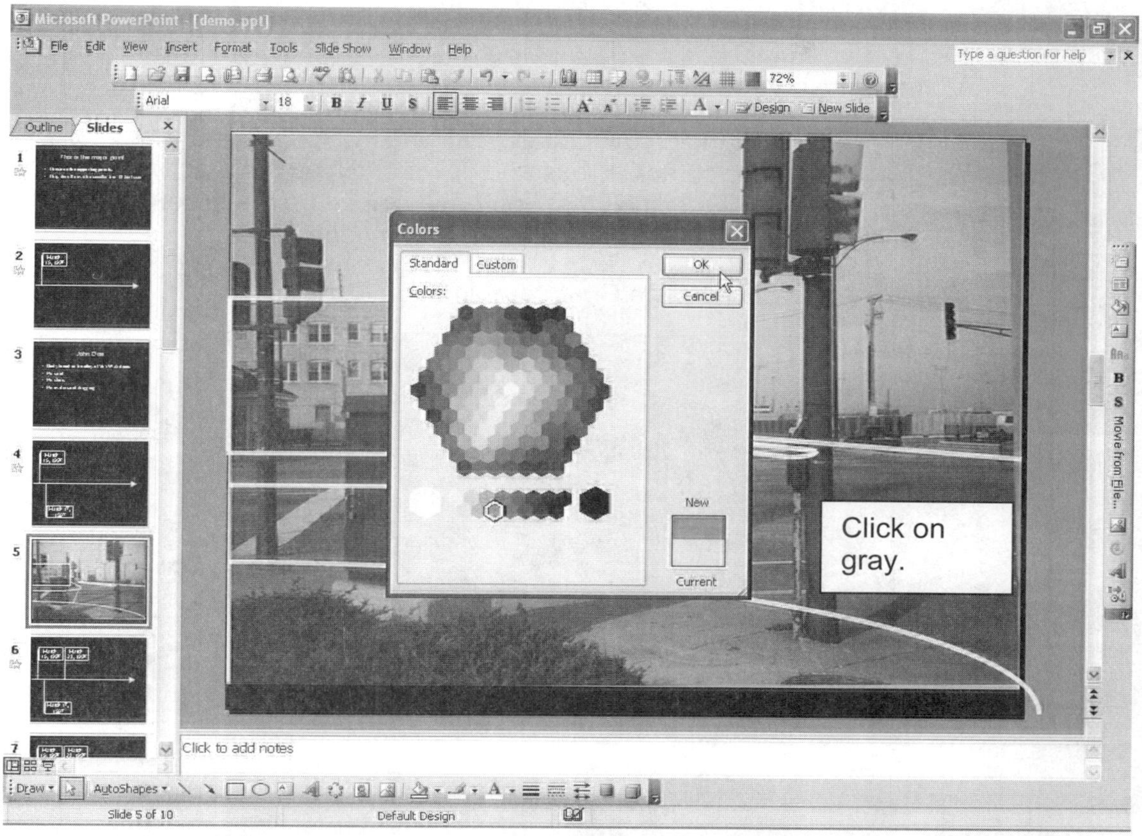
Microsoft PowerPoint - [demo.ppt]
File Edit View Insert Format Tools Slide Show Window Help
Type a question for help
Outline Slides
Colors
Standard Custom
Colors:
OK
Cancel
New
Current
Click on gray.
Click to add notes
Slide 5 of 10
Default Design

Microsoft PowerPoint - [demo.ppt]
File Edit View Insert Format Tools Slide Show Window Help
Type a question for help
Outline Slides
Background
Background fill
Title of Slide
Bullet text
Apply to All
Apply
Cancel
Preview
Omit background graphics from master
Click on Apply.
Click to add notes
Slide 5 of 10
Default Design

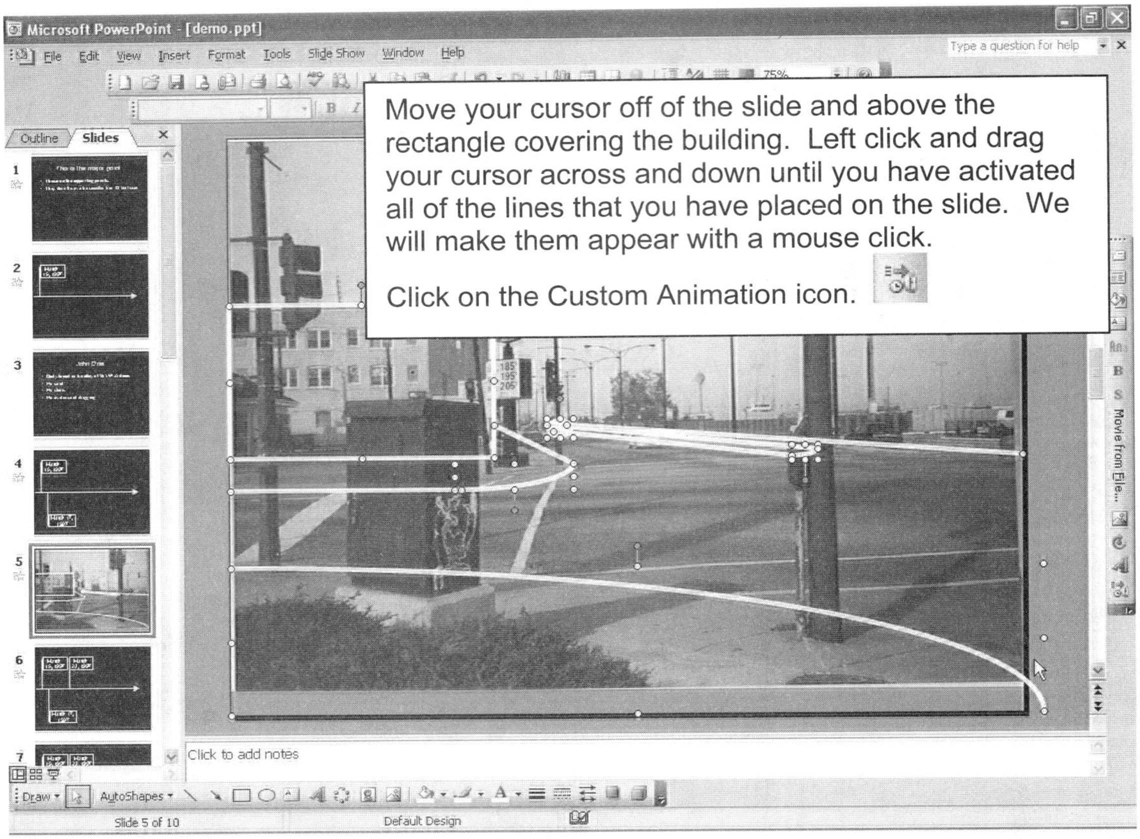
Microsoft PowerPoint - [demo.ppt]
Move your cursor off of the slide and above the rectangle covering the building. Left click and drag your cursor across and down until you have activated all of the lines that you have placed on the slide. We will make them appear with a mouse click.
Click on the Custom Animation icon.
Click to add notes
Slide 5 of 10
Default Design

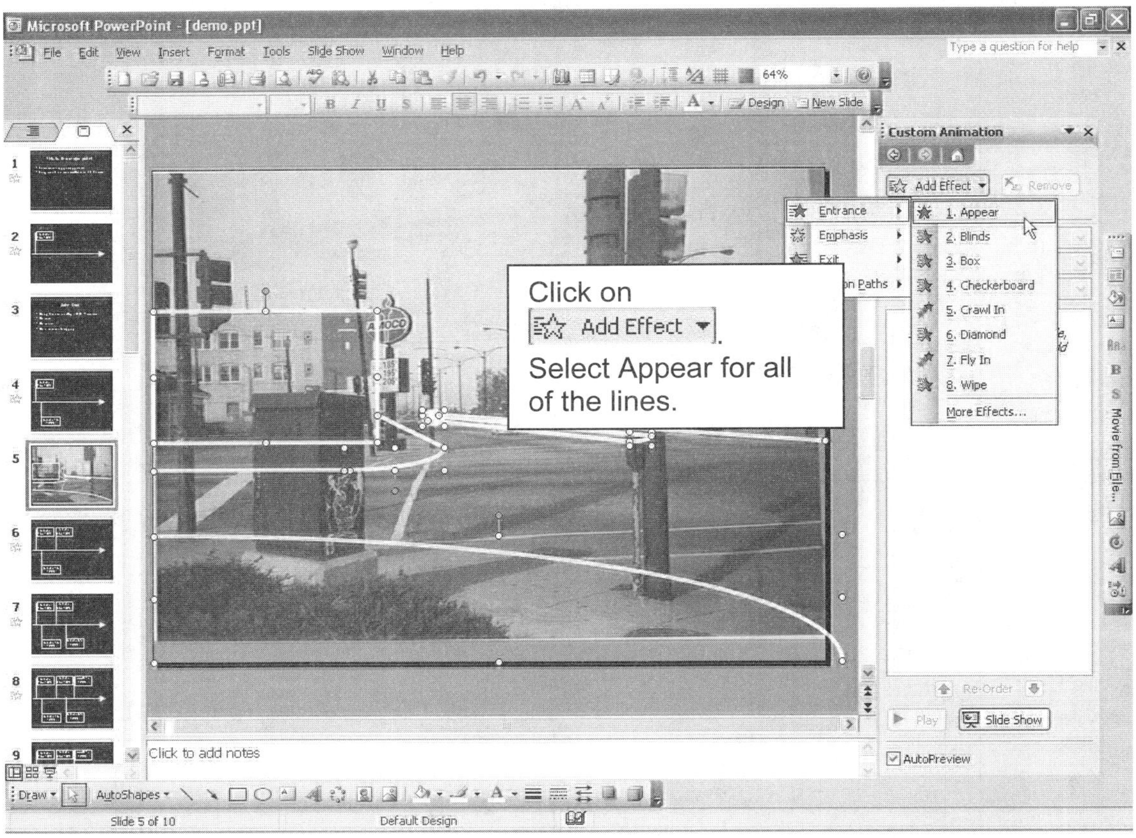
Microsoft PowerPoint - [demo.ppt]
Custom Animation
Add Effect
Entrance
Emphasis
Exit
1. Appear
2. Blinds
3. Box
4. Checkerboard
5. Crawl In
6. Diamond
7. Fly In
8. Wipe
More Effects...
Click on
Add Effect
Select Appear for all of the lines.
Click to add notes
Slide 5 of 10
Default Design

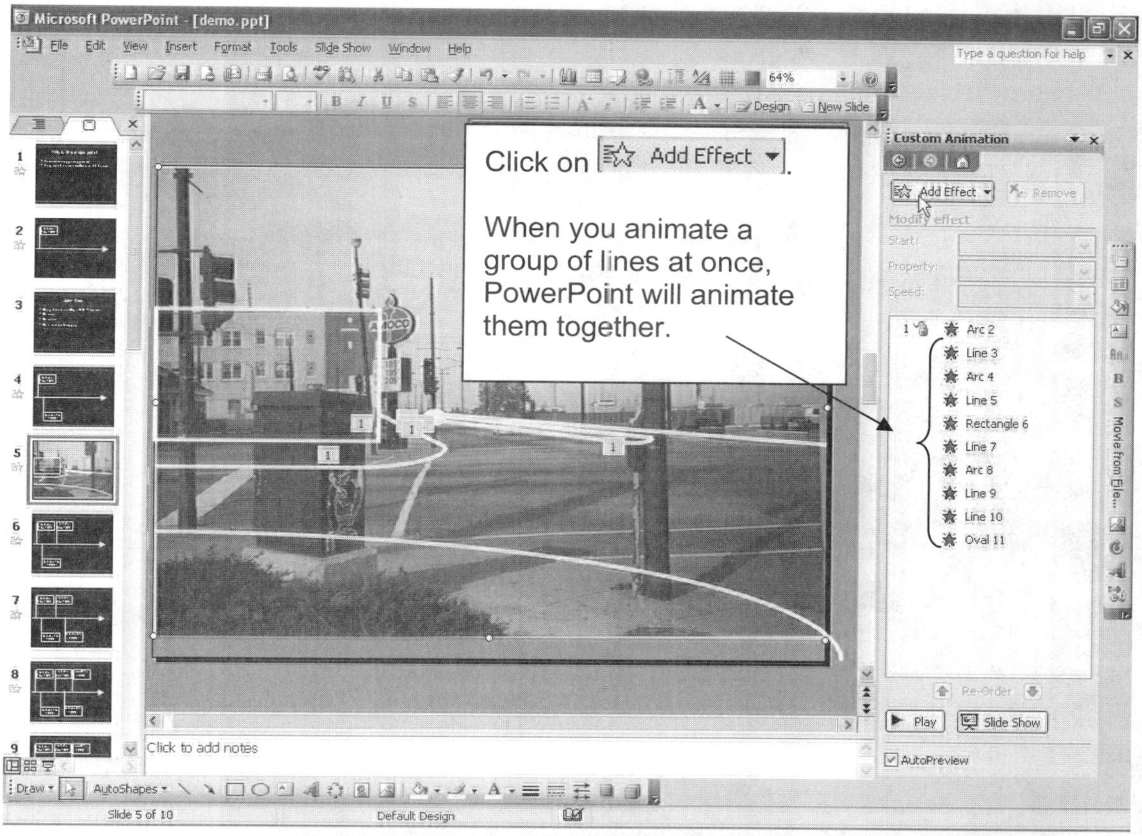
Microsoft PowerPoint - [demo.ppt]
Click on Add Effect.
When you animate a group of lines at once, PowerPoint will animate them together.
Custom Animation
Add Effect
Remove
Arc 2
Line 3
Arc 4
Line 5
Rectangle 6
Line 7
Arc 8
Line 9
Line 10
Oval 11
Play
Slide Show
AutoPreview
Click to add notes
Slide 5 of 10
Default Design

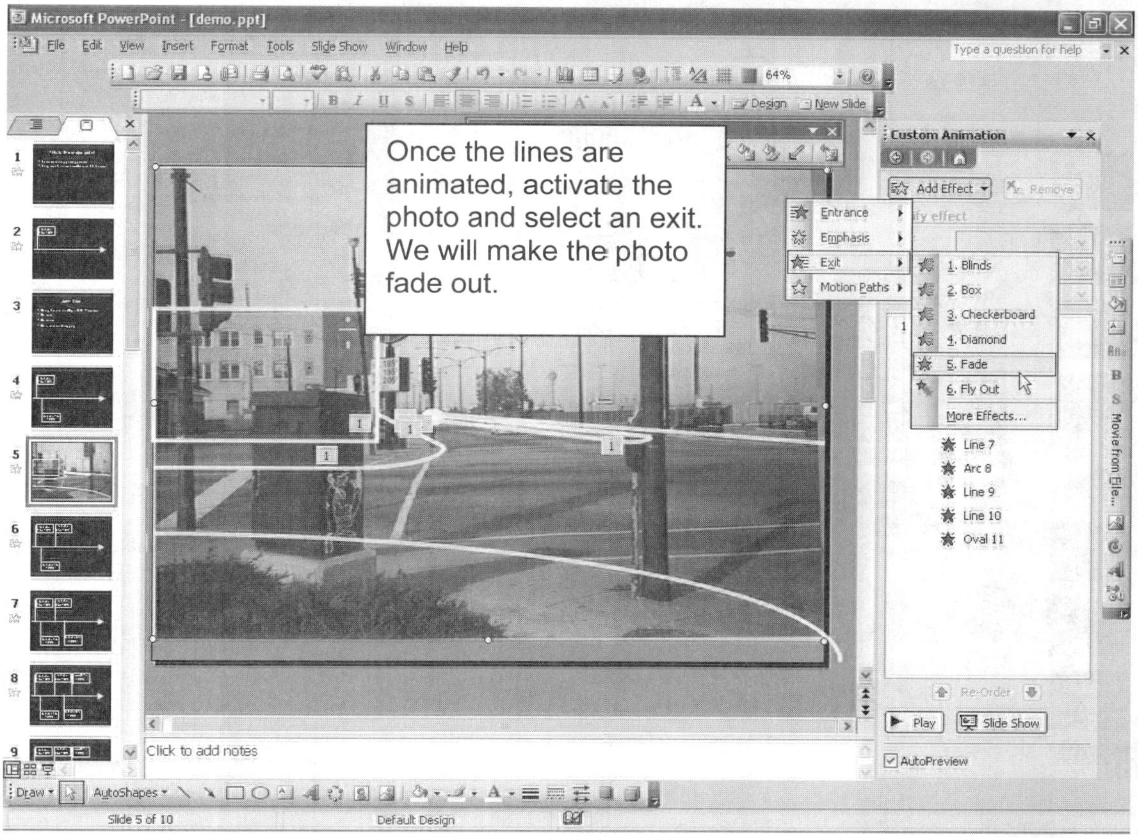
Microsoft PowerPoint - [demo.ppt]
Once the lines are animated, activate the photo and select an exit. We will make the photo fade out.
Custom Animation
Add Effect
Remove
Entrance
Emphasis
Exit
Motion Paths
1. Blinds
2. Box
3. Checkerboard
4. Diamond
5. Fade
6. Fly Out
More Effects...
Line 7
Arc 8
Line 9
Line 10
Oval 11
Play
Slide Show
AutoPreview
Click to add notes
Slide 5 of 10
Default Design

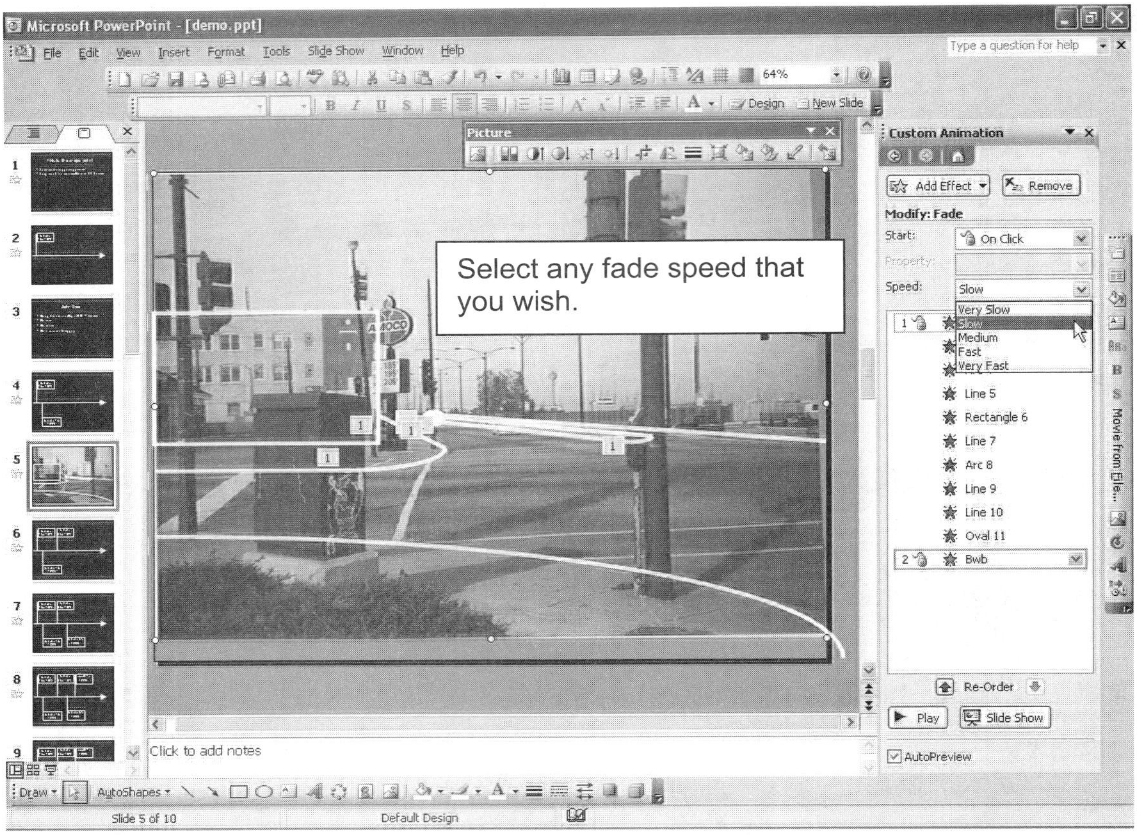
Microsoft PowerPoint - [demo.ppt]
Select any fade speed that you wish.
Custom Animation
Add Effect
Remove
Modify: Fade
Start:
On Click
Property:
Speed:
Slow
Very Slow
Slow
Medium
Fast
Very Fast
Line 5
Rectangle 6
Line 7
Arc 8
Line 9
Line 10
Oval 11
Bwb
Re-Order
Play
Slide Show
AutoPreview
Click to add notes
Slide 5 of 10
Default Design

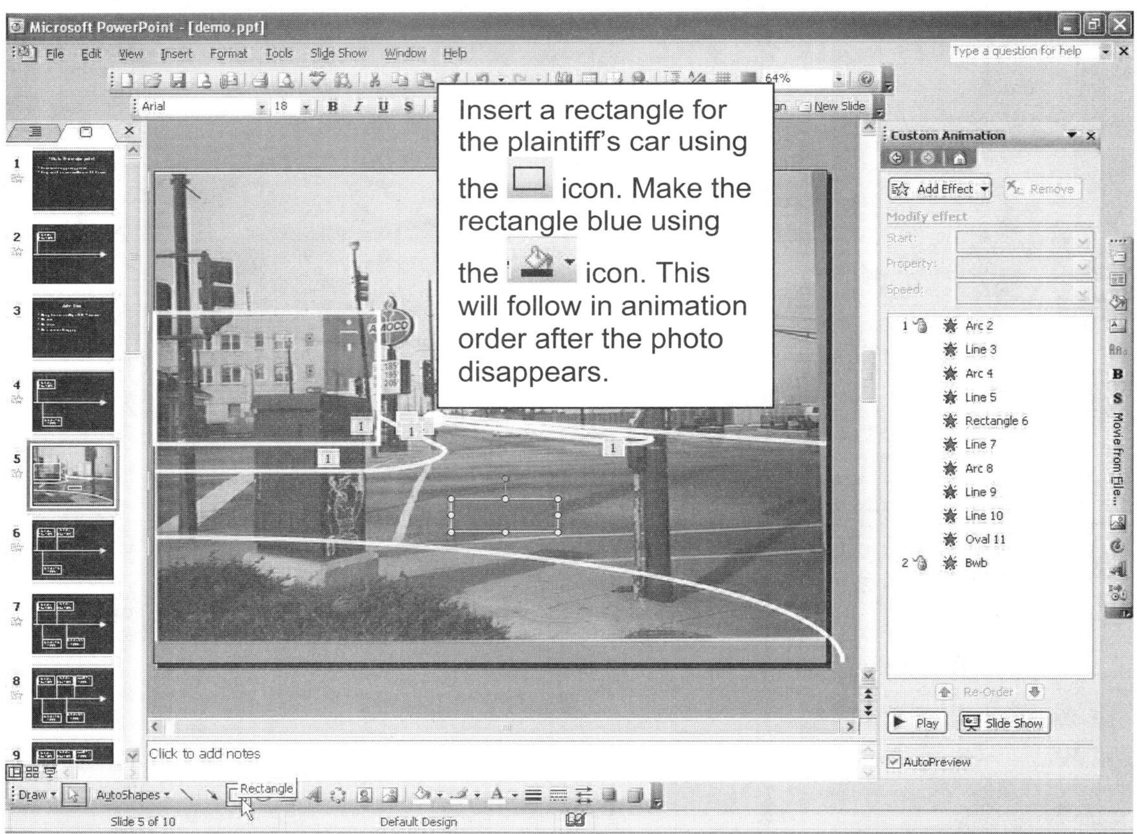
Microsoft PowerPoint - [demo.ppt]
Insert a rectangle for the plaintiff's car using the icon. Make the rectangle blue using the icon. This will follow in animation order after the photo disappears.
Custom Animation
Add Effect
Remove
Modify effect
Arc 2
Line 3
Arc 4
Line 5
Rectangle 6
Line 7
Arc 8
Line 9
Line 10
Oval 11
Bwb
Re-Order
Play
Slide Show
AutoPreview
Click to add notes
Rectangle
Slide 5 of 10
Default Design

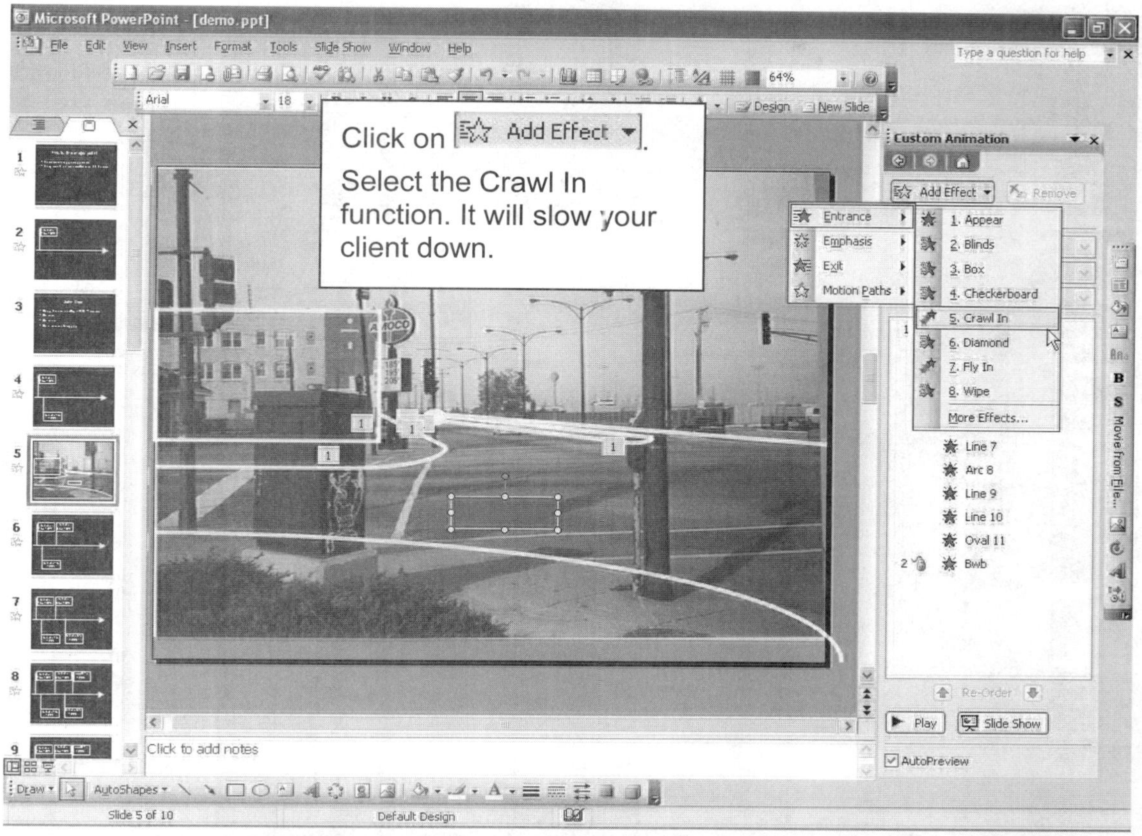
Microsoft PowerPoint - [demo.ppt]
Click on Add Effect.
Select the Crawl In function. It will slow your client down.
Custom Animation
Add Effect
Remove
Entrance
Emphasis
Exit
Motion Paths
1. Appear
2. Blinds
3. Box
4. Checkerboard
5. Crawl In
6. Diamond
7. Fly In
8. Wipe
More Effects...
Line 7
Arc 8
Line 9
Line 10
Oval 11
Bwb
Re-Order
Play
Slide Show
AutoPreview
Click to add notes
Slide 5 of 10
Default Design

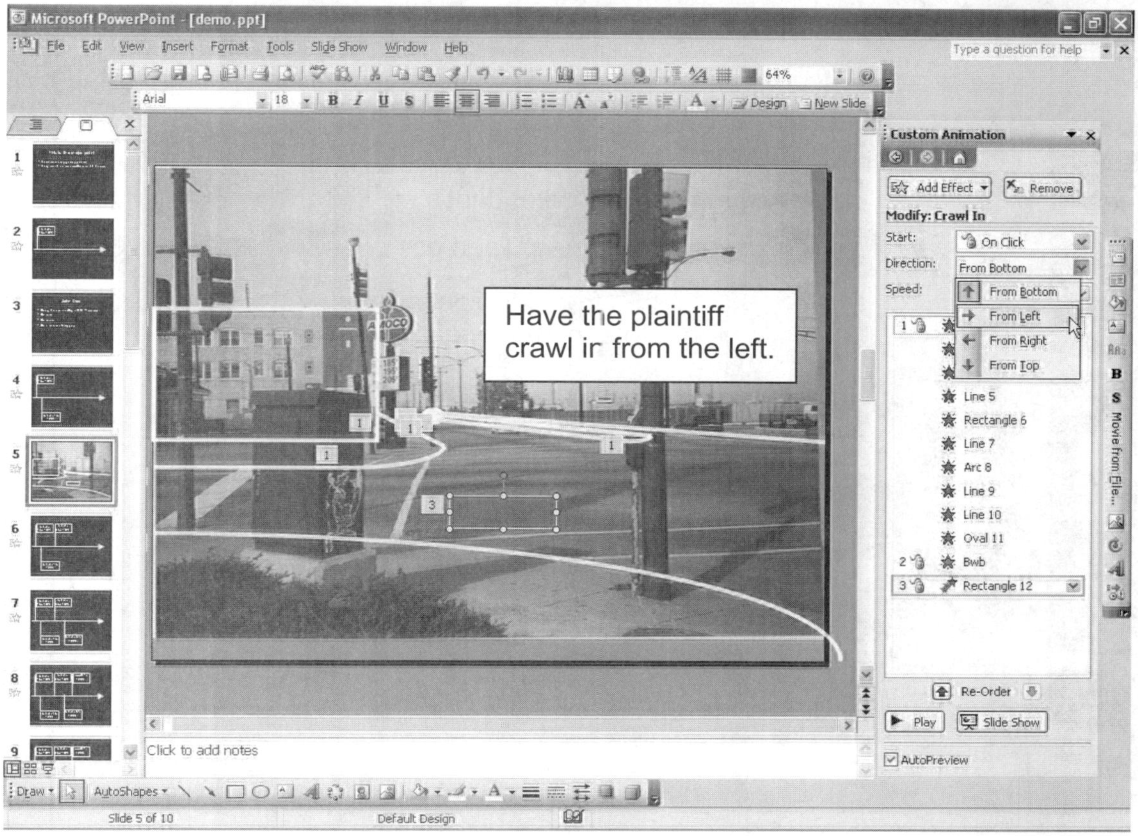
Microsoft PowerPoint - [demo.ppt]
Have the plaintiff crawl in from the left.
Custom Animation
Add Effect
Remove
Modify: Crawl In
Start:
On Click
Direction:
From Bottom
Speed:
From Bottom
From Left
From Right
From Top
Line 5
Rectangle 6
Line 7
Arc 8
Line 9
Line 10
Oval 11
Bwb
Rectangle 12
Re-Order
Play
Slide Show
AutoPreview
Click to add notes
Slide 5 of 10
Default Design

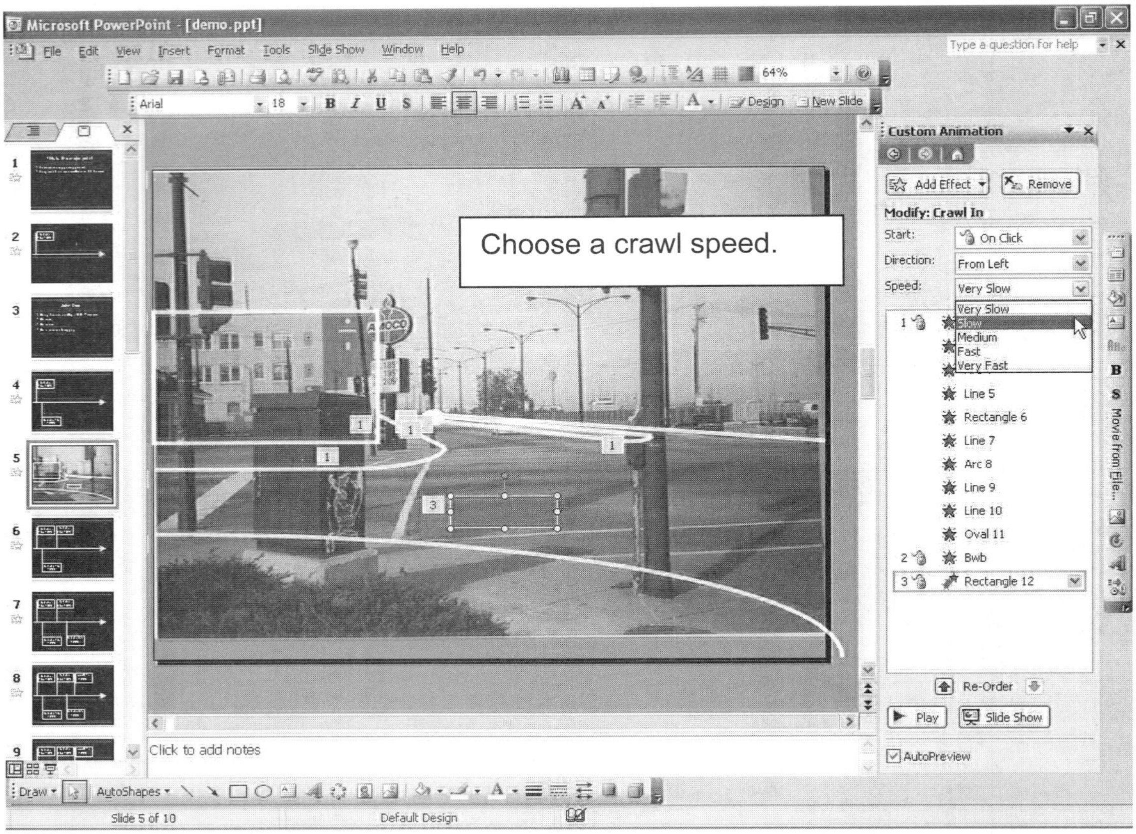
Microsoft PowerPoint - [demo.ppt]
Choose a crawl speed.
Custom Animation
Add Effect
Remove
Modify: Crawl In
Start:
On Click
Direction:
From Left
Speed:
Very Slow
Very Slow
Slow
Medium
Fast
Very Fast
Line 5
Rectangle 6
Line 7
Arc 8
Line 9
Line 10
Oval 11
Bwb
Rectangle 12
Re-Order
Play
Slide Show
AutoPreview
Click to add notes
Slide 5 of 10
Default Design

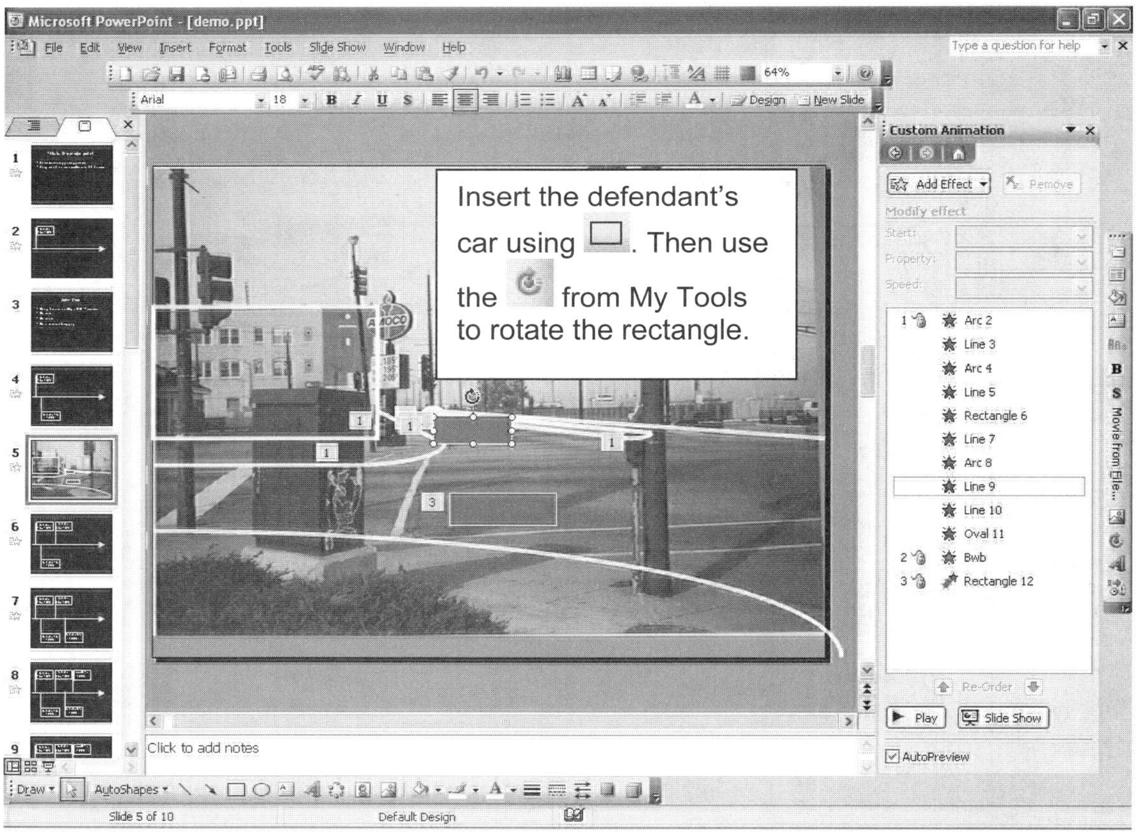
Microsoft PowerPoint - [demo.ppt]
Insert the defendant's car using . Then use the from My Tools to rotate the rectangle.
Custom Animation
Add Effect
Remove
Modify effect
Arc 2
Line 3
Arc 4
Line 5
Rectangle 6
Line 7
Arc 8
Line 9
Line 10
Oval 11
Bwb
Rectangle 12
Re-Order
Play
Slide Show
AutoPreview
Click to add notes
Slide 5 of 10
Default Design

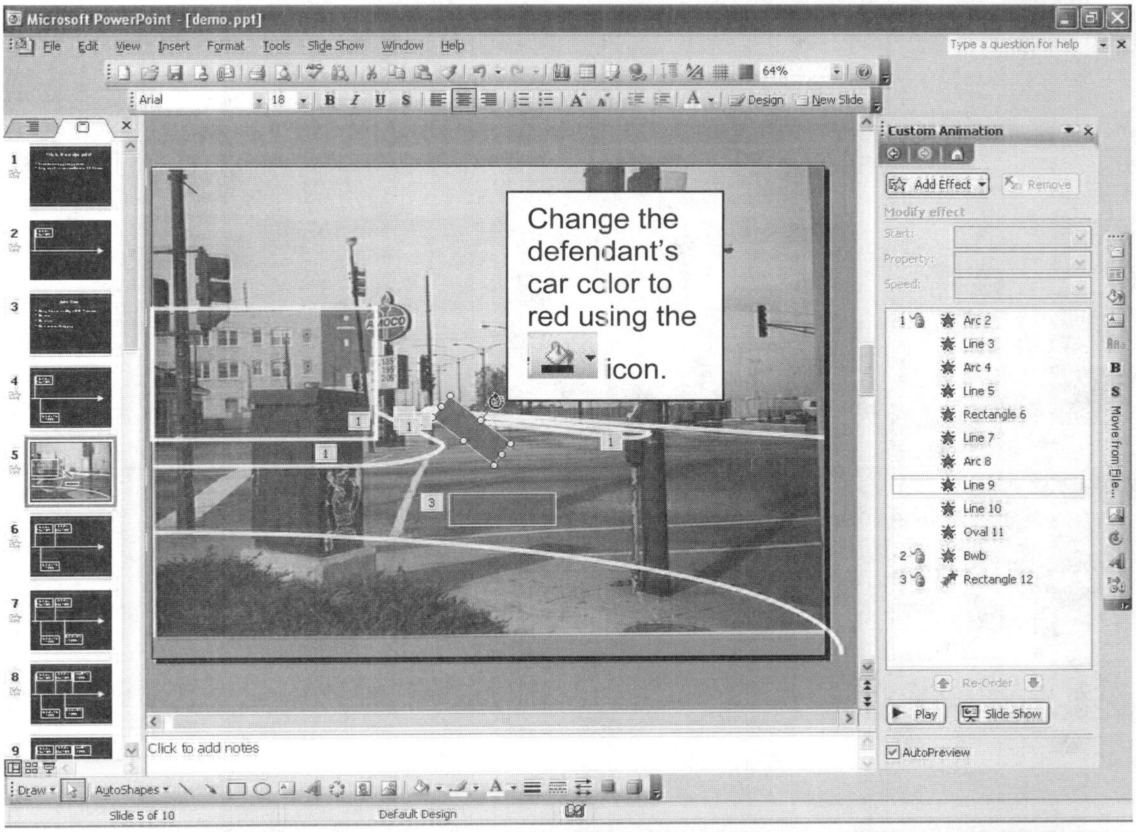
Microsoft PowerPoint - [demo.ppt]
Change the defendant's car color to red using the icon.
Custom Animation
Add Effect
Remove
Arc 2
Line 3
Arc 4
Line 5
Rectangle 6
Line 7
Arc 8
Line 9
Line 10
Oval 11
Bwb
Rectangle 12
Play
Slide Show
AutoPreview
Click to add notes
Slide 5 of 10
Default Design

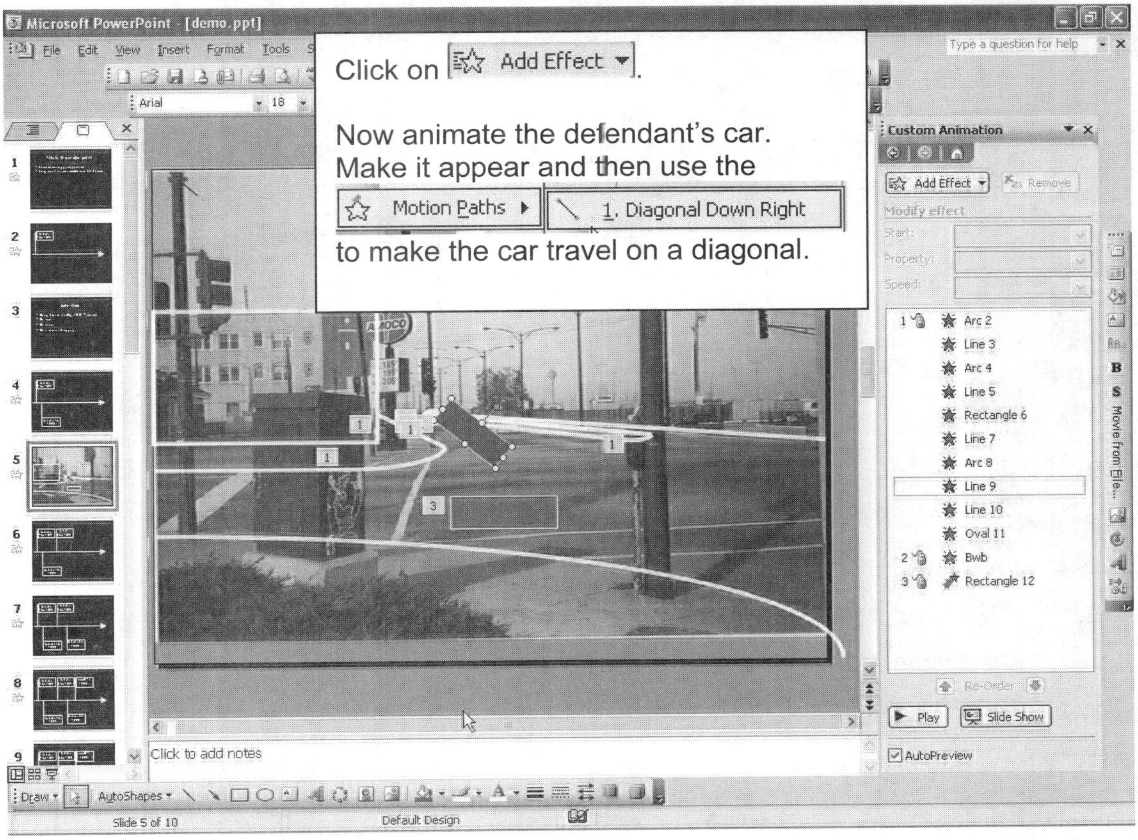
Microsoft PowerPoint - [demo.ppt]
Click on Add Effect.
Now animate the defendant's car. Make it appear and then use the
Motion Paths
1. Diagonal Down Right
to make the car travel on a diagonal.
Custom Animation
Add Effect
Remove
Arc 2
Line 3
Arc 4
Line 5
Rectangle 6
Line 7
Arc 8
Line 9
Line 10
Oval 11
Bwb
Rectangle 12
Play
Slide Show
AutoPreview
Click to add notes
Slide 5 of 10
Default Design

Microsoft PowerPoint - [demo.ppt]
File Edit View Insert Format Tools Slide Show Window Help
Custom Animation
Add Effect
Entrance
Emphasis
Exit
Motion Paths
1. Appear
2. Blinds
3. Box
4. Checkerboard
5. Crawl In
6. Diamond
7. Fly In
8. Wipe
More Effects...
Line 7
Arc 8
Line 9
Line 10
Oval 11
Bwb
Rectangle 12
Re-Order
Play
Slide Show
AutoPreview
Click to add notes
Slide 5 of 10
Default Design

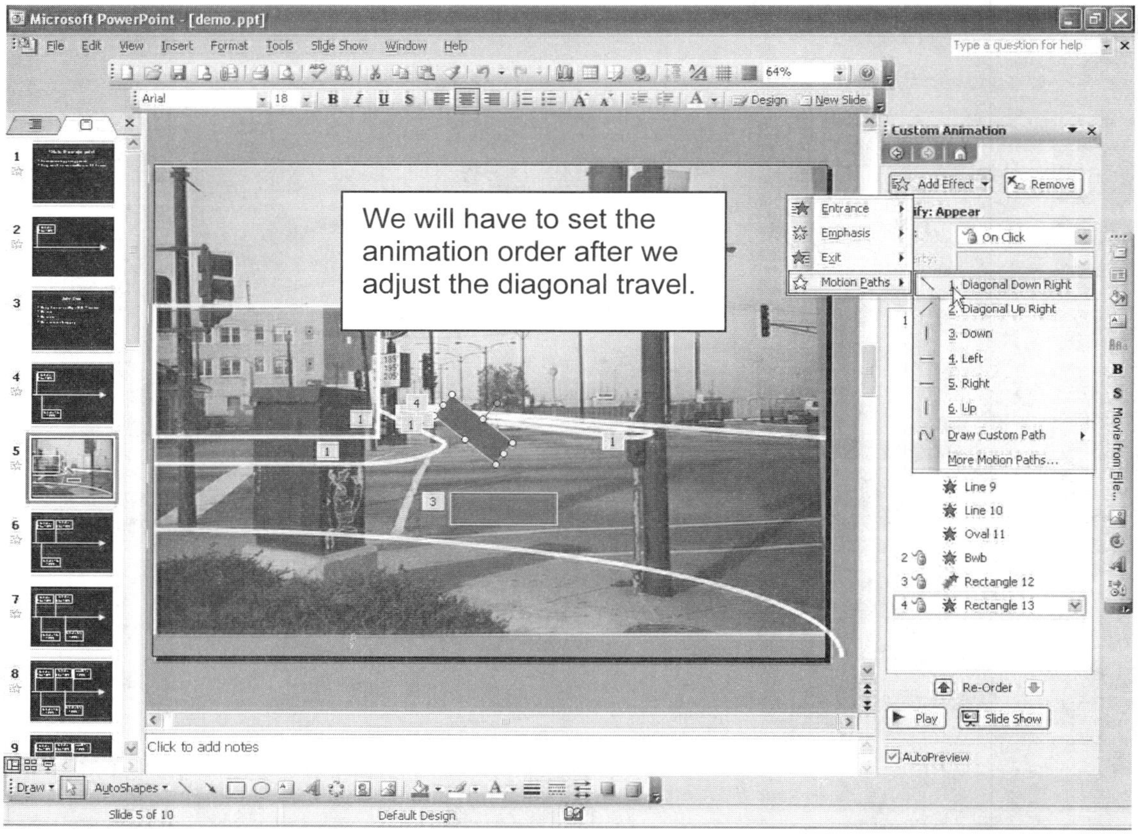
Microsoft PowerPoint - [demo.ppt]
File Edit View Insert Format Tools Slide Show Window Help
We will have to set the animation order after we adjust the diagonal travel.
Custom Animation
Add Effect
Remove
Entrance
Emphasis
Exit
Motion Paths
1. Diagonal Down Right
2. Diagonal Up Right
3. Down
4. Left
5. Right
6. Up
Draw Custom Path
More Motion Paths...
On Click
Line 9
Line 10
Oval 11
Bwb
Rectangle 12
Rectangle 13
Re-Order
Play
Slide Show
AutoPreview
Click to add notes
Slide 5 of 10
Default Design

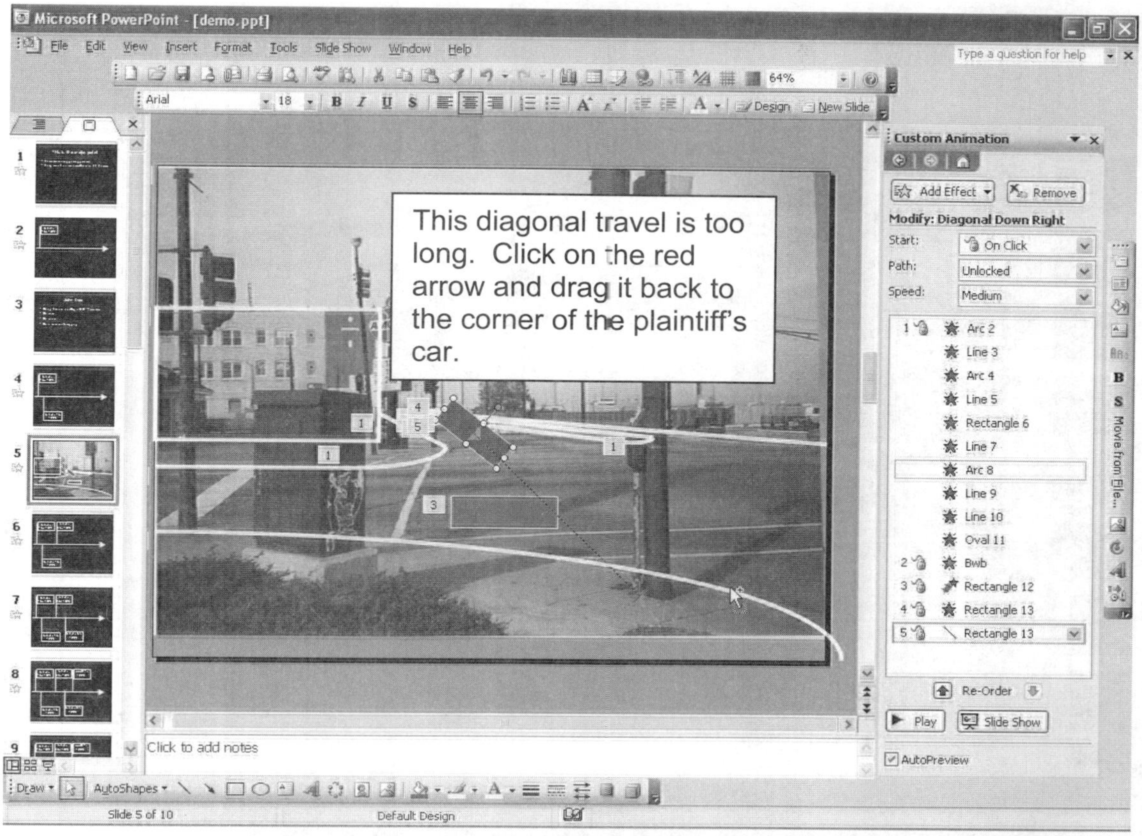
Microsoft PowerPoint - [demo.ppt]
This diagonal travel is too long. Click on the red arrow and drag it back to the corner of the plaintiff's car.
Custom Animation
Modify: Diagonal Down Right
Click to add notes
Slide 5 of 10
Default Design

Microsoft PowerPoint - [demo.ppt]
Custom Animation
Modify: Diagonal Down Right
Click to add notes
Slide 5 of 10
Default Design

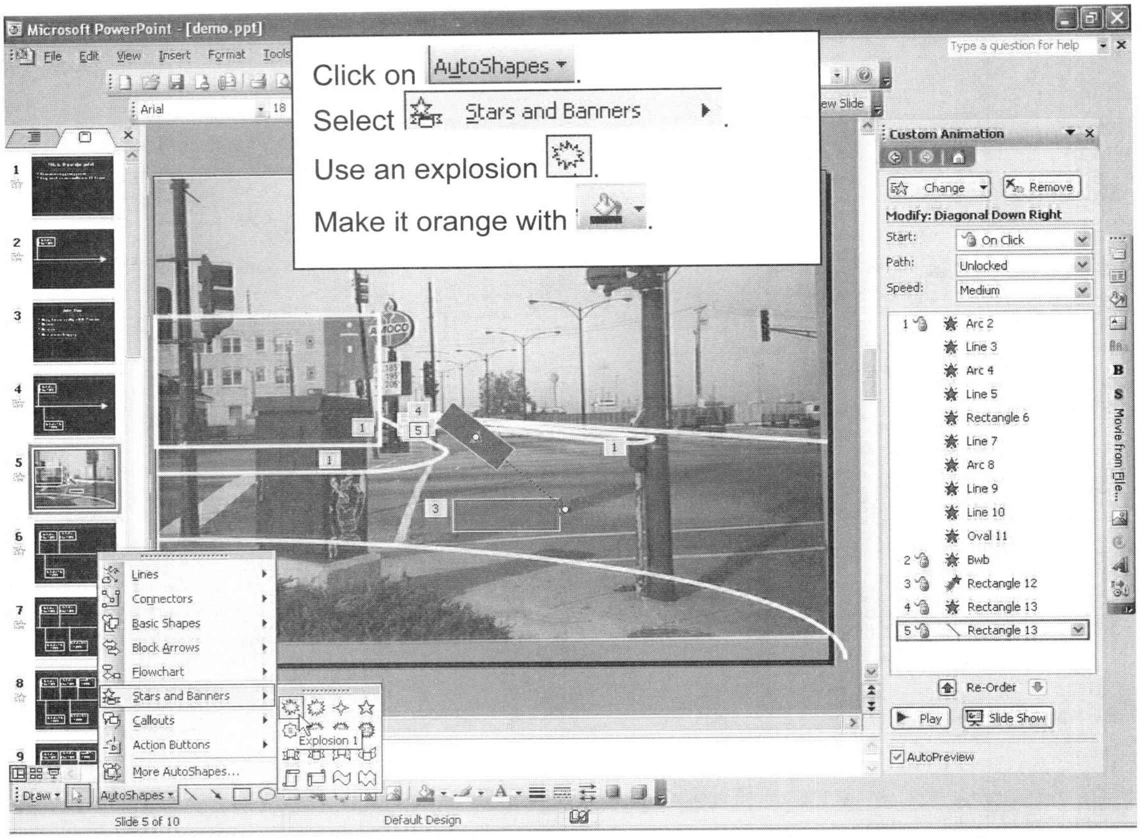
Click on AutoShapes.
Select Stars and Banners.
Use an explosion.
Make it orange with.

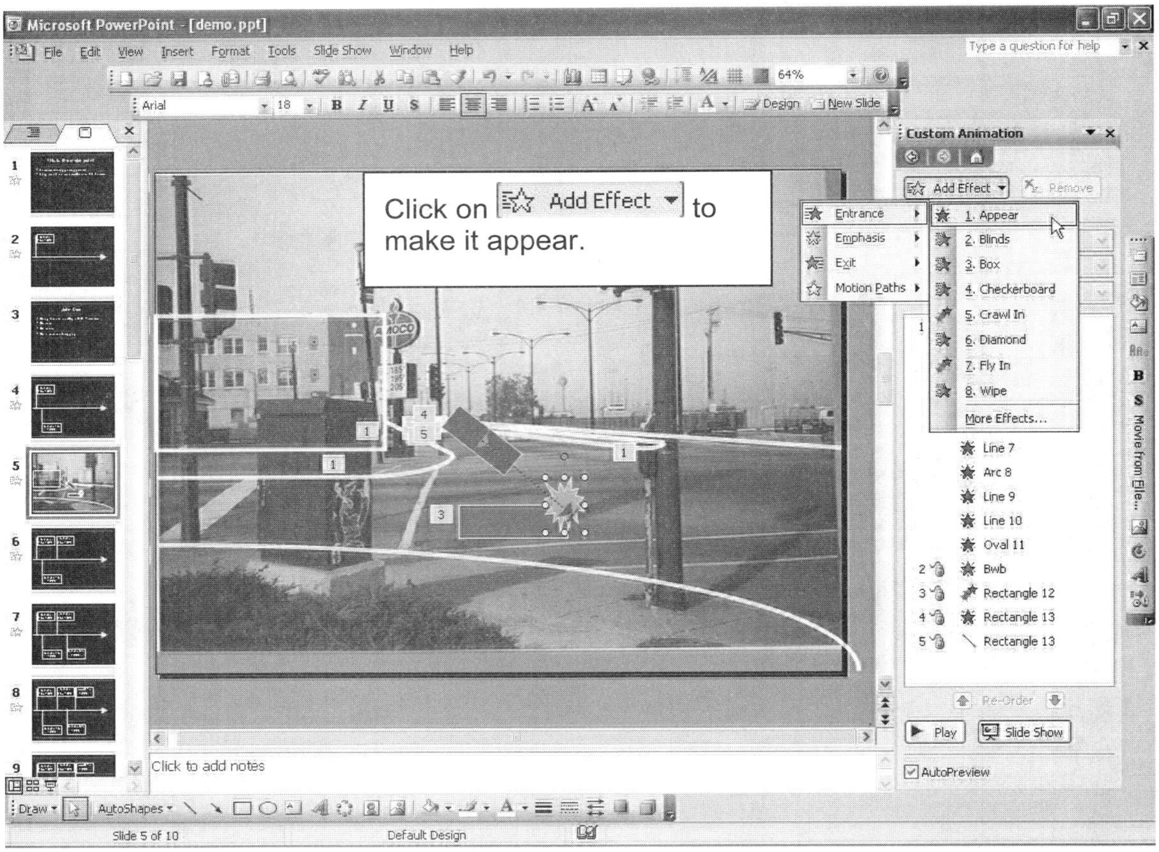
Click on Add Effect to make it appear.

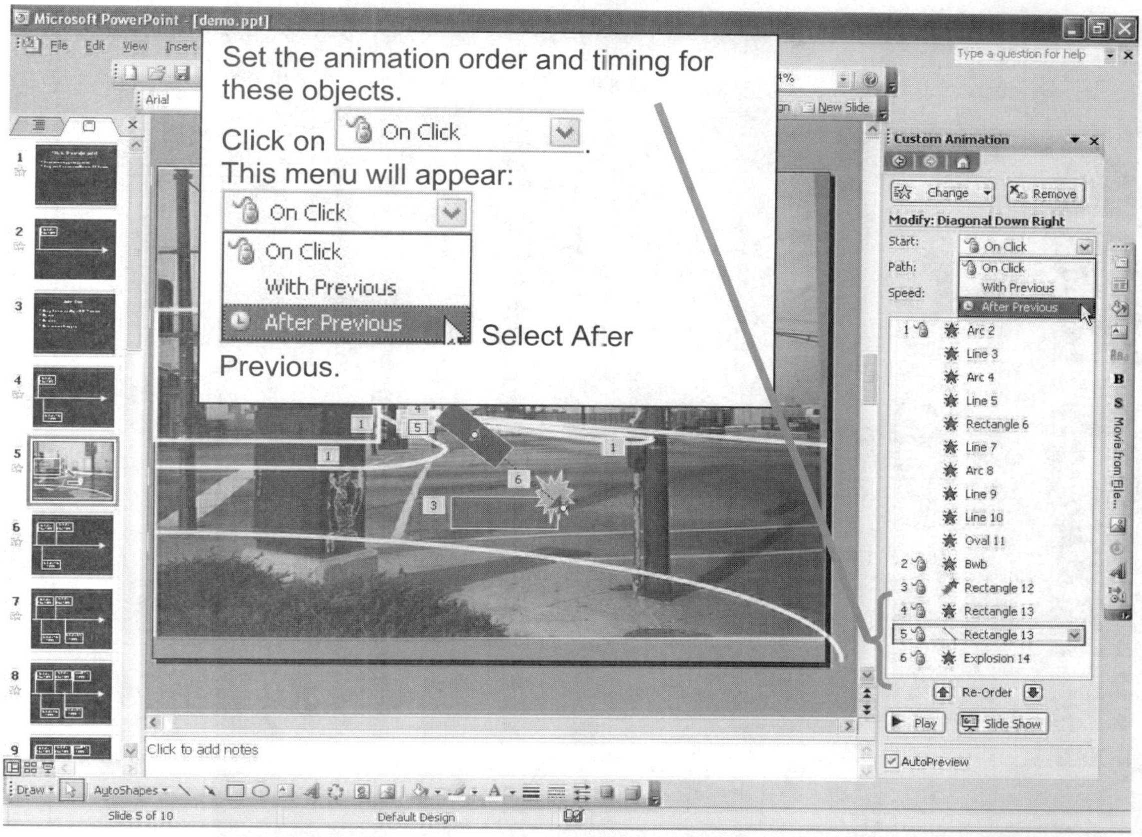
Microsoft PowerPoint - [demo.ppt]
Set the animation order and timing for these objects.
Click on On Click.
This menu will appear:
On Click
On Click
With Previous
After Previous
Select After Previous.
Custom Animation
Change
Remove
Modify: Diagonal Down Right
Start:
Path:
Speed:
Arc 2
Line 3
Arc 4
Line 5
Rectangle 6
Line 7
Arc 8
Line 9
Line 10
Oval 11
Bwb
Rectangle 12
Rectangle 13
Rectangle 13
Explosion 14
Re-Order
Play
Slide Show
AutoPreview
Click to add notes
Slide 5 of 10
Default Design

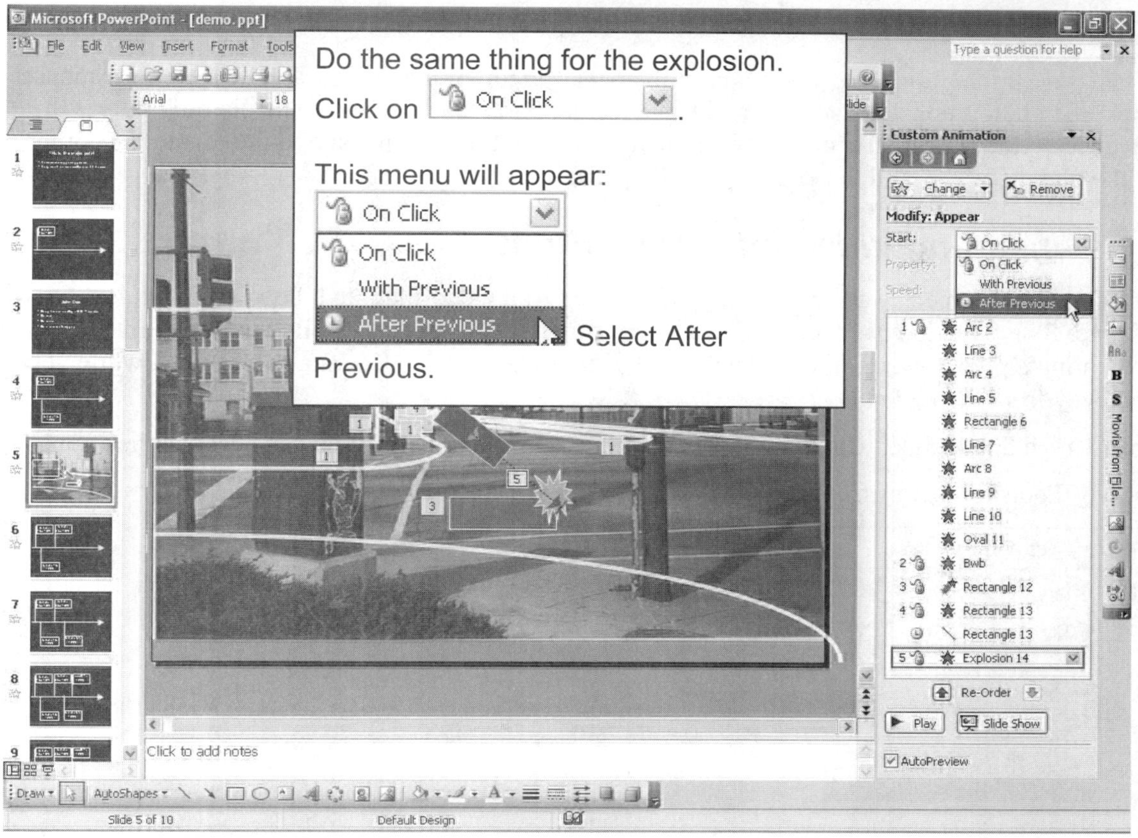
Microsoft PowerPoint - [demo.ppt]
Do the same thing for the explosion.
Click on On Click.
This menu will appear:
On Click
On Click
With Previous
After Previous
Select After Previous.
Custom Animation
Change
Remove
Modify: Appear
Start:
Property:
Speed:
Arc 2
Line 3
Arc 4
Line 5
Rectangle 6
Line 7
Arc 8
Line 9
Line 10
Oval 11
Bwb
Rectangle 12
Rectangle 13
Rectangle 13
Explosion 14
Re-Order
Play
Slide Show
AutoPreview
Click to add notes
Slide 5 of 10
Default Design

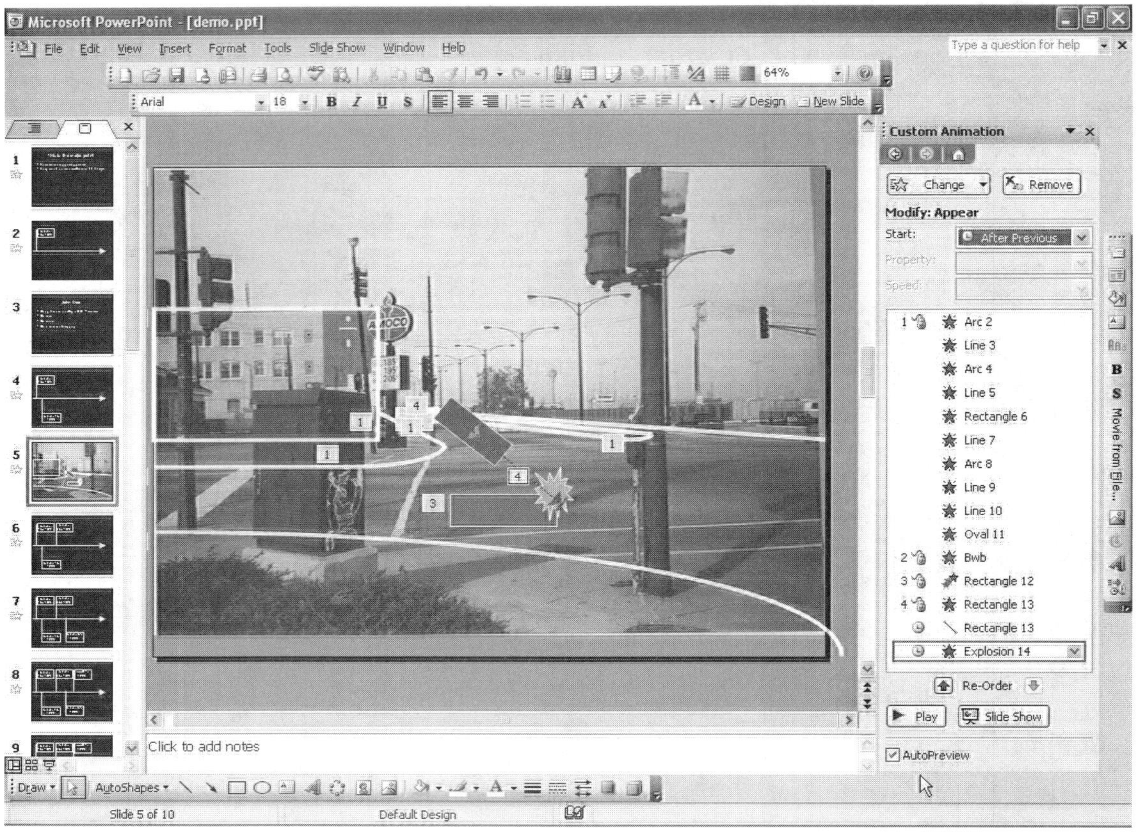

When you run this slide show, the lines will appear on top of the photograph. On the next mouse click, the photograph will fade out and leave the dark gray background. The plaintiff's car will advance on the next mouse click. Then the defendant's car will appear and move into the corner of the plaintiff's car, and the explosion will appear.

Inserting Video into PowerPoint

The following screens walk you through how to insert a video file into a PowerPoint slide. Chapter 8 on Sanction has more useful tips on using video clips, especially when you are presenting a proactive argument or when you want to launch a video on a mouse click while you are away from the laptop.

Start with a blank slide. Click on the Movie from File menu, which you can access either from the My Tools toolbar or from the Insert menu on the standard toolbar.

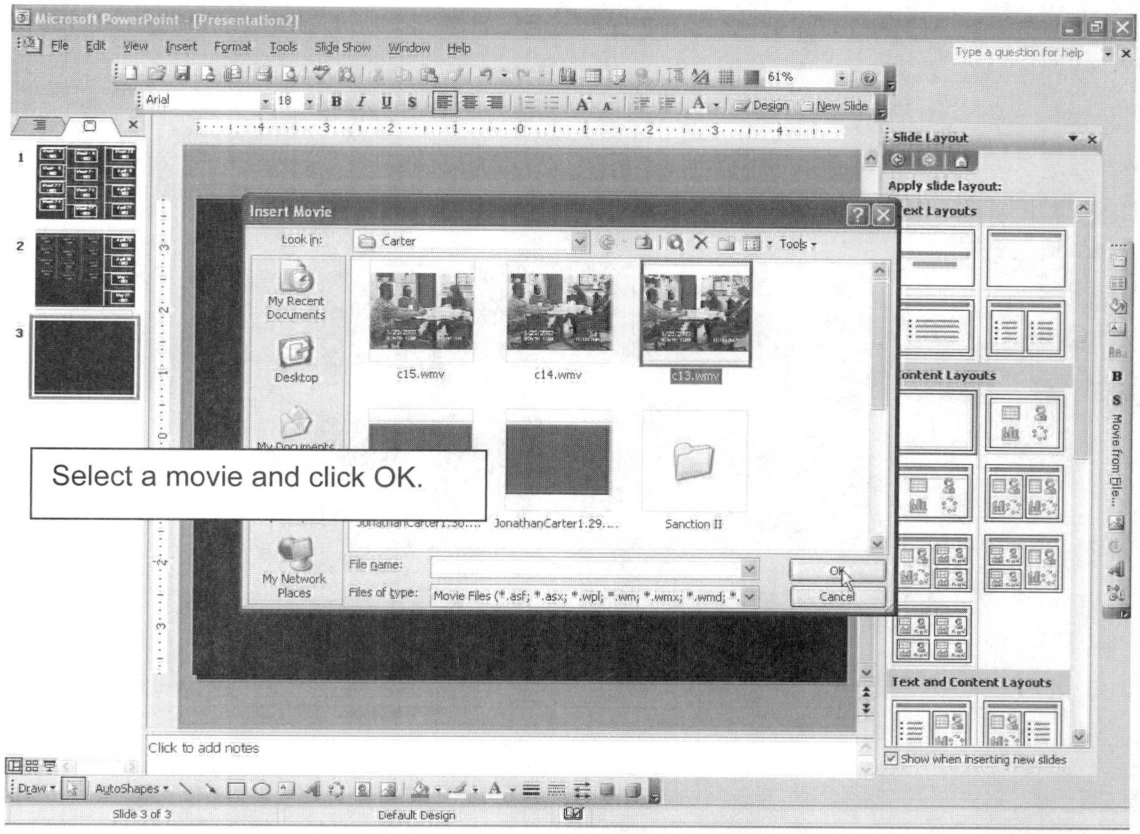
Microsoft PowerPoint - [Presentation2]
Insert Movie
Select a movie and click OK.
c15.wmv
c14.wmv
c13.wmv
Sanction II
Slide Layout
Apply slide layout:
Click to add notes
Slide 3 of 3
Default Design

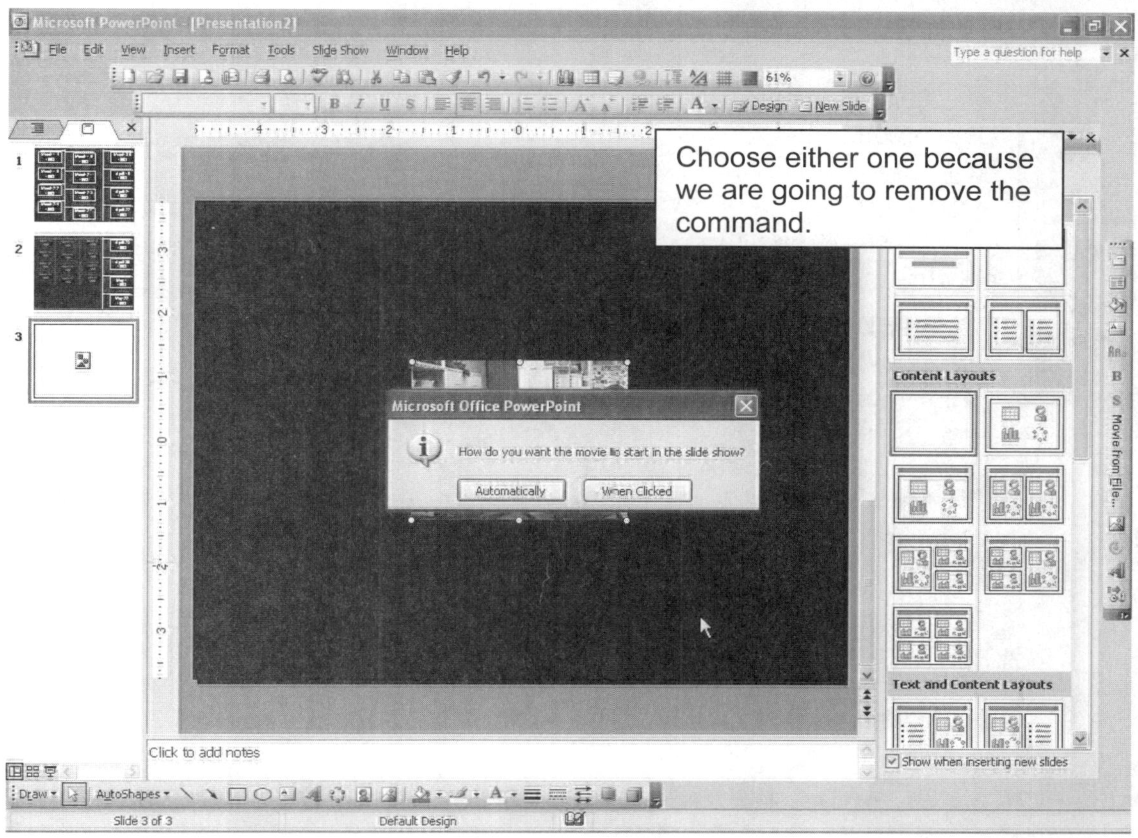
Microsoft PowerPoint - [Presentation2]
Choose either one because we are going to remove the command.
Microsoft Office PowerPoint
How do you want the movie to start in the slide show?
Automatically
When Clicked
Click to add notes
Slide 3 of 3
Default Design

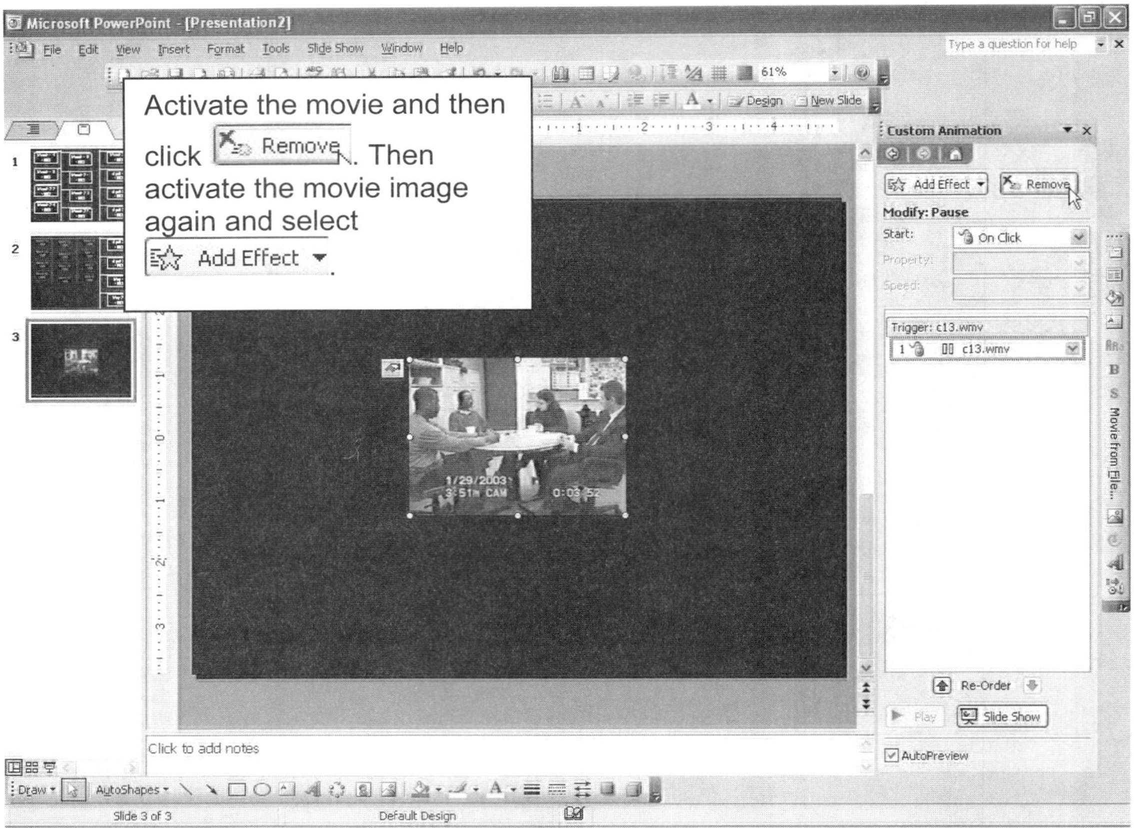
Activate the movie and then click Remove. Then activate the movie image again and select Add Effect.

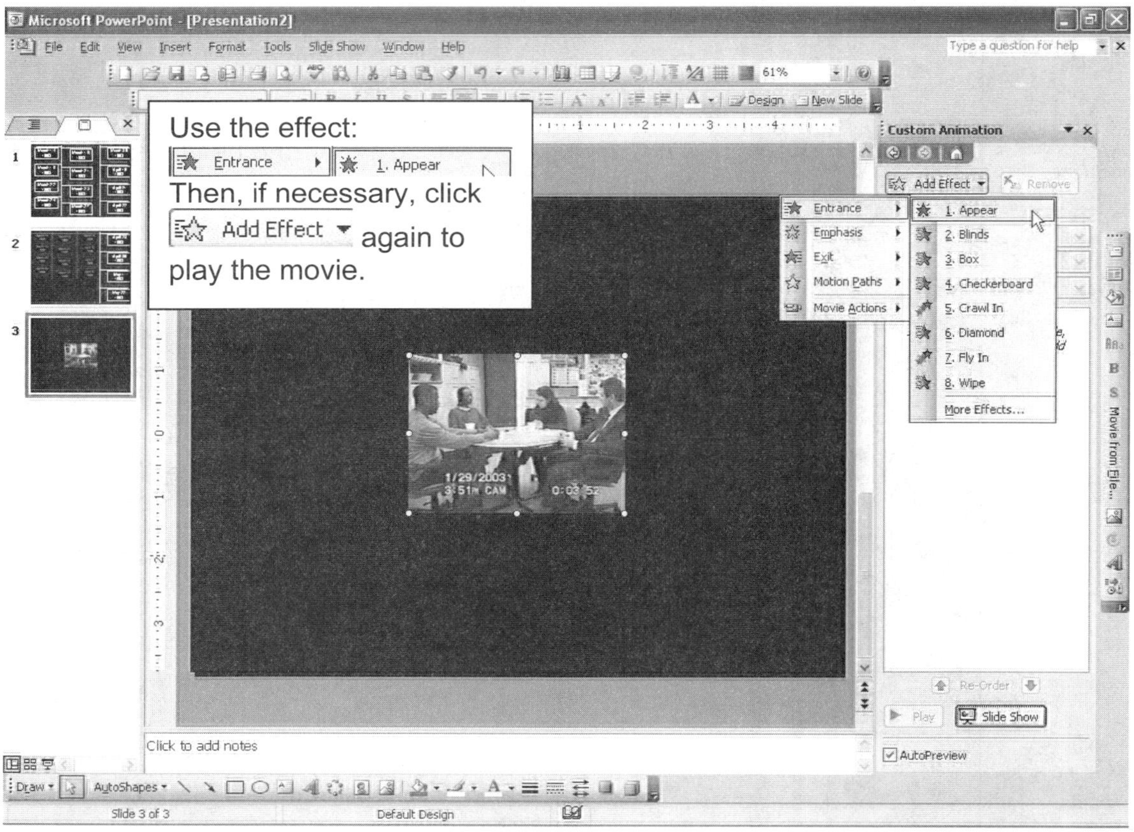
Use the effect: Entrance 1. Appear
Then, if necessary, click Add Effect again to play the movie.

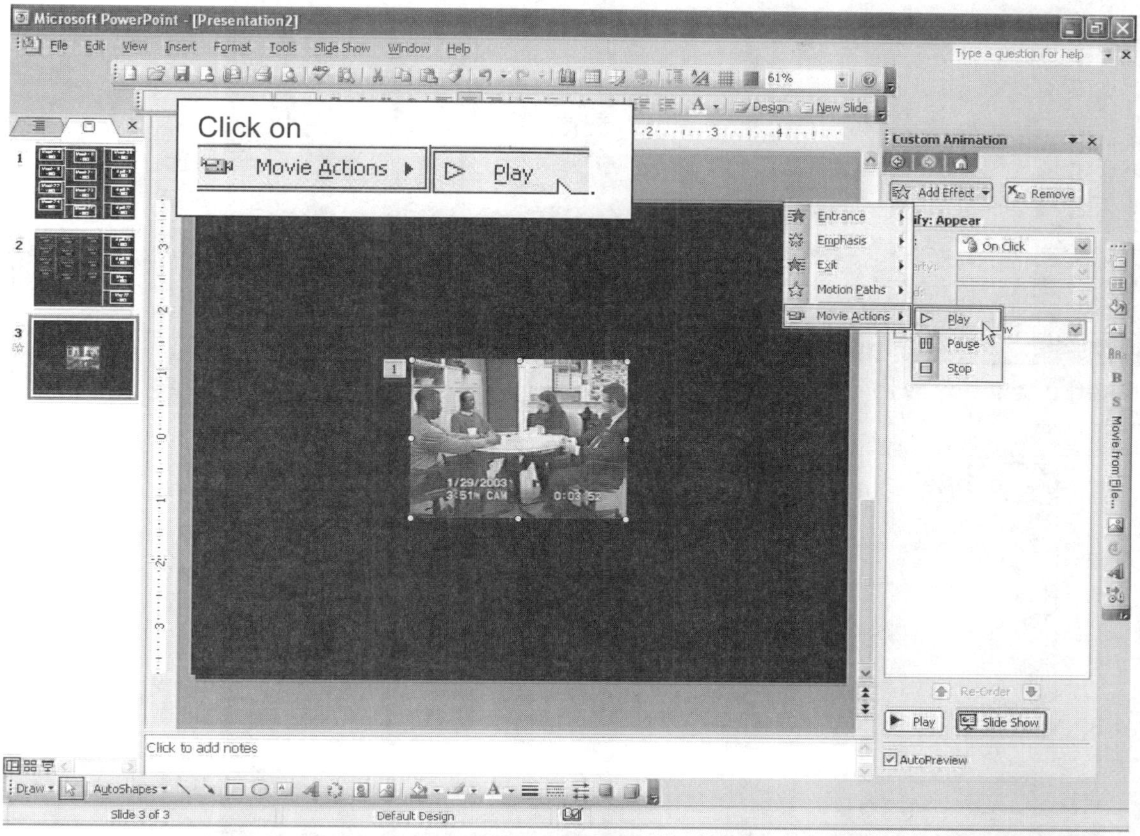
Click on
Movie Actions
Play

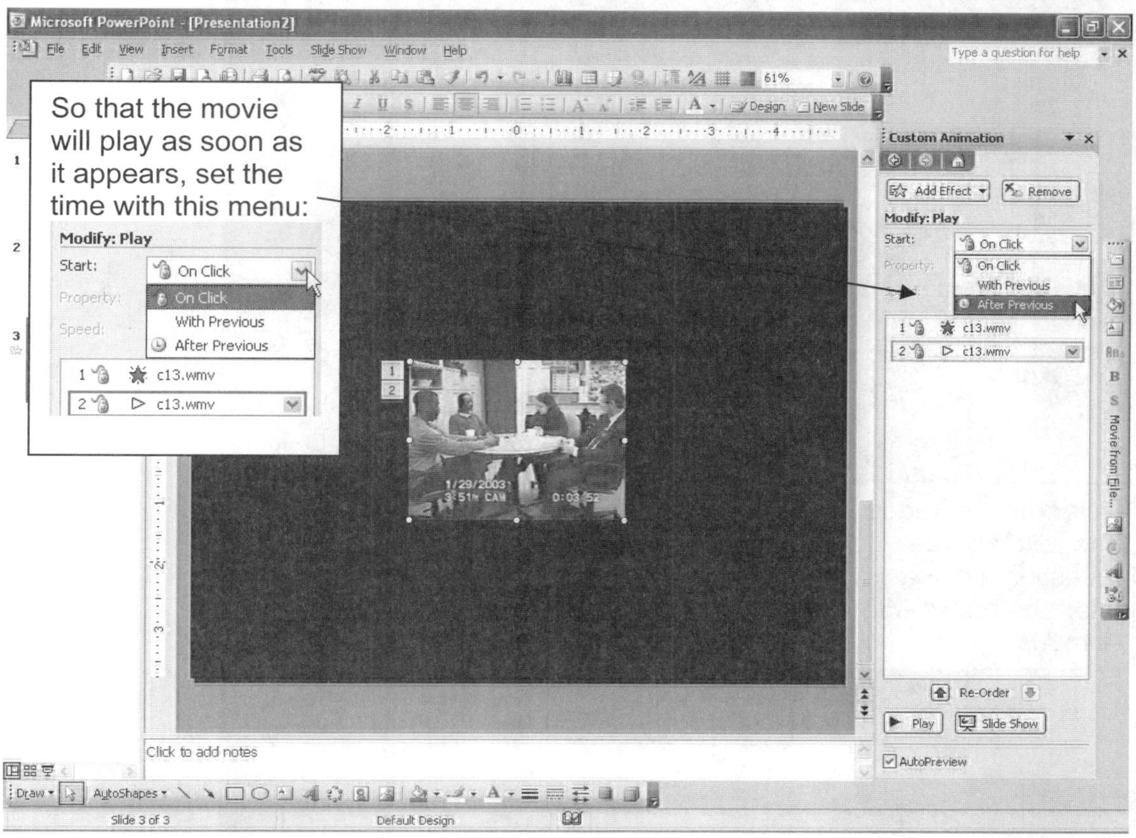
So that the movie will play as soon as it appears, set the time with this menu:
Modify: Play
Start:
On Click
With Previous
After Previous

Microsoft PowerPoint - [Presentation2]
File Edit View Insert Format Tools Slide Show Window Help
Custom Animation
Add Effect
Remove
c13.wmv
c13.wmv
Play
Slide Show
AutoPreview
Insert a text box with
and set the font
10
12
14
16
18
20
24
28
at 32.
Slide 3 of 3
Default Design

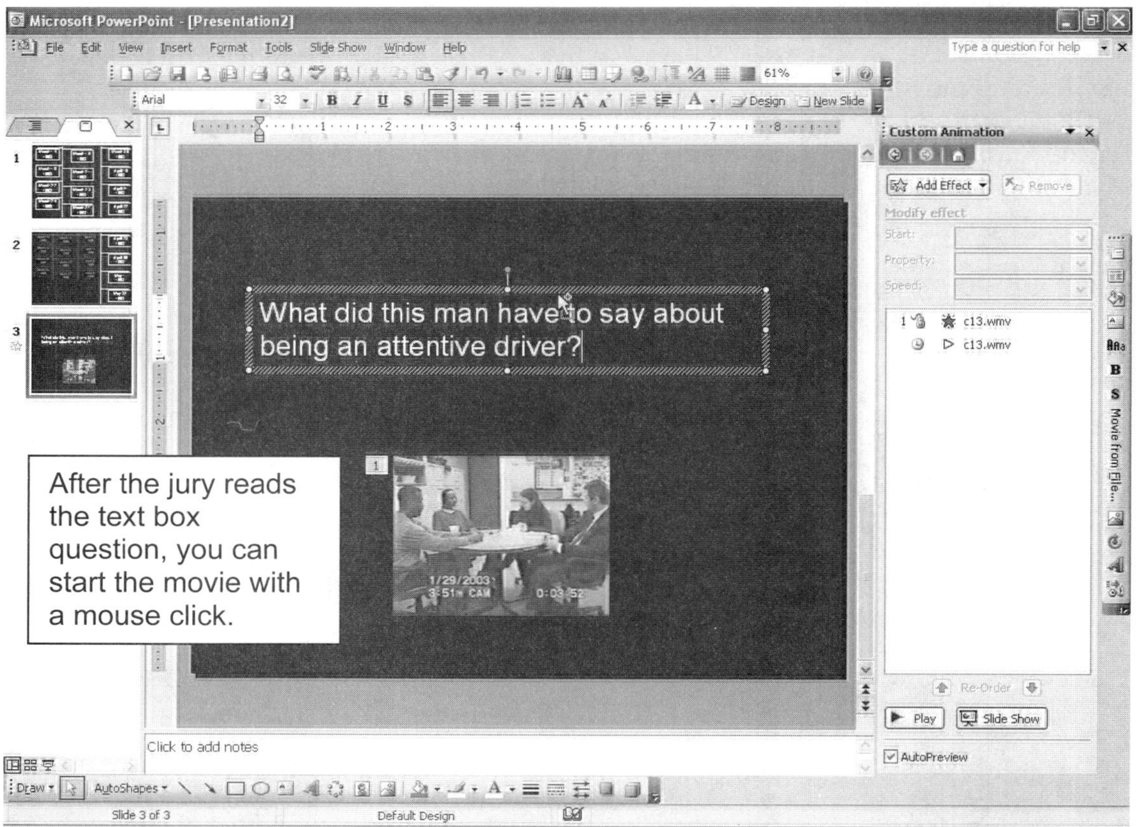
Microsoft PowerPoint - [Presentation2]
File Edit View Insert Format Tools Slide Show Window Help
Custom Animation
What did this man have to say about being an attentive driver?
After the jury reads the text box question, you can start the movie with a mouse click.
Click to add notes
Slide 3 of 3
Default Design

Inserting Sound Files

To insert sound files, go to the  menu and toggle down to

. Select a sound file and insert it on the file slide. You will see an icon like  appear on the slide.

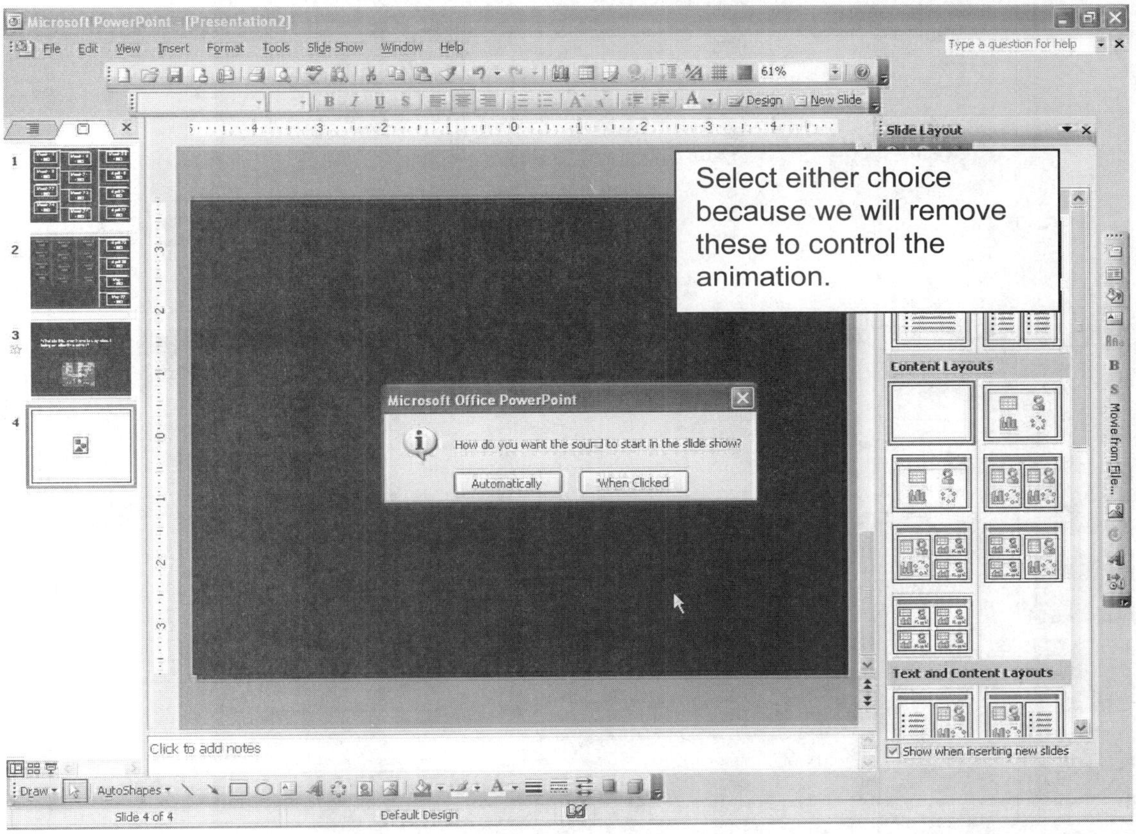

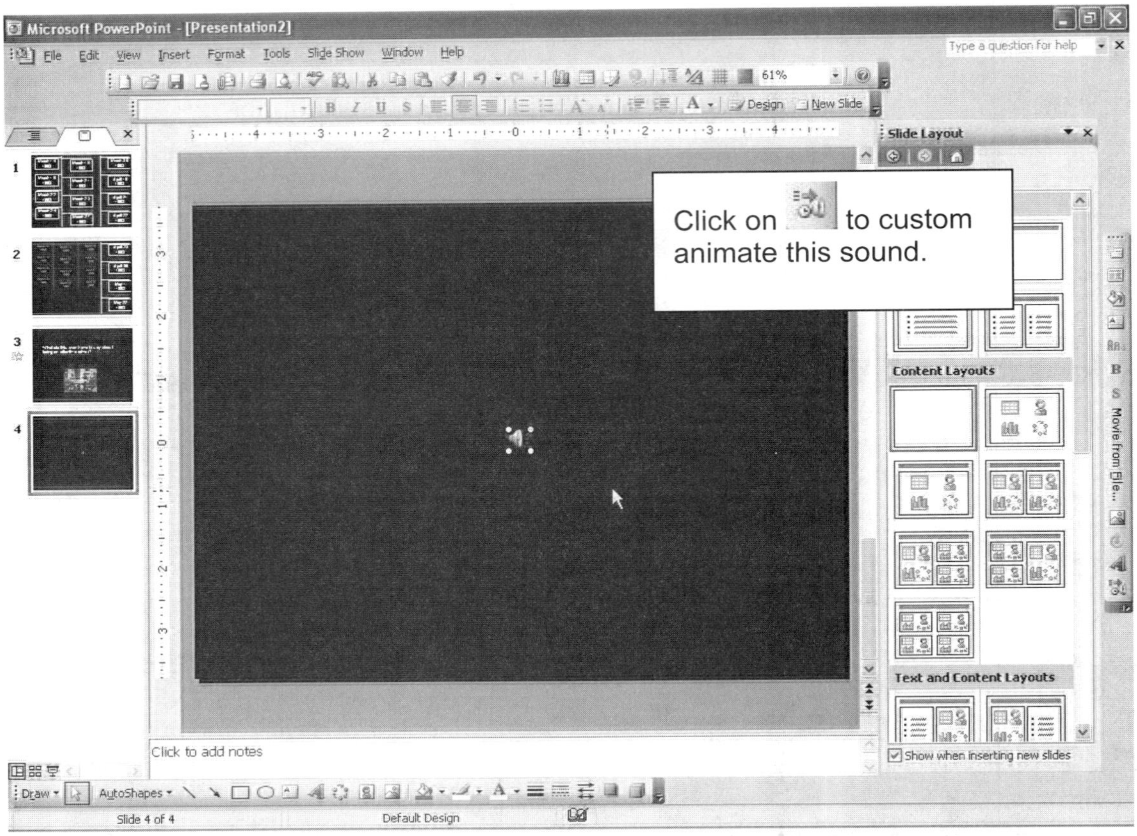
Microsoft PowerPoint - [Presentation2]
Click on to custom animate this sound.
Slide Layout
Content Layouts
Text and Content Layouts
Show when inserting new slides
Click to add notes
Slide 4 of 4
Default Design

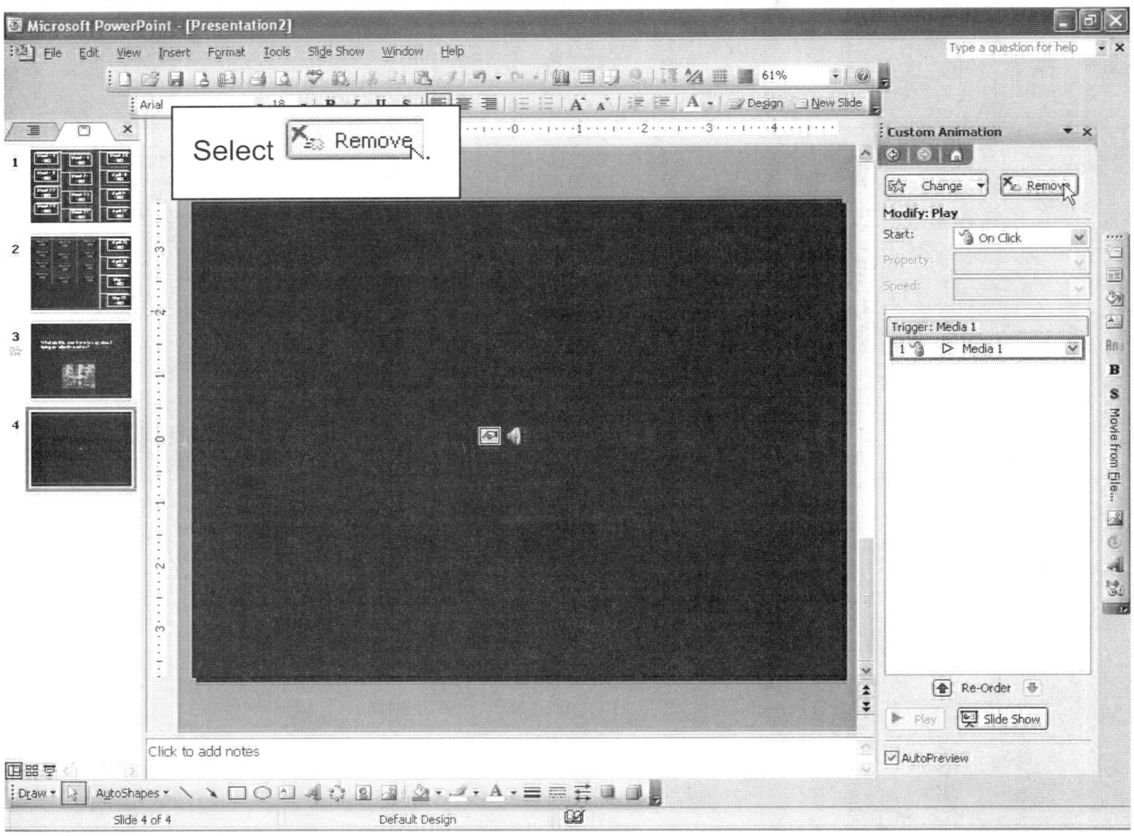
Microsoft PowerPoint - [Presentation2]
Select Remove.
Custom Animation
Change
Remove
Modify: Play
Start:
On Click
Property:
Speed:
Trigger: Media 1
Media 1
Re-Order
Play
Slide Show
AutoPreview
Click to add notes
Slide 4 of 4
Default Design

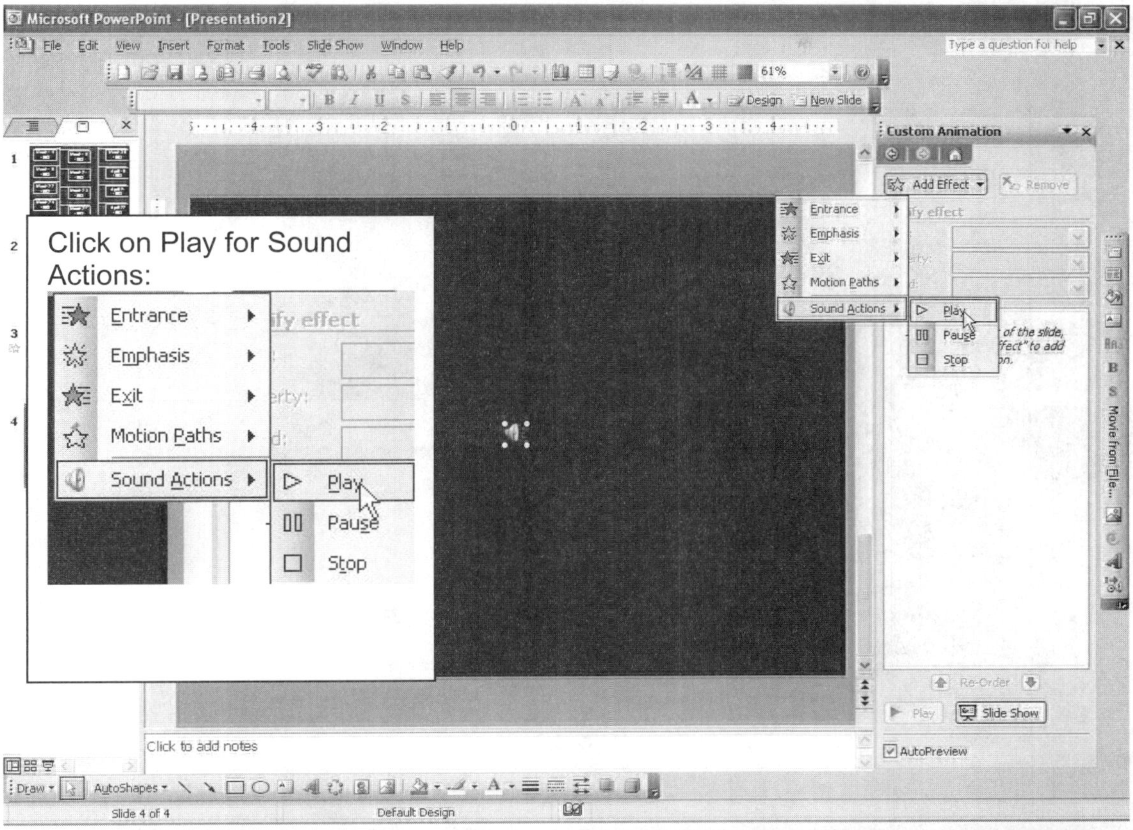
Microsoft PowerPoint - [Presentation2]
Custom Animation
Add Effect
Remove
Click on Play for Sound Actions:
Entrance
Emphasis
Exit
Motion Paths
Sound Actions
Play
Pause
Stop
Click to add notes
Slide 4 of 4
Default Design

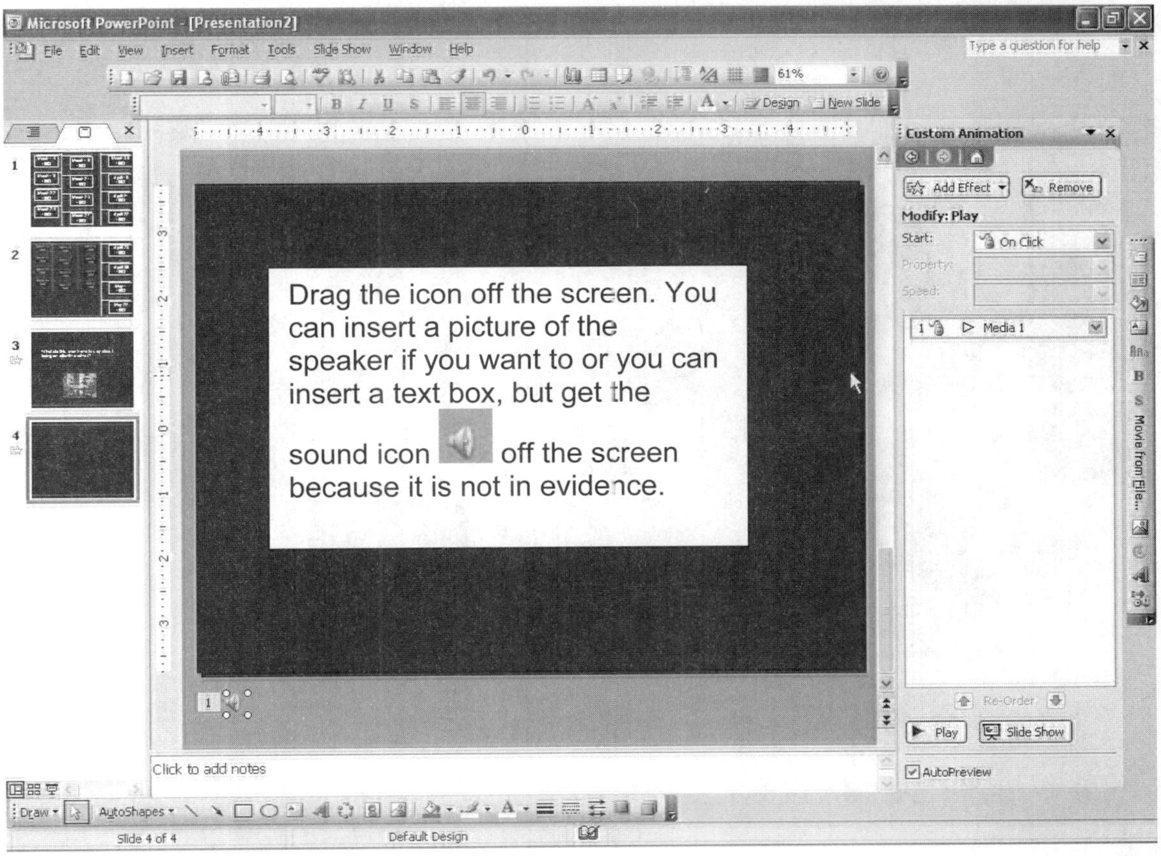
Microsoft PowerPoint - [Presentation2]
Custom Animation
Add Effect
Remove
Modify: Play
Start:
On Click
Media 1
Drag the icon off the screen. You can insert a picture of the speaker if you want to or you can insert a text box, but get the sound icon off the screen because it is not in evidence.
Play
Slide Show
AutoPreview
Click to add notes
Slide 4 of 4
Default Design

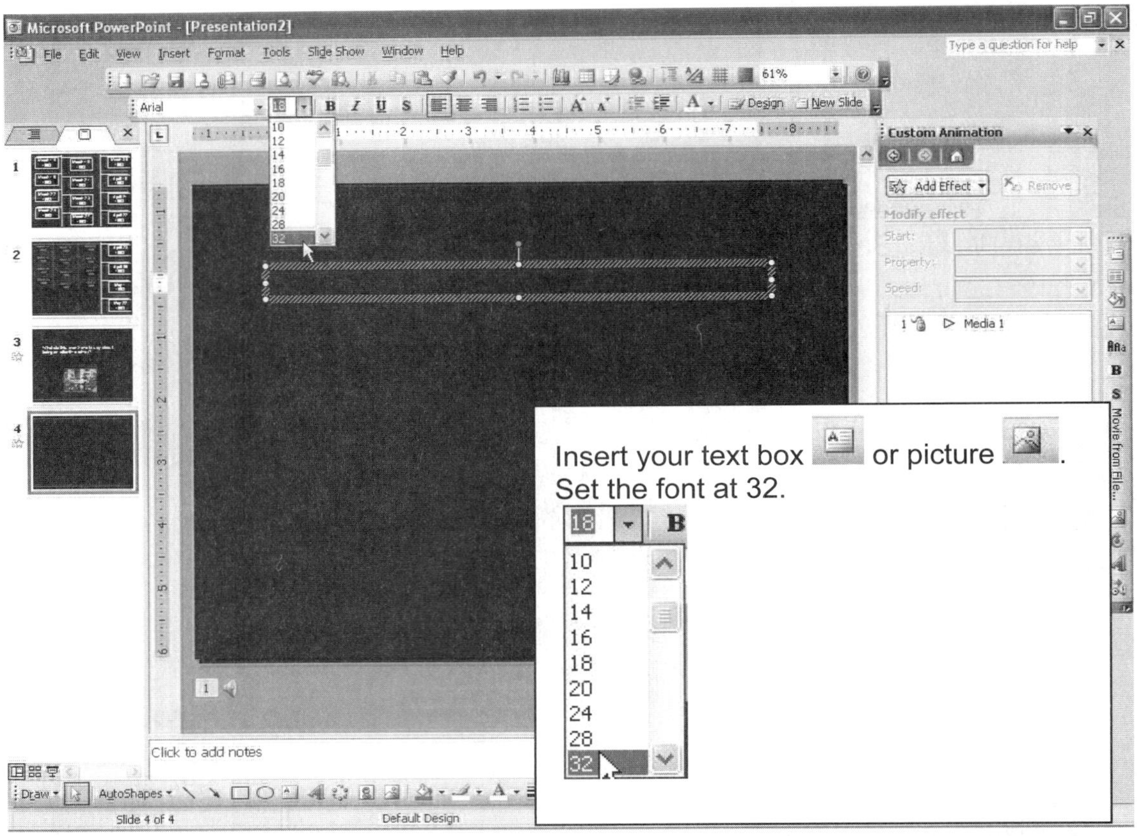
Microsoft PowerPoint - [Presentation2]
Custom Animation
Add Effect
Media 1
Insert your text box or picture.
Set the font at 32.
10
12
14
16
18
20
24
28
32
Click to add notes
Slide 4 of 4
Default Design

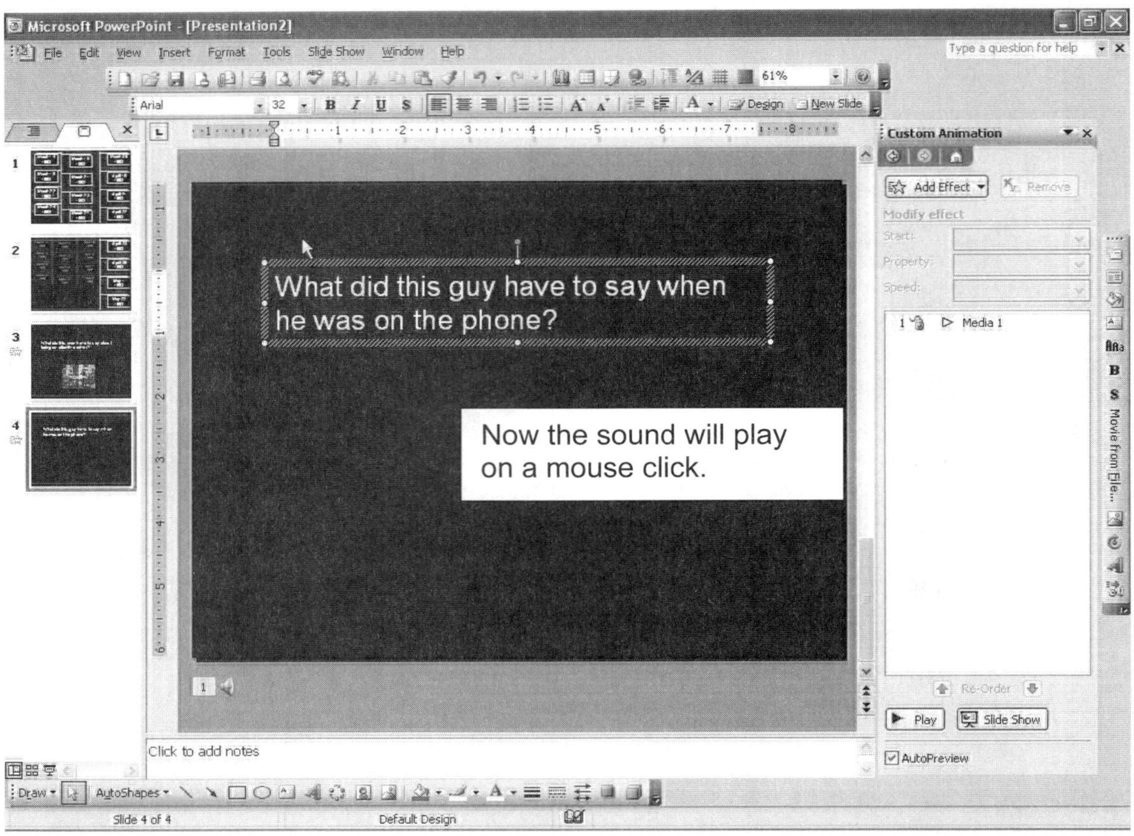
Microsoft PowerPoint - [Presentation2]
Custom Animation
Add Effect
Media 1
What did this guy have to say when he was on the phone?
Now the sound will play on a mouse click.
Play
Slide Show
AutoPreview
Click to add notes
Slide 4 of 4
Default Design

Launching and Running PowerPoint

Launching PowerPoint Independent of Sanction

You can launch a presentation two different ways with PowerPoint, as the next screen shows.

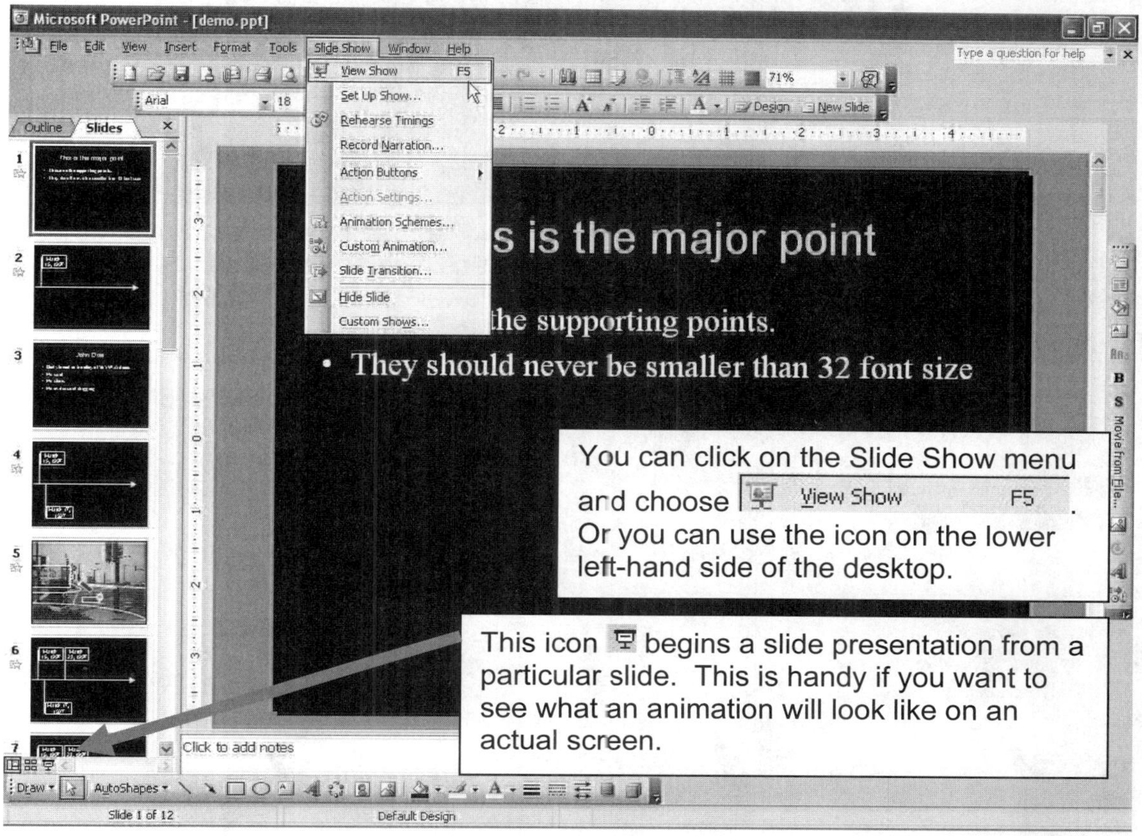

Launching PowerPoint Slide Shows Out of Sanction

Sanction will run a PowerPoint slide show without opening PowerPoint. A PowerPoint slide show is different from a PowerPoint slide presentation. Slide shows are formatted so they will run on computers that do not have PowerPoint. Sanction will run these shows and allow you to use remote mouse clicks so long as you check the 

button on the Sanction toolbar. See Chapter 8 for more on this. To turn a PowerPoint slide presentation into a PowerPoint show, you have to save the file as a PowerPoint Show (.pps) file.

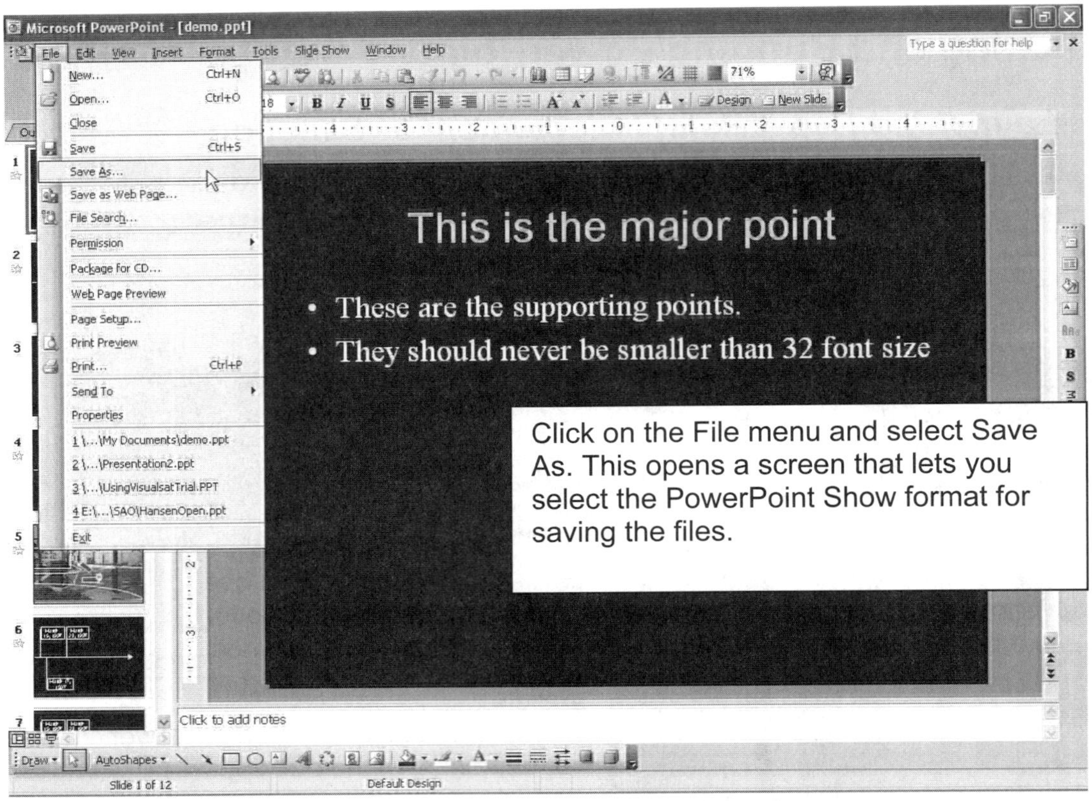
Microsoft PowerPoint - [demo.ppt]
This is the major point
These are the supporting points.
They should never be smaller than 32 font size
Click on the File menu and select Save As. This opens a screen that lets you select the PowerPoint Show format for saving the files.

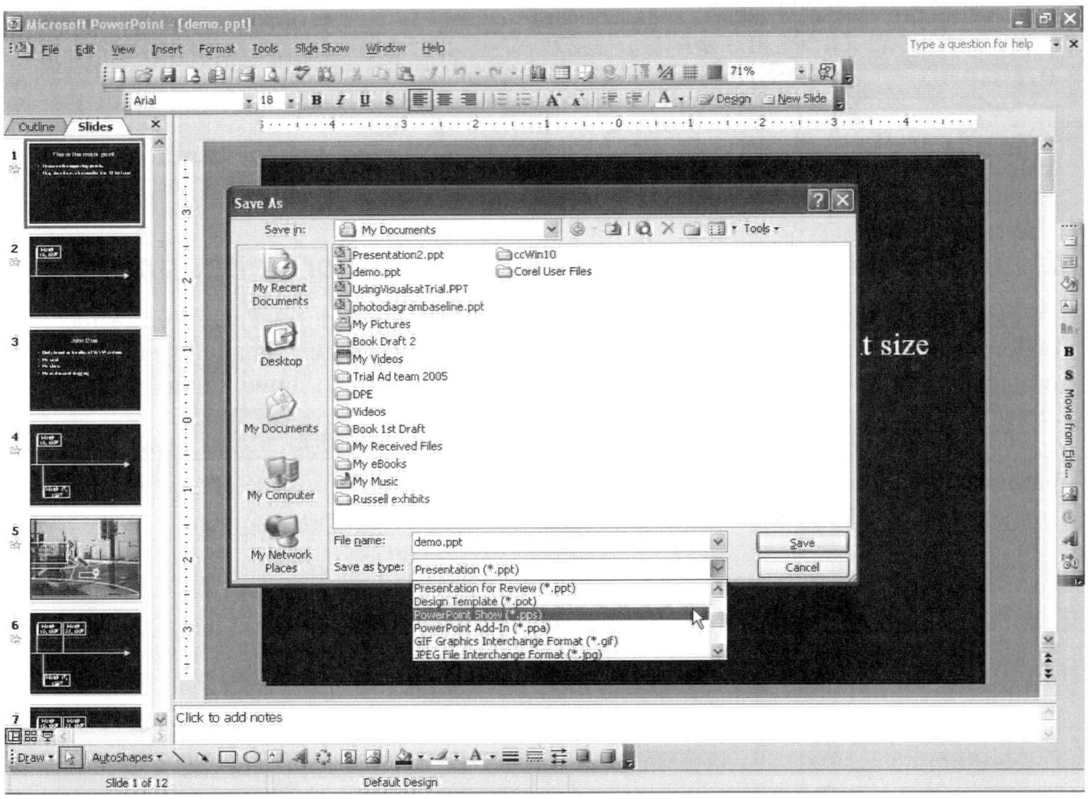
Microsoft PowerPoint - [demo.ppt]
Save As
Save in: My Documents
File name: demo.ppt
Save as type: Presentation (*.ppt)
Presentation for Review (*.ppt)
Design Template (*.pot)
PowerPoint Show (*.pps)
PowerPoint Add-In (*.ppa)
GIF Graphics Interchange Format (*.gif)
JPEG File Interchange Format (*.jpg)

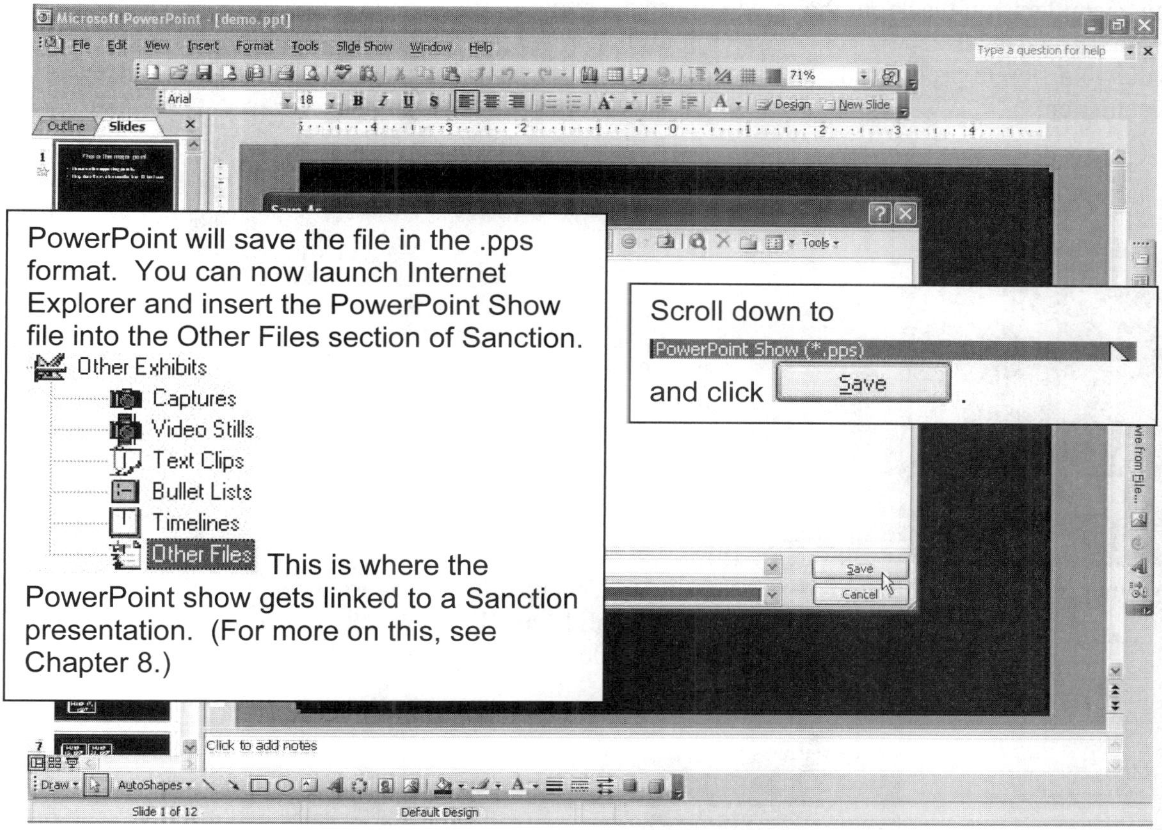

Using Screen Commands When Running a PowerPoint Presentation or Slide Show

When you are running a PowerPoint presentation, you can right click on the screen to bring this menu on the screen.

When you move your cursor to the triangles, the different submenus appear.

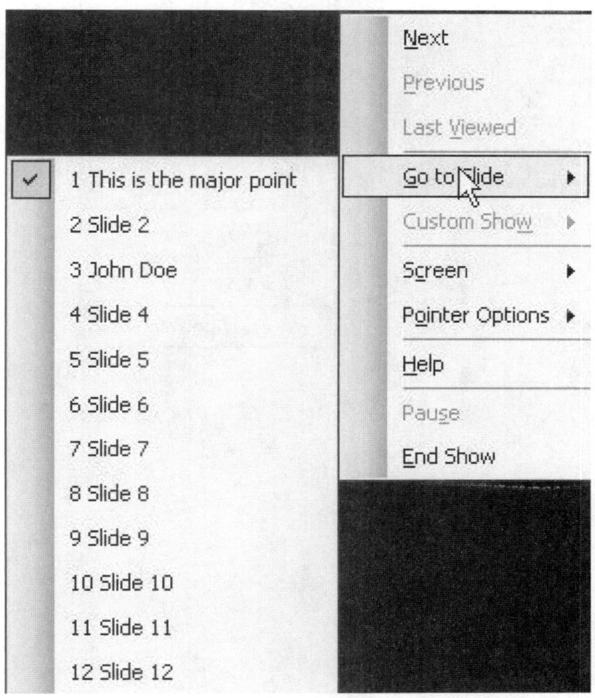

This menu lets you black out the screen or use a white screen. You can also show your speaker notes or switch to different programs in the middle of the presentation.

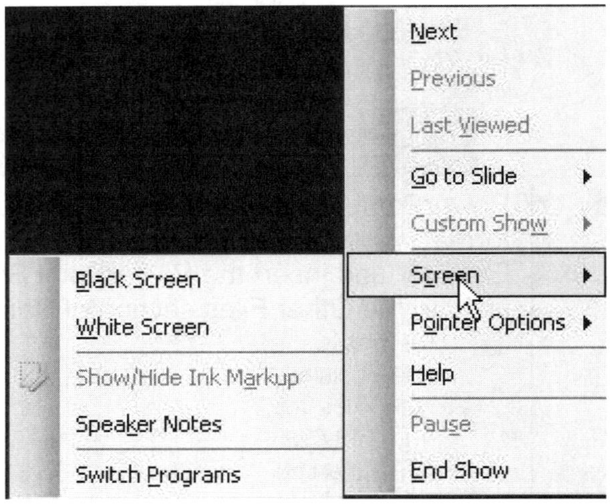

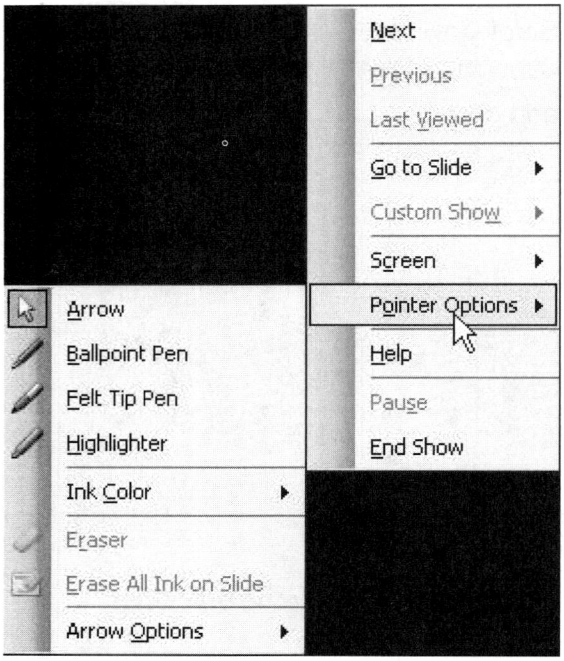

This menu lets you use a pen or highlighter function on a slide, and later prompts you to save the markings. You can do the same things with Sanction and more.

This lets you end the show.

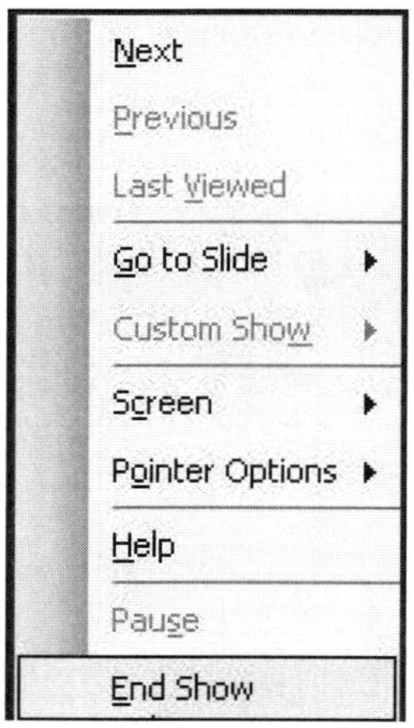

Turning Off a Slide in a Presentation

Assume the judge says you cannot show the jury a slide that is in your presentation. Here is how you can turn a slide off.

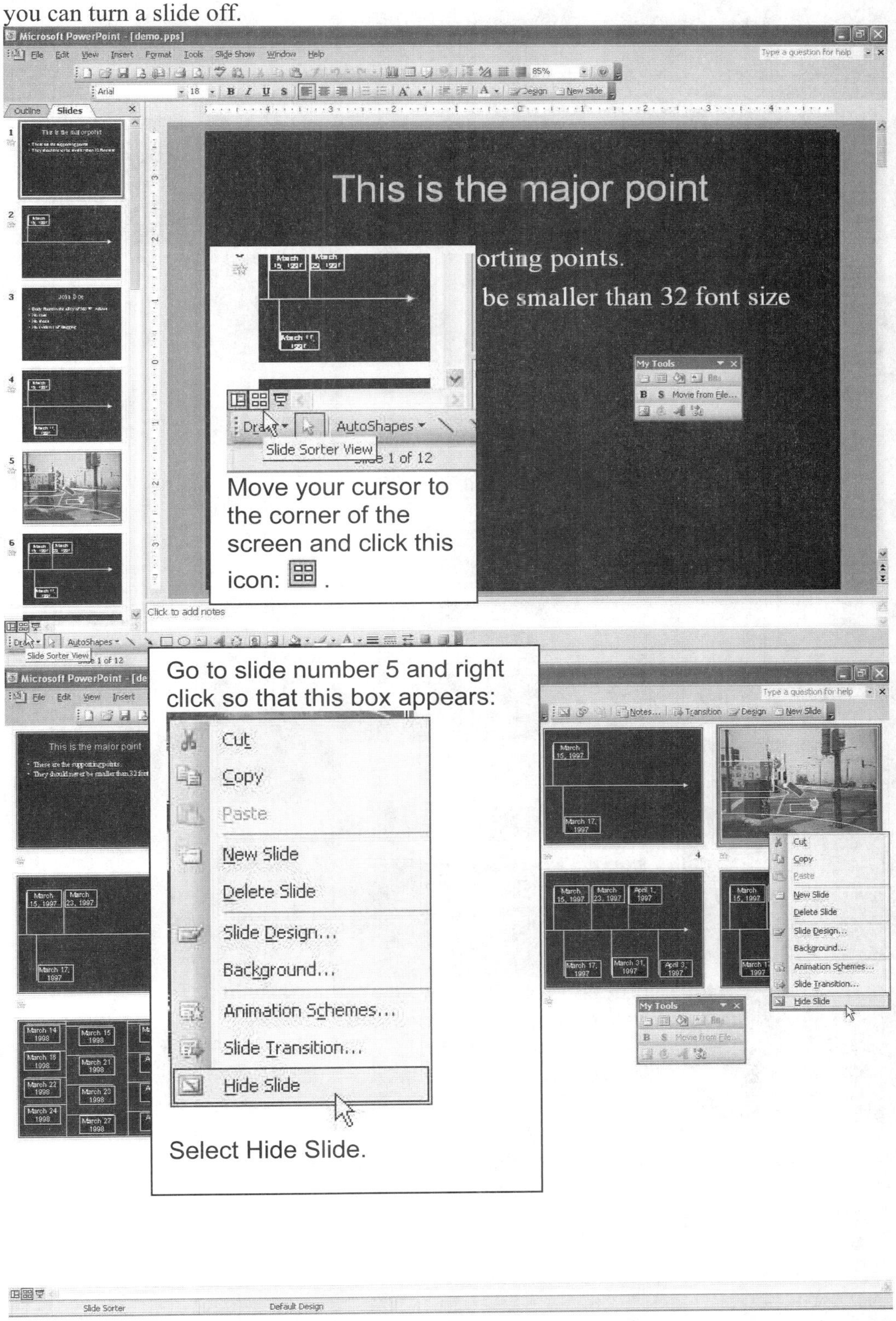

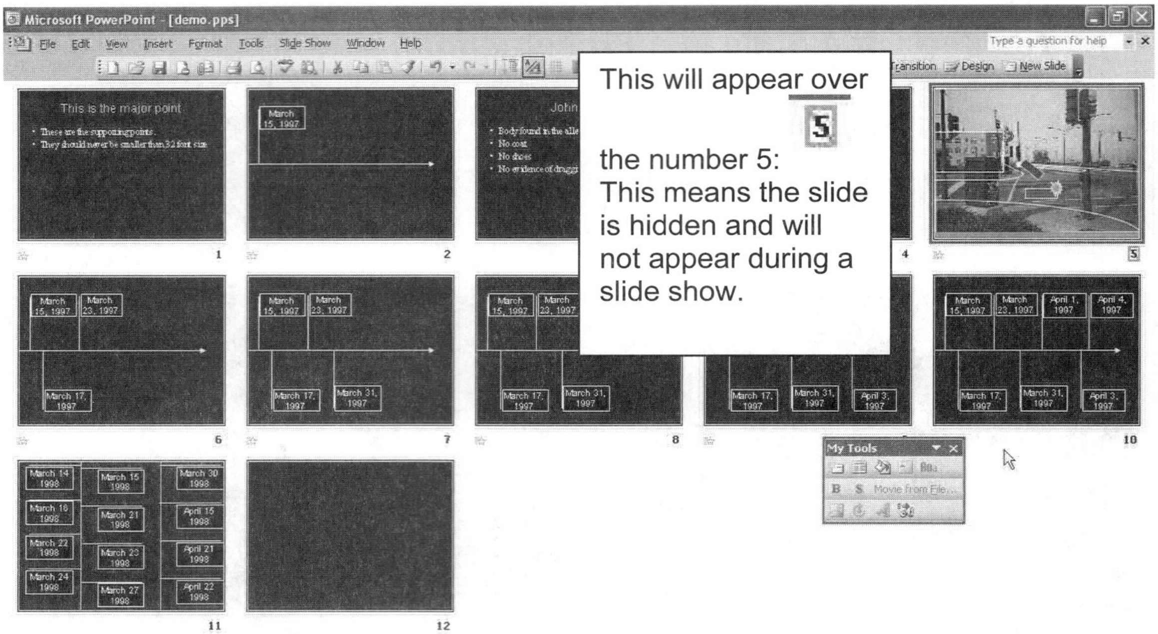
Microsoft PowerPoint - [demo.pps]
This will appear over
5
the number 5:
This means the slide is hidden and will not appear during a slide show.

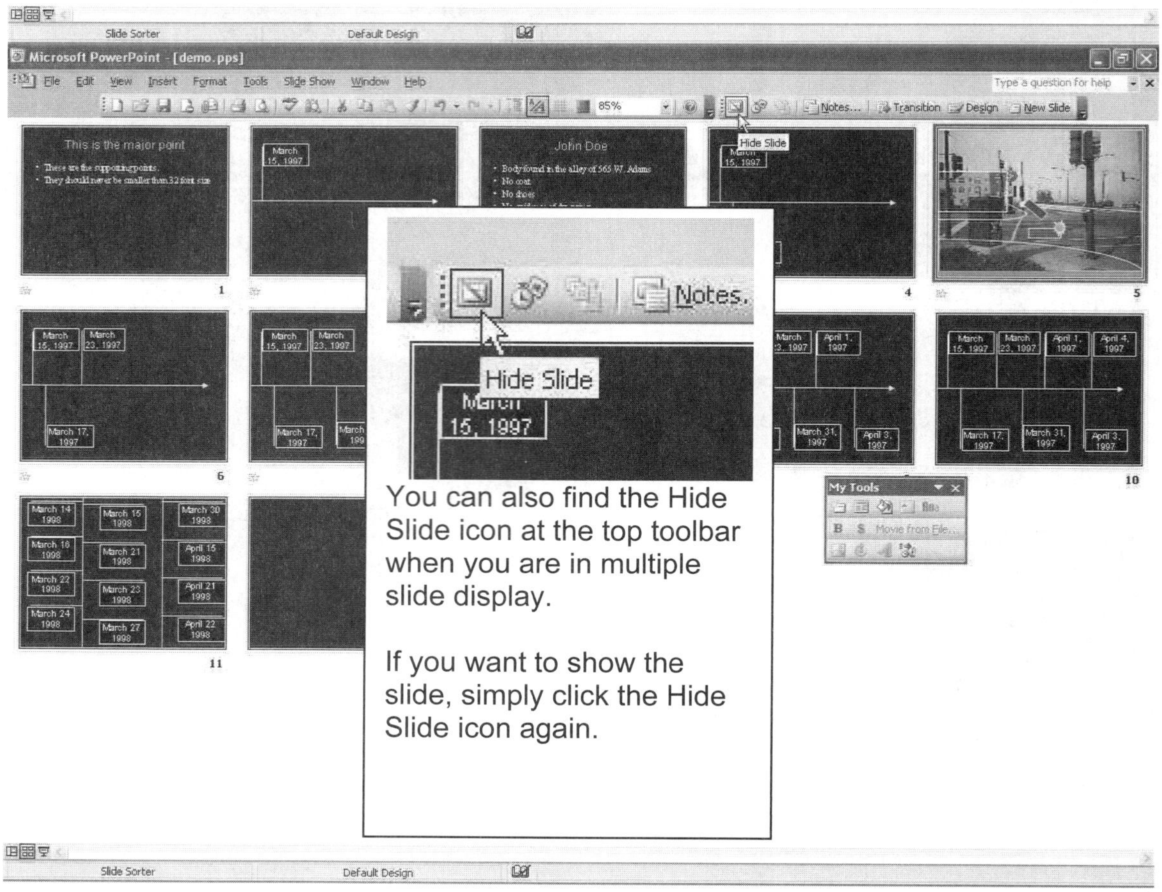
Microsoft PowerPoint - [demo.pps]
Notes.
Hide Slide
You can also find the Hide Slide icon at the top toolbar when you are in multiple slide display.
If you want to show the slide, simply click the Hide Slide icon again.
Slide Sorter
Default Design

Chapter 8

Using Sanction at Trial

This chapter takes you step by step through the process of creating a Sanction case presentation file. The many screen captures and examples in this chapter show Sanction screens, commands, and directions exactly as the software shows them, so place this chapter under or next to your computer screen as you read. If you want to see this chapter in color, download a .pdf file of it from the Litigation Technology website (www.littech.org) and print it in color.

The best way to learn a software package is to get it and use it, so download a demo copy of Sanction from the Sanction website (www.verdictsystems.com or www.sanction.com). If you are a law student, you will have to go through the law student registration process with Sanction to get a one-year license. Sanction gives you this extended license so that you can take your handy work to job interviews. Once that one-year period expires, however, you or your firm will have to purchase a Sanction license. If you are a practicing attorney, you will have to register with Sanction to get your copy of the software. Your copy will launch 30 times before you have to purchase the software.

Reading this chapter does not substitute for reading the Sanction manual. In fact, we borrow passages from the manual and from other Sanction training documents. This chapter merely gives you a visual tutorial as an introduction to the Sanction program. Use this chapter to get started working with the program. Use it in conjunction with the Sanction manual, which you will notice sometimes shows alternative ways to accomplish tasks addressed in this chapter. The choice to teach you to do things differently from some of the manual's procedures is a conscious one. This chapter is an introduction to using an incredibly powerful piece of software. Its objective is to keep the introduction simple and to whet your appetite to encourage you to learn more about Sanction.

This chapter teaches you how to do the following things:

- Open a case
- Insert documents and photos into a presentation
- Insert videos and audio files into a presentation
- Synchronize a transcript with a transcript that you create yourself
- Have transcripts synchronized by a third party
- Create video clips
- Create video clips that also show exhibits that are referred to by a witness on the screen
- Export video clips to Windows media files that play outside of Sanction
- Use the transcript search and find queries
- Create text clips, video stills, bullet lists, and timelines that use Sanction exclusively
- Launch a PowerPoint slide from Sanction
- Run Sanction presentations
- Import another person's Sanction database into your own

Sanction has many advanced features such as the capacity to work with Concordance, Summation, and other litigation management packages. This text, however, does not address those advanced features. See the Sanction manual for more information about these features.

Before you can use Sanction, you need a case file. You can download the Smith case file from the Litigation Technology website (www.littech.org) in the Book Exhibit folder. The file consists of the following:

- A scanned memo from an insurance investigator
- A scanned page of the investigator's notes
- Ten photos of the intersection of 35th and State Street
- A digitized video of the interview of Anthony Smith (the plaintiff)
- A text file transcript for Officer Crumpky that will have no video
- Anthony Smith transcript
- A text file that has page and line breaks
- A .jpg diagram of the intersection of 35th and State Street
- A PowerPoint show labeled Open

Getting Started

Help Resources

If you want to go to another source for information about how to use Sanction, use the Help menu to navigate through any problems.

Using Sanction Help

Sanction provides an extensive Help file that you can access by clicking Help or by pressing Ctrl + H on your keyboard. When you access Help, this menu will appear:

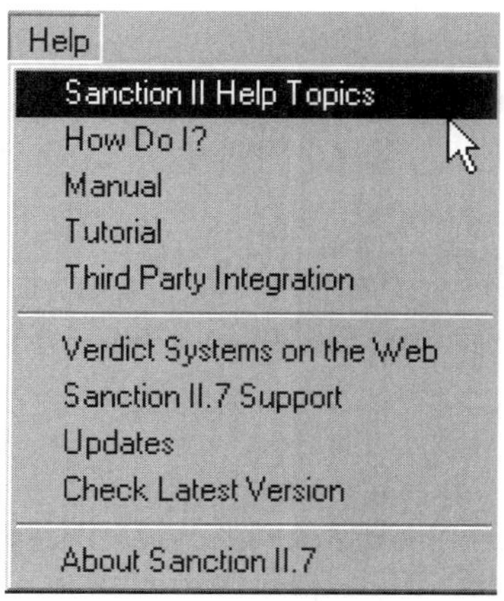

Select Sanction II Help Topics. From the Help Topics window, you may use the Contents, Index, or Find features to find answers to all of your Sanction questions.

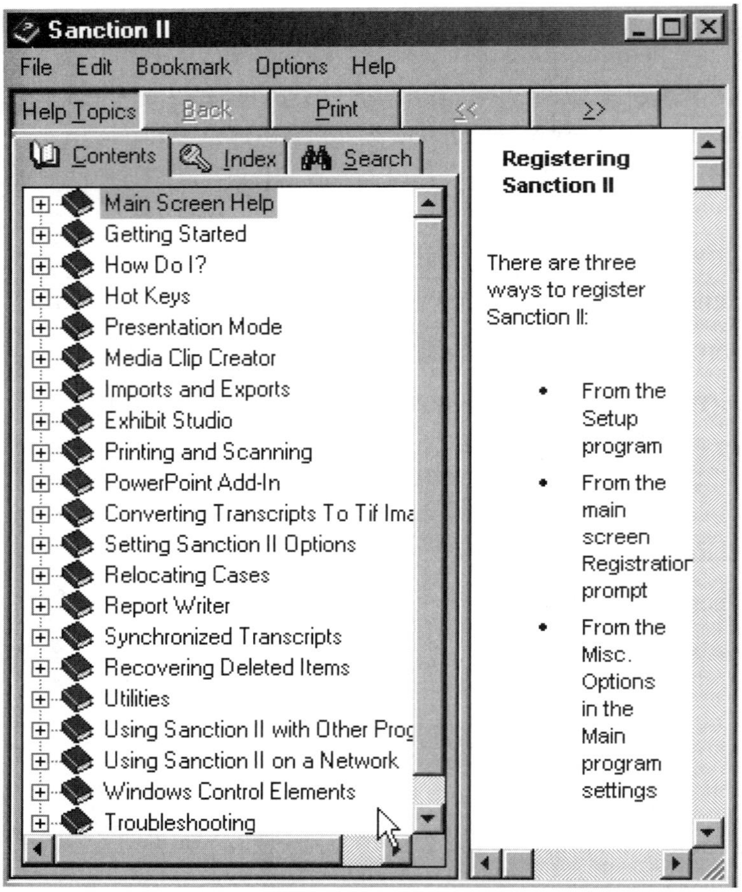

Using the Contents feature: Click on the Contents tab to browse through the Help topics listed in the Help menu.

Using the Index feature: The Help Index feature provides a list of topics arranged alphabetically in the Index list box. In some cases, Windows displays more than one related topic in the topic list, so you can select the topic for which you need more information.

The index is especially useful when you cannot find a particular topic in the Help Contents' list of topics.

To use the Help Index feature, click on the Index tab and type a topic in the text box. The index will scroll to the first entry that most closely matches the typed word. The topic will appear highlighted in the list. If necessary, click a subtopic.

Using the Find feature

You can search for specific words and phrases in a Help topic instead of searching for a topic by category.

To search for words or phrases in a Help topic:

- Type the word you want to find in the first text box at the top of the Search dialog box. The window below will display the first entry that most closely matches the typed word. The word will appear highlighted in the list.
- Click another word in the list to narrow the search if necessary.
- Click a topic in the list, and then click the Display button. Windows will display the selected Help topic.

One More Resource

The Sanction demo case and the tutorial that comes with a Sanction install are excellent resources for learning the program. The videos that are part of the Sanction demo file explain different aspects of the program.

Sanction Desktop

Open Sanction and your desktop will look like this:

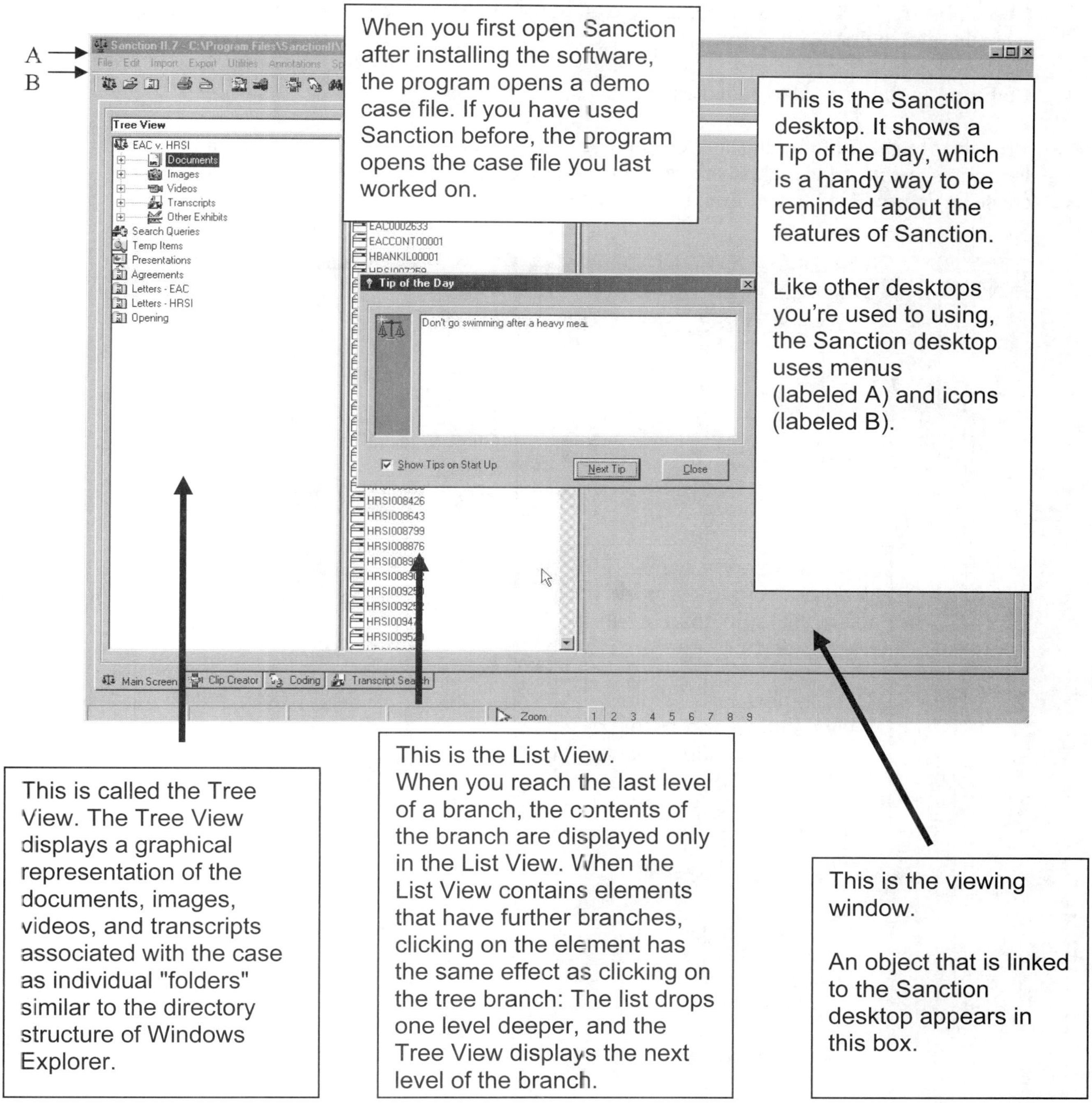

The tabs that appear at the bottom of the desktop are discussed more thoroughly later in the chapter, but here is a brief overview of their functions.

Main Screen: Most of the functions you need to manage presentations are found here. From the Main screen, you can add and delete items, create user folders and presentations, export data, and utilize many special functions.
Clip Creator: The Clip Creator tab leads to all of the necessary features to create media clip segments and multi-clip segments.

Coding: This tab is used to help organize searches in the case.

Transcript Search: From this tab, you may search for words or phrases across multiple transcripts, create .tif text clips, create media clip segments from a highlighted range of text, or create an entire .tif document from the original transcript text.

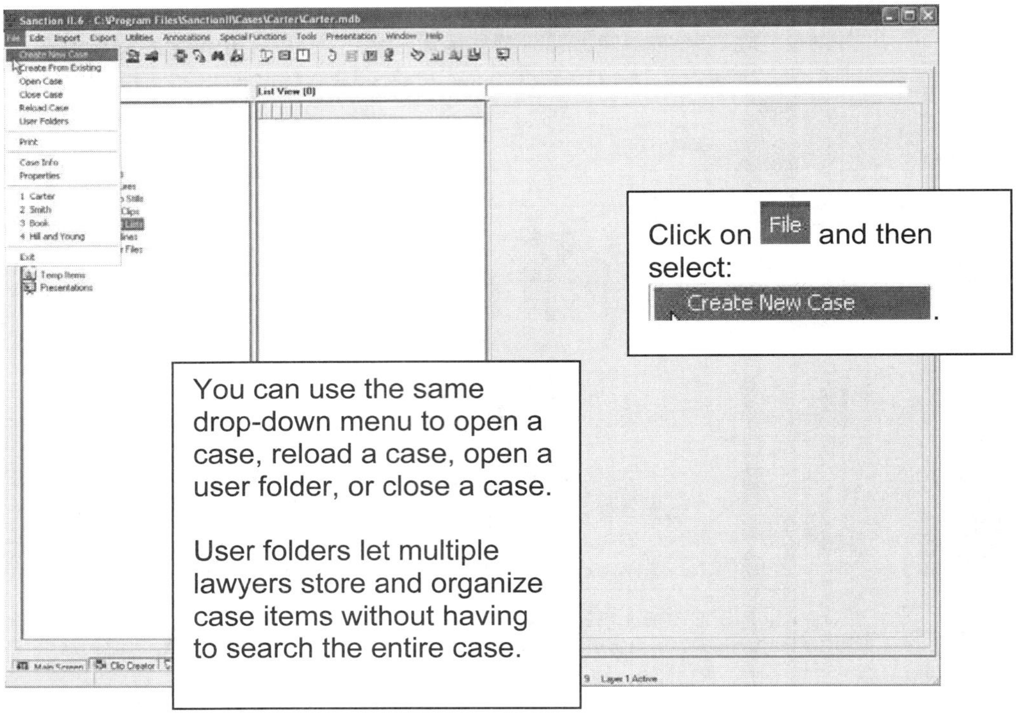

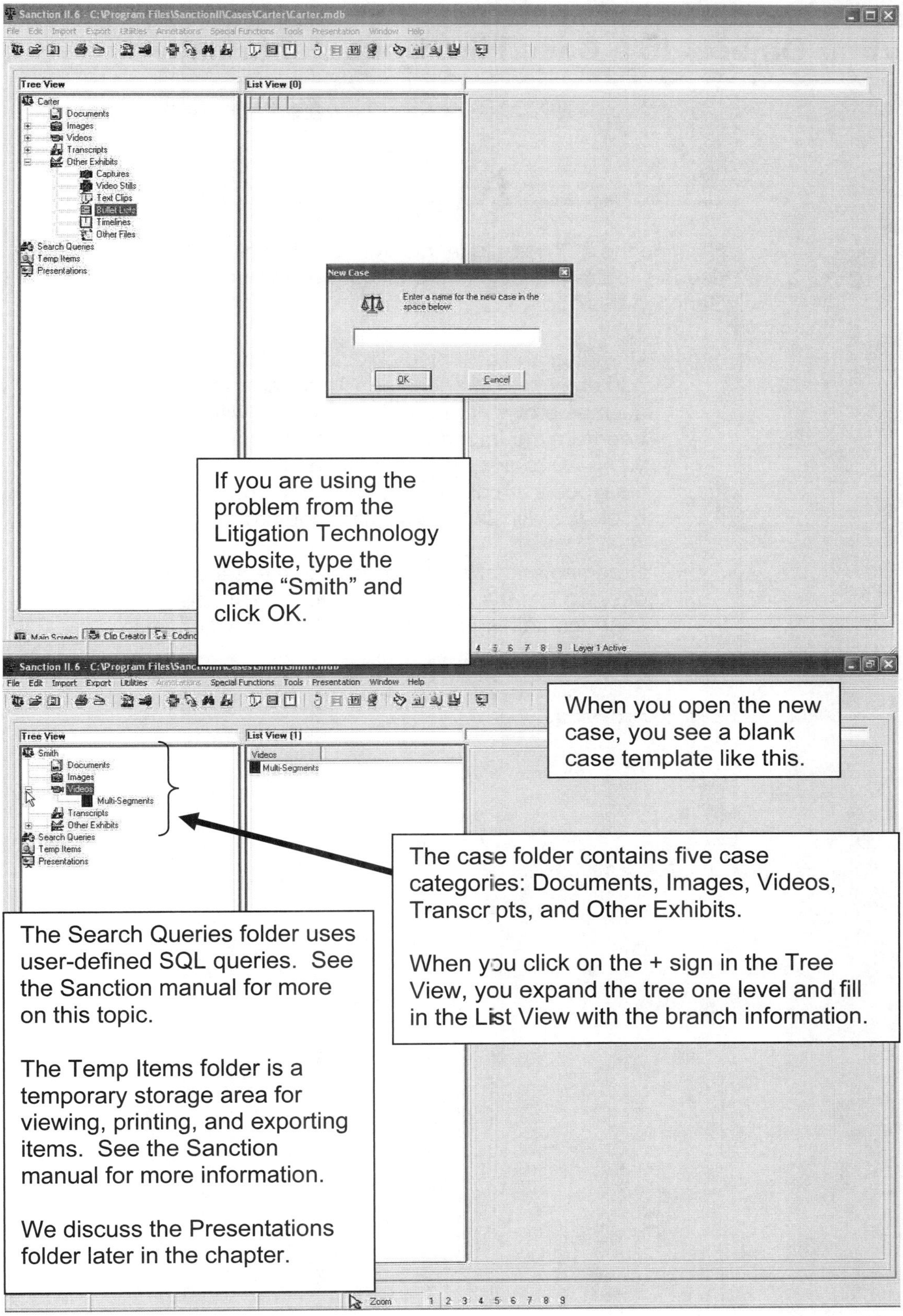
If you are using the problem from the Litigation Technology website, type the name "Smith" and click OK.
When you open the new case, you see a blank case template like this.
The case folder contains five case categories: Documents, Images, Videos, Transcripts, and Other Exhibits.
When you click on the + sign in the Tree View, you expand the tree one level and fill in the List View with the branch information.
The Search Queries folder uses user-defined SQL queries. See the Sanction manual for more on this topic.
The Temp Items folder is a temporary storage area for viewing, printing, and exporting items. See the Sanction manual for more information.
We discuss the Presentations folder later in the chapter.

Adding Objects to a Case File: Document Images

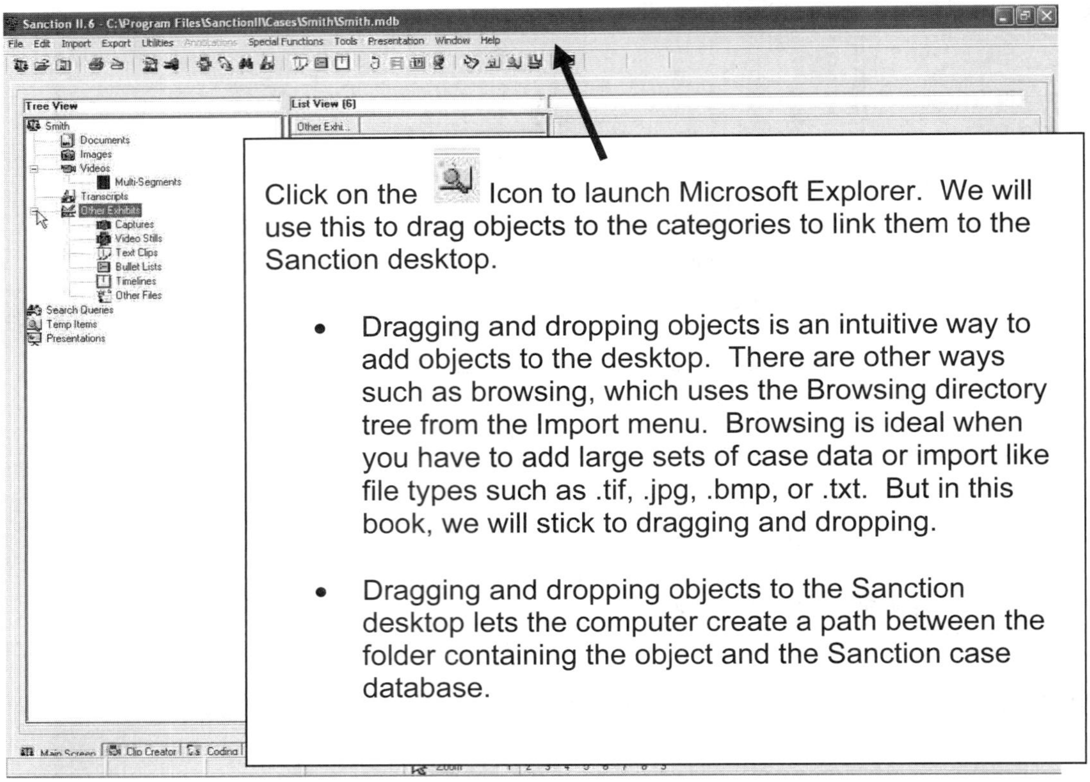

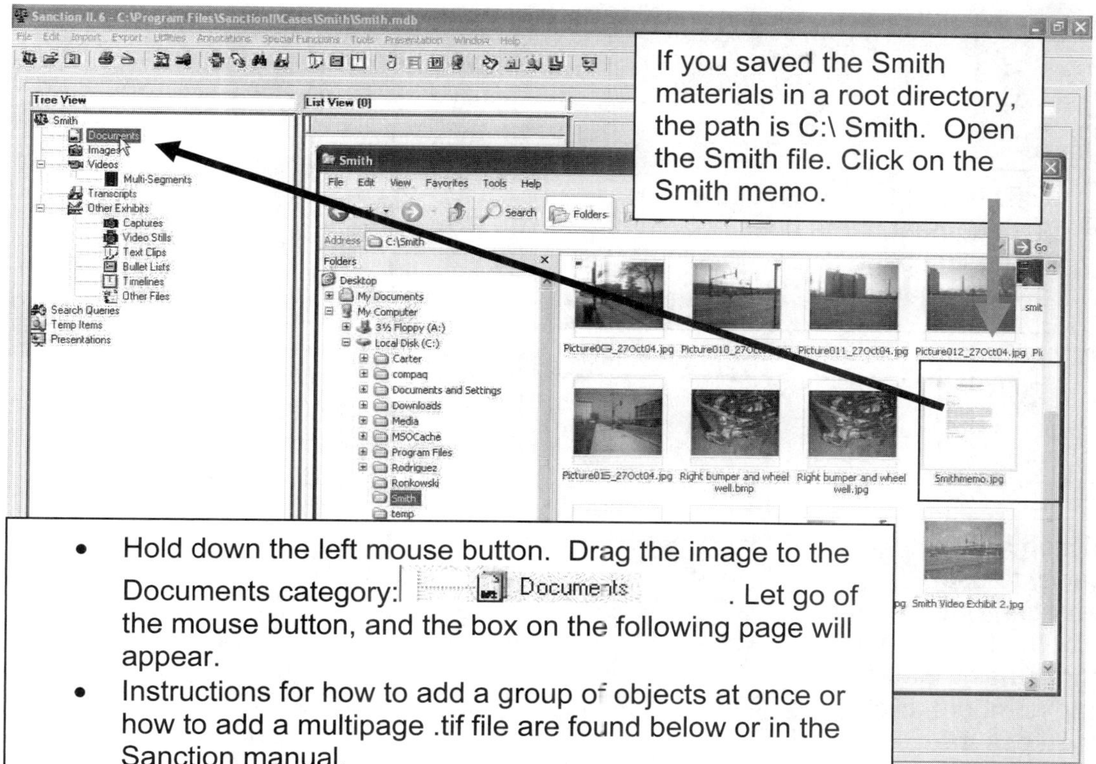

If you saved the Smith materials in a root directory, the path is C:\ Smith. Open the Smith file. Click on the Smith memo.

- Hold down the left mouse button. Drag the image to the Documents category: Documents . Let go of the mouse button, and the box on the following page will appear.
- Instructions for how to add a group of objects at once or how to add a multipage .tif file are found below or in the Sanction manual.

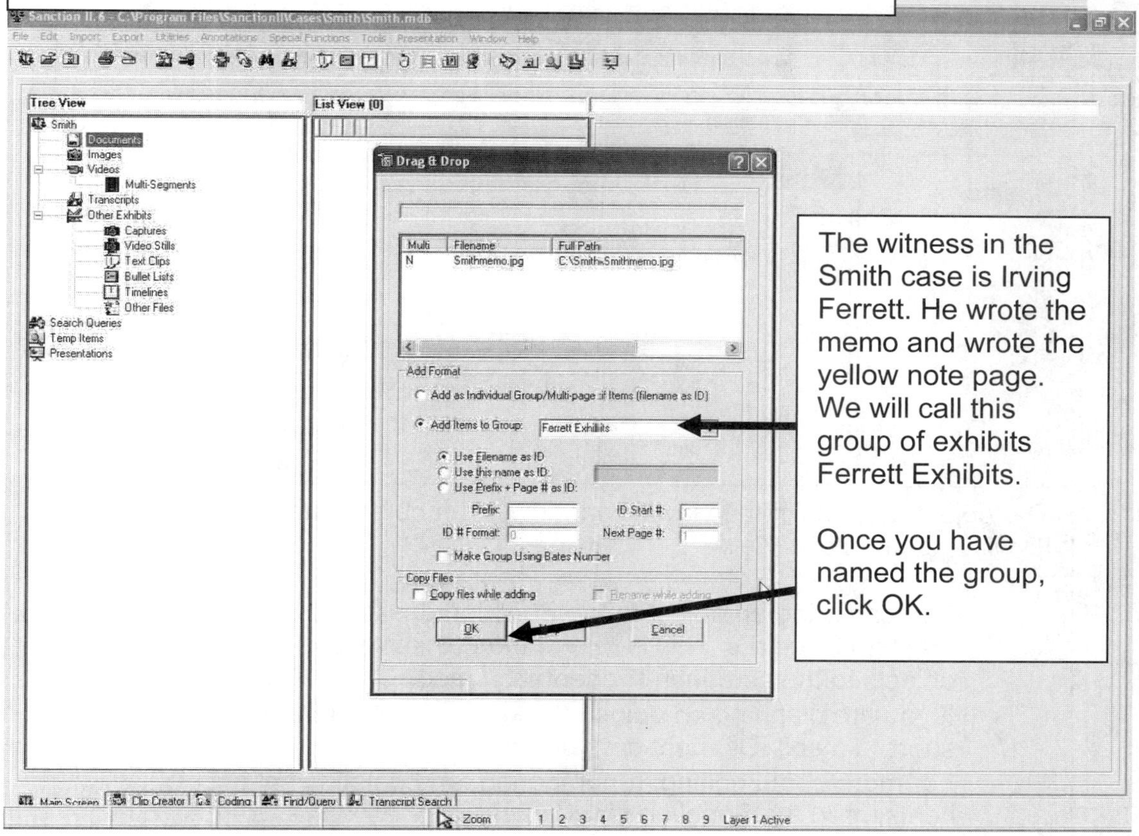

The witness in the Smith case is Irving Ferrett. He wrote the memo and wrote the yellow note page. We will call this group of exhibits Ferrett Exhibits.

Once you have named the group, click OK.

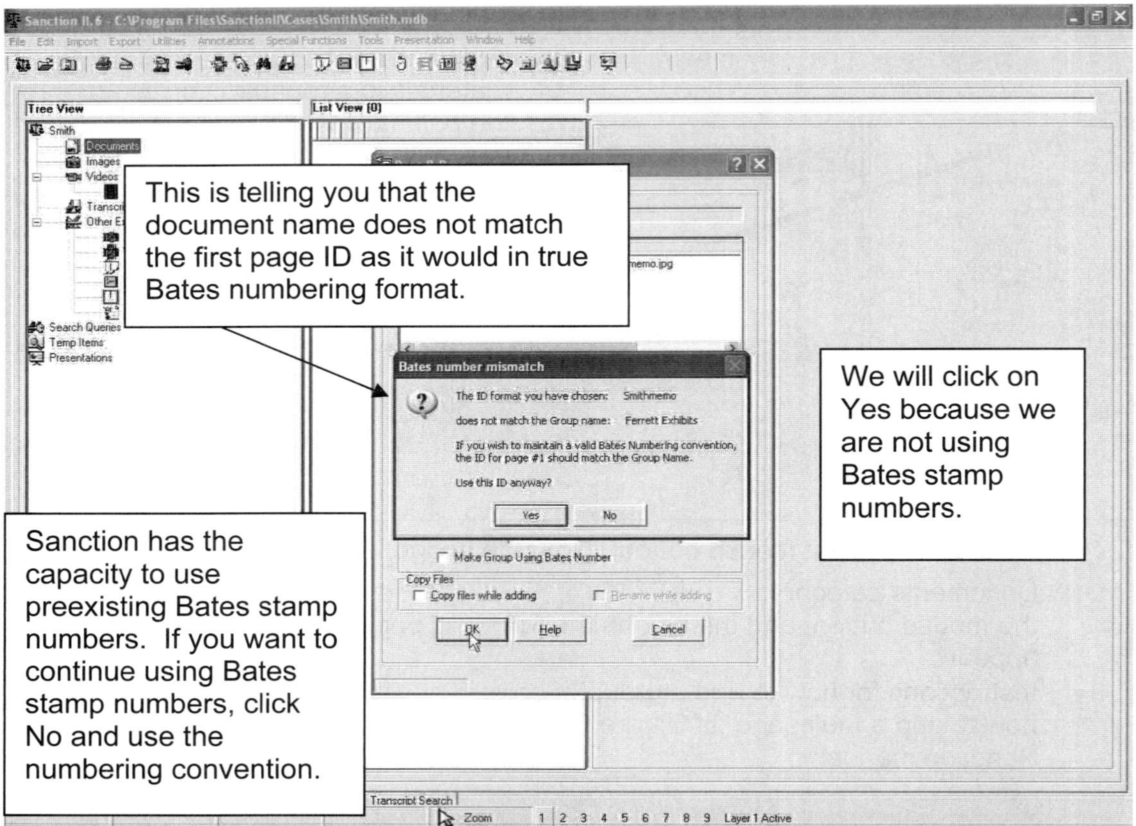
This is telling you that the document name does not match the first page ID as it would in true Bates numbering format.
Bates number mismatch
The ID format you have chosen: Smithmemo
does not match the Group name: Ferrett Exhibits
If you wish to maintain a valid Bates Numbering convention, the ID for page #1 should match the Group Name.
Use this ID anyway?
Yes
No
We will click on Yes because we are not using Bates stamp numbers.
Sanction has the capacity to use preexisting Bates stamp numbers. If you want to continue using Bates stamp numbers, click No and use the numbering convention.

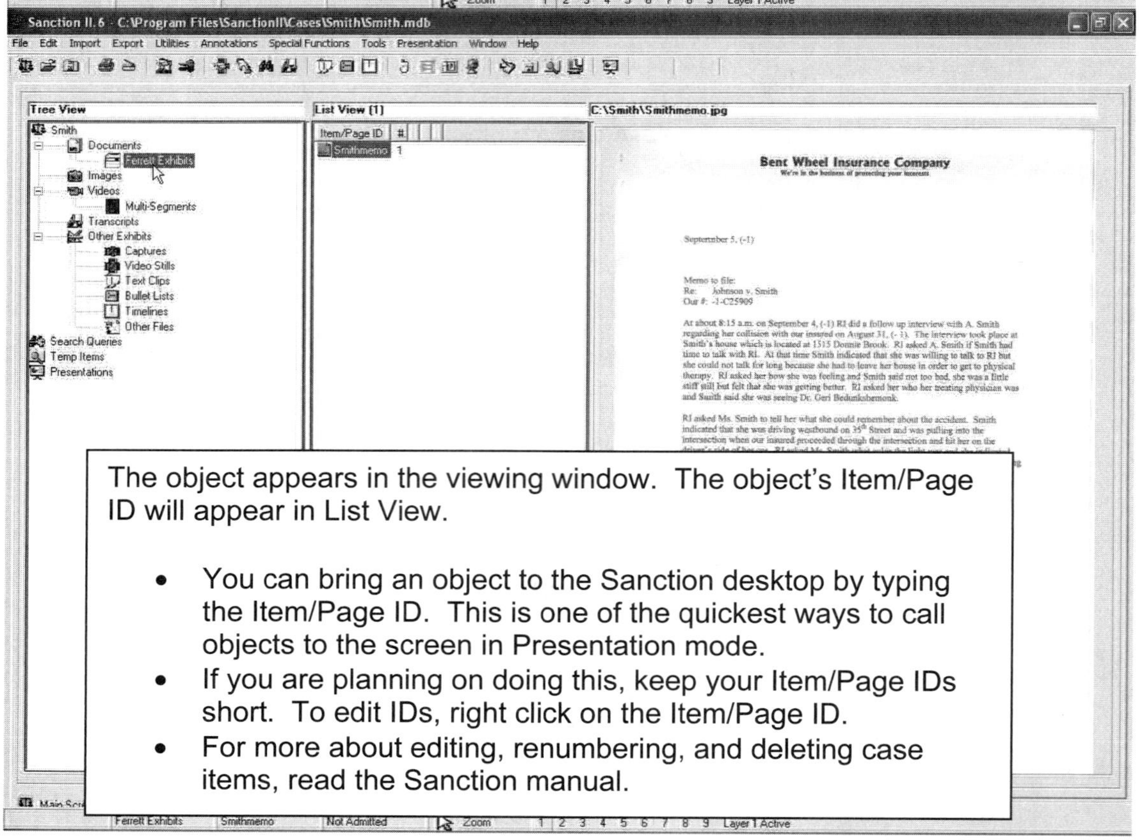
The object appears in the viewing window. The object's Item/Page ID will appear in List View.
• You can bring an object to the Sanction desktop by typing the Item/Page ID. This is one of the quickest ways to call objects to the screen in Presentation mode.
• If you are planning on doing this, keep your Item/Page IDs short. To edit IDs, right click on the Item/Page ID.
• For more about editing, renumbering, and deleting case items, read the Sanction manual.

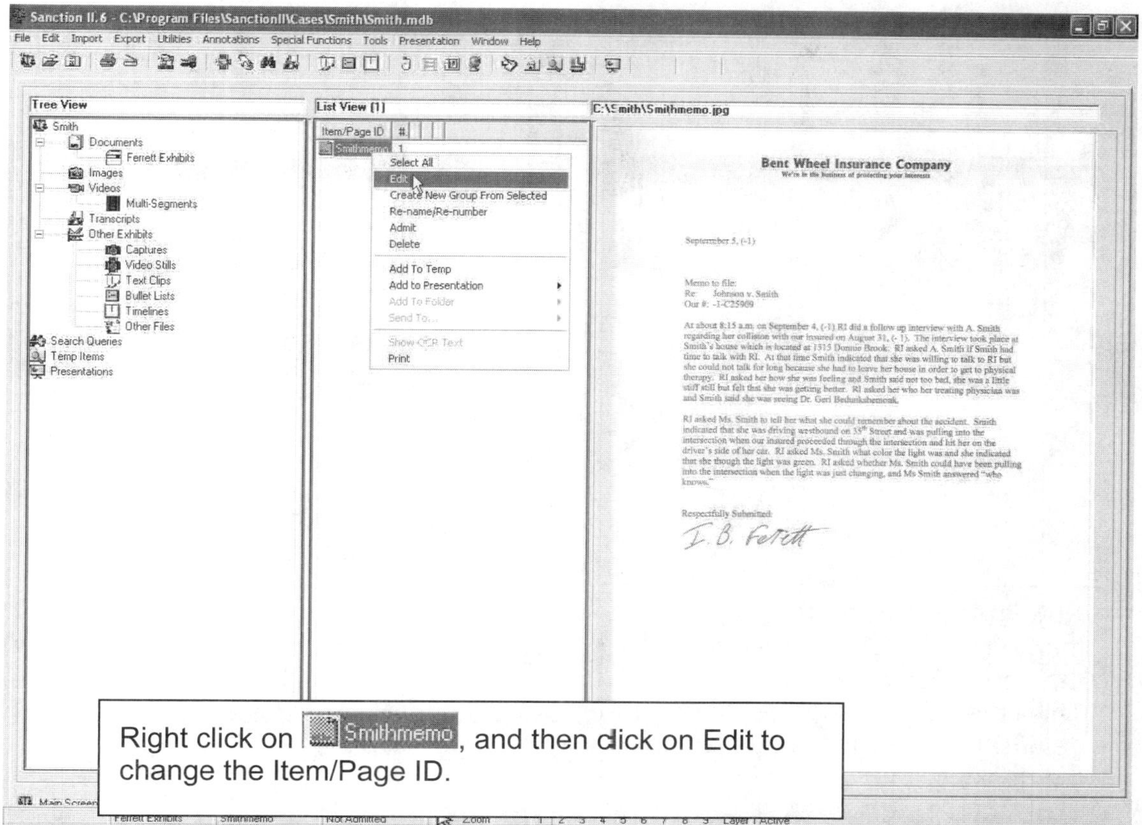

Right click on Smithmemo, and then click on Edit to change the Item/Page ID.

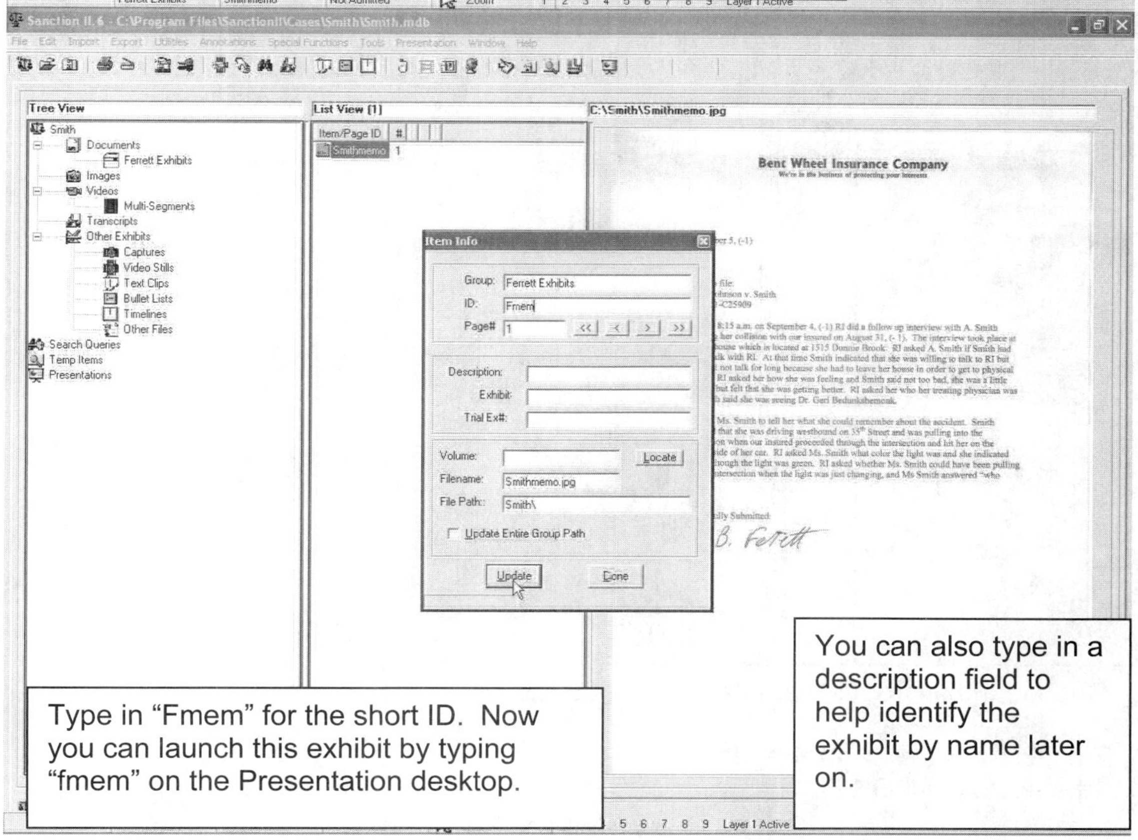

Type in “Fmem” for the short ID. Now you can launch this exhibit by typing “fmem” on the Presentation desktop.

You can also type in a description field to help identify the exhibit by name later on.

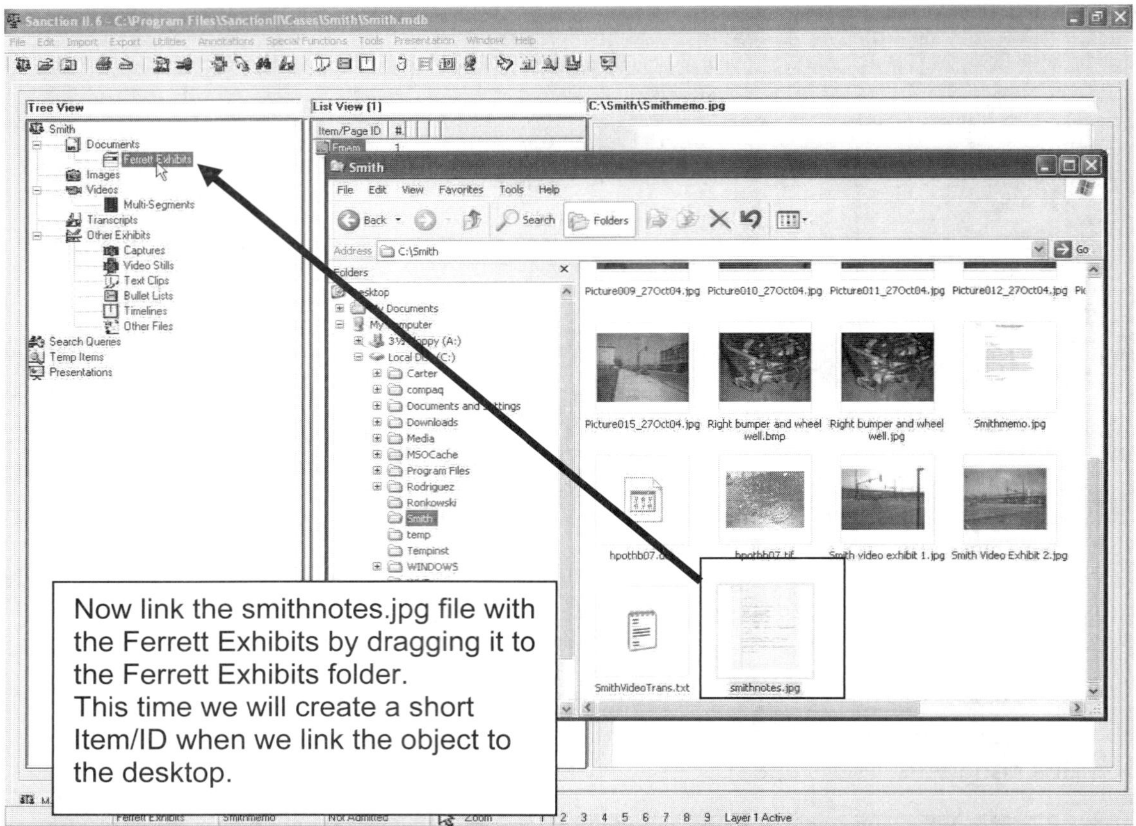
Now link the smithnotes.jpg file with the Ferrett Exhibits by dragging it to the Ferrett Exhibits folder.
This time we will create a short Item/ID when we link the object to the desktop.

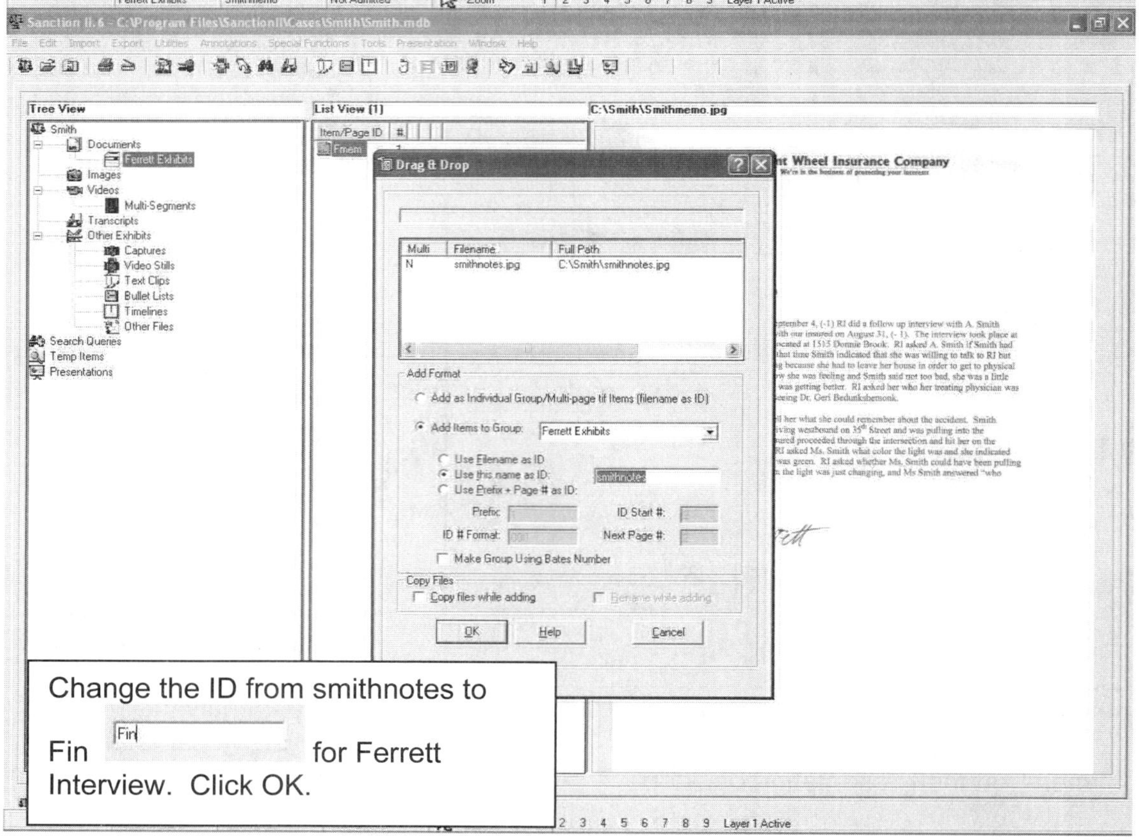
Change the ID from smithnotes to Fin for Ferrett Interview. Click OK.

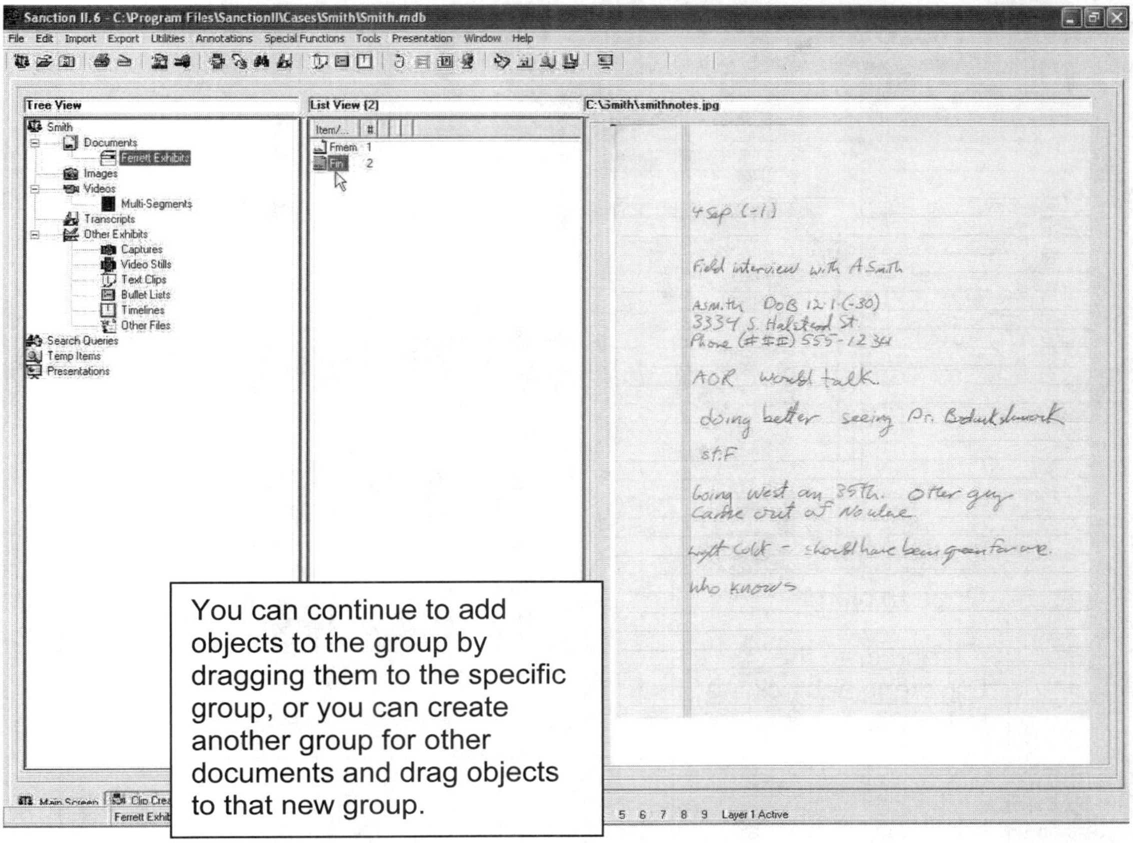
Sanction II.6 - C:\Program Files\SanctionII\Cases\Smith\Smith.mdb
File Edit Import Export Utilities Annotations Special Functions Tools Presentation Window Help
Tree View
Smith
Documents
Ferrett Exhibits
Images
Videos
Multi-Segments
Transcripts
Other Exhibits
Captures
Video Stills
Text Clips
Bullet Lists
Timelines
Other Files
Search Queries
Temp Items
Presentations
List View (2)
Fmem 1
Fin 2
C:\Smith\smithnotes.jpg
You can continue to add objects to the group by dragging them to the specific group, or you can create another group for other documents and drag objects to that new group.
Layer 1 Active

Adding Photos to the Images Folder

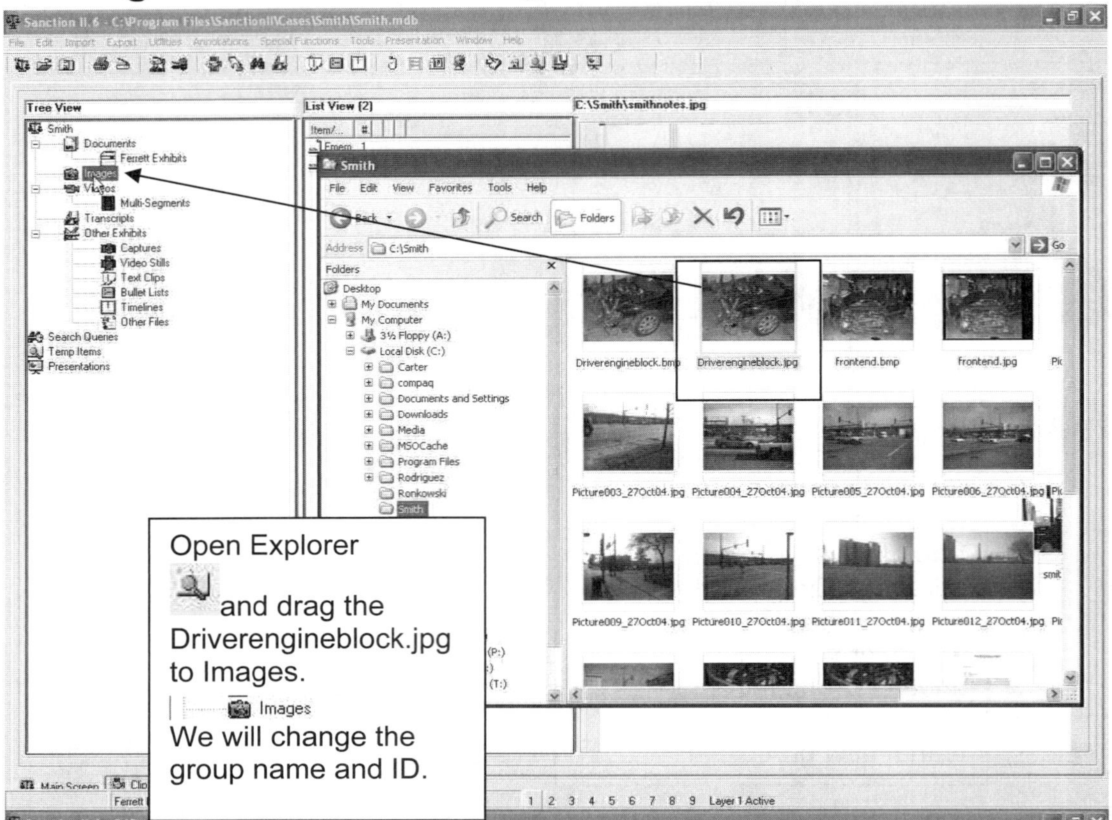

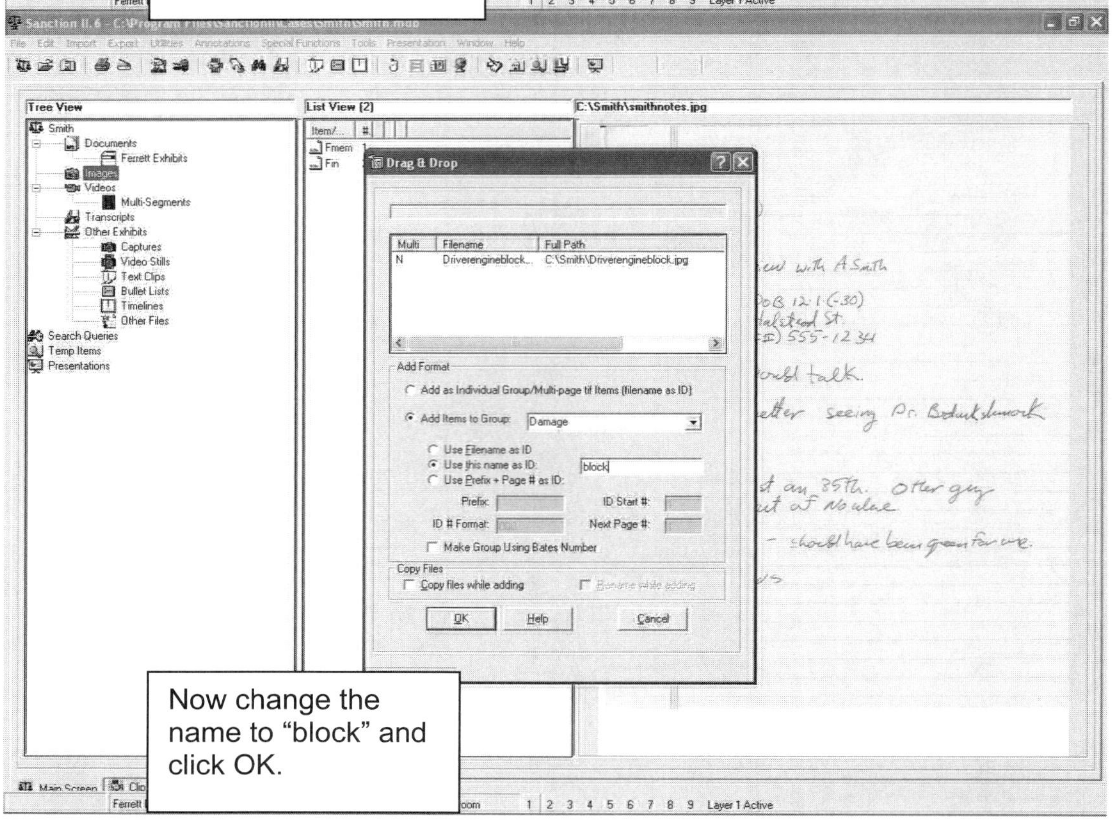

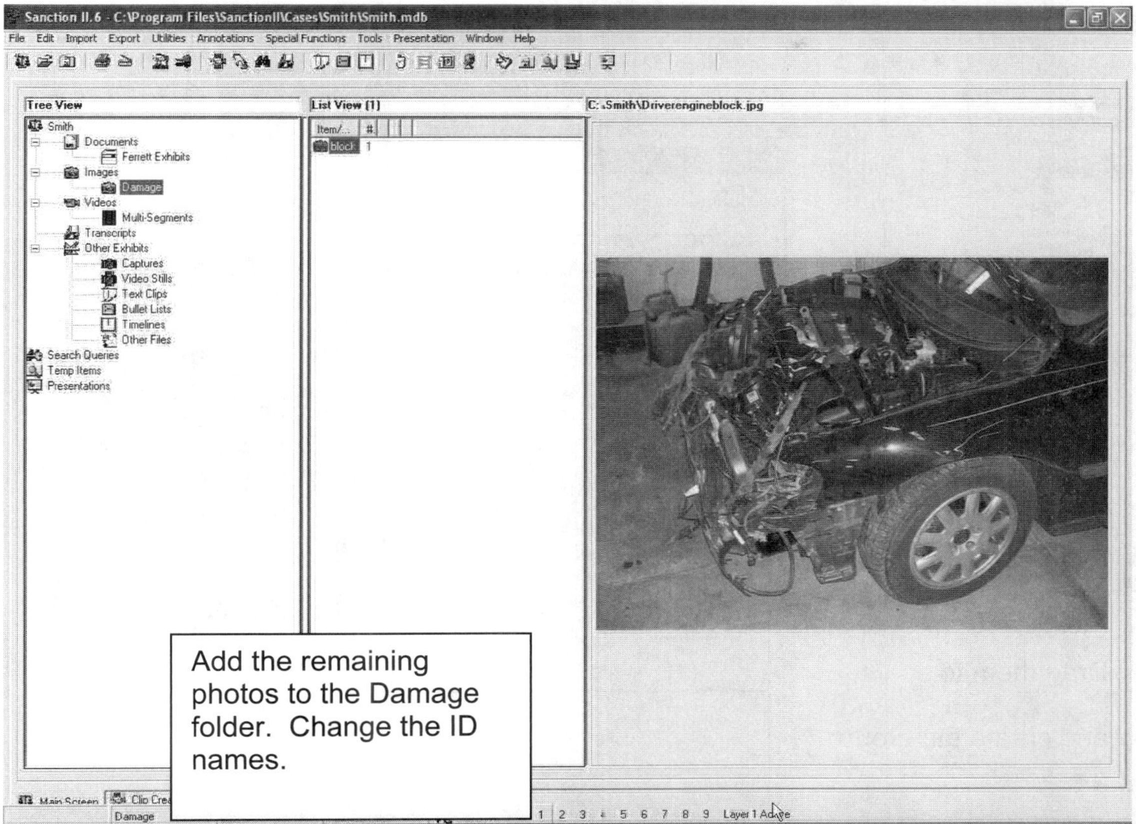
Sanction II.6 - C:\Program Files\SanctionII\Cases\Smith\Smith.mdb
File Edit Import Export Utilities Annotations Special Functions Tools Presentation Window Help
Tree View
Smith
Documents
Ferrett Exhibits
Images
Damage
Videos
Multi-Segments
Transcripts
Other Exhibits
Captures
Video Stills
Text Clips
Bullet Lists
Timelines
Other Files
Search Queries
Temp Items
Presentations
List View (1)
Item/... #
block 1
C:\Smith\Driverengineblock.jpg
Add the remaining photos to the Damage folder. Change the ID names.
Damage
1 2 3 4 5 6 7 8 9 Layer 1 Active

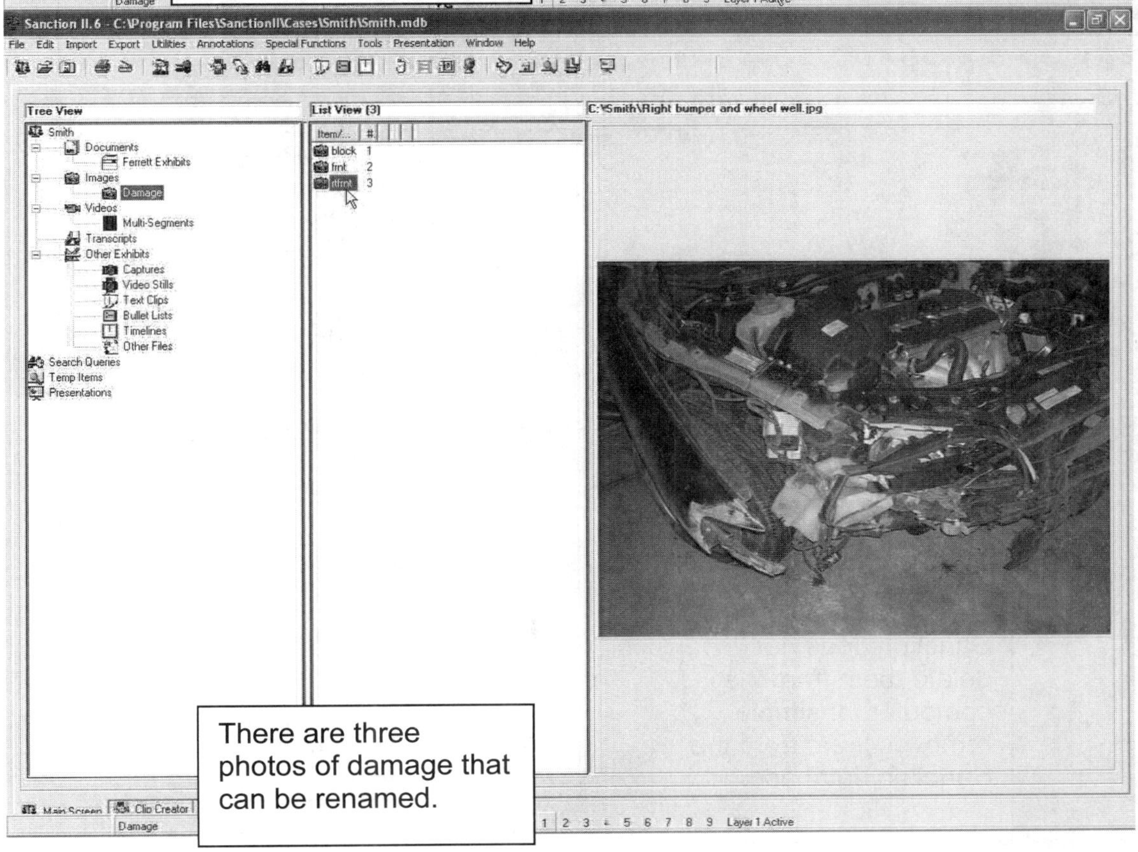
Sanction II.6 - C:\Program Files\SanctionII\Cases\Smith\Smith.mdb
File Edit Import Export Utilities Annotations Special Functions Tools Presentation Window Help
Tree View
Smith
Documents
Ferrett Exhibits
Images
Damage
Videos
Multi-Segments
Transcripts
Other Exhibits
Captures
Video Stills
Text Clips
Bullet Lists
Timelines
Other Files
Search Queries
Temp Items
Presentations
List View (3)
Item/... #
block 1
frnt 2
rtfrnt 3
C:\Smith\Right bumper and wheel well.jpg
There are three photos of damage that can be renamed.
Main Screen
Clip Creator
Damage
1 2 3 4 5 6 7 8 9 Layer 1 Active

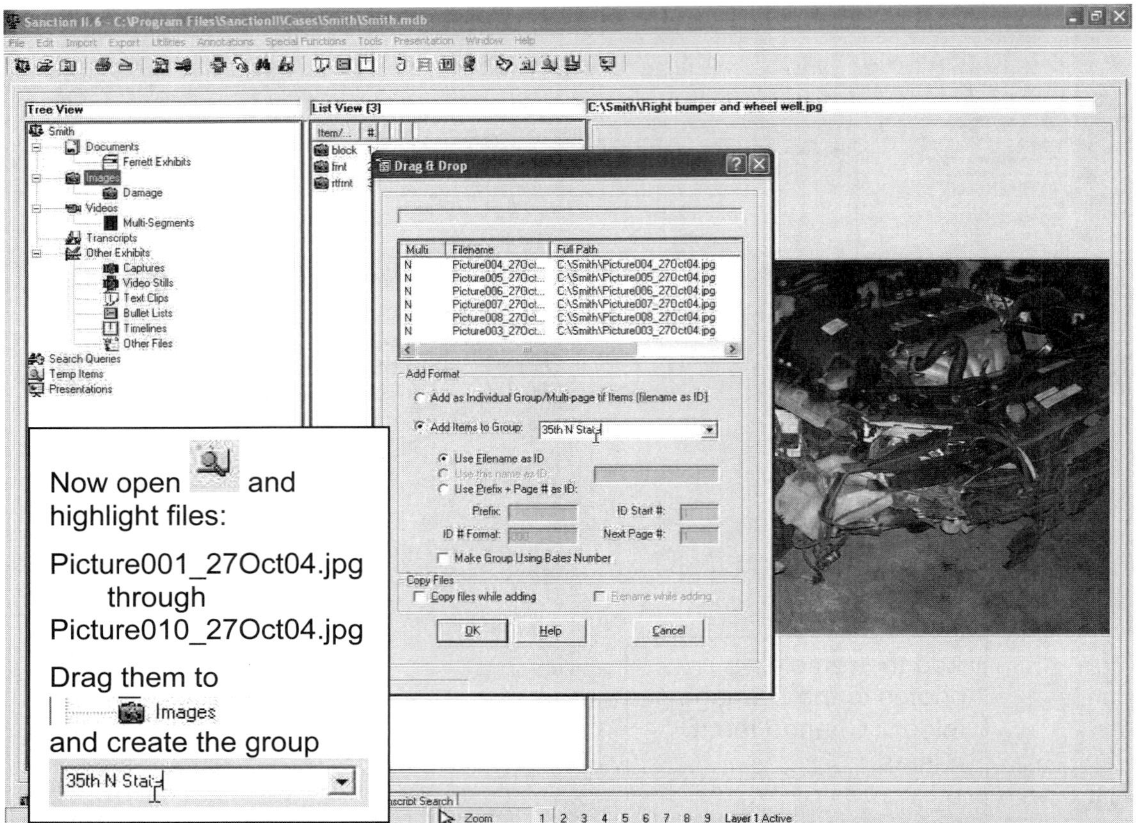
Now open and highlight files:
Picture001_27Oct04.jpg through Picture010_27Oct04.jpg
Drag them to Images
and create the group
35th N State

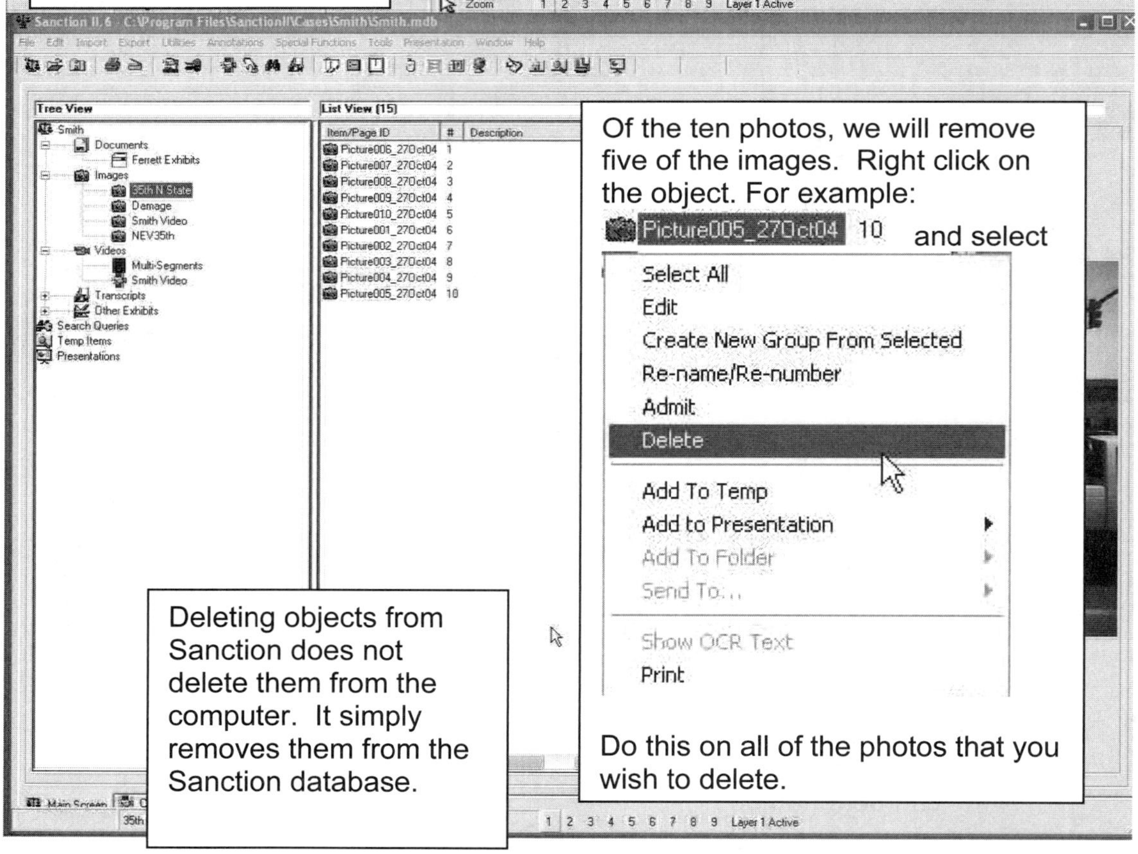
Of the ten photos, we will remove five of the images. Right click on the object. For example:
Picture005_27Oct04 10 and select
Select All
Edit
Create New Group From Selected
Re-name/Re-number
Admit
Delete
Add To Temp
Add to Presentation
Add To Folder
Send To...
Show OCR Text
Print
Do this on all of the photos that you wish to delete.
Deleting objects from Sanction does not delete them from the computer. It simply removes them from the Sanction database.

Adding an Individual Group or a Multipage .tif File

If you want to add an individual group, or if you are using multipage .tif items, Sanction uses the filename of the dragged item(s) as the group name in Tree View and Item/Page ID name in List View. Each file becomes a separate group. Multipage .tif files can be added only by using this option.

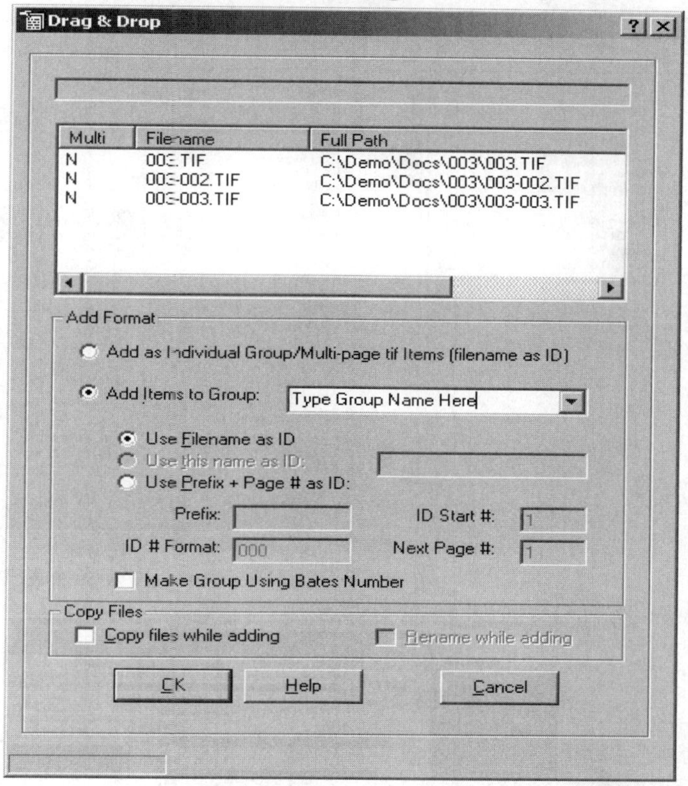

Sanction creates a single group for the dragged item(s) in Tree View based on the group name you type.

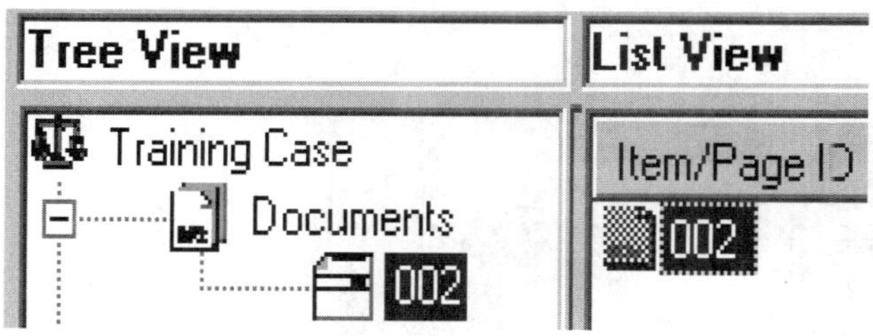

Item/Page IDs in the List View can use the existing filename or be changed by using various format options:

Note: Group and Item/Page ID names are not required to match.

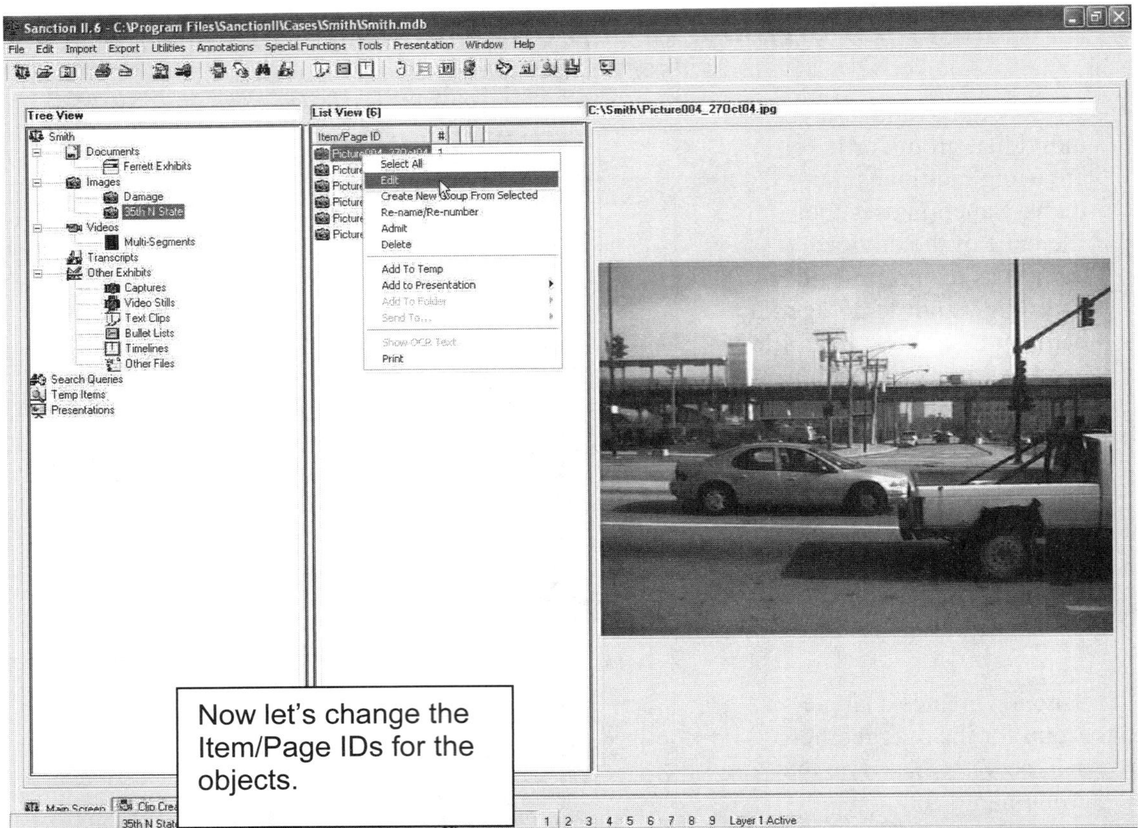

Now let's change the Item/Page IDs for the objects.

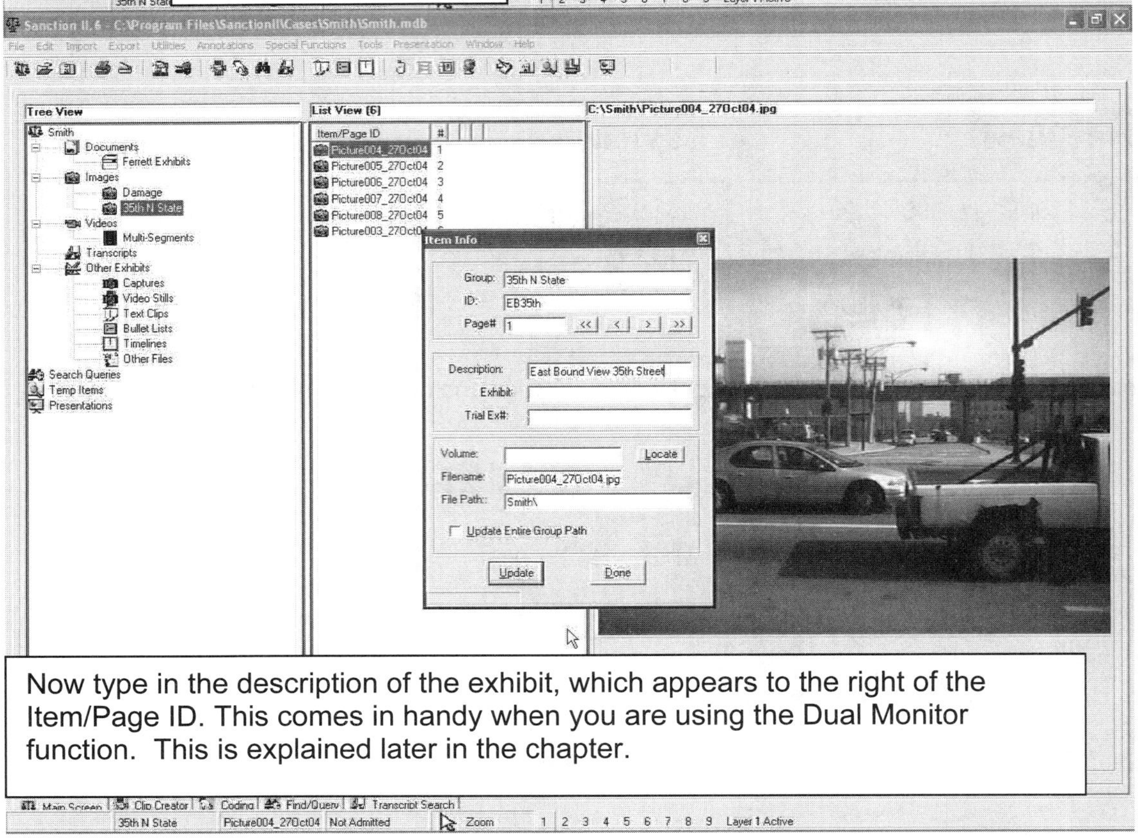

Now type in the description of the exhibit, which appears to the right of the Item/Page ID. This comes in handy when you are using the Dual Monitor function. This is explained later in the chapter.

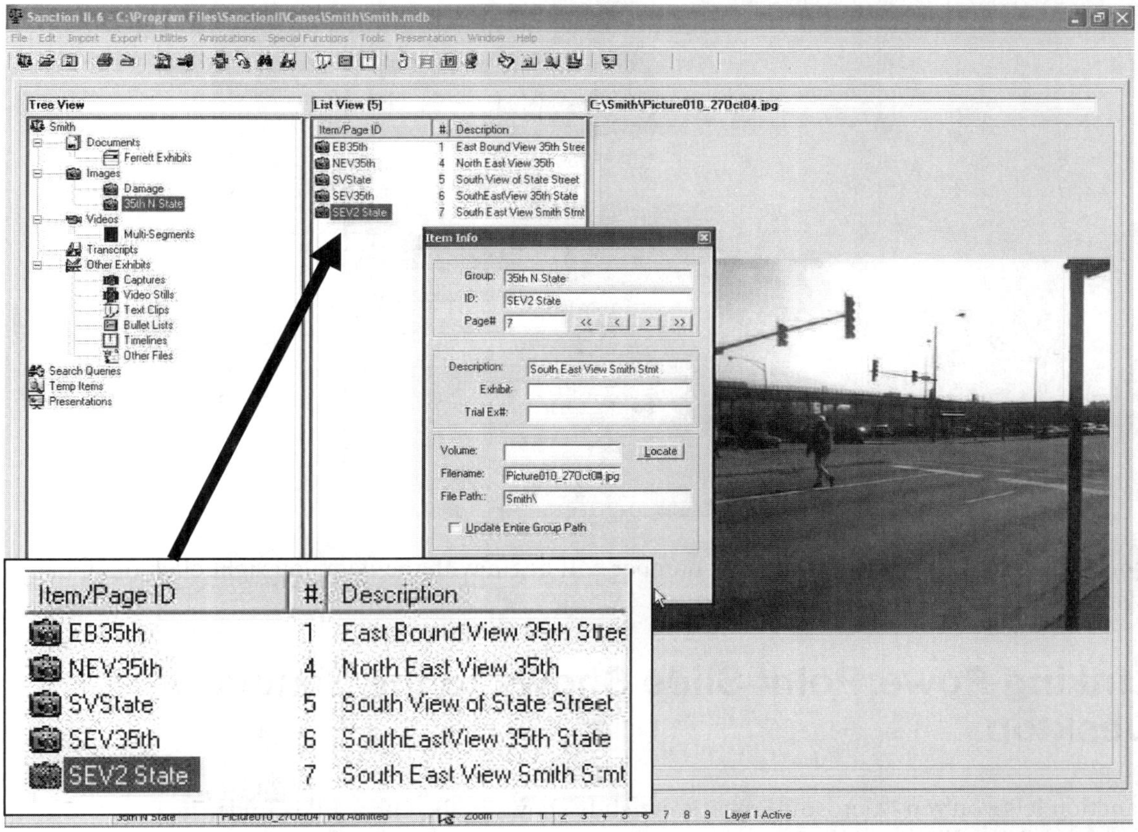

Renaming and Renumbering Case Items

To Rename a Group in Tree View:

- Right click on the group and select Rename.

To Rename Items/Page IDs in List View:

- Right click on the page in the List View that you want to start with and select Rename/Re-number.
- Select Rename Pages and type the desired prefix and format options.

To Renumber Items/Page IDs in List View:

- Right click on the page in the List View that you want to start with and select Rename/Re-number.
- Under Numbering, type the new starting page number in the First New Page# box. Note: This renumbering changes the page number sequence field (#) in List View, not the Item/Page ID field.

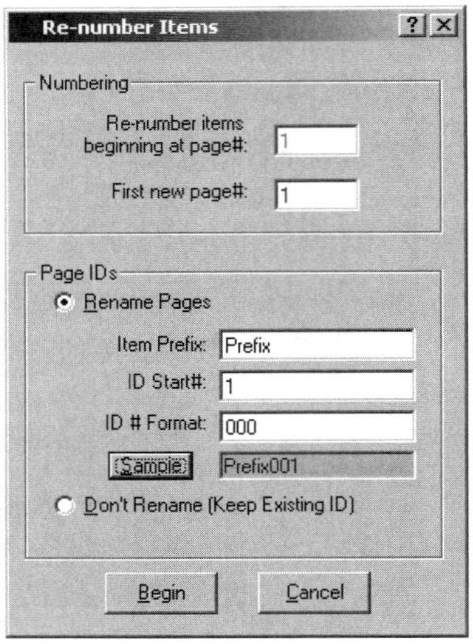

Note: The new Item/Page ID name or number will begin with the item you right click on in the List View.

Linking PowerPoint Slide Shows to the Sanction Desktop

Sanction lets you run Microsoft PowerPoint slide shows in the Other Files folder in Tree View under the Other Exhibits category. Slide shows should be saved from PowerPoint as PowerPoint Show files (.pps) rather than the default Power Point Presentation (.ppt). (See Chapter 7 on PowerPoint.) You will also have to tell Sanction to use source applications. This command lets the PowerPoint show advance through the slide show with animations that can be activated with a cordless presenter mouse click. To activate this command, go to the Tools menu of Sanction and select Settings.

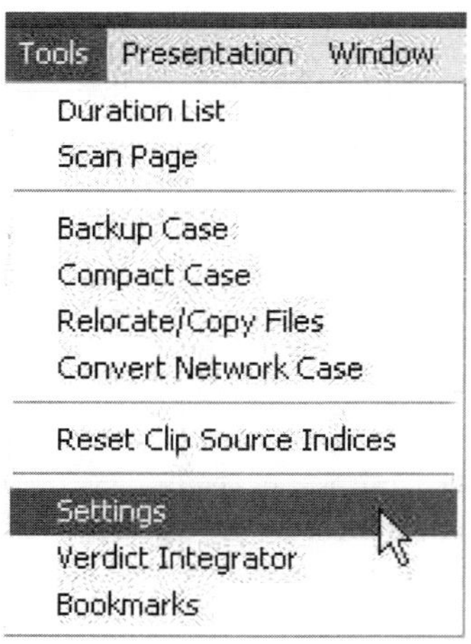

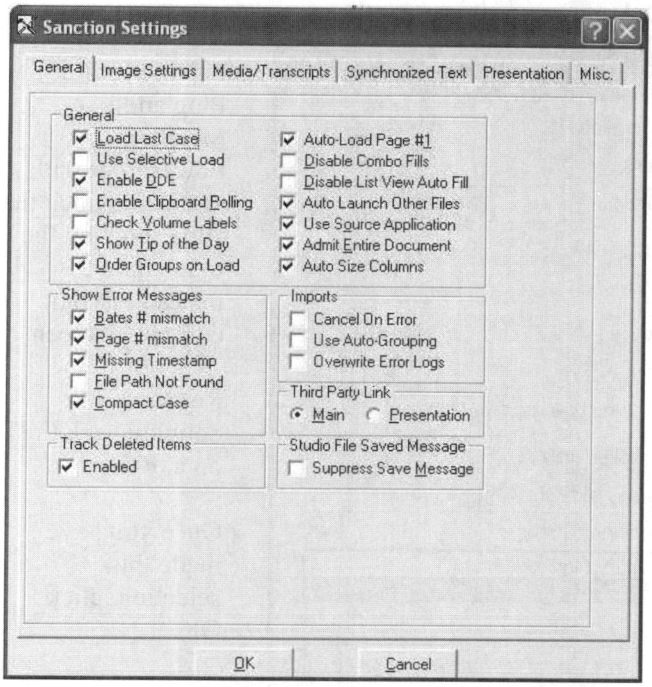

This menu will appear. Check Use ☑ Use Source Application and then OK

Setting Up PowerPoint for Dual Monitor Display

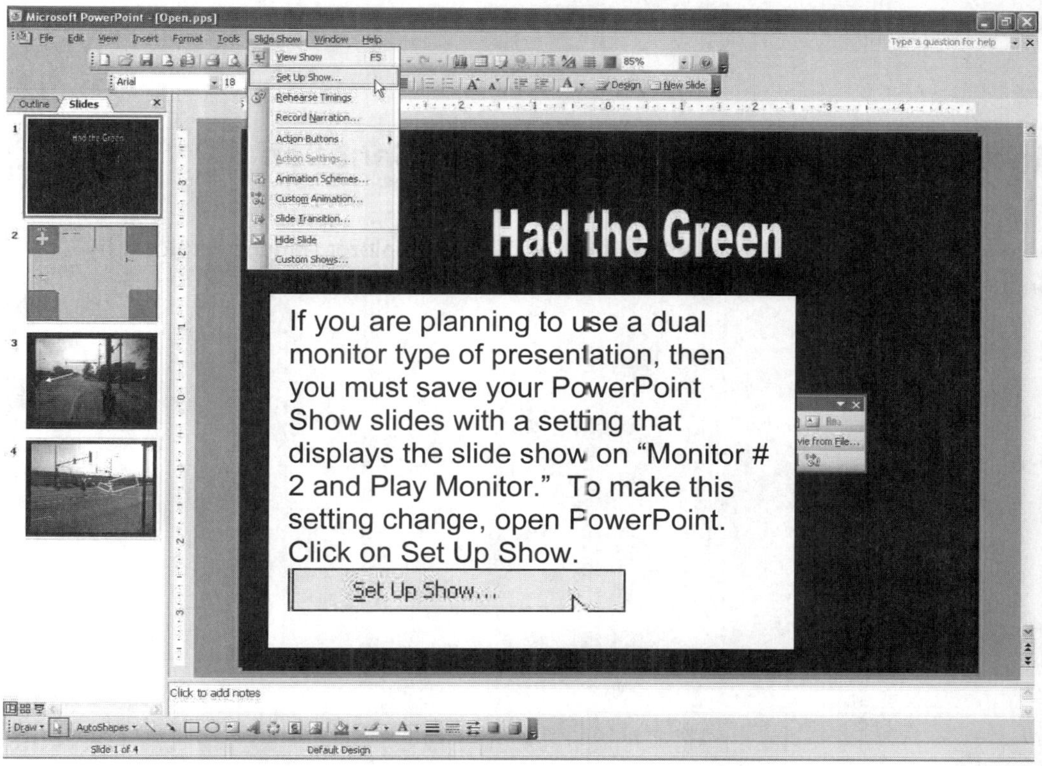

The following window will appear.

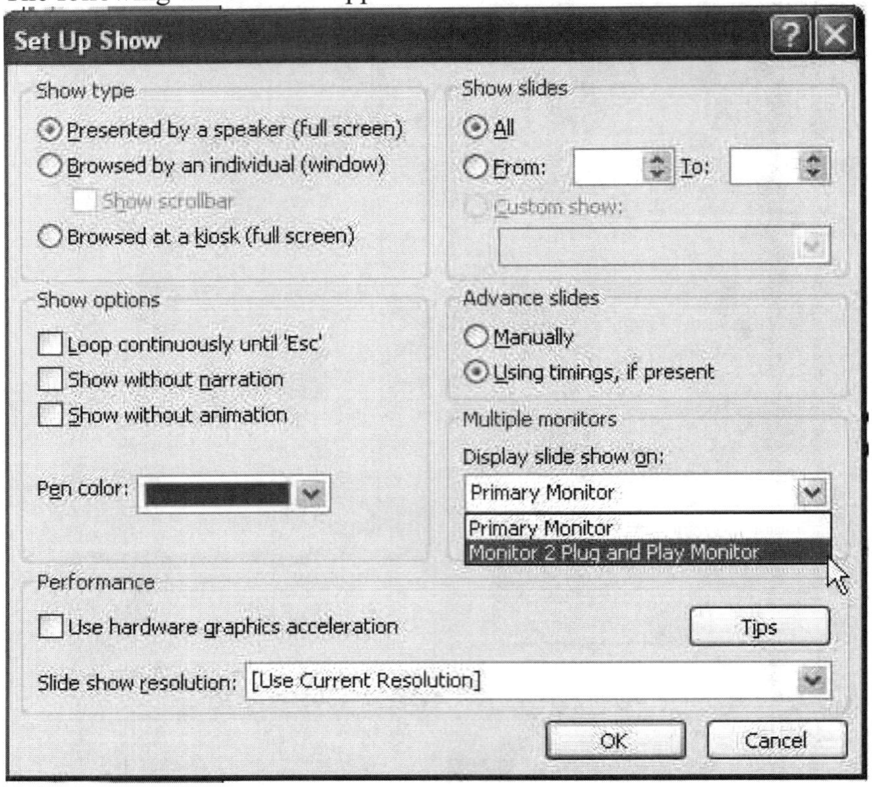

Select Monitor 2 Plug and Play Monitor. PowerPoint will know to launch the slide show on the video monitor instead of your computer screen.

Remember to double-check this on a dry run.

Once you have made this selection, click OK.

Adding a PowerPoint Slide Show to Sanction

Select the PowerPoint Show (.pps) file to add from Windows Explorer (launch Explorer by clicking on the Windows Explorer button on the toolbar in Sanction).

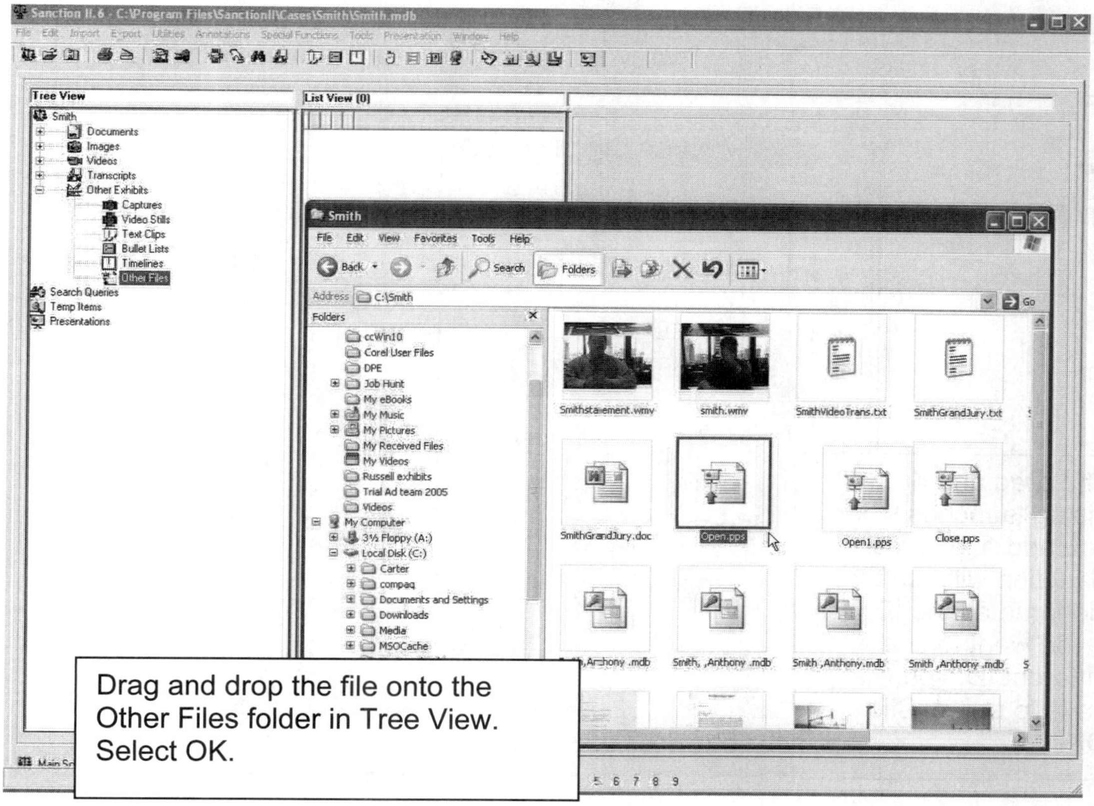

Note: Although the drag and drop dialog launches when you add a .pps file, the information fields are automatically disabled. PowerPoint Slide files are added using their original filenames as their IDs.

Important: When running other programs under Other Files, the native application (Word, Excel, Adobe Acrobat, and so on) must be installed on the computer in order to view them. The program associated with the file type (.doc = Word, .xls = Excel, .pdf = Adobe Acrobat) will open within Sanction and display the file. If this is not desirable, convert the file to a generic .tif, .bmp, or .jpg file before adding to Sanction.

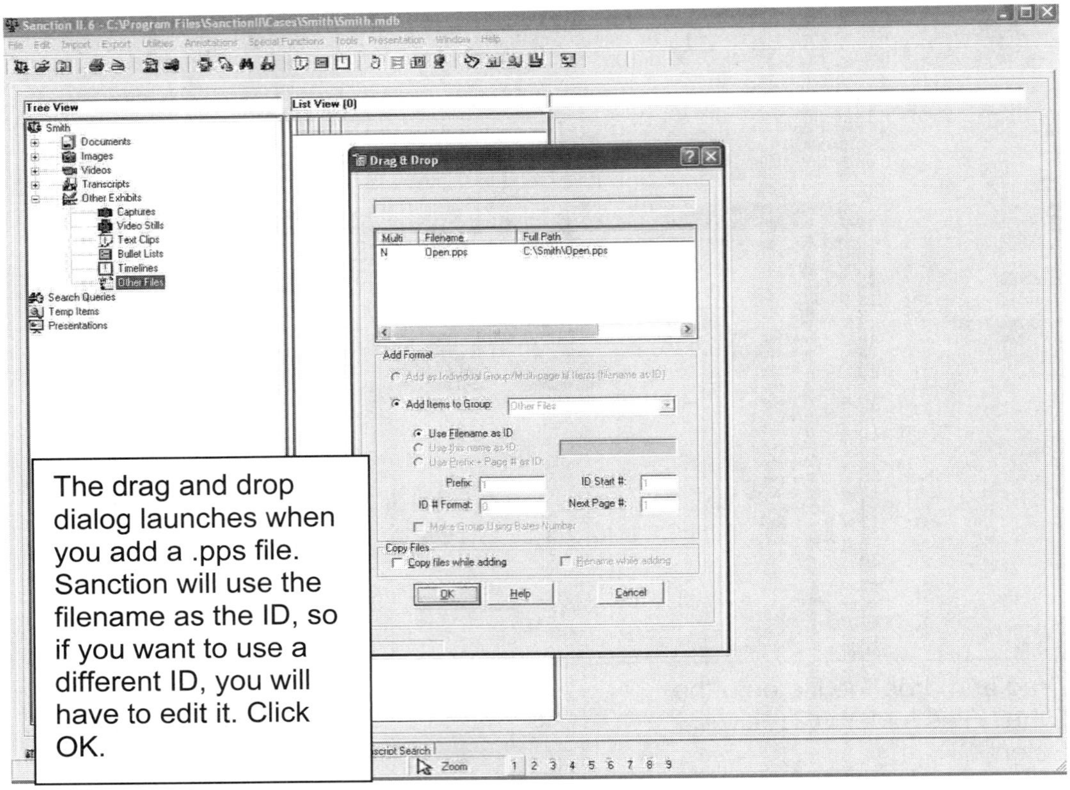

Linking the Video Exhibits to the Video Folder

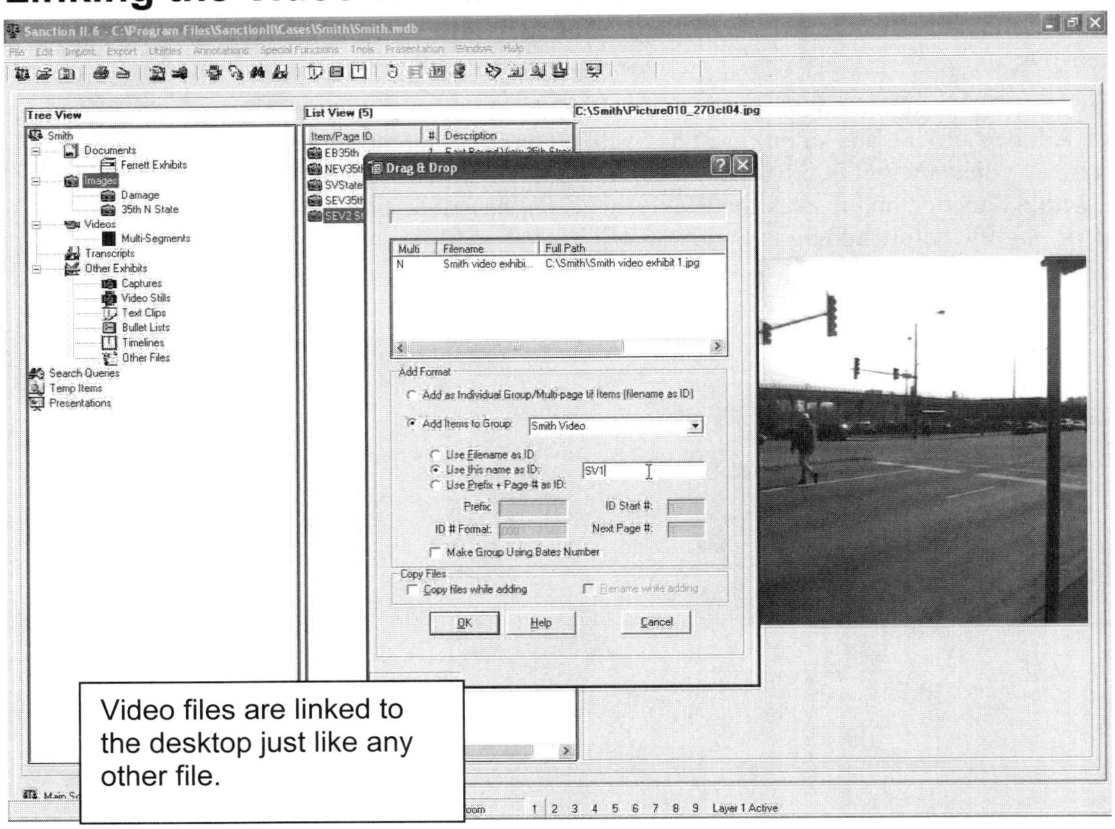

Use Windows Explorer to drag the Smith video to the video desktop.

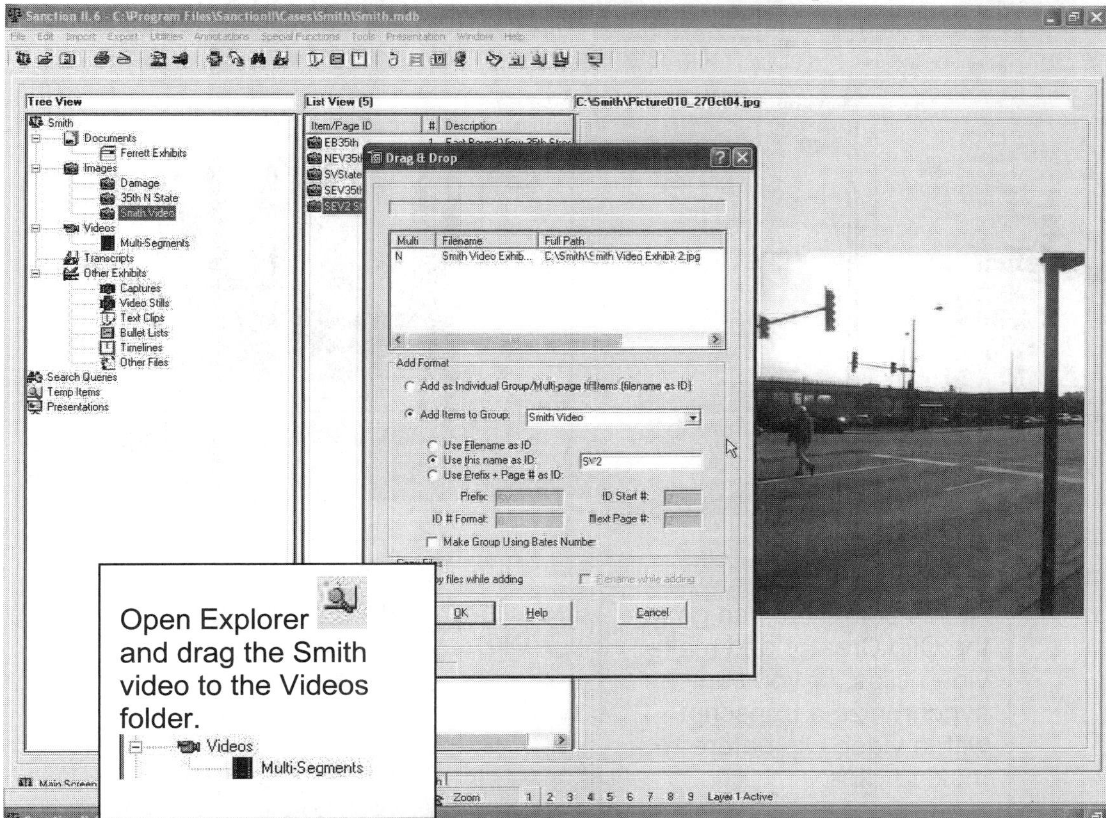

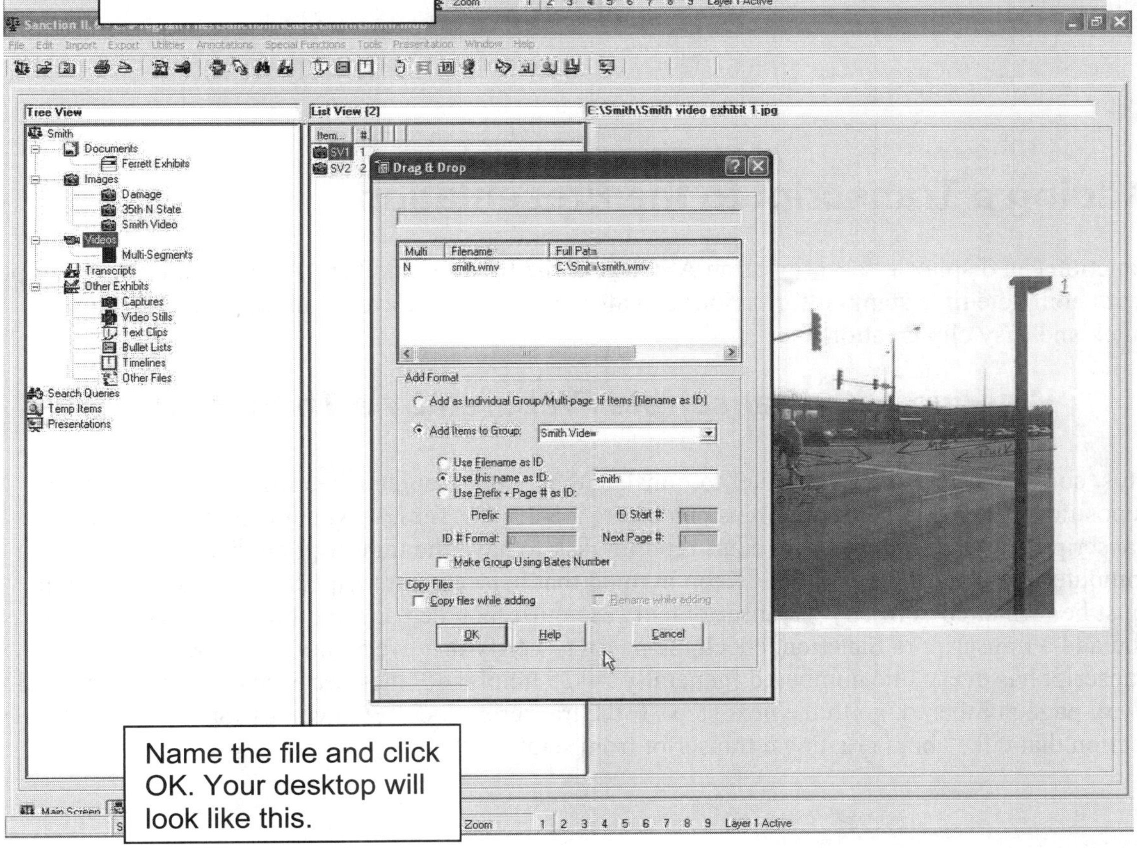

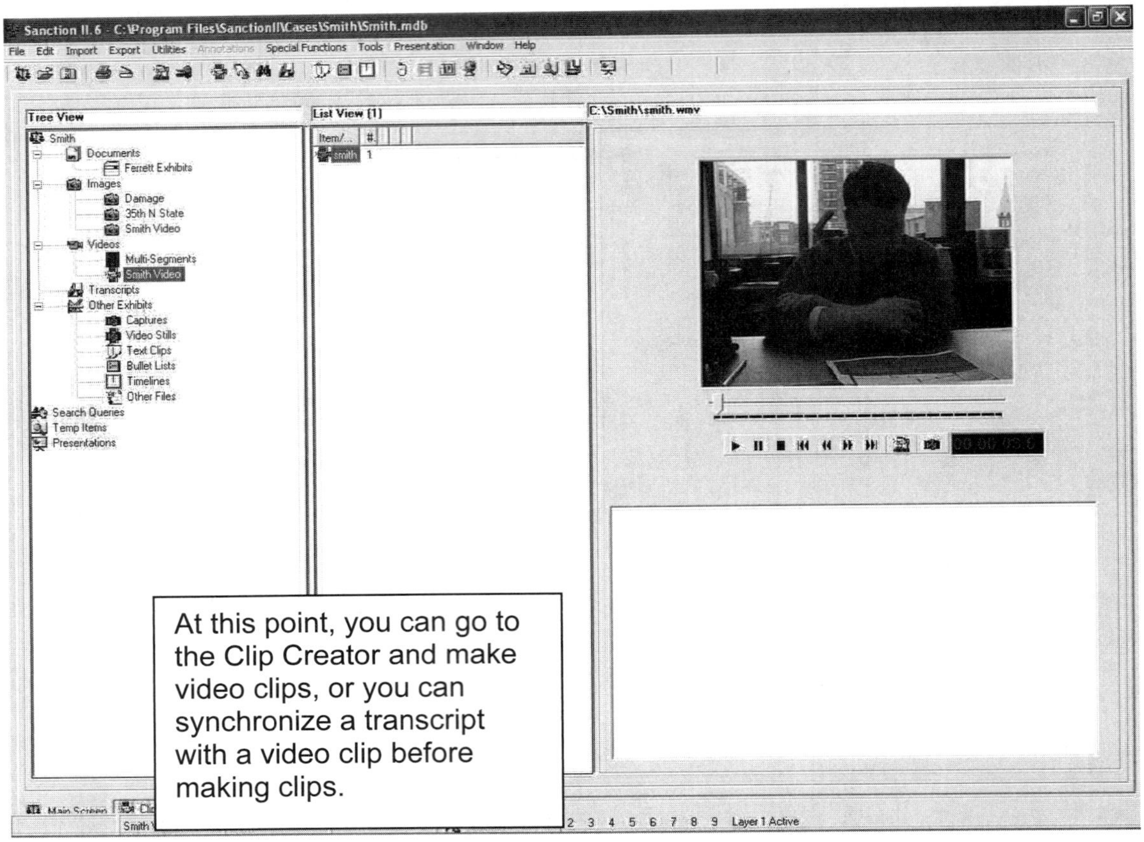

Adding a Transcript to the Presentation

Sanction can display a transcript as an ASCII text file by page number. A synchronized transcript (with complete time stamp information) can also be used with corresponding media files for quick and easy clip creation.

Working with Transcripts Prepared by a Third Party

Most court reporters use a computer to translate their stenographic notes from hearings and depositions. The computer programs can create ASCII text files. If you are going to use a transcript that was prepared by a court reporter, ask to have the transcript on disk. This way your computer can import the text file. Keep in mind that before a transcript can be synchronized, it must be formatted correctly. Transcript text files must include page and line numbers. Before you add a transcript to Sanction, check the pages to verify that every line is numbered. If the transcript has every line numbered (generally 24-25 numbered lines per page on a transcript) and every page numbered, go to the next step. If the transcript does not have this formatting, go to the section that talks about creating a transcript from scratch.

Adding Transcript Text Files That Have Been Previously Formatted

Simply open Windows Explorer, select the deposition text file that you want to add to your presentation, and drag and drop the file onto the Transcripts folder. (Transcripts may also be added from the Import menu by selecting the Transcripts option.) When Sanction adds a transcript, it automatically determines the lines per page, page breaks, and even the deponent name.

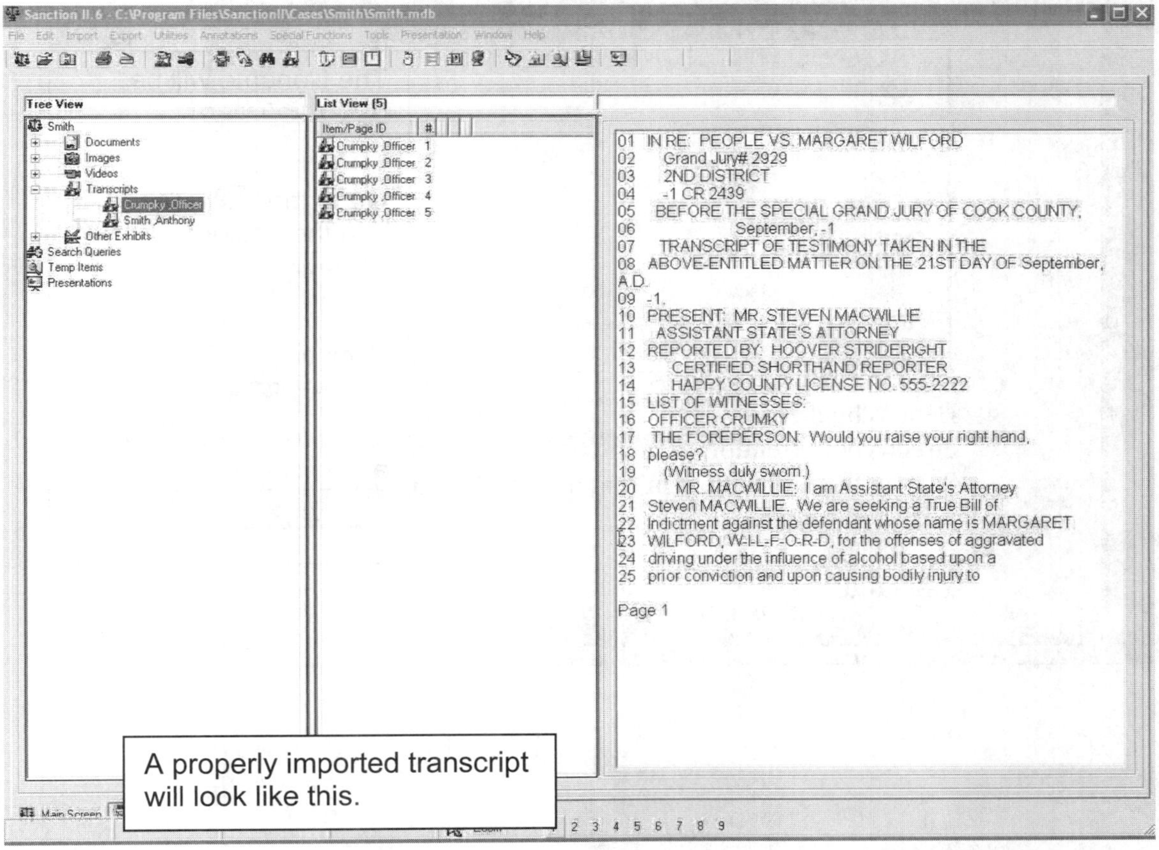

If Sanction is unable to properly identify these settings, use the Transcript Manager utility (described below) to create the proper setting values. Typically, if a transcript imports incorrectly, the page numbers will display incorrectly or clicking on a page displays a blank.

Creating a Transcript from Scratch

Because people will continue to use video cameras and audio recorders in their everyday dealings, you will have to work with transcripts of video or audio files that were transcribed by you or by someone else in your office. This will happen when you get witness interviews on video, voice mail messages, wiretap data, and other types of media files. To use these "transcripts" successfully in Sanction, they must be in the standard court reporter page and line format. While you can use any word processor that you want, we will talk about using Microsoft

Word 2003 since it is the most commonly used word processing software and because it usually comes with the Microsoft Office Suites that include PowerPoint 2003.

Sanction's Transcript Manager converts a plain text file into a page and line numbered transcript. The following two screen captures show you how to save a file as a .txt file in Microsoft Word 2003.

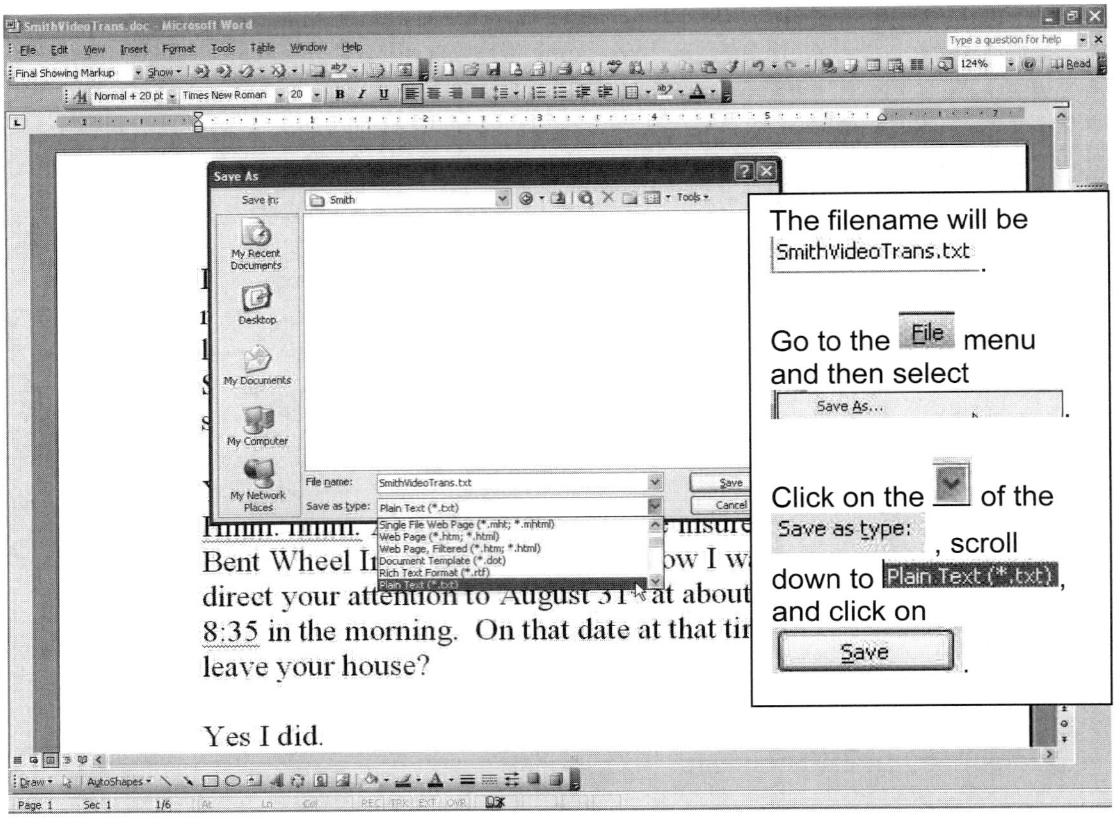

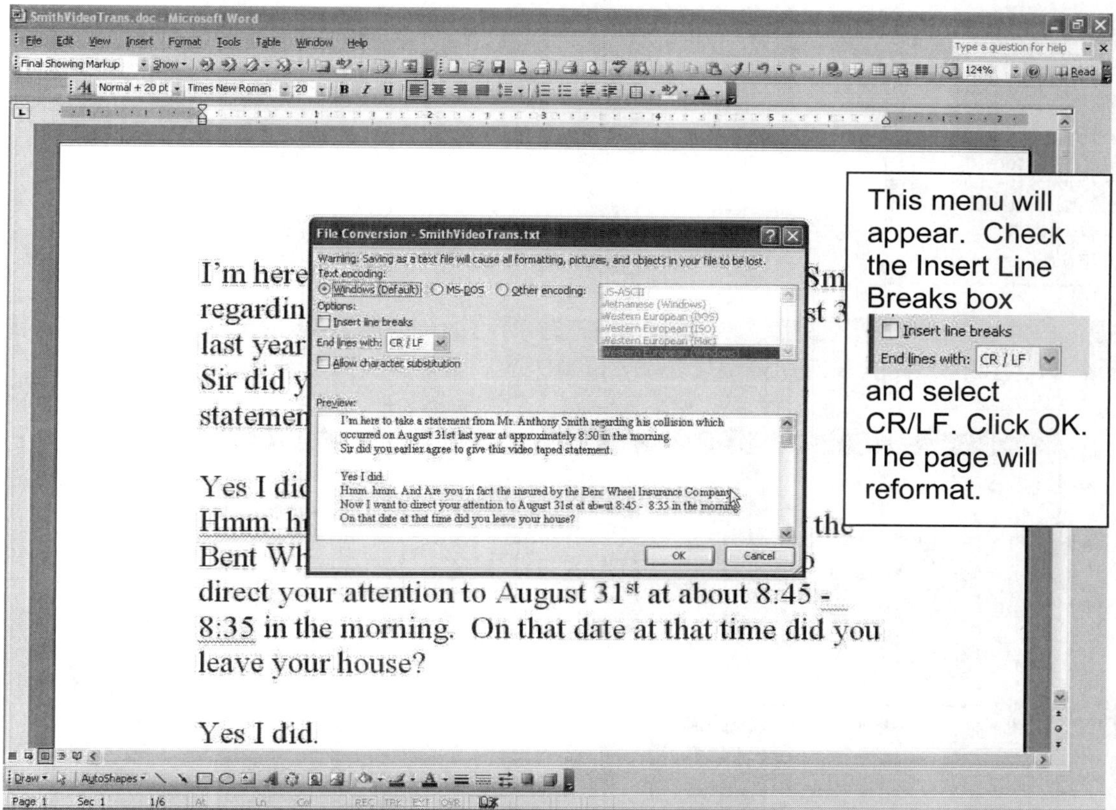
This menu will appear. Check the Insert Line Breaks box
Insert line breaks
End lines with: CR / LF
and select CR/LF. Click OK. The page will reformat.

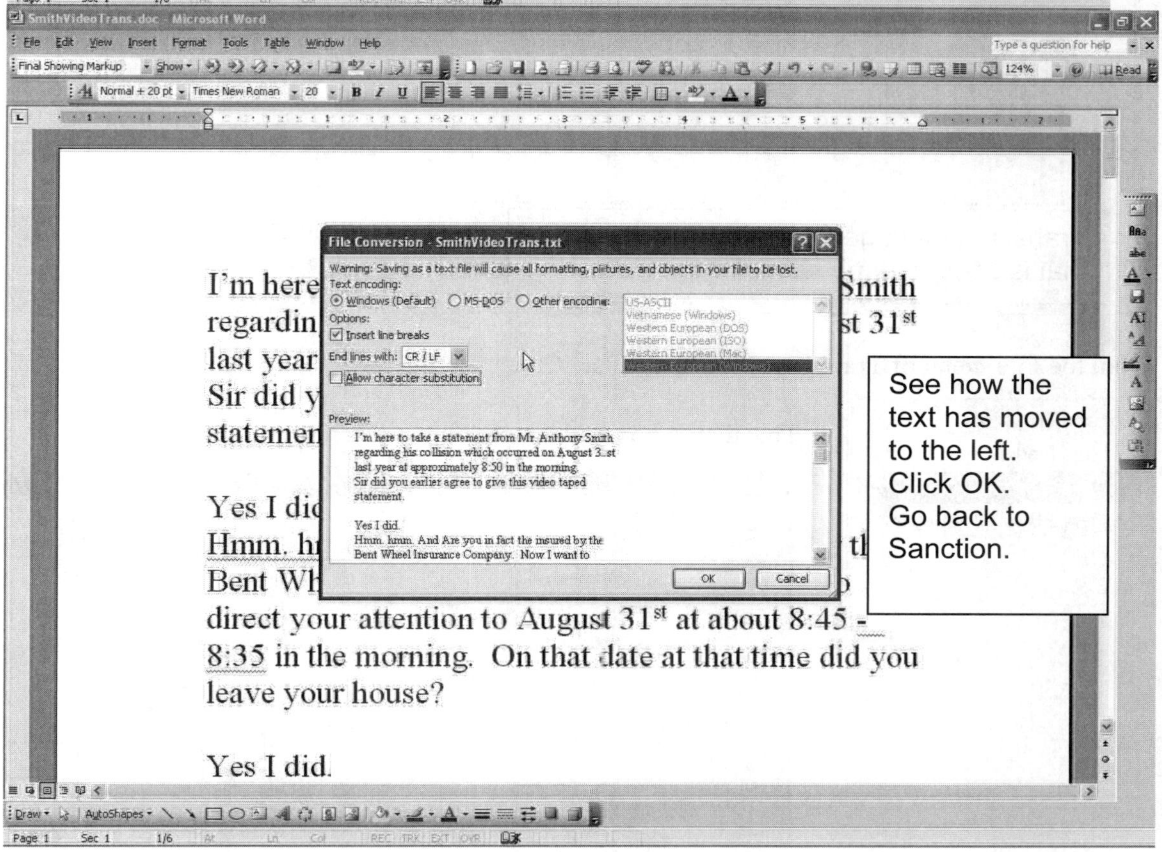
See how the text has moved to the left. Click OK. Go back to Sanction.

Go back to Sanction and open Transcript Manager from the Utilities menu on the toolbar.

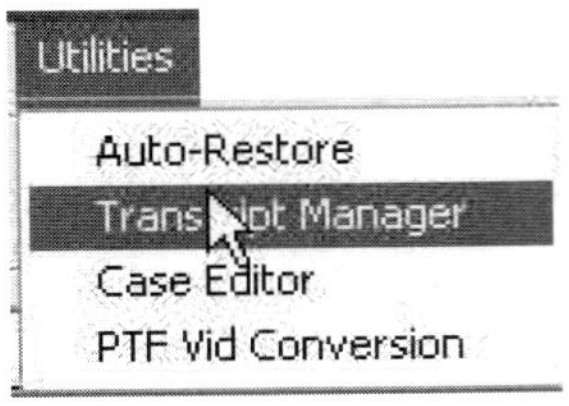

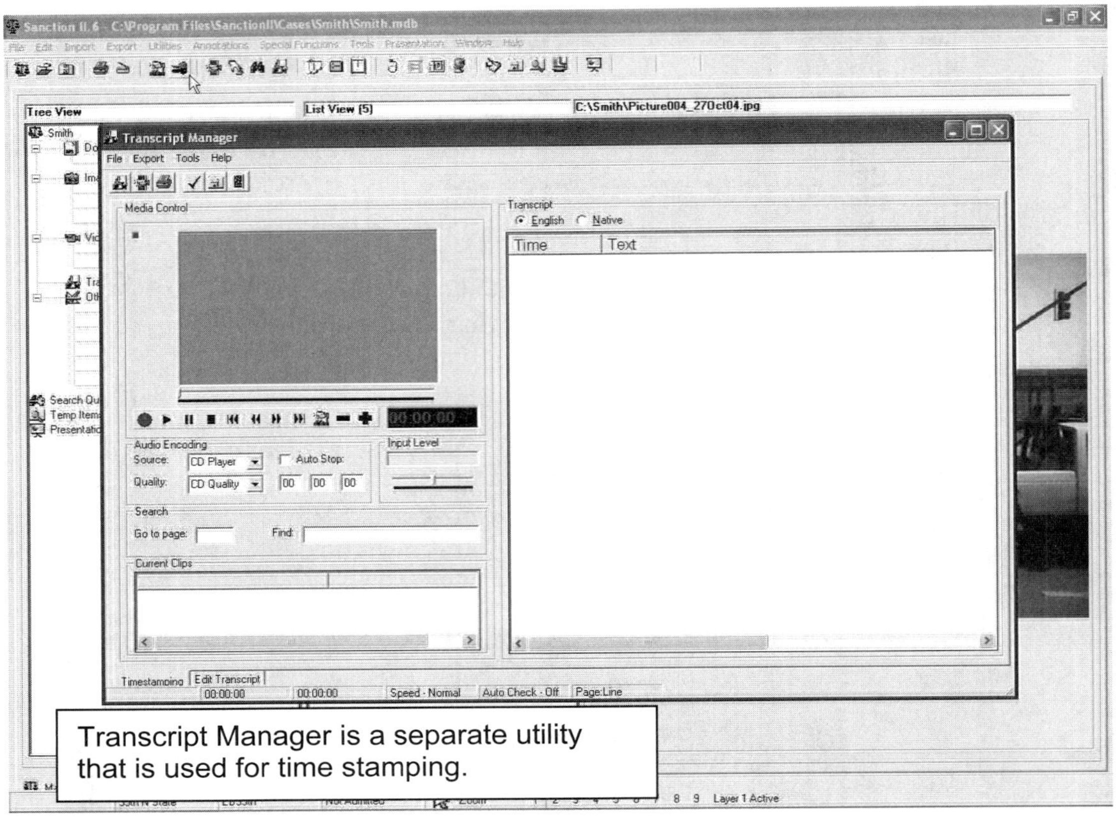

From the File menu of Transcript Manager, select Create from User.

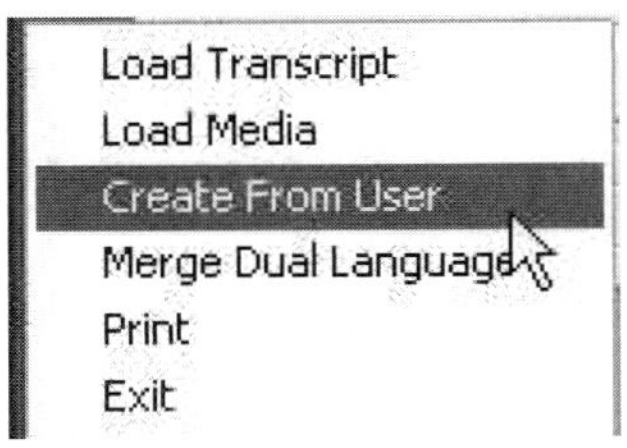

This dialog box will appear on top of Transcript Manager.

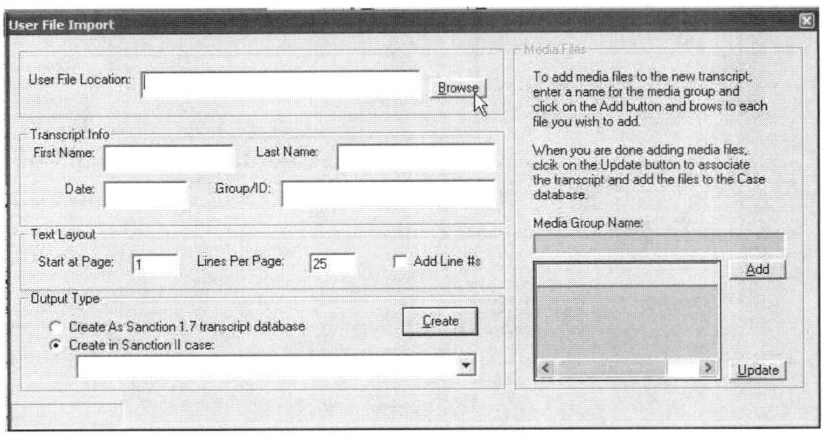

Click on Browse and browse to the location of the saved text file. In our case, the text file is SmithVideoTrans.txt in the Smith folder. Click on the file and select Open.

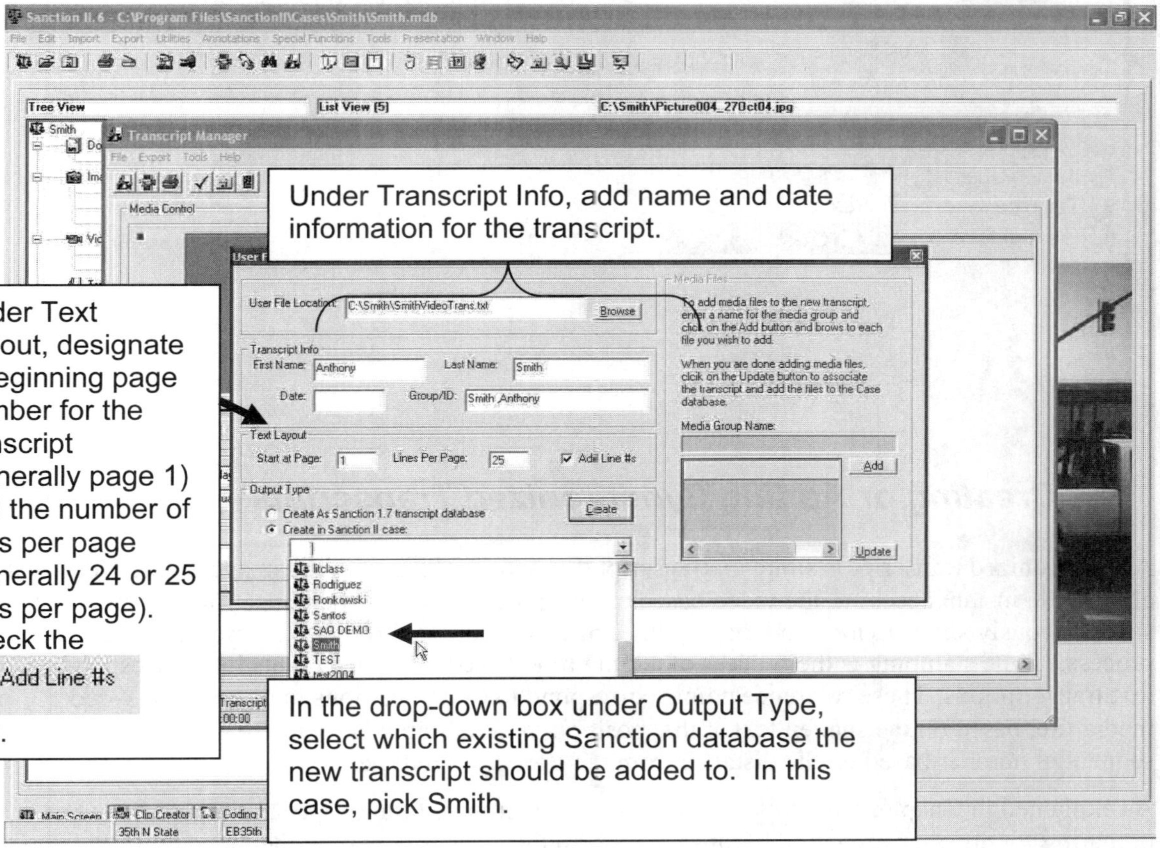

Click on Create. Click on the [minimize] icon to minimize Transcript Manager. Now right click on the Transcripts category on the Main screen within the Sanction Database and select Refresh.

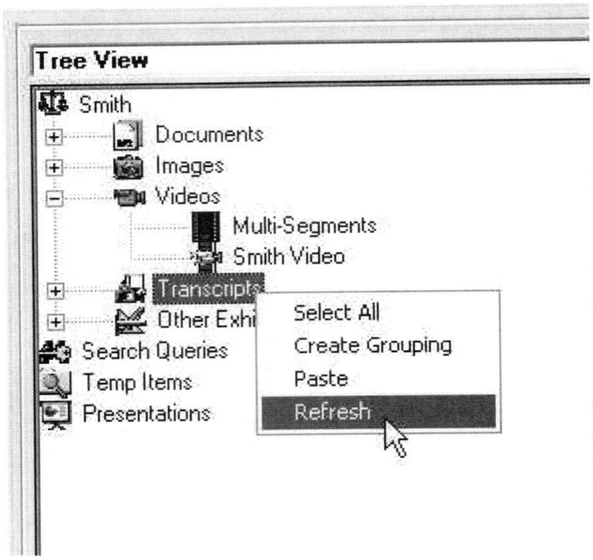

Check the new transcript to verify that the page and line numbers were added correctly.

The new transcript is now ready to be synchronized (or time stamped) to the corresponding audio or video file.

Creating or Adding Synchronized Transcripts

A synchronized transcript is simply a transcript that scrolls along with the image on the video that allows you instant access to the video based on the page and line of the transcript. Sanction will simultaneously show a video and display lines of text if you go through the time stamping process. Time stamping is the process of adding time-based reference points into corresponding text transcriptions. These reference points correspond to exact positions in an audio or video media file, based on the spoken text at that position. A time stamp is basically a progressive, sequential number based on the distance from the start point in time.

As explained in Chapter 5 on cross-examination, synchronized transcripts are imperative when preparing for cross-examination because they form the basis for creating the video clips that you will use during the examination. Time stamping provides two important functions for Sanction. First, if you know the range of text that you want to locate in an audio or video file, you can simply do a text search, either by the actual text or by a page and line number, and the corresponding time stamp will take you to the precise location in the media file where this text is spoken. Second, when a synchronized text and media file are played back, every point in the playing media file can quickly be located and the text displayed from the time stamp references in the synchronized files. This is handy because the Media Clip Creator, which you will be introduced to later in the chapter, allows you to use the page and line numbers of the text file to quickly jump to any point in the media files and create a clip segment from the selected text. Then when Sanction plays the clip back, the media file position determines where in the transcript the current spoken text is located. This synchronized text playback allows the viewer to both hear the spoken words and see the spoken words on the screen.

This section of the chapter takes you step by step through the process of time stamping. If you find this process too frustrating, you can have a transcript time stamped by a service bureau or vendor. If you do use a service bureau or a vendor to do the synchronization, you can simply use the Transcript Manager utility and drag and drop the transcript using the method described previously. (You can contact Verdict Systems on their website at www.verdictsystems.com for a list of vendors who will do this.) The group name is automatically created in Sanction. After the transcript has been successfully loaded, to view a page of the deposition, just click on the desired page number in the List View window. The corresponding page will display in the viewing window.

For those of you who want to synchronize the video yourself, do the following.

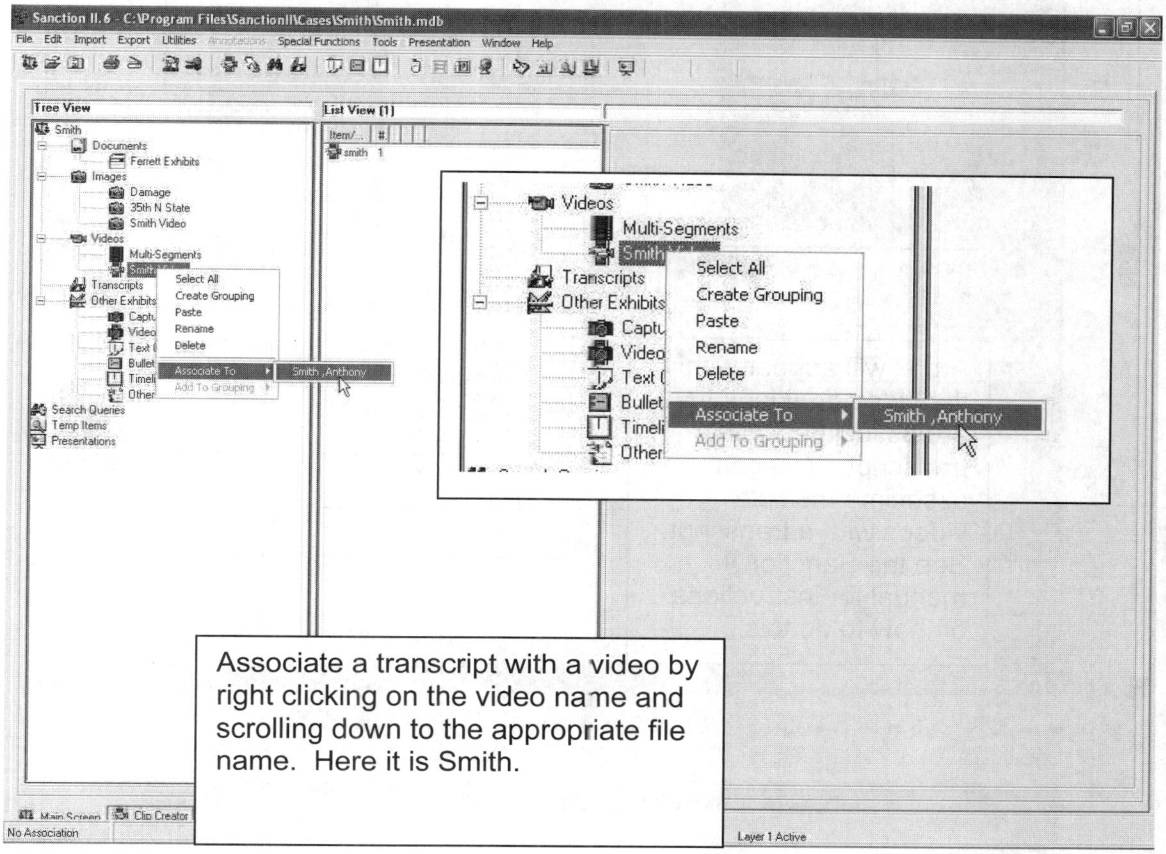

This box will appear:

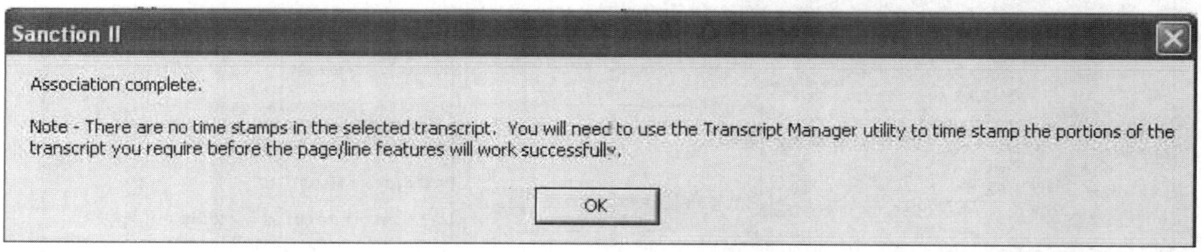

Reopen Transcript Manager. Click on File and then select Load Media. Your screen should look like this:

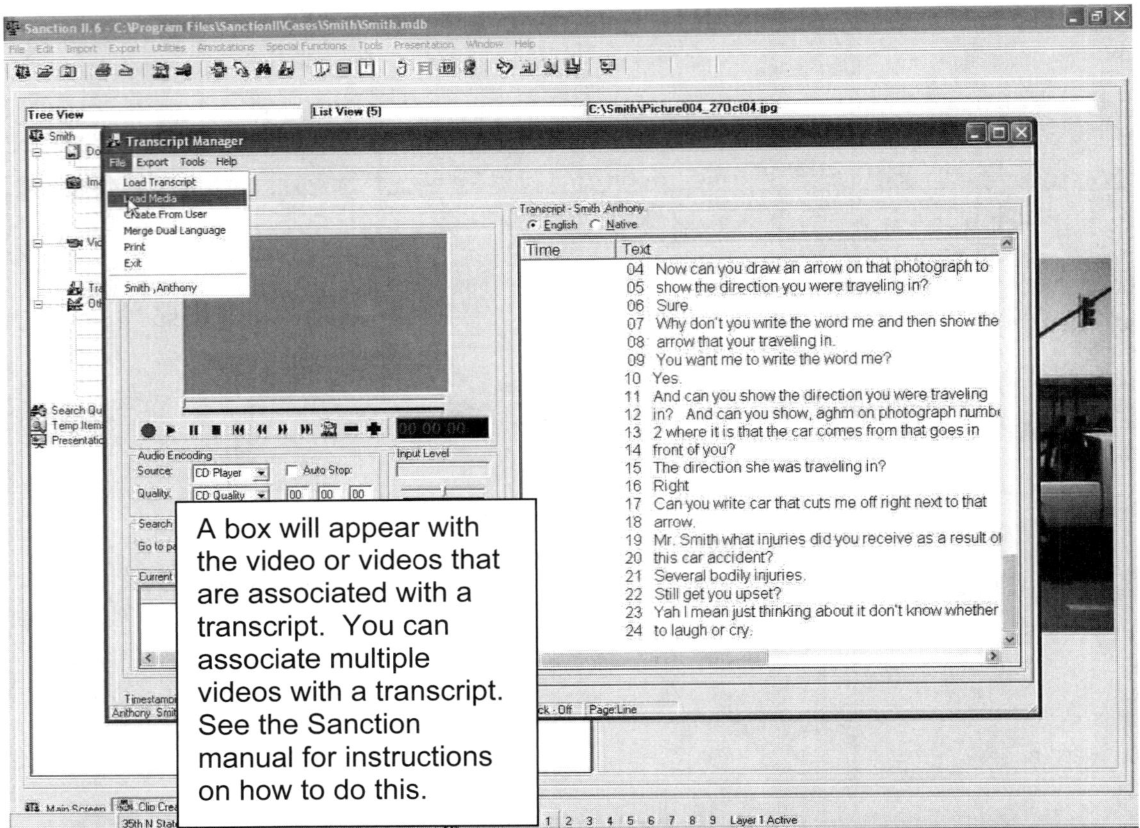
A box will appear with the video or videos that are associated with a transcript. You can associate multiple videos with a transcript. See the Sanction manual for instructions on how to do this.

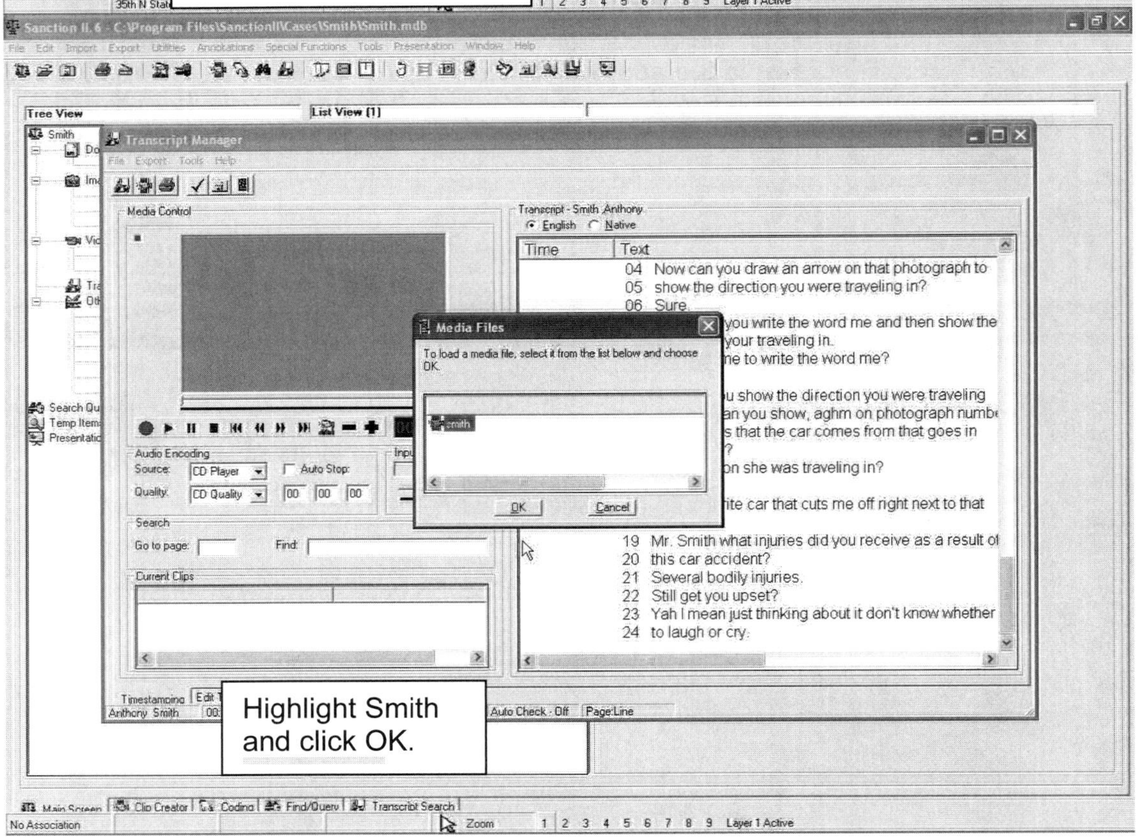
Highlight Smith and click OK.

This is what your desktop should look like once you have loaded the media file and the transcript:

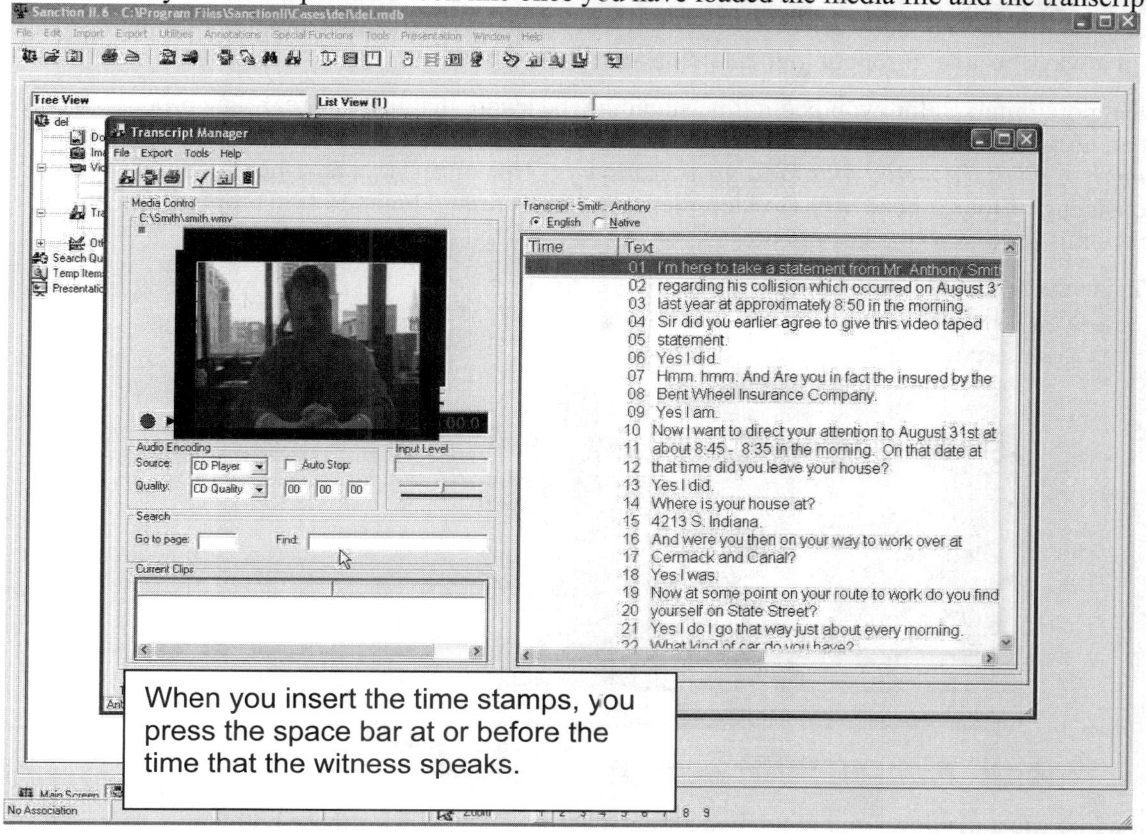

When you push the space bar, Sanction marks the place on the transcript that is supposed to scroll on the screen. In Sanction, the time stamp/text reference is handled by a database table. Each record in the table corresponds to a single line of transcript text. When a time stamp entry is made, the appropriate line in the database table is located, and the current position of the playing media file is entered into the record and automatically updated. Because audio and video files progress sequentially (that is, whenever a media file is played, it is moving forward in time), every time stamp entry in the database table is sequentially equal to or higher than the previous time stamp. While there can be instances where several sequential records (lines of text) could have the same time stamp (for instance, if no individual is speaking or if individuals are talking over each other), no time stamps should ever be "out of order" in a transcript database.If a transcript contains time stamps that are out of order, any attempt to display the synchronized text will result in the wrong line being displayed. Sanction looks for the first match for any time stamp, so if the stamp is out of sequence, the incorrect line will never be displayed. The accuracy of text synchronization is a direct reflection of the accuracy of the time stamp. If a transcript has been poorly synchronized, the text playback will be inaccurate, and clip creation will require the user to search forward and back to "adjust" the clip segment start and stop points. For this reason, it is imperative that anyone involved in the synchronization process understand the level of attention and effort required.

The playback in Sanction is extremely accurate across all supported operating systems, regardless of the computer used to synchronize. However, this accuracy is only as good as the accuracy of the time stamping. Sanction does not "slip" or lose synchronization points. If a range of text displays improperly, it is almost always the result of either poor synchronization or a transcript database that has not been verified properly. Understand how synchronization works, and you will always be able to supply high quality synchronized media.

One more thing: Before you begin time stamping, be aware that this is a real-time process; that is, at an absolute minimum, it requires *as much time to synchronize the media and text as the total length of all of the media files for a given transcript*. This means that an 8-hour deposition consisting of four 2-hour MPEG video files will take at least 8 hours to synchronize. Do not leave this process to the last minute.

This is the Media Control window:

It displays the current video or audio file and allows you to navigate the media file. You will see these buttons:

- ▶ Play the media file (alternatively, press Ctrl + P).
- ❚❚ Pause the media file (alternatively, press Ctrl + S).
- ■ Stop the media file.
- ⏮ Rewind to beginning.
- ◀◀ Rewind several seconds (alternatively, press Ctrl + Z).
- ▶▶ Fast forward several seconds (alternatively, press Ctrl + X).
- ⏭ Jump to end (alternatively, press Ctrl + T).
- Jump to transcript position.
- ✚ and ▬ can speed up playback, but this can compromise your time stamping.

This 00:00:00.0 is the Media Position window. This displays the current cumulative position of the media file. The cumulative position reflects the time elapsed for *all* files in a media group.

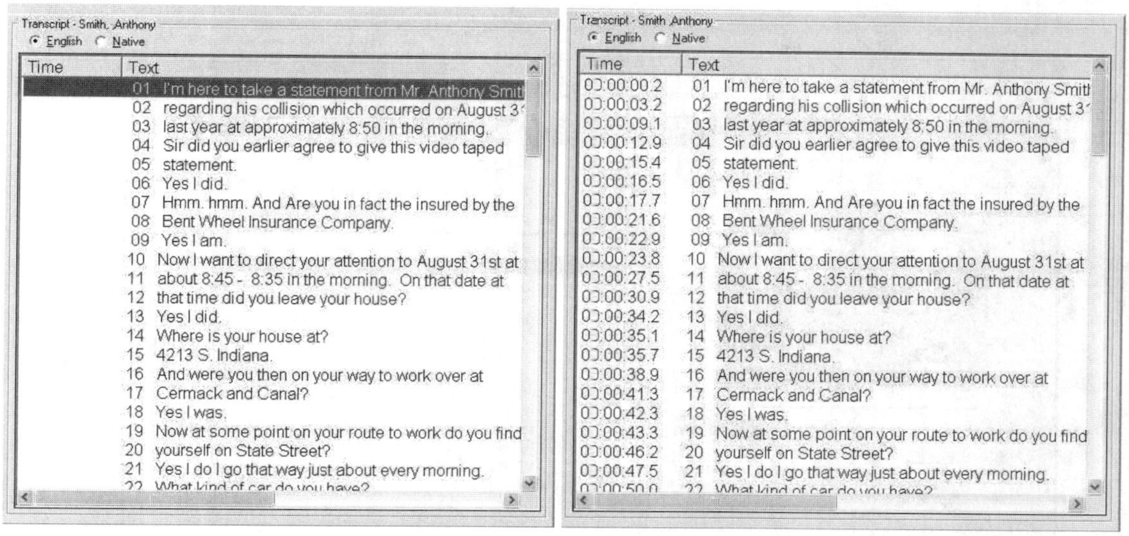

This is the Transcript window before and after time stamps have been added.

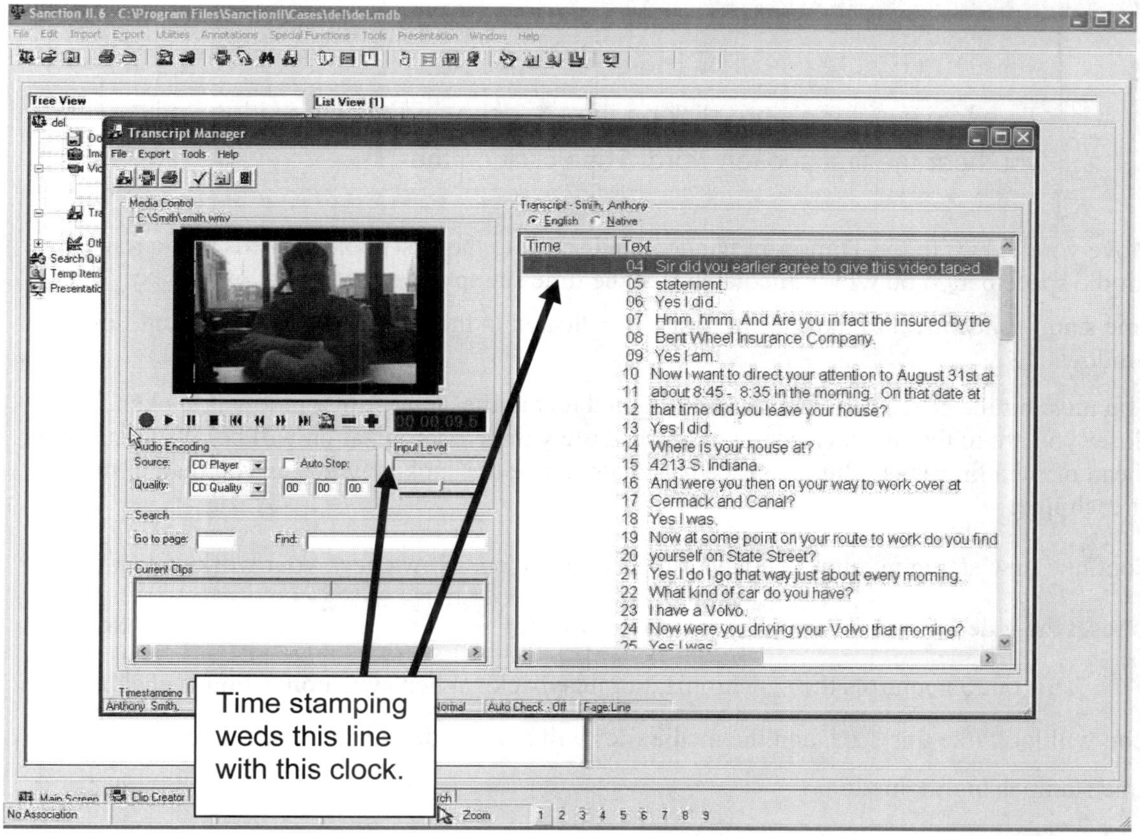

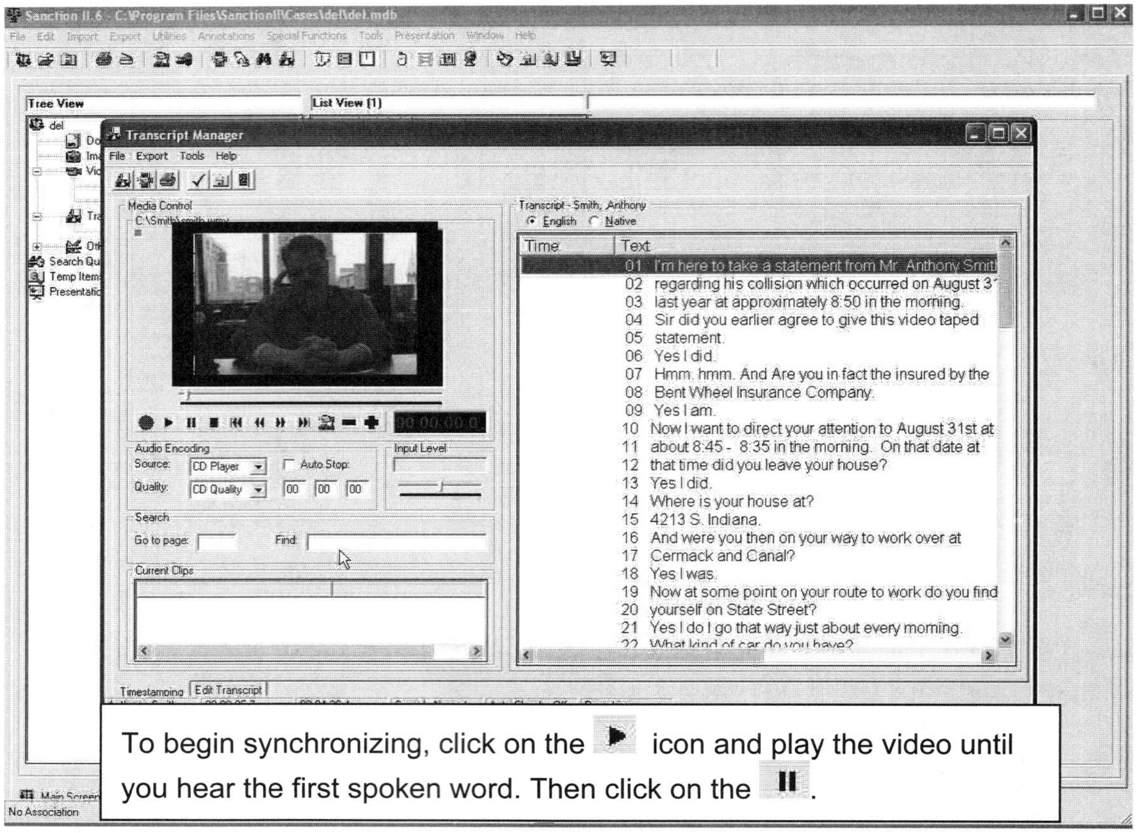

Move your cursor to the Transcript window and scroll to the first spoken words in the transcript. Hit the space bar. You will immediately see the time stamp added to the left of the text. This time stamp is identical to the current position indicated in the 00:00:00.0 Current Position window.

You must hit the space bar when the highlighted text in the Transcript window is spoken. The closer you are to the first words, the more accurate your synchronization will be. You must read ahead of each line as you hit the space bar to anticipate the spoken words as you read to the end of each line.

Continue time stamping until you have finished the video. Now check your work. Click on to reset the video file. Move your cursor to this toolbar and click on . This button controls the synchronization playback. When synchronization is enabled, the icon will look like this , and the media files will play while the text that corresponds to the time stamp is highlighted.

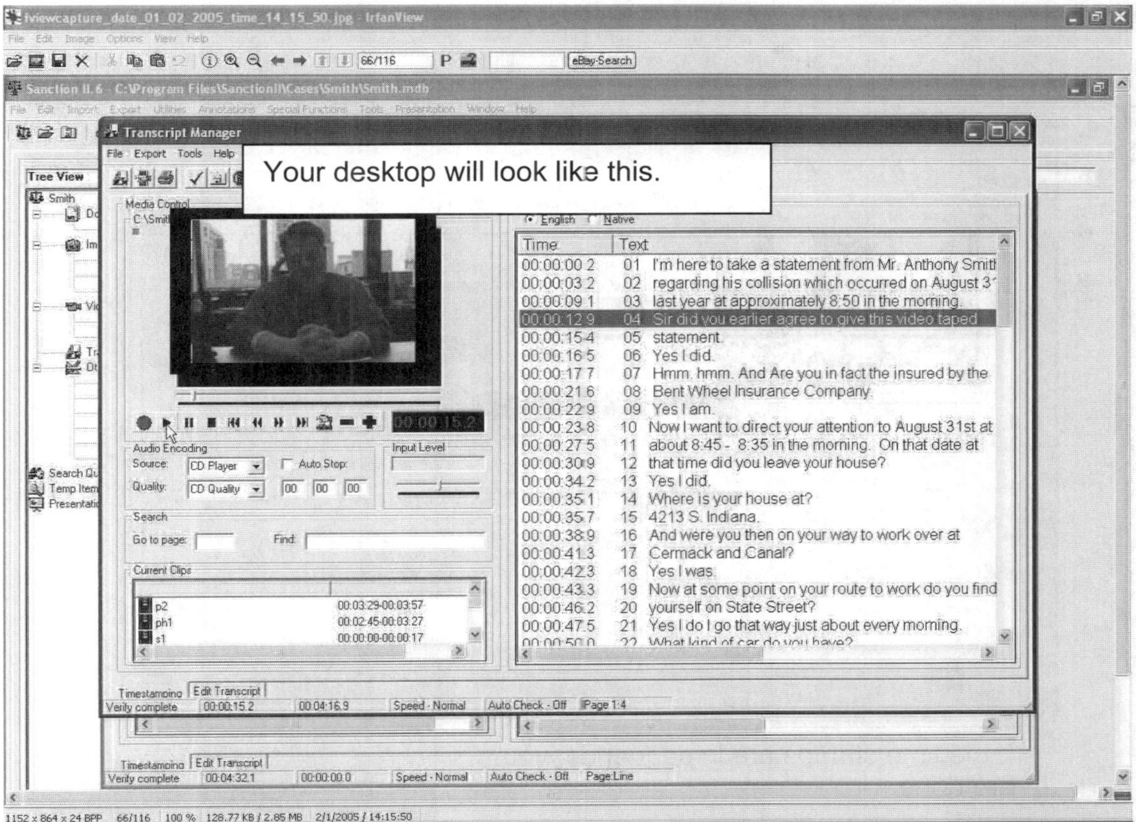
Your desktop will look like this.

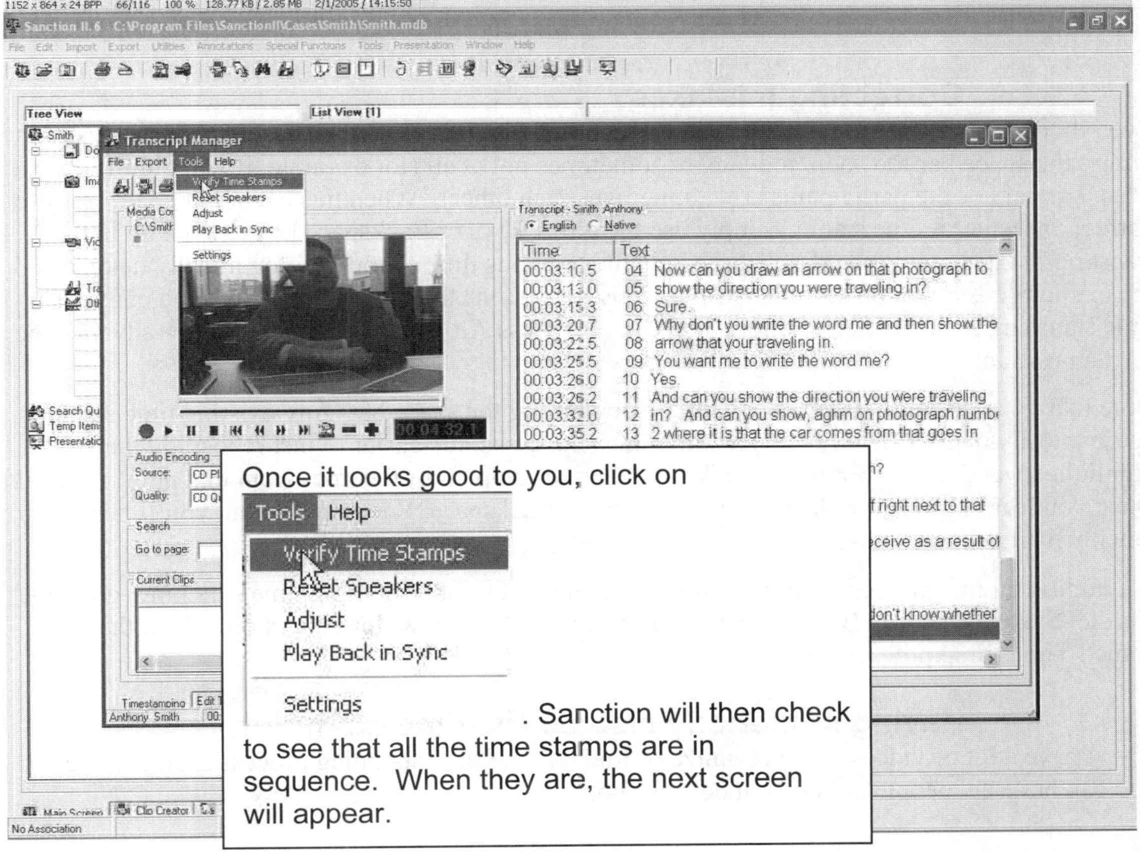
Once it looks good to you, click on
Tools Help
Verify Time Stamps
Reset Speakers
Adjust
Play Back in Sync
Settings
. Sanction will then check to see that all the time stamps are in sequence. When they are, the next screen will appear.

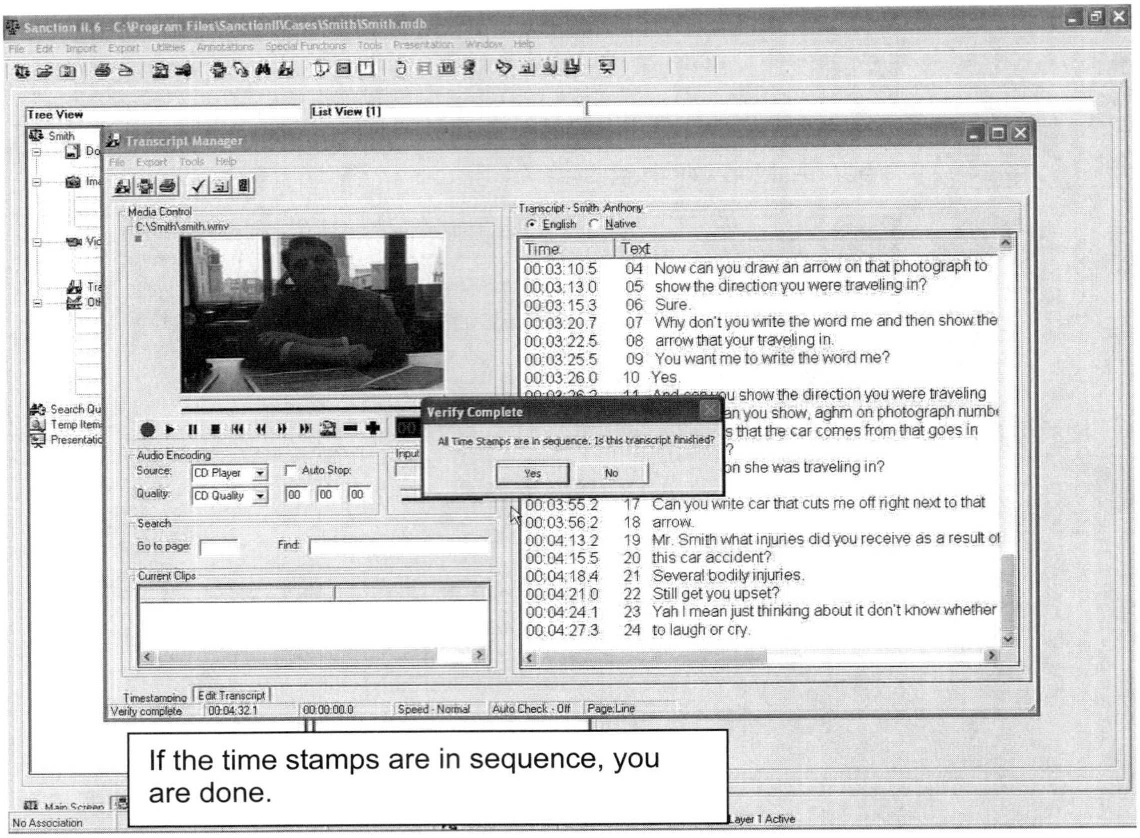

Correcting mistakes

Even though time stamping is a very simple (but tedious) process, you may often find yourself hitting the space bar too soon, too late, or sometimes not at all (for example, if you didn't hear what was said or the participants are talking over each other). When this occurs, it's very easy to correct or reenter a time stamp. Simply use the arrow keys or Backspace key to back up in the transcript. When you hit the Backspace key, the previous time stamp is automatically deleted and the media file is rewound several seconds. This repositions the highlight and lets you continue time stamping at the earlier position. You can also press Alt + < to rewind or Alt + > advance the media position.

Note that you can also "stamp over" any line by hitting the space bar. Any existing time stamp is automatically overwritten by the new time. In some cases, it's easier to just reposition the highlight several lines prior to a mistake and then restamp all of the lines from that point forward. Once you learn how to use the keys such as arrow, Backspace, Enter, and so on, you'll be able to quickly navigate any transcript.

For additional information regarding time stamping and troubleshooting time stamping, go to the Verdict Systems website (www.verdictsystems.com), go to Downloads, and download the file named Timestamp.pdf.

Having somebody else do the time stamping

If you have a lot of videos to synchronize or find that the time stamping process is frustrating, you can have the people at Sanction do it for you.

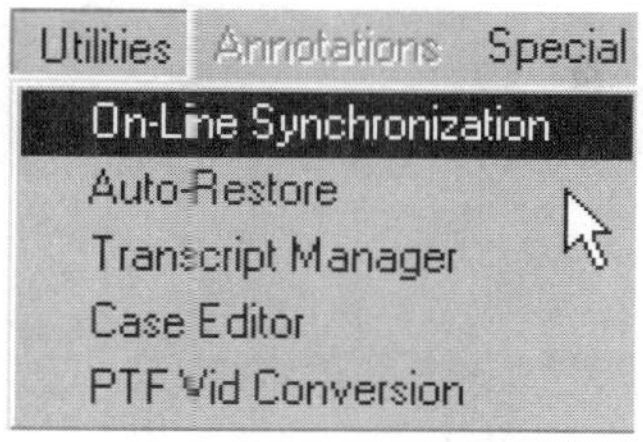

Open this window from the Utilities menu.

The following images were prepared by Dan Bowen from Verdict Systems to explain how to order online synchronization. They are reprinted with his permission.

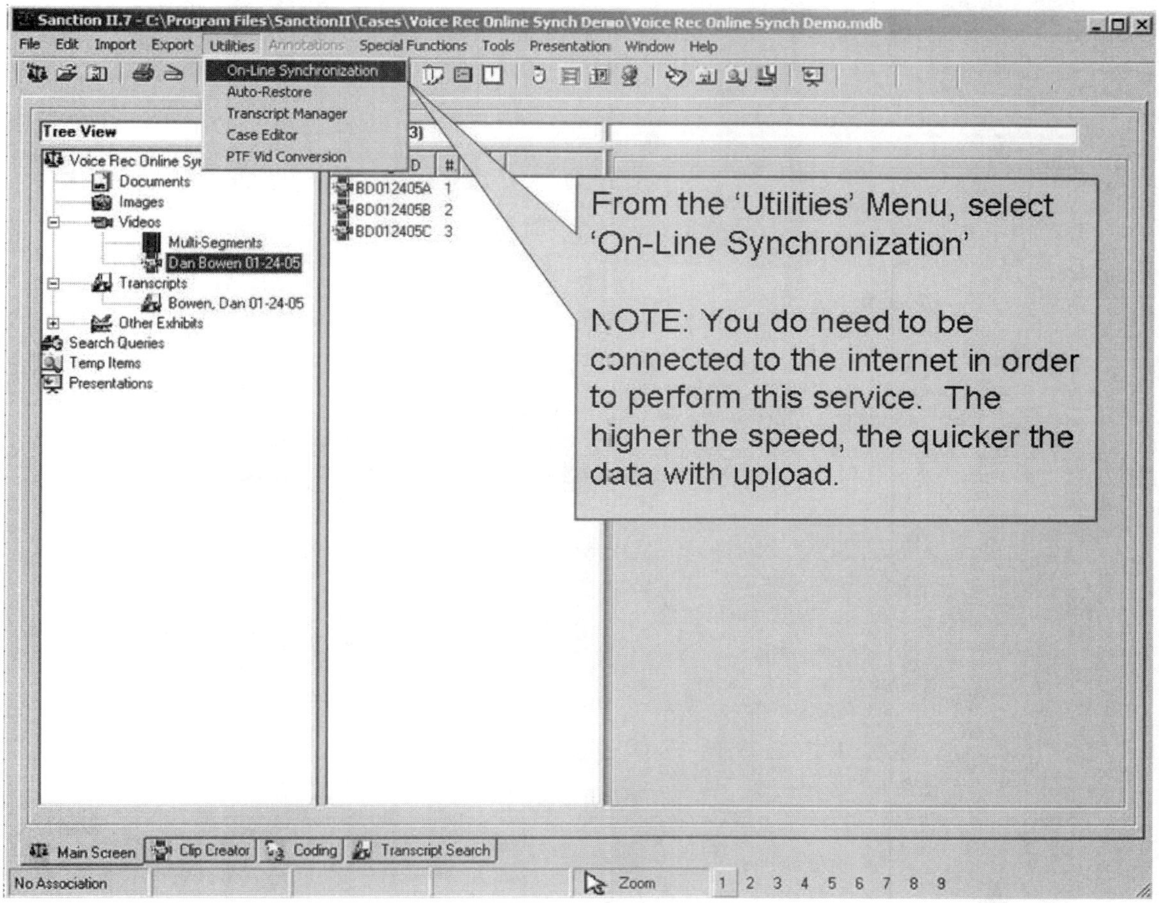

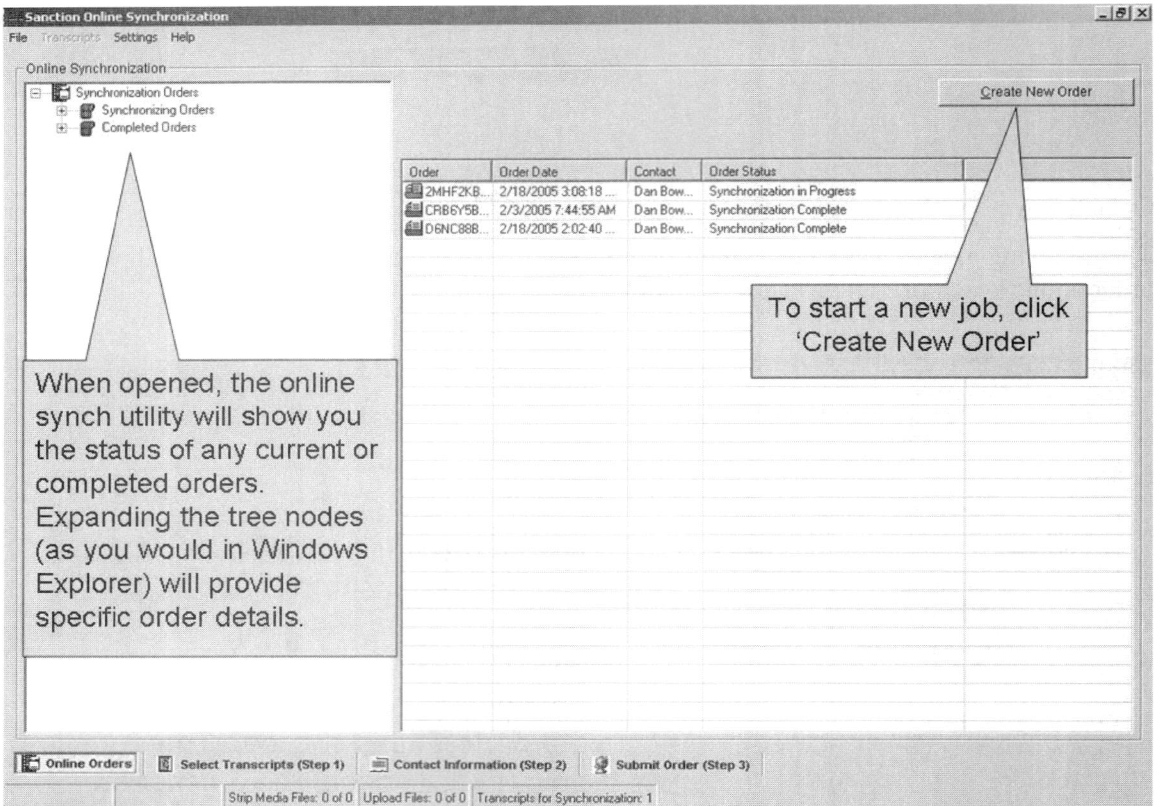
Sanction Online Synchronization
File Transcripts Settings Help
Online Synchronization
Synchronization Orders
Synchronizing Orders
Completed Orders
Create New Order
Order
Order Date
Contact
Order Status
2MHF2KB... 2/18/2005 3:08:18 ... Dan Bow... Synchronization in Progress
CRB6Y5B... 2/3/2005 7:44:55 AM Dan Bow... Synchronization Complete
D6NC88B... 2/18/2005 2:02:40 ... Dan Bow... Synchronization Complete
To start a new job, click 'Create New Order'
When opened, the online synch utility will show you the status of any current or completed orders. Expanding the tree nodes (as you would in Windows Explorer) will provide specific order details.
Online Orders
Select Transcripts (Step 1)
Contact Information (Step 2)
Submit Order (Step 3)
Strip Media Files: 0 of 0
Upload Files: 0 of 0
Transcripts for Synchronization: 1

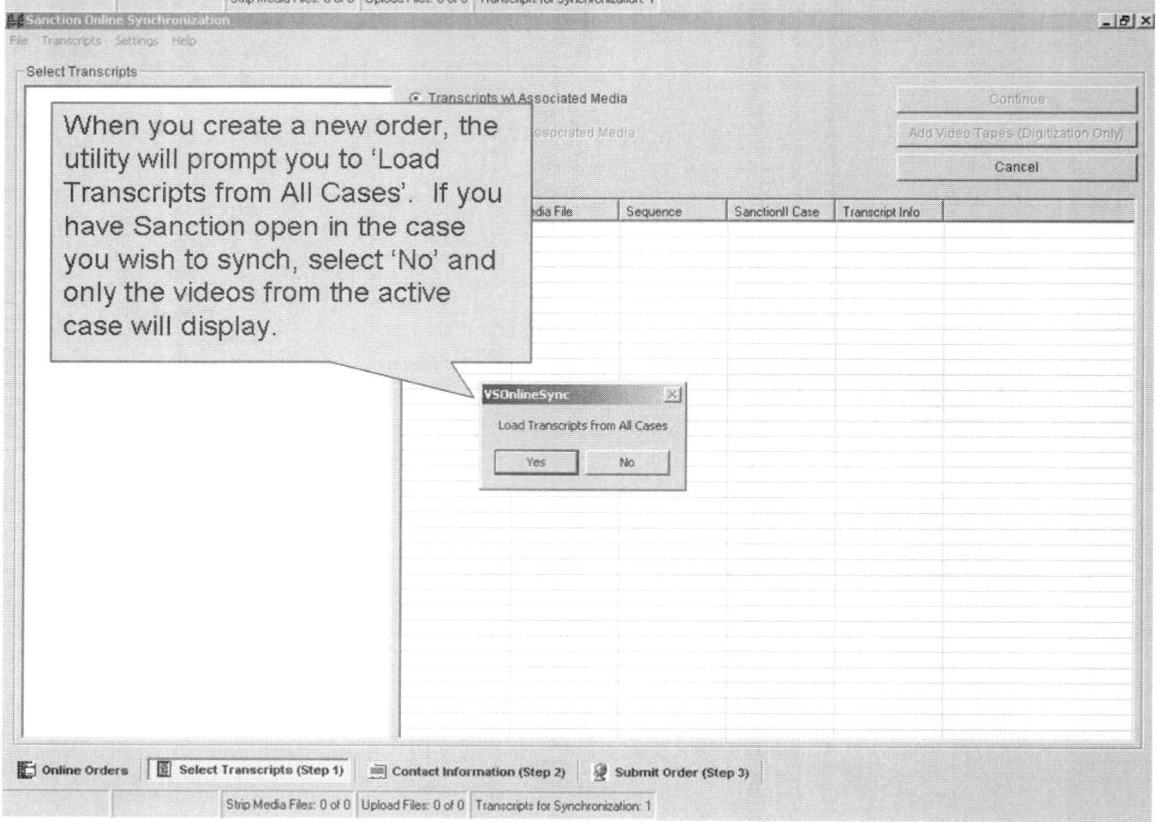
Sanction Online Synchronization
File Transcripts Settings Help
Select Transcripts
Transcripts w\ Associated Media
Continue
Add Video Tapes (Digitization Only)
Cancel
When you create a new order, the utility will prompt you to 'Load Transcripts from All Cases'. If you have Sanction open in the case you wish to synch, select 'No' and only the videos from the active case will display.
Sequence
SanctionII Case
Transcript Info
VSOnlineSync
Load Transcripts from All Cases
Yes
No
Online Orders
Select Transcripts (Step 1)
Contact Information (Step 2)
Submit Order (Step 3)
Strip Media Files: 0 of 0
Upload Files: 0 of 0
Transcripts for Synchronization: 1

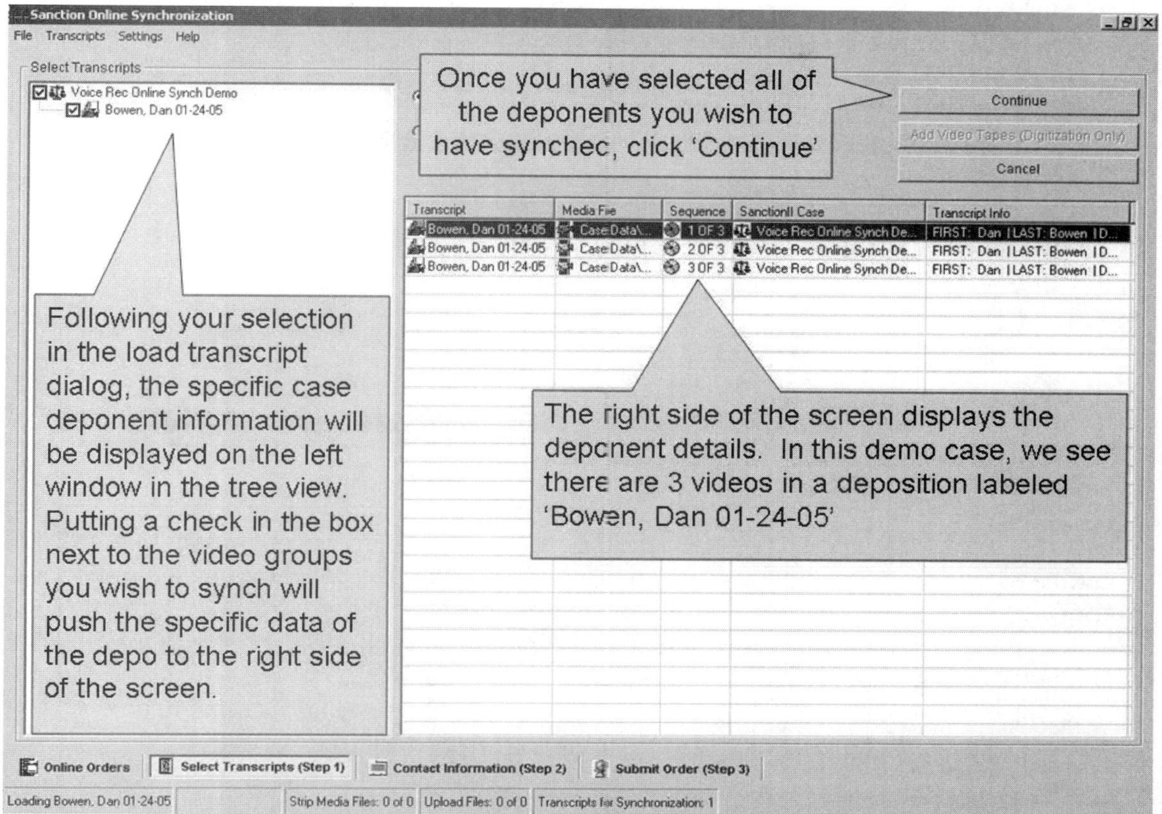
Sanction Online Synchronization
File Transcripts Settings Help
Select Transcripts
Voice Rec Online Synch Demo
Bowen, Dan 01-24-05
Once you have selected all of the deponents you wish to have synchec, click 'Continue'
Continue
Add Video Tapes (Digitization Only)
Cancel
Transcript
Media File
Sequence
SanctionII Case
Transcript Info
Following your selection in the load transcript dialog, the specific case deponent information will be displayed on the left window in the tree view. Putting a check in the box next to the video groups you wish to synch will push the specific data of the depo to the right side of the screen.
The right side of the screen displays the depcnent details. In this demo case, we see there are 3 videos in a deposition labeled 'Bowen, Dan 01-24-05'
Online Orders
Select Transcripts (Step 1)
Contact Information (Step 2)
Submit Order (Step 3)
Loading Bowen, Dan 01-24-05
Strip Media Files: 0 of 0
Upload Files: 0 of 0
Transcripts for Synchronization: 1

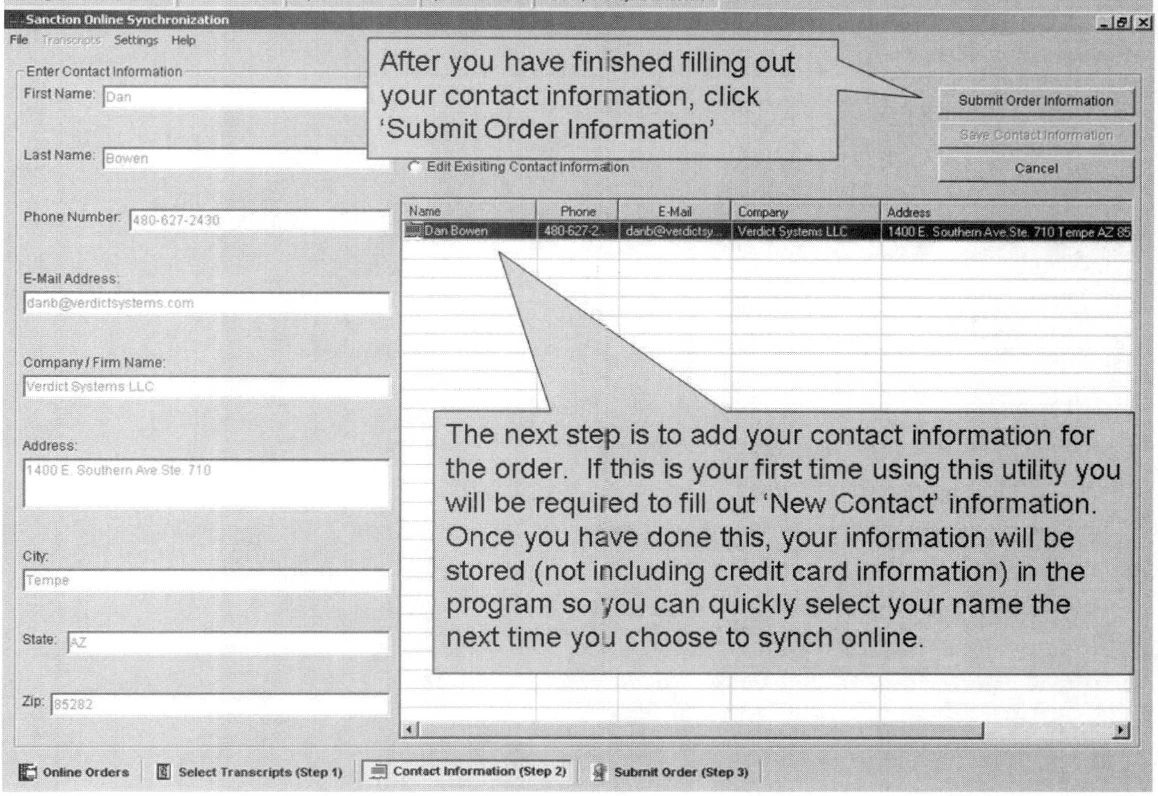
Sanction Online Synchronization
File Transcripts Settings Help
Enter Contact Information
First Name:
Last Name:
Phone Number:
E-Mail Address:
Company / Firm Name:
Address:
City:
State:
Zip:
After you have finished filling out your contact information, click 'Submit Order Information'
Submit Order Information
Save Contact Information
Edit Exisiting Contact Information
Cancel
Name
Phone
E-Mail
Company
Address
The next step is to add your contact information for the order. If this is your first time using this utility you will be required to fill out 'New Contact' information. Once you have done this, your information will be stored (not including credit card information) in the program so you can quickly select your name the next time you choose to synch online.
Online Orders
Select Transcripts (Step 1)
Contact Information (Step 2)
Submit Order (Step 3)

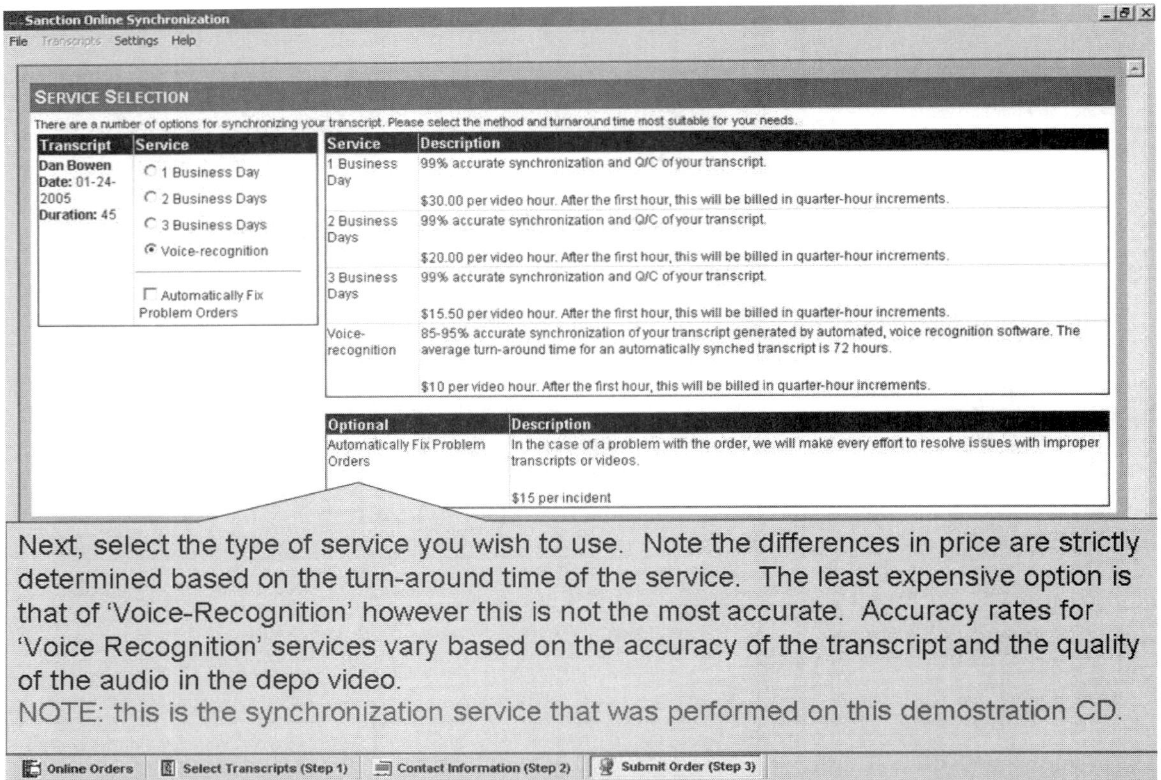
Sanction Online Synchronization
File Transcripts Settings Help
SERVICE SELECTION
There are a number of options for synchronizing your transcript. Please select the method and turnaround time most suitable for your needs.
Transcript
Service
Dan Bowen
Date: 01-24-2005
Duration: 45
1 Business Day
2 Business Days
3 Business Days
Voice-recognition
Automatically Fix Problem Orders
Service
Description
1 Business Day
99% accurate synchronization and Q/C of your transcript.
$30.00 per video hour. After the first hour, this will be billed in quarter-hour increments.
2 Business Days
99% accurate synchronization and Q/C of your transcript.
$20.00 per video hour. After the first hour, this will be billed in quarter-hour increments.
3 Business Days
99% accurate synchronization and Q/C of your transcript.
$15.50 per video hour. After the first hour, this will be billed in quarter-hour increments.
Voice-recognition
85-95% accurate synchronization of your transcript generated by automated, voice recognition software. The average turn-around time for an automatically synched transcript is 72 hours.
$10 per video hour. After the first hour, this will be billed in quarter-hour increments.
Optional
Description
Automatically Fix Problem Orders
In the case of a problem with the order, we will make every effort to resolve issues with improper transcripts or videos.
$15 per incident
Next, select the type of service you wish to use. Note the differences in price are strictly determined based on the turn-around time of the service. The least expensive option is that of 'Voice-Recognition' however this is not the most accurate. Accuracy rates for 'Voice Recognition' services vary based on the accuracy of the transcript and the quality of the audio in the depo video.
NOTE: this is the synchronization service that was performed on this demostration CD.
Online Orders
Select Transcripts (Step 1)
Contact Information (Step 2)
Submit Order (Step 3)

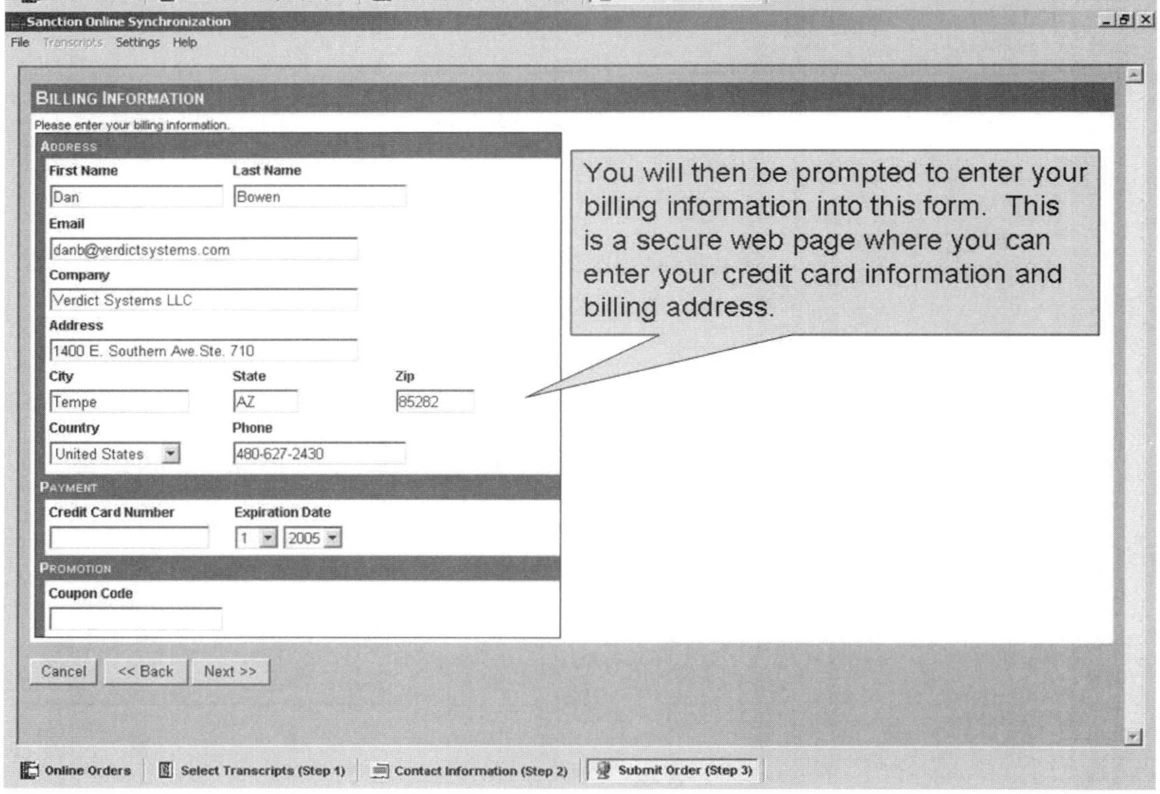
Sanction Online Synchronization
File Transcripts Settings Help
BILLING INFORMATION
Please enter your billing information.
ADDRESS
First Name
Dan
Last Name
Bowen
Email
danb@verdictsystems.com
Company
Verdict Systems LLC
Address
1400 E. Southern Ave.Ste. 710
City
Tempe
State
AZ
Zip
85282
Country
United States
Phone
480-627-2430
PAYMENT
Credit Card Number
Expiration Date
1
2005
PROMOTION
Coupon Code
Cancel
<< Back
Next >>
You will then be prompted to enter your billing information into this form. This is a secure web page where you can enter your credit card information and billing address.
Online Orders
Select Transcripts (Step 1)
Contact Information (Step 2)
Submit Order (Step 3)

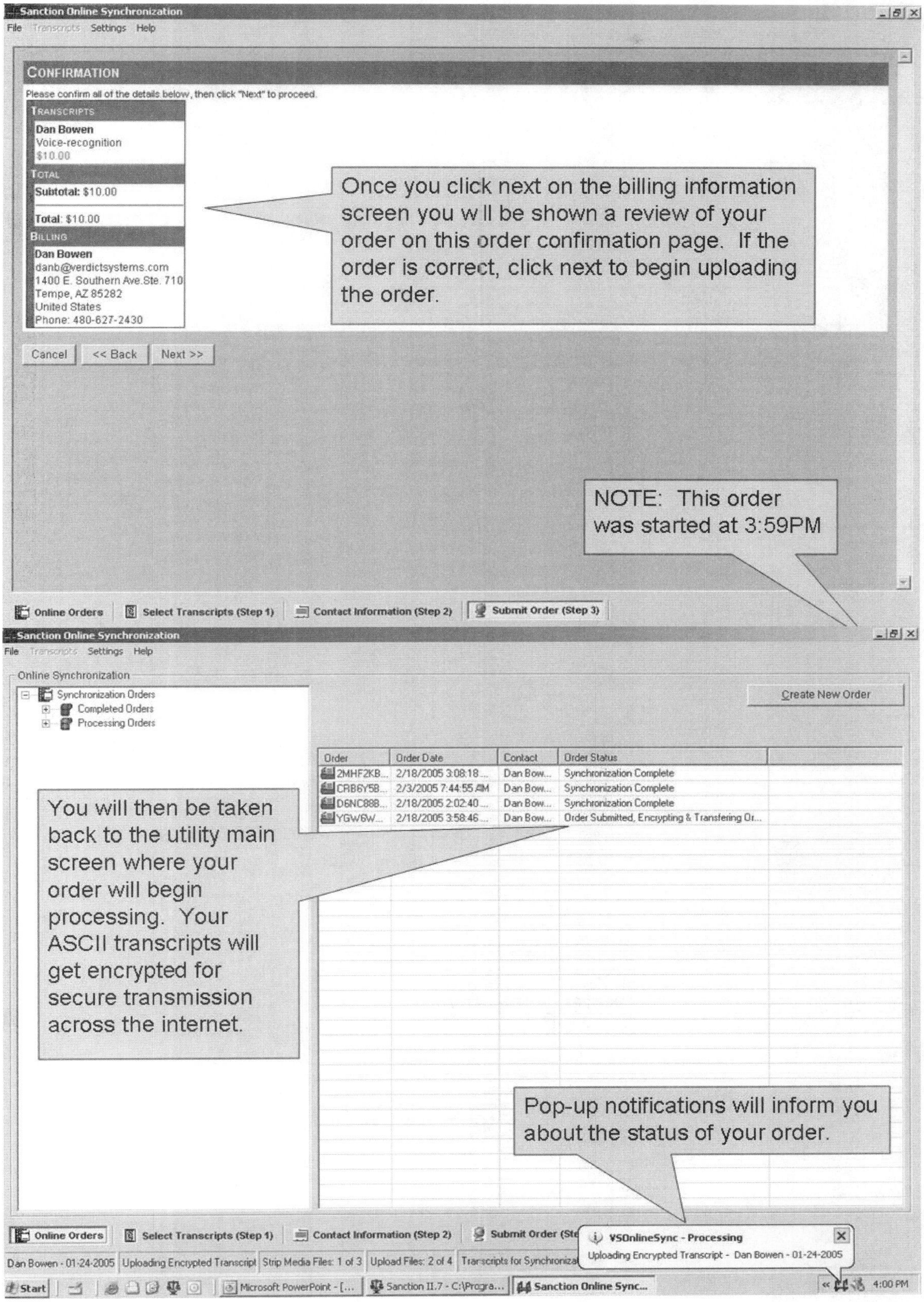
Sanction Online Synchronization
File Transcripts Settings Help
CONFIRMATION
Please confirm all of the details below, then click "Next" to proceed.
TRANSCRIPTS
Dan Bowen
Voice-recognition
$10.00
TOTAL
Subtotal: $10.00
Total: $10.00
BILLING
Dan Bowen
danb@verdictsystems.com
1400 E. Southern Ave.Ste. 710
Tempe, AZ 85282
United States
Phone: 480-627-2430
Once you click next on the billing information screen you w ll be shown a review of your order on this order confirmation page. If the order is correct, click next to begin uploading the order.
Cancel
<< Back
Next >>
NOTE: This order was started at 3:59PM
Online Orders
Select Transcripts (Step 1)
Contact Information (Step 2)
Submit Order (Step 3)
Sanction Online Synchronization
File Transcripts Settings Help
Online Synchronization
Synchronization Orders
Completed Orders
Processing Orders
Create New Order
Order
Order Date
Contact
Order Status
2MHF2KB...
2/18/2005 3:08:18...
Dan Bow...
Synchronization Complete
CRB6Y5B...
2/3/2005 7:44:55 AM
Dan Bow...
Synchronization Complete
D6NC88B...
2/18/2005 2:02:40...
Dan Bow...
Synchronization Complete
YGW6W...
2/18/2005 3:58:46...
Dan Bow...
Order Submitted, Encrypting & Transfering Or...
You will then be taken back to the utility main screen where your order will begin processing. Your ASCII transcripts will get encrypted for secure transmission across the internet.
Pop-up notifications will inform you about the status of your order.
VSOnlineSync - Processing
Uploading Encrypted Transcript - Dan Bowen - 01-24-2005
Dan Bowen - 01-24-2005
Uploading Encrypted Transcript
Strip Media Files: 1 of 3
Upload Files: 2 of 4
Start
Microsoft PowerPoint - [...
Sanction II.7 - C:\Progra...
Sanction Online Sync...
4:00 PM

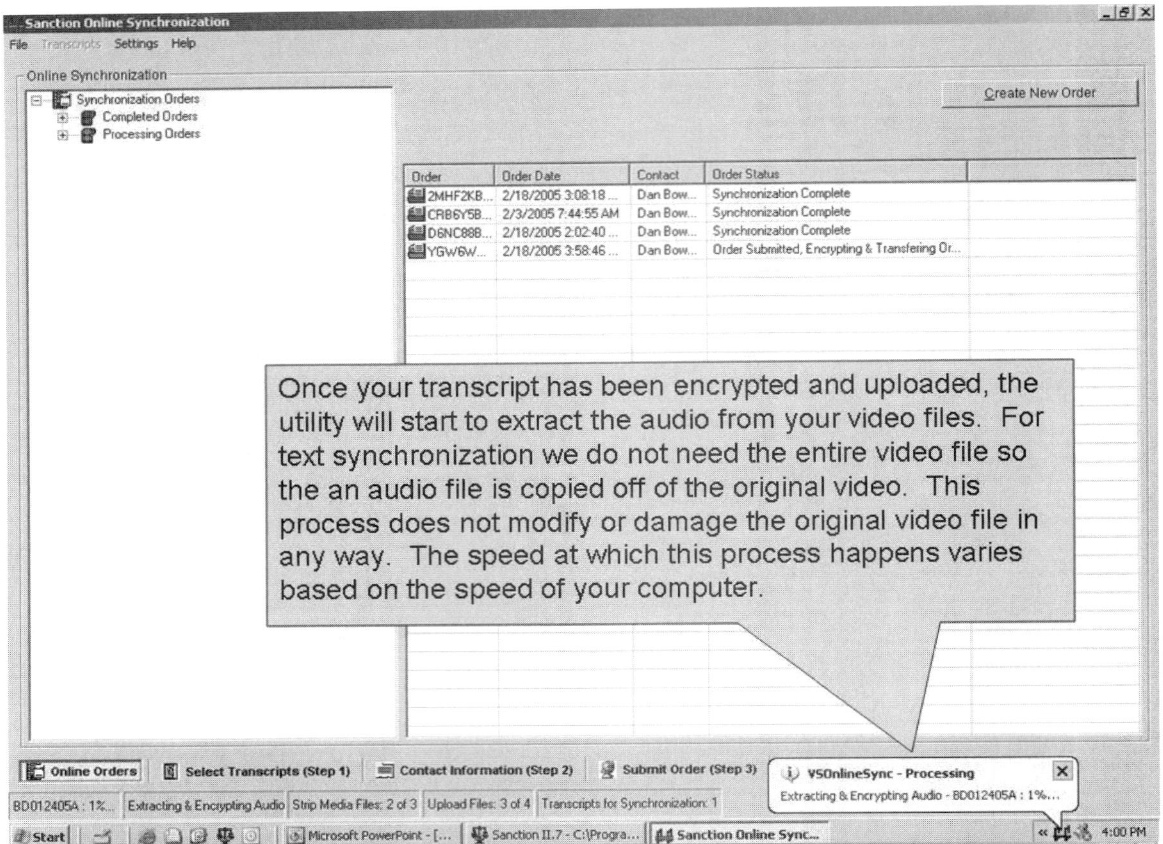
Sanction Online Synchronization
File Transcripts Settings Help
Online Synchronization
Synchronization Orders
Completed Orders
Processing Orders
Create New Order
Order Order Date Contact Order Status
2MHF2KB... 2/18/2005 3:08:18 ... Dan Bow... Synchronization Complete
CRB6Y5B... 2/3/2005 7:44:55 AM Dan Bow... Synchronization Complete
D6NC88B... 2/18/2005 2:02:40 ... Dan Bow... Synchronization Complete
YGW6W... 2/18/2005 3:58:46 ... Dan Bow... Order Submitted, Encrypting & Transfering Or...
Once your transcript has been encrypted and uploaded, the utility will start to extract the audio from your video files. For text synchronization we do not need the entire video file so the an audio file is copied off of the original video. This process does not modify or damage the original video file in any way. The speed at which this process happens varies based on the speed of your computer.
Online Orders
Select Transcripts (Step 1)
Contact Information (Step 2)
Submit Order (Step 3)
VSOnlineSync - Processing
Extracting & Encrypting Audio - BD012405A : 1%...
BD012405A : 1%...
Extracting & Encrypting Audio
Strip Media Files: 2 of 3
Upload Files: 3 of 4
Transcripts for Synchronization: 1
Start
Microsoft PowerPoint - [...
Sanction II.7 - C:\Progra...
Sanction Online Sync...
4:00 PM

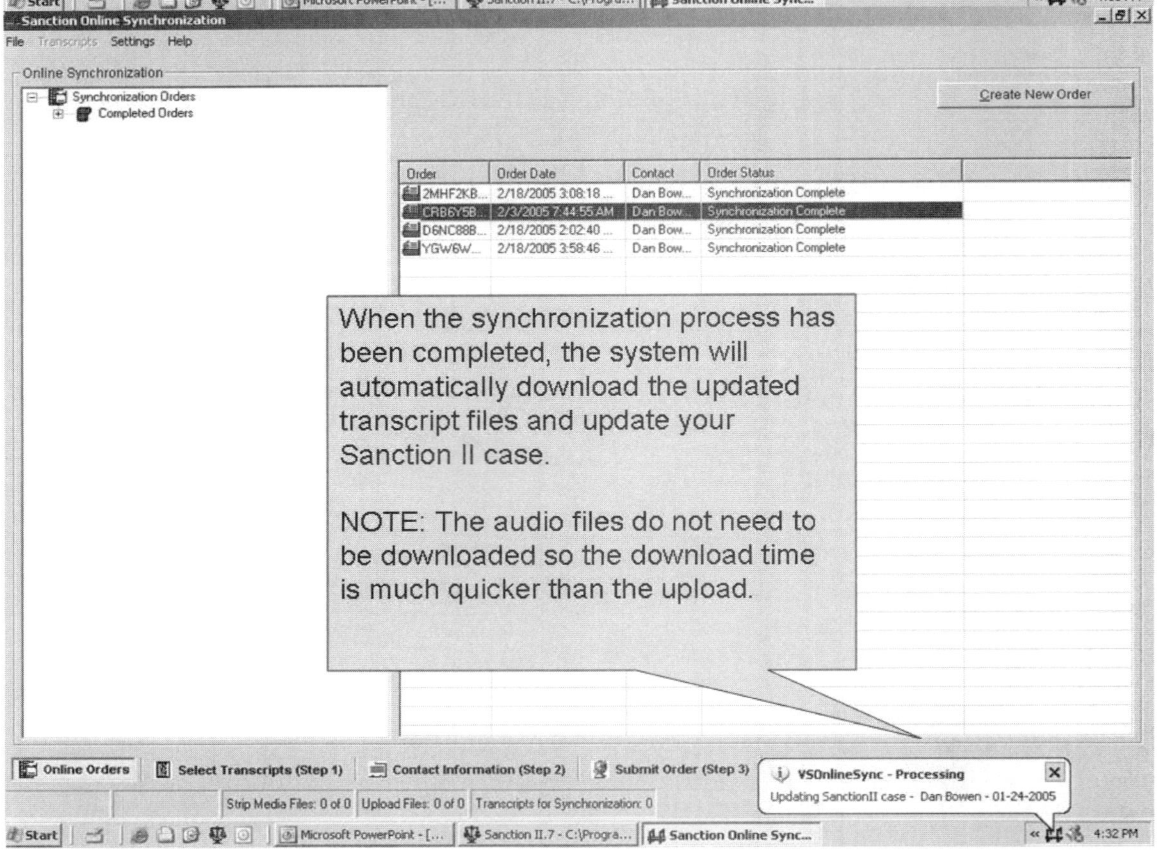
Sanction Online Synchronization
File Transcripts Settings Help
Online Synchronization
Synchronization Orders
Completed Orders
Create New Order
Order Order Date Contact Order Status
2MHF2KB... 2/18/2005 3:08:18 ... Dan Bow... Synchronization Complete
CRB6Y5B... 2/3/2005 7:44:55 AM Dan Bow... Synchronization Complete
D6NC88B... 2/18/2005 2:02:40 ... Dan Bow... Synchronization Complete
YGW6W... 2/18/2005 3:58:46 ... Dan Bow... Synchronization Complete
When the synchronization process has been completed, the system will automatically download the updated transcript files and update your Sanction II case.
NOTE: The audio files do not need to be downloaded so the download time is much quicker than the upload.
Online Orders
Select Transcripts (Step 1)
Contact Information (Step 2)
Submit Order (Step 3)
VSOnlineSync - Processing
Updating SanctionII case - Dan Bowen - 01-24-2005
Strip Media Files: 0 of 0
Upload Files: 0 of 0
Transcripts for Synchronization: 0
Start
Microsoft PowerPoint - [...
Sanction II.7 - C:\Progra...
Sanction Online Sync...
4:32 PM

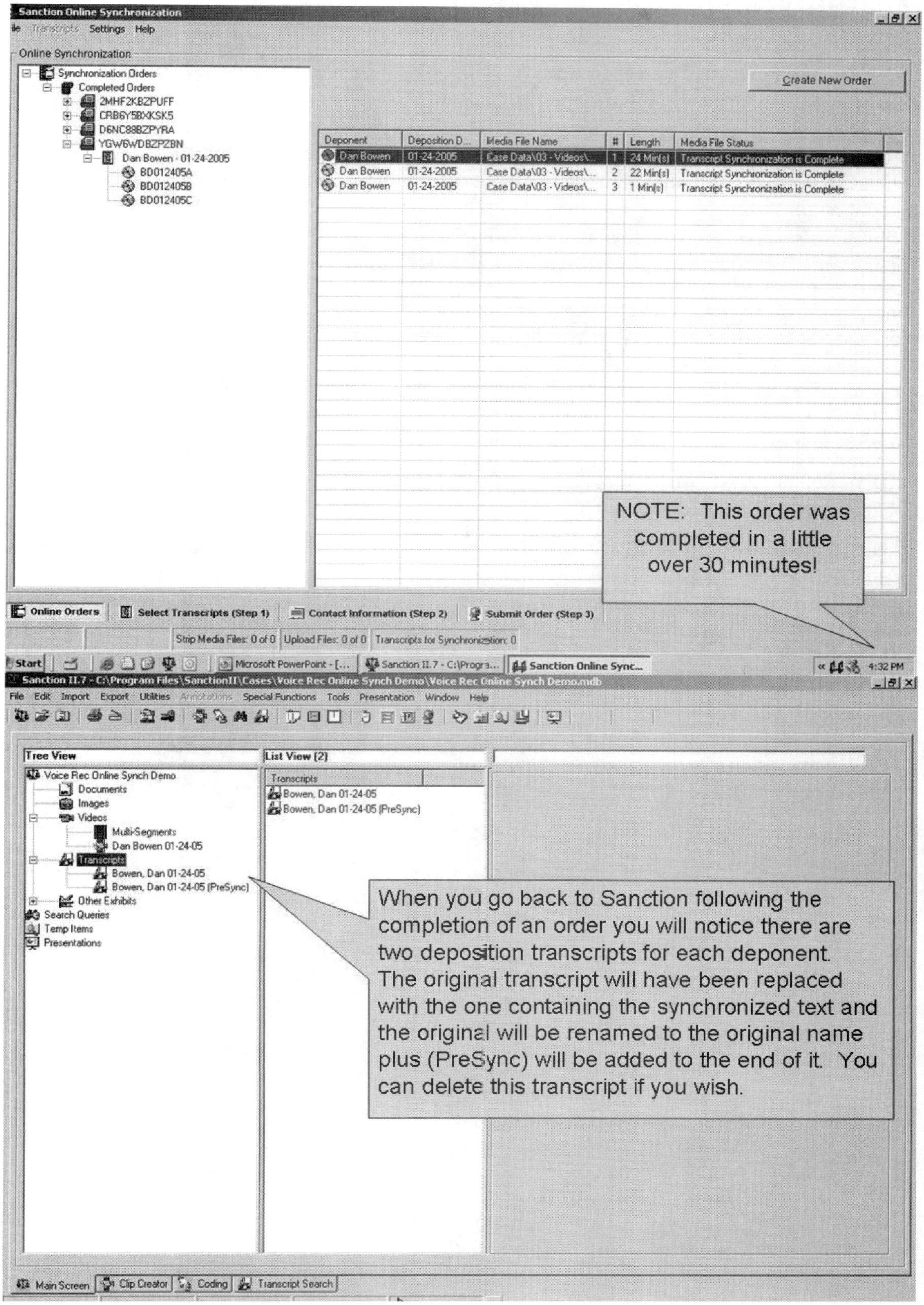
Sanction Online Synchronization
Online Synchronization
Synchronization Orders
Completed Orders
Create New Order
Deponent
Deposition D...
Media File Name
Length
Media File Status
Dan Bowen 01-24-2005 Case Data\03 - Videos\... 1 24 Min(s) Transcript Synchronization is Complete
Dan Bowen 01-24-2005 Case Data\03 - Videos\... 2 22 Min(s) Transcript Synchronization is Complete
Dan Bowen 01-24-2005 Case Data\03 - Videos\... 3 1 Min(s) Transcript Synchronization is Complete
NOTE: This order was completed in a little over 30 minutes!
Online Orders
Select Transcripts (Step 1)
Contact Information (Step 2)
Submit Order (Step 3)
Tree View
List View (2)
Voice Rec Online Synch Demo
Bowen, Dan 01-24-05
Bowen, Dan 01-24-05 (PreSync)
When you go back to Sanction following the completion of an order you will notice there are two deposition transcripts for each deponent. The original transcript will have been replaced with the one containing the synchronized text and the original will be renamed to the original name plus (PreSync) will be added to the end of it. You can delete this transcript if you wish.
Main Screen
Clip Creator
Coding
Transcript Search

Making Video Clips

The video clip feature is one of the most powerful tools in a trial lawyer's arsenal. It can be used with or without synchronized transcripts. This feature helps you to present evidence in your case-in-chief and during cross-examination of opposition witnesses. You can use the video clip to create clips that literally play out of the original video without altering the video. This can help you streamline evidence presentation on direct examination because you can have a witness lay a foundation for the entire video and then testify that the clips in no way altered the original video. Assume you have a case with hours of surveillance video. Assume there are only 20 minutes of video that are relevant to your case. If your videos have been digitized, you can use Clip Creator to make the "best of" clips that your witness can authenticate on the stand. Now think about the concession-based approach to cross-examination that is discussed in Chapter 5. You can create a cross-examination that will let you literally control every word out of a witness's mouth. You can use Sanction to convert the clips that you want to launch in PowerPoint or that were played at the trial from their MPEG format into Windows Media Video files (.wmv). You can then insert the .wmv files into your presentation or burn them onto a CD and impound them with the clerk of the court to preserve your record for appeal since the appellate court does not have Sanction.

Open the Clip Creator tab by clicking this: 

.

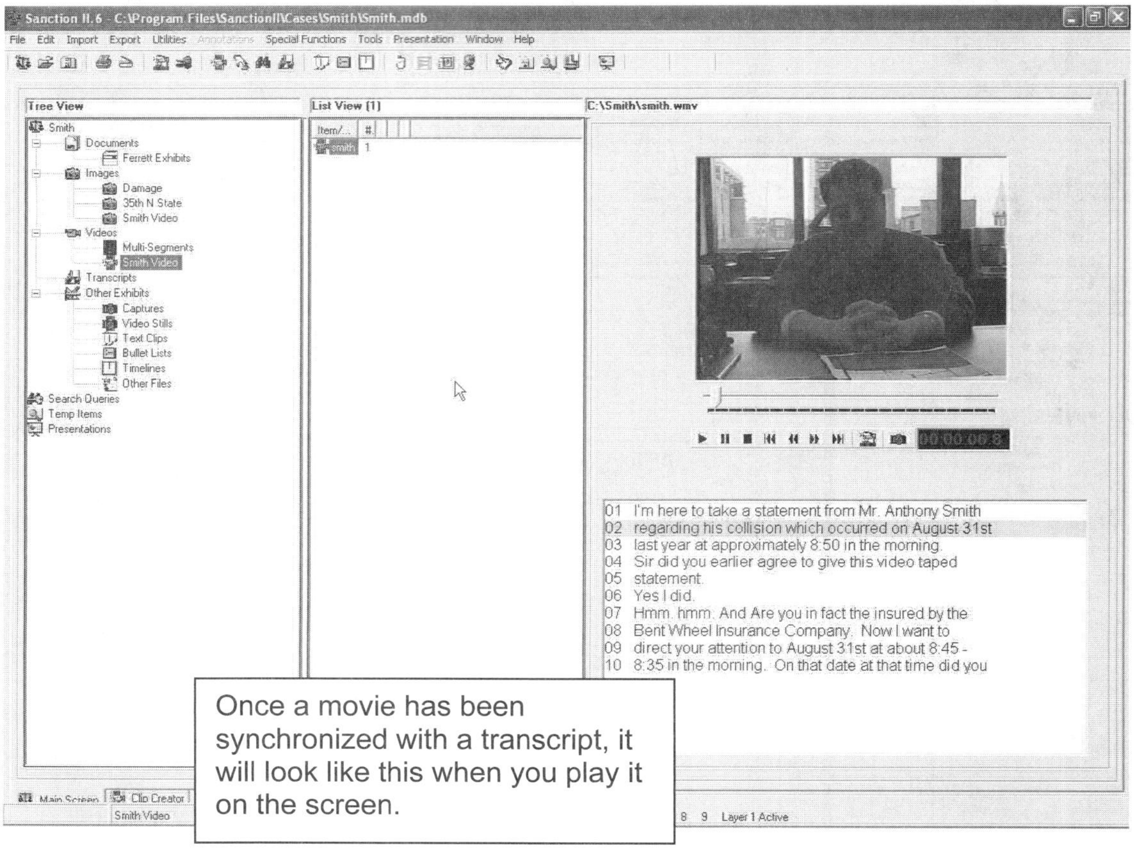

Once a movie has been synchronized with a transcript, it will look like this when you play it on the screen.

This is the desktop under the Clip Creator tab:

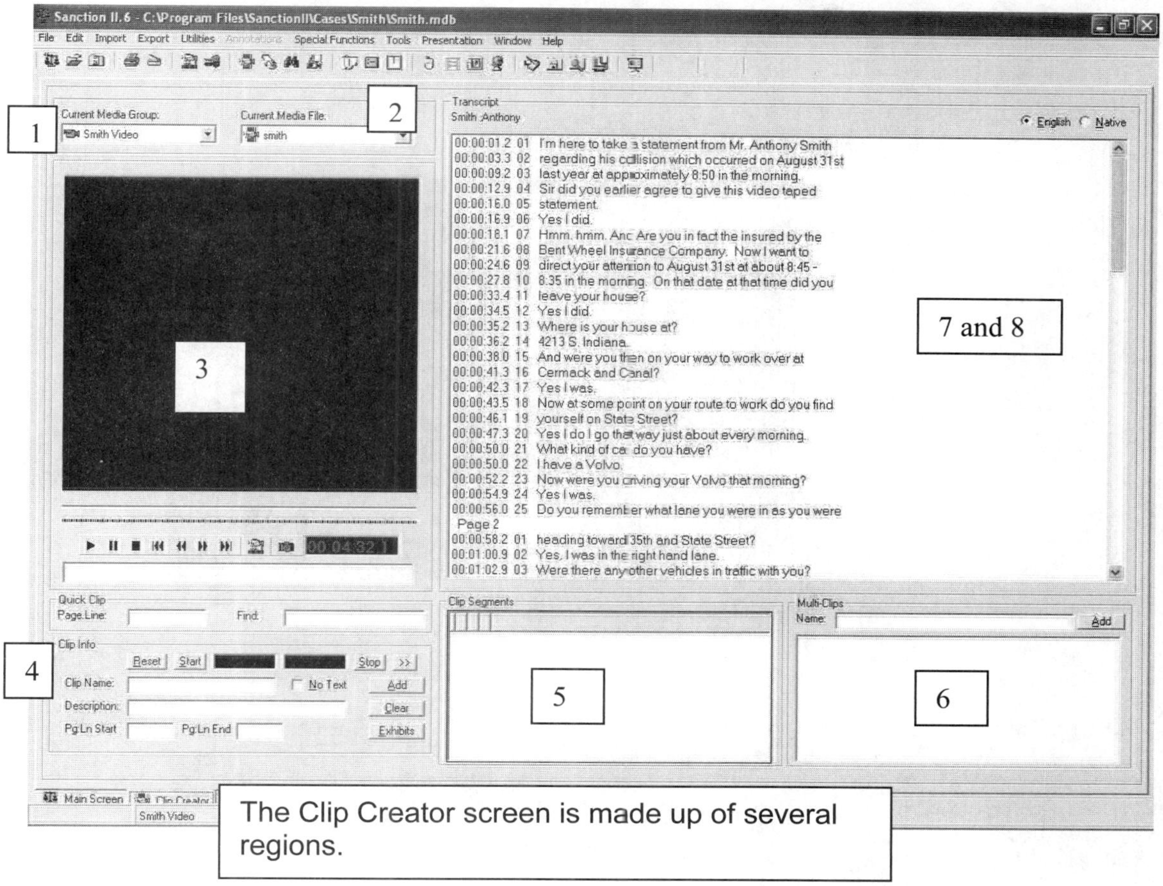

1. Current Media Group: Drop-down list of available media groups.
2. Current Media File: Drop-down list of the root media files for the currently selected group.
3. Media playback screen: Controls for play, pause, rewind, etc.
4. Clip Info editing window: Where you name the clip, describe it, and otherwise edit your clip.
5. Clip Segments window: Lists the clips associated with the loaded media file.
6. Multi-clips tree window: List of multi-clips. This tool helps you link specific clips together in the event that you want to jump around within the media file.
7. Transcript window: Shows the transcript that is associated with the media file and the time stamps.
8. Synchronized Exhibits window: This window appears in the same place as the Transcript window. It contains the list of image groups and files in the current case. Click the Exhibits button to access the window. The next screen shows what it looks like.

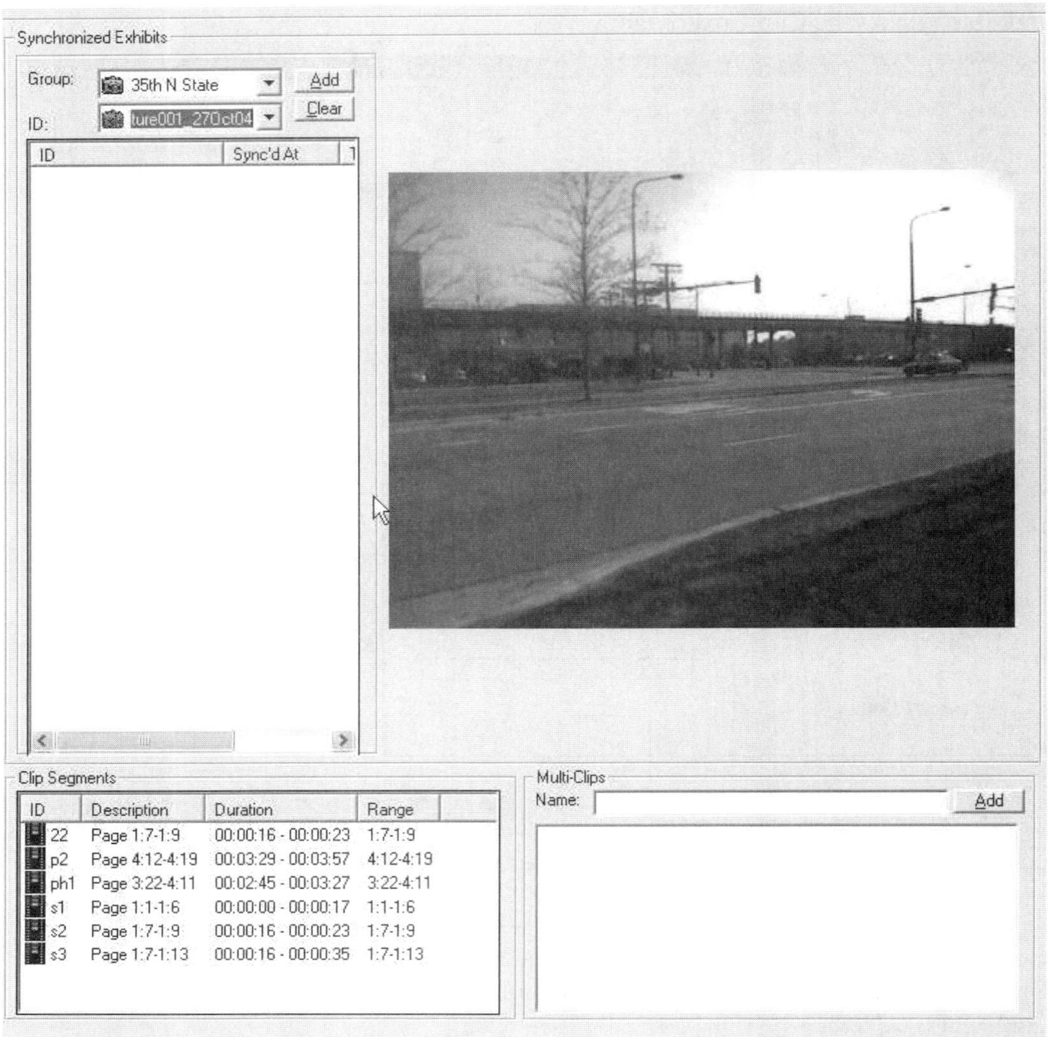

When the current media group has an associated transcript file with valid time stamp information, the synchronized file can be used to create clip segments from any portion of the transcript.

To do this, select a media group for clip creation.

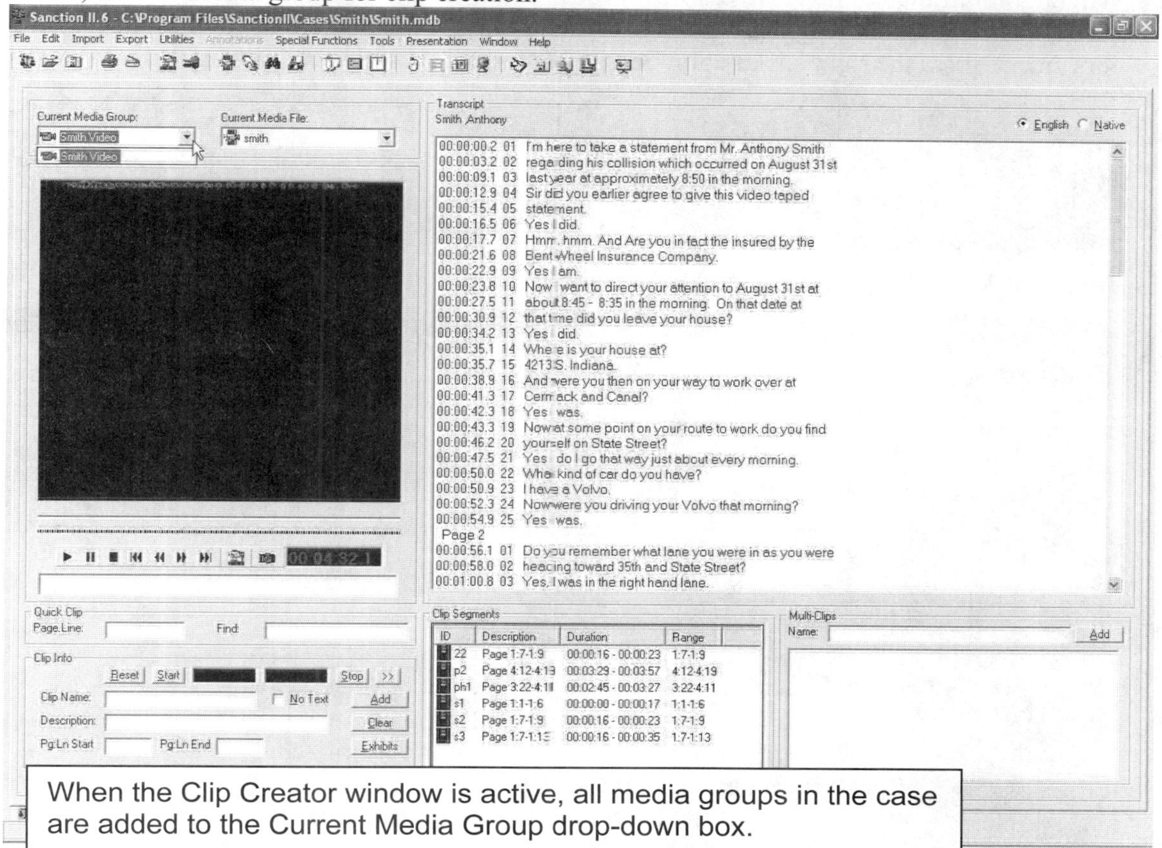

When a media group is selected, each of the root media files is added to the Current Media File drop-down box.

In our case, it is Smith Video 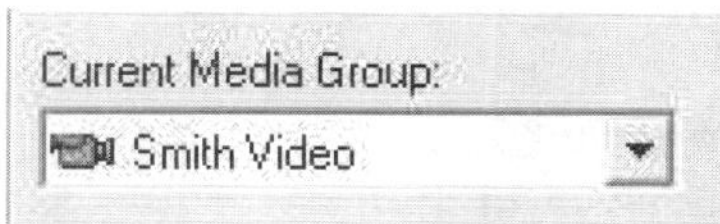

. Select a media file.

The video will load in the media playback screen. The transcript will load in the Transcript window.

Creating Clips from the Media Clip Creator

The easiest way to make a transcript is with Clip Creator. It lets you view the transcript text as you create clips. For experience, make a video clip for every question and answer that a witness gives. Load the transcript by clicking in the Transcript window. (If the Synchronized Exhibits window is currently on the screen, click 

.) The Transcript window will display the entire transcript associated with the media group. Use the up or down arrow key, the Page Up or Page Down key, or the scroll bars to go to a specific page in the transcript.

Highlight the range of text that you want turned into a video clip. Hold down the Shift key and use the arrow button to highlight the text. When you have highlighted the first six lines of the document, press the right click button on your mouse. This is what the highlighted text looks like:

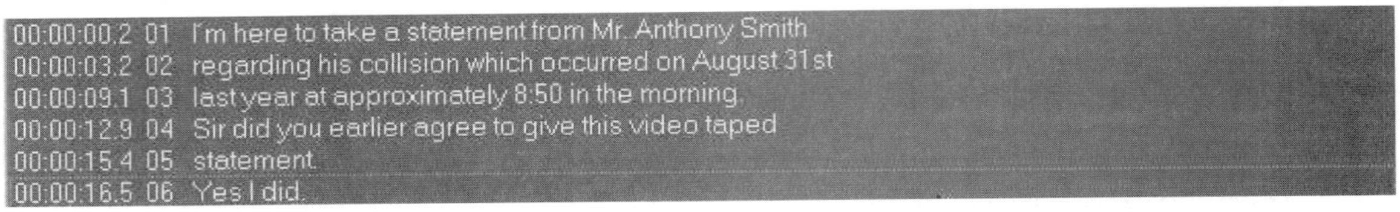

Right click and then select Create Media Clip:

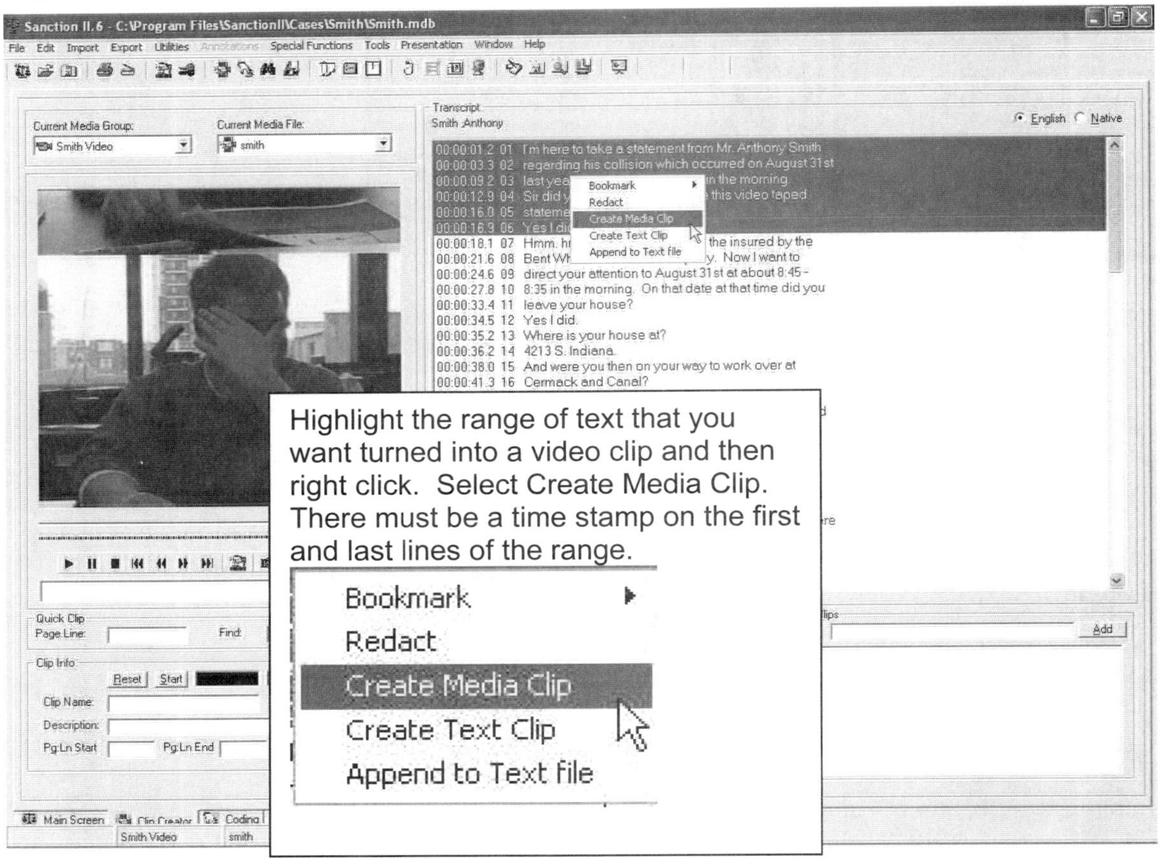

When you select Create Media Clip, the Clip Info box will be populated with this information:

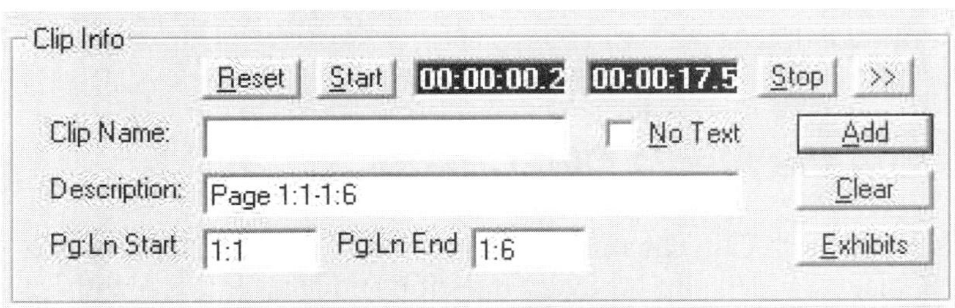

The Media Player will start playing at .00.2 seconds and will play for 17.5 seconds. During that time, page 1, line 1 will scroll through page 1, line 6. Name the clip. If you want to launch clips by typing their clip names, keep the clip names short. For the Smith case, the witness is Smith. Name the clips S# for the number of the clip. Use the duration list to keep track of the clips. You can import the clips as a text file into your notes. See the duration list section that follows. This will help you know what clip number will launch the clip. When you are cross-examining a witness or otherwise playing a clip that has corresponding text, call out the clip number for the court reporter and supply the court reporter with a copy of the transcript. This way the court reporter will have an accurate picture of what you have done.

Adjusting Clip Start and Stop Times

You may find that your time stamped transcript needs adjusting. Sanction lets you adjust clip start and stop times.

To Subtract One Second from the Start/Stop Time:

Click directly on the window with the black background next to either the beginning or end of a clip. 

For greater precision, hold down the Shift key while doing the above, and the adjustment value can be changed from the Sanction Settings option.

To Add One Second to the Start/Stop Time:

Click with the right mouse button on the time in the window next to either the Start or Stop button. 

. For greater precision, hold down the Shift key while doing the above, and the adjustment value can be changed from the Sanction Settings option.

If changes are being made to a new clip, click 

when the adjustments are complete. To save adjustments to an existing clip, click 

.

To Edit Clip Names or Descriptions:

Double click on the clip to be edited in the Clip Segments window. The clip will load.

Make desired changes to the clip and click 

.

Creating a Clip with the Page.Line and Find Text Features

Once you have associated a synchronized transcript with the loaded media files, the Page.Line and Find Text features will be enabled.

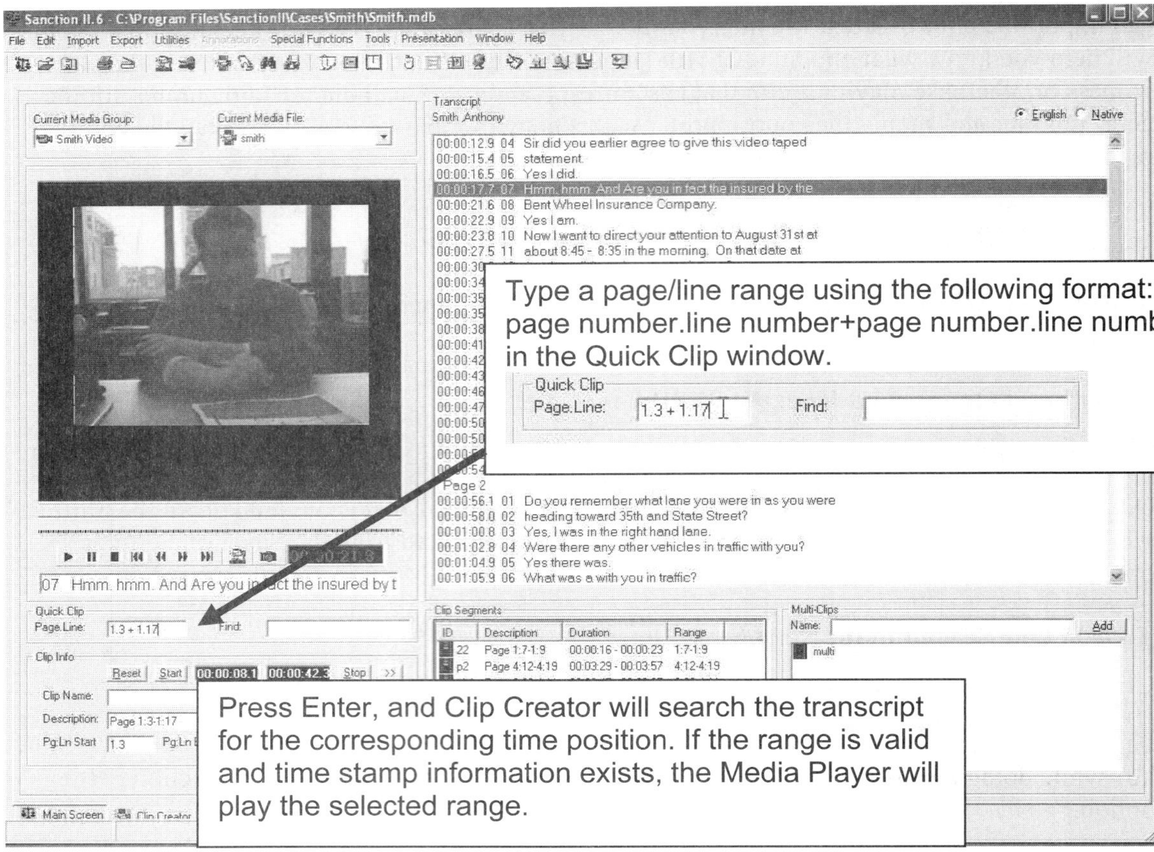

Play the clip and make any adjustments by clicking the Start and Stop buttons. See the "Adjusting Clip Start and Stop Times" section above. When satisfied with the clip adjustments, name the clip and click. The clip will appear in the Clip Segments window.

Note: If you receive the message "No timestamp information ...", this means the line number selected does not have a time stamp entry. Use the next line number up or down and try again. You may then edit the segment to account for the missing time stamp.

Alternatively, you may wish to locate a particular phrase in a transcript and then create your clip segment.

Locating a Phrase or Word with Clip Creator

You can use Clip Creator to search through a transcript for a particular word or phrase.

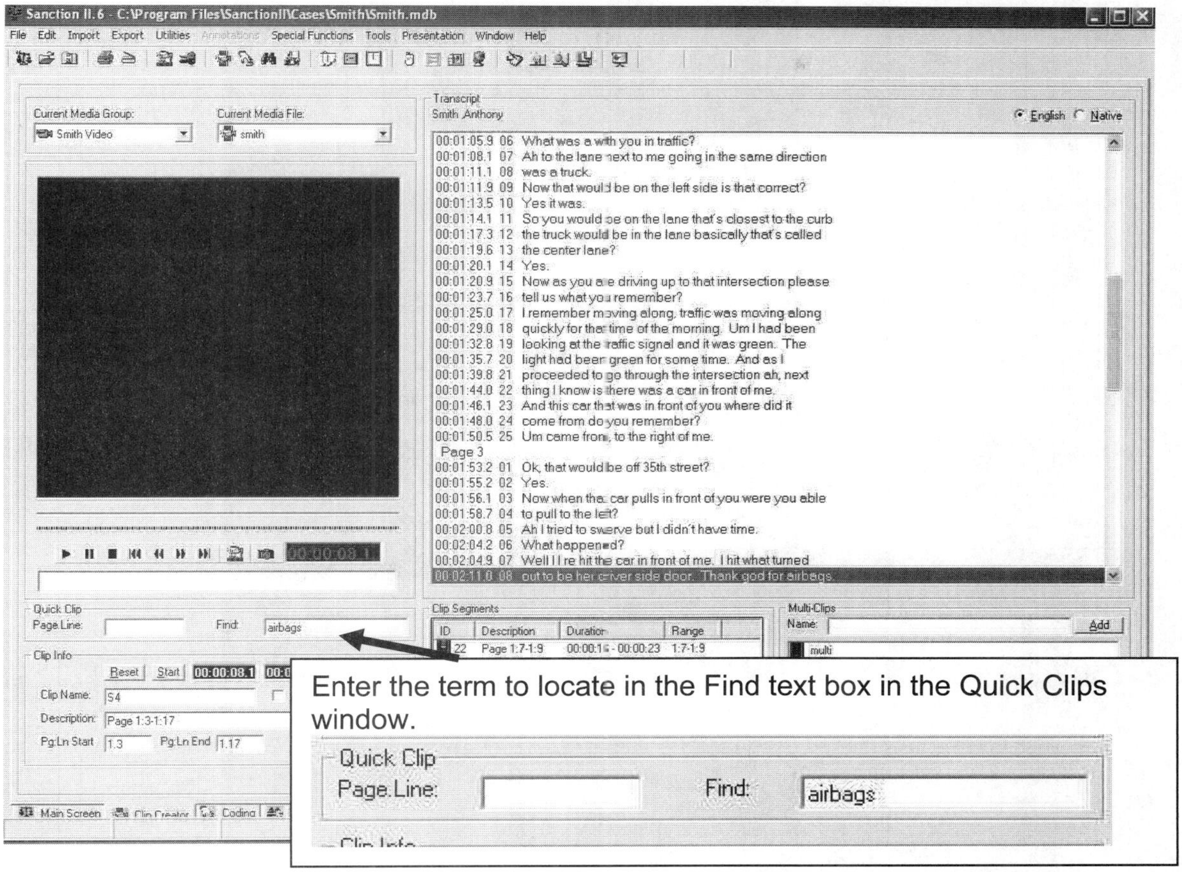

Press Enter. If the search term is located, the transcript line will be highlighted in the Transcript window. Double click on the line to begin playback (if the line has a valid time stamp entry). Press Enter again to continue searching. The start point of the text is automatically updated to the current location each time the term is located and the line is clicked in the Transcript window.

Duration List: Making a Printout of the Clips That You Created

Video clips are great evidence, but they are a type of evidence that can drive judges and court personnel crazy. If you are using video clips of evidence depositions, the judge will want to know how long the clips will take. If you are using the clips during a cross-examination, the court reporter in your trial will hate you unless you provide him or her with a transcript of the video clip that you used during the trial. Sanction has a duration list that lets you create a printout of video clips that will help you solve these problems. You can make a clip that is printed or that you save to your computer. Make sure to save a copy of the clip to the computer because the clips and their codes can be dragged and dropped right into your Cross-Examination Worksheet. Here is how you do it.

Go to the Tool menu and select Duration List.

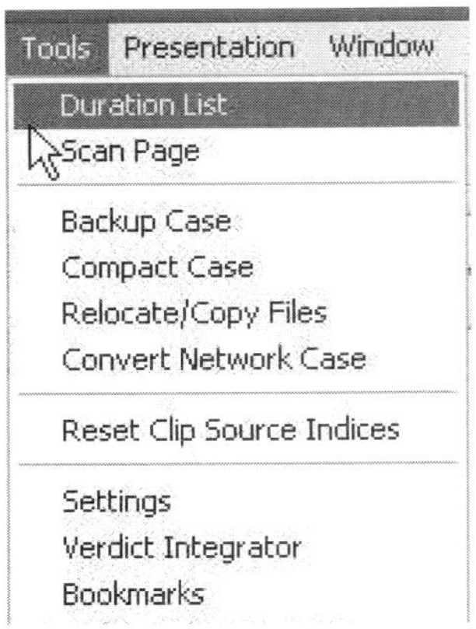

This will launch a utility that lets you make customized lists of the exhibits that will be used at trial.

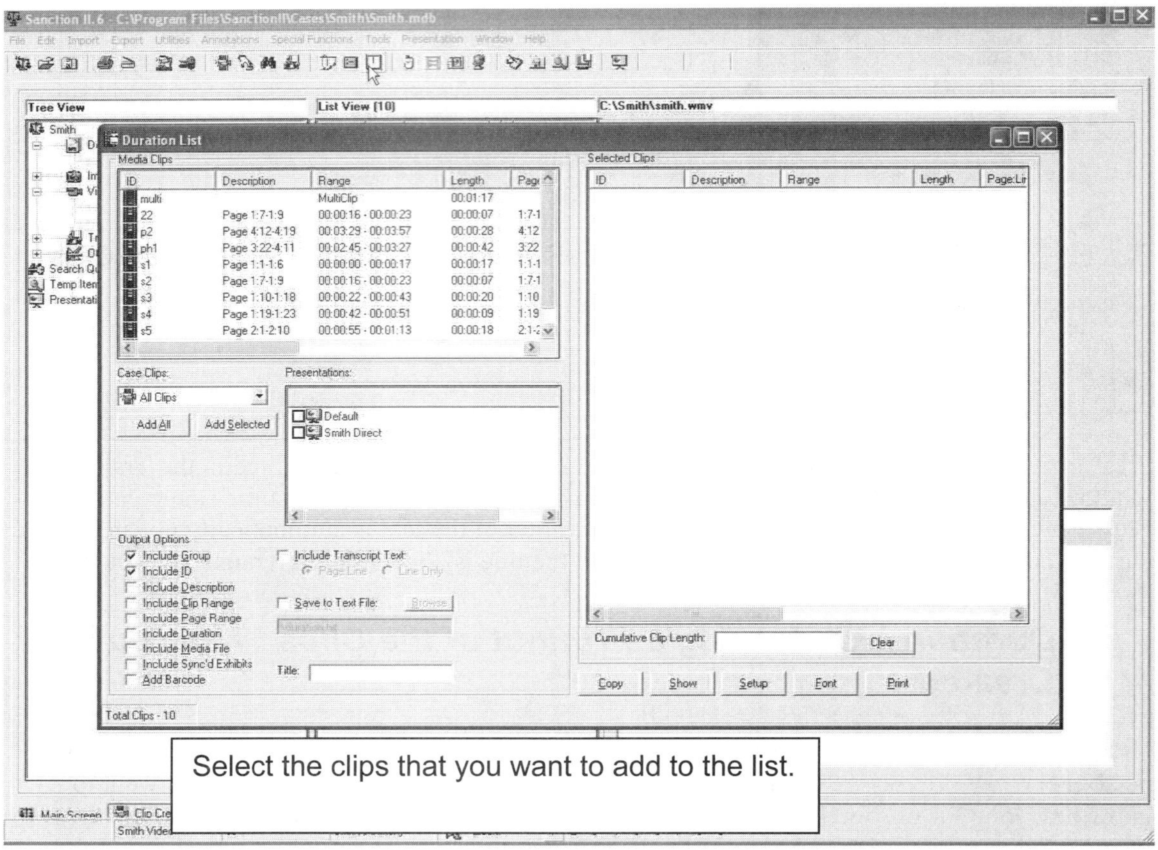

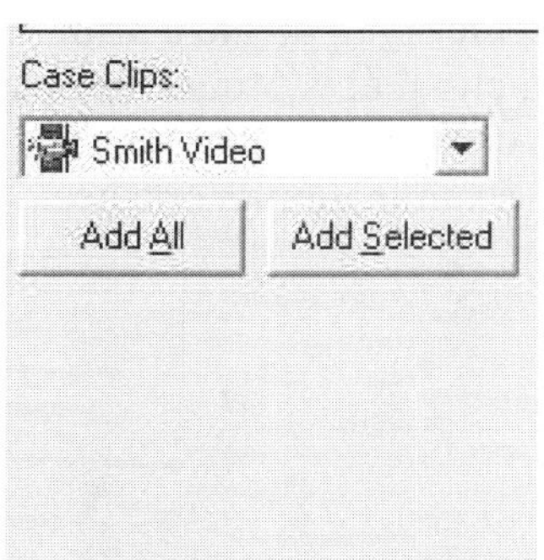

In this case, select Add All for the Smith Video.

Sanction will then add the clips to the Selected Clips box:

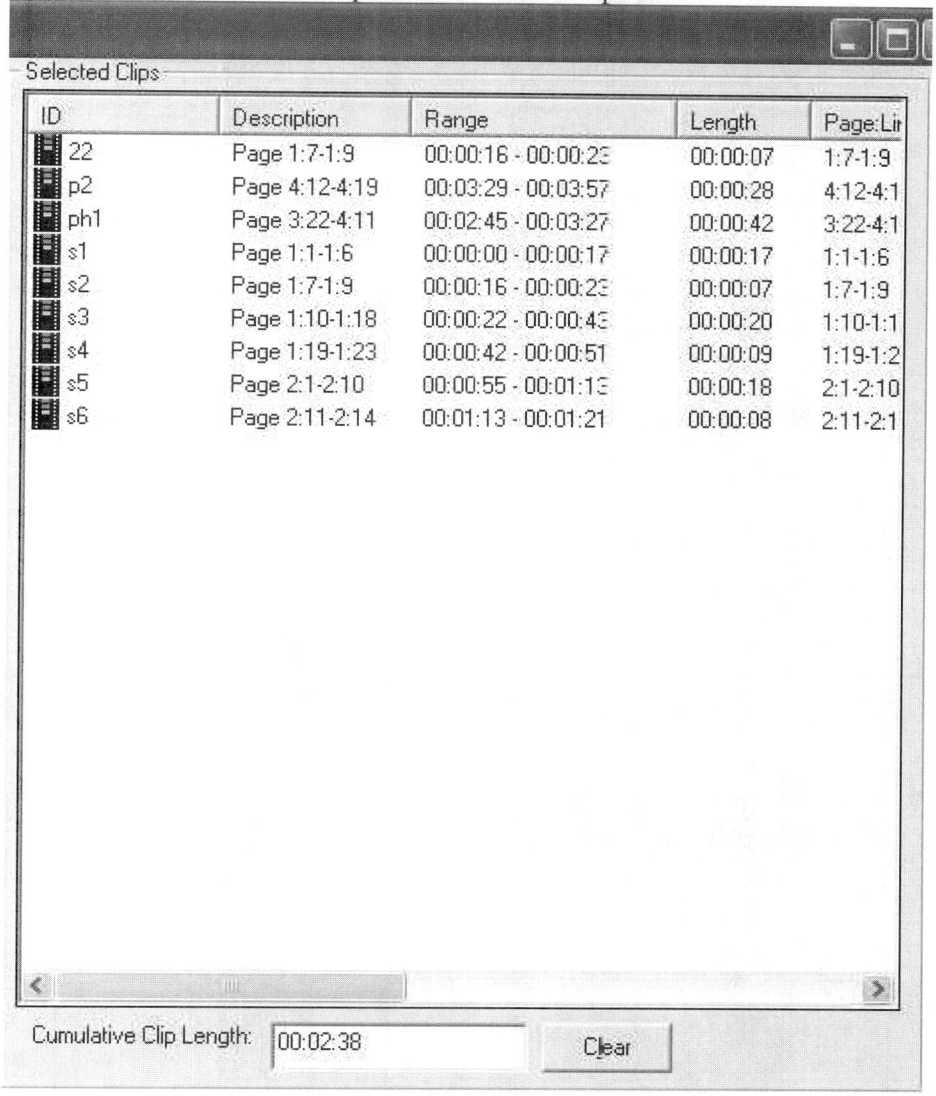

Fill in the boxes of the information that you want to add to the list in the Output Options box:

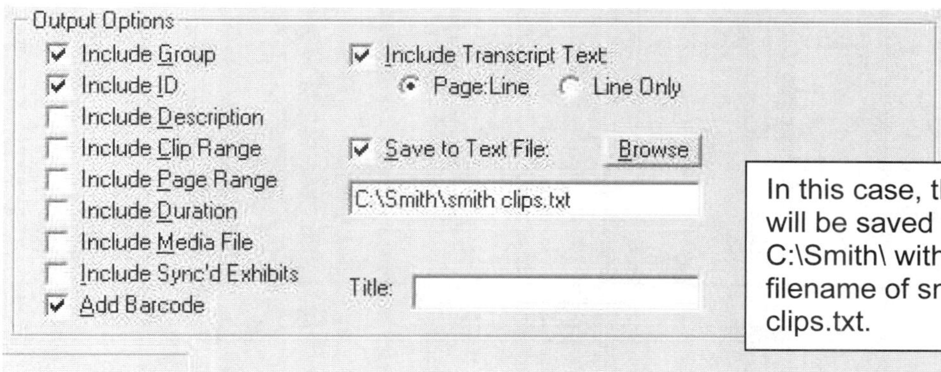

In this case, the text file will be saved to C:\Smith\ with the filename of smith clips.txt.

Click on 

. Sanction will create a text file that tracks all of your clips.

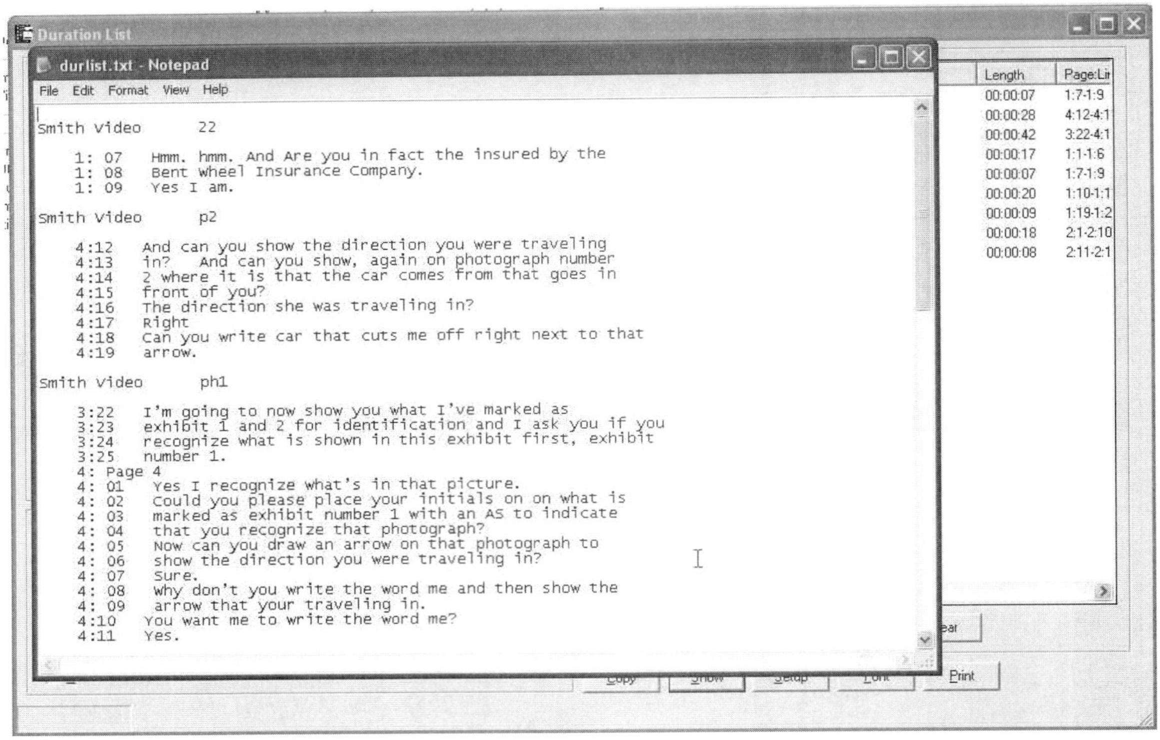
Duration List
durlist.txt - Notepad
File Edit Format View Help
Smith Video 22
1: 07 Hmm. hmm. And Are you in fact the insured by the
1: 08 Bent Wheel Insurance Company.
1: 09 Yes I am.
Smith Video p2
4:12 And can you show the direction you were traveling
4:13 in? And can you show, again on photograph number
4:14 2 where it is that the car comes from that goes in
4:15 front of you?
4:16 The direction she was traveling in?
4:17 Right
4:18 Can you write car that cuts me off right next to that
4:19 arrow.
Smith Video ph1
3:22 I'm going to now show you what I've marked as
3:23 exhibit 1 and 2 for identification and I ask you if you
3:24 recognize what is shown in this exhibit first, exhibit
3:25 number 1.
4: Page 4
4: 01 Yes I recognize what's in that picture.
4: 02 Could you please place your initials on on what is
4: 03 marked as exhibit number 1 with an AS to indicate
4: 04 that you recognize that photograph?
4: 05 Now can you draw an arrow on that photograph to
4: 06 show the direction you were traveling in?
4: 07 Sure.
4: 08 Why don't you write the word me and then show the
4: 09 arrow that your traveling in.
4:10 You want me to write the word me?
4:11 Yes.
Length Page:Li
00:00:07 1:7-1:9
00:00:28 4:12-4:1
00:00:42 3:22-4:1
00:00:17 1:1-1:6
00:00:07 1:7-1:9
00:00:20 1:10-1:1
00:00:09 1:19-1:2
00:00:18 2:1-2:10
00:00:08 2:11-2:1
Print

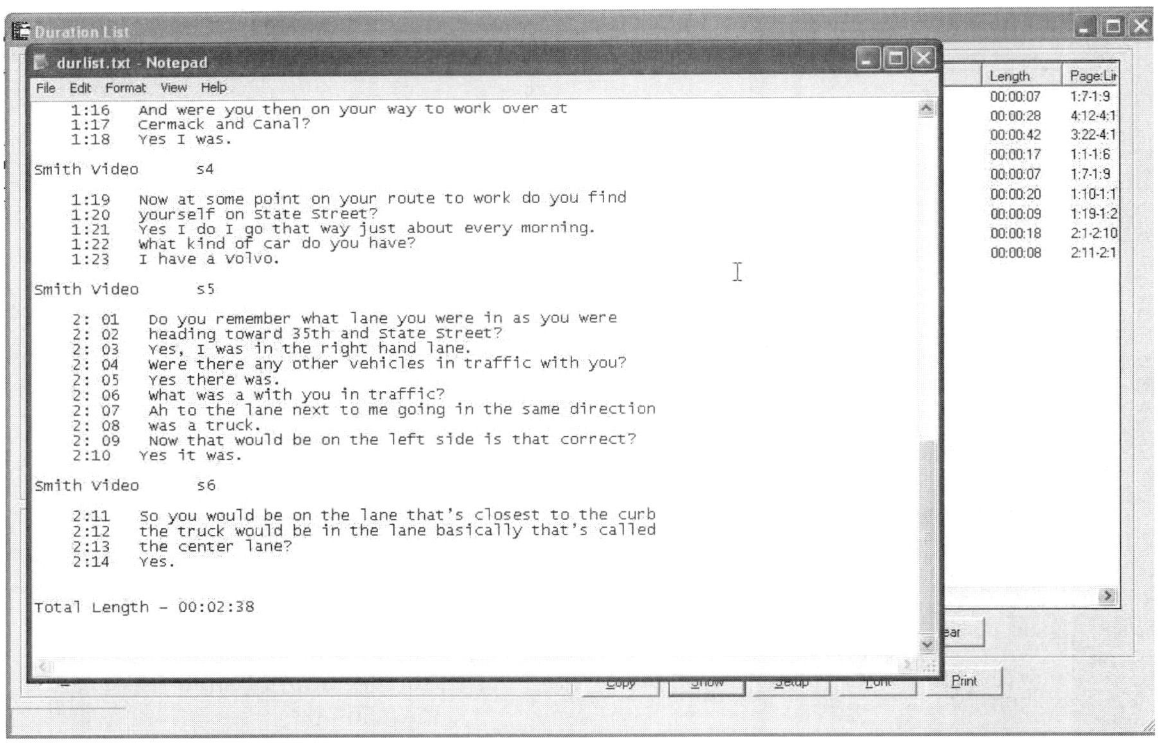
Duration List
durlist.txt - Notepad
File Edit Format View Help
1:16 And were you then on your way to work over at
1:17 Cermack and Canal?
1:18 Yes I was.
Smith Video s4
1:19 Now at some point on your route to work do you find
1:20 yourself on State Street?
1:21 Yes I do I go that way just about every morning.
1:22 What kind of car do you have?
1:23 I have a Volvo.
Smith Video s5
2: 01 Do you remember what lane you were in as you were
2: 02 heading toward 35th and State Street?
2: 03 Yes, I was in the right hand lane.
2: 04 Were there any other vehicles in traffic with you?
2: 05 Yes there was.
2: 06 What was a with you in traffic?
2: 07 Ah to the lane next to me going in the same direction
2: 08 was a truck.
2: 09 Now that would be on the left side is that correct?
2:10 Yes it was.
Smith Video s6
2:11 So you would be on the lane that's closest to the curb
2:12 the truck would be in the lane basically that's called
2:13 the center lane?
2:14 Yes.
Total Length - 00:02:38
Length Page:Li
00:00:07 1:7-1:9
00:00:28 4:12-4:1
00:00:42 3:22-4:1
00:00:17 1:1-1:6
00:00:07 1:7-1:9
00:00:20 1:10-1:1
00:00:09 1:19-1:2
00:00:18 2:1-2:10
00:00:08 2:11-2:1
Print

Manually Creating Media Clips (Without a Synchronized Transcript)

Find the start point of the clip with the Media Playback controls. Click Start.

Find the stop point of the clip with the Media Playback controls. Click . Stop

Type a name for the clip and optional description.

Click to save the clip. The clip will now appear in the Clip Segment List window and also in the Video category on the Main screen under the source media group.

reate Multiple Segment Clips from Existing Clips (Multi-clips), type a name in the Multi-Clips window and choose Add. The new multi-clip folder will appear in the Tree View window.
To add segments to the new multi-clip, drag the segment from the Clip Segments window and drop it on the selected multi-clip name in the Multi-Clips window.

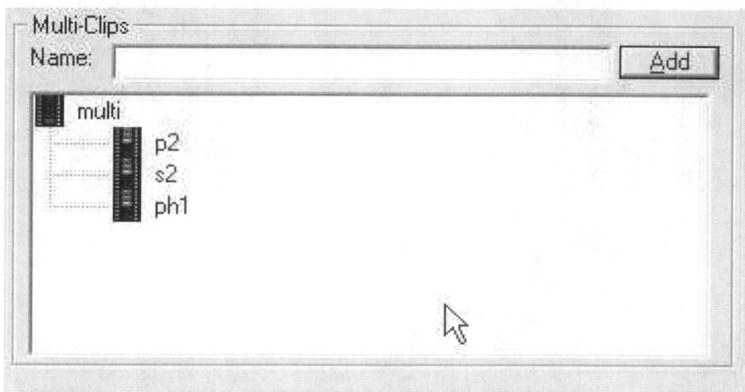

To play a multi-clip, right click on the item and select Play, or type the multi-clip name directly on the screen in Presentation Mode.

To rearrange segments in a multi-clip, drag and drop a segment onto the position immediately above the new location. To reposition a clip as the first clip in the multi-clip, drag and drop the clip onto the multi-clip name. (See diagram above.)

Note: Multi-clips can span media files as well as different media groups. To create a multi-segment containing different media groups, you must load the media group and appropriate root media file from the drop-down combo boxes. You may then drag and drop the desired segments into the multi-clip folder.

See the Sanction manual for explanations on other ways to create video clips with transcripts.

Adding Exhibits/Images for Automatic Display When Clips Are Playing

You can automatically display case exhibits during media clip segment playback. If a witness marked an exhibit or diagram while giving a video or audio statement, you can make Sanction show the exhibit while the witness talks about it on the video. When a segment is played that contains a "synchronized exhibit" in Presentation mode, the media window will shift to the left or top panel when the clip reaches the predetermined exhibit display time (see Presentation mode settings), and the exhibit will be displayed in the opposite panel. If you have included "clear" points, the exhibit will also be removed from the screen in the same manner.

Double click on the segment you wish to add the synchronized exhibit to. (If the Transcript window is currently on screen, click on the Exhibits button to display the Synchronized Exhibits window: Exhibits .) Your screen will change to look like this:

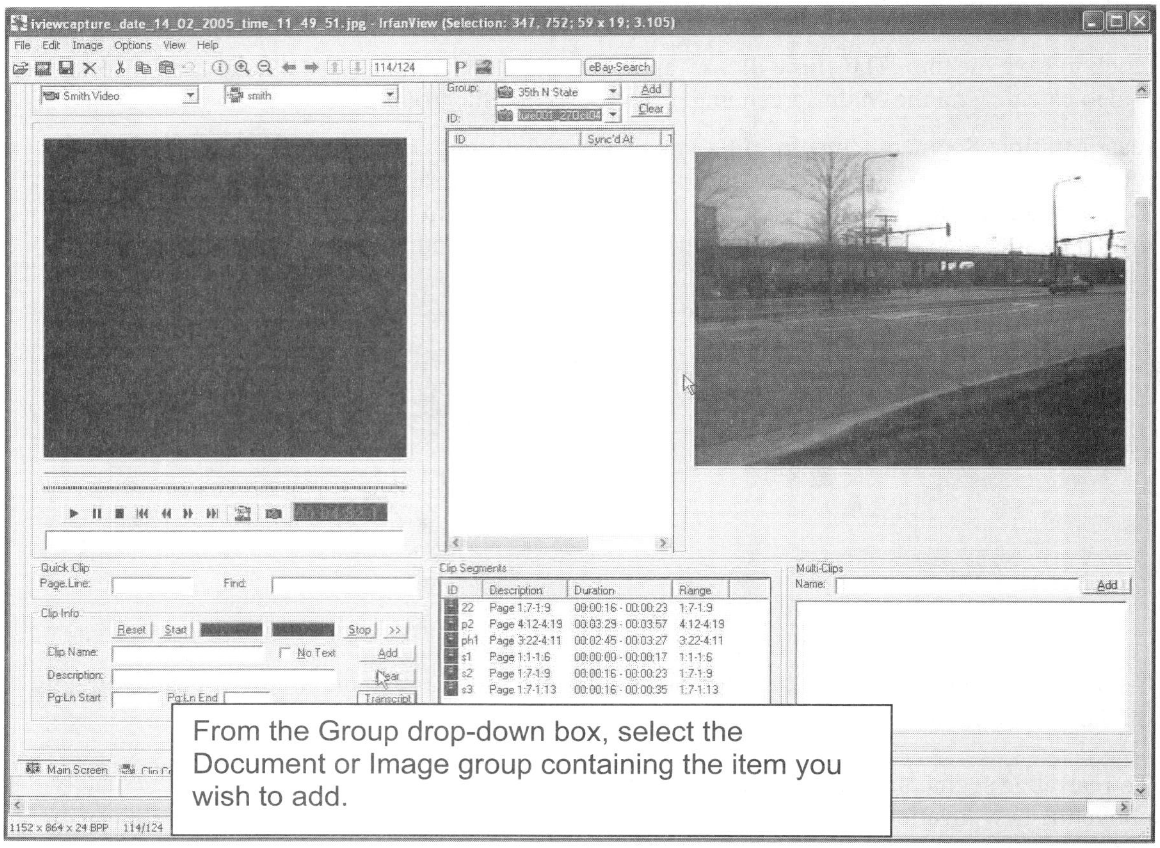

In this case, we will select video clip S2:

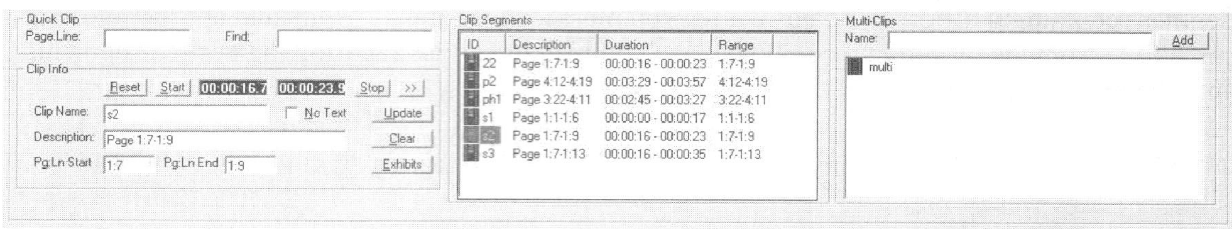

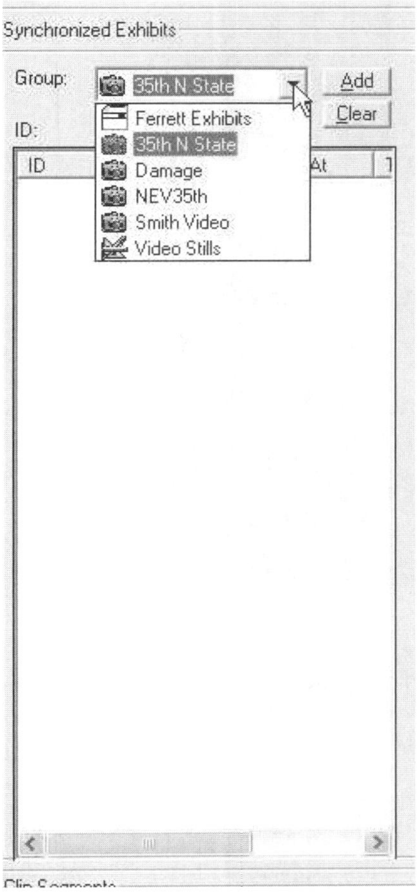

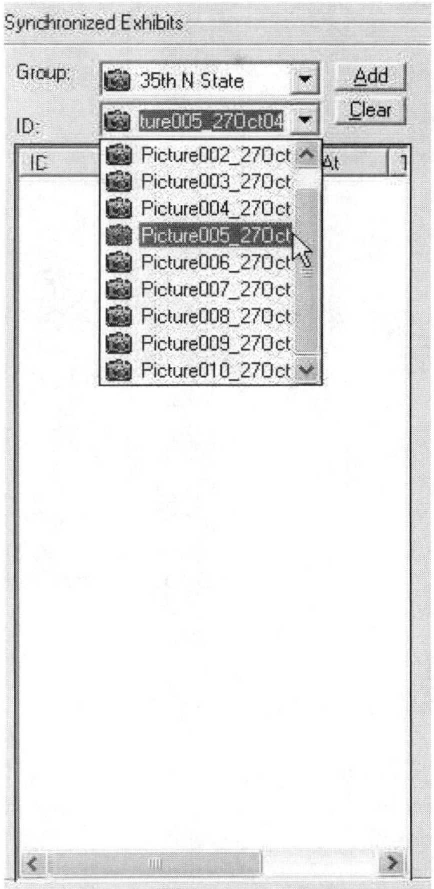

Play the clip segment and pause it at the point you wish the exhibit to be displayed.

The clock will stop, and you can now select your exhibit.

Click on the Add button in the Synchronized Exhibits window to add the exhibit at the selected time point. To add a "clear point" to the clip segment (to clear the current exhibit), click on the Clear button, and then select Update.

To remove a synchronized exhibit entirely, right click on the exhibit in the Synchronized Exhibits list and choose Remove Sync Item. To change the current sync point for an exhibit, right click on the exhibit in the Synchronized Exhibits list and choose Re-Sync. The exhibit sync time will be updated to reflect the current position of the Media Player.

Important: If you wish to delete clip segments, do so from the Clip Creator tab only. If you delete a clip from the Main screen and it is included in a multi-clip elsewhere, it is possible that the multi-clip may no longer play correctly.

Exporting Video and Video Clips to Windows Media File Format

You may need to share video or audio files and clips with co-counsel, expert witnesses, judges, or others who don't own Sanction. You can convert Sanction media clip segments into Windows media files that will play outside Sanction. Sanction's Clip Splitter feature allows users to make smaller .wmv (video) or .wma (audio) files from any media clip created in Sanction. If the media file is synchronized to a transcript, the converted clips can also display synchronized text within Windows Media Player.

Components Required for Use of Sanction Clip Splitter

Windows Media Encoder

To successfully create .wmv and .wma files using Sanction, Windows Media Encoder runtime files must be installed on your computer. Although these files are not installed automatically as part of Sanction, the Windows Media Encoder executable file is located in the Sanction subdirectory. To install the Windows Media Encoder runtime files, follow the next screen.

- Launch Windows Explorer.

  Go to your 

  menu and select Explore.

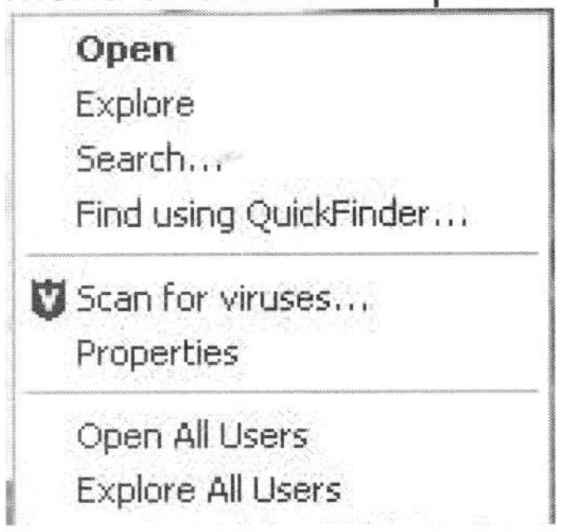

- Browse to the Sanction program directory (typically found at C:\Program Files\Sanction).
- Double click on the WMEDist.exe file to run the installation. 

Windows Media Player

Sanction's Clip Splitter feature requires that Windows Media Player 6.4 or higher be installed on the computer. For a free update to Windows Media Player, visit www.microsoft.com/downloads.

Converting Sanction Media Clips to Windows Media Files

Media clips must first be created using one of Sanction's standard Clip Creator features (see previous discussion in this chapter). Go to the Clip Creator and select Convert Media Clips, as the next screen capture shows.

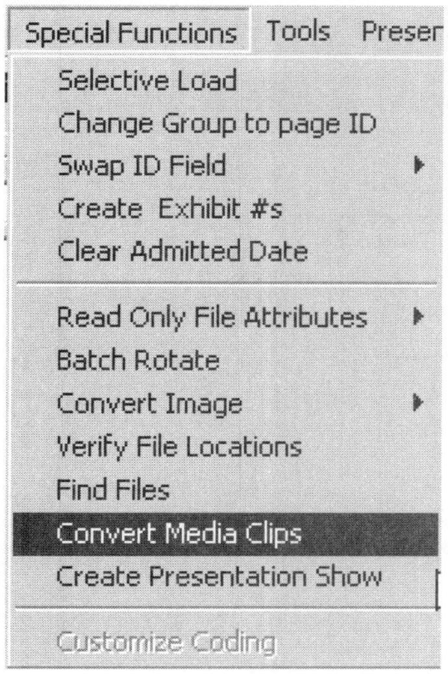

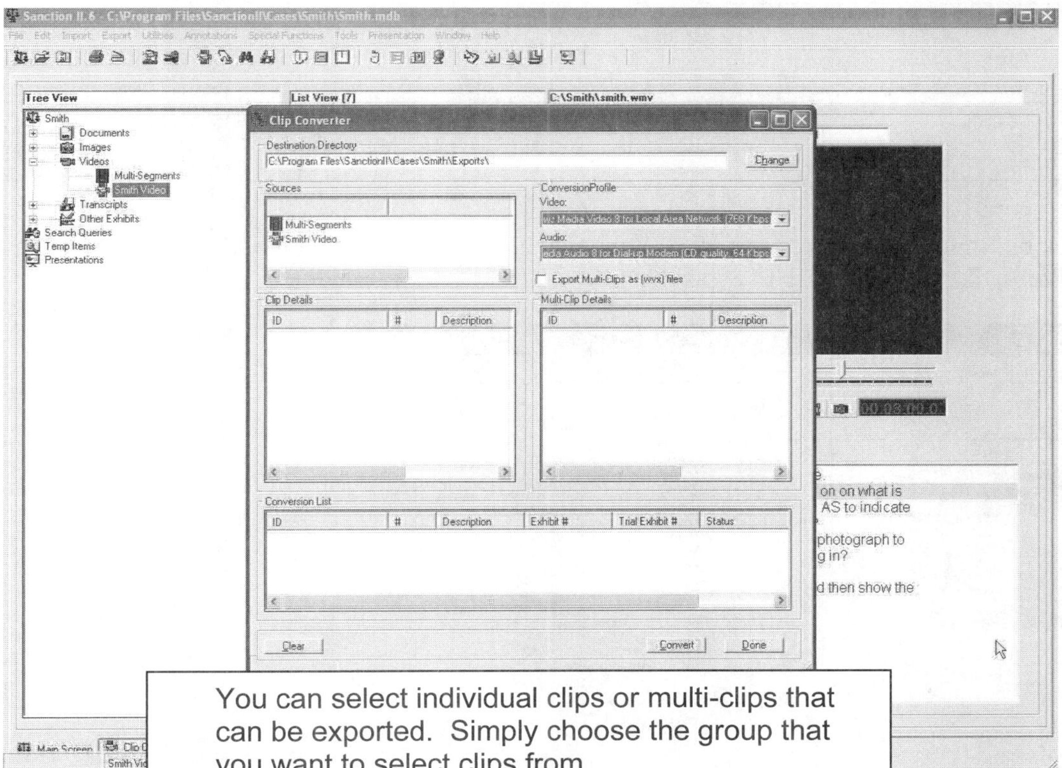

You can select individual clips or multi-clips that can be exported. Simply choose the group that you want to select clips from.

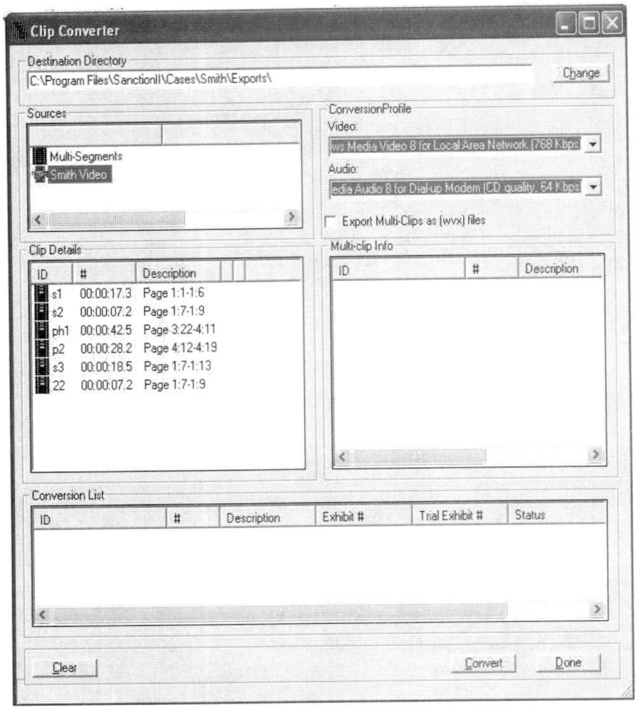

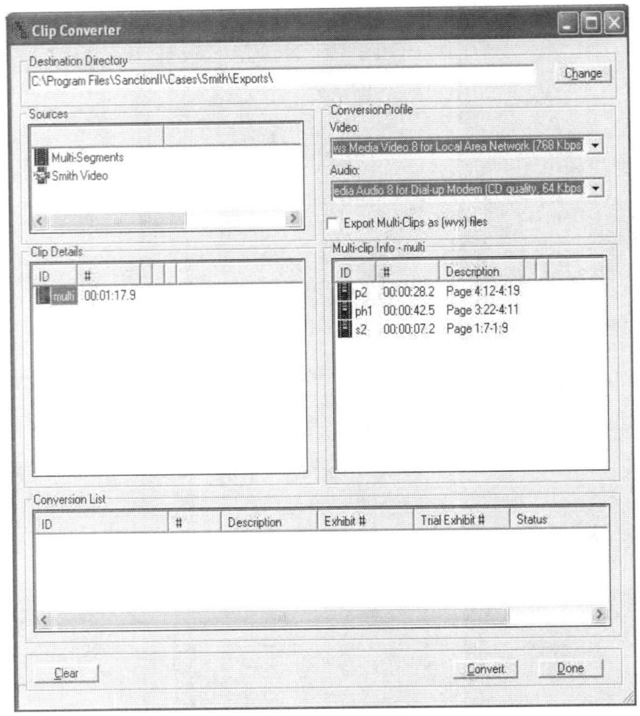

Click on Smith. We will export clip s2; the other screen shows what the Multi-Segments clips will look like if you choose to export them.

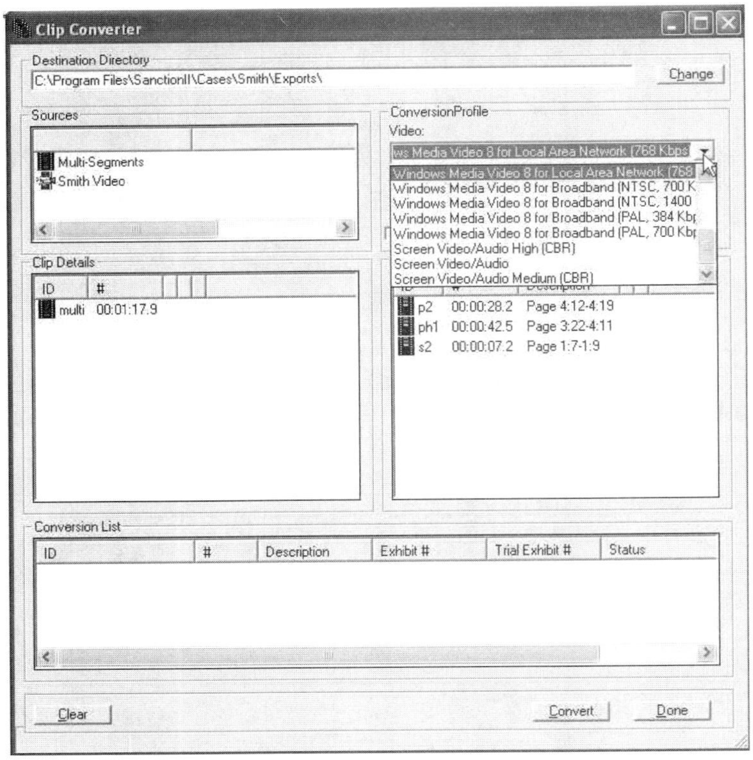

You can use these drop-down menus to select a file size. The larger the file size, the higher the quality of the image.

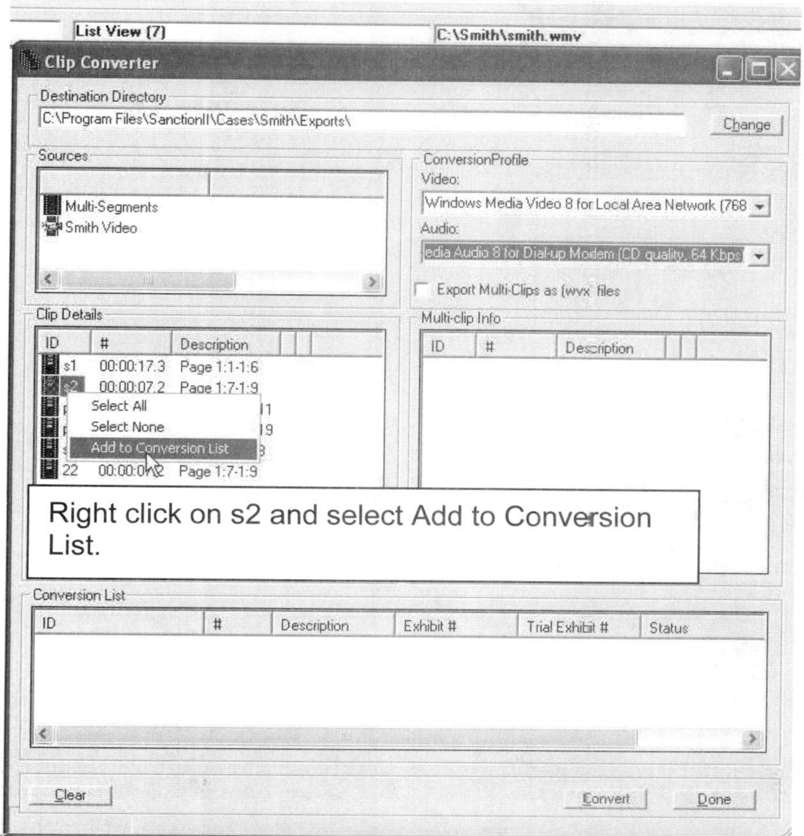
Clip Converter
Right click on s2 and select Add to Conversion List.

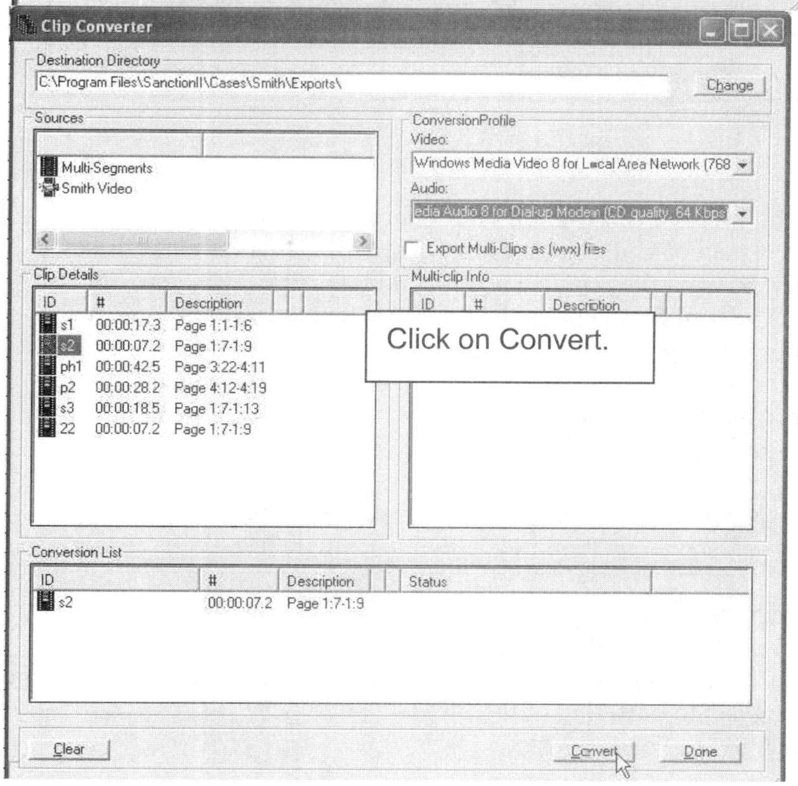
Clip Converter
Click on Convert.

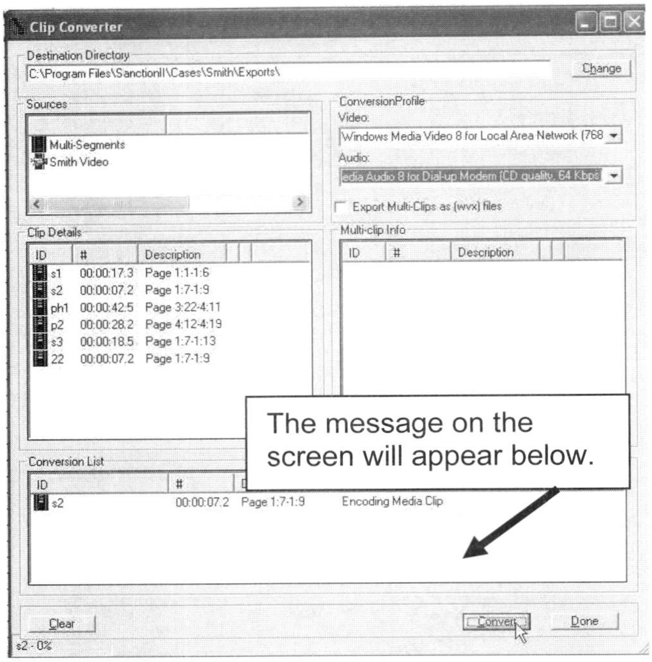

The newly converted clips will be saved in C:\Program Files\SanctionII\Smith\Exports\ subdirectory. (Sanction will use a path of C:\Program Files\SanctionII\Cases for all of these exports.) In addition to the .wmv or .wma files created and saved in this directory, you will also find files with a .smi extension. The .smi files contain the transcript text that corresponds with each media file (if the media files were synchronized). When the captioning option is enabled in Windows Media Player, the .smi file allows the transcript text to display as the media clip plays. When distributing the Windows Media Files, be sure to copy the .wmv/.wma files and the .smi file so the transcript text is included with the media files.

Note: If you are using Windows Media Encoder 9, the .wmv file contains the text in it. A .smi file is no longer created.

Important: Using Windows media files (.wmv/.wma) within Sanction is *not supported.* Windows media files should *never* be used in place of Sanction's standard synchronized media clips. Windows media files are a "streaming" format, and any synchronization applied to this type of file is highly inaccurate and subject to buffering of the file.

Searching in Sanction

There are a number of different ways to search for things in Sanction.

Using the Coding Tab

Sanction has a Coding tab that is a powerful way to find and retrieve exhibits or other information. The Coding feature allows data entry into "objective" coding fields for future search and query. Any item in the main case categories can be coded with information using various fields including document type, authors, recipients, and descriptions. You can even customize the coding fields for more types of searches. The coding feature can eliminate the need for larger, more expensive case management products because data may be imported directly into the Sanction coding fields. Once data is entered in the coding table, whether manually or through an import file, powerful compound searches can be created using the Query function to pinpoint the exact information sought. You can also import data from one of the popular document management database programs that exist in the legal industry by using the Field Importer feature. If you want to learn more about this type of function, see the Sanction manual.

No matter what you decide about using the custom coding feature, you should use the preset coding fields to search case categories for specific information based on the individual case item fields, such as ID, Group, Descriptions, Exhibit #s, TrialEx #s, or by using powerful SQL-based searches. Found items can be added to the Temp, User, or Presentation folders with a simple right click. You can search through different fields in the case database. See the Sanction manual for an explanation on how to use this feature.

Using the Transcript Search Tab

The Transcript Search feature provides a quick and easy way to search multiple transcripts for specific words and phrases. Entire transcripts or portions of the transcript can be viewed from the Transcript Search tab. By selecting or highlighting a range of text within a transcript and right clicking, several options become available. You should read this section of the Sanction manual carefully once you start working with larger files. The more information you have to sift through, the more you will appreciate the program's ability to help you find things. The following are just a few of the features that the Transcript Search tab can help you with.

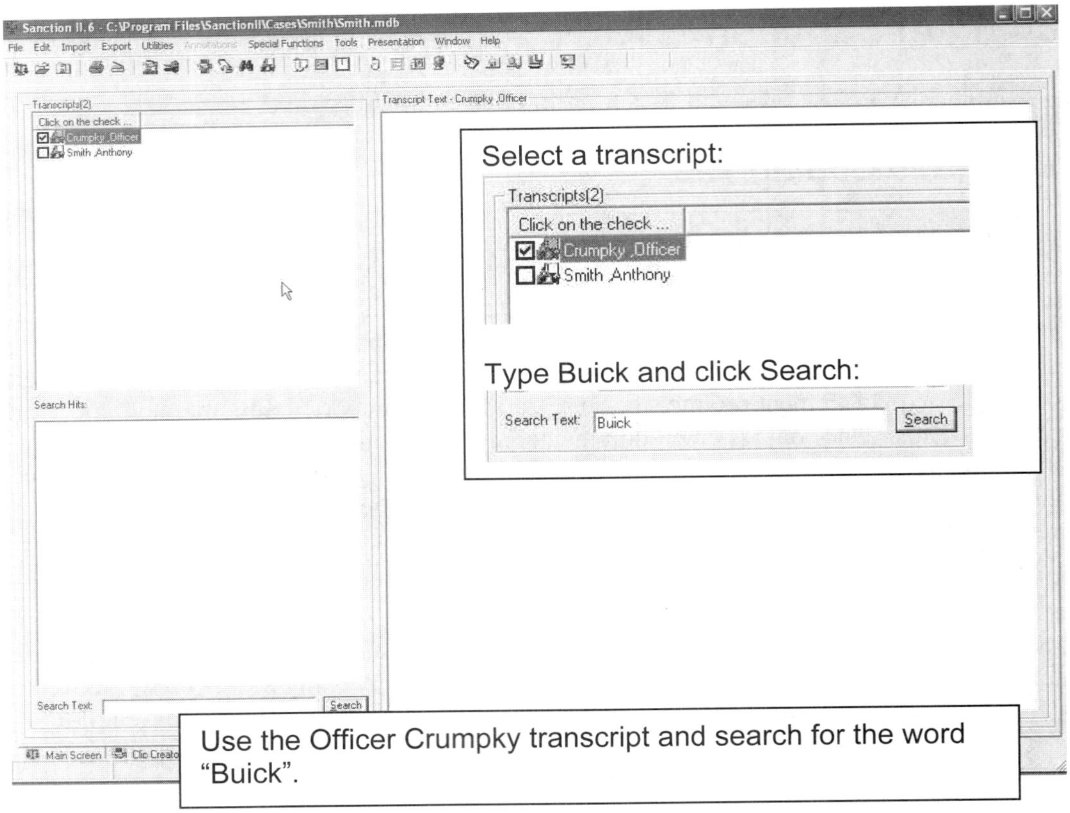
Sanction II.6 - C:\Program Files\SanctionII\Cases\Smith\Smith.mdb
Select a transcript:
Transcripts(2)
Click on the check ...
Crumpky ,Officer
Smith ,Anthony
Type Buick and click Search:
Search Text: Buick
Search
Use the Officer Crumpky transcript and search for the word "Buick".

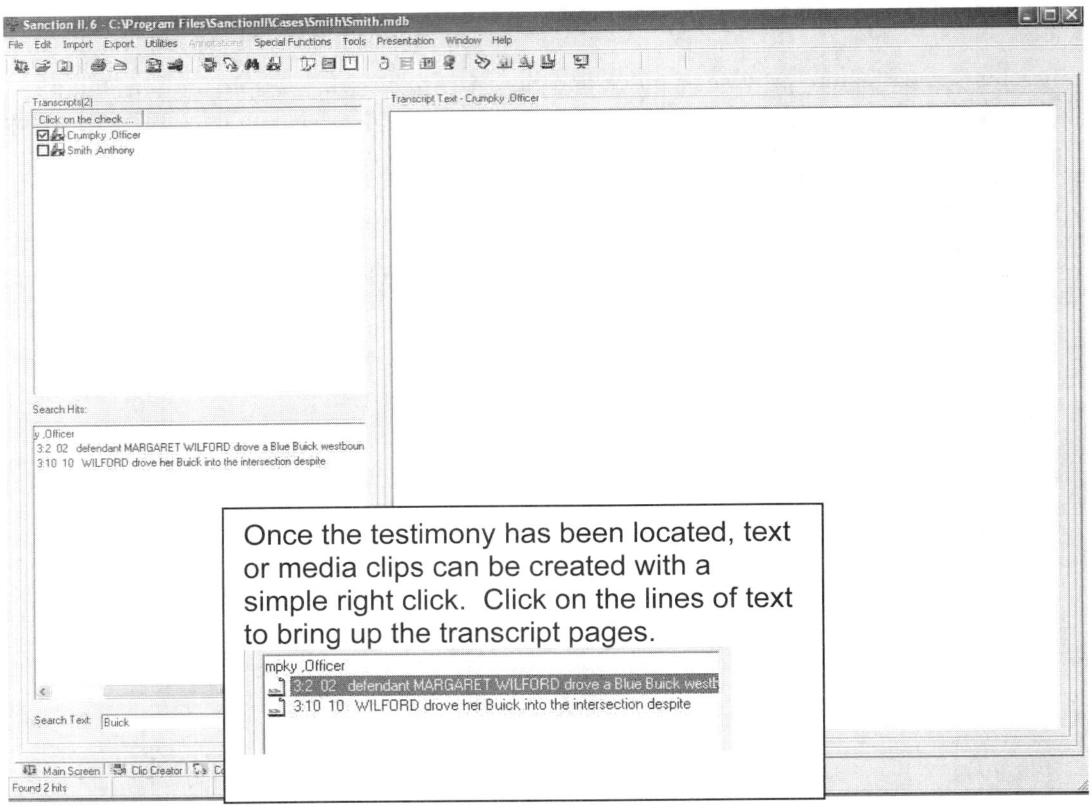
Sanction II.6 - C:\Program Files\SanctionII\Cases\Smith\Smith.mdb
Once the testimony has been located, text or media clips can be created with a simple right click. Click on the lines of text to bring up the transcript pages.
mpky ,Officer
3:2 02 defendant MARGARET WILFORD drove a Blue Buick westb
3:10 10 WILFORD drove her Buick into the intersection despite
Found 2 hits

In the Transcript window, highlight the range for the text. Right click on the highlighted text and choose Create Text Clip.

The new text clip will automatically save in Text Clips. Once saved, right click on it in List View and select Edit.Line numbers of the highlighted range (ex: 0C00301)

Selected transcript pages can be printed or even converted to individual .tif image files and saved as a new group under the Documents category. These image files can be annotated just like any other image, eliminating the need for expensive image scanning of transcript documents.

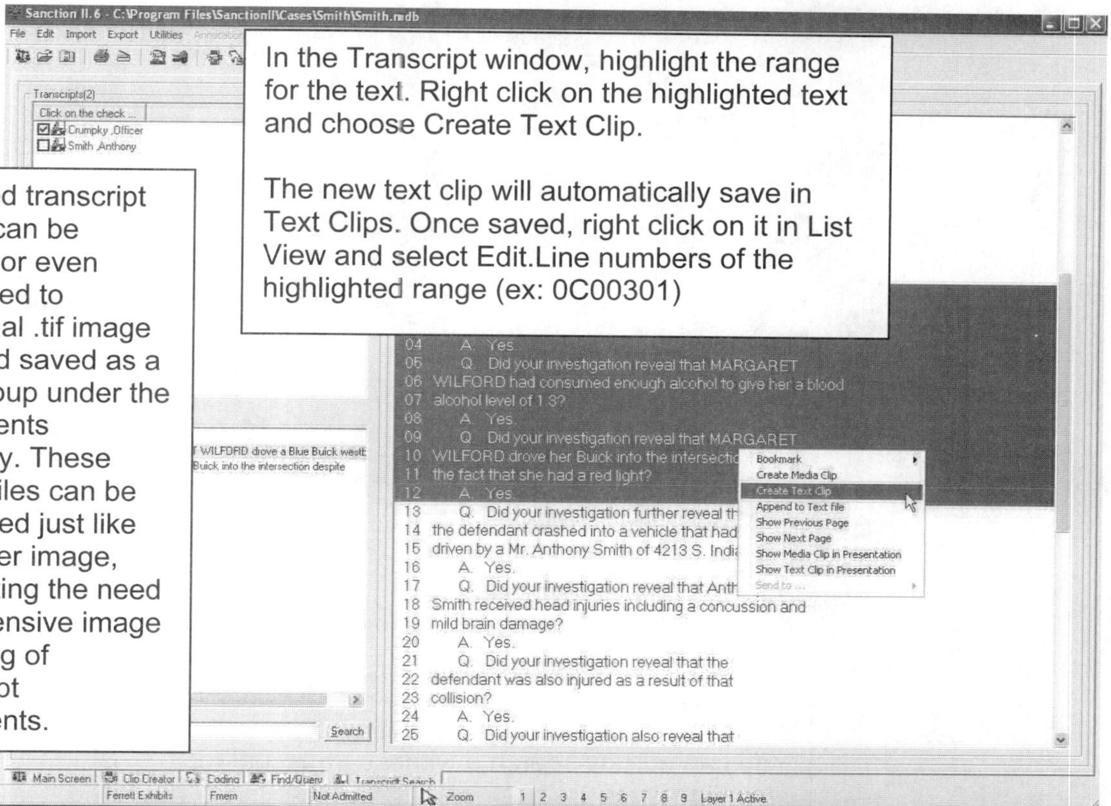

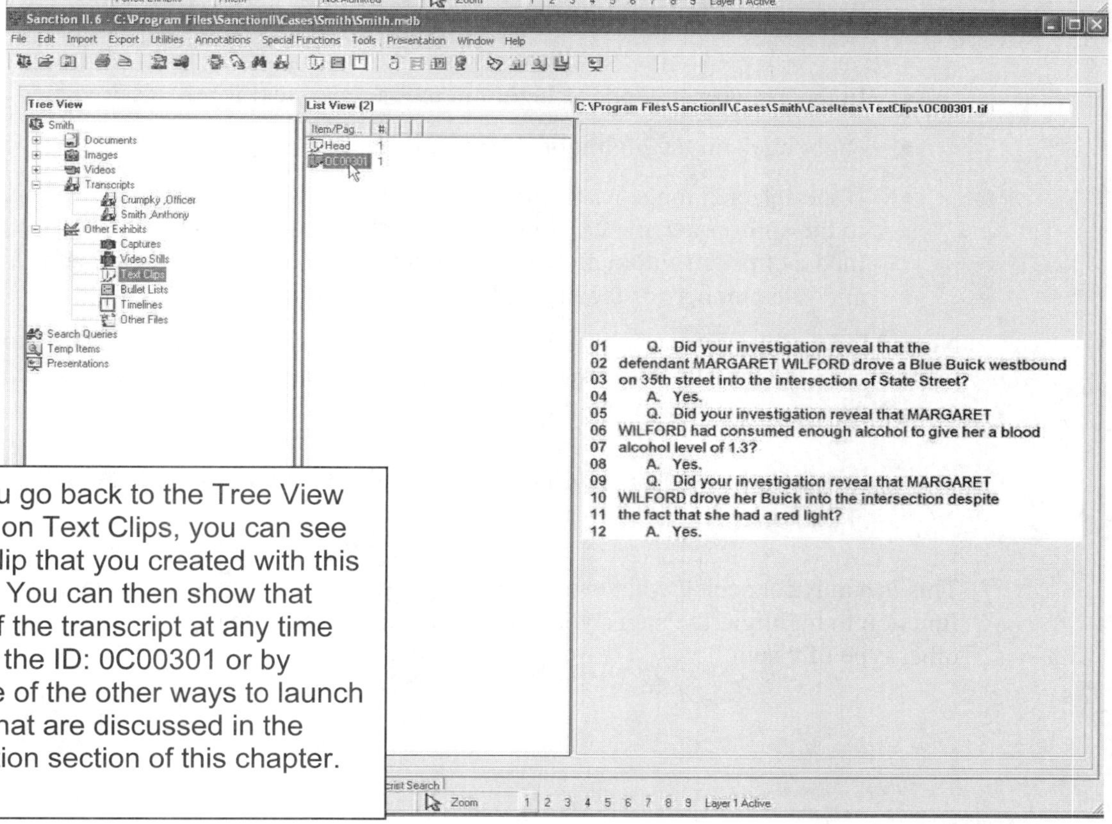

When you go back to the Tree View and click on Text Clips, you can see the text clip that you created with this function. You can then show that section of the transcript at any time by typing the ID: 0C00301 or by using one of the other ways to launch exhibits that are discussed in the presentation section of this chapter.

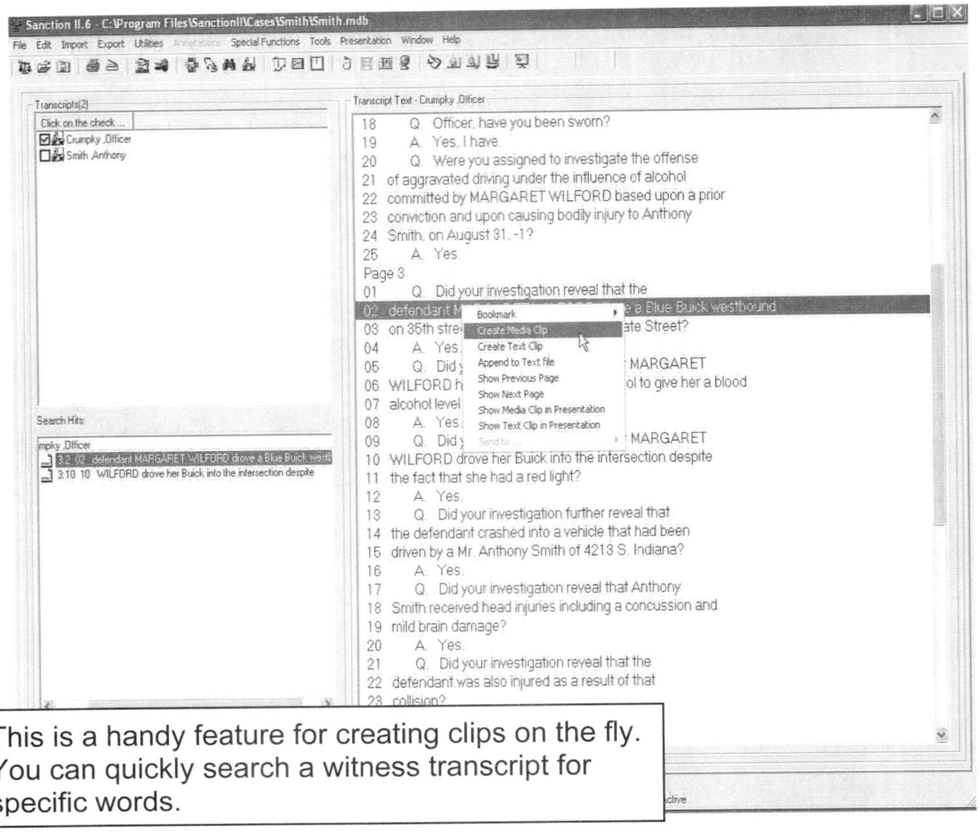

This is a handy feature for creating clips on the fly. You can quickly search a witness transcript for specific words.

- In the Transcript window, highlight the range of text for the desired media clip.
- Right click on the highlighted text and choose Create Media Clip.
- If the selected range has valid time stamp information, the clip will be created and added to the appropriate media group under the Videos category on the Main screen. New media clips are automatically named pursuant to the media group name and the first page and line numbers of the highlighted range.

Note: Media clips created from the Transcript Search tab must be edited for accuracy in the same manner as any other clip. When you are done creating clips, be sure to check each clip for the correct start and stop time using the Clip Creator tab.

Searching for Words and Phrases Across Multiple Transcripts

This is handy for seeing what every witness has to say about a particular fact or event. Use this function to highlight the pages you want to search. If video exists, you can create clips or any other type of visual.

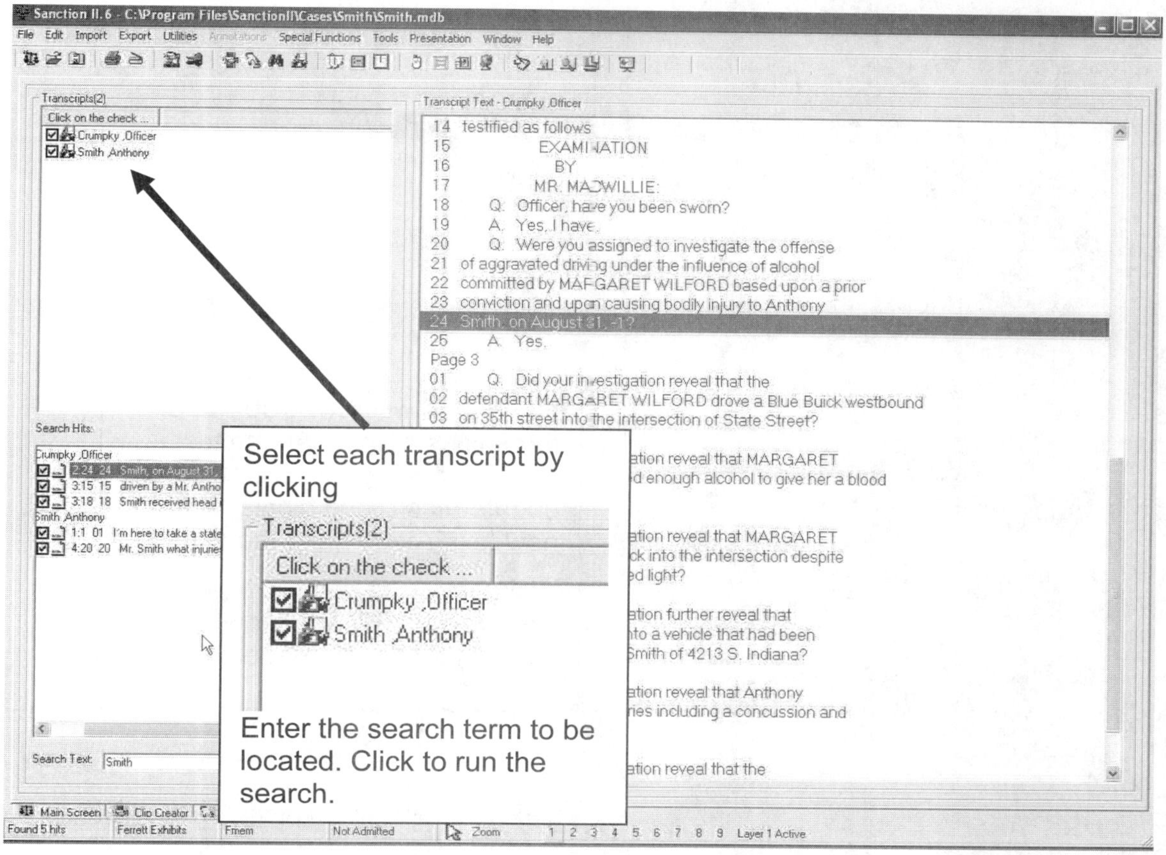

Making Exhibits That Organize Images

You can make three kinds of custom exhibits with Sanction if you choose to install CaseSoft's TimeMap Program. The first two feature tabs are included in the Sanction program: text clips and bullet points.

Creating a Text Clip

Click this icon: .

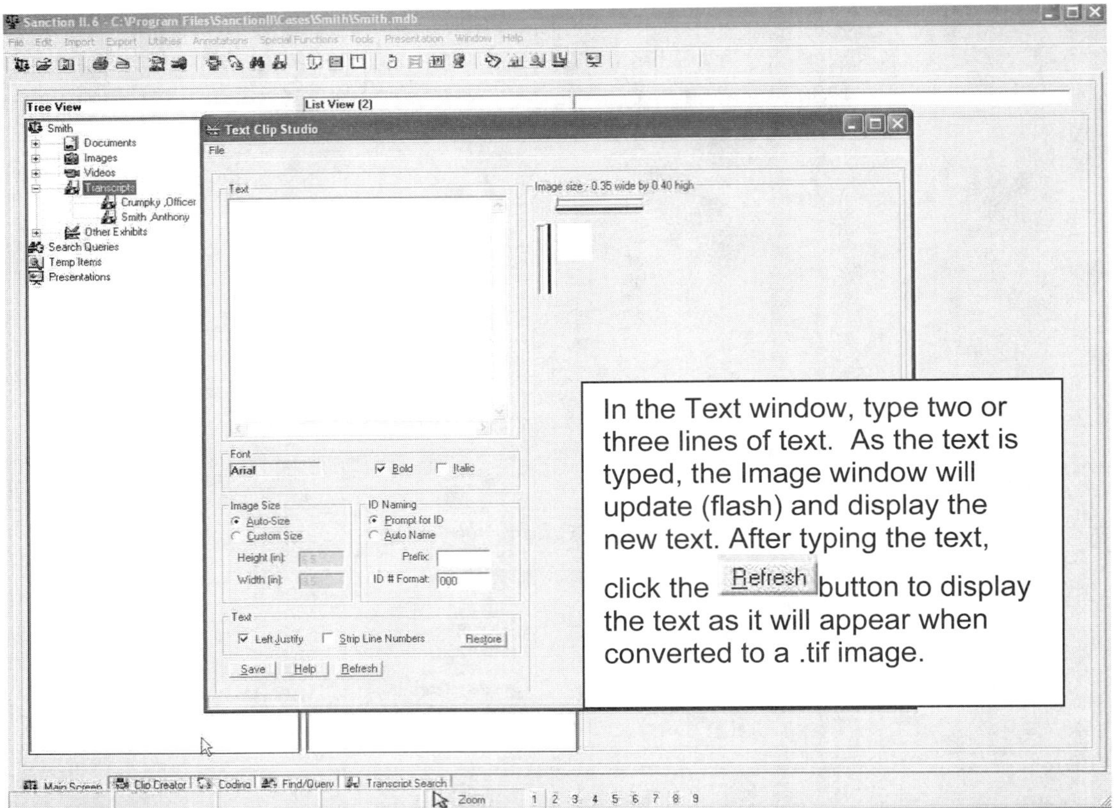
Text Clip Studio
In the Text window, type two or three lines of text. As the text is typed, the Image window will update (flash) and display the new text. After typing the text, click the Refresh button to display the text as it will appear when converted to a .tif image.

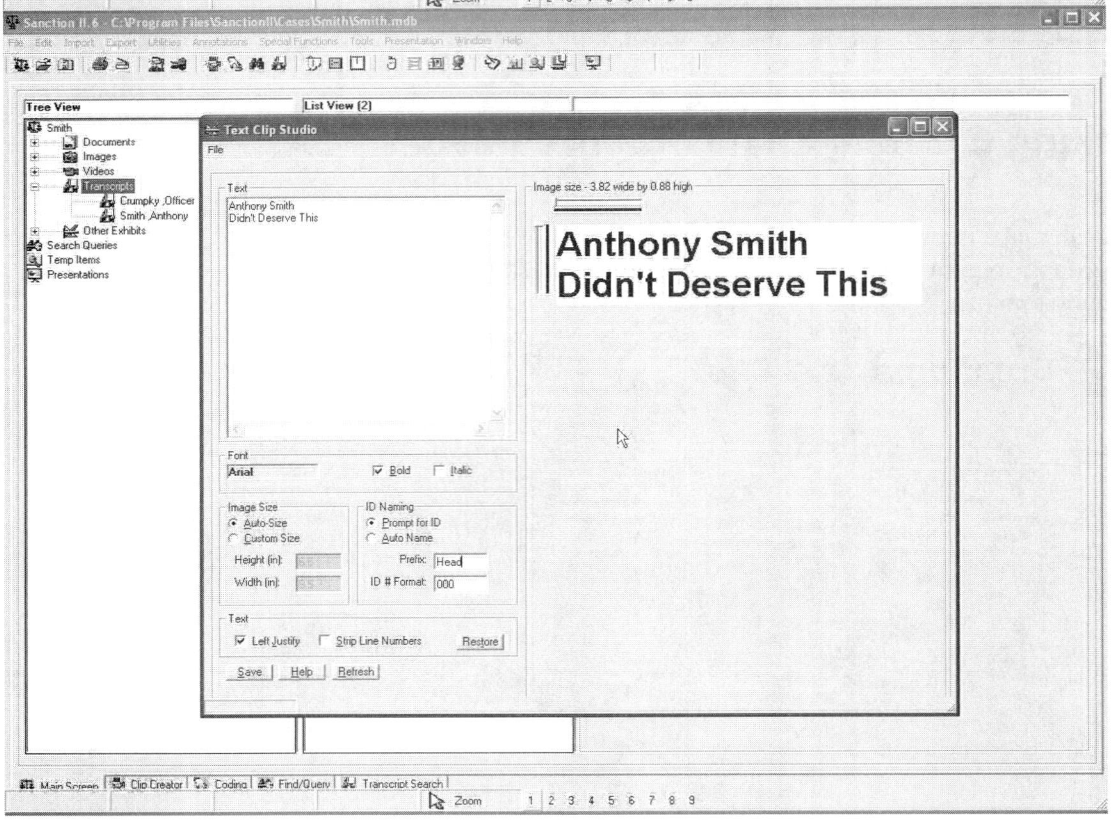
Text Clip Studio
Anthony Smith
Didn't Deserve This

See the Sanction manual for instructions on how to format your text clip. Once you are satisfied with the work, click on Save. You will be prompted for a name in a box like the one below. Use a short name for the ID. Click OK, and the box on the right will appear.

When you go back to the Sanction desktop and click on Text Clips in Other Exhibits, you can see what your clip looks like.

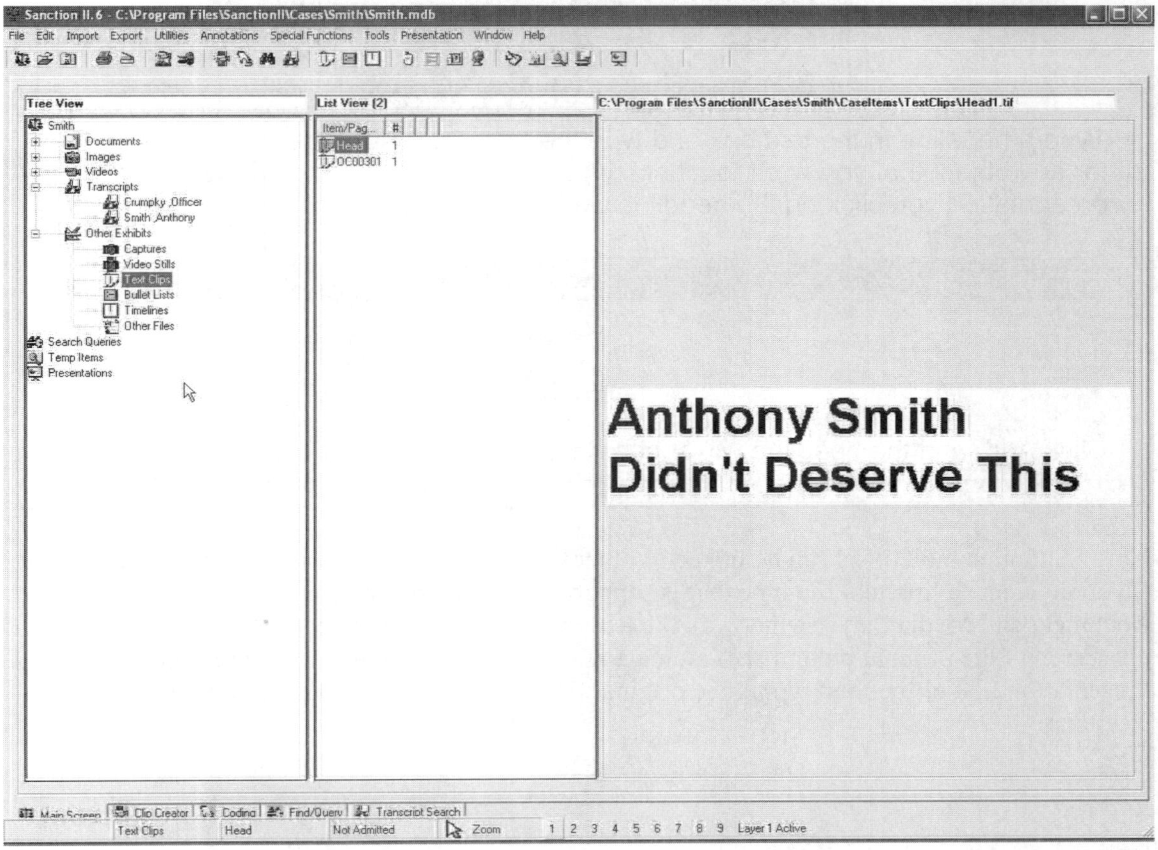

To learn about more advanced Clip Creator features, see the Sanction manual.

Creating Bullet Lists

Bullet lists consist of three major elements — a heading (optional), the actual bullet items, and optional hyperlinked case items. Creating a bullet list is probably one of the simplest tasks in Sanction: just type the text in the appropriate text box and press the Enter key.

To create a bullet list, click on the  icon. The following window will appear:

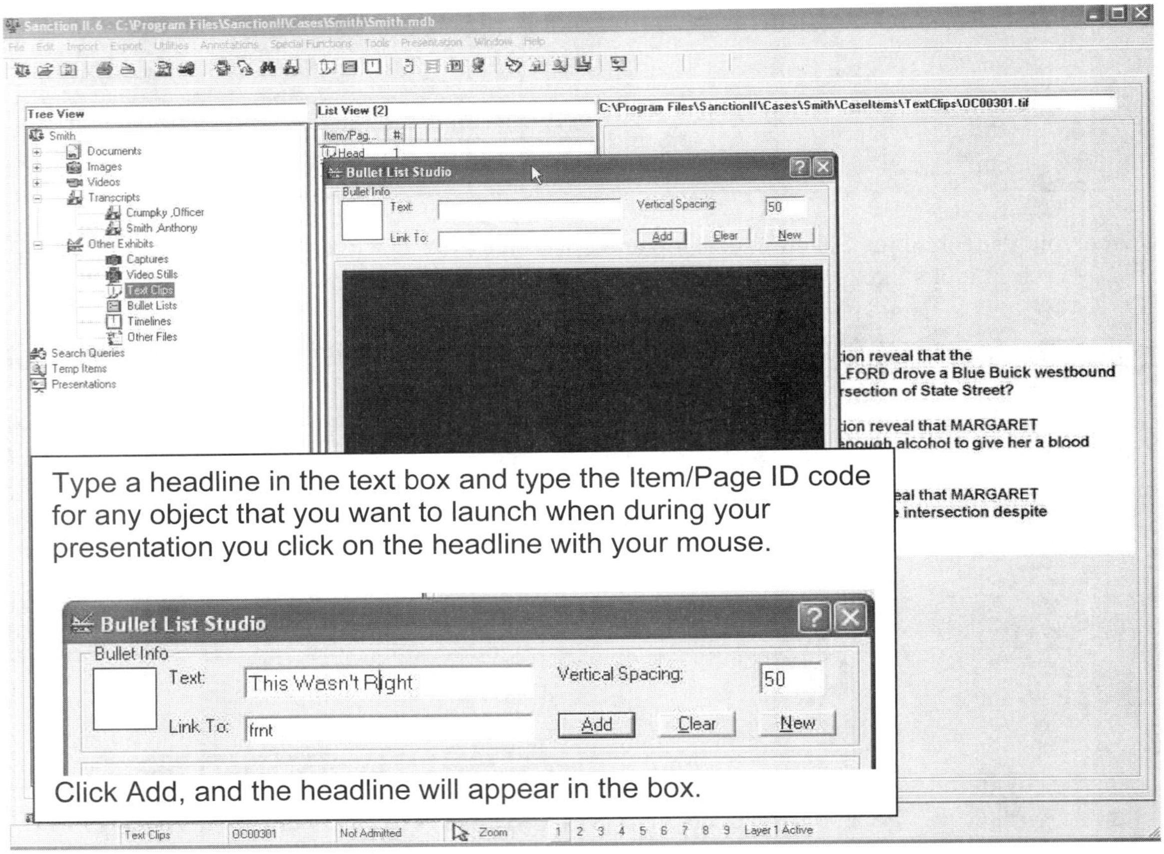

Note: Although bullet lists can be linked to other hyperlink documents, this is not recommended. If you do create a link to a file type that is supported only by the browser (as opposed to the Document and Media Player windows), the Restore Hyperlink button cannot be used to restore the screen to the original bullet list. You must reload the bullet list manually either from the Presentation List or by blind typing the original ID. (More on blind typing appears later in this chapter.)

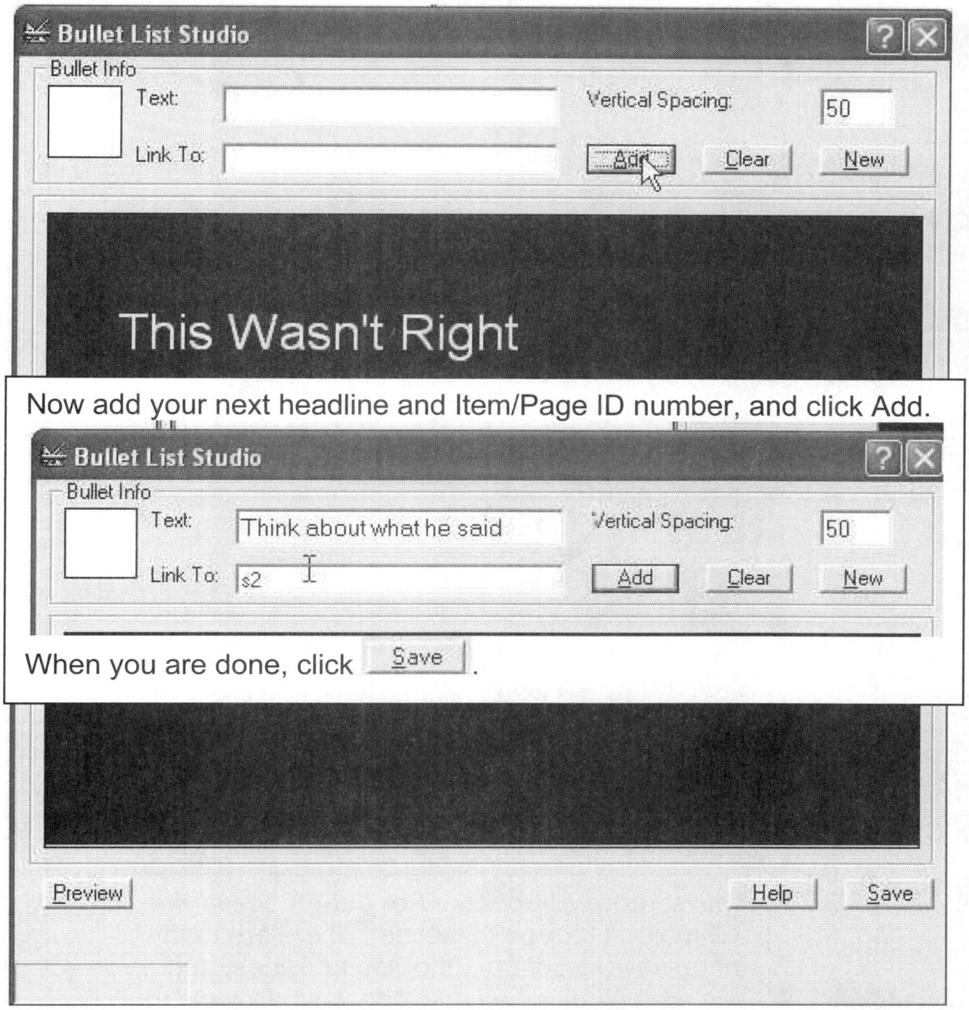

If you want to learn more about changing font color or background color, or about indenting and spacing bullet lists, see the Sanction manual. When you go back to the Sanction desktop and click on Bullet Lists in Other Exhibits, you can see what your clip looks like.

Using a TimeMap Timeline in Sanction

Sanction allows you to launch a TimeMap timeline from within Sanction.

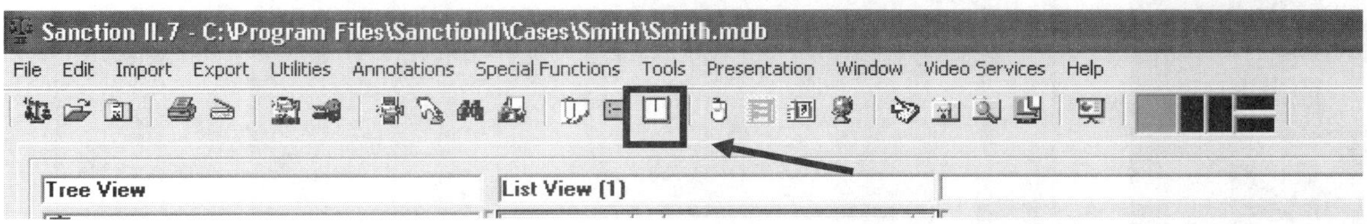

If you have TimeMap installed on your machine, you will have this icon on your Sanction toolbar. Sanction will look for a copy of it on your machine and include this icon if you do.

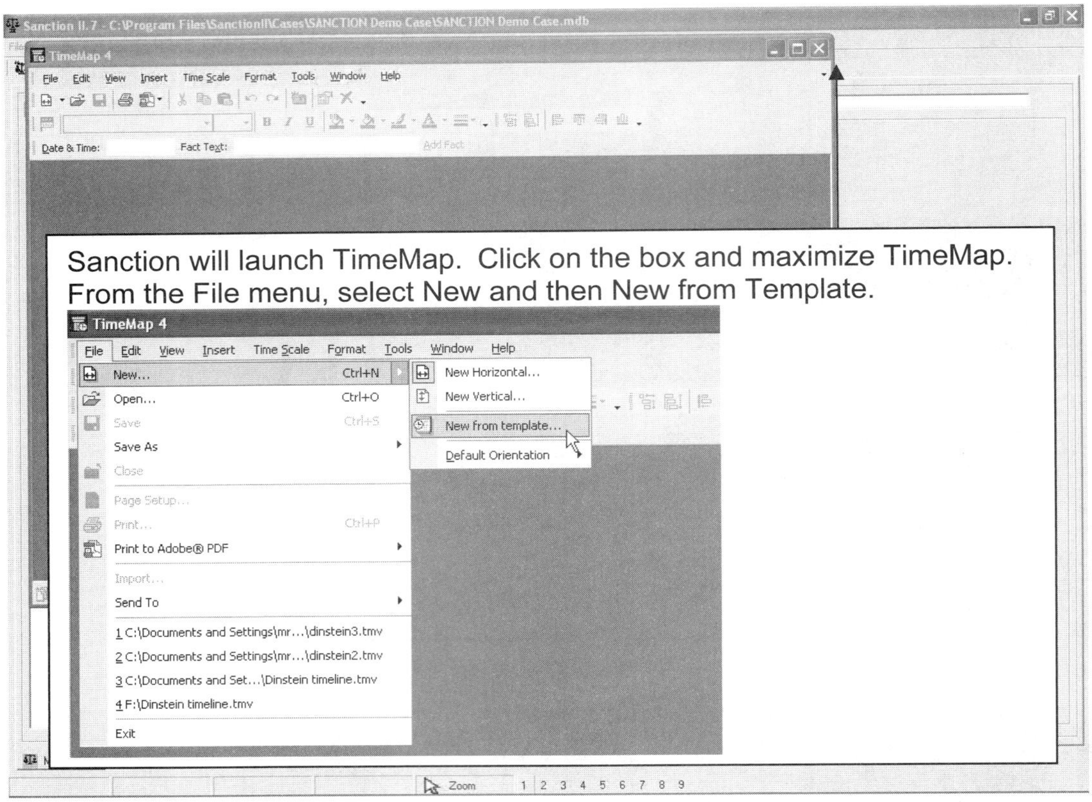
Sanction will launch TimeMap. Click on the box and maximize TimeMap.
From the File menu, select New and then New from Template.
TimeMap 4
File Edit View Insert Time Scale Format Tools Window Help
New... Ctrl+N
Open... Ctrl+O
Save Ctrl+S
Save As
Close
Page Setup...
Print... Ctrl+P
Print to Adobe® PDF
Import...
Send To
Exit
New Horizontal...
New Vertical...
New from template...
Default Orientation

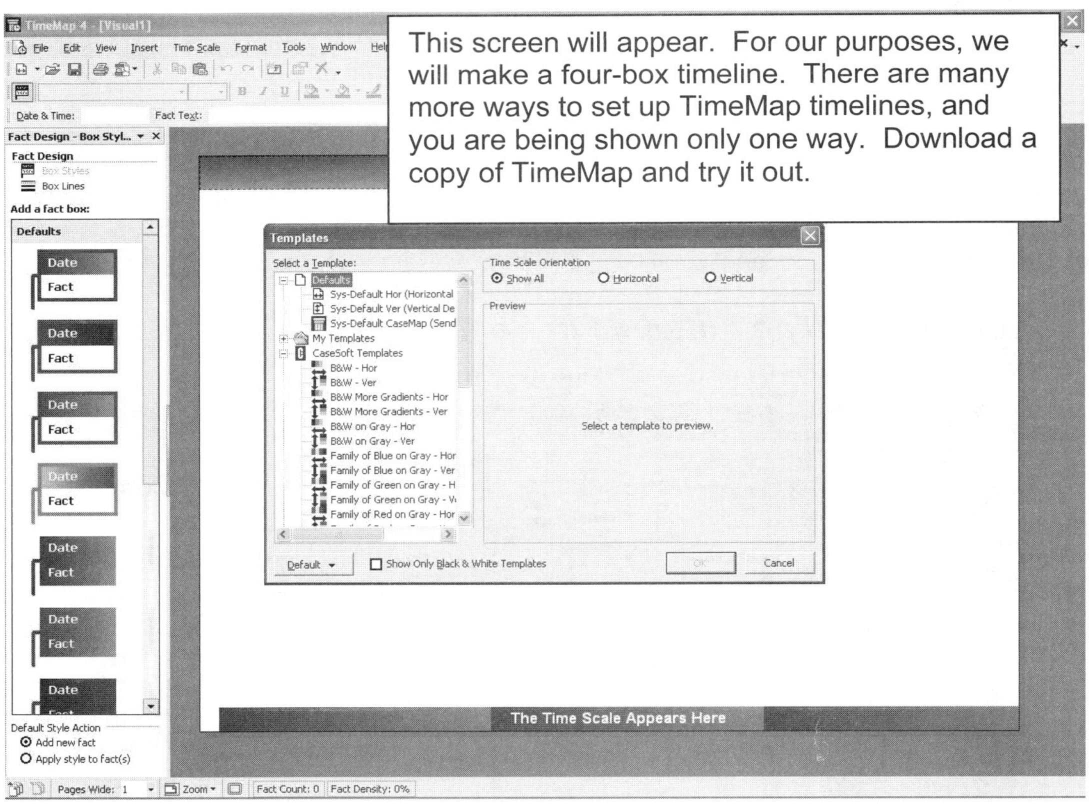
This screen will appear. For our purposes, we will make a four-box timeline. There are many more ways to set up TimeMap timelines, and you are being shown only one way. Download a copy of TimeMap and try it out.
Templates
Select a Template:
Time Scale Orientation
Show All
Horizontal
Vertical
Preview
Select a template to preview.
Show Only Black & White Templates
Cancel
The Time Scale Appears Here

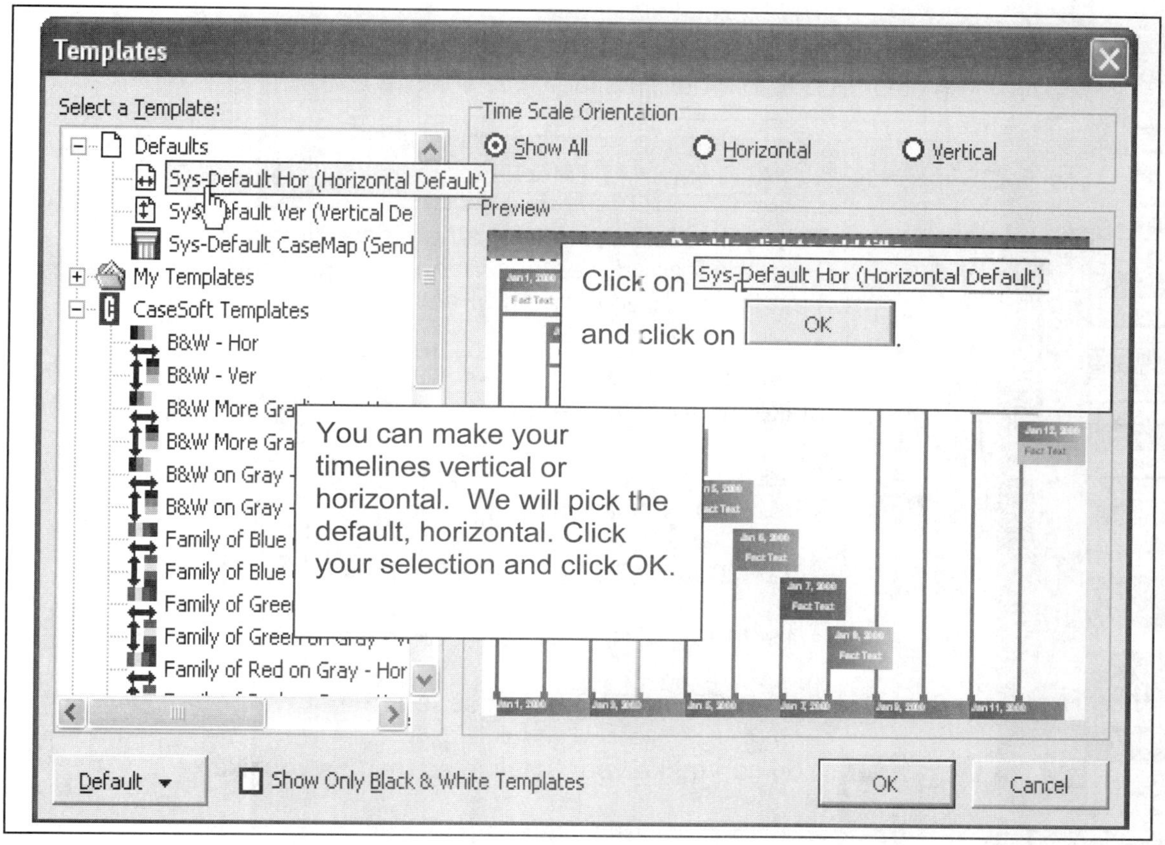
Templates
Select a Template:
Defaults
Sys-Default Hor (Horizontal Default)
Sys-Default CaseMap (Send
My Templates
CaseSoft Templates
B&W - Hor
B&W - Ver
Family of Red on Gray - Hor
Time Scale Orientation
Show All
Horizontal
Vertical
Preview
Click on Sys-Default Hor (Horizontal Default)
and click on OK.
You can make your timelines vertical or horizontal. We will pick the default, horizontal. Click your selection and click OK.
Default
Show Only Black & White Templates
OK
Cancel

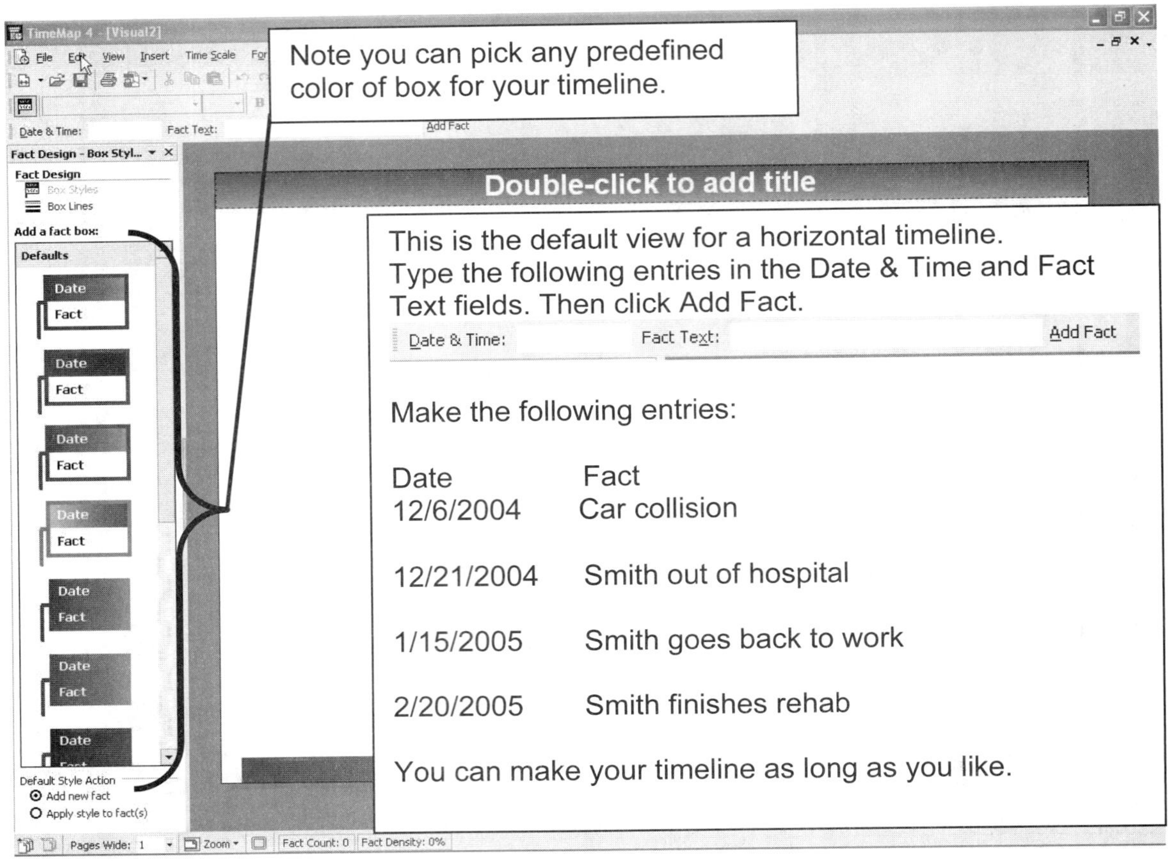
TimeMap 4 - [Visual2]
File Edit View Insert Time Scale
Note you can pick any predefined color of box for your timeline.
Date & Time: Fact Text: Add Fact
Fact Design - Box Styl...
Fact Design
Box Styles
Box Lines
Add a fact box:
Defaults
Date
Fact
Default Style Action
Add new fact
Apply style to fact(s)
Double-click to add title
This is the default view for a horizontal timeline. Type the following entries in the Date & Time and Fact Text fields. Then click Add Fact.
Date & Time: Fact Text: Add Fact
Make the following entries:
Date Fact
12/6/2004 Car collision
12/21/2004 Smith out of hospital
1/15/2005 Smith goes back to work
2/20/2005 Smith finishes rehab
You can make your timeline as long as you like.
Pages Wide: 1
Zoom
Fact Count: 0
Fact Density: 0%

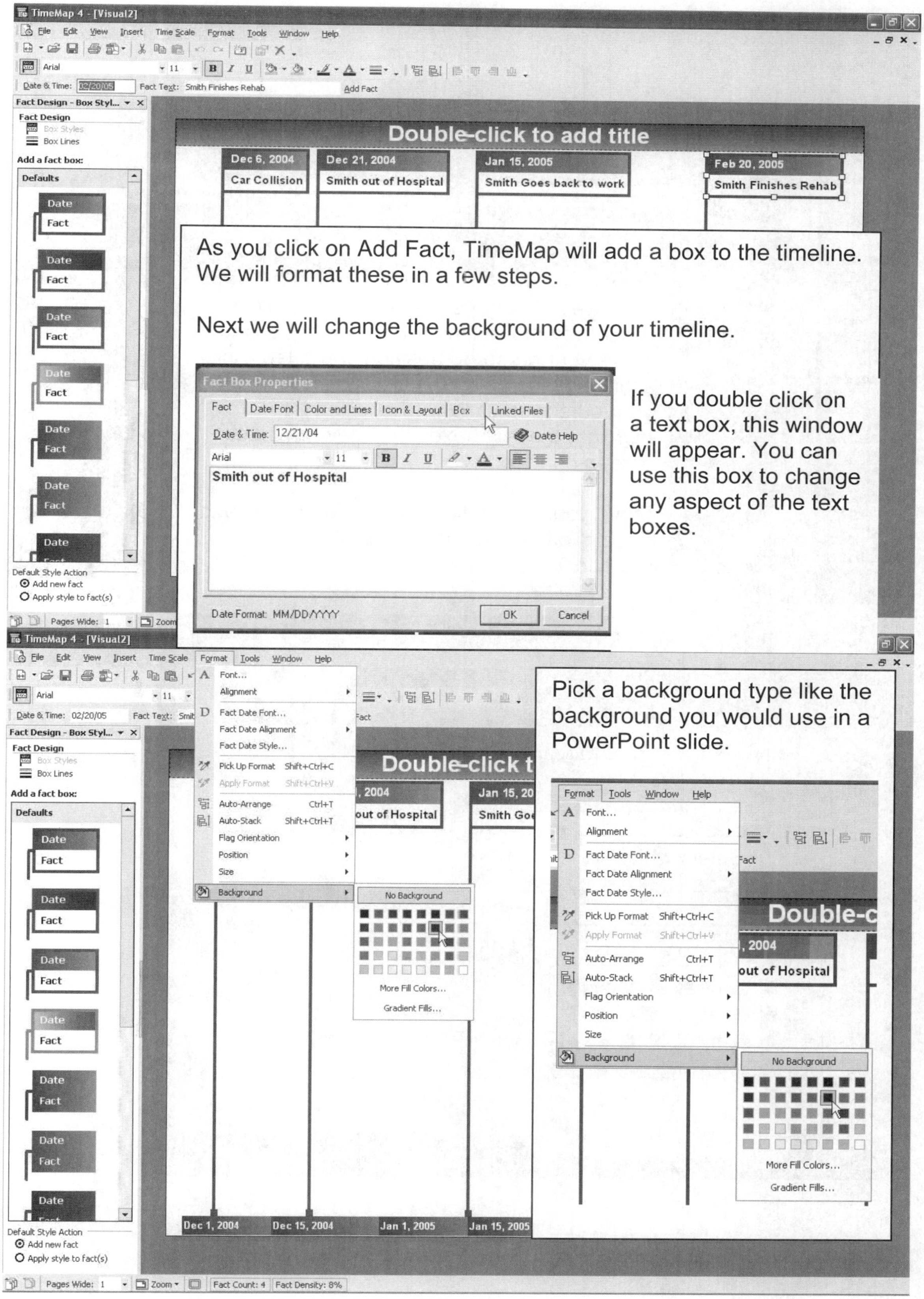
As you click on Add Fact, TimeMap will add a box to the timeline. We will format these in a few steps.
Next we will change the background of your timeline.
If you double click on a text box, this window will appear. You can use this box to change any aspect of the text boxes.
Pick a background type like the background you would use in a PowerPoint slide.

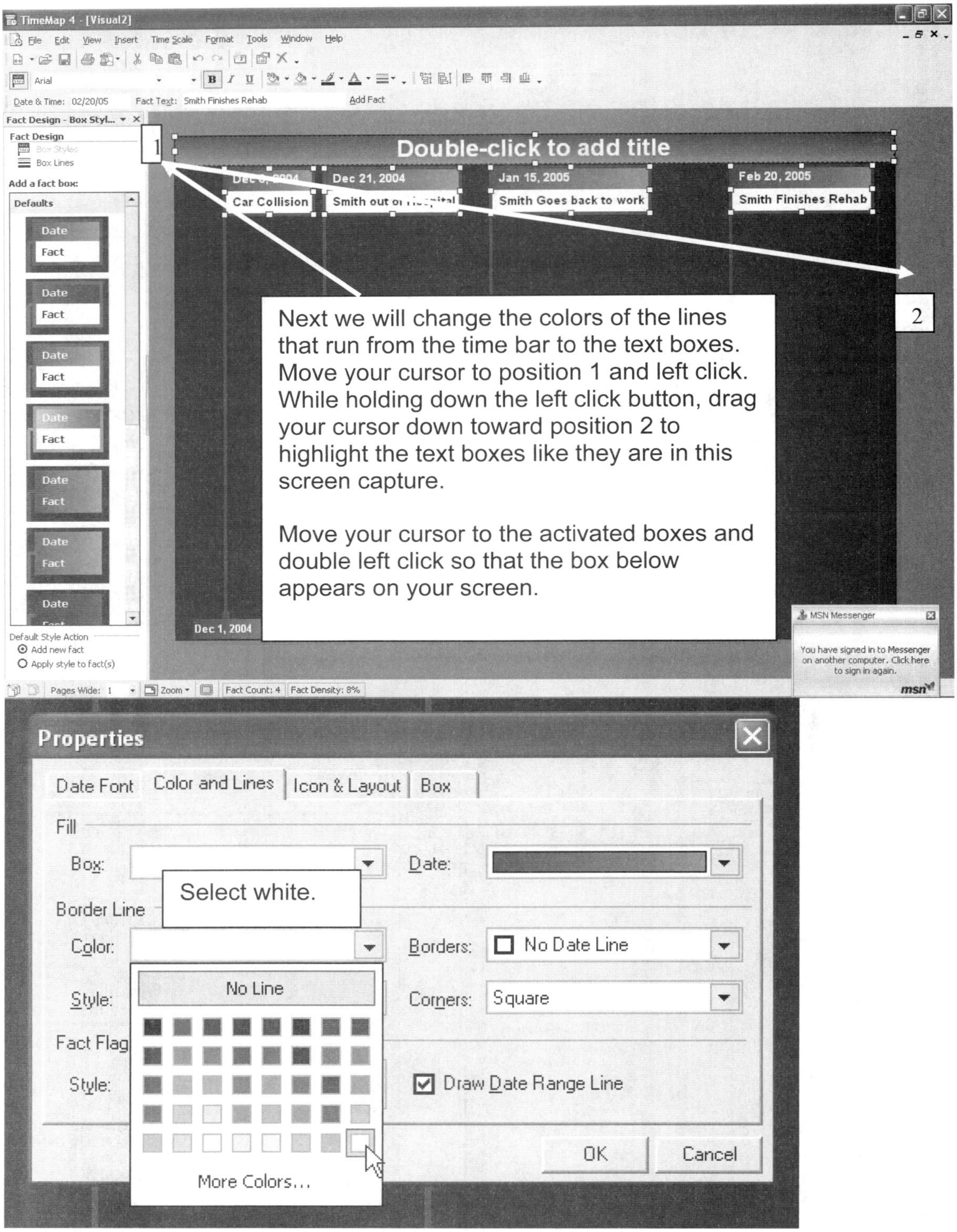
TimeMap 4 - [Visual2]
Double-click to add title
Dec 21, 2004
Jan 15, 2005
Feb 20, 2005
Car Collision
Smith Goes back to work
Smith Finishes Rehab
1
2
Next we will change the colors of the lines that run from the time bar to the text boxes. Move your cursor to position 1 and left click. While holding down the left click button, drag your cursor down toward position 2 to highlight the text boxes like they are in this screen capture.
Move your cursor to the activated boxes and double left click so that the box below appears on your screen.
Dec 1, 2004
Properties
Date Font
Color and Lines
Icon & Layout
Box
Fill
Box:
Date:
Select white.
Border Line
Color:
Borders:
No Date Line
No Line
Style:
Corners:
Square
Fact Flag
Style:
Draw Date Range Line
More Colors...
OK
Cancel

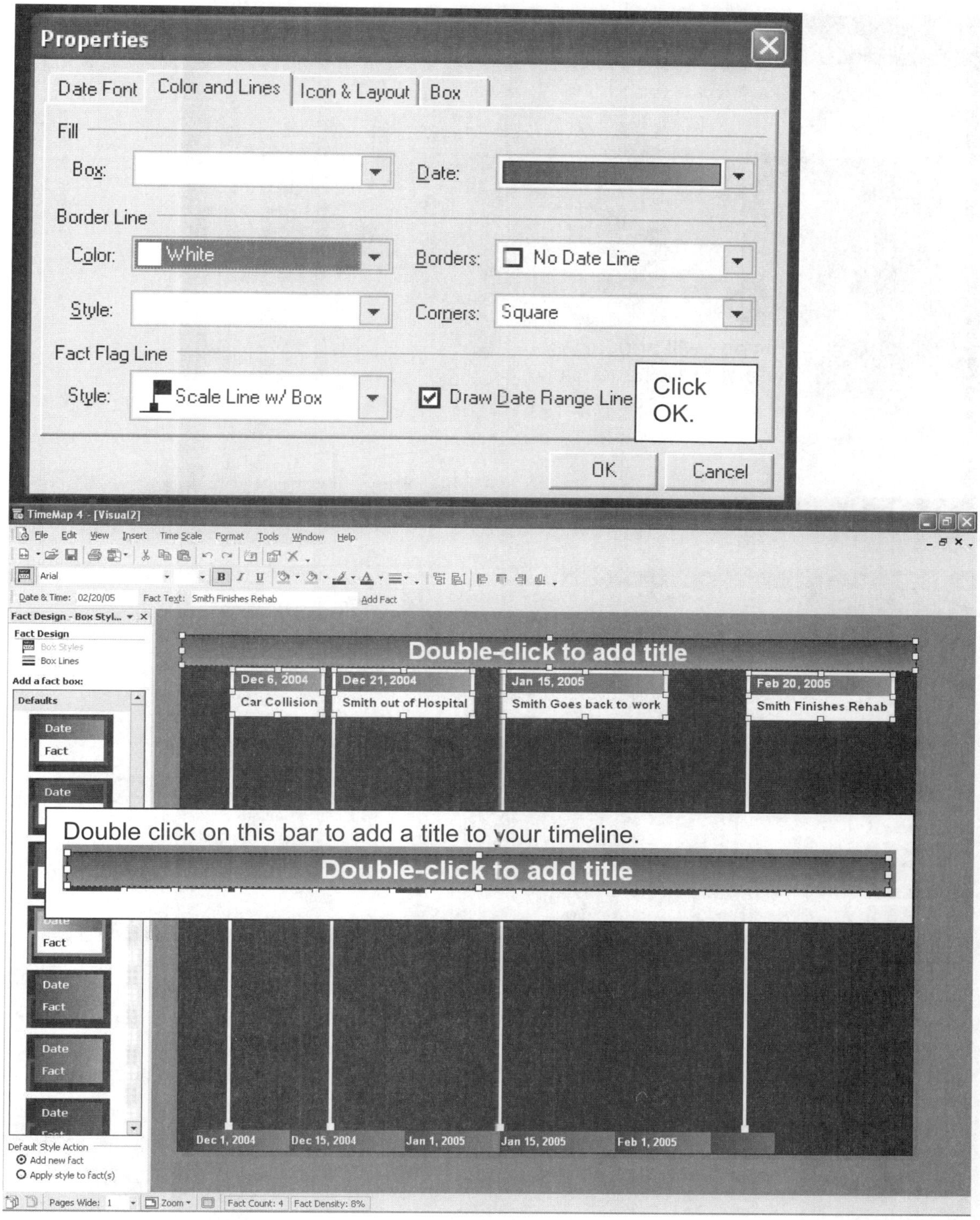
Properties
Date Font
Color and Lines
Icon & Layout
Box
Fill
Box:
Date:
Border Line
Color:
White
Borders:
No Date Line
Style:
Corners:
Square
Fact Flag Line
Style:
Scale Line w/ Box
Draw Date Range Line
Click OK.
OK
Cancel
TimeMap 4 - [Visual2]
Double-click to add title
Dec 6, 2004
Car Collision
Dec 21, 2004
Smith out of Hospital
Jan 15, 2005
Smith Goes back to work
Feb 20, 2005
Smith Finishes Rehab
Double click on this bar to add a title to your timeline.
Double-click to add title
Dec 1, 2004
Dec 15, 2004
Jan 1, 2005
Jan 15, 2005
Feb 1, 2005

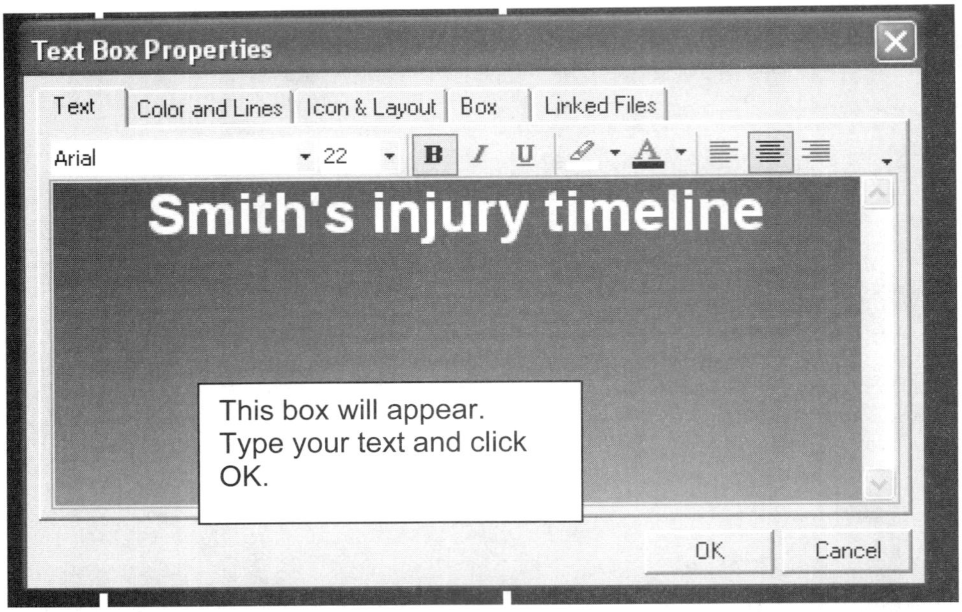
Text Box Properties
Text
Color and Lines
Icon & Layout
Box
Linked Files
Arial
22
Smith's injury timeline
This box will appear. Type your text and click OK.
OK
Cancel

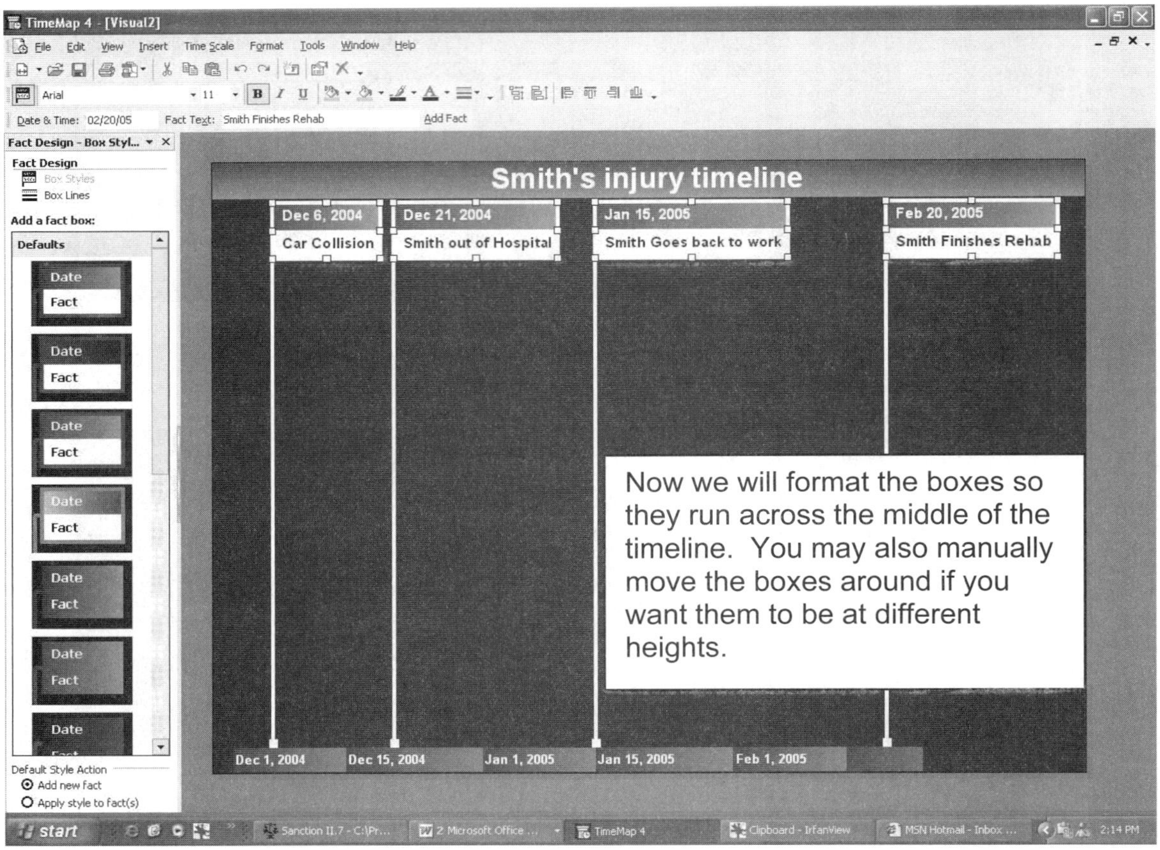
TimeMap 4 - [Visual2]
File
Edit
View
Insert
Time Scale
Format
Tools
Window
Help
Date & Time: 02/20/05
Fact Text: Smith Finishes Rehab
Add Fact
Fact Design - Box Styl...
Fact Design
Box Styles
Box Lines
Add a fact box:
Defaults
Date
Fact
Default Style Action
Add new fact
Apply style to fact(s)
Smith's injury timeline
Dec 6, 2004
Car Collision
Dec 21, 2004
Smith out of Hospital
Jan 15, 2005
Smith Goes back to work
Feb 20, 2005
Smith Finishes Rehab
Now we will format the boxes so they run across the middle of the timeline. You may also manually move the boxes around if you want them to be at different heights.
Dec 1, 2004
Dec 15, 2004
Jan 1, 2005
Jan 15, 2005
Feb 1, 2005
start
TimeMap 4
2:14 PM

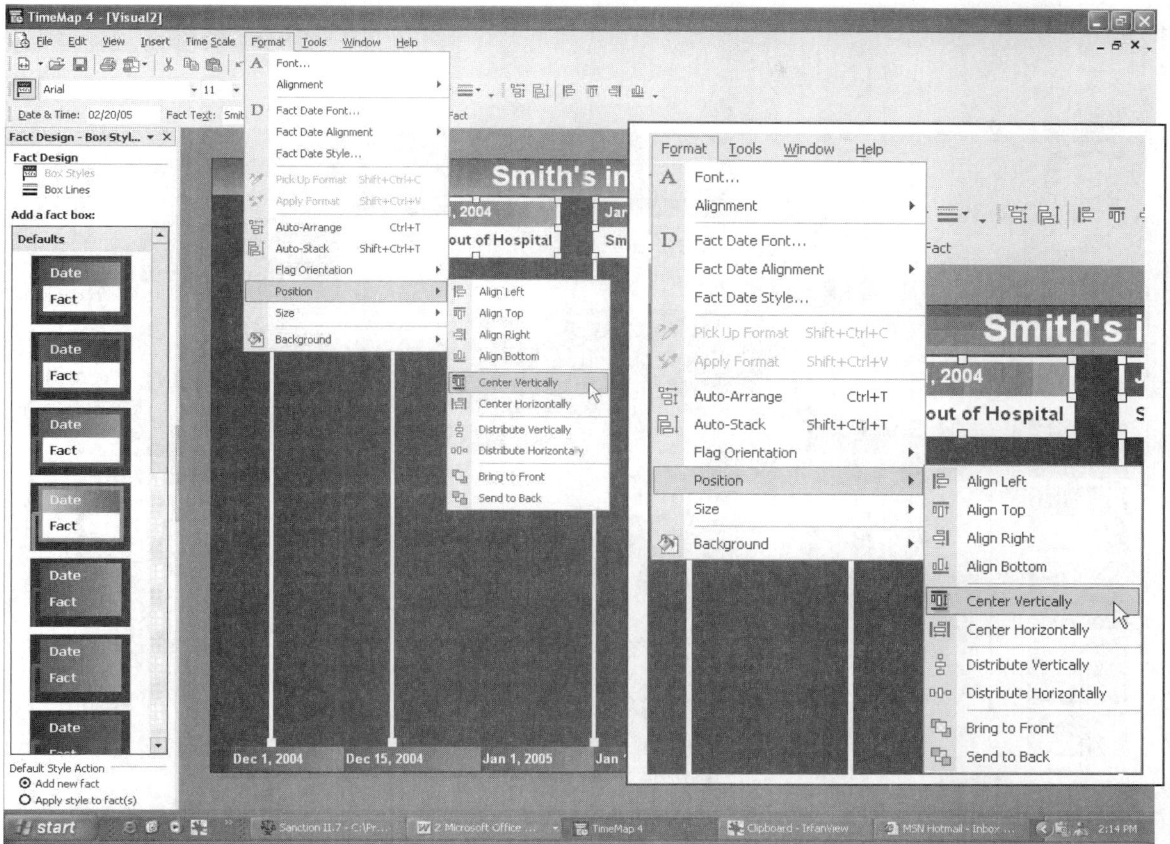
TimeMap 4 - [Visual2]
File Edit View Insert Time Scale Format Tools Window Help
Font...
Alignment
Fact Date Font...
Fact Date Alignment
Fact Date Style...
Pick Up Format Shift+Ctrl+C
Apply Format Shift+Ctrl+V
Auto-Arrange Ctrl+T
Auto-Stack Shift+Ctrl+T
Flag Orientation
Position
Size
Background
Align Left
Align Top
Align Right
Align Bottom
Center Vertically
Center Horizontally
Distribute Vertically
Distribute Horizontally
Bring to Front
Send to Back
Smith's i
out of Hospital
Dec 1, 2004
Dec 15, 2004
Jan 1, 2005
Fact Design - Box Styl...
Fact Design
Box Lines
Add a fact box:
Defaults
Date
Fact
Default Style Action
Add new fact
Apply style to fact(s)

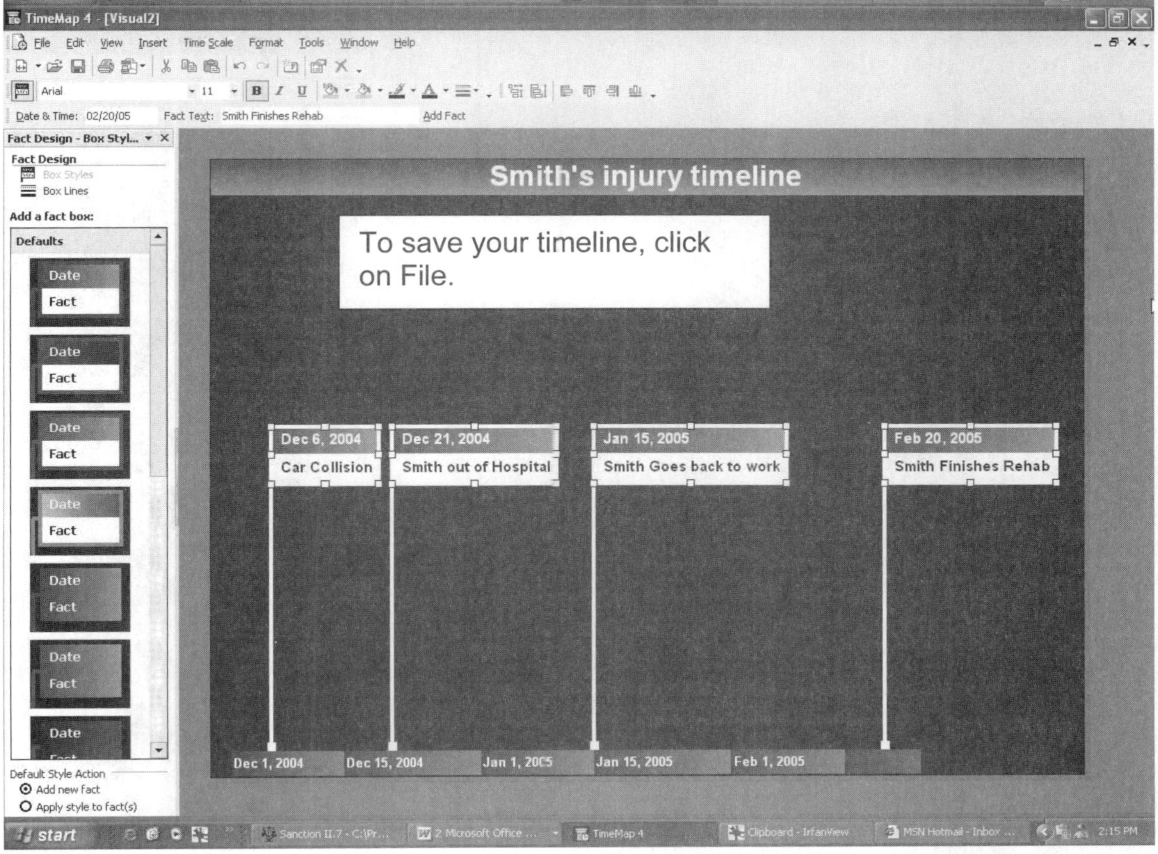
TimeMap 4 - [Visual2]
File Edit View Insert Time Scale Format Tools Window Help
Date & Time: 02/20/05
Fact Text: Smith Finishes Rehab
Add Fact
Smith's injury timeline
To save your timeline, click on File.
Dec 6, 2004
Car Collision
Dec 21, 2004
Smith out of Hospital
Jan 15, 2005
Smith Goes back to work
Feb 20, 2005
Smith Finishes Rehab
Dec 1, 2004
Dec 15, 2004
Jan 1, 2005
Jan 15, 2005
Feb 1, 2005
Fact Design - Box Styl...
Fact Design
Box Lines
Add a fact box:
Defaults
Date
Fact
Default Style Action
Add new fact
Apply style to fact(s)

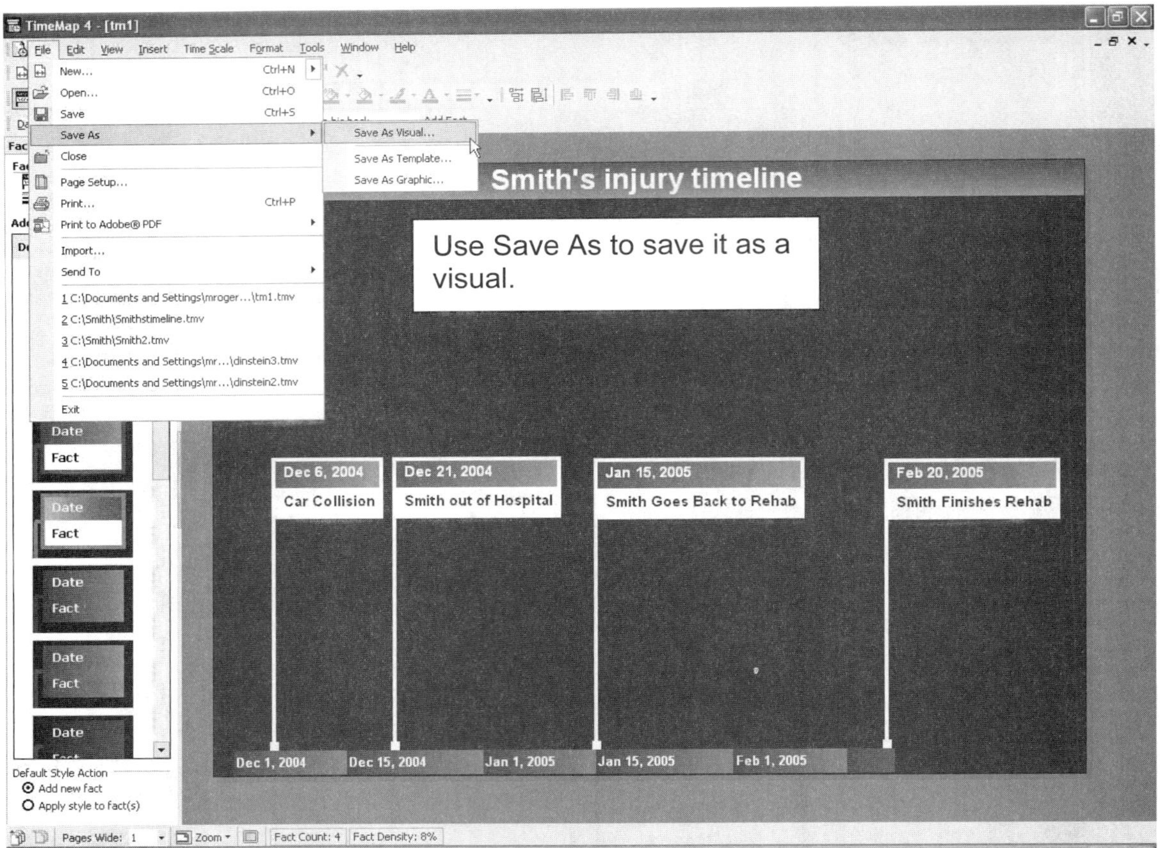
TimeMap 4 - [tm1]
File Edit View Insert Time Scale Format Tools Window Help
New... Ctrl+N
Open... Ctrl+O
Save Ctrl+S
Save As
Save As Visual...
Save As Template...
Save As Graphic...
Close
Page Setup...
Print... Ctrl+P
Print to Adobe® PDF
Import...
Send To
1 C:\Documents and Settings\mroger...\tm1.tmv
2 C:\Smith\Smithstimeline.tmv
3 C:\Smith\Smith2.tmv
4 C:\Documents and Settings\mr...\dinstein3.tmv
5 C:\Documents and Settings\mr...\dinstein2.tmv
Exit
Smith's injury timeline
Use Save As to save it as a visual.
Dec 6, 2004
Car Collision
Dec 21, 2004
Smith out of Hospital
Jan 15, 2005
Smith Goes Back to Rehab
Feb 20, 2005
Smith Finishes Rehab
Dec 1, 2004
Dec 15, 2004
Jan 1, 2005
Jan 15, 2005
Feb 1, 2005
Default Style Action
Add new fact
Apply style to fact(s)
Pages Wide: 1
Zoom
Fact Count: 4
Fact Density: 8%

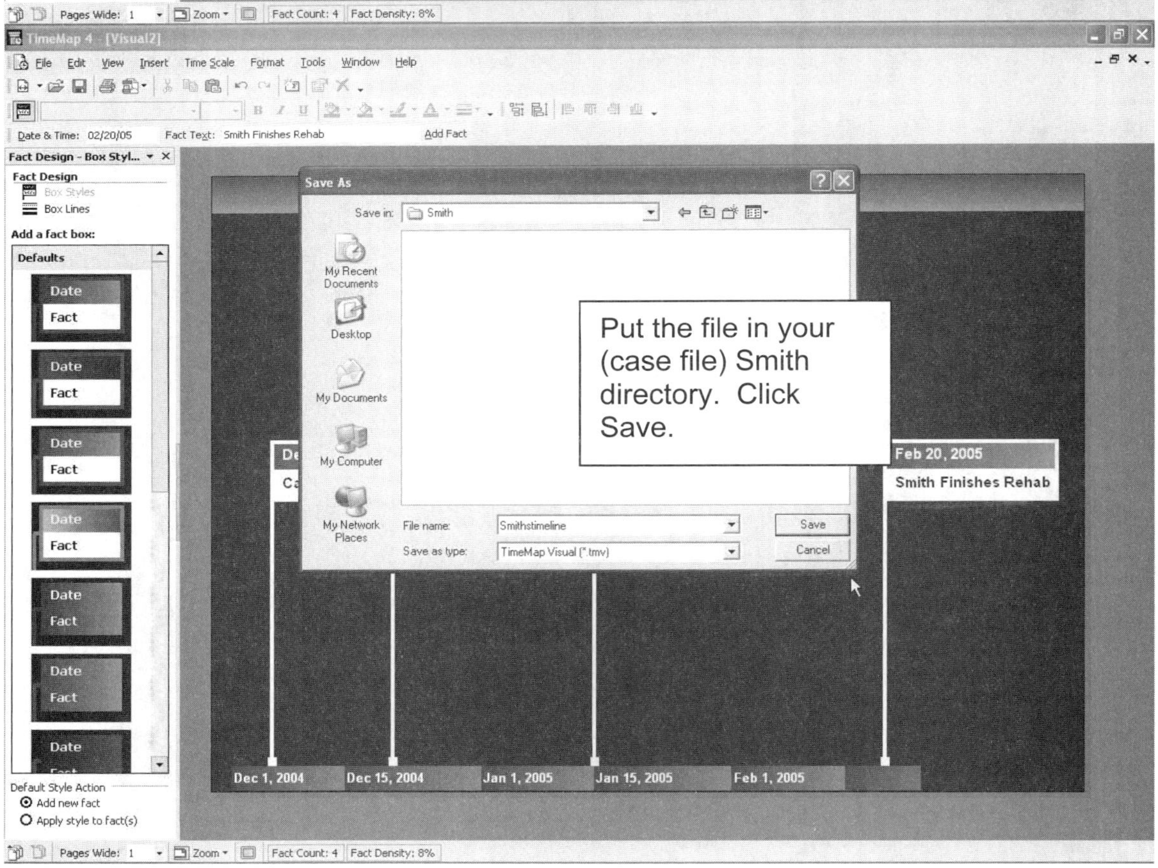
TimeMap 4 - [Visual2]
File Edit View Insert Time Scale Format Tools Window Help
Date & Time: 02/20/05
Fact Text: Smith Finishes Rehab
Add Fact
Fact Design - Box Styl...
Fact Design
Box Styles
Box Lines
Add a fact box:
Defaults
Save As
Save in: Smith
My Recent Documents
Desktop
My Documents
My Computer
My Network Places
File name: Smithstimeline
Save as type: TimeMap Visual (*.tmv)
Save
Cancel
Put the file in your (case file) Smith directory. Click Save.
Feb 20, 2005
Smith Finishes Rehab
Dec 1, 2004
Dec 15, 2004
Jan 1, 2005
Jan 15, 2005
Feb 1, 2005
Default Style Action
Add new fact
Apply style to fact(s)
Pages Wide: 1
Zoom
Fact Count: 4
Fact Density: 8%

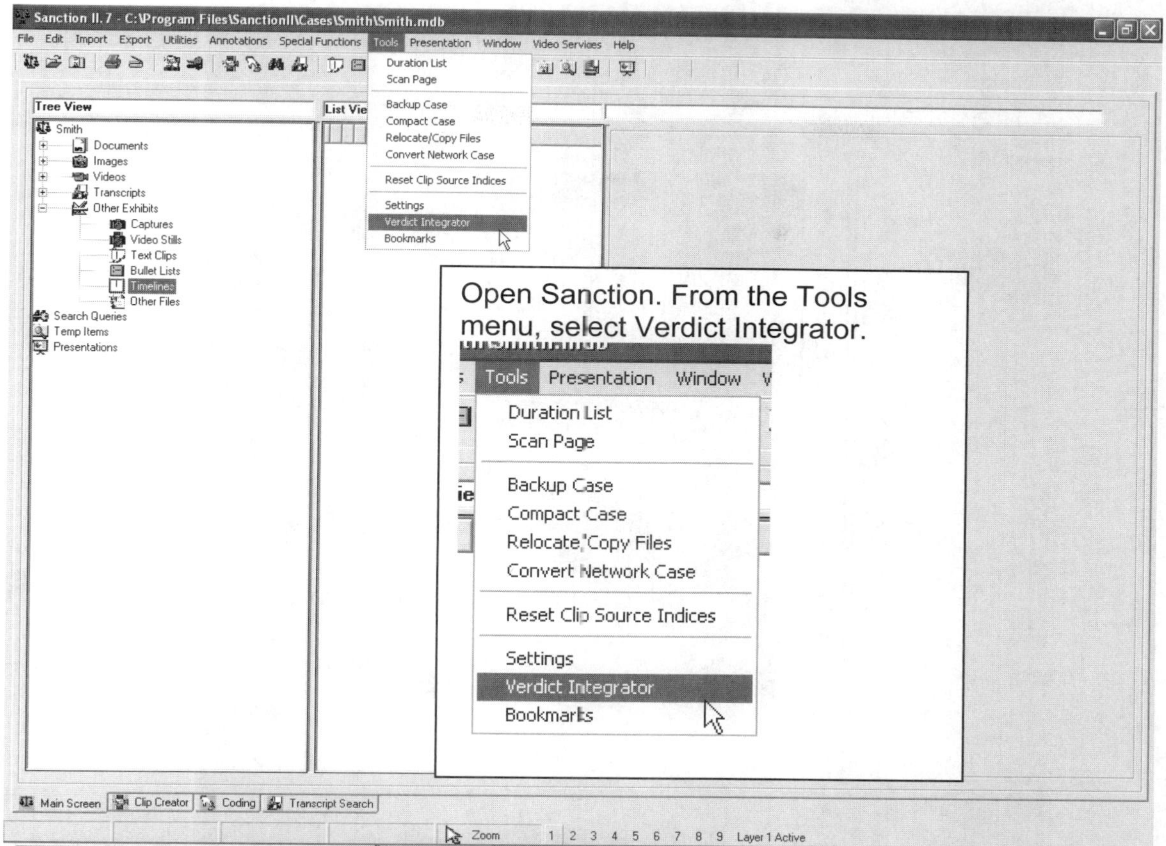

Open Sanction. From the Tools menu, select Verdict Integrator.

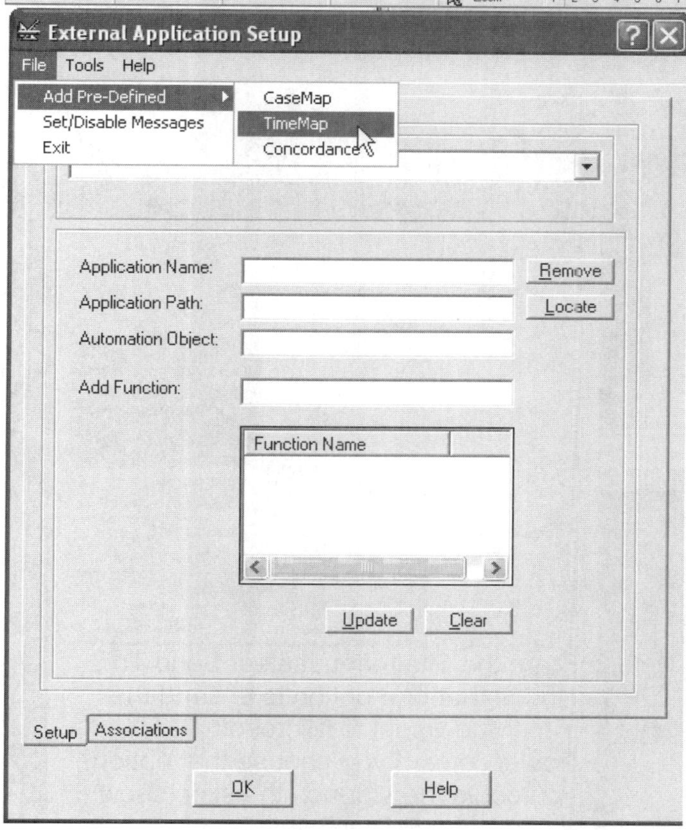

This window will appear. From the File menu, select Add Pre-Defined. Then select TimeMap. Click OK.

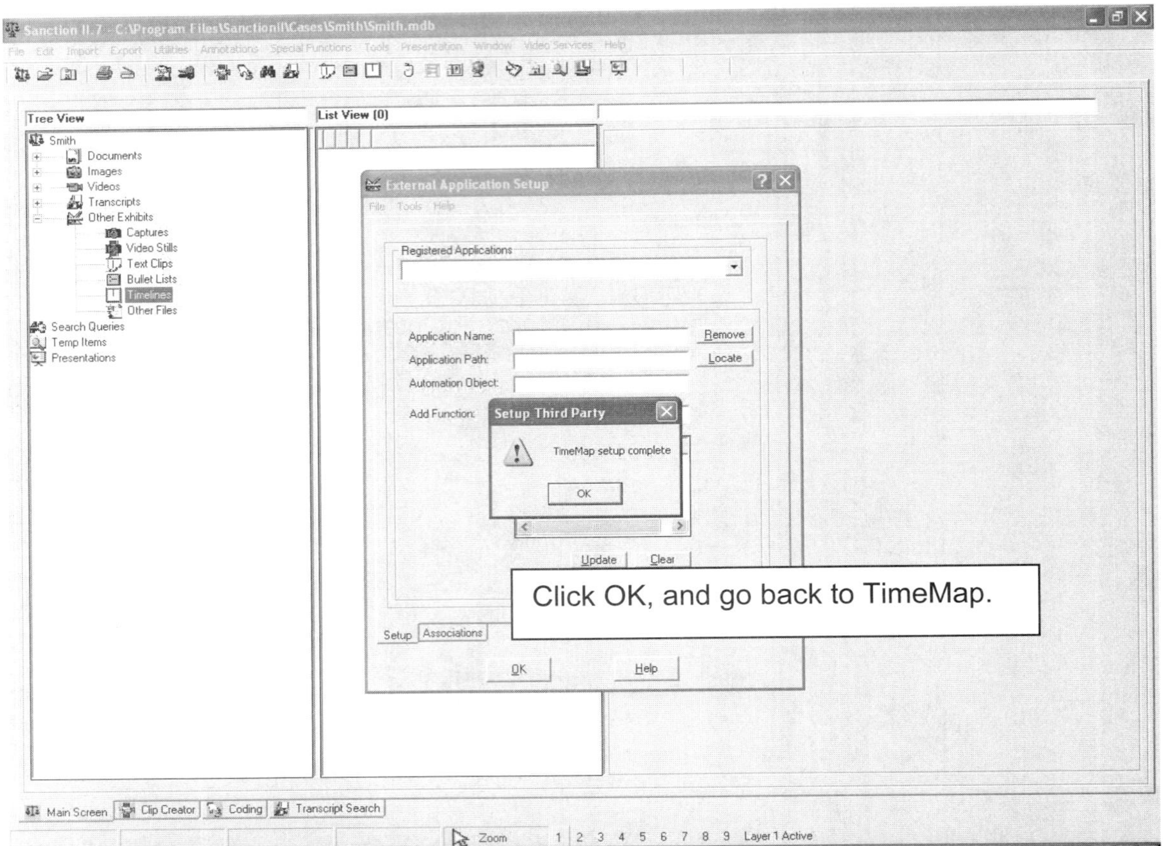
Click OK, and go back to TimeMap.

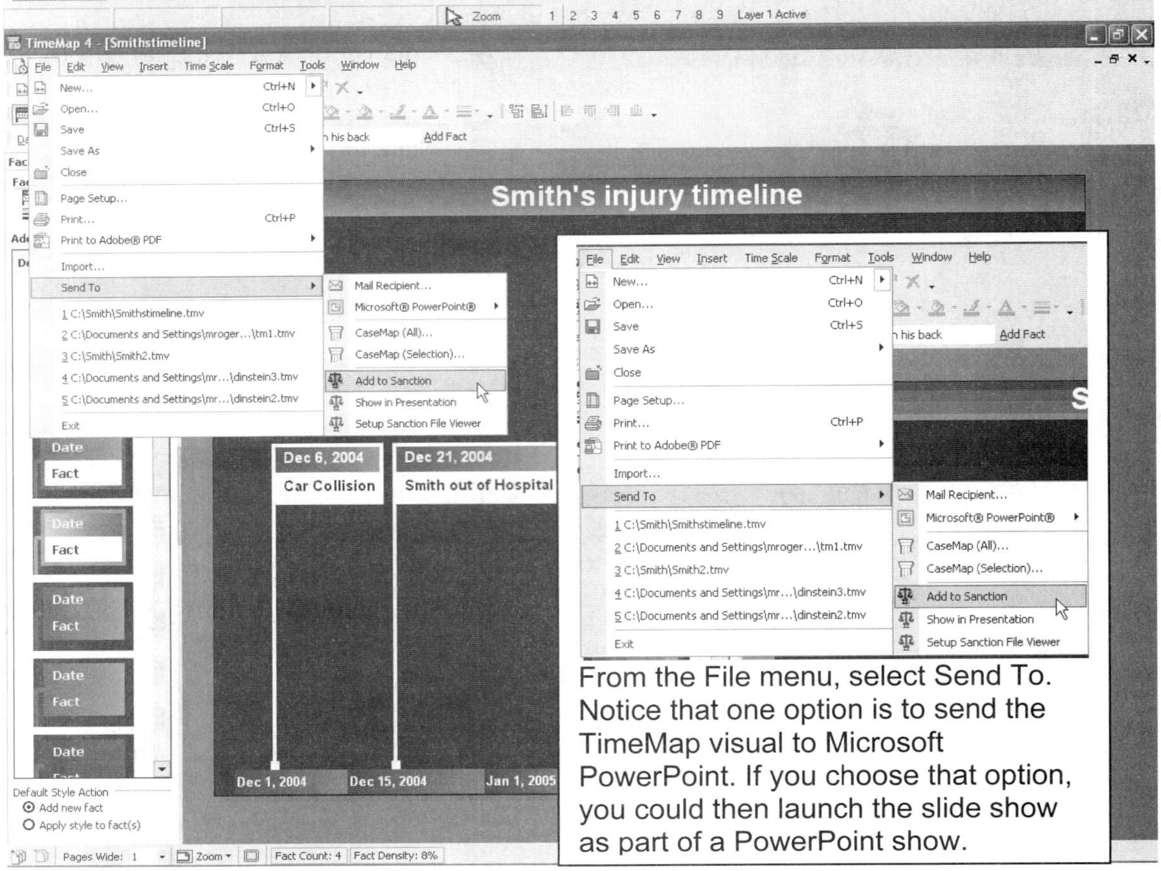
From the File menu, select Send To. Notice that one option is to send the TimeMap visual to Microsoft PowerPoint. If you choose that option, you could then launch the slide show as part of a PowerPoint show.

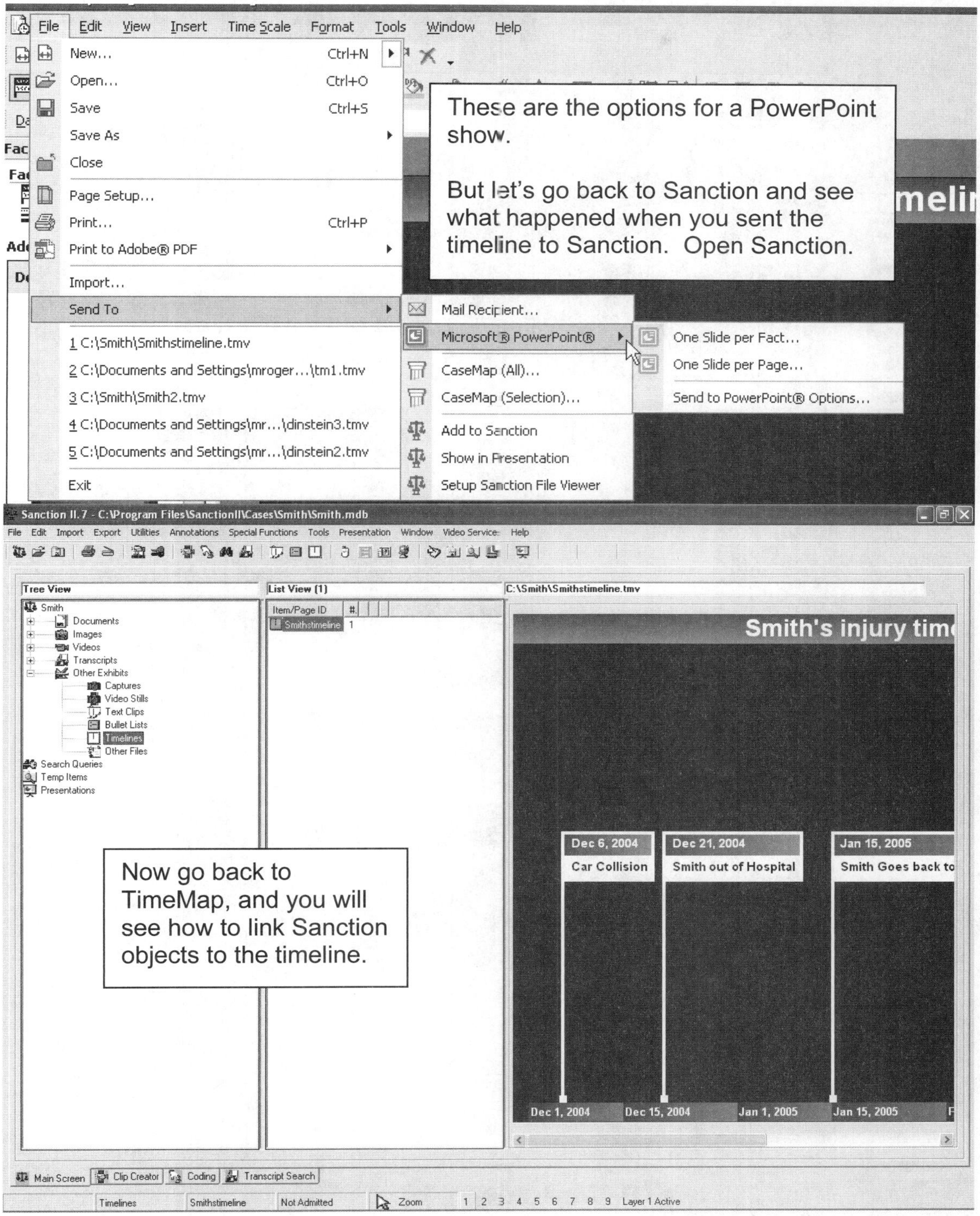
File Edit View Insert Time Scale Format Tools Window Help
New... Ctrl+N
Open... Ctrl+O
Save Ctrl+S
Save As
Close
Page Setup...
Print... Ctrl+P
Print to Adobe® PDF
Import...
Send To
1 C:\Smith\Smithstimeline.tmv
2 C:\Documents and Settings\mroger...\tm1.tmv
3 C:\Smith\Smith2.tmv
4 C:\Documents and Settings\mr...\dinstein3.tmv
5 C:\Documents and Settings\mr...\dinstein2.tmv
Exit
Mail Recipient...
Microsoft® PowerPoint®
CaseMap (All)...
CaseMap (Selection)...
Add to Sanction
Show in Presentation
Setup Sanction File Viewer
One Slide per Fact...
One Slide per Page...
Send to PowerPoint® Options...
These are the options for a PowerPoint show.
But let's go back to Sanction and see what happened when you sent the timeline to Sanction. Open Sanction.
Sanction II.7 - C:\Program Files\SanctionII\Cases\Smith\Smith.mdb
Tree View
List View (1)
C:\Smith\Smithstimeline.tmv
Smith
Documents
Images
Videos
Transcripts
Other Exhibits
Captures
Video Stills
Text Clips
Bullet Lists
Timelines
Other Files
Search Queries
Temp Items
Presentations
Item/Page ID
Smithstimeline
Smith's injury tim
Dec 6, 2004
Car Collision
Dec 21, 2004
Smith out of Hospital
Jan 15, 2005
Smith Goes back to
Dec 1, 2004
Dec 15, 2004
Jan 1, 2005
Jan 15, 2005
Now go back to TimeMap, and you will see how to link Sanction objects to the timeline.
Main Screen
Clip Creator
Coding
Transcript Search
Timelines
Smithstimeline
Not Admitted
Zoom
Layer 1 Active

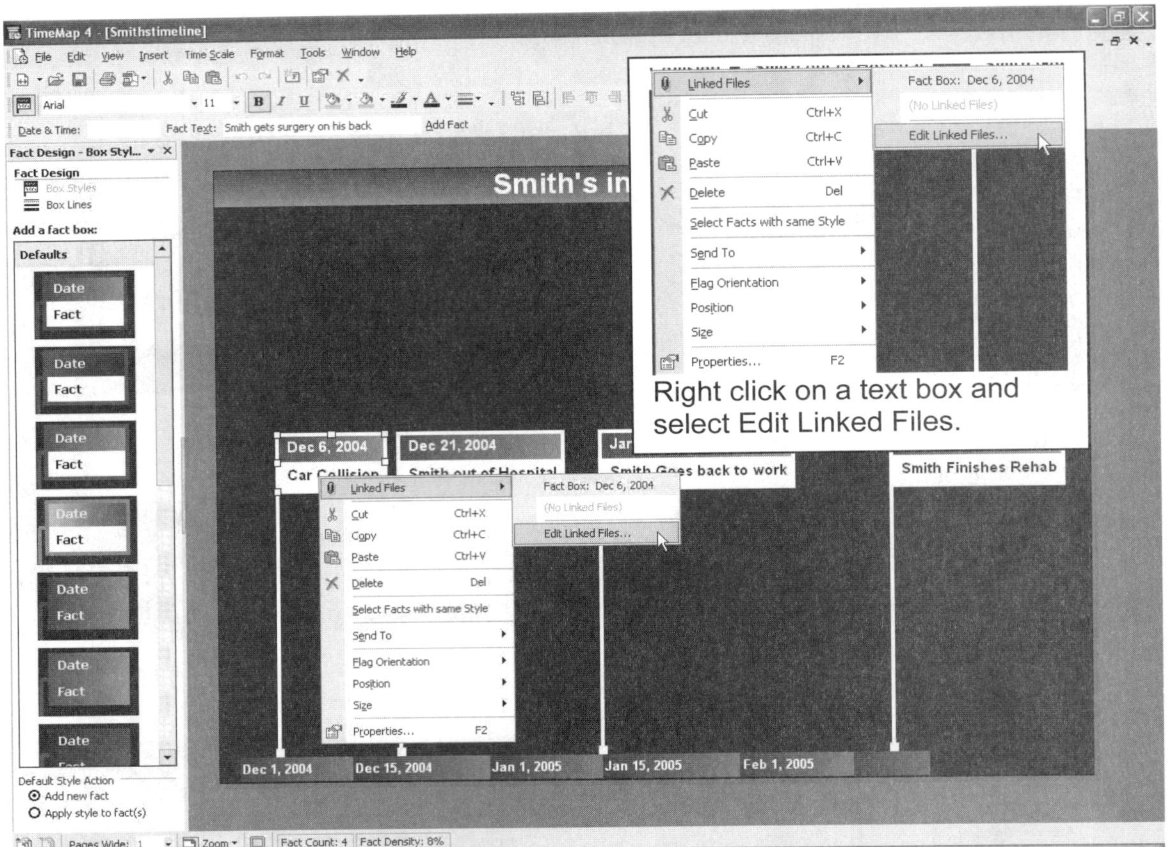
Right click on a text box and select Edit Linked Files.

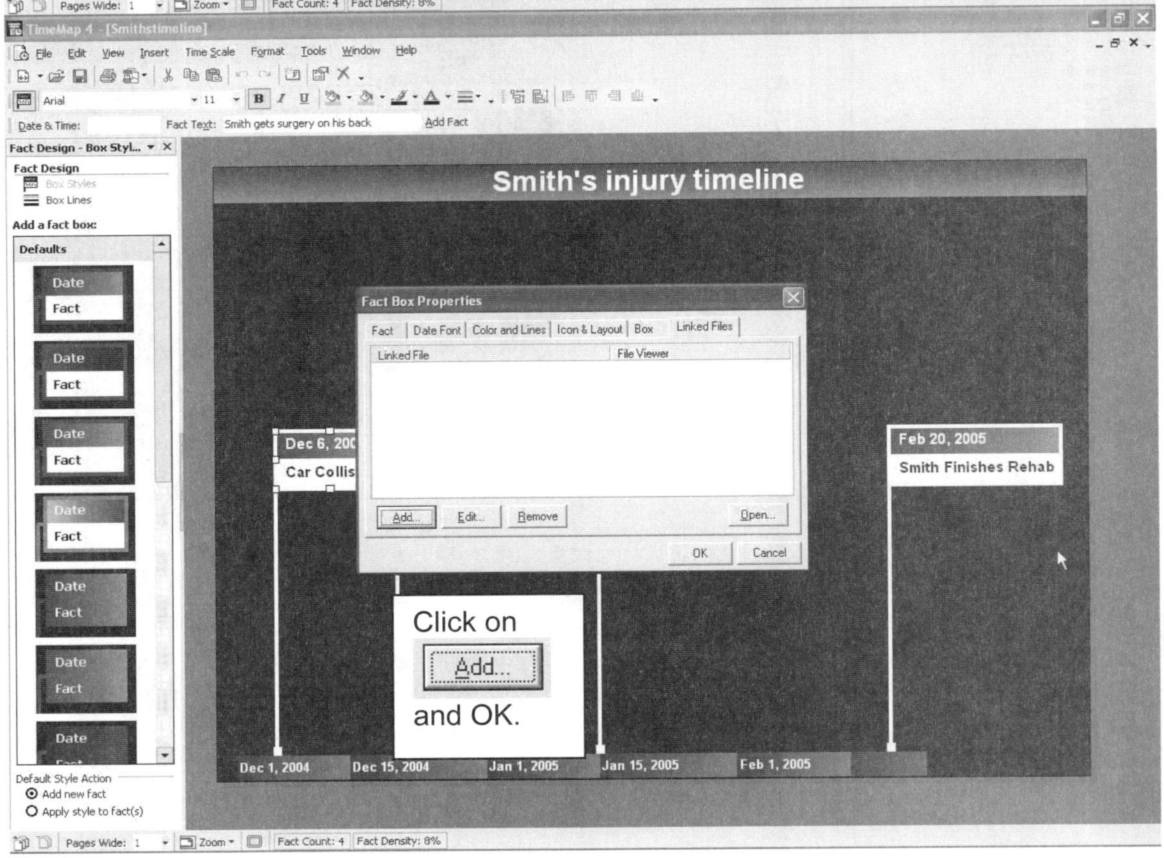
Click on Add... and OK.

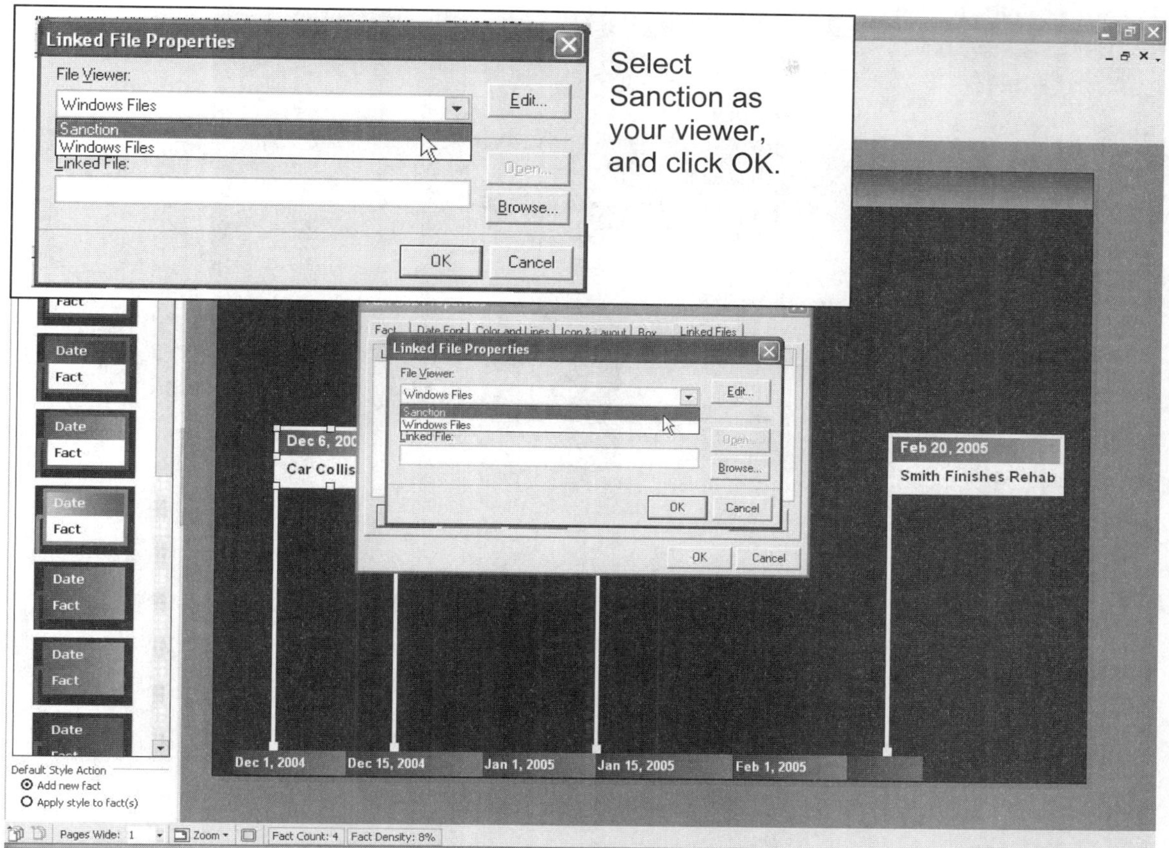
Linked File Properties
File Viewer:
Windows Files
Sanction
Windows Files
Linked File:
Edit...
Open...
Browse...
OK
Cancel
Select Sanction as your viewer, and click OK.
Feb 20, 2005
Smith Finishes Rehab
Dec 1, 2004
Dec 15, 2004
Jan 1, 2005
Jan 15, 2005
Feb 1, 2005

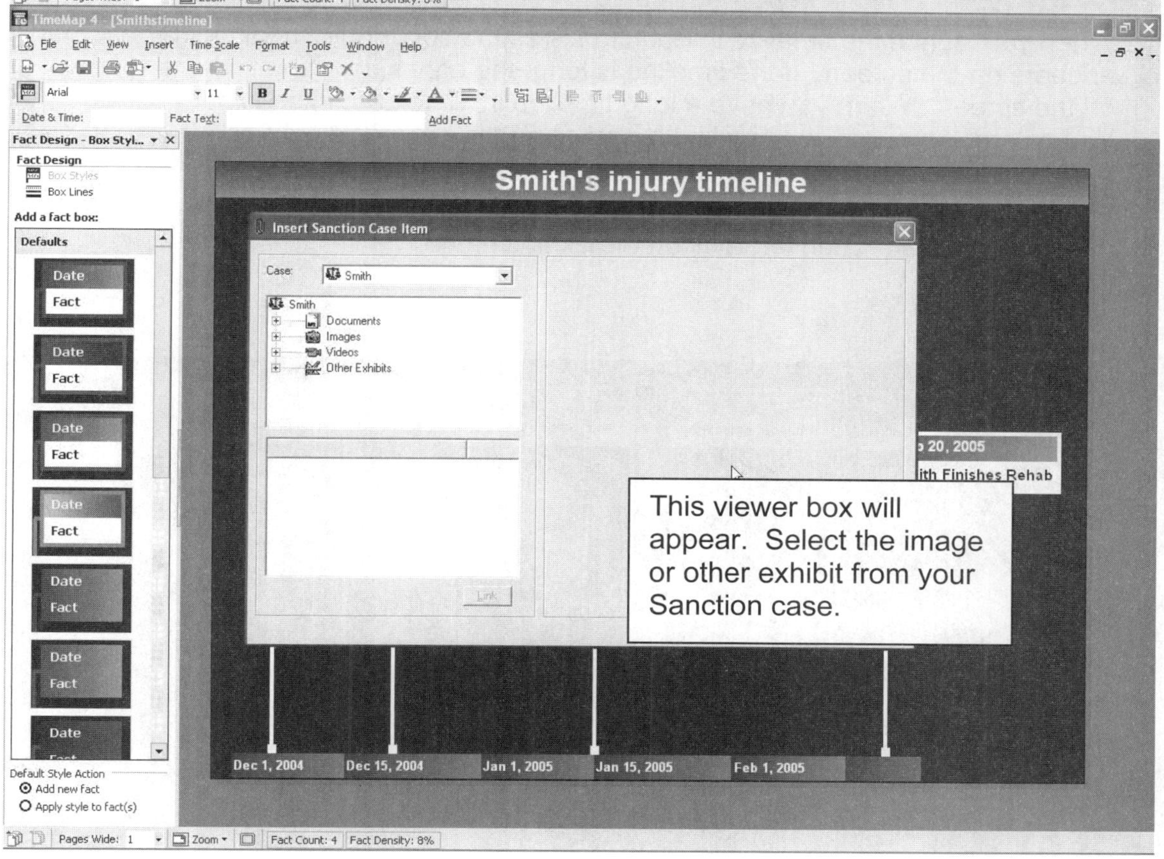
TimeMap 4 - [Smithstimeline]
Smith's injury timeline
Insert Sanction Case Item
Case:
Smith
Documents
Images
Videos
Other Exhibits
This viewer box will appear. Select the image or other exhibit from your Sanction case.
Dec 1, 2004
Dec 15, 2004
Jan 1, 2005
Jan 15, 2005
Feb 1, 2005

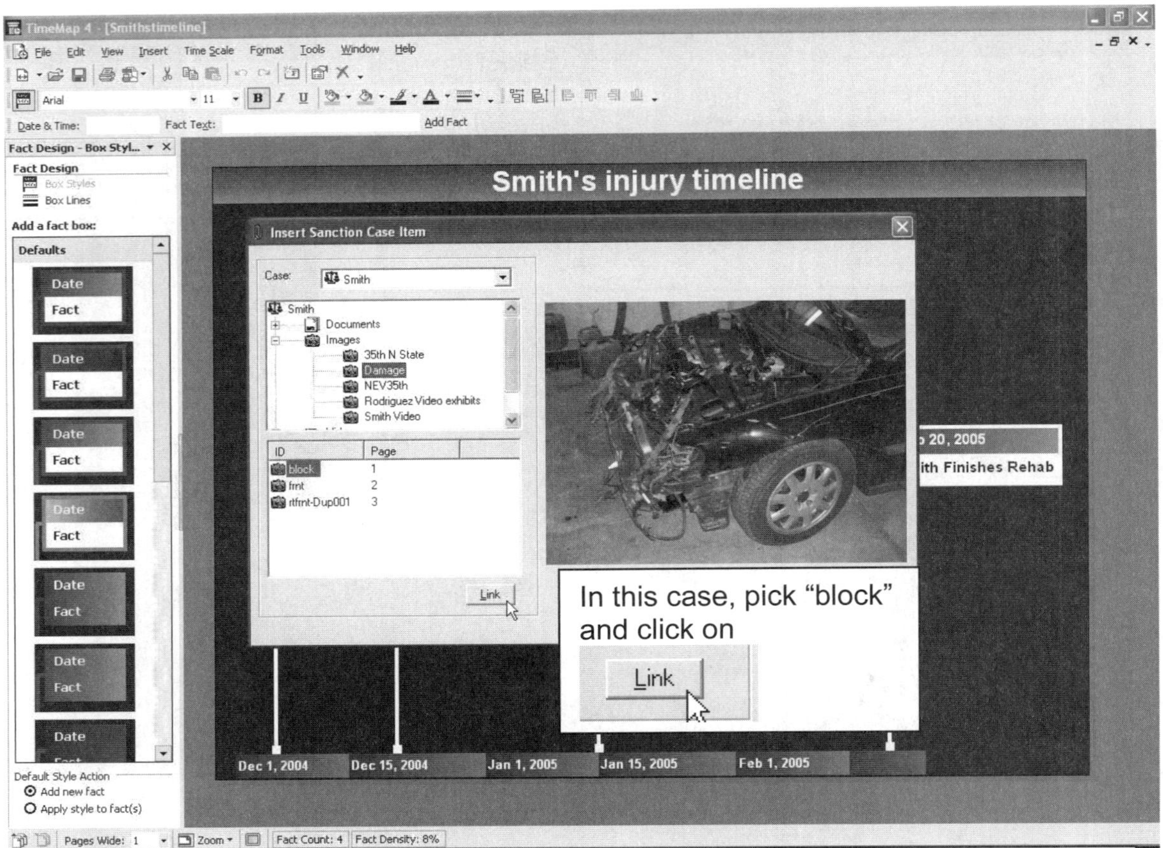

When you launch the timeline in Sanction Presentation mode, the timeline appears on the screen. If the timeline is long, the right side of the timeline will run off the screen. When you have a long timeline in TimeMap, this toolbar appears. You can move though the timeline by dragging the bar to the right or left.

To bring the linked exhibit to the screen, right click on the box and the exhibit name will appear. Then left click on the exhibit name.

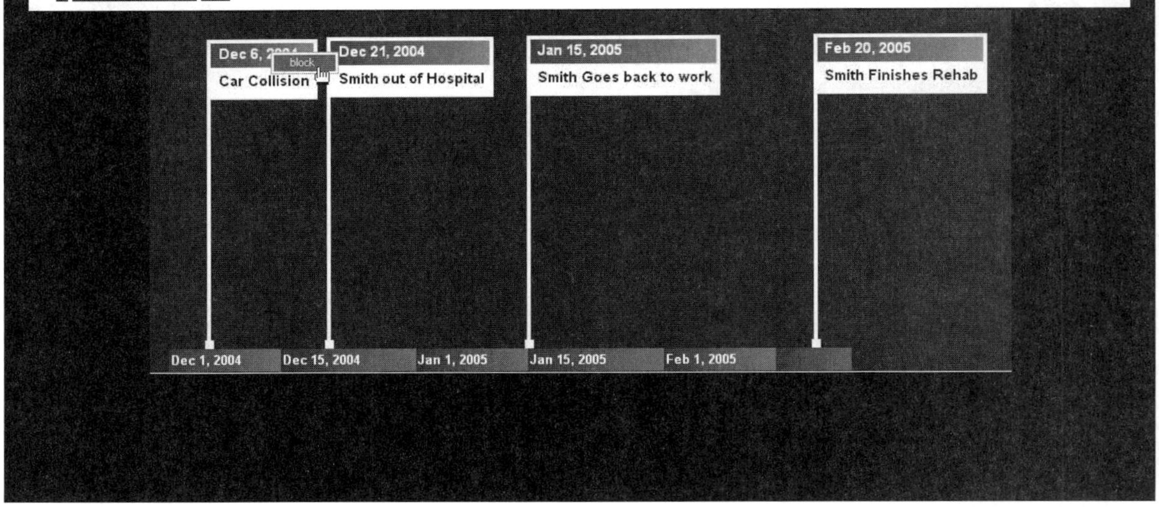

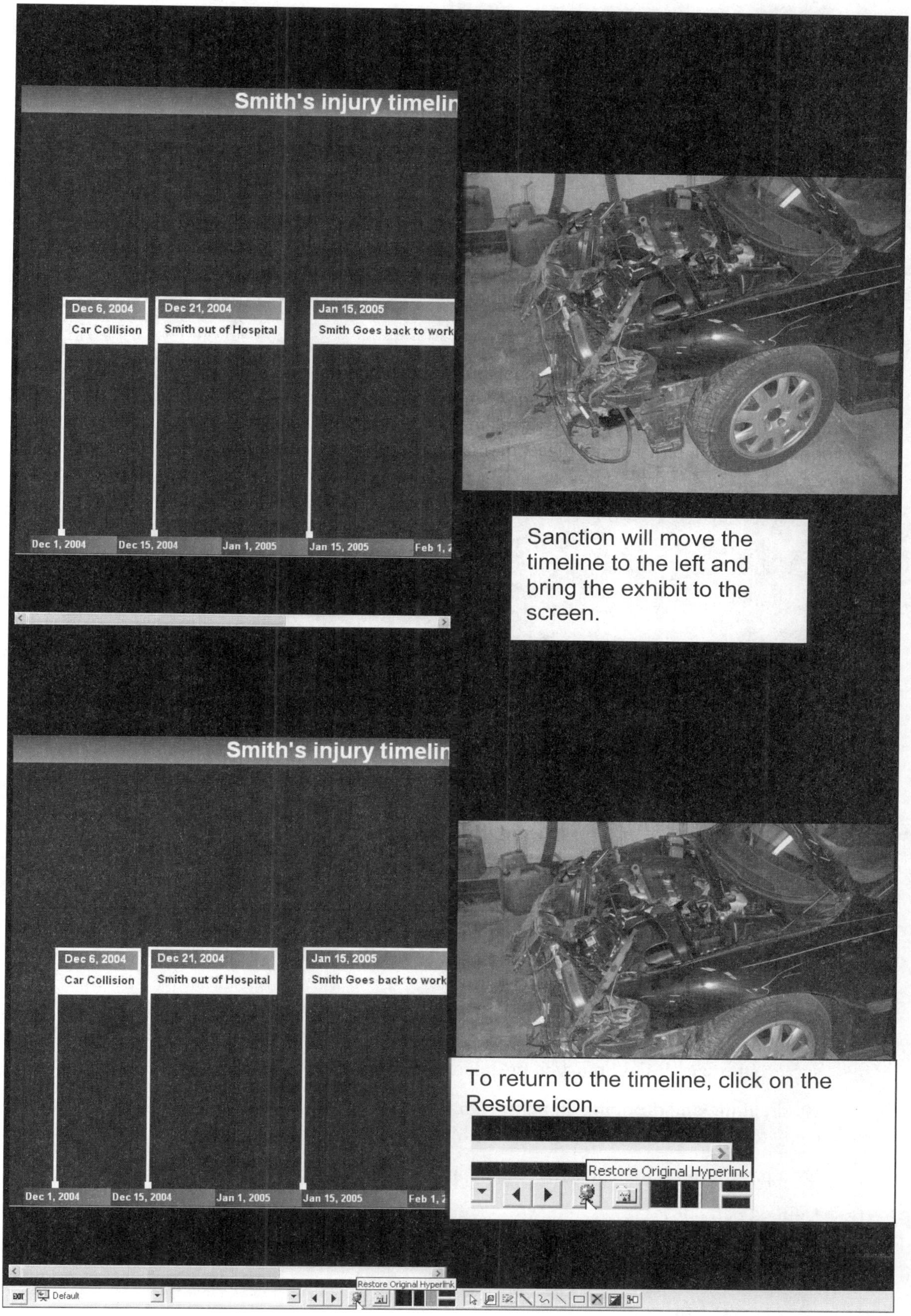
Smith's injury timelin
Dec 6, 2004
Car Collision
Dec 21, 2004
Smith out of Hospital
Jan 15, 2005
Smith Goes back to work
Dec 1, 2004
Dec 15, 2004
Jan 1, 2005
Jan 15, 2005
Sanction will move the timeline to the left and bring the exhibit to the screen.
Smith's injury timelin
Dec 6, 2004
Car Collision
Dec 21, 2004
Smith out of Hospital
Jan 15, 2005
Smith Goes back to work
Dec 1, 2004
Dec 15, 2004
Jan 1, 2005
Jan 15, 2005
To return to the timeline, click on the Restore icon.
Restore Original Hyperlink
Default
Restore Original Hyperlink

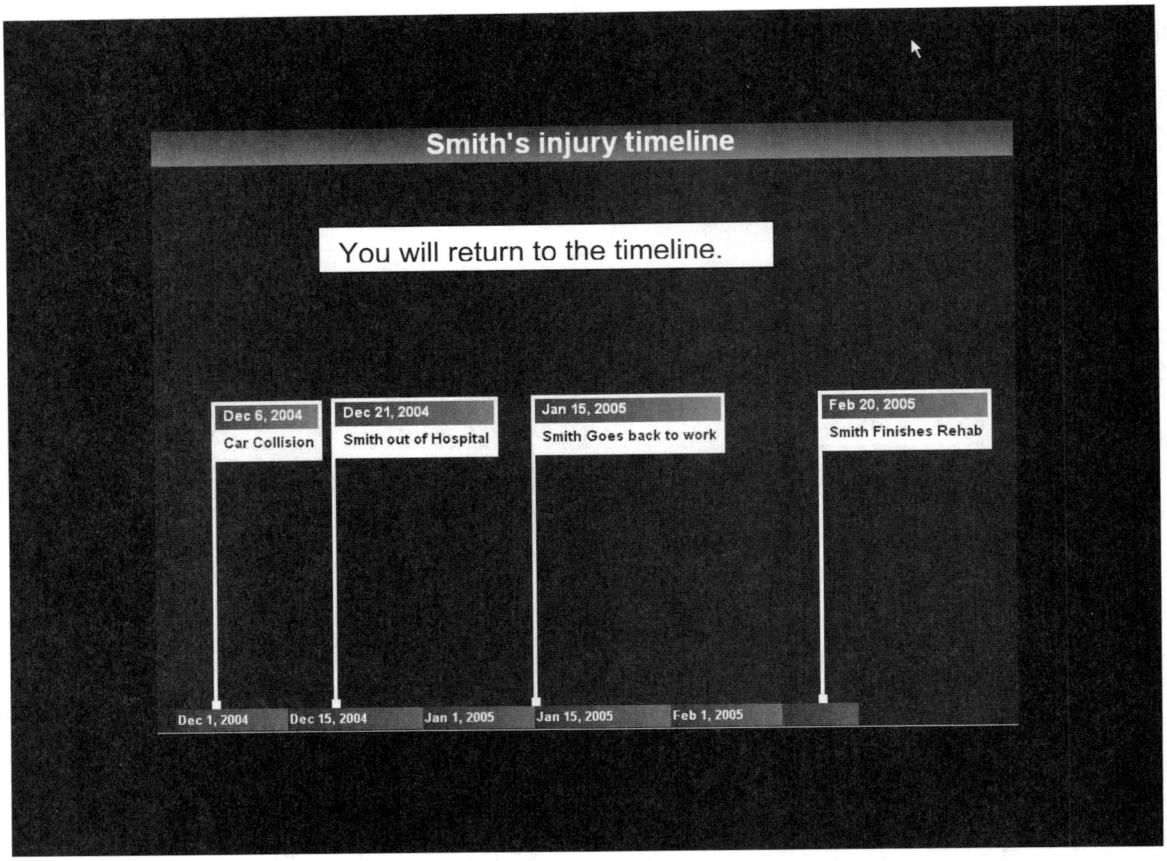

Using Sanction in Presentation Mode

When you are using Sanction in Presentation mode, it's show time! There are a number of ways to launch exhibits during a Sanction presentation.

Items can be displayed in Presentation mode using any of the following methods:

- In the order they appear in the selected Presentation folder using the forward and back control buttons
- By selecting items individually from the drop-down combo box
- Using Presentation hot keys
- Using a direct/blind search by typing ID, Exhibit#, Trial Exhibit#, or Description on the screen (the search field must be preselected)
- By dragging and dropping an item from the Main screen onto the Presentation screen (only available when working in Dual Monitor mode)
- By a page jump if the currently loaded image is in the same group
- Using a barcode

Introduction to the Presentation Mode Control Toolbar

To enter the Presentation mode, click on the  icon or click on the 

menu. The Presentation screen launches. It looks like this:

When Presentation mode is active, the program screen changes to a black display background. At the bottom of the screen is the Presentation control toolbar. The toolbar is made up of various control buttons that access different functions. Some of the buttons are used to draw on images, while others allow you to control clip segment playback and even change the various settings in Presentation mode.

The toolbar is made of several drop-down boxes, buttons, and panels. The first button on the toolbar is the Exit button: 

. Clicking Exit closes the Presentation screen and returns to the Sanction Main screen.

Next to the button is the Presentation folder drop-down box: 

. Any saved presentations will be displayed in this list. You can create presentations that organize exhibits for every aspect of the trial.

The next box to the right is the Presentation item crop-down box: . This combo box contains all items within the selected Presentation folder. Clicking an item in the Presentation list will display it on the Presentation screen.

 These are the forward and backward buttons that move from exhibit to exhibit in a particular presentation.

 This is the Restore Hyperlink button.

 This is the Toolbar Settings icon. You can use this to customize Sanction.

 These icons tell you where your exhibit will appear. You can put an exhibit in the middle of the screen, or on the left side, right side, top or bottom of the screen.

 These are command icons.

By default, when Sanction is installed, the Presentation toolbar is set to always be visible on the screen. To change this setting so the toolbar is visible only when the mouse passes over it, deselect the Control Toolbar Always Visible option from the Presentation Toolbar Settings pop-up menu.  When you click on this, the following menu will appear.

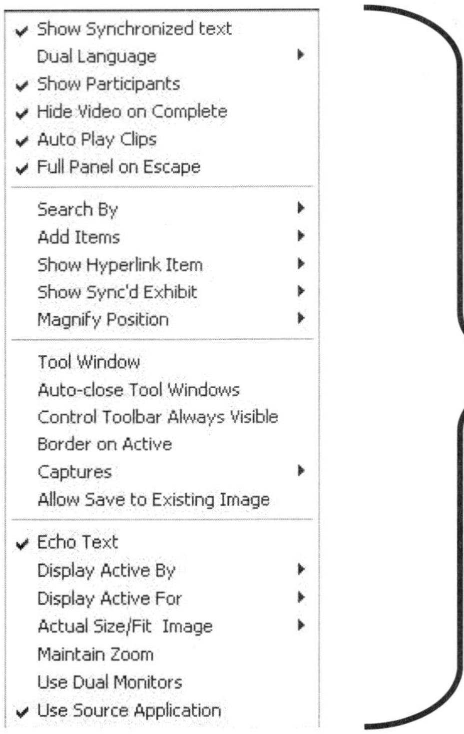

Control Toolbar Always Visible has been deactivated on this menu. When you click on this, the toolbar will disappear from the screen until you activate it by running your mouse over it. Turn this toolbar off once you are comfortable with Sanction. It is an unnecessary distraction on the screen when you are not using the Sanction program.

Customizing the Toolbar

Buttons may be configured or customized by double clicking at the end of the toolbar to display the Customize Toolbar screen. Note that the drop-down lists, Exit, Navigation, Restore Hyperlink, Settings, and active panel buttons cannot be customized and must always remain on. To customize your toolbar, double click on the gray area on the toolbar.

The window that appears will let you customize your toolbar. Simply click on the icon for a particular command that you want to add to your toolbar and the select window will appear.

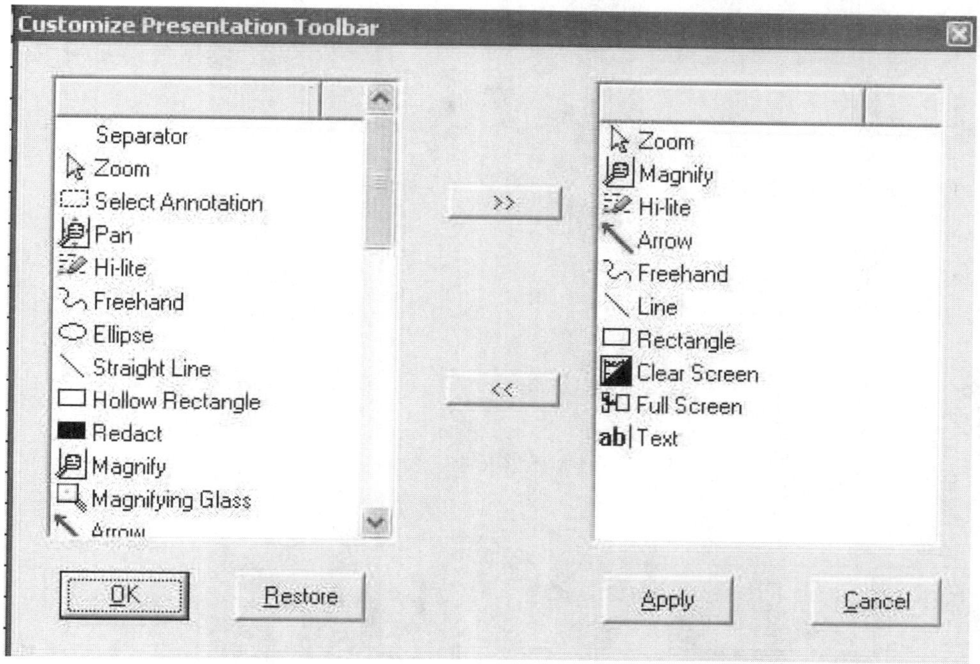

Select the additional commands that you want to add to the toolbar. Here, Text has been added to the toolbar. Click Apply and then OK to save the changes to your toolbar.

Displaying Items Using the Forward and Back Buttons

To use the  buttons, you must have at least one item in the Presentation folder. Presentation folder items follow a specific order. The buttons will allow you to move to the next item or previous item in the list of items in the Presentation folder.

Setting Up Presentation Folders to Use the Forward and Back Buttons

You should use the Presentation folders to prepare a predetermined list of presentation items. Presentation folders are a repository for items you wish to present in court each day or that you want to use with a particular witness. Presentation folders can be arranged in a specific order, and items can be added to more than one specific presentation. This way, different witnesses can have their own presentations.

Creating a Presentation folder

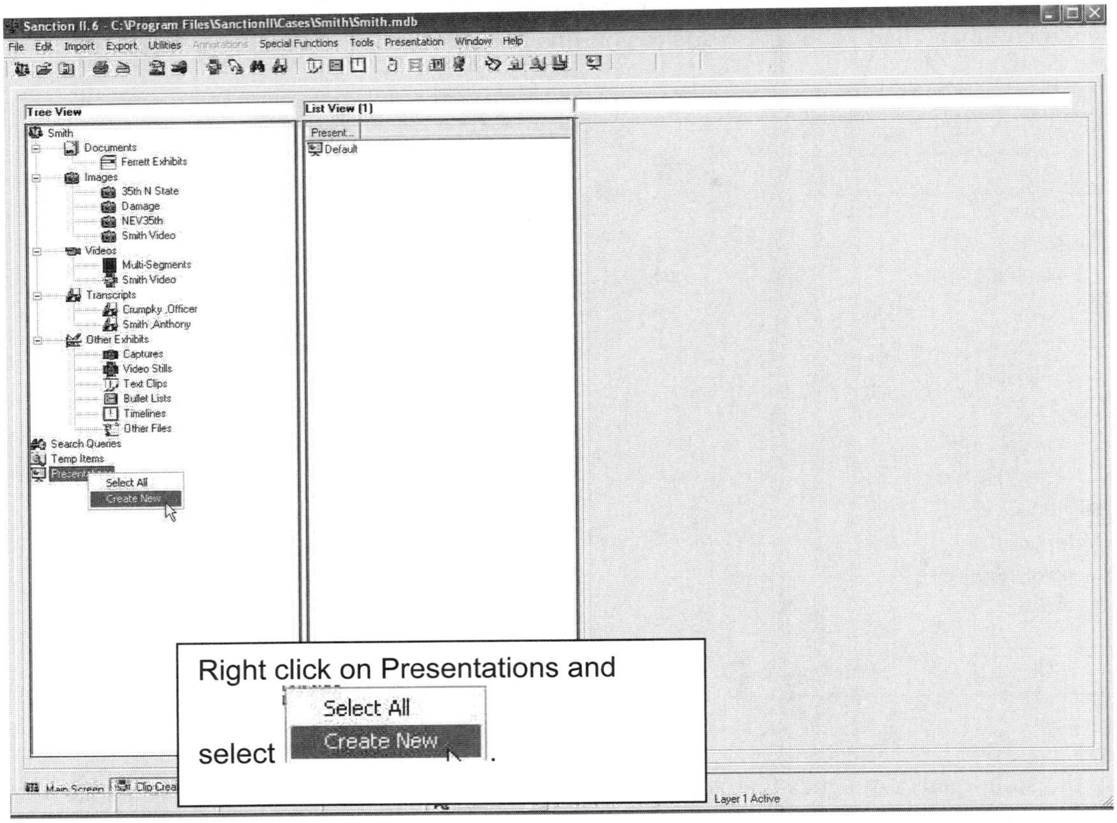

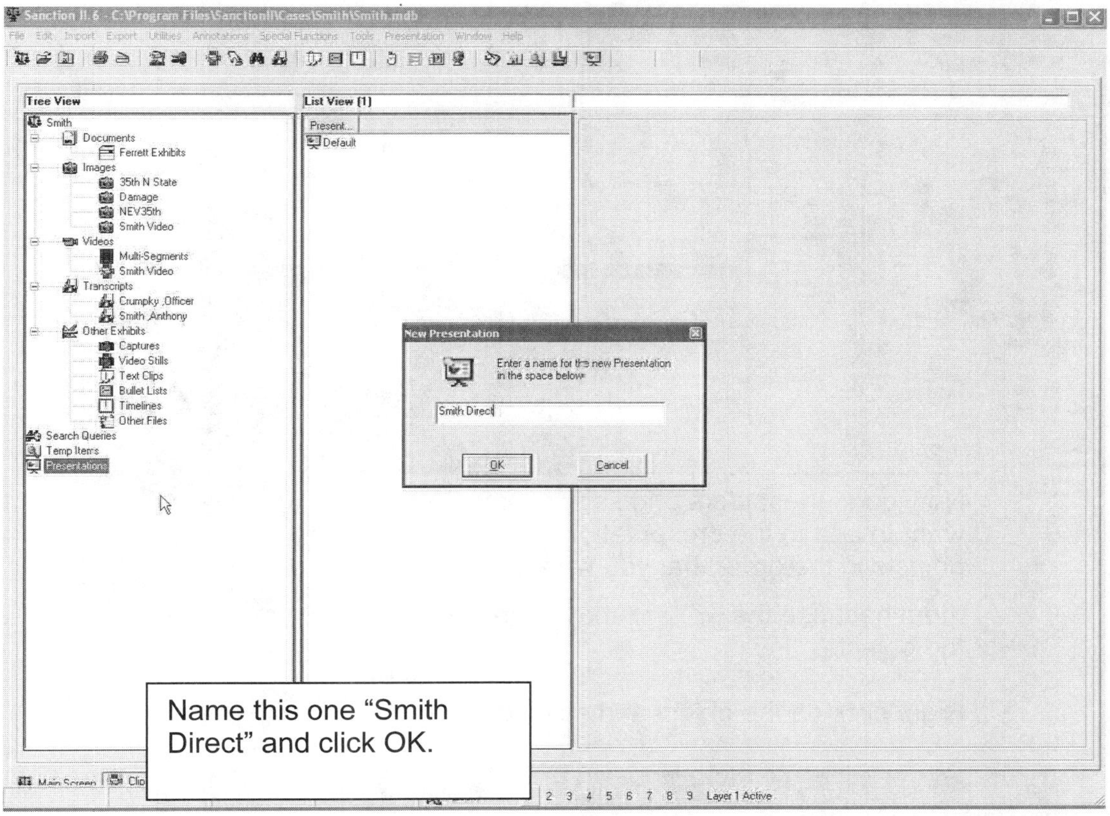
New Presentation
Enter a name for the new Presentation in the space below
Smith Direct
OK
Cancel
Name this one "Smith Direct" and click OK.

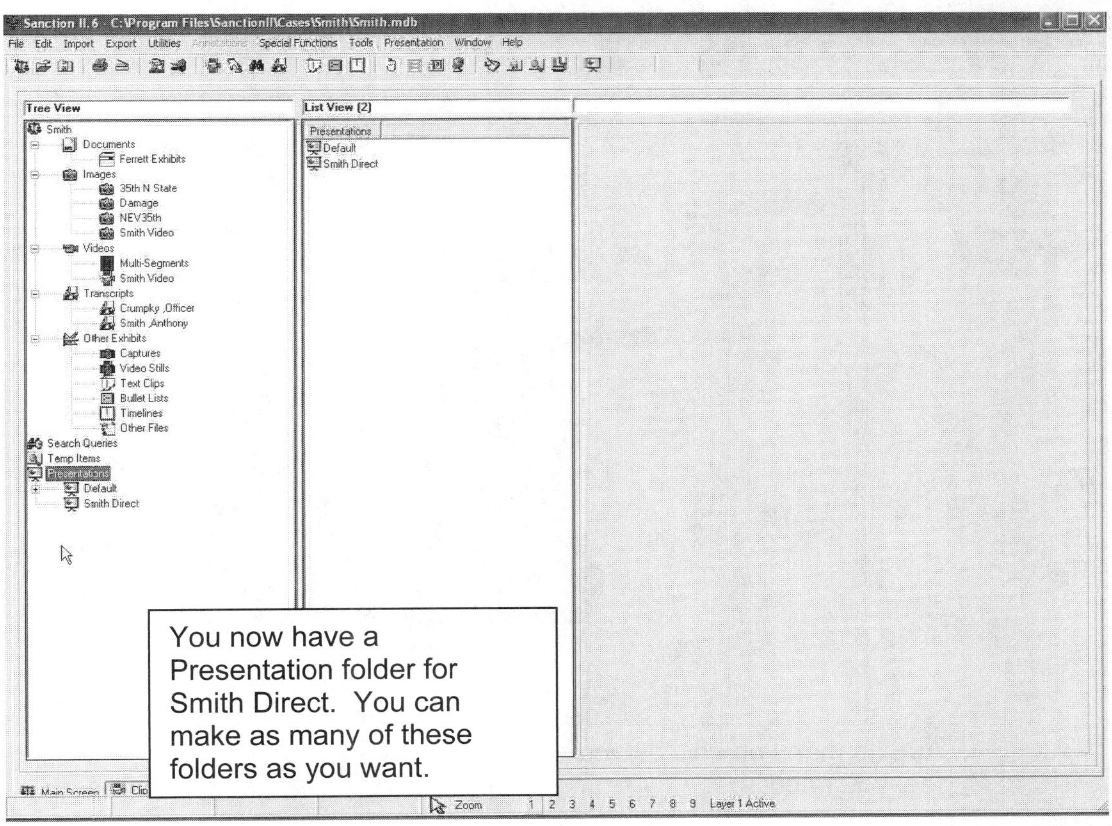
You now have a Presentation folder for Smith Direct. You can make as many of these folders as you want.

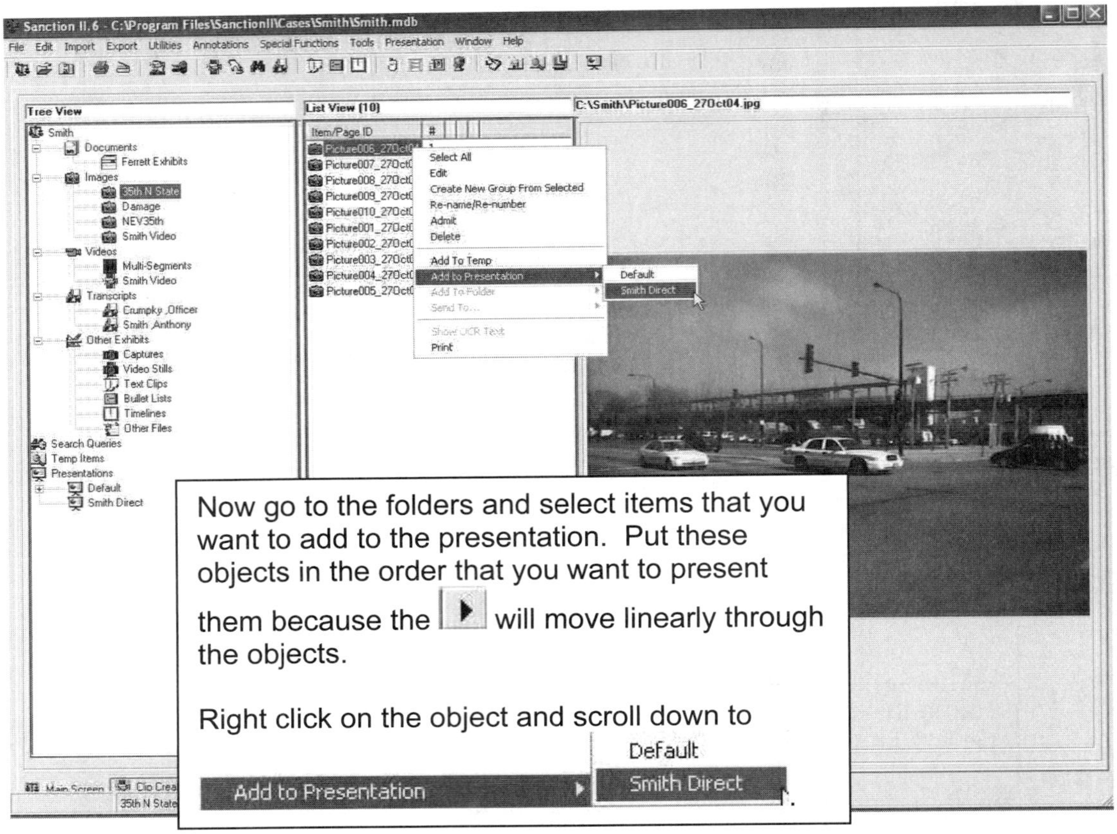
Now go to the folders and select items that you want to add to the presentation. Put these objects in the order that you want to present them because the ▶ will move linearly through the objects.
Right click on the object and scroll down to
Add to Presentation
Default
Smith Direct

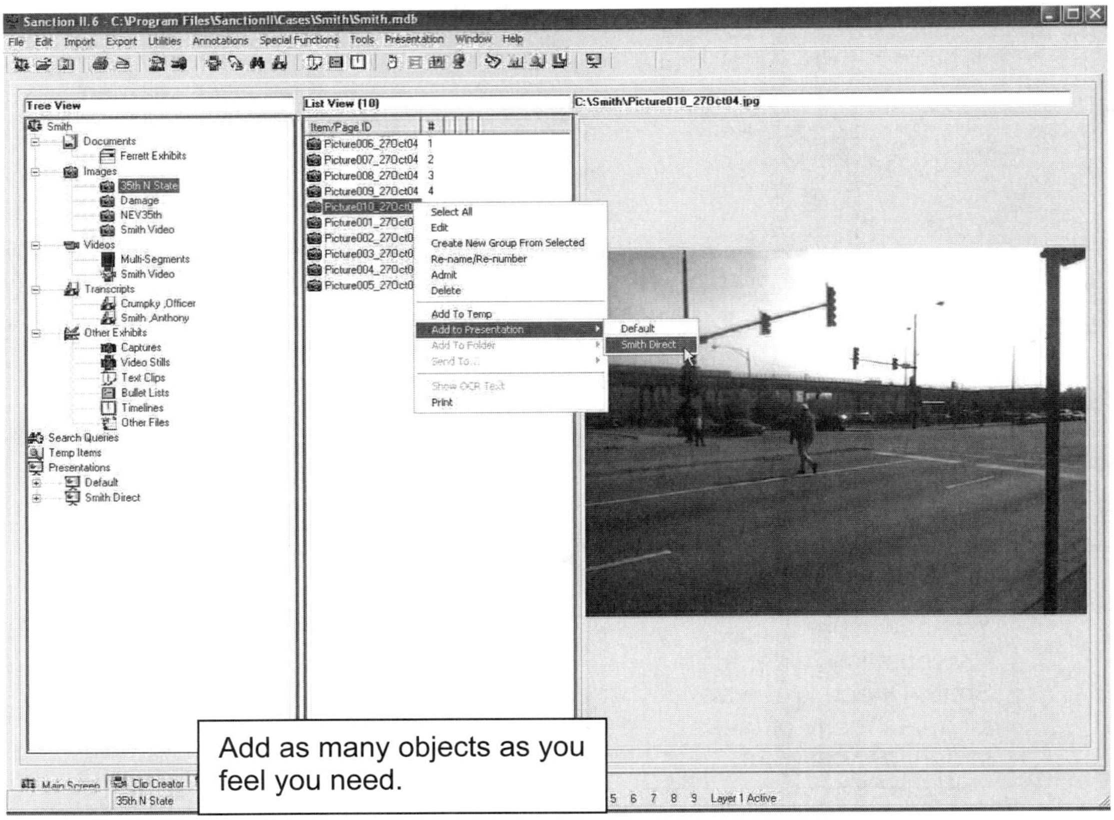
Add as many objects as you feel you need.

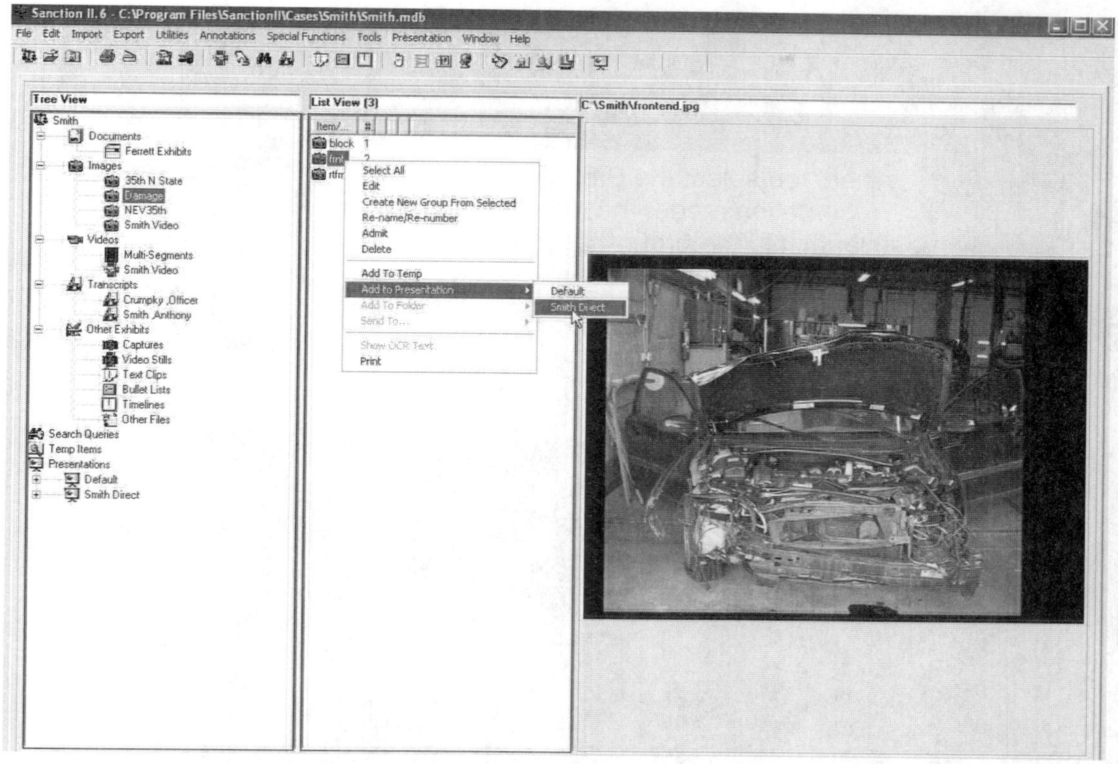

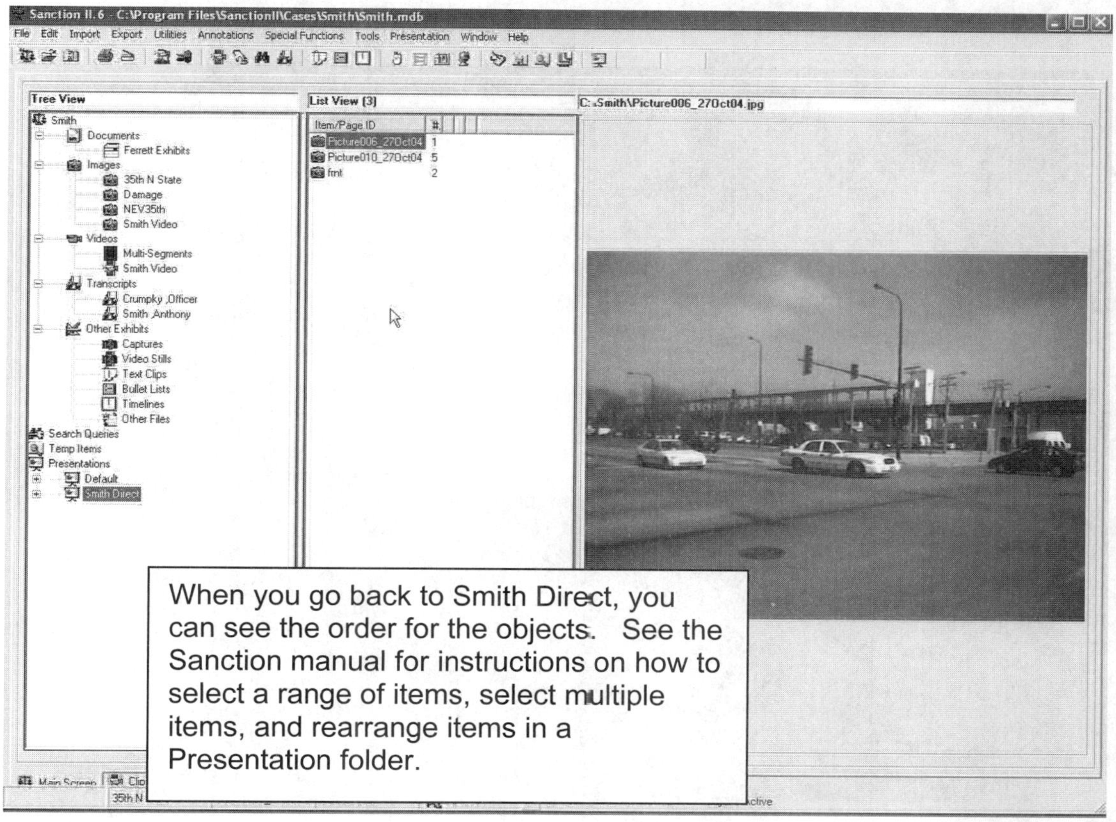

When you go back to Smith Direct, you can see the order for the objects. See the Sanction manual for instructions on how to select a range of items, select multiple items, and rearrange items in a Presentation folder.

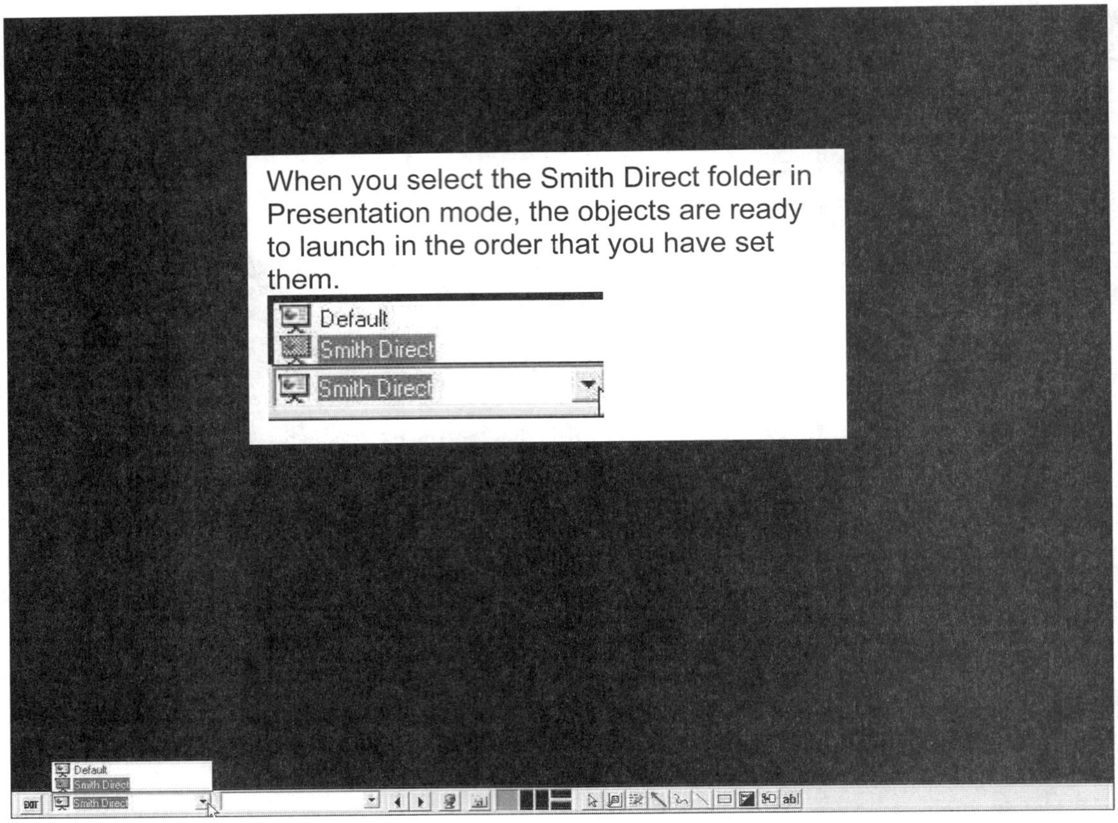
When you select the Smith Direct folder in Presentation mode, the objects are ready to launch in the order that you have set them.
Default
Smith Direct
Smith Direct

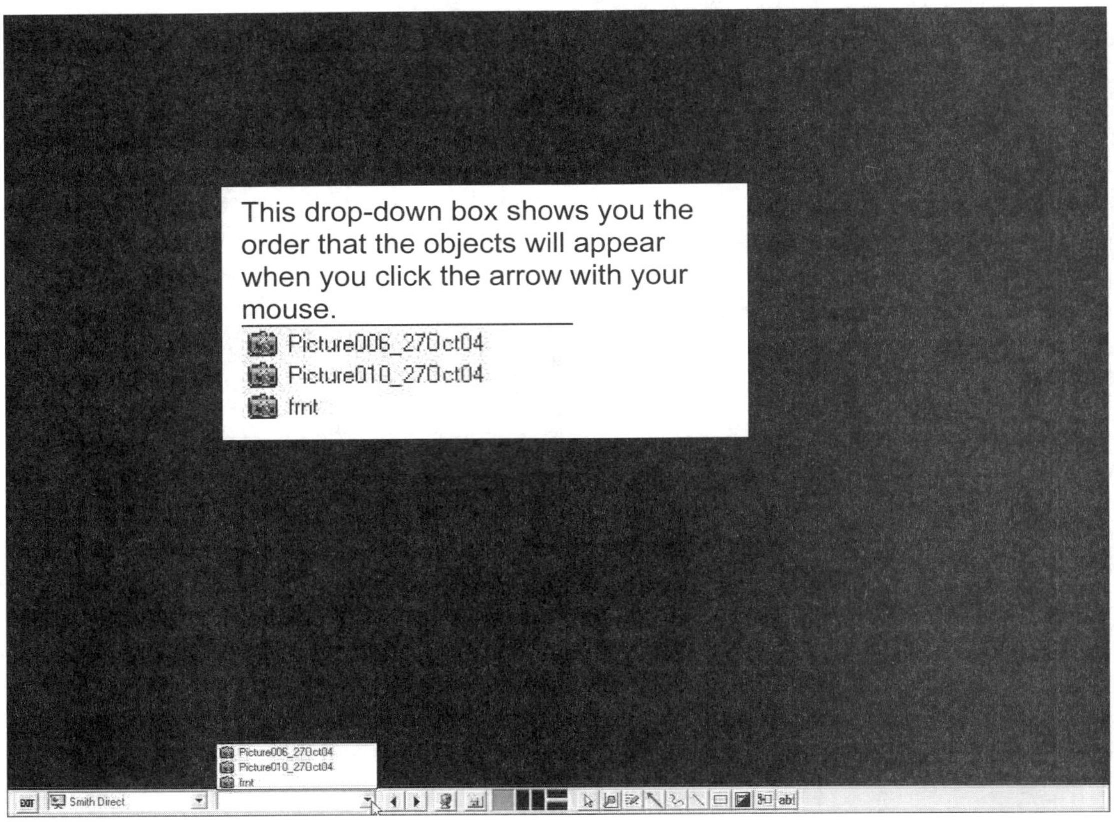
This drop-down box shows you the order that the objects will appear when you click the arrow with your mouse.
Picture006_27Oct04
Picture010_27Oct04
frnt
Smith Direct

Whatever item is currently selected on the screen, clicking on the  button will move to the next item in sequence. Clicking on the  button will move to the previous item. If the current item is already the first item and you select , or the item is already last in the sequence and you select , nothing will happen. The + key and the - key also control the  and  buttons.

Displaying Items Using the Drop-Down Combo List

The items in the selected Presentation folder will appear in the combo box in the same order they are saved in the folder. Select any item in the combo box to display it on the Presentation screen.

Direct Searching (Blind Searching) by ID, Exhibit#, Trial Exhibit#, or Description

Any item that is part of the case can be displayed on the Presentation screen by typing the ID in the combo box or directly on the screen. Simply type the ID and press the Enter key. The Search By field option can be changed to either the Exhibit#, Trial Exhibit#, or Description field using the Settings icon.

Remember the pop-up box that you used to edit IDs? Right click on the object and click on the Edit button.

You can launch an object by typing the Description, Exhibit, or Trial Ex# so long as you filled in the appropriate box.

Keep in mind that if you attempt to search the Exhibit field, but have not added exhibit numbers to case items, no object will launch when you type something.

To change the Search By field, click  on the Presentation toolbar and select Search By from the menu items.

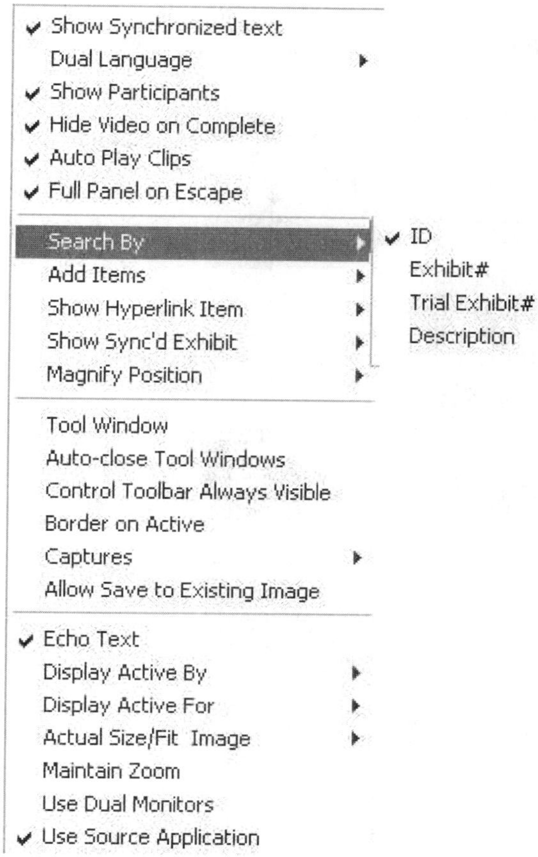

Select the desired option, and Sanction will perform subsequent searches using the selected field.

Important: When the Search By field is changed to something other than ID, be sure that *all case items* have an entry in the selected field. For example, if you attempt to search the Exhibit field, but have not added exhibit numbers to case items, the status indicator will continually show "red" (as no item could be located based on the search field).

Note: Using the Description field for blind searching is not recommended. A blind/direct search will fail if the item ID has a " | " (pipe) character in the ID name. If you must use the pipe character, place the item in a Presentation folder and select it from the drop-down combo box. In general, it is best to avoid using the pipe character in naming items.

Add item settings by default

If an item is located by blind search, it will be recorded as part of the active presentation folder (typically the Default folder). This feature is helpful in recording items that are displayed during a presentation. However, if numerous items are allowed to accumulate in the Default presentation folder during the course of a trial, the time it takes to display items on the screen in Presentation mode may increase dramatically. Be sure to either periodically clear the Default presentation folder or save the contents to another presentation folder.

Dragging and Dropping Objects When Using the Dual Monitor Feature

The Dual Monitor feature is the easiest way to use Sanction. When you use this feature, you can launch objects by simply dragging or grabbing the item from the List View on the Main screen, dragging it to the second monitor displaying Presentation mode, and then dropping the item.

To set up Sanction to run in Dual Monitor mode, follow these steps:

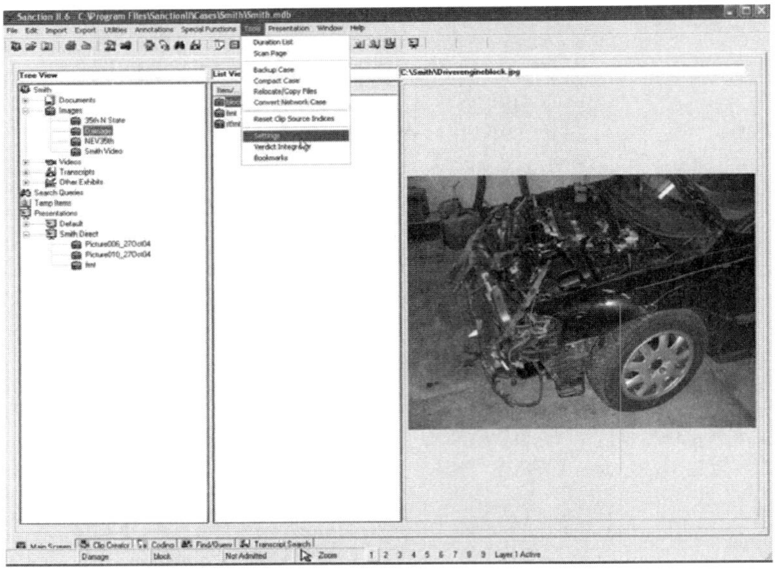

From the Tools menu, select Settings:

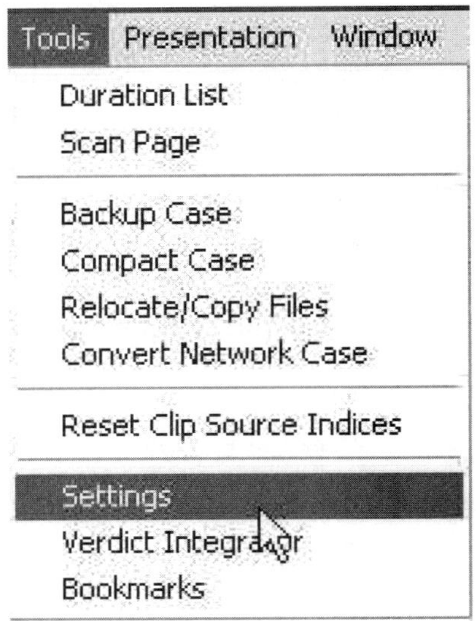

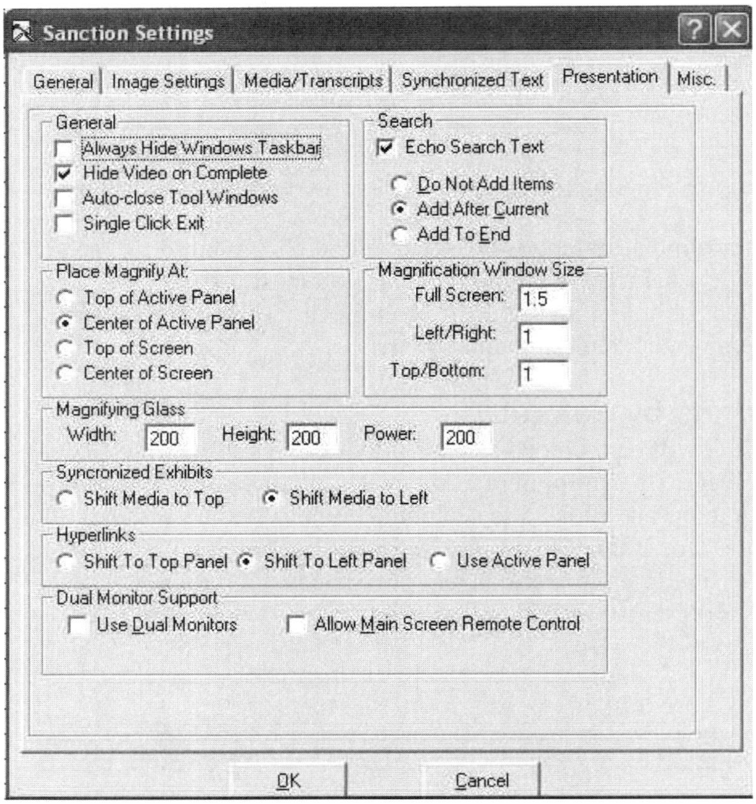

Check the

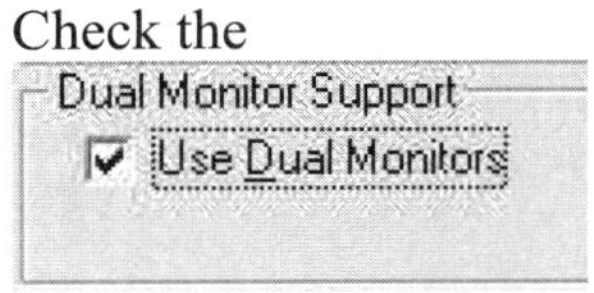

and click OK. Then when you launch the presentation, the Sanction screen will appear on your laptop and the Presentation screen will appear on your video monitor.

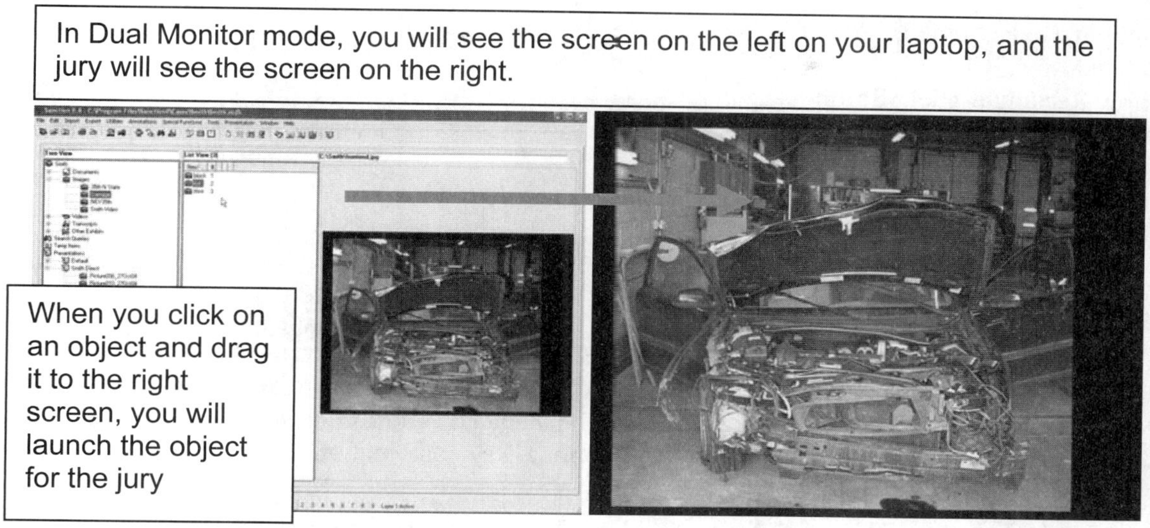

Simply grab the item from the List View on the Main screen, drag it to the second monitor displaying Presentation mode, and drop the item.

Displaying Items Using the Presentation Hot Keys

While in Presentation mode, you can use the following hot keys to execute commands:
Clear Panel: F4
Clear All Panels: Esc
Capture: F7
Capture to Group: Ctrl + F7
Show Edit Tool Window: F11
Save Image: Ctrl + S
Next Page: Page Down
Previous Page: Page Up
Scroll Image Up: Up arrow
Scroll Image Down: Down arrow
Scroll Image Right: Right arrow
Scroll Image Left: Left arrow
Auto-Delete: F5
Next Item in Combo List: + (Forward Button)
Previous Item in Combo List: - (Back Button)
Activate Left Pane View: Shift + left arrow
Activate Right Pane View: Shift + right arrow
Activate Top Pane View: Shift + up arrow
Activate Bottom Pane View: Shift + down arrow
Activate Full Pane View: Shift + Home
Admit Item: Ctrl + A

Note: For the following image commands, media files must be paused or hot keys will not respond.

Zoom Tool: Ctrl + Z; Shift F2
Magnify Tool: Ctrl + M; Shift F4
Select Annotation: Shift F3

Highlight Tool: Ctrl + H; Shift F5
Freehand Line: Ctrl + F
Hollow Rectangle Tool: Shift F8
Filled Rectangle Tool: Shift F9
Rotate Left: Ctrl + L
Rotate Right: Ctrl + R
Invert (flip): Ctrl + I
Increment Layer: F12 Shift F6
Remove Layer: Shift + F12

Important: Hot keys work for the active pane in Presentation mode. If several items are displayed, or an image is magnified and you have clicked elsewhere on screen, it is possible to lose the focus. If a function key does not perform the intended action, click on the image, transcript, or video window and then use the appropriate key combination.

Displaying Text Clips, Bullet Lists, and Timelines in Presentation Mode

Text clips can be displayed just like any other image file. Bullet lists have the additional functionality of linking to other case items. Therefore, in Presentation mode, you have several options for how linked items will be displayed. When you load a bullet list in the full screen panel in Presentation mode and click on a linked item, you have three viewing options: replace the bullet list in the full screen with the linked item, automatically shift the bullet list to the left panel and display the linked item in the right panel, or automatically shift the bullet list to the top panel and display the linked item in the bottom panel.

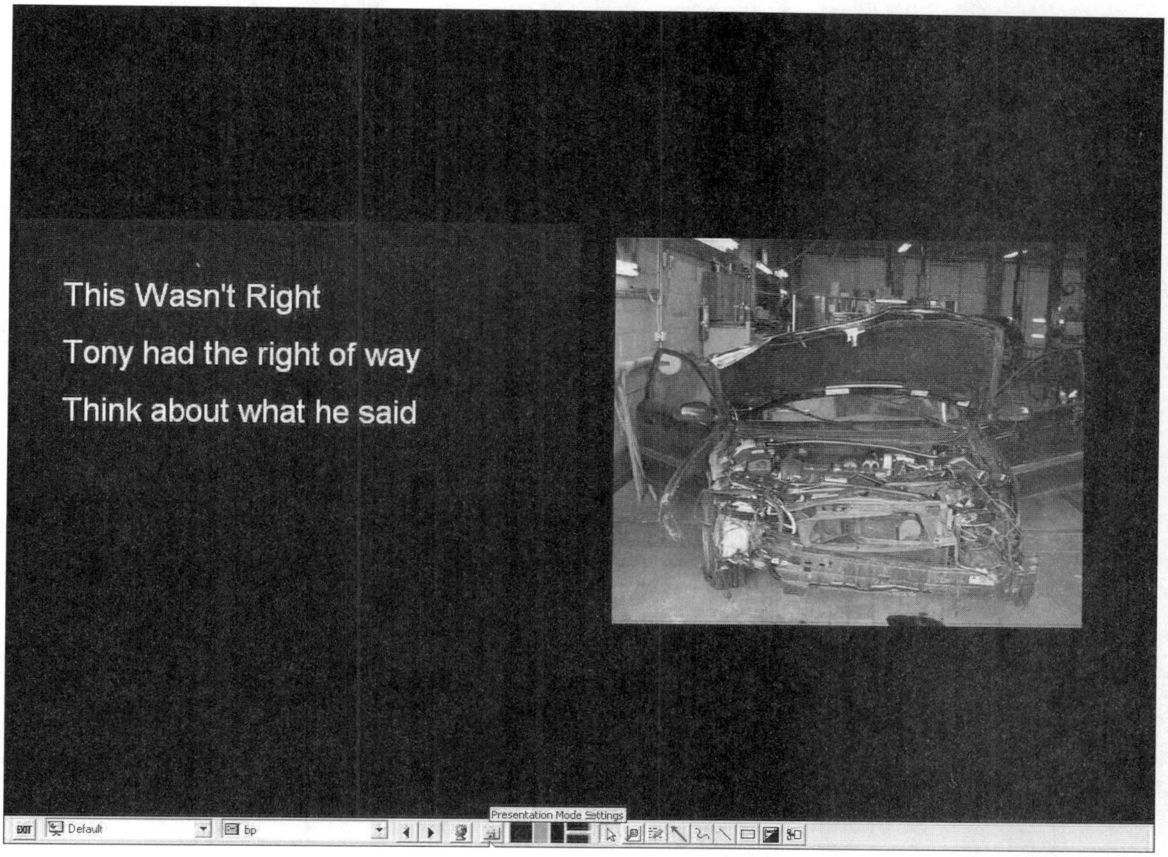

The display choice for linked items can be set from either the Main Screen Presentation Settings or by clicking on the Settings icon in Presentation mode.

If you choose to have linked items replace the bullet list or timeline in Full Screen mode, you can return to the bullet list by clicking on the Restore Hyperlink toolbar icon.

Bullet lists, timelines, and text clips can provide very powerful visual guidance in a presentation. Take time to learn how to use each of these features by practicing with the various settings to see how they affect the output files. Once you are familiar with how Exhibit Studio items are created and modified, you will find them indispensable!

Importing a Sanction Database into an Existing Database

If you are working with another person on a case and that person has created a separate Sanction database, you can import that database into your own. Do not simply copy the database from the other person's computer. That will overwrite your existing database and erase all of your work. Instead, use the Import function to import the other database into your own.

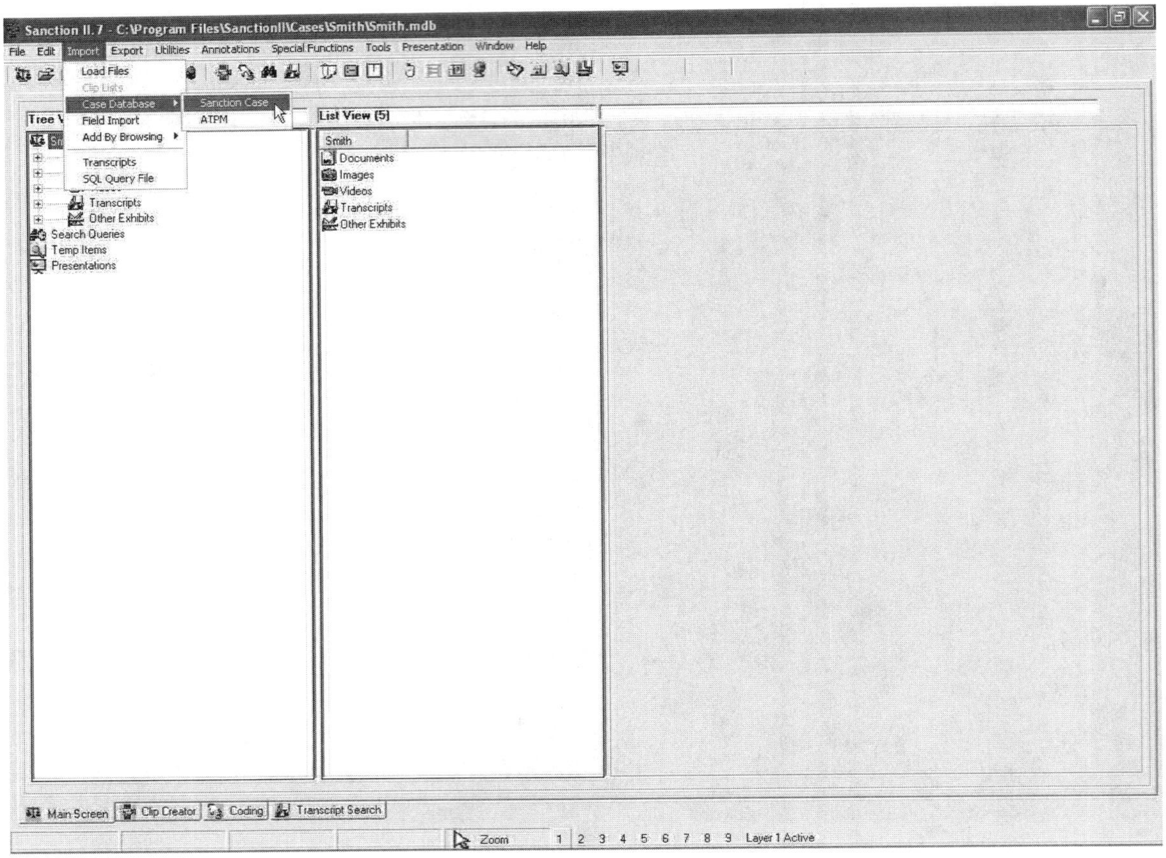
Sanction II.7 - C:\Program Files\SanctionII\Cases\Smith\Smith.mdb
File Edit Import Export Utilities Annotations Special Functions Tools Presentation Window Help
Load Files
Clip Lists
Case Database
Sanction Case
ATPM
Field Import
Add By Browsing
Transcripts
SQL Query File
List View (5)
Smith
Documents
Images
Videos
Transcripts
Other Exhibits
Search Queries
Temp Items
Presentations
Main Screen
Clip Creator
Coding
Transcript Search
Zoom
Layer 1 Active

Chapter 9

Tips for Choosing and Using Computer Equipment in the Courtroom

This chapter assumes that you *are not* working in a high-tech courtroom. In fact, it assumes that you are working in a courthouse that is verging on dilapidated. One of the biggest mistakes you can make when planning your computer-assisted courtroom presentation is to assume that you will have access to anything more than electricity. (In fact, the smart thing to do is to bring an extra power strip so that you can share electricity with the courtroom clerk or the court reporter!)

This chapter first shares tips for choosing and setting up your computer presentation equipment. It then gives you time-tested presentation tips to use once your trial begins.

Equipment

Get a decent laptop. A decent laptop contains the following equipment:

1. The largest hard drive you can afford (60 gigabytes or larger)
2. Lots of RAM (Random Access Memory)
3. As large a co-processor as is available (if 64-bit co-processors are available in laptops at the time you are reading this book, get a 64-bit co-processor instead of a 32-bit co-processor; more bits are faster)
4. Ability to show an image on the computer screen and on the monitor
5. A DVD drive that can burn RW/R (rewritable/ recordable) compact discs

Get a backup laptop. It never hurts to have a second laptop waiting to be swapped into the trial if the first laptop develops problems. If you cannot afford two laptops, borrow one from somebody. You will feel more confident simply knowing that you have a backup machine available.

Get a high-resolution video monitor. These are not televisions. Televisions have a resolution of less than 800 x 600 DPI (dots per inch). The resolution of a television is not very good when you are showing a full-sized document on the screen. A high-resolution video monitor has a resolution of 1024 x 768 DPI, which is the optimal resolution to use with Sanction on the extended desktop screen. This type of resolution shows detail. This means that you can put a document on the screen and be able to read it without having to zoom in on portions of the document. It is important because a lower resolution makes the text appear blurred. If you are dealing with a cynical juror looking for a reason to distrust you, this blurriness is the kind of excuse he or she needs to think you are hiding or, worse yet, altering something. If possible, get a video monitor that has an RCA audio and video out plug on the back of the monitor. In this way, you can connect a smaller television that faces the judge or your opponent so that he or she can see the objects you are showing the jury.

Think twice about using RGB or computer projectors. While many people like projectors for presentations, they are not the best tool for the visual trial in a courtroom, unless you are trying multiple simultaneous jury trials. Projectors make noise and heat. They make noise because the cooling fan makes a constant whirring sound, and they make heat because the bulb in the projector is extremely bright and consequently creates a lot of heat. Projectors also take up valuable courtroom space. If you are going to use a projector in a courtroom, then it should have an extremely bright bulb. The stronger the bulb inside the projector, the higher the projector's lumen or candlepower rating. The brighter a projector is, the better it can compete with light in the courtroom. Try to get the temperature in the courtroom lowered to compensate for the heat that will be thrown by the projector. Also try to avoid turning off lights in the courtroom, as a well-lighted courtroom helps jurors and judges stay awake.

What do projectors do? They put a high-resolution image on a screen or wall. Red, green, and blue lights are blended to send an image that is composed of pixels. Think of a grid sitting on top of a picture of a pencil. Each box of the grid is a pixel location. The grid is colored red, green, or blue depending on what the computer analyzing the grid decides. Higher resolutions use a greater number of pixels per square inch. These images can be highly detailed depending on the resolution of the projector. Image resolution can range from 640 x 480 pixels to 1280 x 1024 pixels, or greater, as the technology improves.

The advantage of a projector is Resolution, Resolution, and Resolution! Projectors can show detail. Their resolution is better than a television monitor, so the images projected onto the screen look crisp. For instance, a scanned image of an 8 1/2″ x 11″ sheet of paper that has handwriting on it will look clear and crisp when projected onto a screen or wall. The same image will look distorted and fuzzy on a television. The detail of the writing will not show up on a television until you zoom in on a portion of the document.

You will also need to get long cables that can carry your video signal from your computer to the monitor. The cables should be long enough to enable you to move your cart with ease around the room as the trial progresses. Do not expect the judge to give you five minutes to move your cart from the opening statement position to the place where you intend to use it during direct examination. You must be prepared to move your equipment quickly.

This is an S Video plug. It carries a fairly high-resolution image to the monitor or projector.

This is an RCA cable. It is a common video port that carries an image to the projector or monitor.

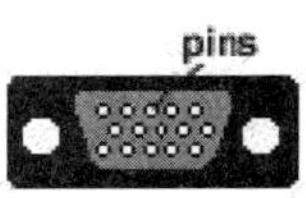

This is an RGB plug. Most laptops have a plug like this for carrying a signal to a projector.

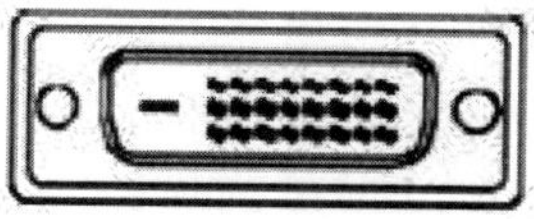

This is a DVI or digital video plug. It carries a high-resolution signal to monitors and projectors.

Get cables with the appropriate endings that are long enough to run across the room in places that are out of the way from foot traffic so that they can be placed in the courtroom where no one can trip on them.

Consider going wireless. As technology improves and as costs come down, wireless transmission of video and audio signals to monitors and projectors will become more affordable. Just make sure that the wireless technology does not conflict with law enforcement radio equipment that is worn by courtroom personnel.

Know how to hook up your own equipment. Learn what plug goes where and why. Consider pre-marking your cables and plugs on your equipment with colored tape. When your equipment does not work, you will lose credibility. When you are in the middle of trial and a witness stumbles over your wires (or opposing counsel accidentally pulls your cords out), you are not going to remember that the yellow plug on a red, yellow, and white RCA plug is historically the video cable. Finally, use tape to secure your cables to the floor so that jurors and court personnel do not trip over them.

If you are planning to work with videotaped evidence, you will need a video capture card for your computer. Make sure it has sound. If you expect to work with video frequently, get a desktop machine that has the proper features. If possible, get one with two co-processors, a 200 gigabyte or larger hard drive, and a gigabyte of RAM. The machine should have a sound card and speakers so that you can listen to the quality of video and audio files while working with them. Make sure the machine has a CD drive that can burn CDs for your laptop.

Get a cordless presentation device. Obtain a Bluetooth presentation device. Bluetooth wireless technology is an industry-standard protocol that provides short-range wireless connections between Bluetooth devices, such as a keyboard and a computer mouse. It also uses a radio transmission that is not on the same frequency as most courtroom deputy and bailiff radios. (I found a good cordless presentation device at www.logitech.com.) These devices allow you to advance slides without having to stand by your computer and press a button. This will make your life easier during opening statement, closing argument, or whenever you want to run a series of slides during the trial.

Get a scanner and digital camera. A scanner is a type of digital camera that allows you to digitize photographs and documents. The resolution of the image you create will affect the size of the file that the scanner creates. Digital photographs are images that are captured and stored in digital form on a computer or other type of electronic media without the use of film or paper. Digital images are any visual data stored in a computer that can be used by a computer. They can include digital photographs, scanned analog photographs, video files, or any other data you can think of.

Equipment Checklist

- Laptop
- Backup laptop (Sanction, PowerPoint, and case file using the same path as the laptop)
- Video monitor (Do you need a second monitor for the judge and opponent?)
- Video signal cables
- Audio cable that converts headphone jack to RCA audio
- A surge suppressor
- Extra power strips
- Extra video cable connectors
- External speakers for your laptop if you are not using the video monitor for audio
- Cordless presenter
- Second cordless presenter
- Electrical tape
- Duct tape
- Pliers
- Screwdrivers
- Cart for monitor and document camera
- Document camera (Can it fit on the same cart as the monitor?)
- Table or cart for laptop

Equipment Placement

Consider the strategic placement of your equipment in your courtroom. You do not want your equipment competing with your jury's attention. Get a cart on which you can roll your equipment around the room. For an ideal presentation, technology should be easily moved around the courtroom. For example, technology used during opening statement or closing argument should be to off to the side of the attorney when the attorney presents his or her argument.

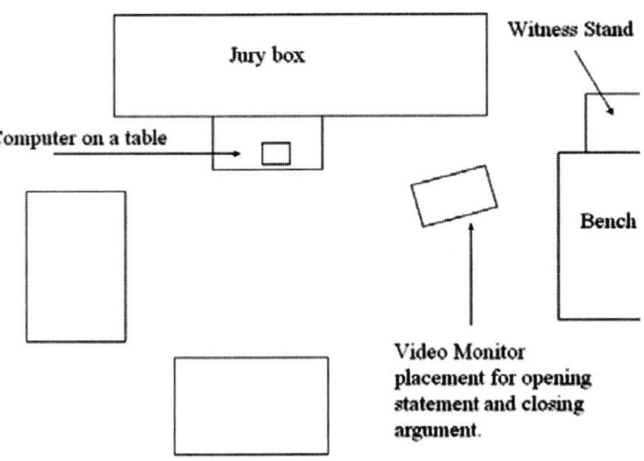

You want the monitor off to the side during your opening statement or closing argument. In the location depicted here, a right-handed person can gesture naturally toward the monitor.

Jurors can look at the lawyer and then look at the information on the screen. This puts the lawyer in the position of teacher while making the presentation.

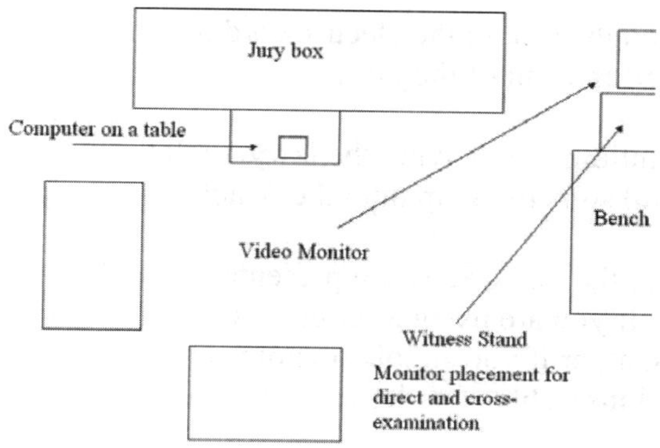

Putting the monitor next to the witness stand focuses the jurors' attention on the witness and the exhibit that is being displayed.

Imagine how much a witness will shrink as he or she is confronted with inconsistent video that is sitting right next to the witness stand.

Set up the equipment before the trial and experiment with different locations. Sit in various seats in the jury box to make sure that all the jurors can see the monitors or screens.

Presentation Tips

Find out if the judge is going to require you to provide the court or your opponent with a video monitor before you bring your equipment to court. See if you can get the judge to order your opponent to bring his or her own video display.

Go to the Litigation Technology website (www.littech.org) and check what the state of the law is for your jurisdiction regarding the use of technology at trial.

If you are working with RCA plugs: Buy three RCA video signal splitters from an electronic supply store. Buy four more RCA plug connectors than you think you need.

Bring electrical tape and duct tape to court. Buy 36-foot RCA audio cable and split the cables, giving you a 72-foot video cable if you use one of your RCA connectors. Now you can have your laptop at your table and the video monitor 72 feet away from you.

Run your cables across the room in places that are out of the way from foot traffic so that no one trips on them. Tape the cables to the floor. Tape the RCA connectors to the cables so that they are unlikely to get unplugged.

When the courtroom is empty, sit in the jury seats and make sure you can see the video monitor in its location for opening statement and closing argument and for direct and cross-examination.

Bring a surge suppressor to the courthouse. Plug it in by the court reporter if no other electricity is available in the courtroom. Make sure the power light on the surge suppressor is on. Make sure your laptop is plugged in. Most laptop batteries will not last the entire day.

Bring two more electric cords than you think you need.

Put new batteries in your Bluetooth presentation device every day. Keep extra batteries in your briefcase. Test your presenter and make sure it is working outside the presence of the jury.

If you are doing an opening statement and then moving into calling witnesses without taking a break, make sure that you have practiced moving the cart to the position that it will be in for direct and cross before the jury comes out. Leave enough slack in the electric cord that supplies the equipment on the cart so you can maneuver the cart in front of the jury.

Work your own computer. Nothing looks more pretentious than having the lawyer tell the "computer guy" to advance to the next screen or to call something up onto the Sanction desktop.

Use a blank screen (in PowerPoint, press the B key) or the black Sanction presentation desktop when you do not want the jury looking at the screen. If you are using a series of slides but want to talk about something that is not supported by a visual, or if you simply do not want to use visuals at every step of the argument, then you should insert blank slides at the appropriate places in the presentation.

Use a blue blank screen at the beginning of your presentation. This way, you can look at the jury's video monitor and know that your computer signal is getting to the video monitor.

Use No Effect for Image Settings on Sanction. This way you will not have documents zooming in or sliding onto the screen like the text at the beginning of a Star Wars movie.

Click on the Settings icon:

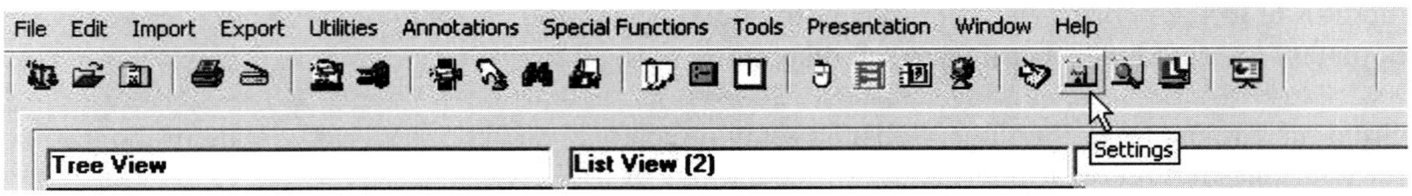

Go to the Image Settings tab and select No Effect:

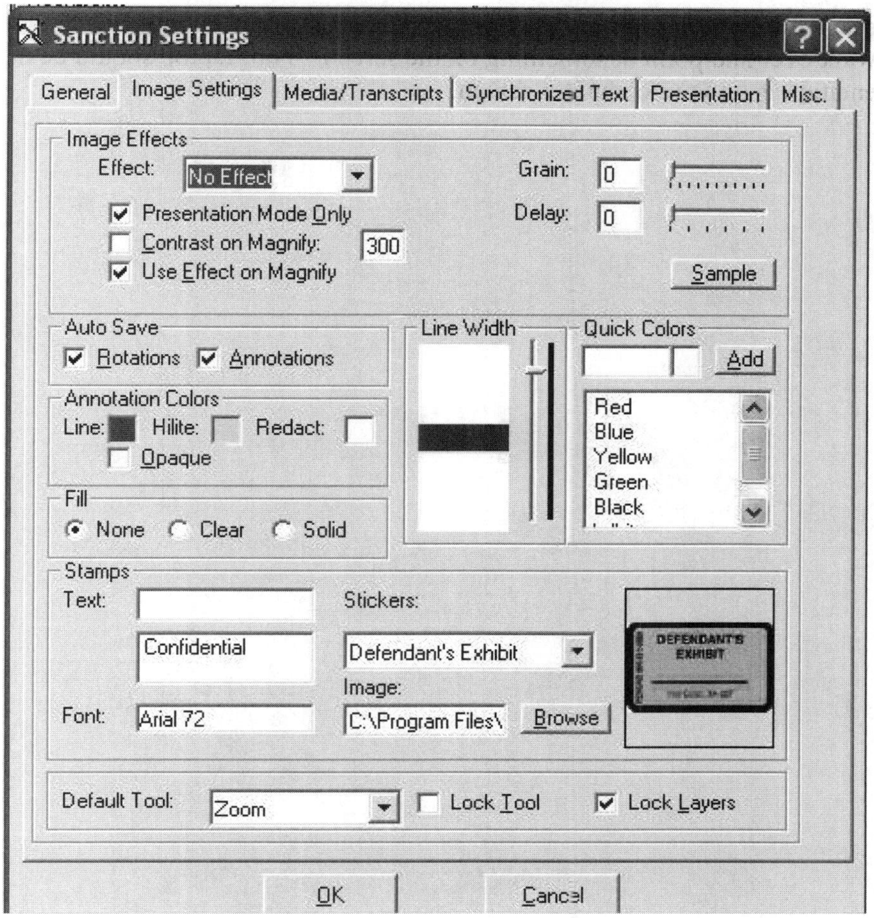

Hide the Sanction toolbar on the presentation screen because it distracts from your presentation. Follow these steps:

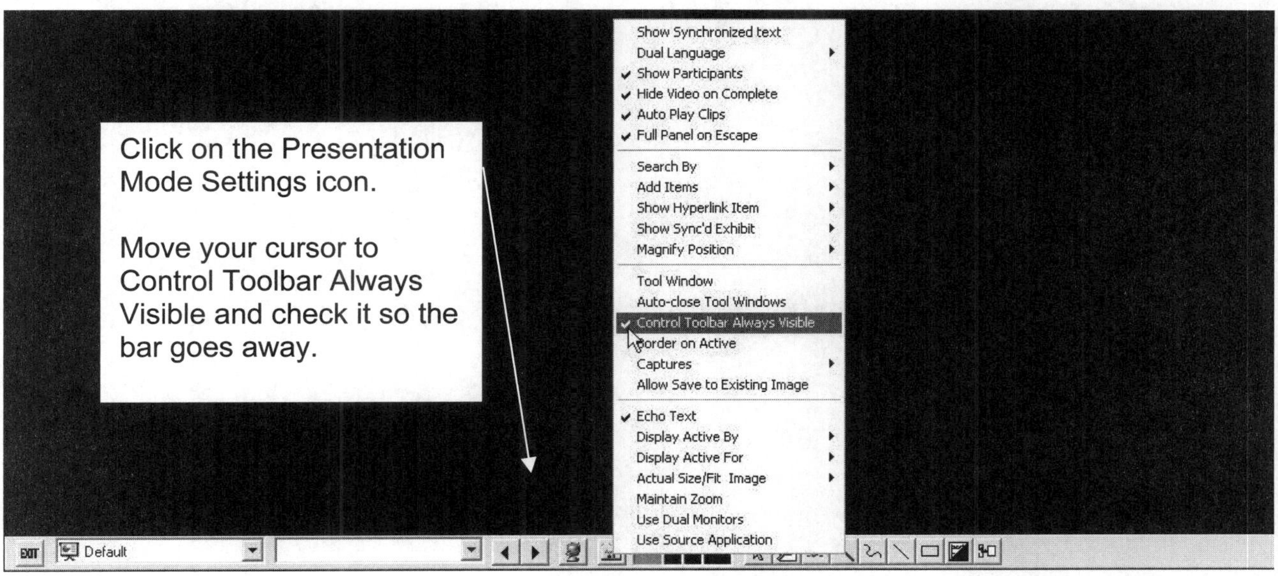

Once you begin your presentation, avoid checking the video monitor that is off to your side unless you are going to walk over and point at something on the screen. Your laptop should be in front of you. Your presentation is on your computer screen.

Index of PowerPoint Terms and Commands

Evidence points to or away from, 171-172

Index of Sanction Terms and Commands